Annotated Edition

PowerPoint 97

A PROFESSIONAL APPROACH

Margaret Marple
MMPC
Norwalk, CT

Sharon Fisher-Larson
Elgin Community College
Elgin, IL

Glencoe
McGraw-Hill

New York, New York   Columbus, Ohio   Woodland Hills, California   Peoria, Illinois

This program has been prepared with the assistance of Gleason Group, Inc., Norwalk, CT.

Editorial Director: Pamela Ross

Developmental Editor: Thomas Cain

Copy Editor: Beth Conover

Composition: PDS Associates, Creative Ink

Screens were captured using CaptureEze 97 from Application Techniques, Inc., Pepperell, MA.

Glencoe/McGraw-Hill

A Division of The McGraw·Hill Companies

PowerPoint 97: A Professional Approach
Student Edition
ISBN 0-02-803323-X

PowerPoint 97: A Comprehensive Approach
Student Edition
ISBN 0-02-803351-5

PowerPoint 97: A Professional Approach
Annotated Instructor's Edition
ISBN 0-02-803327-2

PowerPoint 97: A Comprehensive Approach
Teacher's Annotated Edition
ISBN 0-02-803358-2

Copyright © 1999 by The McGraw-Hill Companies, Inc. All rights reserved. Printed in the United States of America. Except as permitted under the United States copyright Act of 1976, no part of this publication may be reproduced or distributed in any form or by any means, or stored in a data base or retrieval system, without the prior written permission of the publisher.

1 2 3 4 5 6 7 8 9 10 027 03 02 01 00 99 98 97

Microsoft, PowerPoint, and Windows are either registered trademarks or trademarks of Microsoft Corporation in the United States and/or other countries.

PostScript is a registered trademark of Adobe Systems, Inc.

Contents

Program Components	*T-4*
Classroom Resources	*T-4*
Inside the Annotated Edition	*T-5*
Introduction	*T-5*
Teaching Plan	*T-5*
Prepare	*T-5*
Teach	*T-5*
Close	*T-6*
Assess	*T-7*
Teaching Resources	*T-8*
Assessment Resources	*T-9*
Using the Case Study	*T-10*
Using the Appendices	*T-11*
Teaching a Lesson	*T-12*
Using the Portfolio Builder	*T-13*
Course Schedules	*T-14*
Two-Quarter Schedule	*T-14*
Two-Semester Schedule	*T-15*
One-Semester Schedule	*T-16*

PROGRAM COMPONENTS

Classroom Resources

Annotated Edition with Student Template CD-ROM

TEACHING RESOURCES

- Classroom Presentations with Presentations CD-ROM
- School-to-Work Strategies
- Internet Manual
- Cross-Curriculum Guide
- Spanish Glossary
- Certification Procedures
- Instructional Video

ASSESSMENT RESOURCES

Assessment Resources Binder

- Test Bank with Test Bank CD-ROM
- Mid-Term and Final Exams with Exams Disk
- Alternative Assessment Guide

- Solutions Manual with Solutions CD-ROM
- Projects Manual with Projects Disk
- Portfolio Builder with Portfolio Template Disk

T-4

Inside the Annotated Edition

Introduction

The Annotated Edition of PowerPoint 97 is a comprehensive resource designed to make teaching easy and efficient, whether you're a novice instructor or have many years of experience. You'll find icons on the left of the student page and extensive annotations at the bottom of the page. The annotations contain a wealth of ideas, including helpful strategies for teaching the basic skills that form the core of this course. You'll want to tailor your teaching to your own preferences and to your students' interests and abilities by choosing among the many activities offered for each unit and lesson. The *Annotated Edition* also shows you how to integrate the various components in the *Classroom Resources* into your teaching.

Teaching Plan

For each lesson, the *Annotated Edition* presents a four-step teaching plan: Prepare, Teach, Close, and Assess.

PREPARE

Focus students' attention on the Objectives—the key skills taught in a lesson. Each heading in a lesson correlates to an Objective.

Prepare your computer by making sure that the files required in the lesson are loaded on your computer and the computers used by your students.

Note that the Estimated Time applies only to self-study situations. It represents the estimated time that a student will take to complete a lesson. It does not include time spent for such end-of-lesson activities as Using Help, Concepts Review, Skills Review, or Lesson Applications.

TEACH

The TEACH portion of the teaching plan represents the heart of the lesson. It always begins with a list of the **Teaching Resources**. Use this list to preview and choose among the program components available for use with the lesson.

An **Objective Number** identifies the Objective associated with each heading.

An Icon identifies the key screen images included in the **Classroom Presentation** for the lesson. These slide shows include many of the screens that students will encounter in the lesson. Using a Presentation rather than working through the lesson in front of the class gives you more time for hands-on teaching. Presentations correlate to the lesson number (Presentation #1 is used with Lesson 1, and so on).

A **Checked Objective Number** indicates that an assignment can be given after teaching the Objective. An **Objective Assignment** annotation identifies the **Skills Review Exercises** or the **Lesson Applications Exercises** that relate to the Objective being taught. This becomes particularly important when a lesson must be taught over a number of class periods. It ensures that students have the opportunity to reinforce their learning prior to finishing the lesson in class.

NOTE Notes appear throughout the **Annotated Edition**. A Note icon at the left of the student page marks text that is referenced by a Note annotation at the bottom of the page. Notes provide helpful teaching strategies, suggestions for reteaching, or teaching alternatives. They can also help you troubleshoot computer problems in the classroom, making sure that students' computers have the correct settings and

INSIDE THE ANNOTATED EDITION

CLOSE

CLOSE, the third step in the teaching plan, is used to determine whether students have mastered the Objectives of the lesson. Providing students with a variety of ways to demonstrate what they have learned gives you the opportunity to evaluate their progress and to identify students who need additional reinforcement through reteaching and practice.

TEST BANK The Test Bank, in the **Assessment Resources** binder, provides additional questions for reviewing lesson concepts.

True/False Questions and **Short Answer Questions** allow students to quickly check their understanding.

Critical Thinking asks students to examine the way they work, to connect their learning with their experiences, and to move outside the textbook into the real world for answers.

Skills Review provides guided practice for students. When a skill taught in the lesson is introduced in a Skills Review Exercise, students are guided through the particular skill using "a, b, c" steps.

A **Disk Icon** appearing opposite the first step in the Exercise indicates that the student will load files in the Exercise. An **Exercise Annotation** found at the bottom of the page indicates which Objectives are taught in the Exercise, which files are required to complete the Exercise, and which files are shown in the **Solutions Manual** and on the **Solutions Disk**.

ASSESS

The final step in the teaching plan is to evaluate student understanding of the concepts and procedures presented. The ASSESS part of the teaching plan always

that all of the required components are installed.

Two Notes that occur at the end of the lesson are especially significant. One focuses on the Command Summary—a feature that shows students how to use a toolbar button, a menu choice, or a keyboard command to accomplish a specific task. You may need to help students understand their choices and select the method appropriate for the task at hand.

Often, the last Note in the lesson highlights the Using Help feature. Because software companies no longer provide extensive documentation, any software user must know how to use the Help system. Using Help familiarizes students with PowerPoint's Help system and introduces advanced topics related to the lesson content.

T-6

begins with a list of **Assessment Resources**. Use this list to preview and choose among the resources available in the **Classroom Resources** box.

💾 **Lesson Applications** provide independent practice for students. As with the

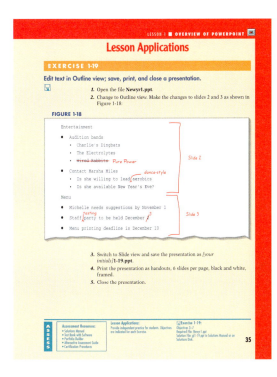

Skills Review Exercises, a **Disk Icon** opposite the first step indicates that the student will load and save files in the Lesson Application. An **Exercise Annotation** at the bottom of the page indicates which Objectives are taught by the Lesson Application, which files are required by the Application, and which files are shown in the **Solutions Manual** and on the **Solutions Disk**.

Lesson Applications are arranged by level of difficulty. The first Lesson Application will be less challenging for most students than the second Lesson Application, and so on.

📁 At least two Lesson Applications will be marked with the **Portfolio Icon**, indicating that the document produced in the Application may be added to a student's portfolio. Currently many schools are using student portfolios, into which students place samples of their work. The **Portfolio Builder** manual in the **Classroom Resources** discusses this method of assessment in detail.

At the end of each unit, **Unit Applications** provide an additional opportunity to assess students. They begin with a list detailing the appropriate **Assessment Resources**. Use this list to preview and choose among the resources available in the **Classroom Resources** box.

Annotations indicate which **Project** can be assigned to students upon completion of the Unit Applications. The **Project Manual** in the **Classroom Resources** includes a challenging project for each unit in the student edition. These projects may be assigned as a means of additional assessment or used as extra-credit assignments.

If appropriate, annotations will indicate that a **Mid-Term Exam** or a **Final Exam** can be assigned after completion of the Unit Applications. The **Mid-Term and Final Exams** booklet in the **Assessment Resources** binder contains exams for use throughout the course.

Just as with the Skills Review Exercises, a **Disk Icon** appearing opposite the first step indicates that the student will load and save files in the Application. The **Exercise Annotation** at the bottom of the page indicates which files are required by the Application, and which files are shown in the **Solutions Manual** and on the **Solutions Disk**.

With this system you'll have more teaching resources at your fingertips than have ever been assembled for a computer-applications course. We hope it makes your teaching experience easier and more rewarding.

T-7

Teaching Resources

Annotated Edition

The *Annotated Edition* provides a variety of teaching strategies and support aids using marginal Notes and Annotations at the bottom of the page. You can use the ideas provided to develop and enhance your lesson plans. The *Annotated Edition* references all the Teaching Resources and the Assessment Resources in the *Classroom Resource* box. This information makes the *Annotated Edition* your indispensable master guide.

PowerPoint Classroom Presentations

A PowerPoint Classroom Presentation is available for every lesson in the student text. Each Presentation lists the Objectives for the lesson and includes the important graphic screens that students will encounter in the lesson. The PowerPoint Classroom Presentations booklet explains how to integrate the Presentations into various classroom and lab settings.

School-to-Work Strategies Manual

Computer-applications instructors, more than most other instructors, are keenly aware of the need to prepare their students for the workforce. This booklet outlines the issues associated with the federal Tech Prep/Applied Academics Reform Initiative. It also describes many programs and strategies for teaching students who will go directly into the workforce. Use this booklet as a resource to help students avail themselves of helpful programs. You may also use the information to set up programs for this purpose within your school and community.

Internet Manual

The *Internet Manual* provides a brief introduction to the Internet and suggests Internet projects related to computer applications. The projects can be used as enrichment material or extra-credit assignments. They may also be used by those students who will be working in an environment that will require knowledge of the Internet.

Spanish Glossary

A major segment of the U.S. population speaks Spanish as a first language. The *Spanish Glossary* lists English computer terms followed by their Spanish translation and definition.

Certification Procedures

Certification Procedures describes the existing certification procedures from professional associations and from Microsoft for students, instructors, and trainers using Microsoft PowerPoint.

Instructional Video

An instructional video describes how to use all the components of the *Classroom Resources* box in conjunction with the *Annotated Edition*.

Assessment Resources

Assessment Resources Binder

The *Assessment Resources Binder* collects three valuable assessment tools in a single easy-to-access binder: the *Test Bank*, the *Mid-Term and Final Exams* booklet, and the *Alternative Assessment Guide*.

TEST BANK

Test-preparation software enables you to develop tailor-made lesson, unit, mid-term, or final exams. You can customize your tests as desired, choosing from the bank of questions provided or adding your own questions. The *Test Bank* guide fully describes how to use the test-preparation software.

MID-TERM AND FINAL EXAMS

Mid-term and final exams are provided in both reproducible form and on disk. The *Mid-Term and Final Exams* guide also contains a key for all the exams and a reproducible Certificate of Completion (which is also included on the Exams disk).

ALTERNATIVE ASSESSMENT GUIDE

The *Alternative Assessment Guide* is a collection of articles that examine many of the alternative assessment methods available to the computer-applications instructors. It includes an overview of various assessment methods and specific discussions of authentic assessment, rubrics, portfolios, and criteria-based evaluations.

Solutions Manual

The *Solutions Manual* shows the solution documents for every Exercise in the student text. Solution files are included on Solution disks. For assessment purposes, you can print a solution file on an acetate. You can then lay the acetate over your students' work to correct it.

Projects Manual

The *Projects Manual* contains challenging projects for each unit in the student text. The *Projects Manual* also shows the solution documents for each project. For assessment purposes, the solution files are included on a Projects disk. The Projects Manual also includes an "Assessment Checklist" for each project.

Portfolio Builder

The *Portfolio Builder* provides assistance in implementing the portfolio assessment method in your classroom. It includes a discussion of the capstone "Portfolio Builder" project.

Using the Case Study

Many of your students won't have extensive business experience, or experience with computer applications. They'll be learning a skill without a context in which to apply it. That's why the student text includes a Case Study.

All the lessons in the student edition relate to Good 4 U, a fictional restaurant located in New York City.

Encourage students to read about Good 4 U on page 2. Every effort has been made to make the company realistic. The presentations on which the students will work refer to on-going work at Good 4 U.

Review page 3 with students. This page establishes the students as "interns" at Good 4 U. Take time to discuss the three "foundation skills" and five "competencies" identified by the Secretary of Labor (and introduced in the *SCANS Report for America 2000*).

Page 4 identifies the key people at Good 4 U. Reviewing these profiles will heighten the students' sense of reality as they develop presentations for Good 4 U.

Review with students the "Tips for Designing Presentations" on page 5. Because many students have no experience with a presentations graphic program, it may be helpful to review the presentation on pages 6 and 7 with them.

Finally, tell students that the Preview on page 8 represents actual presentations, handouts, and notes that they will produce in the course.

Using the Appendices

If students haven't used the latest version of Windows before, but they have used an earlier version, suggest that they review Appendix A: "Windows Tutorial." If your entire class is unfamiliar with the latest version of Windows, you may want to review Appendix A together.

Appendix B: "Using the Mouse" and Appendix C: "Using Menus and Dialog Boxes" are recommended for students who have never used Windows in any version.

Appendix D: "PowerPoint Toolbars" shows the most widely used PowerPoint toolbars. Each button on the toolbar is identified. This is a helpful reference for students who may forget what toolbar contains a specific button.

Appendix E: "File Management" explains how information is stored in Windows and introduces students to the Windows Explorer. File management is extremely important in this course and experience with the Windows Explorer will make the job of managing files easier.

Appendix F: "Proofreader's Marks" should be referred to whenever students are asked in the student text to edit text that contains proofreader's marks. The ability to understand and interpret proofreader's marks is an important skill in any computer applications course.

Appendix G: "Multimedia and Pack and Go" describes how to add video and audio clips to a presentation. It also describes how to use PowerPoint's Pack and Go feature.

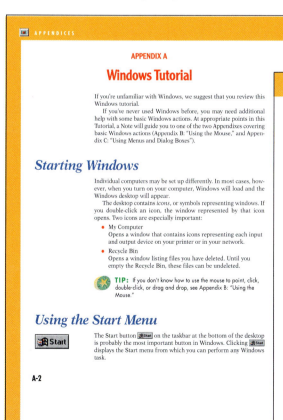

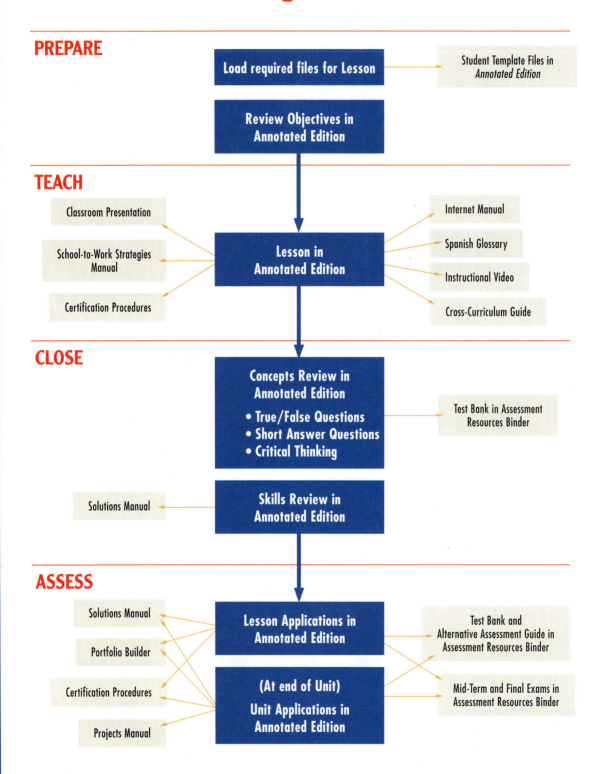

Using the Portfolio Builder

What Is a Portfolio?

A portfolio is an organized collection of documents used by the student and the instructor to reflect on the development of a student's content knowledge, skills, and use of learning strategies.

The two most common types of portfolios are:

- Developmental portfolios
- Representational portfolios.

Developmental portfolios document a student's growth over a period of time. This type of portfolio provides an opportunity for students to begin assessing their level of skill, to make them aware of the need for that skill in the work world, and to help them identify and plan for improving their skills. Developmental portfolios are often used as an alternative means of assessment. The *Portfolio Builder* manual discusses developmental portfolios in detail.

A representational Portfolio Builder is also included in *PowerPoint 97: A Professional Approach*.* This type of Portfolio Builder contains only the best work created by the student and can be used for employment purposes. The *Portfolio Builder* also can be effectively used as a capstone project, allowing students to evaluate their individual skill level in relation to a targeted employment goal.

The Portfolio Builder

To further assist students in their employment search and interview process, the Portfolio Builder guides students through the preparation of a resume and an application letter. It discusses what students will encounter in a job interview and helps them focus their job search on prospective local employers.

All of the documents prepared by the student for their representational portfolio are aimed at specific local employers that the student has researched. Sample documents are illustrated and possible types of documents are suggested for inclusion in the portfolio. Ultimately, the representational Portfolio Builder can increase the employment chances for your students. It may be assigned as an extra-credit project, a capstone project for assessment, or as a self-study project for students who want to collect a representational portfolio of their work for employment purposes.

---

* In the *PowerPoint 97: A Comprehensive Approach* program, the representational Portfolio Builder is included in a reproducible format in the *Portfolio Builder* manual.

Two-Quarter Schedule

(90-minute periods for 11 weeks, meeting twice a week, for 33 class-contact hours per quarter)

UNITS	LESSONS	CLASS PERIODS
UNIT 1 **Introduction to PowerPoint**	*1* Overview of PowerPoint	3
	2 Creating a Presentation Automatically	3
	Project 1	2
UNIT 2 **Working with Presentations**	*3* Starting with a Blank Presentation	3
	4 Using Outline View	3
	Mid-Term Exam 1	1
	5 Working with Text**	3
	Project 2	1
UNIT 3 **Customizing a Presentation**	*6* Working with PowerPoint Objects	3
	7 Working with Lines, Fills, and Colors	3
	8 Manipulating PowerPoint Objects**	4
	Project 3	2
END OF QUARTER	Final Exam 1	1
UNIT 4 **Customizing—Beyond the Basics**	*9* Advanced Text Manipulation	4
	10 Advanced Drawing Techniques**	4
	Project 4	2
UNIT 5 **Advanced Topics**	*11* Creating a Chart	3
	12 Creating a Table	3
	Mid-Term Exam 2	1
	13 Creating Flowcharts and Organization Charts	4
	14 Animation and Slide Show Effects	3
	15 Using the Internet**	4
	Project 5	2
	Capstone Project: Portfolio Builder	2
	Final Exam 2	1

END OF QUARTER

* To increase in-class lecture time, Projects may be assigned for completion outside class.

** Includes completion of Unit Applications.

COURSE SCHEDULES

Two-Semester Schedule

(90-minute periods for 16 weeks, meeting twice a week, for 48 class-contact hours per semester)

UNITS	LESSONS	CLASS PERIODS
UNIT 1 **Introduction to PowerPoint**	*1* Overview of PowerPoint	4
	2 Creating a Presentation Automatically**	4
	Project 1	3
UNIT 2 **Working with Presentations**	*3* Starting with a Blank Presentation	4
	4 Using Outline View	5
	Mid-Term Exam 1	2
	5 Working with Text**	4
	Project 2	3
UNIT 3 **Customizing a Presentation**	*6* Working with PowerPoint Objects	5
	7 Working with Lines, Fills, and Colors	4
	8 Manipulating PowerPoint Objects**	5
	Project 3	3
END OF SEMESTER	Final Exam 1	2
UNIT 4 **Customizing—Beyond the Basics**	*9* Advanced Text Manipulation	5
	10 Advanced Drawing Techniques**	6
	Project 4	3
UNIT 5 **Advanced Topics**	*11* Creating a Chart	5
	12 Creating a Table	4
	Mid-Term Exam 2	2
	13 Creating Flowcharts and Organization Charts	5
	14 Animation and Slide Show Effects	4
	15 Using the Internet**	6
	Project 5	3
	Capstone Project: Portfolio Builder	3
	Final Exam 2	2

END OF SEMESTER

* To increase in-class lecture time, Projects may be assigned for completion outside class.

** Includes completion of Unit Applications.

T-15

One-Semester Schedule

CORE LESSONS

UNIT 1
Introduction to PowerPoint
 1 Overview of PowerPoint
 2 Creating a Presentation Automatically

UNIT 2
Working with Presentations
 3 Starting with a Blank Presentation
 4 Using Outline View
 5 Working with Text

UNIT 3
Customizing a Presentation
 6 Working with PowerPoint Objects
 7 Working with Lines, Fills, and Colors

UNIT 5
Advanced Topics
 14 Creating Slide Show Effects

OPTIONAL LESSONS

UNIT 3
Customizing a Presentation
 8 Manipulating PowerPoint Objects

UNIT 4
Customizing—Beyond the Basics
 9 Advanced Text Manipulation
 10 Advanced Drawing Techniques

UNIT 5
Advanced Topics
 11 Creating a Chart
 12 Creating a Table
 13 Creating Flowcharts and Organization Charts
 15 Using the Internet

SKILL EMPHASIS

By adding two or more "Optional" Lessons to the "Core" Lessons, individual one-semester courses can be tailored to particular student or class requirements.

Emphasis on Advanced Text and Drawing
 8 Manipulating PowerPoint Objects
 9 Advanced Text Manipulation
 10 Advanced Drawing Techniques

Emphasis on Charts and Tables
 11 Creating a Chart
 12 Creating a Table
 13 Creating Flowcharts and Organization Charts

Annotated Edition

PowerPoint 97

A PROFESSIONAL APPROACH

Margaret Marple
MMPC
Norwalk, CT

Sharon Fisher-Larson
Elgin Community College
Elgin, IL

New York, New York   Columbus, Ohio   Woodland Hills, California   Peoria, Illinois

This program has been prepared with the assistance of Gleason Group, Inc., Norwalk, CT.

Editorial Director: Pamela Ross

Developmental Editor: Thomas Cain

Copy Editor: Beth Conover

Composition: PDS Associates, Creative Ink

Screens were captured using CaptureEze 97 from Application Techniques, Inc., Pepperell, MA.

Glencoe/McGraw-Hill
A Division of The **McGraw·Hill** *Companies*

PowerPoint 97: A Professional Approach
Student Edition
ISBN 0-02-803323-X

PowerPoint 97: A Comprehensive Approach
Student Edition
ISBN 0-02-803351-5

PowerPoint 97: A Professional Approach
Annotated Instructor's Edition
ISBN 0-02-803327-2

PowerPoint 97: A Comprehensive Approach
Teacher's Annotated Edition
ISBN 0-02-803358-2

Copyright © 1999 by The McGraw-Hill Companies, Inc. All rights reserved. Printed in the United States of America. Except as permitted under the United States copyright Act of 1976, no part of this publication may be reproduced or distributed in any form or by any means, or stored in a data base or retrieval system, without the prior written permission of the publisher.

1 2 3 4 5 6 7 8 9 10 027 03 02 01 00 99 98 97

Microsoft, PowerPoint, and Windows are either registered trademarks or trademarks of Microsoft Corporation in the United States and/or other countries.

PostScript is a registered trademark of Adobe Systems, Inc.

Contents

Preface	ix
Installation Requirements	xii
Case Study	*1*

UNIT 1

Introduction to PowerPoint — 9

Lesson 1 ***Overview of PowerPoint*** — *10*

Starting PowerPoint	10
Navigating in PowerPoint	13
Keying Text on a Slide	17
Using the View Buttons	18
Naming and Saving a Presentation	22
Printing Slides and Handouts	24
Closing Presentations and Exiting PowerPoint	26
USING HELP	27
CONCEPTS REVIEW	29
SKILLS REVIEW	30
LESSON APPLICATIONS	35

Lesson 2 ***Creating a Presentation Automatically*** — *39*

Using the AutoContent Wizard	39
Changing Sample Text in Slide View	41
Using the Spelling Checker and Style Checker	44
Making Changes in Slide Sorter View	48
Adding Headers and Footers	51
Choosing Print Options	54
USING HELP	56
CONCEPTS REVIEW	57
SKILLS REVIEW	58
LESSON APPLICATIONS	63
UNIT 1 APPLICATIONS	**69**

CONTENTS

UNIT 2

Working with Presentations — 75

Lesson 3 Starting with a Blank Presentation — 76

- Choosing a Slide Layout — 76
- Adding New Slides in Slide View — 78
- Changing Bullet Levels — 80
- Changing Slide Layouts — 82
- Changing the Design Template — 83
- Working with Speaker's Notes — 86
- USING HELP — 88
- CONCEPTS REVIEW — 90
- SKILLS REVIEW — 91
- LESSON APPLICATIONS — 96

Lesson 4 Using Outline View — 102

- Starting a Presentation in Outline View — 103
- Adding a New Slide in Outline View — 104
- Promoting and Demoting Outline Entries — 105
- Expanding a Slide — 107
- Creating a Summary Slide — 109
- Moving Bulleted Items in Outline View — 109
- Moving Slides in Outline View — 111
- Importing a Word Outline into PowerPoint — 113
- USING HELP — 117
- CONCEPTS REVIEW — 118
- SKILLS REVIEW — 119
- LESSON APPLICATIONS — 126

Lesson 5 Working with Text — 131

- Applying Text Attributes to Selected Text — 131
- Applying Attributes to Text Placeholders — 135
- Controlling Presentation Fonts — 137
- Working with Bullets — 138
- Changing Text Alignment — 140
- Changing Size and Position of Text Placeholders — 140
- Using Master Slides to Format Text — 144
- USING HELP — 149
- CONCEPTS REVIEW — 151
- SKILLS REVIEW — 152
- LESSON APPLICATIONS — 157
- **UNIT 2 APPLICATIONS** — 163

CONTENTS

UNIT 3

Customizing a Presentation 169

Lesson 6 Working with PowerPoint Objects 170

Using Clip Art 171
Format and Crop Clip Art 174
Using WordArt for Special Effects 176
Working with Floating Text Boxes 178
Rotating Text 180
Working with Basic Drawing Tools 182
Using Basic AutoShapes 186
Placing Text in a Graphic Object 188
USING HELP 190
CONCEPTS REVIEW 192
SKILLS REVIEW 193
LESSON APPLICATIONS 200

Lesson 7 Working with Lines, Fills, and Colors 206

Changing the Line Color and Style of Objects 206
Changing the Fill Color of Objects 209
Adding Patterns, Shading, and Textures 210
Using the Format Painter Tool 214
Adding Fill and Shading Effects to Master Slides and Backgrounds 215
Changing the Colors of a Clip Art Object 218
Changing a Presentation Color Scheme 219
Changing Black and White Settings 222
USING HELP 224
CONCEPTS REVIEW 225
SKILLS REVIEW 226
LESSON APPLICATIONS 233

Lesson 8 Manipulating PowerPoint Objects 238

Selecting Multiple Objects 238
Aligning, Flipping, and Distributing Objects 241
Grouping and Ungrouping Objects 244
Working with Layers of Objects 246
Applying Object Shadows and 3-D Effects 247
Using the Duplicate Command 250
Advanced Clip Art Editing 251

v

CONTENTS

USING HELP	254
CONCEPTS REVIEW	255
SKILLS REVIEW	256
LESSON APPLICATIONS	264
UNIT 3 APPLICATIONS	**271**

UNIT 4

Customizing—Beyond the Basics 281

Lesson 9 Advanced Text Manipulation 282

Working with Indents	282
Working with Tabs	285
Controlling Line Spacing	289
Working with Text Box Settings	290
Working with Page Setup Options	294
Customizing Handout and Notes Masters	296
CONCEPTS REVIEW	298
SKILLS REVIEW	299
LESSON APPLICATIONS	305

Lesson 10 Advanced Drawing Techniques 310

Using Guides to Position and Measure Objects	310
Using Zoom	313
Exploring the Snap and Nudge Features	314
Using the Freeform Tool	316
Editing a Freeform Drawing	320
Using the Curve Tool	321
CONCEPTS REVIEW	324
SKILLS REVIEW	325
LESSON APPLICATIONS	332
UNIT 4 APPLICATIONS	**336**

UNIT 5

Advanced Topics 341

Lesson 11 Creating a Chart 342

Inserting a Chart	342
Changing Sample Data	343
Viewing the New Chart	346

Editing a Chart	*347*
Formatting a Chart	*348*
Adding Shapes and Text Objects	*353*
Creating a Pie Chart	*354*
CONCEPTS REVIEW	*358*
SKILLS REVIEW	*359*
LESSON APPLICATIONS	*365*

Lesson **12** *Creating a Table* — *368*

Creating a Word Table	*368*
Keying Text in the Table	*370*
Using the Word Tables and Borders Toolbar	*371*
Working with Column Alignment	*374*
Recoloring a Word Table	*376*
Making Changes to a Table	*377*
CONCEPTS REVIEW	*379*
SKILLS REVIEW	*380*
LESSON APPLICATIONS	*385*

Lesson **13** *Creating Flowcharts and Organization Charts* — *390*

Drawing Flowchart AutoShapes	*390*
Connecting Flowchart AutoShapes	*391*
Inserting an Organization Chart	*394*
Adding Placeholder Boxes	*396*
Rearranging and Formatting Boxes	*398*
CONCEPTS REVIEW	*402*
SKILLS REVIEW	*403*
LESSON APPLICATIONS	*408*

Lesson **14** *Animation and Slide Show Effects* — *412*

Creating Transition Effects	*412*
Creating Text Animations	*415*
Creating Object Animations	*417*
Creating Chart Animations	*418*
Adding Animation Effects to a Template Design	*418*
Adding Hyperlinks	*419*
Timing Slides	*421*
CONCEPTS REVIEW	*423*
SKILLS REVIEW	*424*
LESSON APPLICATIONS	*427*

Lesson 15 Using the Internet — 430
Create Hyperlinks to Internet Sites — 430
Using an Internet Hyperlink — 432
Browsing the Web — 433
Creating a Presentation to Publish on the Internet — 436
Using Help — 441
UNIT 5 APPLICATIONS — 442

Portfolio Builder* P-1

Appendices

Appendix A: Windows Tutorial — A-2

Appendix B: Using the Mouse — A-11

Appendix C: Using Menus and Dialog Boxes — A-12

Appendix D: PowerPoint Toolbars — A-14

Appendix E: File Management — A-16

Appendix F: Proofreader's Marks — A-18

Appendix G: Multimedia and Pack and Go — A-19

Glossary — G-1
Index — I-1

*Available in *PowerPoint 97: A Professional Approach*

Preface

PowerPoint 97 has been written to help you master Microsoft PowerPoint for Windows. The text is designed to take you step-by-step through the features in PowerPoint that you are likely to use in both your personal and business life.

Case Study

Learning about the features of PowerPoint is one thing, but applying what you've learned is another. That's why a *Case Study* runs throughout the text. It offers you the opportunity to learn PowerPoint within a realistic business context. Take the time to read the Case Study about Good 4 U, a fictional restaurant set in New York City. All of the presentations for this course will deal with this restaurant business.

Organization of the Text

The text includes five *units*. Each unit is divided into smaller *lessons*. There are 15 lessons, each building on previously learned procedures. This building block approach, together with the Case Study and the features listed below, enables you to maximize your learning process.

Features of the Text

- ☑ *Objectives* are listed for each lesson
- ☑ The *estimated time* required to complete the lesson is stated
- ☑ Within a lesson, each *heading* corresponds to an objective
- ☑ *Exercises* that walk you through all procedures in a lesson are titled for easy reference
- ☑ *Key terms* are italicized and defined as they are encountered
- ☑ Extensive *graphics* display screen contents
- ☑ *Toolbar buttons* and *keyboard keys* are shown in the text when they are used

PREFACE

- *Large toolbar buttons in the margins* provide easy-to-see references
- Lessons contain important *Notes* and useful *Tips*
- A *Command Summary* lists the commands learned in the lesson
- *Using Help* introduces you to a Help topic related to the content of a lesson
- *Concepts Review* includes True/False, Short Answer, and Critical Thinking questions to focus on lesson content
- *Skills Review* provides skill reinforcement for each lesson
- *Lesson Applications* ask you to apply your skills in a more challenging way
- *Unit Applications* give you the opportunity to use all of the skills you learned throughout the unit
- Appendices
- Glossary
- Index

Conventions Used in the Text

This text uses a number of conventions to help you learn the program and save your work.

- Text that you are asked to key appears either in **boldface** or as a separate figure.
- Filenames appear in **boldface**.
- You will be asked to save each presentation with your initials, followed by the exercise name. For example, an exercise may end with the instruction: "Save the presentation as *[your initials]***5-12.ppt**."
- Menu letters you can key to activate a command are shown as they appear on screen, with the letter underlined (example: "Choose P̲rint from the File menu."). Dialog box options are also shown this way (example: "Click Fra̲me Slides in the Print dialog box.").

x

PREFACE

Applying the Read-Only Attribute

After loading and decompressing the files on the Student disks, we strongly recommend that you apply the read-only attribute to these files. This ensures that you do not write over a file that may be used in another exercise. It also requires that you to use the Save As command and rename the file using the naming convention specified in the text.

To apply the read-only attribute, select all the files in the Windows Explorer, choose Properties from the File menu, check the Read-only box, and click OK.

If You Are Unfamiliar with Windows

If you're unfamiliar with Windows, you'll want to work through *Appendix A: "Windows Tutorial"* before beginning Lesson 1. You may also need to review *Appendix B: "Using the Mouse"* and *Appendix C: "Using Menus and Dialog Boxes"* if you've never used a mouse or Windows before.

Screen Differences

As you read about and practice each concept, illustrations of the screens have been provided to help you follow the instructions. Don't worry if your screen has a somewhat different appearance than the screen illustration. These differences result from variations in system and computer configurations.

Acknowledgments

We would like to thank the many reviewers of this text, and those students and teachers who have used this book in the past, for their valuable assistance.

INSTALLATION REQUIREMENTS

Installation Requirements

To work with this textbook, you need Microsoft PowerPoint 97 installed on an IBM or IBM-compatible microcomputer's hard drive (or on a network). To properly install PowerPoint, refer to the PowerPoint manual that came with the program. Use the following checklist to evaluate the PowerPoint installation requirements.

Hardware

- ☑ Personal computer with a 486 or higher processor
- ☑ Hard disk drive
- ☑ 3.5-inch diskette drive
- ☑ 8 MB of RAM
- ☑ 26-58 MB of hard disk space; 48 MB required for a "Typical" installation
- ☑ VGA or higher-resolution video monitor (SVGA 256-color recommended)
- ☑ Printer (laser or ink-jet recommended)
- ☑ Mouse

Optional

- ☑ CD-ROM drive*
- ☑ 9600 baud or higher modem (14.4 baud recommended) and Internet functionality
- ☑ Multimedia computer required for sound and other multimedia effects

*The CD-ROM used to install PowerPoint 97 contains items used in this text, such as Microsoft Internet Explorer and extra clip art, which are not available on 3.5-inch diskettes.

Software

- ☑ PowerPoint 97 or Microsoft Office 97
- ☑ Windows 95

INSTALLATION REQUIREMENTS

What's Installed with PowerPoint 97

If PowerPoint is already installed, you may need to add components from the CD-ROM. For example, this textbook uses design templates and clip art that may not be on your computer. See the table on page xvi for a list of components installed during a "Typical" installation and others available when you perform a "Custom" installation.

To install a component:

1. Load the CD-ROM originally used for installation.
2. Click the Windows Start button, click Settings, and click Control Panel.
3. Double-click the Add/Remove Programs icon.
4. On the Install/Uninstall tab, click Add/Remove or Install, whichever is available.
5. Follow the Setup instructions. Click the item listed in the Options list in Setup. If you need to see more options for an item you selected, click the Change Option button.

Locating Design Templates

This textbook uses design templates from two template folders that should be on your hard drive: Presentation Designs and Presentations. Once you open the Design Template dialog box, click the Up One Level button to switch between these folders to locate a particular template.

To make sure both folders are easily accessible, add them to the Favorites folders. Then you can click Look in Favorites in the Design Template dialog box to locate the folders. To add a folder to the Favorites folders list, locate the folder, double-click its name, and click the Add to Favorites button.

If the design templates used in this textbook are not in either template folder on your computer, you can install them from the PowerPoint or Microsoft Office CD-ROM. See the previous instructions for installing a new component. Or, copy individual template files from the following locations on the CD-ROM:

\Template\Designs
\Template\Content
\Valupack\Template\Designs
\Valupack\Template\Present

xiii

INSTALLATION REQUIREMENTS

Adding Additional Clip Art

This textbook uses clip art provided on the Microsoft Office 97 CD-ROM. You can choose any available clip art or use the suggested clip art, which is identified by keyword. You find clip art by keyword using the Microsoft Clip Gallery. (The suggested clip art must be loaded in the Clip Gallery.)

There are three ways to access the clip art suggested in the textbook:

- Access the clip art directly from the CD-ROM (insert the disk before opening the Microsoft Clip Gallery.

- Install categories of clip art from the CD-ROM onto your hard drive. To do this, insert the CD-ROM into your disk drive. In the Clipart folder on the CD-ROM, double-click the file **setup.exe** to start the Microsoft Clipart Extra installation program. Click Custom. Under Options, check Office, Popular, and PowerPoint and clear the remaining check boxes. This method, which requires 125 MB disk space, installs over 3,000 images directly into the Microsoft Clip Gallery.

- Copy from the CD-ROM only the files used in this textbook, which are listed by filename and path in the following table. (Ask your instructor if you can access these files from a folder on a server.) You can then insert the file by filename using the Insert, Picture, From File command. (You'll be able to view the picture in the Insert Picture dialog box before inserting it.) Alternatively, you can open the Microsoft Clip Gallery, click the Import Clips button, and locate the filename. This method adds the image to the Clip Gallery. You can include a keyword for future reference and place the picture in a category. You can then insert the picture in your presentation.

INSTALLATION REQUIREMENTS

Clip Art Used in Textbook

Filename	Path	Where Used
1stplace.wmf	D:\Clipart\Office\1stplace.wmf	Lesson 6
Couple3.wmf	D:\Clipart\Office\Couple3.wmf	Unit 3
Dancers.wmf	D:\Clipart\Office\Dancers.wmf	Unit 3
Frtbskt1.wmf	D:\Clipart\Office\Frtbskt1.wmf	Lesson 6
Grapes6.wmf	D:\Clipart\Office\Grapes6.wmf	Lesson 8
Handshk1.wmf	D:\Clipart\Office\Handshk1.wmf	Unit 4
Jogger3.wmf	D:\Clipart\Office\Jogger3.wmf	Unit 3
Jogger4.wmf	D:\Clipart\Office\Jogger4.wmf	Unit 3
Jogger5.wmf	D:\Clipart\Office\Jogger5.wmf	Unit 3
Laward.wmf	D:\Clipart\Office\Laward.wmf	Unit 3
Meal2.wmf	D:\Clipart\Office\Meal2.wmf	Lesson 6
Pencil.wmf	D:\Clipart\Office\Pencil1.wmf	Unit 3
Phonesym.wmf	D:\Clipart\Office\Phonesym.wmf	Lesson 13
Sailing.wmf	D:\Clipart\Office\Sailing.wmf	Lesson 8
Sailing4.wmf	D:\Clipart\Office\Sailing4.wmf.	Lesson 6
Sandtoys.wmf	D:\Clipart\Office\Sandtoys.wmf	Lesson 8
Sprint.wmf	D:\Clipart\Office\Sprint.wmf	Lesson 8
Writegrp.wmf	D:\Clipart\Office\Writegrp.wmf	Lesson 7
Meeting.wmf	D:\Clipart\Popular\Meeting.wmf	Unit 3
Basebal2.wmf	D:\Clipart\Powerpnt\Basebal2.wmf	Lesson 9
Circarro.wmf	D:\Clipart\Powerpnt\Circarro.wmf	Lesson 8
Coins3.wmf	D:\Clipart\Powerpnt\Coins3.wmf	Lesson 6
Disk.wmf	D:\Clipart\Powerpnt\Disk.wmf	Lesson 6
Firewks.wmf	D:\Clipart\Powerpnt\Firewks.wmf	Unit 3
Gldngate.wmf	D:\Clipart\Powerpnt\Gldngate.wmf	Lesson 7
Globewst.wmf	D:\Clipart\Powerpnt\Globewst.wmf	Lesson 14
People1.wmf	D:\Clipart\Powerpnt\People1.wmf	Lesson 6
Plum.wmf	D:\Clipart\Powerpnt\Plum.wmf	Lesson 6
Puzzle.wmf	D:\Clipart\Powerpnt\Puzzle.wmf	Lesson 6
Soup.wmf	D:\Clipart\Powerpnt\Soup.wmf	Lesson 6
Wheat.wmf	D:\Clipart\Powerpnt\Wheat.wmf	Lesson 7
Lecture.wmf	D:\Clipart\Powerpoint\Lecture.wmf	Unit 3
Agree.wmf	D:\Program Files\Microsoft Office\Clipart\Popular\Agree.wmf	Lesson 6
Car.wmf	D:\Program Files\Microsoft Office\Clipart\Popular\Car.wmf	Lesson 10
Dancers2.wmf	D:\Program Files\Microsoft Publisher\Clipart\Dancers2.wmf	Lesson 6

For current information about the components included in PowerPoint 97, see the **Ppread8.txt** file in your Microsoft Office\Office folder (or Microsoft Office folder if you installed stand-alone PowerPoint).

XV

INSTALLATION REQUIREMENTS

PowerPoint Component	Installed Option with Typical?	Office Setup Option	PowerPoint Setup
PowerPoint Program Files	Yes	PowerPoint; PowerPoint Program Files	PowerPoint Program Files
Templates:			
Typical content	Yes	PowerPoint; Typical Content Templates	Typical Content Templates
Additional content	No	PowerPoint; Additional Content Templates	Additional Content Templates
Design templates	Yes	PowerPoint; Design Templates	Design Templates
Web publishing tools	No	Web Page Authoring (HTML)	Web Page Authoring (HTML)
Help	Yes	PowerPoint; Help; Help for PowerPoint	Help; Help for PowerPoint
Sounds	Yes	PowerPoint; Animation Effects Sounds	Animation Effects Sounds
Clip art	Yes	PowerPoint; PowerPoint Program Files	PowerPoint Program Files
Office tools:			
Office Assistant	Yes	Office Tools	Office Assistant
Spelling Checker	Yes	Office Tools	Proofing Tools
Clip Gallery	Yes	Office Tools; Clip Gallery	Clip Gallery
Organization Chart	Yes	Office Tools; Organization Chart	Organization Chart
Microsoft Graph	Yes	Office Tools; Microsoft Graph	Microsoft Graph
Microsoft Graph Help	Yes	Office Tools; Microsoft Graph Help	Microsoft Graph Help
Equation Editor	No	Office Tools; Equation Editor	Equation Editor
Microsoft Photo Editor	No	Office Tools; Microsoft Photo Editor	Microsoft Photo Editor
TrueType fonts	Yes	Office Tools; Microsoft TrueType Fonts	Microsoft TrueType Fonts
Graphics import and export filters	Some	Converters and Filters; Graphics Filters	Graphics Filters
Getting Results Book	Yes	Getting Results Book	Not available

CASE STUDY

There's more to learning a presentation graphics program like Microsoft PowerPoint than simply keying text on colored backgrounds and calling the result a "presentation." You need to know how to use PowerPoint in a real-world situation. That's why all the lessons in this book relate to everyday business tasks.

As you work through lessons, imagine yourself working as an intern for Good *4 U*, a fictional New York restaurant featuring healthy food and promoting an active life-style.

CASE STUDY
Good 4 U
900 Central Park South
New York, NY 10019
(212) 555-4663

Good 4 U has been in business for only a little over three years—but it's been a success from the time it served its first veggie burger. The restaurant—which features healthy food and has a theme based on the "everyday active life"—seems to have found an award-winning recipe for success.

The food at Good 4 U is all low-fat. While not vegetarian, the menu features lots of vegetables (all organic, of course!), as well as fish and chicken. The restaurant doesn't serve alcohol, instead offering fruit juices and sparkling water.

Good 4 U's theme of "everyday active life" is reflected on the restaurant's walls, which are covered with in-line skating, running, tennis, and bicycling memorabilia. (The pictures opening each unit in the text depict some of the sports activities enjoyed by regular customers.)

CASE STUDY

Working As an Intern

You'll be working as an intern at Good 4 U. This position involves assisting with a few different projects until you've had a chance to experience working with most of the company's departments. You'll be working primarily with Roy Olafsen, the Marketing Manager (see "Key People at Good 4 U," on the next page). Good 4 U management stresses that this experience is your "trial period" in which you have an opportunity to demonstrate your skills.

Good 4 U, like other businesses, expects that any incoming employee will have a solid foundation of skills* that includes:

Basic Skills
Reading, writing, arithmetic/mathematics, listening, and speaking

Thinking Skills
Creative thinking, decision making, problem solving, being able to visualize problems and solutions, knowing how to learn, and reasoning

Personal Qualities
Responsibility, self-esteem, sociability, self-management, and integrity/honesty

In addition, Good 4 U believes that the five competencies identified below are the keys to job-performance.

Keys to Successful Job-Performance*

1. Resources: Identifies, organizes, plans, and allocates resources

A. *Time*—Selects goal-relevant activities, ranks them, allocates time, and prepares and follows schedules
B. *Money*—Uses or prepares budgets, makes forecasts, keeps record, and makes adjustments to meet objectives
C. *Material and Facilities*—Acquires, stores, allocates, and uses materials or space efficiently
D. *Human Resources*—Assesses skills and distributes work accordingly, evaluates performance and provides feedback

2. Interpersonal: Works with others

A. *Participates as a Member of a Team*—Contributes to the group effort
B. *Teaches Others New Skills*
C. *Serves Clients/Customers*—Works to satisfy customers' expectations
D. *Exercises Leadership*—Communicates ideas to justify a position, persuades and convinces others, responsibly challenges existing procedures and policies
E. *Negotiates*—Works toward agreements involving exchanges of resources, resolves differing interests
F. *Works with Diversity*—Works well with men and women from diverse backgrounds

3. Information: Acquires and uses information

A. *Acquires and Evaluates Information*
B. *Organizes and Maintains Information*
C. *Interprets and Communicates Information*
D. *Uses Computers to Process Information*

4. Systems: Understands complex relationships

A. *Understands Systems*—knows how social, organizational, and technological systems work and operates effectively with them
B. *Monitors and Corrects Performance*—Distinguishes trends, predicts impacts on system operations, diagnoses systems' performance and corrects malfunctions
C. *Improves or Designs Systems*—Suggests modifications to existing systems and develops new or alternative systems to improve performance

5. Technology: Works with a variety of technologies

A. *Selects Technology*—Chooses procedures, tools or equipment including computers and related technologies
B. *Applies Technology to Task*—Understands overall intent and proper procedures for setup and operation of equipment
C. *Maintains and Troubleshoots Equipment*—Prevents, identifies, or solves problems with equipment, including computers and other technologies

* These skills and competencies were identified by the Secretary of Labor and the Secretary's Commission on Achieving Necessary Skills (SCANS). They are included in the report *What Work Requires of Schools: A SCANS Report for America 2000*, published in June, 1991, by the U.S. Department of Labor.

CASE STUDY

Key People at Good 4U

In your work as an intern, you'll have a chance to meet many of the people who work at Good 4 U. You will certainly interact with the four key people profiled here. In fact, you'll be doing most of your work for Roy Olafsen, the Marketing Manager.

Gus Irvinelli
Co-owner

Gus Irvinelli was formerly a New York real-estate developer. He's an avid tennis player and was selected for the U.S. Amateur team. When he's not working at the restaurant or playing tennis, Gus runs an adoption program for greyhounds that have been retired from dog tracks. He can often be seen running in Central Park with one of his three greyhounds.

Julie Wolfe
Co-owner

Julie Wolfe led the New York Flash to two Women's Professional Basketball Association championships in her ten years with the team. When she retired, she started Good 4 U, explaining that "it was the sort of restaurant that I wanted to go to, but could never find." Today Julie keeps active by running in marathons. She's run in the New York City Marathon every year since she retired from basketball.

Michele Jenkins
Head Chef

Michele started her cooking career at the Culinary Institute of America in Hyde Park, New York. After working for five years in an upscale restaurant in New York, she quit to take a position in a small restaurant in the Provence region of France. While in France, Michele began long-distance bicycling. Now, she rides ten miles every day in and around Central Park.

Roy Olafsen
Marketing Manager

Two years ago, Roy Olafsen was a marketing manager for a large hotel chain. He was overweight and out-of-shape. In the same week that his doctor told him to eat better and exercise regularly, Roy received a job offer from Good 4 U. "It was too good to pass up," he says. "It was my chance to combine work and a healthy life style." On weekends or weeknights, Roy can be seen with his family skating in the park.

In your first meeting with Roy Olafsen, he gave you the following tips for designing presentations. These tips can be applied to any presentation, but can be modified, as needed.

Tips for Designing Presentations

- ✓ Every presentation should have a title slide. Make sure the title relates to the presentation content.
- ✓ Maintain a consistent color scheme throughout the presentation.
- ✓ Keep the background simple, making sure the text can be seen clearly.
- ✓ Avoid long lines of text. Avoid too many lines of text. No line should consist of more than seven words; no slide should consist of more than seven lines.
- ✓ Avoid small text. Text on slides should be no smaller than 24 points, text for overheads should be no smaller than 18 points.
- ✓ For bulleted text, avoid using a single bullet or more than five bullets per slide. Don't use more than two levels of bullets.
- ✓ Use consistent wording in bulleted text.
- ✓ Use clip art that relates to the content and doesn't distract from the message. Avoid the temptation to "jazz up" a slide show with too much clip art.
- ✓ Keep charts simple. The most effective charts are pie charts with three or four slices and column charts with three or four columns.
- ✓ Provide some form of handout so your audience can keep track of the presentation.
- ✓ Your final slide should provide a recommendation or summary.

CASE STUDY

Sample PowerPoint Presentation

This is a sample presentation to be delivered onscreen (on a computer) in a conference room. The audience includes Good *4 U* sales and marketing staff and the restaurant owners.

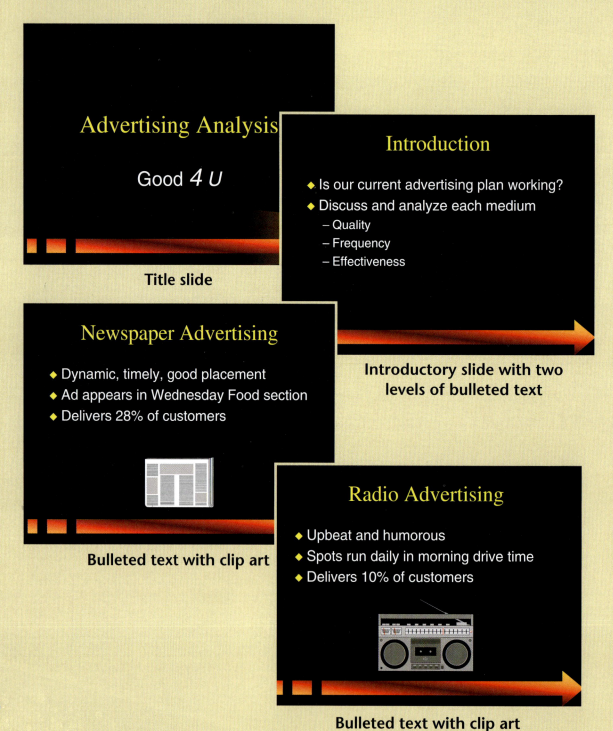

CASE STUDY

Mailers

- Two-for-one lunch coupons
- Mailers sent six times a year
- Delivers 12% of customers

Bulleted text with clip art

Yellow Pages

- Attractive display, prominent placement
- Ad appears in all metro editions
- Delivers 6% of customers

Bulleted text with clip art

Advertising Analysis

	% Customers Delivered	% Total Revenue
Newspaper	28%	30%
Radio	10%	5%
Mailers	12%	18%
Yellow Pages	6%	12%

Slide with a table

Advertising Budget

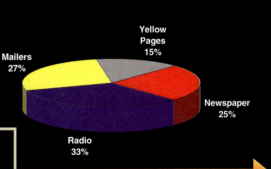

Yellow Pages 15%
Mailers 27%
Newspaper 25%
Radio 33%

Slide with a pie chart

Next Steps

- Evaluate current ad design/copy
- Meet with account executives
- Distribute customer questionnaire
- Submit media plan by next month

Closing slide

CASE STUDY

Preview

As you learn Microsoft PowerPoint, you'll produce professional presentations and handouts for Good *4 U*. You'll learn all the important PowerPoint features, from keying slide text and working with fills and colors to using templates and clip art.

You'll learn how to create charts and tables, and you'll display your presentations with an array of dazzling slide show effects. By "working" as an intern at Good *4 U*, you'll gain experience that you can apply to real-world business.

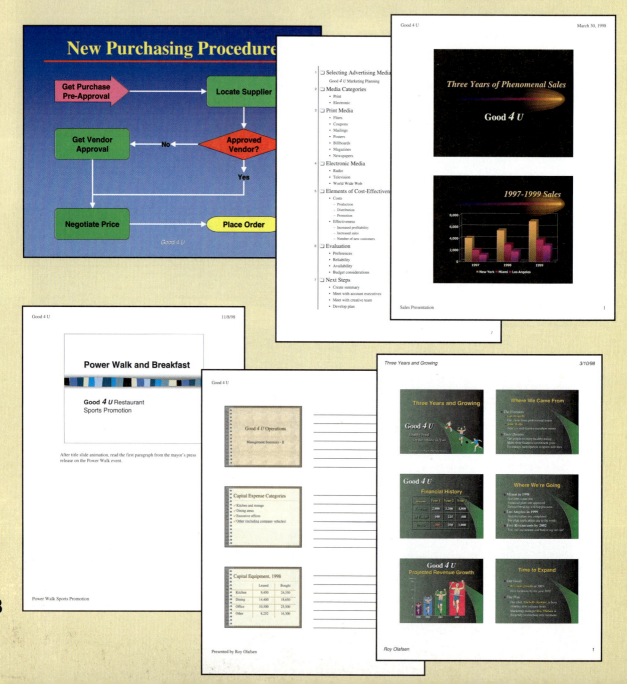

UNIT 1

Introduction to PowerPoint

LESSON 1 Overview of PowerPoint
LESSON 2 Creating a Presentation Automatically

LESSON 1
Overview of PowerPoint

OBJECTIVES After completing this lesson, you will be able to:
1. Start PowerPoint.
2. Navigate in PowerPoint.
3. Key text on a slide.
4. Use the view buttons.
5. Name and save a presentation.
6. Print slides and handouts.
7. Close a presentation and exit PowerPoint.

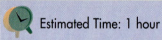
Estimated Time: 1 hour

Microsoft PowerPoint is a powerful but easy-to-use graphics program that you use to create professional-quality slide presentations. This lesson begins with an overview of many PowerPoint features and provides a road map of the five PowerPoint screen views.

Objective 1
Starting PowerPoint

NOTE

FIGURE 1-1
Shortcut icon to start PowerPoint

You can start PowerPoint several ways, depending how your system is set up. For example, you can use the Start button on the Windows taskbar or Windows Explorer. If a shortcut icon to start PowerPoint is on your Windows desktop, you can double-click it.

PREPARE
Point out to students that the learning objectives show what they will learn in the lesson. Each heading in the lesson correlates to a learning objective.
Required Files
Growing1.ppt

TEACH
Teaching Resources:
- PowerPoint Classroom Presentations
- School-to-Work Strategies Manual
- Internet Manual
- Spanish Glossary
- Methodology Video
- Certification Procedures

NOTE
Every computer in the classroom should access PowerPoint the same way. You may want to provide a handout to students describing how to access PowerPoint. This is especially true in a networked environment.

10

LESSON 1 ■ **OVERVIEW OF POWERPOINT**

  NOTE: Windows allows great flexibility in starting applications. If you have problems, ask your instructor for help.

EXERCISE 1-1 Start PowerPoint

1. Turn on your computer to load Windows.
2. Click the Start button on the Windows taskbar and point to Programs.

FIGURE 1-2
Starting PowerPoint from the Windows taskbar

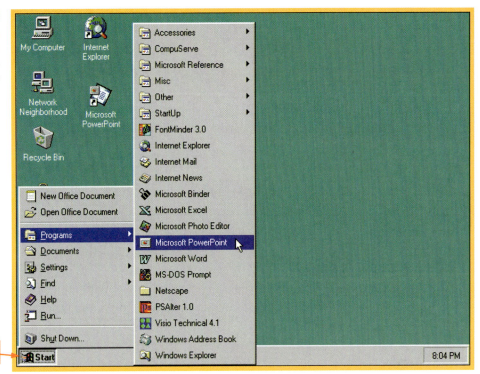

FIGURE 1-3
PowerPoint opening dialog box

3. On the submenu, click Microsoft PowerPoint. A dialog box opens in the PowerPoint window prompting you to create a new presentation or open an existing one (see Figure 1-3).

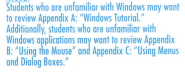
Students who are unfamiliar with Windows may want to review Appendix A: "Windows Tutorial." Additionally, students who are unfamiliar with Windows applications may want to review Appendix B: "Using the Mouse" and Appendix C: "Using Menus and Dialog Boxes."

Use PowerPoint Classroom Presentation #1 to display screens from the lesson, including this one, in a slide-show format.

UNIT 1 ■ INTRODUCTION TO POWERPOINT

EXERCISE 1-2 **Open an Existing Presentation**

1. In the PowerPoint opening dialog box, choose Open an existing presentation (next to the yellow file folder icon). Click OK or press the Enter key [Enter]. The Open dialog box appears. (Opening a PowerPoint presentation is similar to opening an Excel spreadsheet or Word document.)

2. Click the down arrow to the right of the Look in box to choose the appropriate drive and folder.

FIGURE 1-4
Files listed in the Open dialog box

Presentation files

NOTE: Your instructor will advise you which drive and folder to use in this course.

3. Locate and then click the filename **Growing1.ppt**. Click the Preview button to get a quick look at the presentation's first slide before opening it.

4. Click Open. (You can also double-click the filename to open the file.)

TABLE 1-1 **Open Dialog Box Buttons**

BUTTON	BUTTON NAME	PURPOSE
	Up One Level	Moves up one level in the hierarchy of folders or drives on your computer, or on computers connected to your computer.

continues

NOTE
Make sure students know where files for this course are located. All files are included on the "Student Template Disk." You can load these files on a hard disk or on a network. If this has not already been done, it will be necessary to load the files from the Student disk to a location where the students can access them.

In PowerPoint Classroom Presentation #1.

NOTE
Throughout the text, file extensions (".ppt") are displayed. If a computer doesn't show extensions, open Windows Explorer, choose Options from the View menu, and make sure the following option is not selected: "Hide MS-DOS file extensions for file types that are registered."

NOTE
You may want to review the buttons in the Open dialog box. These buttons are helpful for locating and viewing files. The same buttons appear in the Save As dialog box.

LESSON 1 ■ OVERVIEW OF POWERPOINT

TABLE 1-1   Open Dialog Box Buttons *continued*

BUTTON	BUTTON NAME	PURPOSE
	Search the Web	Opens the Search page of your Internet browser so you can search the Web for information.
	Look in Favorites	Goes to the location you designate as your "favorites" with the Add Favorites button.
	Add to Favorites	Adds the file or folder to the location where you have your most-used documents.
	List	Lists all folders and files by name.
	Details	Lists files with additional details, such as file size or last date modified.
	Properties	Lists more file details, such as author, date created, date modified, and number of revisions.
	Preview	Displays a thumbnail view of the first slide in the selected presentation.
	Commands and Settings	Use to perform other functions such as sorting the file list and printing.

Objective 2
Navigating in PowerPoint

If you are already familiar with other Windows programs, you'll feel right at home with PowerPoint. Although a number of new buttons appear in the PowerPoint window (see Figure 1-5 on the next page), it's easy to recognize similarities to the Microsoft Word and Microsoft Excel windows.

TABLE 1-2   Parts of the PowerPoint Window

PART	PURPOSE
Title bar	Contains the name of the presentation.
Menu bar	Displays the names of menus that you use to perform various tasks. You can open menus using the mouse or the keyboard.
Toolbars	Rows of buttons that give you instant access to a wide range of commands. Each button displays an icon and is accessed using the mouse. PowerPoint opens with the Standard, Formatting, Drawing, and Common Tasks toolbars displayed.

continues

NOTE
PowerPoint stores toolbar settings in a file called *[computer name]*.pcb in the Windows folder. For example, if a user on a computer named LAB42 changes the toolbars, PowerPoint creates lab42.pcb. It's a good idea to make a backup .pcb file right after installing PowerPoint and setting up the toolbars as you want your students to see them. Save it as default.pcb so you can restore the original toolbar settings at any time by copying default.pcb to *[computer name]*.pcb. (Under Windows NT 3.51, PowerPoint uses the user name rather than the machine name for the .pcb file, and will create multiple .pcb files, one for each user who logs on to the system and uses PowerPoint.)

UNIT 1 ■ INTRODUCTION TO POWERPOINT

TABLE 1-2 Parts of the PowerPoint Window *continued*

PART	PURPOSE
Scroll bars	Used with the mouse to move right or left and up or down within a slide. You can also use the vertical scroll bar to move from slide to slide.
View buttons	Five buttons located on the left side of the horizontal scroll bar, that you use to change the way you view a PowerPoint presentation.
Slide changer	Two double-arrow buttons—Previous Slide and Next Slide—located at the bottom of the vertical scroll bar, that are used to navigate from slide to slide.
Status bar	Displays information about the presentation you're working on.
Slide area	The area where you create, edit, and display presentation slides.
Office Assistant	Provides tips as you work and suggests Help topics related to the work you're doing.

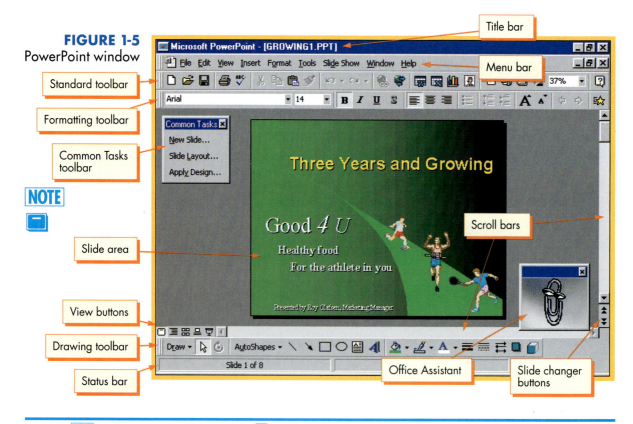

FIGURE 1-5
PowerPoint window

NOTE
The presentation name appears as "Growing1.ppt [Read-Only]" in the title bar. You may want to explain that all files loaded from the Student disk have the read-only protection to preserve the original file. Students must use Save As instead of Save, as explained in the section "Naming and Saving a Presentation" in this lesson.

In PowerPoint Classroom Presentation #1.

LESSON 1 ■ **OVERVIEW OF POWERPOINT**

EXERCISE 1-3 Display and Hide Toolbars

You can access most of PowerPoint's features from buttons on the toolbars. You can show or hide the toolbars and move them around the screen.

1. Using the right mouse button, click any visible toolbar to see the Toolbars menu. If it's not already visible, select Common Tasks to display the Common Tasks toolbar.

FIGURE 1-6
Toolbars menu

 NOTE: You can also choose Toolbars from the View menu to show or hide toolbars.

2. Move the mouse pointer over the title bar of the Common Tasks toolbar and drag the toolbar to the other side of your screen. This is an example of a "floating" toolbar.

3. Convert the Formatting toolbar from a "docked" toolbar to a "floating" toolbar. Click the two vertical gray bars at the left of the Formatting toolbar and drag it downward. You can now position it anywhere on your screen.

4. Return the Formatting toolbar to its docked position by double-clicking its title bar. You can also dock a toolbar by dragging it to the top, bottom, or side of the screen.

5. Hide the Office Assistant by clicking its Close button ⊠. Drag the Common Tasks toolbar to the upper left corner of the screen (below the Formatting toolbar).

TIP: Another way to hide the Office Assistant is to right-click it and choose Hide Assistant from the shortcut menu. You can also use the shortcut menu to choose another animated character.

EXERCISE 1-4 Identify Toolbar Buttons and Menu Items

NOTE

Some parts of the PowerPoint screen, such as toolbar buttons, are identified when you point to them with the mouse.

FIGURE 1-7
Identifying a toolbar button

1. Move the mouse pointer over the Increase Font Size button  toward the right side of the Formatting toolbar. PowerPoint displays a ToolTip—a box under the button that contains the button name. (In Lesson 5, you use this button to increase the size of text.)

NOTE
Point out that displayed toolbars appear on the Toolbars menu with a check mark. If you choose a toolbar with a check mark from the menu, you "uncheck" the toolbar and hide it from view.

In PowerPoint Classroom Presentation #1.

NOTE
You may want students to leave the Office Assistant activated or to hide the Common Tasks toolbar.

NOTE
To display a ToolTip, remind students they must point to the toolbar button and hold the pointer still. PowerPoint doesn't display tips unless the mouse hasn't moved for a second or so.

15

UNIT 1 ■ INTRODUCTION TO POWERPOINT

2. Move the mouse pointer to the Next Slide button ▼ at the bottom of the vertical scroll bar. Click this button to move to the next slide in the presentation.

NOTE

3. Point to other toolbar buttons to identify them by name.

4. To see more information about a toolbar button, press Shift + F1 and click a toolbar button. To close the information box, click it or press Esc.

5. Click File on the menu bar. Notice that many of the commands available from the File menu are the same as those found on the File menu in other Windows programs.

6. To close the File menu, click a blank area on the screen or press Esc.

NOTE

7. Explore other menus on the menu bar. Notice that the menus contain commands unique to PowerPoint, as well as commands common to other Windows applications.

EXERCISE 1-5 Move from Slide to Slide

PowerPoint provides several ways to move to other slides in a presentation using the mouse or the keyboard.

NOTE

1. Drag the vertical scroll box to the bottom of the scroll bar. Notice the boxes that display slide numbers and slide titles.

FIGURE 1-8
Dragging the vertical scroll box to move to another slide

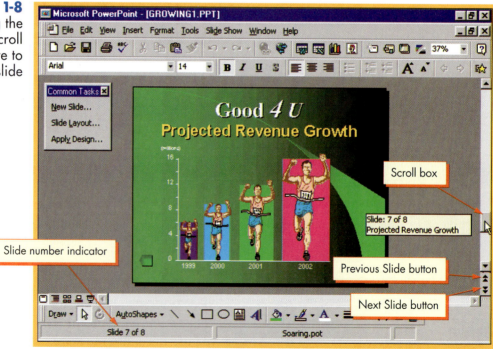

NOTE Point out that some toolbar icons appear in gray. For example, the Cut icon is gray unless something is selected.

NOTE Until students become used to Windows and the method of moving among menus, they may accidentally click the mouse button. This may also happen when moving the pointer over a toolbar button. You may have to instruct students how to close a dialog box or stop a procedure.

NOTE Students may be unfamiliar with the process of dragging screen elements. You might take this opportunity to demonstrate how to drag and ask the students to practice.

In PowerPoint Classroom Presentation #1.

16

LESSON 1 ■ **OVERVIEW OF POWERPOINT**

When you release the mouse button, slide 8 appears on your screen. Drag the scroll box up to display slide 7. Notice that the slide number is indicated on the left side of the status bar.

2. Click the Previous Slide ▲ button several times to move back in the presentation. Use the Next Slide ▼ button to move forward.

NOTE

3. As an alternative to clicking ▼ and ▲, press PgDn and PgUp several times. Use this method to move to slide 3.

Objective 3
Keying Text on a Slide

Editing text in PowerPoint is just like editing text in a word processor. You click to position the insertion point where you want to key new text and drag the pointer to select existing text. The keys Enter, Delete, and Backspace also work the same way.

EXERCISE 1-6 Edit Text on a Slide

1. With slide 3 displayed, click anywhere on the line containing the text "Gus came from a tennis background." Notice the box that surrounds the text. All PowerPoint text is contained in *text boxes*. The wide border made up of tiny diagonal lines indicates the text box is activated and in edit mode, meaning you can edit and insert text.

NOTE

2. Without clicking, move the mouse off the text box and then back on again. Notice that the pointer changes to an arrow outside a text box and to an I-beam inside it.

NOTE

3. Drag the I-beam across the text "a tennis background" to select it. (See Figure 1-9 on the next page.)

4. Key **professional tennis** to replace the selected text. As you can see, replacing text in PowerPoint is just like replacing text in Word.

5. To insert a new line, click the insertion point to the right of the words "healthy eating" near the bottom of the slide and press Enter. Notice that a new bullet appears at the beginning of the new line.

6. On the new blank bullet line, key **Make their financial investment grow**

7. Instead of a title, slide 3 contains a *placeholder*—a dotted box that is holding a place for the title. Click the placeholder text ("Click to add title") to activate the placeholder and key the title **Where We Came From**

8. Click a blank part of the slide area to deactivate the text box. To make sure you're clicking a blank area, click when the pointer is an arrow, not an I-beam.

NOTE
Another way to move from slide to slide is to click above or below the scroll box on the vertical scroll bar.

NOTE
Explain to students that if they click when they see an I-beam, they activate a text box for editing. To deactivate a text box, click outside the text box (when the pointer is an arrow).

NOTE
Students may be unfamiliar with the process of dragging the I-beam. You might take this opportunity to demonstrate how to drag and ask the students to practice. If necessary, refer students to Appendix B: "Using the Mouse."

17

UNIT 1 ■ INTRODUCTION TO POWERPOINT

FIGURE 1-9
Use the same methods to edit text as in a word processor.

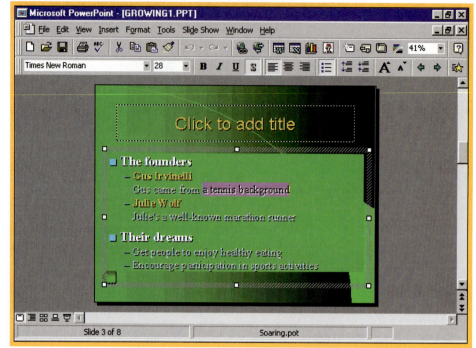

Objective 4
Using the View Buttons

You use the view buttons, located on the left side of the horizontal scroll bar, to work with your presentation in different ways. Until now, you have been working in Slide view. You can also work in Outline view, Slide Sorter view, and Notes Pages view, or you can view your presentation as a slide show. Each view has special features to help you create a polished presentation.

EXERCISE 1-7   Use Outline View

1. Click the Outline View button in the lower left corner of the screen (the left side of the horizontal scroll bar). Close the Common Tasks toolbar so you have a better view of the outline. Outline view displays only the text of the presentation and includes a miniature version of the slide you're working on.

   NOTE: If you don't see the slide miniature, right-click anywhere in the outline and choose Slide Miniature or choose View, Slide Miniature from the menu bar.

In PowerPoint Classroom Presentation #1.

18

LESSON 1 ■ OVERVIEW OF POWERPOINT

2. While still in Outline view, scroll down until you see the text for slide 5.

FIGURE 1-10
Working in Outline view

NOTE

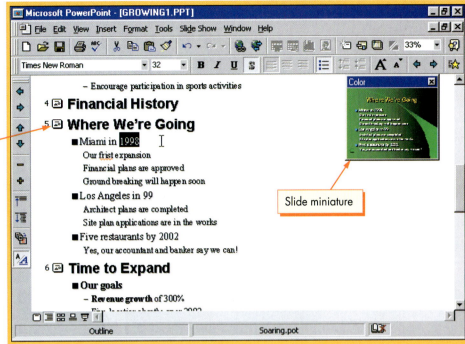

3. Using normal text editing methods, change "Miami in 99" to read "Miami in 1998." Change "99" in the next bulleted item to read "1999." When you edit text in Outline view, the changes are also reflected in Slide view. In fact, you can key an entire slide show in Outline view if that's the way you like to work. The slide miniature shows you a preview of the slide as you enter or edit text.

4. Notice the wavy red underline beneath the word "frist." Like Word, PowerPoint checks your spelling as you work. It uses the same red underline to indicate mistakes. Right-click "frist" and choose "first" from the shortcut menu.

5. Double-click the slide 5 icon to return to Slide view. (You can also click the Slide View button ▢ or choose View, Slide from the menu.) You learn to use all the Outline view features in Lesson 4.

EXERCISE 1-8 Use Slide Sorter View

1. Click the Slide Sorter View button ▦, located to the right of the Outline View button. You can now see several slide miniatures on the screen. In this view you can rearrange your slides or apply special slide show effects.

In PowerPoint Classroom Presentation #1.

You may want to have students click the Show Formatting button in Outline view to view the outline text without formatting. You may also have students increase the zoom so they can see the text they're editing more clearly.

19

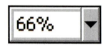

UNIT 1 ■ INTRODUCTION TO POWERPOINT

2. On the Standard toolbar, click the down arrow next to the Zoom box and choose 66% from the drop-down list so you can see all eight slides in this presentation at the same time.

NOTE: You may need to experiment with the zoom percentage to see all eight slides. Depending on your screen resolution, 66% or 50% will be the right choices.

3. In Slide Sorter view, you can rearrange the order of your slides. To move slide 7 before slide 6, click slide 7 and drag it to the left of slide 6. As you drag a slide, a vertical line indicates the slide's new position. If you are familiar with Word, you'll recognize the drag-and-drop pointer.

FIGURE 1-11
Slide sorter view

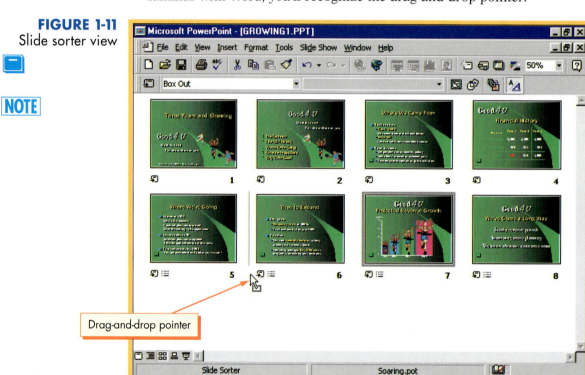

4. Double-click slide 6 to look at it in Slide view.

EXERCISE 1-9 Use Notes Page View

 1. Click the Notes Page View button 🖳. Change the zoom setting to "Fit" so you can see the entire page. You see a standard 8½" × 11" page with a slide

In PowerPoint Classroom Presentation #1.

NOTE
If students are not familiar with the drag-and-drop pointer, review its use and appearance. Stress the importance of noticing the changes in the pointer's appearance to be sure the correct procedure is being performed.

LESSON 1 ■ **OVERVIEW OF POWERPOINT**

on the top half of the page and a text box on the bottom half. In notes page view, you can key notes for the speaker to use during a presentation.

2. Move to Notes 3: by dragging the vertical scroll box.

3. Change the zoom to 75% magnification and scroll so you can see the notes text box on the bottom half of the page. Notice that this slide already contains note text.

4. Click ▢ to return to Slide view and move to slide 1.

NOTE

 TIP: In all views except Slide Show view, you can use the keyboard commands [Ctrl]+[Home] and [Ctrl]+[End] to move to the first or last slide in a presentation.

EXERCISE 1-10 Run a Slide Show

1. Click the Slide Show button 🖳. After a few moments, the first slide in the presentation fills the screen.

2. Click the left mouse button to move to slide 2. Click it again to move to slide 3. The left mouse button is one of many ways to move forward in a slide presentation.

3. Press [P] on the keyboard to move back to slide 2.

TIP: As an alternative to clicking the left mouse button, you can press [N] to move forward through the slides. [N] means "Next" and [P] means "Previous." You can also use the right and left arrow keys and [PgUp] and [PgDn] to move backward and forward in a slide show.

4. Move the mouse pointer over one of the round buttons to the left of "The Founders" and notice that the pointer changes to a hand. This indicates the button contains a *hyperlink* that causes PowerPoint to do something special when you click it. Try it now by clicking the bullet to the left of "Where We're Going."

5. The hyperlink takes you to a slide titled "Where We're Going" in the presentation. Click anywhere to see a sample of a PowerPoint text animation. Click twice more to see the remaining text on this slide.

6. Notice that there's a button shaped like a left-pointing arrow at the lower left of the screen. This button contains another hyperlink that takes you back to slide 2. Click it now.

7. Explore the other slides in the presentation using the hyperlink buttons on slide 2 and in the lower left of each of the other slides.

NOTE
You can also use [Home] and [End] in all views but Slide Show and Outline to move to the first/last slide in a presentation respectively. The [Ctrl] key modifier is only necessary in Outline view.

UNIT 1 ■ INTRODUCTION TO POWERPOINT

NOTE

8. Right-click anywhere on the screen to display the shortcut menu, which provides a variety of options related to the slide show. Click Next.

FIGURE 1-12
Click the right mouse button to see a slide show menu.

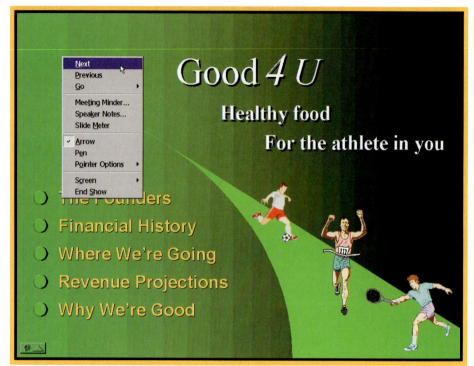

NOTE

9. Using the left mouse button, display each slide in the show, until you return to the main PowerPoint window. You can end a slide show at any time by pressing Esc.

NOTE: If your computer is equipped for sound, you'll hear the audio effects contained on slides 6 and 8.

Objective 5
Naming and Saving a Presentation

In PowerPoint, presentations are saved as files. When you create a new presentation or make changes to an existing one, you must save the presentation to make your changes permanent. Until your changes are saved, they can be lost if there's a power failure or a computer problem.

NOTE

The first step in saving a document is to give it a *filename*. In Windows 95, filenames can be up to 255 characters long and are followed by a period and a three-character extension. Filename extensions distinguish different types of files. For example, PowerPoint presentations have the extension .ppt and Word documents have the extension .doc.

NOTE
Clicking the Control Panel button, which appears in the bottom left corner of a slide in Slide Show view, is another way to open the slide show menu.

 In PowerPoint Classroom Presentation #1.

NOTE
At this point in the lesson, you may want to engage students in a discussion about real-life uses for presentations. Cull from your class a list of outside activities, such as clubs, organizations, and cultural groups to which students belong. Determine how they can use PowerPoint to make presentations for these groups or for their employers.

NOTE
Although a filename can be 255 characters long, the drive and path names are part of this character count. That is, you could save a 250+ character filename to C:\, but you'd have to shorten the name to save it to C:\PowerPoint Files\Jane Doe\Unit 1\Lesson 2\.

LESSON 1 ■ OVERVIEW OF POWERPOINT

Throughout the exercises in this book, your document filenames will consist of three parts:

NOTE

- *[Your initials]*, which may be your initials or an identifier that your instructor asks you to use, such as **rst**
- The number of the exercise, such as **3-1**
- The **.ppt** extension that PowerPoint uses automatically for presentations. An example of a filename is **rst3-1.ppt**

NOTE

Before you save a new presentation, you must decide where you want to save it. Unless you specify otherwise, PowerPoint saves the presentation in the current drive and folder. For example, to save a presentation to a diskette, you need to change to the appropriate drive.

 NOTE: Your instructor will advise you of the proper drive to use in this course.

 When working with an existing file, choosing the <u>S</u>ave command (or clicking the Save button on the Standard toolbar) replaces the file on the disk with the one you are working on. After saving, the old version of the file no longer exists and the new version contains all your changes.

NOTE

When you give an existing presentation a new name using the Save <u>A</u>s command, the original presentation remains on the disk unchanged and a second presentation is saved on the disk as well.

EXERCISE 1-11   Name and Save a Presentation

1. Click <u>F</u>ile to open the <u>F</u>ile menu and choose Save <u>A</u>s. The Save As dialog box appears.

FIGURE 1-13
Save As
dialog box

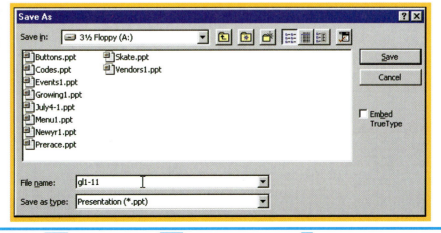

NOTE
Throughout the text, students are told to save their files using their initials and the Exercise number. If using student initials presents a problem (if, for example, students with the same initials save files in a shared folder on a hard drive), assign a unique identifier to each student saving files within a particular folder.

NOTE
You will need to tell students which drive to use to save their files. Typically, students save their files on a formatted disk (the "student disk").

NOTE
Emphasize the difference between Save and Save As. This concept is very important for students who are new to computers.

In PowerPoint Classroom Presentation #1.

23

UNIT 1 ■ INTRODUCTION TO POWERPOINT

2. In the File name text box, key *[your initials]***1-11**. You don't have to key the filename extension, .ppt. PowerPoint adds it automatically.

NOTE: To name files, you can use uppercase letters, lowercase letters, or a combination of both. Filenames can also include spaces. For example, a file can be named "Good 4 U - Three Years and Growing".

3. If necessary, change the drive to your data disk by clicking the down arrow in the Save in drop-down list box and choosing the appropriate drive. If you are saving the file on a diskette, make sure a formatted disk is in the drive.

4. Click Save and your document is saved and named for future use. Notice that the title bar displays the new filename.

Objective 6
Printing Slides and Handouts

Although many times the primary way of viewing a presentation will be as a slide show, you can also print PowerPoint slides, just as you print Word documents or Excel spreadsheets. PowerPoint provides a variety of print options, including printing each slide on a separate page, printing several slides on the same page, printing an outline, and printing notes pages. You can start printing in one of three ways:

- Choose Print from the File menu.
- Press Ctrl + P.
- Click the Print button.

The first two methods open the Print dialog box where you can choose printing options. If you click, the default print options control the printed format.

Throughout this book you are instructed to print handouts instead of full-size slides. *Handouts* contain several scaled-down slide images on each page; they are often given to an audience during a presentation. Printing handouts saves both paper and printing time.

EXERCISE 1-12 Print a Slide

1. To print the third slide in your presentation, move to slide 3 and choose Print from the File menu. The Print dialog box displays PowerPoint's default settings and indicates the designated printer.

NOTE: Long filenames are not compatible with older computer systems. Additionally, long filenames may be truncated by some dialog boxes, making it difficult to distinguish between similarly named files. A truncated filename removes spaces and punctuation and uses the first 6 characters, followed by a tilde (~) and a number. For example, the truncated filename GOOD4U~3.ppt can be either Good 4 U Sales Report or Good 4 U Contest. You'd have to open it to find out.

LESSON 1 ■ **OVERVIEW OF POWERPOINT**

FIGURE 1-14
The Print dialog box offers many printing options.

2. In the Print range option box, choose Current Slide.

3. From the Print what drop-down list box, choose Slides (without animations) and click the Black & white checkbox, if necessary.

4. Click OK to start printing. As the print job proceeds, you see the animated printer icon on the PowerPoint status bar. You also see a printer icon on the far right side of the Windows taskbar.

 **TIP:** If you start a large print job by accident, you can usually stop it by double-clicking the animated printer icon on the PowerPoint status bar.

EXERCISE 1-13 Print a Presentation Handout

Printing several slides on a single page is a handy way to review your work and to create audience handouts. It's also a convenient way to print class assignments.

1. Press Ctrl+P to open the Print dialog box.
2. Choose All as the Print range option.
3. From the Print what drop-down list box, choose Handouts (6 slides per page).

In PowerPoint Classroom Presentation #1.

NOTE
The Black & white print setting optimizes the look of color slides for printing on a black and white printer. Do not use this setting if a color printer is available in your classroom.

NOTE
PowerPoint prints faster if you turn off background printing (Tools, Options, Print tab). If you do this, make students aware that they will see a standard print progress message box while PowerPoint prints rather than the animated print icon mentioned in the text.

25

UNIT 1 ■ INTRODUCTION TO POWERPOINT

NOTE

4. Choose <u>B</u>lack & white, if necessary. Click the Fra<u>m</u>e slides checkbox to select it and click OK. PowerPoint prints the entire presentation on two pages (six framed slide images on the first page and two on the second page).

Objective 7

Closing Presentations and Exiting PowerPoint

After you finish working on a presentation and save it, you can close it and open another file or you can exit the program.

The easiest ways to close a presentation and exit PowerPoint include the following:

- Use the <u>F</u>ile menu.
- Use keyboard shortcuts. Ctrl+W closes a presentation and Alt+F4 exits PowerPoint.
- Use the Close buttons ✕ in the upper right corner of the window.

FIGURE 1-15
Close buttons

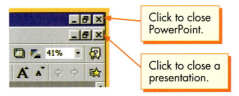

 NOTE

EXERCISE 1-14 **Close a Presentation and Exit PowerPoint**

1. Choose <u>C</u>lose from the <u>F</u>ile menu to close the presentation.
2. Click <u>Y</u>es to save the presentation again. (After printing a presentation, you are prompted to save it before closing.)

3. Click the Close button ✕ in the upper right corner of the screen to close PowerPoint and display the Windows desktop.

NOTE
To save printing time and paper, students are instructed to print handouts, 6 slides per page, black and white, framed, throughout this course (unless they are being taught other print options).

Objective 7 Assignment:
Exercises 1-15 through1-18 (Skills Review) and Exercises 1-19 through 1-22 (Lesson Applications) can be assigned after completing Objective 7.

In PowerPoint Classroom Presentation #1.

NOTE
The Close buttons are the easiest way to close a document or exit the program. Emphasize that the top Close button exits PowerPoint, while the bottom button closes the document window.

LESSON 1 ■ OVERVIEW OF POWERPOINT

COMMAND SUMMARY

NOTE

FEATURE	BUTTON	MENU	KEYBOARD
Next Slide	▼		PgDn
Previous Slide	▲		PgUp
Zoom Control	66%	View, Zoom	
Next (Slide Show)	Left mouse button	Right-click, Next	N
Previous (Slide Show)		Right-click, Previous	P
End a slide show		Right-click, End Show	Esc
Save	💾	File, Save	Ctrl+S
Save As		File, Save As	
Print	🖨	File, Print	Ctrl+P
Close a presentation	✕	File, Close	Ctrl+W or Ctrl+F4
Exit PowerPoint	✕	File, Exit	Alt+F4

USING HELP

NOTE

The Office Assistant is your guide to Word online Help. The Office Assistant provides tips based on the kind of work you're doing and directs you to relevant Help topics. It may also amuse you with its animated movements. If you find it annoying, you can hide it or choose another character.

Get acquainted with the Office Assistant:

1. Start PowerPoint, if necessary. Click Cancel in the opening PowerPoint dialog box.

2. If the Office Assistant is not displayed, click the Office Assistant button 📋 on the Standard toolbar.

3. Click the Office Assistant figure. A balloon appears with the question "What would you like to do?"

4. Key **How do I use Office Assistant?** in the text box and click Search. The Office Assistant locates Help topics related to your question.

5. Review the displayed topics and click "See more" to display additional related topics.

NOTE
Point out that the Command Summary lists a variety of ways to accomplish a specific task. Students can decide which method they prefer. Review keyboard combinations with students. Make sure they master this skill and understand how it will be represented in this text.

NOTE
Encourage students to follow the steps in "Using Help." Software companies are increasingly using online Help systems—rather than printed documentation—to train users and assist in answering user questions.

27

6. Click the topic "Ways to get assistance while you work." A PowerPoint Help window with the same topic name is displayed. This window provides a general overview of Help.

FIGURE 1-16
Getting Help while you work

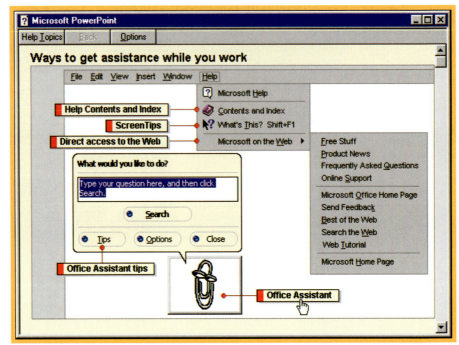

7. Click the topic Office Assistant to display a descriptive box. Review the description and then click the box to close it. Click the topic Office Assistant tips and review the description.

8. Explore other topics in the Help window. Click the window's Close button to close Help. Close the Office Assistant.

In PowerPoint Classroom Presentation #1.

LESSON 1 ■ OVERVIEW OF POWERPOINT

TEST BANK

Concepts Review

TRUE/FALSE QUESTIONS

Each of the following statements is either true or false. Indicate your choice by circling **T** or **F**.

T **(F)** 1. You can use the horizontal scroll bar to move to a new slide.

T **(F)** 2. If you double-click a slide in Outline view, you can move it to a different location.

(T) F 3. You can edit text in Slide view or Outline view.

(T) F 4. You can easily move a slide to a new location in Slide Sorter view.

(T) F 5. Editing text in PowerPoint is similar to editing text in a word processor.

T **(F)** 6. When viewing a slide show, pressing the right mouse button moves to the next slide.

(T) F 7. A handout is a page with more than one slide printed on it.

T **(F)** 8. If you click 🖨, you can choose exactly which items to print.

SHORT ANSWER QUESTIONS

Write the correct answer in the space provided.

1. Where on the PowerPoint screen are the view buttons located?
   Left side of horizontal scroll bar

2. In Slide Sorter view, what happens when you drag a slide?
   Changes the slide order in the presentation

3. What are the names of the five view buttons?
   Slide, Outline, Slide Sorter, Notes Page, Slide Show

4. What shape does the mouse pointer have when you move it over a text box?
   I-beam

5. Which key do you press to stop a slide show?
   The Escape (Esc) key

CLOSE

Concepts Review: Allows students to check their understanding.

TEST BANK Consider using the Test Bank to provide an additional review of lesson concepts.

UNIT 1 ■ INTRODUCTION TO POWERPOINT

6. Besides handouts and slides, what other formats can you print in PowerPoint?

   Notes Pages, Outline

7. What is the maximum number of slides you can print on a handouts page?

   Six

8. Which menu and menu option would you use to save a copy of your presentation under a new filename?

   File, Save As

CRITICAL THINKING

Answer these questions on a separate page. There are no right or wrong answers. Support your answers with examples from your own experience, if possible.

1. Think about the different ways you can move from one slide to another in Slide view, Slide Sorter view, and Outline view. Which options do you prefer and why?

2. PowerPoint and other Microsoft Office applications for Windows allow filenames that can be 255 characters in length. In previous versions of Microsoft Office applications, only 8 characters were allowed. Some people think the 8-character system is better because it forces you to create a set of rules for naming files. What do you think?

3. You can produce screen shows, printouts, overhead transparencies, 35mm slides, and other presentation media with PowerPoint. How might you choose among these options for any particular presentation? Why would you choose one medium over another? What factors would influence your decision?

Skills Review

EXERCISE 1-15

Open a file; identify parts of the PowerPoint screen; key text; save, print, and close the file.

1. If PowerPoint is already open, skip to Step 2. Otherwise, start PowerPoint by following these steps:

Critical Thinking Questions:
Answers will vary based on students' preferences, observations, experiences, and research.

Skills Review:
Provides guided practice for students. Objectives are indicated for each Exercise.

Exercise 1-15:
Objectives 1–3, 5–7
Required File: Buttons.ppt
Solution File: gl1-15.ppt in Solutions Manual or on Solutions Disk

LESSON 1 ■ **OVERVIEW OF POWERPOINT**

NOTE

    a. Click the Start button [Start] on the Windows taskbar.

    b. Point to Programs, point to Microsoft PowerPoint and click it.

    c. Click Cancel to close the PowerPoint dialog box.

2. Open a presentation by following these steps:

    a. Click the Open button [icon] on the Standard toolbar.

    b. Choose the appropriate drive and folder, if necessary.

NOTE

    c. Double-click the file **Buttons.ppt**.

3. Click anywhere on the text "Click to add subtitle" and key your full name.

4. Select the two question marks in the text "Exercise 1-??" by dragging the I-beam across them. Key the number of this exercise.

5. To move to slide 2, click the Next Slide button [icon] at the bottom of the vertical scroll bar.

6. Key the answers to the questions on slide 2 by following these steps:

    a. Click to position the insertion point after the word "*Answer*:"

    b. Press [Spacebar] to insert a space after the colon and key the answer

7. Save the presentation as *[your initials]***1-15.ppt** by following these steps:

    a. Choose Save As from the File menu to open the Save As dialog box.

    b. Choose the appropriate drive and folder, if necessary.

    c. Key the filename *[your initials]***1-15** in the File name text box. (Remember, you don't have to key the filename extension, .ppt.)

    d. Click Save.

8. Print the presentation by following these steps:

    a. Choose Print from the File menu.

    b. Choose All in the Print range option box, if necessary.

    c. Choose Handouts (2 slides per page) from the Print what drop-down list.

    d. Make sure the options Black & White and Frame Slides are selected and click OK.

9. Close the presentation by clicking the lower Close button [X] in the upper right corner of the window.

EXERCISE 1-16

Edit text on a slide and move a slide in Slide Sorter view.

1. Open the file **Menu1.ppt**.

2. Move to slide 2 by dragging the vertical scroll box.

NOTE
Because some students may already have PowerPoint open and some may not, students are instructed to close the opening PowerPoint dialog box in step 1, and then use the Open button on the Standard toolbar to open a file. You may want to remind them that they can also open the file from the PowerPoint opening dialog box.

NOTE
In the Skills Review and Lesson Applications, students open presentations that have varying degrees of formatting. Advise students that they will learn how to apply formatting in the coming lessons. In addition, students open presentations that are of varying length (some presentations have only one slide). You may want to explain the uses for single-slide presentation files.

Exercise 1-16:
Objectives 2–7
Required File: Menu1.ppt
Solution File: gl1-16.ppt in Solutions Manual or on Solutions Disk

UNIT 1 ■ INTRODUCTION TO POWERPOINT

3. Make the corrections as shown in Figure 1-17.

FIGURE 1-17

NOTE

4. Change the position of slides 2 and 3 by following these steps:
   a. Click the Slide Sorter View button.
   b. Click slide 3 and drag it to the left of slide 2.
5. Save the presentation as *[your initials]***1-16.ppt**.
6. Print the presentation as handouts, 6 slides per page, black and white, framed.
7. Close the presentation.

EXERCISE 1-17

View a presentation in all views, move a toolbar, save and print a presentation.

1. Open the file **Codes.ppt**.
2. Click ▤ to view the presentation in Outline view.
3. Click 🖳 to view the presentation in Notes Pages view.
4. Click 🏛 to view the presentation in Slide Sorter view.
5. Double-click slide 1 in Slide Sorter view to change to Slide view.
6. Move a toolbar by following these steps:

NOTE
This figure contains proofreading marks. You may want to review Appendix F: "Proofreader's Marks" with students.

💾 **Exercise 1-17:**
Objectives 2–7
Required File: Codes.ppt
Solution File: File gl1-17.ppt in Solutions Manual or on Solutions Disk.

LESSON 1 ■ **OVERVIEW OF POWERPOINT**

    a. Point to the two vertical gray bars at the left of the Drawing toolbar (which should be docked at the bottom of the screen).

 NOTE: If the Drawing toolbar is not docked at the bottom of the screen, drag it by its title bar below the view buttons.

    b. Hold down the left mouse button and drag the toolbar by the vertical bars until it is raised above the view buttons and slightly to the right, making it a floating toolbar.

    c. Double-click the title bar of the Drawing toolbar to restore it to its docked position.

7. Click the I-beam to the right of "Training Session" on slide 1 and press [Enter] to start a new line. Key today's date.

8. Run a slide show of the presentation by following these steps:

    a. Click the Slide Show button 🖵.

    b. After slide 1 appears in Slide Show view, click the left mouse button to advance to the next slide.

    c. Continue to click the left mouse button until you return to Slide view.

9. Save the presentation as *[your initials]***1-17.ppt**.

10. Print the presentation as handouts, 6 slides per page, black and white, framed.

11. Close the presentation.

EXERCISE 1-18

Key text on a slide, make changes in Outline view, and print the slide.

1. Open the file **Events1.ppt**.

2. Insert a new line of bulleted text by following these steps:

    a. Click the I-beam to the right of the word "team" at the end of the line "National In-Line Skate demo team."

    b. Press [Enter] to start a new line with an automatic bullet.

    c. Key **Autograph session with Marsha Miles**

3. Make changes in Outline view following these steps:

    a. Click 📄 to switch to Outline view.

    b. Click the I-beam between the words "with" and "Marsha" to position the insertion point.

    c. Key **aerobic video star** and insert any necessary spaces.

Exercise 1-18:
Objectives 3–7
Required File: Events1.ppt
Solution File: File gl1-18.ppt in Solutions Manual or on Solutions Disk.

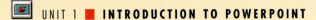

UNIT 1 ■ INTRODUCTION TO POWERPOINT

4. Save the presentation as *[your initials]***1-18.ppt**.

5. Since this is a one-slide presentation, print the slide full-size by following these steps:

   a. Choose Print from the File menu.

   b. Choose Slides from the Print what drop-down list box.

   c. If necessary, choose Black & White and choose Frame Slides.

   d. Click OK.

6. Close the presentation.

LESSON 1 ■ **OVERVIEW OF POWERPOINT**

Lesson Applications

EXERCISE 1-19

Edit text in Outline view; save, print, and close a presentation.

1. Open the file **Newyr1.ppt**.
2. Change to Outline view. Make the changes to slides 2 and 3 as shown in Figure 1-18:

FIGURE 1-18

```
Entertainment
  • Audition bands
      • Charlie's Dingbats
      • The Electrolytes
      • Wired Rabbits   Pure Power                 } Slide 2
  • Contact Marsha Miles         dance-style
      • Is she willing to lead ⌃ aerobics
      • Is she available New Year's Eve?
Menu
  • Michelle needs suggestions by November 1
         tasting                      5
  • Staff ⌃ party to be held December 2           } Slide 3
  • Menu printing deadline is December 10
```

3. Switch to Slide view and save the presentation as *[your initials]***1-19.ppt**.
4. Print the presentation as handouts, 6 slides per page, black and white, framed.
5. Close the presentation.

Assessment Resources:
• Solutions Manual
• Test Bank with Software
• Portfolio Builder
• Alternative Assessment Guide
• Certification Procedures

Lesson Applications:
Provide independent practice for students. Objectives are indicated for each Exercise.

Exercise 1-19:
Objectives 3–7
Required File: Newyr1.ppt
Solution File: gl1-19.ppt in Solutions Manual or on Solutions Disk.

35

UNIT 1 ■ INTRODUCTION TO POWERPOINT

EXERCISE 1-20

Work in Slide Sorter view to change the order of slides in a presentation.

1. Open the presentation **July4-1.ppt**.
2. Change to Slide Sorter view.
3. Change the order of slides to correspond to the list shown in Figure 1-19:

FIGURE 1-19

Slide Number	Slide Title
1	Fourth of July Celebration
2	Entertainment
3	Special Menu Items
4	In-Line Skate Race in the Park
5	In-Line Skate Race Rules

4. Run a slide show of the presentation.
5. Save the presentation as *[your initials]***1-20.ppt**.
6. Print the presentation as handouts, 6 slides per page, black and white, framed.
7. Close the presentation.

EXERCISE 1-21

Edit text in Outline view and Slide view and print slides.

1. Open the presentation **Codes.ppt**.
2. On slide 1, key the word **Personnel** to the left of "Training" so the title reads "Personnel Training Session."
3. Change to Outline view and locate the last line of text on slide 2 (which begins "Under no circumstances"). Position the insertion point at the end of that line and key **while on the job**
4. Locate the last line of text on slide 3. Position the insertion point between "Good 4 U" and "test" and key **proficiency** (the phrase should read "Good 4 U proficiency test").

Exercise 1-20:
Objectives 4–7
Required File: July4-1.ppt
Solution File: gl1-20.ppt in Solutions Manual or on Solutions Disk.

Exercise 1-21:
Objectives 2–7
Required File: Codes.ppt
Solution File: gl1-21.ppt in Solutions Manual or on Solutions Disk

The completed presentation for this Exercise may be used in a student's portfolio.

LESSON 1 ■ **OVERVIEW OF POWERPOINT**

NOTE

5. Change to Slide view and move to slide 4. Delete the periods at the end of the two sentences that begin "Guests."
6. Below the third bullet, change "Shirts are" to **T-shirts will be**
7. Save the presentation as *[your initials]***1-21.ppt**.
8. Print the presentation as handouts, 6 slides per page, black and white, framed.
9. Close the presentation.

EXERCISE 1-22

Edit, rearrange, and print slides.

1. Open the presentation **Prerace.ppt**.
2. In Slide view, edit slide 2 as shown in Figure 1-20.

FIGURE 1-20

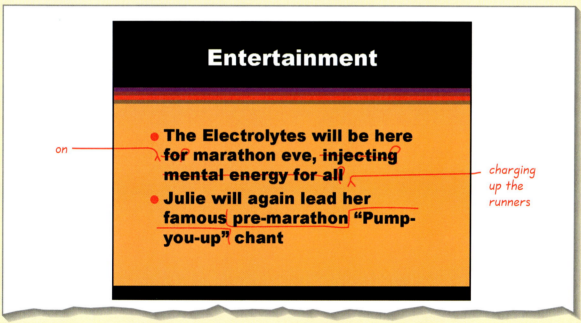

NOTE

3. In Outline view, edit slide 3 as shown in Figure 1-21 (on the next page).
4. Working in Slide Sorter view, move slide 3 before slide 2.
5. Display slide 1 in Slide view and run a slide show of the presentation.
6. Save the presentation as *[your initials]***1-22.ppt**.
7. Print the presentation as handouts, 6 slides per page, black and white, framed.
8. Close the presentation.

NOTE
In this Exercise, students are asked to delete the periods for consistency. In the next lesson, students will learn how to have PowerPoint check for and remove inconsistent punctuation by performing a style check.

Exercise 1-22:
Objectives 2–7
Required File: Prerace.ppt
Solution File: gl1-22.ppt in Solutions Manual or on Solutions Disk.

The completed presentation for this Exercise may be used in a student's portfolio.

NOTE
This figure contains proofreading marks. You may want to review Appendix F: "Proofreader's Marks" with students.

37

UNIT 1 ■ INTRODUCTION TO POWERPOINT

FIGURE 1-21

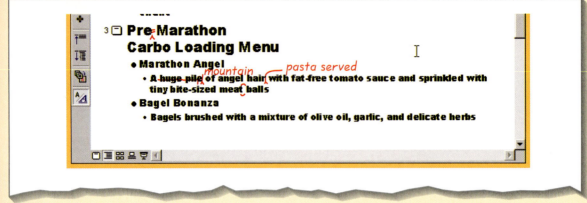

NOTE

NOTE
This figure contains proofreading marks. You may want to review Appendix F: "Proofreader's Marks" with students.

38

Creating a Presentation Automatically

LESSON 2

OBJECTIVES

After completing this lesson, you will be able to:
1. Use the AutoContent Wizard.
2. Change sample text in Slide view.
3. Use the spelling checker and style checker.
4. Make changes in Slide Sorter view.
5. Add headers and footers.
6. Choose printing options.

 Estimated Time: 1½ hours

PowerPoint offers a variety of methods to create a presentation. You can begin from scratch and create a new presentation, use an existing template that contains color or style enhancements, or get step-by-step help using a wizard. A *wizard* is an online guide that helps you complete a task.

Objective 1
Using the AutoContent Wizard

The quickest way to create a presentation is with the AutoContent Wizard. It asks a series of questions and uses your answers to develop the framework for a new presentation.

PREPARE
Point out to students that the learning objectives show what they will learn in the lesson. Each heading in the lesson correlates to a learning objective.
Required Files
July4-2.ppt

TEACH
Teaching Resources:
• PowerPoint Classroom Presentations
• School-to-Work Strategies Manual
• Internet Manual
• Spanish Glossary
• Methodology Video
• Certification Procedures

UNIT 1 ■ INTRODUCTION TO POWERPOINT

EXERCISE 2-1 Use the AutoContent Wizard

1. Start PowerPoint. Close the Office Assistant, if it is displayed.
2. In the PowerPoint opening dialog box, choose <u>A</u>utoContent Wizard and click OK. The AutoContent Wizard opening dialog box appears.

FIGURE 2-1
AutoContent Wizard icon

NOTE: If PowerPoint was already open when you started this lesson, you may need to locate the AutoContent Wizard. Choose <u>N</u>ew from the <u>F</u>ile menu, click the Presentations tab, and double-click the AutoContent Wizard icon.

3. In the AutoContent Wizard opening dialog box, click <u>N</u>ext. Notice the "road map" in the dialog box. As you move from one dialog box to the next, a green square indicates where you are in the process. You move forward and backward by clicking the <u>N</u>ext and <u>B</u>ack buttons or by clicking the gray boxes.

FIGURE 2-2
AutoContent Wizard opening screen

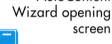

4. In the Presentation type dialog box, the wizard asks what kind of presentation you want to give and shows you a list of presentation types. You can click one of the buttons to the left of the list to show only specific types of presentations. Click <u>G</u>eneral and choose Recommending a Strategy from the list. Click <u>N</u>ext. The green square moves to Output options.

5. In the Output options dialog box, you tell the wizard how you plan to use this presentation. Choose <u>P</u>resentations, informal meetings, handouts. Click Next to move to Presentation style.

6. In the Presentation style dialog box, choose On-<u>s</u>creen presentation and choose <u>N</u>o where it asks "Will you print handouts?" Click <u>N</u>ext.

Use PowerPoint Classroom Presentation #2 to display screens from the lesson, including this one, in a slide-show format.

You may want to review presentation types and their uses with students.

40

LESSON 2 ■ CREATING A PRESENTATION AUTOMATICALLY

7. In the Presentation options dialog box, select the text "Title goes here" in the first text box and key **Good 4 U Restaurant** in its place. Press Tab to move to the second text box and key your name. Delete any text that appears in the Additional information text box.

8. Click Next to move to the last dialog box. Click Finish. PowerPoint creates an eight-slide strategy presentation for you and displays it in Outline view with the title slide selected. Notice the presentation design and color, as shown in the title slide miniature

FIGURE 2-3
Presentation created using the AutoContent Wizard

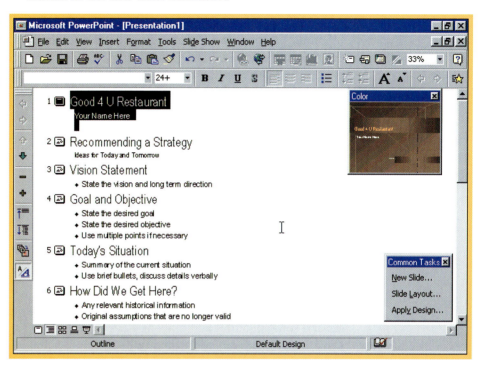

Objective 2
Changing Sample Text in Slide View

NOTE

The AutoContent Wizard creates a presentation based on a suggested outline using sample text. You can replace the sample text with your own content using basic editing techniques. As you learned in Lesson 1, editing presentation text is much the same as editing text in a word processor.

EXERCISE 2-2 Edit Sample Text in a Title Placeholder

Each slide in the sales presentation contains a title placeholder with sample text. For example, slide 2 is titled "Recommending a Strategy," and slide 3 is named "Vision Statement." You can select and then edit these sample text objects.

In PowerPoint Classroom Presentation #2.

Objective 2 Assignment:
Exercise 2-11 (Skills Review) can be assigned after completing Objective 2.

NOTE
Make sure students review the sample text in the "Recommending a Strategy" presentation. Point out that this sample text is there to suggest slide content.

41

UNIT 1 ■ INTRODUCTION TO POWERPOINT

1. Click the slide icon next to slide 2 and press Delete to delete the slide.

2. Double-click the slide icon next to the new slide 2 (titled "Vision Statement") to switch to Slide view. Click at the bottom of the vertical scroll bar to view slide 3. Notice the sample text for the title and bulleted list. As you examine each slide, note how the sample text suggests the content for a sales presentation.

3. Display slide 4. (Remember, you can drag the scroll box, click , or press PgDn.) Notice that the slides are numbered in the bottom right corner.

4. In slide 4, move the pointer over the title placeholder ("Today's Situation") until it becomes an I-beam. Click the I-beam to activate the title placeholder.

5. Drag the I-beam over the sample title text to select it. Key the new title **Good 4 U Provides** in place of the selected text.

6. Click outside the title placeholder to deactivate it.

 NOTE: After you edit placeholder text, deactivate the placeholder by clicking elsewhere on the screen. Be sure you see the white arrow pointer when you click.

EXERCISE 2-3   Edit Sample Text in a Text Placeholder

In this presentation, all the slides contain sample text, some in title placeholders and some in bullet text placeholders. You can edit sample text in bullet text placeholders and add additional bullets.

1. Return to slide 3 (titled "Goal and Objective"). With the I-beam pointer, click the bulleted list to activate the text placeholder.

2. At the right of the first bullet, drag to select the text "State the desired goal" and key **Encourage corporations to use Good 4 U for special events**

3. Press Enter to add a new bullet and key **Provide healthy food that tastes good**

4. Triple-click the text "State the desired objective" to select it and press Delete to remove it.

5. Select the last bullet line on slide 4 and key **Provide "something different"** (include the quotation marks).

 NOTE: When you select bulleted text, the bullet character is not highlighted.

NOTE
The AutoContent Wizard creates a presentation in which slides 2 through 8 are numbered 1 through 7. To avoid confusion, students delete the slide numbered "1" at the beginning of this Exercise.

LESSON 2 ■ **CREATING A PRESENTATION AUTOMATICALLY**

FIGURE 2-4
Editing sample text on slide 3

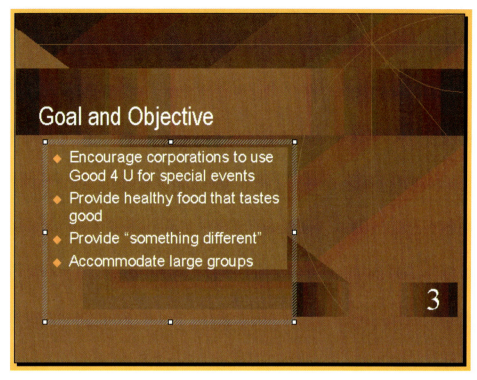

6. Press Enter to create another bulleted item and key **Accommodations for large groups**

7. In slide 4, select and delete all bulleted text from "Summary" through "verbally." Key the following four bulleted items, pressing Enter to start each new item:

   ♦ **Low-fat, natural foods**
   ♦ **Innovative menu**
   ♦ **Three stars from the New York Times**
   ♦ **Private dining for 25 to 500 people**

8. Save the presentation as *[your initials]***2-3.ppt** and leave it open.

TABLE 2-1 Selecting Text

METHOD	RESULT
Click and drag	Selects text with the mouse
Double-click a word	Selects the entire word
Ctrl +click text	Selects the sentence
Triple-click text	Selects the paragraph

In PowerPoint Classroom Presentation #2.

NOTE
Although students learn how to apply text attributes in Lesson 5, you might ask them to italicize the publication title "New York Times."

NOTE
Students save the partially completed presentation and leave it open so they can use it in Exercise 2-8.

NOTE
You may want to review the text selecting and editing methods listed in Tables 2-1 and 2-2, most of which will be familiar to students who know how to use Word.

43

UNIT 1 ■ INTRODUCTION TO POWERPOINT

TABLE 2-2 Editing Text

METHOD	RESULT
Arrow key	Moves the insertion point right, left, up, or down within the text
Backspace	Deletes characters to the left of the insertion point
Ctrl + Backspace	Deletes the word to the left of the insertion point
Delete	Deletes characters to the right of the insertion point
Ctrl + Delete	Deletes the word to the right of the insertion point

Objective 3

Using the Spelling Checker and Style Checker

NOTE

PowerPoint provides three tools to improve your spelling and the overall appearance of your presentation:

- A spelling checker, which corrects spelling by comparing words to an internal dictionary file.
- AutoCorrect, which corrects common spelling and capitalization errors automatically as you key text.
- A style checker, which checks a presentation for visual clarity and consistency of case and punctuation.

EXERCISE 2-4 Use the Spelling Checker

The spelling checker in PowerPoint works much the same as it does in other Microsoft Office applications. As you type, it flags misspelled words with a red wavy underline. It will also check an entire presentation at once.

1. Without closing the current presentation, open the file **July4-2.ppt**.
2. To start the spelling checker, click the Spelling button on the Standard toolbar or press F7. PowerPoint highlights "Registraton," the first word it doesn't find in its dictionary. It displays the word in the Spelling dialog box and suggests a corrected spelling. (See Figure 2-5 on the next page.)
3. Click Change to apply the correct spelling of "Registration."
4. When the spelling checker locates "jalapenos," click Ignore because this word is spelled correctly. Do the same for "Slurpee."

Objective 3 Assignment:
Exercise 2-12 (Skills Review) can be assigned after completing Objective 3.

NOTE
Advise students to review a presentation after they style-check and spell-check. The style checker may make an unwanted change, such as changing an uppercase letter to lowercase. The spelling checker will not catch words that are spelled correctly but misused (such as using "desert" for "dessert").

NOTE
At this point, students have two presentations open at the same time. They learn how to use the Window menu to switch between presentations.

NOTE
You may want to point out the spelling icon on the status bar, which appears as an open book. The icon contains an "x" when it detects spelling errors in the file. You can click this icon to start the spelling checker. The "x" is replaced by a check mark after completing a spelling check (assuming that no words exist in the presentation that PowerPoint does not recognize).

44

LESSON 2 ■ **CREATING A PRESENTATION AUTOMATICALLY**

FIGURE 2-5
Using the spelling checker

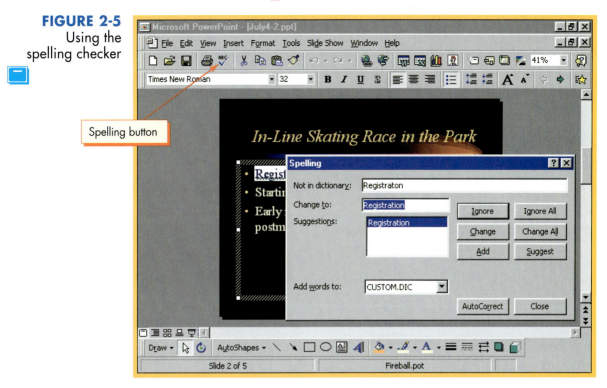

 NOTE: If the Spelling dialog box is hiding a misspelled word in your presentation, move the dialog box to a different position by dragging its title bar.

5. Click Change to correct the spelling of "raspberries."
6. Notice that there are two choices for the correct spelling of "gurdian." Select the first choice ("guardian"), if necessary, and click Change. Click OK when the spelling check is complete.

EXERCISE | **2-5** | **Use AutoCorrect**

If you key "teh" instead of "the," or "tuesday" instead of "Tuesday," AutoCorrect corrects the word automatically as you key. The correction takes place after you press Spacebar, Enter, or enter punctuation, such as a period.

1. Display slide 2 of the active presentation (**July4-2.ppt**).
2. Choose AutoCorrect from the Tools menu. If necessary, turn on the AutoCorrect feature by checking Replace text as you type.

In PowerPoint Classroom Presentation #2.

45

UNIT 1 ■ INTRODUCTION TO POWERPOINT

FIGURE 2-6
AutoCorrect dialog box

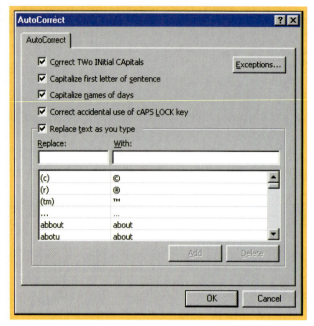

3. Scroll through the Replace text as you type list to see the changes that AutoCorrect will make automatically. Click OK.

4. Position the insertion point to the immediate left of "June" in the last bulleted item. Key **saturday** and press Spacebar. The word is automatically corrected to "Saturday." Leave the file open for the next exercise.

> **TIP:** You can customize AutoCorrect to catch your own common typos or to expand abbreviations. Just key the error or abbreviation (for example, **asap**) in the Replace box and then key the correction (for example, **as soon as possible**) in the With box. Next, click Add to put your entry on the list. For example, you could create an entry to replace your company's initials with its full name. To delete a Replace With entry, select it in the list and click Delete.

EXERCISE 2-6   Use the Style Checker

The style checker looks for consistency, balance, and overall readability of your presentation. For example, it will correct or notify you of a bulleted item that ends with a period or a title that is uppercase when all other titles are in title case. You can choose style checker options that change all slides in your presentation.

In PowerPoint Classroom Presentation #2.

46

LESSON 2 ■ **CREATING A PRESENTATION AUTOMATICALLY**

1. In the active presentation (**July4-2.ppt**), display slide 1.
2. Choose Style Checker from the Tools menu to display the Style Checker dialog box.

FIGURE 2-7
Style Checker dialog box

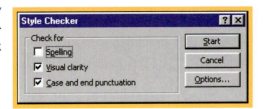

3. Click the Spelling check box to clear it, as you have already performed this function.
4. Click Options to review the style checker options available. Click the Visual Clarity tab. These settings are designed to make the presentation easy to read.
5. Click the Case and End Punctuation tab. Notice the default case settings: title case for slide titles and sentence case for body text. Under End Punctuation, notice the settings that will remove periods.
6. Change the Slide title style to UPPERCASE. Clear the check mark next to Body text style to deselect that option and click OK.

FIGURE 2-8
Style Checker options

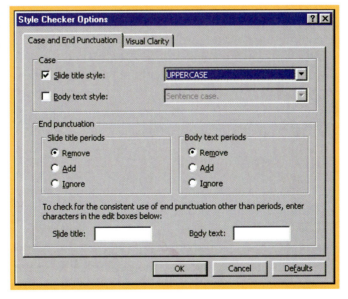

NOTE: When PowerPoint changes body text to sentence case, it may change proper nouns like names or days of the week to lowercase. If you use this option, check your presentation carefully afterward.

In PowerPoint Classroom Presentation #2.

NOTE
Once you run a spelling check, PowerPoint remembers and doesn't recheck words you already corrected or okayed. Therefore, it's not really necessary to uncheck Spelling in the Style Checker dialog box. However, students are instructed to do so to illustrate that they can perform any or all of these functions.

NOTE
Students change a Style Checker default setting, but then reset the default at the end of the Exercise (see step 10).

NOTE
This dialog box presents opportunities for discussion about the elements of good presentation design.

47

UNIT 1 ■ INTRODUCTION TO POWERPOINT

7. Click **S**tart. The style checker changes the titles of the slides to uppercase and questions a period at the end of paragraph 3 on slide 2.

8. Click **C**hange to delete the period. The style checker continues reviewing slides and displays a summary with references to slides 1 and 2. (For our purposes, these slides are okay.) Click OK.

9. Click to switch to Slide Sorter view. Notice that all slides now have uppercase titles.

10. Choose St**y**le Checker from the **T**ools menu again, click **O**ptions, and click De**f**aults to reset the default settings. Click OK and then click Cancel. The current presentation is not affected, but the style checker defaults are ready for use in future presentations.

NOTE

TIP: If the style checker changes the case for a proper name (for example, changes "Good 4 U" to "good 4 u"), you can use the Find and Replace commands to locate and correct the text. Choose **R**eplace from the **E**dit menu, key **good 4 u** in the Fi**n**d what box, key **Good 4 U** in the Re**p**lace with box, check the Match **C**ase box, and click Replace **A**ll (or click **F**ind Next to review each occurrence before replacing).

Objective 4

Making Changes in Slide Sorter View

Slide Sorter view provides an overview of your entire presentation by displaying a miniature version of the slides in the order they appear.

In Lesson 1, you learned how to rearrange slides in Slide Sorter view by dragging. In this lesson, you continue to practice dragging and you also rearrange slides using the Cut, Copy, and Paste commands.

EXERCISE 2-7 Move Slides by Dragging

1. With the presentation **July4-2.ppt** in Slide Sorter view, click slide 3 to select it.

2. Position the arrow pointer within the selected slide's borders, press the left mouse button, and drag the pointer between the first and second slides. Notice the vertical line and the drag-and-drop pointer as you drag. (See Figure 2-9 on the next page.)

3. Release the mouse button. Slide 3, titled "SPECIAL MENU ITEMS," becomes slide 2.

4. Save the presentation as *[your initials]***2-7.ppt** and leave it open for the next exercise.

Objective 4 Assignment:
Exercise 2-13 (Skills Review) can be assigned after completing Objective 4.

NOTE
Most students are familiar with Find and Replace from their word-processing program. You may want to point out the various uses for the Find and Replace commands, particularly in a long presentation.

LESSON 2 ■ CREATING A PRESENTATION AUTOMATICALLY

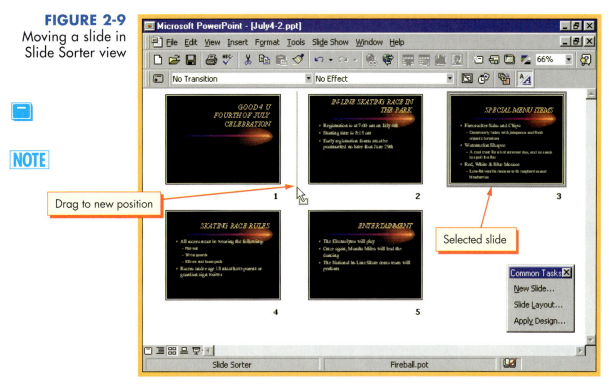

FIGURE 2-9
Moving a slide in Slide Sorter view

EXERCISE 2-8   Cut, Copy, and Paste Slides

NOTE

You can apply the Cut, Copy, and Paste commands to text, graphics or entire slides. For example, you can use Cut, Copy and Paste to move a bulleted list from one slide to another or use the same commands to move entire slides from one presentation to another.

You can paste material within a presentation, between presentations, and even between a presentation and another application—like a word processing document. In this exercise, you learn how to view two different presentations at once in Slide Sorter view and copy slides between them.

1. Choose *[your initials]***2-3.ppt** from the Window menu to display the presentation.

2. Switch to Outline view.

3. On slide 3, select the first bulleted item (which begins "Encourages corporations"). Click the Cut button on the Standard toolbar. This deletes the text and places it on the Clipboard.

In PowerPoint Classroom Presentation #2.

NOTE
Point out the appearance of the drag-and-drop pointer so students become accustomed to recognizing it.

NOTE
Reinforce the concept of cut, copy, and paste for students who are not familiar with these operations. In addition, review the keyboard shortcuts for these commands, which some students may prefer to the toolbar buttons or shortcut menu.

49

UNIT 1 ■ INTRODUCTION TO POWERPOINT

NOTE

 NOTE: The Clipboard is a Windows feature that can store text or graphics temporarily for pasting. Each time you cut or copy an item, it replaces the previously stored item. Unlike the Cut command, Delete does not save items to the Clipboard.

 4. On slide 2, select the sample bulleted text (which begins "State the vision") and click the Paste button .

TIP: You can also use the keyboard shortcuts Ctrl+X to cut and Ctrl+V to paste.

NOTE

5. Switch to Slide Sorter view. Choose Arrange All from the Window menu. Both presentations appear side-by-side, each within its own window in Slide Sorter view. Each window's title bar displays the name of the presentation it contains. The active presentation, *[your initials]***2-3.ppt**, should appear in the left window.

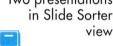

FIGURE 2-10
Two presentations in Slide Sorter view

6. In the right window, right-click slide 2 (titled "SPECIAL MENU ITEMS"). This activates the right presentation as it selects the slide and displays the shortcut menu.

7. Choose Copy from the shortcut menu to copy the slide to the Clipboard.

  TIP: You can also use the keyboard shortcut Ctrl+C to copy or click the Copy button on the Standard toolbar.

NOTE
Explain the use of the Clipboard for students who are not familiar with it. Point out that the Cut and Copy commands replace what was previously stored on the Clipboard.

NOTE
The presentation that is active when you choose Arrange All always appears on the left after arranging. Make sure students verify the position of their arranged presentations (2-3 should be on the left and 2-7 on the right).

 In PowerPoint Classroom Presentation #2.

50

LESSON 2 ■ **CREATING A PRESENTATION AUTOMATICALLY**

8. Right-click between slides 5 and 6 in the left presentation, *[your initials]***2-3.ppt**, and choose <u>P</u>aste from the shortcut menu. The slide is pasted from one presentation into the other. Notice that the pasted slide takes on the design of the presentation into which it is copied.

> **NOTE:** You can also move slides between presentations by dragging. Using the left mouse button, simply drag a slide from one window to the other, positioning the slide with the drag-and-drop pointer (and the vertical line). Using the right mouse button, drag and position the slide. A pop-up menu asks if you want to <u>M</u>ove Here or <u>C</u>opy Here (or C<u>a</u>ncel).

9. Maximize the left presentation by clicking the Maximize button on its title bar.

10. Display the new slide 6 in Slide view. Delete the text that describes the watermelon slurpee to make the text fit the slide. Change the slide title to **Sample Menu Items for Special Event** (using uppercase and lowercase letters).

11. In Slide Sorter view, select slide 5 (titled "How Did We Get Here?") and press Delete. Delete the last slide (titled "Recommendations").

> **TIP:** To delete more than one slide at a time in Slide Sorter view, select the first slide, hold down Shift, select additional slides, and press Delete.

12. In Slide view, edit slide 6 ("Available Options") by changing its title to **Next Steps**. Replace the sample bulleted text with the following text:
    ♦ **Develop mailing list for targeted companies**
    ♦ **Develop price plan based on group size and level of service**
    ♦ **Send promotional mailer to target companies**
    ♦ **Prepare sales force for telephone follow-up**

13. Check spelling in the presentation and save it as *[your initials]***2-8.ppt**. Leave both presentations open.

Objective 5

Adding Headers and Footers

You can add identifying information to your presentation, such as header or footer text, the date, or a slide or page number. These elements appear in special header and footer placeholders on slides and on notes and handout pages.

NOTE
Make sure students understand how to maximize a window.

NOTE
You can also delete a slide by selecting the slide and choosing <u>E</u>dit, <u>D</u>elete Slide from the menu.

51

UNIT 1 ■ INTRODUCTION TO POWERPOINT

TABLE 2-3   **Adding Identifying Information to Presentations**

INFORMATION	DESCRIPTION
Date and Time	The current date—updated automatically or fixed
Header	Descriptive text on notes and handout pages only
Page Number	Number placed in the lower right corner of notes and handout pages by default
Slide Number	Number you can place in the lower right corner of slides
Footer	Descriptive text for use on either slides or notes and handout pages

EXERCISE 2-9   Add Footers, Dates, and Page Numbers

1. Display *[your initials]***2-7.ppt** (the Fourth of July presentation). Choose Header and Footer from the View menu. Note the tabs in the Header and Footer dialog box—one for adding information to slides and one for adding information to notes and handouts.

FIGURE 2-11
Header and Footer dialog box, Slide tab

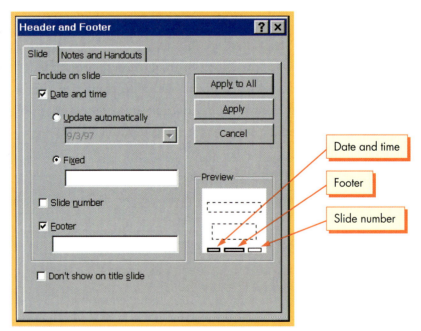

In PowerPoint Classroom Presentation #2.

52

LESSON 2 ■ CREATING A PRESENTATION AUTOMATICALLY

2. In the Preview box, notice the positions for the elements you can place on a slide. As you enable each element by selecting its check box, PowerPoint indicates where it will print with a bold outline in the Preview box.

3. Click the Slide number box to select it. Click the check box at the bottom of the dialog box so the page number does not appear on the title slide. Click Apply to All. Scroll through the document in Slide view and notice the numbers at the bottom right of each slide except the title slide.

4. Open the Header and Footer dialog box again and display the Notes and Handouts tab. Under the Date and Time option, click Update automatically to add today's date. Each time you print the file, it will include the current date. You can choose different date and time formats from the drop-down list.

FIGURE 2-12
Header and Footer dialog box, Notes and Handouts tab

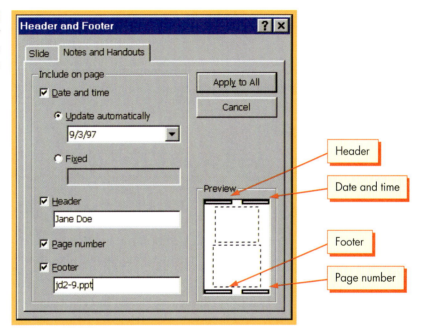

5. Check Header, if necessary. Position the insertion point in the Header text box and key your name. The header appears in the upper left corner of the page.

6. Check Page Number, if necessary. Page numbers appear at the bottom right of the page.

7. Check Footer, if necessary. Key the filename *[your initials]***2-9.ppt** in the Footer text box. Click Apply to All to add this information to all handout pages (but not to individual slides).

8. Save the presentation as *[your initials]***2-9.ppt**. You print it in the next exercise.

NOTE
You may want to explain that although the Date and time and Footer boxes are checked on the Slide tab of the dialog box, these items do not appear on the slide unless text is entered in the Fixed and Footer text boxes.

NOTE
Discuss the advantages of entering a fixed date versus updating automatically.

In PowerPoint Classroom Presentation #2.

NOTE
Stress the difference between adding identifying information to slides and to notes/handouts. The slide information appears directly on the slide, while the notes/handout information appears on the notes/handout sheets.

53

UNIT 1 ■ INTRODUCTION TO POWERPOINT

Choosing Print Options

☑ **Objective 6**

As Lesson 1 demonstrated, PowerPoint provides many ways to print an entire presentation or a portion of a presentation. For example, in the Print dialog box you can select:

- Individual slides, the current slide, or a range of slides
- Slides, handouts (2, 3, or 6 to a page), notes, or outlines
- Multiple copies

Additionally, there are two options for printing in black and white. The Black & white option converts the presentation colors to shades of gray. The Pure black & white option converts all colors to either black or white, eliminating all shades of gray. In complex presentation designs where shades of gray may obscure your text, this setting is preferable.

NOTE: Because the Pure black & white option simplifies your presentation graphics, it also speeds up printing time.

EXERCISE 2-10 Choose Print Dialog Box Options

1. With the Fourth of July presentation displayed, choose Print from the File menu.
2. Under Print Range, click Slides and key **1,2** in the text box to print only slides 1 and 2. Make sure the Black & white option box is checked.

NOTE

TIP: To print consecutive slides, you can use a hyphen. For example, enter **2-4** to print slides 2 through 4. To print a combination of slides, you can key the range **1,3,5-9,12** to print slides 1, 3, 5 through 9, and 12.

3. Choose Slides from the Print what drop-down list, if necessary, and click OK. Only slide 2 is numbered.
4. Open the Print dialog box again. Choose All to print all slides. From the Print what drop-down list, choose Handouts (3 slides per page).

FIGURE 2-13
Print what drop-down list

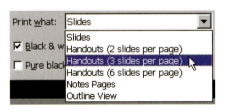

☑ **Objective 6 Assignment:**
Exercise 2-14 (Skills Review) and Exercises 2-15 through 2-18 (Lesson Applications) can be assigned after completing Objective 6.

NOTE
You can also enter a slide range in a particular order. For example, key the range **4-1** to print slides 4 through 1 in reverse order.

In PowerPoint Classroom Presentation #2.

54

LESSON 2 ■ CREATING A PRESENTATION AUTOMATICALLY

5. Make sure the Black & white and Frame slides option boxes are checked and click OK. The presentation prints on three handout sheets that include the header and footer information you added to notes and handout pages: your name, the date, the filename, and the page number.

6. Click to save the presentation, then close it.

7. With *[your initials]***2-8.ppt** displayed, view the presentation in Slide view. Notice that the date appears on the title slide and that the slides contain slide numbers (except for slide 5, which was pasted from another presentation). These elements were created by the AutoContent Wizard.

8. Open the Header and Footer dialog box. On the Slide tab, clear the Date and Time check box and click Apply. The date is no longer on slide 1.

9. Open the Print dialog box. Make sure Frame slides is checked and check the Pure black & white option. This presentation would be difficult to read if you print it with shades of gray.

10. Set the Print what dialog box to print handouts, 6 slides per page, and click OK. Slide 1 prints without the date. Notice that the handout prints with a header (your name) and a footer (the presentation title). These elements were added automatically by the AutoContent Wizard.

11. Close the presentation. Click Yes when you are asked to save changes.

NOTE **NOTE:** Some presentations created with the AutoContent Wizard print with headers and footers on the handouts automatically using the text you key in the title slide. This text is part of the master slide. Master slides and handout masters are discussed in Lessons 5 and 9.

COMMAND SUMMARY

NOTE

FEATURE	BUTTON	MENU	KEYBOARD
Spelling checker	ABC✓	Tools, Spelling	F7
Style checker		Tools, Style Checker	
Cut	✂	Edit, Cut	Ctrl+X
Copy	📋	Edit, Copy	Ctrl+C
Paste	📋	Edit, Paste	Ctrl+V
Choose next open presentation		Window	Ctrl+Tab
Header and footer		View, Header and Footer	

NOTE
A presentation created with the AutoContent Wizard contains automatic headers and footers that cannot be altered without working with the handout master. Students will notice these headers and footers when they print their presentations.

NOTE
Point out that the Command Summary lists a variety of ways to accomplish a particular task. Students can decide which method they prefer to use.

UNIT 1 ■ INTRODUCTION TO POWERPOINT

USING HELP

NOTE   PowerPoint's online Help feature is like an interactive teaching tool. One way to explore online Help is to display a list of Help topics. After you choose a topic, PowerPoint displays information or provides a demonstration.

To display a list of Help topics, make sure a presentation is active and then choose Contents and Index from the Help menu. Choose a topic by double-clicking (or click the topic and then click the Open button).

Follow these steps to learn more about getting help in PowerPoint:

1. Open any presentation file.

2. Choose Contents and Index from the Help menu. Click the Contents tab, if necessary.

3. Browse through the list of Help categories, each of which is represented by a book icon 📕.

4. Double-click the category "Printing Presentations." A list of topics appears, each preceded by a question mark page icon ❓.

FIGURE 2-14
Help Topics screen in PowerPoint

5. Click the topic "Print slides, notes, handouts, and outlines" and click Display.

6. Review the Help window and click the button to the left of "Show me" for a demonstration. PowerPoint shows you how to open the Print dialog box and points you to the appropriate dialog box area.

7. Click Cancel to close the dialog box. Close the presentation.

NOTE
Encourage students to follow the steps in "Using Help." Software companies are increasingly using their online Help systems—rather than printed documentation—to train users and assist in answering user questions.

In PowerPoint Classroom Presentation #2.

LESSON 2 ■ CREATING A PRESENTATION AUTOMATICALLY

TEST BANK

Concepts Review

TRUE/FALSE QUESTIONS

Each of the following statements is either true or false. Indicate your choice by circling T or F.

(T) F 1. The AutoContent Wizard begins a presentation with the title slide.

T (F) 2. The title slide in a presentation is limited to one line.

(T) F 3. Before editing text in a placeholder, you must click the placeholder to activate it.

T (F) 4. You can activate the spelling checker by pressing F1.

(T) F 5. The style checker can review spelling as well as style.

(T) F 6. The style checker can be used to change the case of slide titles.

(T) F 7. To move a slide while in Slide Sorter view, you can drag it or use the Cut and Paste commands.

(T) F 8. You can use either Delete or ✂ to remove a selected slide from a presentation.

SHORT ANSWER QUESTIONS

Write the correct answer in the space provided.

1. When using the AutoContent Wizard, what are the two methods for moving forward to the next dialog box?
   Click Next or click the gray box

2. In Slide view, what shape is the pointer when it is placed outside a text box?
   White arrow

3. Which feature in PowerPoint, if turned on, replaces commonly misspelled words with the correct words as you key?
   AutoCorrect

4. What function does 📋 perform?
   Copies the selection to the Windows Clipboard

Concepts Review: Allows students to check their understanding.

TEST BANK Consider using the Test Bank to provide an additional review of lesson concepts.

57

UNIT 1 ■ INTRODUCTION TO POWERPOINT

5. Which dialog box must you open to add the date at the top of every handout page?

   Header and Footer

6. When you add slide numbers to a presentation, where do the numbers appear on the slides?

   Lower right corner

7. How would you use the Print dialog box to print only slides 1, 3, and 5 of a presentation?

   Key the print range 1,3,5 in the Slides text box

8. How many slides can you print per handout page (state all options)?

   _2, 3, or 6_

CRITICAL THINKING

Answer these questions on a separate page. There are no right or wrong answers. Support your answers with examples from your own experience, if possible.

1. The AutoContent Wizard, spelling checker, and style checker help you create a uniform presentation. What are the advantages and disadvantages of uniformity for the audience? For the presenter?

2. You can use headers and footers to identify your slides, handouts, and notes. What information is most important to include? Why?

Skills Review

EXERCISE 2-11

Create a new presentation using the AutoContent Wizard and change sample text in the presentation.

1. Create a new presentation using the AutoContent Wizard by following these steps:

   a. Start PowerPoint. In the opening dialog box, choose the AutoContent Wizard option and click OK. (If PowerPoint is already active, choose New from the File menu, click the Presentations tab, and double-click the AutoContent Wizard icon.)

   b. In the AutoContent Wizard dialog box, click Next.

Critical Thinking Questions:
Answers will vary based on students' preferences, observations, experiences, and research.

Skills Review:
Provides guided practice for students. Objectives are indicated for each Exercise.

Exercise 2-11:
Objectives 1–2
Required File: None
Solution File: gl2-11.ppt in Solutions Manual or on Solutions Disk

58

LESSON 2 ■ CREATING A PRESENTATION AUTOMATICALLY

    c. Click <u>G</u>eneral for type of presentation and pick Generic from the list at the right of the dialog box. Click <u>N</u>ext.

    d. Choose <u>P</u>resentations, informal meetings, handouts. Click <u>N</u>ext

    e. Choose On-<u>s</u>creen presentation for type of output and choose <u>Y</u>es to print handouts. Click <u>N</u>ext.

    f. Key **Advertising Analysis** in the <u>P</u>resentation title text box, key your name in the second text box, and key **Good 4 U** in the <u>A</u>dditional information text box. Click <u>N</u>ext.

    g. In the last dialog box, click <u>F</u>inish.

2. Change the sample title text by following these steps:

    a. Switch to Slide view and use `PgDn` or `▼` to go to slide 4. Click the title text placeholder, select the text "Topic One," and key **Newspaper Advertising**. Click outside the text box to deselect it.

    b. Change the title text in slide 5 to **Radio Advertising**

    c. Skip to slide 7 and change the title text to **Yellow Pages**

3. Change the sample body text by following these steps:

    a. Click the bulleted text on slide 7 to activate the placeholder.

    b. Drag to select all bulleted text, from "Give" through "appropriate." Press `Delete`.

    c. Key the following text, pressing `Enter` at the end of each new bulleted item:

    ▪ **Attractive display, prominent placement**

    ▪ **Ad appears in all metro editions**

    ▪ **Delivers 6% of customers**

4. Change the sample body text of slide 3 to the following bulleted items:

    ▪ **Quality**

    ▪ **Frequency**

    ▪ **Effectiveness**

5. In Slide Sorter view, delete the slides with these titles: "Introduction," "Topic Three," and "What This Means."

6. Save the presentation as *[your initials]***2-11.ppt**.

7. Print the presentation as handouts, 6 slides per page, black and white, framed. (Because this type of presentation is preset for headers and footers, the handouts will contain your name as a header, the date, a page number, and the presentation title as a footer.)

8. Close the presentation.

NOTE
Students create a partial draft (containing sample text) based on AutoContent's Generic format. Ask students to notice the sample text that comes with a generic presentation. Other versions of this presentation are used in Exercises 2-12, 2-13, and 2-14.

UNIT 1 ■ INTRODUCTION TO POWERPOINT

EXERCISE 2-12

Use the spelling checker and style checker.

1. Open the file **Advert1.ppt**.
2. Run the spelling checker by following these steps:
   a. Click [ABC✓].
   b. Click Change to correct the spelling of "advertising."
   c. Click Change to correct the spelling of "humorous."
   d. Click Ignore to skip over "vs."
   e. Click OK when the spelling check is complete and return to slide 1.
3. Run the style checker by following these steps:
   a. Choose Style Checker from the Tools menu.
   b. Click Options to view the options. Make sure the Slide title style is set to Title Case and the Body text style is set to Sentence case. Click OK.
   c. Clear the Spelling check box and click Start.
   d. When the style checker locates end punctuation in slide 2, paragraph 2, click Change.
   e. When the style checker locates end punctuation in slide 7, paragraph 1, click Change to delete it.
   f. Click OK when style checking is complete.
4. Check slide 4. If necessary, change "Wednesday" to an uppercase "W." Check slide 9. If necessary, change the word "cost" to a lowercase "c."
5. Move to slide 1. Replace "Student's Name" with your name.
6. Save the presentation as *[your initials]***2-12.ppt**.
7. Print the presentation as handouts, 6 slides per page, black and white, framed.
8. Close the presentation.

EXERCISE 2-13

Reorder a presentation in Slide Sorter view.

1. Open the file **Advert2.ppt**.
2. In slide 1, replace "Student's Name" with your own name.
3. Switch to Slide Sorter view.
4. Move slide 7 to the left of slide 5 by selecting and dragging it.
5. Cut and paste to move a slide by following these steps:

Exercise 2-12:
Objective 3
Required File: Advert1.ppt
Solution File: gl2-12.ppt in Solutions Manual or on Solutions Disk

Exercise 2-13:
Objectives 2, 4
Required File: Advert2.ppt
Solution File: File gl2-13.ppt in Solutions Manual or on Solutions Disk.

LESSON 2 ■ **CREATING A PRESENTATION AUTOMATICALLY**

   a. Right-click slide 7 ("Mailers").
   b. Choose Cut from the shortcut menu to cut the slide.
   c. Right-click between slides 5 and 6 and choose Paste to paste the slide.
6. Copy a slide by following these steps:
   a. Select slide 1 and press Ctrl+C to copy it.
   b. Scroll to the bottom of the presentation. Position the insertion point after slide 9.
   c. Press Ctrl+V to paste the slide. (The copied slide should be slide 10.)
7. Edit slide 10 by changing the title to **Good 4 U**. Delete the text in the placeholder below the title and key **Successful Advertising Planning for the 21st Century**
8. Delete slide 8, "What This Means."
9. Save the presentation as *[your initials]***2-13.ppt**.
10. Print the presentation as handouts, 6 slides per page, black and white, framed.
11. Close the presentation.

EXERCISE 2-14

Add headers and footers to a presentation and choose printing options.

1. Open the file **Advert2.ppt**.
2. In slide 1, replace "Student's Name" with your name.
3. Add a footer and slide numbers by following these steps:
   a. Choose Header and Footer from the View menu.
   b. Click the Slide tab, if necessary.
   c. Check Slide number.
   d. Check Footer and key your name as a footer.
   e. Check Don't show on title slide so the footer and slide number do not print on slide 1.
   f. Click Apply to All.
4. Scroll through the presentation in Slide view to check the footer and slide numbers.
5. Add a date and footer to handout pages by following these steps:
   a. Open the Header and Footer dialog box.
   b. Click the Notes and Handouts tab.
   c. Check Date and Time and Update Automatically.

Exercise 2-14:
Objectives 4–6
Required File: Advert2.ppt
Solution File: File gl2-14.ppt in Solutions Manual or on Solutions Disk.

UNIT 1 ■ INTRODUCTION TO POWERPOINT

   d. Check *F*ooter and key *[your initials]***2-14.ppt** in the *F*ooter text box.
   e. Make sure *P*age number is checked.
   f. Click Apply to All.
6. Delete slides with these titles: "Topics of Discussion," "Yellow Pages," and "What This Means."
7. Save the presentation as *[your initials]***2-14.ppt**.
8. Print slides 1 and 3 only by following these steps:
   a. Choose *P*rint from the *F*ile menu.
   b. Click Sl*i*des and key **1,3** in the text box.
   c. Choose Slides from the Print *w*hat drop-down list, choose *B*lack & white, and click OK.
9. Print all the slides in the presentation as handouts, 3 slides per page, black and white, framed.
10. Save the file again and close it.

Assessment Resources:
- Solutions Manual
- Test Bank with Software
- Portfolio Builder
- Alternative Assessment Guide
- Certification Procedures

LESSON 2 ■ CREATING A PRESENTATION AUTOMATICALLY

Lesson Applications

EXERCISE 2-15

Create a presentation using the AutoContent Wizard, change it in Slide view and Slide Sorter view, and check the spelling.

1. Start the AutoContent Wizard to create a presentation. When choosing a presentation type, click Corpora<u>t</u>e and choose **Company Meeting** from the list at the right of the dialog box. Click <u>N</u>ext.

2. Complete the rest of the steps in the wizard, choosing <u>P</u>resentations, informal meetings, handouts, On-<u>s</u>creen presentation, and <u>Y</u>es for handouts. Key **Good 4 U Power Bars** as the <u>P</u>resentation title, your name for <u>Y</u>our name, and **Brainstorming Session** for <u>A</u>dditional information. Click <u>F</u>inish when you get to the last step of the wizard.

3. Working in Slide view, go to slide 2 and key the following text in the bulleted text placeholder:

   Talk about Good 4 U developing and marketing a power bar (healthy "candy" bar)

4. On slide 4, change the title to read **Product Development**. Replace the current body text with the following four bulleted items:

   - **Features of the product**
   - **Packaging**
   - **Naming**
   - **Promotion**

5. On slide 7, change the title to **Marketing Overview**. Change the body text to:

   - **Customer profile**
   - **Market research**
   - **Advertising budget**

6. Switch to Slide Sorter view and delete slide 3. Delete the renumbered slides 4 and 5. Delete the remaining slides 5 through 9, leaving the "Summary" slide.

7. Check spelling in the presentation.

8. Save the presentation as *[your initials]***2-15.ppt**.

9. Print the presentation as handouts, 6 slides per page, pure black and white, framed.

Lesson Applications:
Provide independent practice for students. Objectives are indicated for each Exercise.

Exercise 2-15:
Objectives 1–4, 6
Required File: None
Solution File: gl2-15.ppt in Solutions Manual or on Solutions Disk.

NOTE
You may want to recommend that students look at completed presentations in Slide Show view. Some presentations created using the AutoContent Wizard contain transition effects and animations, which may be particularly interesting for students.

63

UNIT 1 ■ INTRODUCTION TO POWERPOINT

NOTE: As part of the AutoContent Wizard formatting, the presentation prints using the title slide information in the header and footer.

10. Close the presentation.

EXERCISE 2-16

Create a presentation using the AutoContent Wizard, change sample text, delete and reorder slides, add slide numbers and a footer, and run the spelling checker and style checker.

1. Use the AutoContent Wizard to create a presentation. For the presentation type, choose Product/Services Overview from the Sales/Marketing category. The output will be an on-screen presentation with handouts. On the title slide, include the title **Customer Relations Training** and your name. Delete any additional information.
2. Change the sample text for slides 2 through 5 as shown in Figure 2-15.

FIGURE 2-15

Slide 2
```
Overview
  ▪ How you greet and seat people is critical
  ▪ Effective handling of special events guarantees success
```

Slide 3
```
Agenda
  ▪ Receiving customers
  ▪ Handling special events
```

Slide 4
```
Special Events
  ▪ Usher celebrities to their tables
  ▪ Direct reporters to their station
  ▪ Consult with event planner for details
```

Slide 5
```
Receiving Customers
  ▪ Be professional, courteous
  ▪ Guide skaters and cyclists to equipment storage area
  ▪ Practice now by role playing
```

Exercise 2-16:
Objectives 1–6
Required File: None
Solution File: gl2-16.ppt in Solutions Manual or on Solutions Disk.

64

LESSON 2 ■ **CREATING A PRESENTATION AUTOMATICALLY**

3. Delete remaining slides 6 and 7.
4. Reverse the positions of slides 4 and 5 so "Receiving Customers" comes before "Special Events."
5. Run the style checker with the spelling checker, using the style checker to change slide titles to uppercase.
6. Add slide numbers and a footer that contains the text **Good 4 U** to each slide except the title slide. (This presentation will print handouts with headers, footers, and page numbers automatically.)
7. In Slide view, select the text "Your Logo Here" and key **Good 4 U** in its place.
8. Save the presentation as *[your initials]***2-16.ppt**.
9. Print the presentation as handouts, 6 slides per page, pure black and white, framed.
10. Close the presentation.

EXERCISE 2-17

Change slide text, copy a slide, use the spelling checker and style checker, add and remove headers and footers, and choose print options.

1. Open the file **Events2.ppt**.
2. Move slide 6 to the slide 1 position and delete slide 2 (formerly slide 1).
3. On slide 2, create a line break before the word "Good" by pressing Shift + Enter.

 TIP: Pressing Shift + Enter creates a line break within a paragraph. Pressing Enter before the word "Good" would create a new bulleted item.

4. Change the title of slide 2 to **Objectives** and add the following bullet point after the existing one:
   ▪ **Increase bookings of special events from entertainment and sports industries**
5. Change the title of slide 3 to read **What does everyone want?**
6. Change the third bulleted item on slide 4 to **Award-winning service and cuisine**
7. Add a new first bullet to slide 4 that reads **High-energy, high-profile atmosphere**
8. Change slide 5 to read as follows:

Exercise 2-17:
Objectives 2–6
Required File: Events2.ppt
Solution File: gl2-17.ppt in Solutions Manual or on Solutions Disk

The completed presentation for this Exercise may be used in a student's portfolio.

UNIT 1 ■ INTRODUCTION TO POWERPOINT

Next Steps - Sports
- **Develop list of ideas for special events**
- **Target sports-promotion companies**
- **Contact professional sports organizations**
- **Ask investors to call on sports-star friends**

9. Copy slide 5. Paste it at the end of the presentation to create slide 6.
10. Change slide 6 to read as follows:

   Next Steps - Entertainment
   - **Develop list of ideas for special events**
   - **Contact press agents**
   - **Contact public relations firms**
   - **Ask investors to call on celebrity friends**

11. Run the style checker with the spelling checker. Make sure the style checker options are set for title case for slide titles. (At completion, click OK in the Style Checker Summary box—you change slide 1 in the next step.)
12. Edit slide 1 so the words "Food," "Health," and "Century" begin with uppercase letters.
13. Check that the title of slide 3 appears in title case. (Note how it was keyed in step 4.) On slide 2, change "Good 4 U" to uppercase "G" if necessary.
14. Add slide numbers to all slides. Add a handout header that contains the completed filename, *[your initials]***2-17.ppt**. Add a handout footer that contains your name.
15. Save the presentation as *[your initials]***2-17.ppt**.
16. Print the presentation as handouts, 6 slides per page, black and white, framed.
17. Close the presentation.

EXERCISE 2-18

Create a presentation using the AutoContent Wizard, change sample text, delete and reorder slides, add slide numbers, and use the spelling checker and style checker.

1. Use the AutoContent Wizard to create a Generic on-screen presentation with handouts. On the title slide, include the topic **Premium Items** and your name. For additional information, key **Good 4 U**.

The completed presentation for this Exercise may be used in a student's portfolio.

LESSON 2 ■ CREATING A PRESENTATION AUTOMATICALLY

2. Delete slide 2.

3. Edit slides 2 through 5 as shown in Figure 2-16.

FIGURE 2-16

```
         Topics of Discussion
Slide 2    ■ Introduce new premium items to give away at special events
           ■ All premium items will contain the Good 4 U logo

         Item 1: Water Bottle
Slide 3    ■ Made of durable plastic
           ■ Excellent for outdoor sports and indoor workouts

         Item 2: Knee Pads
Slide 4    ■ Made of durable vinyl/foam
           ■ Essential protection for skaters

         Item 3: Visor
Slide 5    ■ Made of white cotton blend
           ■ Adjustable, one size fits all
           ■ Ideal for tennis, running, walking, skating
```

4. Delete slides 6 through 8.

5. Move the Item 3 slide before the Item 2 slide. Change the item numbers in the slide titles to be consecutive.

6. Open the file **Products.ppt**. Use the <u>W</u>indow menu to arrange both presentations, displaying them both in Slide Sorter view. (Remember, each window has its own view buttons.)

7. Copy slide 3 ("Next Steps") from the Products.ppt presentation. Paste the slide after slide 5 in your Premium Items presentation.

8. Run the style checker with the spelling checker. Make sure the slide title style is set to title case.

9. On slide 1, change the first letter of your last name to uppercase, if necessary.

10. Add slide numbers and the footer **Good 4 U** to all slides except the title slide. (Handouts will print with headers and footers automatically.)

11. Save the presentation as *[your initials]***2-18.ppt**.
12. Print the presentation as handouts, 6 slides per page, black and white, framed.
13. Print only slides 1 and 2 as handouts, 2 slides per page, using the pure black and white setting.
14. Close the presentation.

UNIT 1 ■ APPLICATIONS

Unit 1 Applications

APPLICATION 1-1

Copy and delete slides, copy and edit slide text, and add header and footer information to handouts.

1. Open the file **Growing2.ppt**.
2. In Slide Sorter view, move slide 2 after slide 7.
3. Delete the newly numbered slide 2.
4. Move slide 3 ("Financial History") after slide 5.
5. Copy the slide 3 title "Where We're Going" and paste it into the slide 2 title placeholder. Edit the slide 2 title to read **Who We Are**.
6. Copy slide 2 and paste it between slides 2 and 3.
7. On the new slide 3, change the title to **What We Want**. Delete all the text in the bullet placeholder and key these bulleted items:
   - **To encourage healthy eating**
   - **To promote participation in sports activities**
   - **To expand our market base**
8. On slide 2, delete the text "Their dreams" and the subtext below it.
9. Check spelling in the presentation.
10. Save the file as *[your initials]***u1-1.ppt**.
11. On the handouts, include today's date as a fixed date, add your name as the header, and add the filename as the footer.
12. Print the presentation as handouts, 6 slides per page, pure black and white, framed.
13. Save the file again and close it.

APPLICATION 1-2

Copy and move slides, edit slide text, use the spelling checker and style checker, add slide numbers, and add handout headers and footers.

1. Open the file **Menu1.ppt**.
2. Copy slide 3 ("Pasta Delights") and paste it at the end of the presentation.
3. Move slide 2 ("Just Sweet Enough") to the end of the presentation after the slide you just copied.

ASSESS

Assessment Resources:
- Solutions Manual
- Test Bank with Software
- Portfolio Builder
- Alternative Assessment Guide
- Certification Procedures
- Projects Manual

Unit Applications:
Provide independent practice of the skills acquired from each lesson in the Unit.

Project:
After students complete Unit 1, you can assign Project #1 from the Projects Manual.

Unit Application 1-1:
Required File: Growing2.ppt
Solution File: glu1-1.ppt in Solutions Manual or on Solutions disk

Unit Application 1-2:
Required File: Menu1.ppt
Solution File: glu1-2.ppt in Solutions Manual or on Solutions disk

69

4. On the "Just Sweet Enough" slide, change "desert" to **dessert** and delete the sentence that begins "The striking lime flavor."

5. Change the text on slide 3 (the second "Pasta Delights" slide) to match the text shown in Figure U1-1.

FIGURE U1-1

```
Salad Delights

• Corn, Black Bean, and Mango Salad

  The sweetness of mango and fresh corn, blended with savory beans and
  a hint of cilantro

• Michelle's Cobb Salad

  Roast turkey breast, cucumber, tomato, baby corn, avocado, sprouts,
  and black olives over a bed of romaine lettuce with a side of
  vinaigrette
```

6. Copy slide 1 and paste it at the end of the presentation. Change the text "New Additions to our Menu" to **A New Experience in Dining**

7. Check spelling and style in the presentation, setting the options so body text style is not checked (clear the check box). Remove any periods that the style checker locates. Ignore the Style Checker Summary.

8. Reset the style checker to its default option settings. (Open the Style Checker dialog box, click Options, click Defaults, click OK, and click Cancel.)

9. Save the file as *[your initials]***u1-2.ppt**.

10. Add slide numbers to all slides. Add a handout header that contains your name, add a handout footer that contains the filename, and add today's date as a fixed date.

11. Print slide 3 of the presentation in black and white.

12. Print the entire presentation as handouts, 6 slides per page, black and white, framed.

13. Save the presentation again and close it.

UNIT 1 ■ APPLICATIONS

APPLICATION 1-3

Use the AutoContent Wizard to create a new presentation, edit slide text, delete and copy slides, add slide numbers, add handout headers and footers, and use the spelling checker and style checker.

1. Use the AutoContent Wizard to start a new presentation. For presentation type, choose Status from the Projects category. The presentation will be for an informal meeting and an on-screen presentation. Choose No for the print handouts question (this prevents the Wizard from automatically applying handout headers and footers). Clear all the title page text boxes before finishing with the Wizard.

2. In Outline view, delete slide 1.

3. On the new slide 1, keep the title ("Status Summary"), but change the body text to the following:
   - **Currently have at least one special event scheduled per month**
   - **Some events are dependent on weather and other factors**

4. Change the title and body text of slide 2 to read as follows:

   1st Quarter Events
   - **January:**
   - **February:**
   - **March:**

5. In Slide Sorter view, copy slide 2 and paste it before slide 3. Paste the same slide two additional times, so four copies of the same slide appear as slides 2, 3, 4, and 5. (*Tip:* You can copy just once and paste repeatedly.)

6. Delete all slides after slide 5 except the last slide ("Goals for Next Review").

7. Edit slides 2 through 6 as shown in Figure U1-2.

FIGURE U1-2

```
        1st Quarter Events
Slide 2  • January: All-Stars' New Year's Day party
         • February: Westchester Girls' Gymnastics demonstration and lunch
         • March: National In-Line Skaters' warm-up party

        2nd Quarter Events
Slide 3  • April: Health Expo brunch
         • May:
         • June:
```
continues

Unit Application 1-3:
Required File: None
Solution File: glu1-3.ppt in Solutions Manual or on Solutions disk

The completed presentation for this Application may be used in a student's portfolio.

71

UNIT 1 ■ INTRODUCTION TO POWERPOINT

continued

Slide 4
- 3rd Quarter Events
  - July: Autograph session with aerobic video star Marsha Miles
  - August: Autograph session with marathon runner Steve Forbo
  - September:

Slide 5
- 4th Quarter Events
  - October: Tour de France bicyclers' dinner
  - November:
  - December: Holiday party for Special Olympics

Slide 6
- Next Steps
  - Confirm dates
  - Make necessary schedule shifts
  - Draft schedule for ad copy
  - Post schedule on Internet

8. Check spelling and style in the presentation, changing the slide title style to uppercase but clearing the body text style box so the style checker doesn't check this style. The Style Checker Summary will find inconsistencies with slides 2 and 6. Click OK.

9. To correct the inconsistencies, change the gymnastics event on slide 2 to end **demonstration/lunch**. On slide 6, in the second bullet, move the word "shifts" to the next line by clicking just before the word and pressing [Shift] + [Enter].

10. Run the style checker again.

11. Restore the style checker defaults. (Be sure you don't apply the defaults to the presentation by starting the style checker again.)

12. Rearrange the event schedule by moving the in-line skaters event from March to May and the gymnastics event from February to March.

13. Change the first bullet in slide 1 to read **Currently have two special events scheduled per quarter**

14. Save the presentation as *[your initials]***u1-3.ppt**.

15. Add slide numbers to all slides and remove the date. To the handouts, add a header that contains your name, add a footer that contains the filename, and add today's date as a fixed date.

UNIT 1 ■ APPLICATIONS

16. Print the presentation as handouts, 6 slides per page, black and white, framed.
17. Save and close the presentation.

APPLICATION 1-4

Write your own presentation using the AutoContent Wizard, change sample text, copy and paste a slide, use the style checker and spelling checker, and add a slide footer.

1. Use the AutoContent Wizard to create a new Generic presentation, which you will customize to discuss launching a new Good 4 U restaurant in your hometown. You'll create an on-screen presentation and print handouts. Key **Good 4 U** in the Presentation title box. Key your name in the Your name box and key the name of your home town in the Additional information box.
2. Delete the "Introduction" slide.
3. On the "Topics of Discussion" slide, use two bulleted items: one to explain the idea and the other to state the proposed street or neighborhood location.
4. On the "Topic One" slide, key **Meeting the Needs** in place of the existing title text and replace the body text with the following bulleted items:
   - **Neighborhood has no restaurant that supports healthy food, sports, and fitness**
   - **Health and fitness are important concerns in the community**
5. Delete the slides titled "Topic Two," "Topic Three," and "Real Life."
6. Change the title of the "What This Means" slide to **Key Benefits**, then list three ways your town would benefit from having a restaurant that promotes healthy eating and fitness.
7. Copy the "Key Benefits" slide and paste it between slides 4 and 5. Change the title to **Key Concerns** and change the body text to the following:
   - **How will community react to a high-profile "health food" restaurant?**
   - **Can we find a large enough space for a reasonable rent?**
   - **How quickly can we locate investors?**
8. On the "Next Steps" slide, list what you think the next three steps are for launching the new restaurant (for example, finding investors and a location).

Unit Application 1-4:
Required File: None
Solution File: sample glu1-4.ppt in Solutions Manual or on Solutions disk

NOTE
In this Application, students are asked to write some of their own slide content. Consequently, students' solution files will vary. A sample file is shown in the Solutions Manual and on the Solutions disk.

The completed presentation for this Application may be used in a student's portfolio.

73

9. Add a footer to all slides except the title slide. Use the text **Prepared by** and key your name.
10. Run the spelling checker and style checker. Use the default settings, except for body text style, which you should clear. Ignore or correct inconsistencies listed in the Style Checker Summary box as needed.
11. Save the presentation as *[your initials]***u1-4.ppt**.
12. Print the presentation as handouts, 6 slides per page, black and white, framed.
13. Close the presentation.

UNIT 2

Working with Presentations

LESSON 3 Starting with a Blank Presentation
LESSON 4 Using Outline View
LESSON 5 Working with Text

LESSON 3
Starting with a Blank Presentation

OBJECTIVES After completing this lesson, you will be able to:
1. Choose a slide layout.
2. Add new slides in Slide view.
3. Change bullet levels.
4. Change slide layouts.
5. Change design templates and color schemes.
6. Work with speaker's notes.

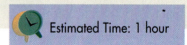
Estimated Time: 1 hour

The AutoContent Wizard is a great tool for creating standard presentations, but you will soon want the freedom to design your own slides and layouts. PowerPoint guides you through this process with features like AutoLayout and Design Template. In this lesson, you start with a blank presentation and create black and white slides. You then add colorful backgrounds to enhance their impact.

Objective 1
Choosing a Slide Layout

PowerPoint gives you great flexibility in choosing your slide layout. The layout is determined by the slide's contents, which can consist of bulleted text, tables,

---

PREPARE
Point out to students that the learning objectives show what they will learn in the lesson. Each heading in the lesson correlates to a learning objective.

Required Files
None

TEACH
Teaching Resources:
- PowerPoint Classroom Presentations
- School-to-Work Strategies Manual
- Internet Manual
- Spanish Glossary
- Methodology Video
- Certification Procedures

LESSON 3 ■ STARTING WITH A BLANK PRESENTATION

charts, or a simply a title for the presentation. Most presentations include at least two slide layouts: one for a title slide and one for the body of the presentation. You can choose an AutoLayout that is appropriate for the content of your presentation.

EXERCISE 3-1   Choose Slide Layouts

1. Start PowerPoint.
2. In the opening PowerPoint dialog box, choose **B**lank presentation and click OK. The New Slide dialog box appears with the Title Slide AutoLayout selected.

  NOTE: If PowerPoint is already active, close any open presentations and click the New button on the Standard toolbar to open a blank presentation and activate the New Slide dialog box.

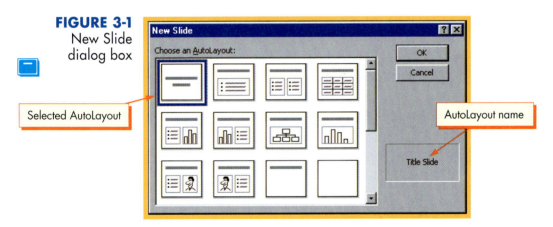

FIGURE 3-1
New Slide dialog box

3. Use the arrow keys to highlight each available AutoLayout Notice that the layout name changes in the lower right corner of the dialog box.

 NOTE: Don't double-click an AutoLayout unless you want to open it.

4. Click the Title Slide (the first one) and click OK. A slide with two placeholders appears. (See Figure 3-2 on the next page.)
5. Activate the title placeholder and key **Good 4 U Restaurant**. Remember, to activate a placeholder, move the mouse pointer over the text until it becomes an I-beam and then click.

NOTE
The New button on the Formatting toolbar is the equivalent of choosing **N**ew from the **F**ile menu (or pressing Ctrl+N) and choosing Blank Presentation from the General tab.

Use PowerPoint Classroom Presentation #3 to display screens from the lesson, including this one, in a slide-show format.

NOTE
If a student accidentally opens the wrong AutoLayout slide, he or she should click the Slide Layout button on the Common Tasks toolbar. In the Slide Layout dialog box, choose the correct AutoLayout.

77

UNIT 2 ■ **WORKING WITH PRESENTATIONS**

FIGURE 3-2
Title slide

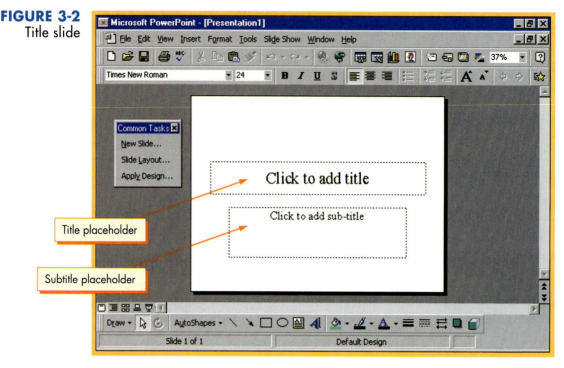

> **NOTE:** If the Common Tasks toolbar is not displayed, choose View, Toolbars, Common Tasks.

6. Click the subtitle placeholder and key **For the Pleasure of Your Company**
7. Click outside the subtitle box to deactivate it.

☑ Objective 2
Adding New Slides in Slide View

The body of most presentations requires a different layout than the title slide. Once you begin a presentation, you can add slides with different AutoLayouts by opening the New Slide dialog box. To open this dialog box, you can:

- Click New Slide on the Common Tasks toolbar.
- Click the New Slide button 🔲 on the Standard toolbar.
- Choose New Slide from the Insert menu or press Ctrl+M.

In a new slide you can activate a placeholder by clicking it or by pressing Ctrl+Enter. Pressing Ctrl+Enter repeatedly cycles through each object on the slide. After cycling through each slide object, pressing this keyboard combination again inserts a new slide.

In PowerPoint Classroom Presentation #3.

☑ **Objective 2 Assignment:**
Exercise 3-9 (Skills Review) can be assigned after completing Objective 2.

LESSON 3 ■ STARTING WITH A BLANK PRESENTATION

EXERCISE 3-2 Insert New Slides

FIGURE 3-3
Bulleted List
AutoLayout icon

1. Click the New Slide button on the Standard toolbar. The New Slide dialog box appears with the Bulleted List AutoLayout selected. It is the default AutoLayout after a title slide.
2. Click OK.
3. Press `Ctrl`+`Enter` to activate the title placeholder (or click the title placeholder) and key **Excellent Service**

NOTE

4. Press `Ctrl`+`Enter` or click the bulleted text placeholder to activate it and key the following text:
   - **We put your employees and guests at ease**
   - **We make your company look good**
   - **Schedules maintained**
   - **Professional and courteous staff**
   - **Guaranteed customer satisfaction**

5. Press `Ctrl`+`Enter` to create a new slide using the same AutoLayout.
6. Key **A Delightful Menu** as the title and then key the following text:
   - **High-quality, healthy food**
   - **Variety to appeal to a broad range of tastes**

7. Choose New Slide from the Common Tasks toolbar and double-click the Bulleted List icon. Another new slide appears.

NOTE

8. Key **High-Energy Fun** as the title and then key the following text:
   - **Athletic decor**
   - **Sports promotions**

 NOTE: Notice that AutoCorrect automatically adds the accent mark to the word "décor."

9. Press `Ctrl`+`M` to open the New Slide dialog box. Choose the Bulleted List AutoLayout.
10. Key **A Healthy Atmosphere** as the title and key the following text:
    - **Smoke-free**
    - **Alcohol optional**
    - **We sell none**
    - **We'll gladly serve your own**
11. Check spelling and then save the presentation as *[your initials]***3-2.ppt**. Leave it open for the next exercise.

NOTE
Pressing Ctrl+Enter is a convenient way to activate a placeholder or to insert a new slide. New slides inserted using Ctrl+Enter use the default layout—that is, Bulleted List after the Title Slide, or the currently selected body slide. Students open the New Slide dialog box in steps 7 and 9 for practice. Point out that Ctrl+Enter is the best method for inserting a slide with the same layout, whereas opening the dialog box is necessary to choose a different layout.

NOTE
Students in the habit of pressing Enter at the end of a line may add extra lines to their text boxes without realizing it. These extra lines change the size of placeholders and possibly the placement. For example, if you press Enter after keying a title, the title will be two lines tall. In later lessons, when students apply formatting to a text box, the results will be different than expected. Make students aware of this and show them how to delete an extra line.

79

UNIT 2 ■ WORKING WITH PRESENTATIONS

Changing Bullet Levels
☑ Objective 3

In PowerPoint you can change the level of importance assigned to bulleted items. You can show supporting ideas under main ideas, just as they would be in an outline. You can *demote* a bullet, indenting it to the right, or *promote* a bullet, raising its level.

EXERCISE 3-3 Promote and Demote Bullet Levels

NOTE

1. In slide 2, select the text "We make your company look good," and click the Demote button ➡ on the Formatting toolbar. The text is reduced in size, indented to the right, and the bullet shape changes.

2. Return the text to its original size and placement by clicking the Promote button ⬅.

3. Position the insertion point anywhere in the next item ("Schedules maintained") and click ➡. The item is demoted.

4. In the next item, position the insertion point between the bullet and the word "Professional." Do not select the text. Press [Tab]. The bullet is demoted.

5. With the insertion point between the bullet and the text, press [Shift]+[Tab]. The bullet is promoted.

> **NOTE:** If you press [Tab] or [Shift]+[Tab] when text is selected, the text is deleted. Use ⬅ and ➡ to promote and demote selected text. Additionally, if you press [Tab] when the insertion point is within the text, you insert a tab character.

6. Select the last two items and click to demote them.

FIGURE 3-4
Demoting bulleted text

> Excellent Service
> • We put your employees and guests at ease
> • We make your company look good
>   – Schedules maintained
>   – Professional and courteous staff
>   – Guaranteed customer satisfaction

☑ Objective 3 Assignment:
Exercise 3-10 (Skills Review) can be assigned after completing Objective 3.

NOTE
You may want to show students how to drag a selected bullet left or right to promote or demote it. This method takes some practice, however.

In PowerPoint Classroom Presentation #3.

80

LESSON 3 ■ STARTING WITH A BLANK PRESENTATION

7. In Slide Sorter view, move slide 5 ("A Healthy Atmosphere") to become slide 4.

8. Double-click the new slide 4 to change to Slide view. Select and demote the last two bullets, making them subtext under "Alcohol optional."

EXERCISE 3-4 Use Undo and Redo

The Undo button on the Standard toolbar reverses the last action you took. You can undo a series of editing actions, including keying or deleting text, promoting or demoting items, or changing formats and text attributes. You can undo up to 20 actions. The Redo button reapplies editing commands in the order you undid them.

TIP: You can increase the number of actions PowerPoint can undo by choosing Tools, Options, Edit tab, and changing the Maximum number of undos.

1. In slide 2, select the bulleted text "We make your company look good" and its three sub-bullets.

2. Click three times. The items are indented and reduced in size by three levels.

FIGURE 3-5
Creating third level bullets

3. Choose Undo Demote from the Edit menu. The last demotion is undone.
4. Click the Undo button. Another level of demotion is undone.
5. Press Ctrl+Z. The first level of demotion is undone.
6. Press Ctrl+Y. The most recent demotion is redone.

In PowerPoint Classroom Presentation #3.

NOTE
The Undo/Redo options can rescue a presentation. Students practice these options in later exercises. You may want to point out the usefulness of Undo. Emphasize, however, that Undo and Redo work best if carried out immediately after an edit.

81

UNIT 2 ■ WORKING WITH PRESENTATIONS

7. Click the Redo button . The previous level of demotion is redone.

8. Choose <u>R</u>edo Demote from the <u>E</u>dit menu. The final level of demotion is redone.

9. Undo the three demotions so the slide matches Figure 3-4. Deselect the selected text.

> **NOTE:** Undo and Redo are cleared when you save a presentation. After saving, you cannot undo or redo actions performed prior to the saving.

Objective 4
Changing Slide Layouts

You can try out different layouts on existing slides. If you don't like your changes, you can reverse them using the Undo option. You change the layout of the active slide with the Slide Layout dialog box. There are three ways to open the dialog box:

- Click Slide <u>L</u>ayout button on the Common Tasks toolbar.
- Click the Slide Layout button on the Standard toolbar.
- Choose Slide <u>L</u>ayout from the shortcut menu or the F<u>o</u>rmat menu.

EXERCISE 3-5 Change a Slide Layout

1. Move to slide 5 ("High-Energy Fun") and click Slide <u>L</u>ayout on the Common Tasks toolbar. The Slide Layout dialog box appears. (Notice its similarity to the New Slide dialog box.)

FIGURE 3-6
2 Column Text icon

2. Select the 2 Column Text layout and click <u>A</u>pply. The layout of the slide changes with the two existing bullets appearing in a left-column placeholder.

3. Select the second bullet ("Sports promotions") and cut it.

4. Click "Click to add text" to activate the right-column placeholder (or press Ctrl + Enter) and then paste. One bullet appears in each column.

5. Add the following item to the left column:
   - **Energetic staff**

6. Add the following item to the right column:
   - **Special event tie-ins**

7. Press Ctrl + Enter . A new slide appears with the 2 Column Text layout.

> **NOTE**
> When students explore the different layouts, they will come across layouts with clip art and object placeholders. You may want to discuss these features and note that they will be explained in later lessons.

LESSON 3 ■ STARTING WITH A BLANK PRESENTATION

8. Using the arrow pointer, right-click a blank area of the slide (an area outside of a text placeholder) to display the shortcut menu. Choose Slide Layout.
9. Double-click the Bulleted List layout icon to change layouts.

NOTE

10. Begin the title of the new slide by keying **Special Events that are** and press Enter to start a new title line.
11. Complete the title by keying **Good 4 U** and then key the following bulleted text:
    - **High-energy meetings**
    - **Productive lunches**
    - **Company celebrations**
12. Add the footer **Good 4 U Restaurant** on every slide except the title.
13. Spell-check the presentation and save it as *[your initials]***3-5.ppt.**
14. Create headers and footers for Notes and Handouts. Include the date and your name at the top of the page and the page number and filename at the bottom.
15. Print the presentation as handouts, 6 slides per page, black and white, framed.
16. Save the presentation again and leave it open.

Objective 5
Changing the Design Template

NOTE

You can apply a *design template* that adds a uniform color and design scheme to your presentation. The Default Design you have been using produces black and white slides on a plain background. PowerPoint provides many attractive, professional templates you can choose in the Apply Design dialog box. To open the dialog box, you can:

- Click Apply Design on the Common Tasks toolbar.
- Click the Apply Design button on the Standard toolbar.
- Choose Apply Design from the Format menu or the shortcut menu.
- Double-click the existing template name on the status bar.

EXERCISE 3-6 Change the Design Template

1. With the presentation *[your initials]***3-5.ppt** open, choose Apply Design from the Common Tasks toolbar. The Apply Design dialog box appears.

NOTE
You can press Enter in the title placeholder to start a new title line. Shift+Enter is used for bulleted list text to avoid creating another bullet.

Objective 5 Assignment:
Exercise 3-11 (Skills Review) and Exercises 3-13 and 3-15 (Lesson Applications) can be assigned after completing Objective 5.

NOTE
Changing design templates changes all standard template colors used in the presentation. Clip art colors and other non-standard colors do not change when a design template changes.

83

UNIT 2 ■ WORKING WITH PRESENTATIONS

FIGURE 3-7
Apply Design
dialog box

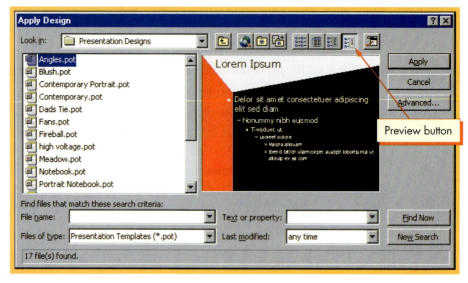

NOTE: You can find design templates in different locations on both the hard drive and the Microsoft Office CD-ROM. This lesson uses templates from the hard drive location C:\Program Files\Microsoft Office\Templates\Presentation Designs. If "Presentation Designs" doesn't appear in the Look in box of the Apply Design dialog box, ask your instructor how to locate it.

2. Click the Preview button, if necessary. Scroll the list of design template filenames (which have the extension .pot) in the dialog box and click one of the filenames. The preview box illustrates the template's features.

3. Preview two or three different designs and then choose **Professional.pot**. Click Apply. In a few seconds, your presentation is reformatted with the new design. Notice that the template name appears on the status bar.

4. Click ↶▾ to restore the Default Design.

5. Double-click "Default Designs" on the status bar to reopen the Apply Design dialog box, choose the **Pulse.pot** design, and click Apply.

FIGURE 3-8
Using the status
bar to apply a
design template

6. Review the presentation in Slide Sorter view.

7. Review the presentation in Slide Show view, using your preferred method to advance from slide to slide (such as the left mouse button or PgDn). Notice that this design includes animation effects, which can only be seen

In PowerPoint Classroom Presentation #3.

The Apply Design dialog box does not necessarily open to the Presentation Designs folder, which contains the designs used in this lesson. Show students how to use the Look in box to navigate to C:\Program Files\Microsoft Office\Templates\Presentation Designs. Or, refer to the Installation Requirements section at the beginning of this text to show students how to add this folder to the Favorites folder on their computers.

Remind students how to start a slide show, advance to the next slide, and quit a slide show. Remind them also to start the show from slide 1 by selecting slide 1 before clicking the Slide Show View button.

84

LESSON 3 ■ STARTING WITH A BLANK PRESENTATION

in Slide Show view. Many of PowerPoint's built-in designs have animation effects.

 NOTE: Animation effects are discussed in "Lesson 15: Creating Slide Show Effects."

8. Return to Slide view.

EXERCISE 3-7 Change the Template Color Scheme

You can apply new colors to the current design template by changing the template's color scheme. Using the Color Scheme dialog box, you can choose from several standard color schemes and apply a scheme to a single slide or to all slides in a presentation. You open the Color Scheme dialog box from either the F̲ormat menu or the shortcut menu.

1. Change the design template to **Ribbons.pot**.
2. Using the arrow pointer, right-click a blank area of a slide and choose Slide C̲olor Scheme from the shortcut menu. Click the Standard tab, if necessary. The Color Scheme dialog box appears.

FIGURE 3-9
Color Scheme dialog box

3. Select the third color scheme in the first row and click P̲review.

 NOTE: You can also customize color schemes, as you'll learn in "Lesson 7: Working with Lines, Fills, and Colors."

In PowerPoint Classroom Presentation #3.

NOTE
Point out the tip in the Color Scheme dialog box.
Light backgrounds work best for overheads. Dark backgrounds are recommended for screen presentations and slides.

85

UNIT 2 ■ WORKING WITH PRESENTATIONS

4. Drag the dialog box out of the way so you can see the effect on the slide.
5. Click Apply to All. The color scheme of all slides in the presentation is changed.
6. Click [↶]. The previous color scheme is restored.
7. Click [↷]. The new color scheme is restored.
8. In Slide view, scroll through the slides to review the color change.
9. Click the Black and White View button [▨] on the Standard toolbar. A version of the current slide is displayed as it would be printed in black and white. A miniature of the color slide is also displayed.
10. Click [▨] again to return to the color display.

NOTE

TIP: It's a good idea to check your presentation in Black and White view if you'll be distributing black and white printed slides or handouts. You learn how to control the shading and contrast of black and white printouts in Lesson 7.

Objective 6
Working with Speaker's Notes

Speakers often use notes to guide their presentations. In PowerPoint, a notes page contains a small picture of the slide above a text section. The text can include a script, comments, or reminders. To key notes for a slide, switch to Notes Page view or choose Speaker Notes from the View menu.

EXERCISE 3-8 Create Notes and Print Notes Pages

1. Display slide 2 and click [▨] to switch to Notes Page view.
2. Open the Zoom drop-down list box on the Standard toolbar and choose 100%. Scroll down to the notes text placeholder.

FIGURE 3-10
Zoom drop-down list box

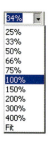

3. Click the notes text placeholder to activate it and key the following text:

   **Your choice of a meeting place says a lot about your organization.
   Good 4 U focuses on service for two reasons:
   1. We want you, your employees, and your guests (friends, clients, investors) to feel at ease.
   2. We want our professionalism to mirror yours.
   (Review bulleted points.)**

NOTE
You may want to discuss the value of reviewing slides in Black and White view. This practice becomes more important in later lessons when students work with text, autoshapes, and fills.

Objective 6 Assignment:
Exercises 3-12 (Skills Review) and 3-16 (Lesson Applications) can be assigned after completing Objective 6.

In PowerPoint Classroom Presentation #3.

LESSON 3 ■ **STARTING WITH A BLANK PRESENTATION**

4. While still in Notes Page view, display slide 3 and key the following notes text:

   Distribute menus.
   Point out vegetarian and meat dishes.

5. Switch to Slide view and choose Spea<u>k</u>er Notes from the <u>V</u>iew menu. You use the Speaker Notes dialog box to create, view, or edit speaker notes.

FIGURE 3-11
Speaker Notes dialog box

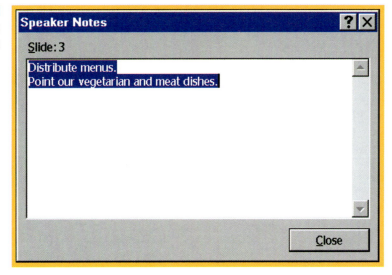

6. Add the note **Point out healthy beverages.** Close the Speaker Notes dialog box.

7. Check spelling and style in the presentation.

8. Display slide 1 in Slide view and choose Fit from the Zoom box, if necessary.

9. Save the presentation as *[your initials]***3-8.ppt**.

10. Edit the Notes and Handouts footer to reflect the new filename.

11. Choose <u>P</u>rint from the <u>F</u>ile menu, click Sl<u>i</u>des, and key **2-3** in the text box.

12. From the Print <u>w</u>hat drop-down list, choose Notes Pages, and then choose the print options for black and white and framed slides. Click OK to print the notes pages for slides 2 and 3.

13. Save and close the presentation.

In PowerPoint Classroom Presentation #3.

NOTE
After working on a presentation in different views, it's a good idea to display slide 1 in Slide view with the Zoom set to "Fit" before saving the presentation. That way, the presentation opens with slide 1 in Slide view.

NOTE
Step 12 asks students to print in black and white to save time. To verify that students changed color schemes, you might have them print a notes page in color or you might check their answer files.

87

UNIT 2 ■ **WORKING WITH PRESENTATIONS**

COMMAND SUMMARY

NOTE

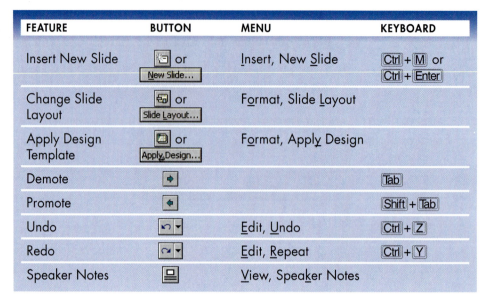

USING HELP

NOTE

Your choice of color schemes can affect the tone of your presentation. Help is available to remind you of your options.

Exploring color schemes in Help:

1. Click [?] to display the Office Assistant.
2. Key **color schemes** in the text box and click Search.
3. Click the first topic, "How color schemes work." (See Figure 3-12 on the next page.)
4. Click "Color schemes" and read about the topic.
5. Review the topics "Customize color schemes" and "Combine color schemes."

 NOTE: If the "Combine color schemes" topic is not displayed, enlarge the Help window by dragging the bottom right corner.

6. Close the Help window when you finish. Close the Office Assistant.

NOTE
Point out that the Command Summary lists a variety of ways to accomplish a particular task. Students can decide which method they prefer to use.

NOTE
Encourage students to follow the steps in "Using Help." Software companies are increasingly using their online Help programs—rather than printed documentation—to train users and assist in answering user questions.

88

LESSON 3 ■ **STARTING WITH A BLANK PRESENTATION**

FIGURE 3-12
Using Help to understand color scheme options

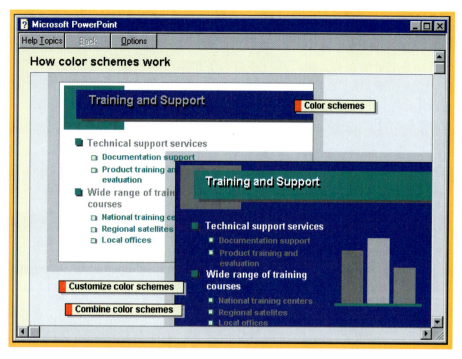

In PowerPoint Classroom Presentation #3.

89

UNIT 2 ■ WORKING WITH PRESENTATIONS

TEST BANK

Concepts Review

TRUE/FALSE QUESTIONS

Each of the following statements is either true or false. Indicate your choice by circling **T** or **F**.

T **(F)** 1. When you open a blank presentation, the Slide Layout dialog box appears.

(T) F 2. The AutoLayout dialog box shows the name of each layout.

T **(F)** 3. You can add a new slide by pressing Ctrl+Y.

(T) F 4. You can promote and demote bullets using the left and right arrow buttons on the Formatting toolbar.

(T) F 5. You can undo a task by pressing Ctrl+Z.

T **(F)** 6. You can change a design template in the Slide Layout dialog box.

T **(F)** 7. A template color scheme is predefined and cannot be changed.

(T) F 8. You can print speaker's notes in either black and white or color.

SHORT ANSWER QUESTIONS

Write the correct answer in the space provided.

1. Which Common Tasks toolbar item can you use to change a slide from a title slide to a bulleted list slide?

   Slide Layout

2. How do you add a new slide to a presentation?

   New Slide button; Insert, New Slide; Ctrl+Enter; or Ctrl+M

3. You just promoted a bullet. Name two ways you can use the mouse to return it to its original size and position.

   Click Undo, click Demote

4. What happens when you press Ctrl+M?

   The new Slide dialog box opens

5. If you insert a new slide while working on a title slide, what slide layout is automatically chosen for you?

   Bulleted List

Concepts Review: Allows students to check their understanding.

TEST BANK Consider using the Test Bank to provide an additional review of lesson concepts.

LESSON 3 ■ STARTING WITH A BLANK PRESENTATION

6. Which tab do you click in the Color Scheme dialog box to choose a predefined color scheme?
   Standard

7. How can you add or edit speaker notes without changing to Notes Page view?
   Choose View, Speaker Notes to open the Speaker Notes dialog box

8. In what drop-down list in the Print dialog box do you find the option to print notes pages?
   Print what

CRITICAL THINKING

Answer these questions on a separate page. There are no right or wrong answers. Support your answers with examples from your own experience, if possible.

1. You can make the slides for your presentation white with black text or you can add color and graphics. Why might you include some plain slides? Review the design templates. In what kinds of presentations might you use the different templates?

2. What are some advantages of starting with a blank presentation instead of using the AutoContent Wizard? Which method do you prefer and why?

Skills Review

EXERCISE 3-9

Choose slide layouts and add new slides in Slide view.

1. Open a new blank presentation and choose the layout for the title slide by following these steps:
   a. Start PowerPoint. Select <u>B</u>lank Presentation and click OK. (If PowerPoint is already running, click the New button.)
   b. In the New Slide dialog box, choose the Title Slide layout and click OK.

2. Complete the title slide by following these steps:
   a. Press [Ctrl]+[Enter] (or click the I-beam pointer on "Click to add title").
   b. Key **Healthy Eating** and press [Enter] to start a new title line.
   c. Key **for Young Athletes** to complete the title.

Critical Thinking Questions:
Answers will vary based on students' preferences, observations, experiences, and research.

Skills Review:
Provides guided practice for students. Objectives are indicated for each Exercise.

Exercise 3-9:
Objectives 1–2
Required File: None
Solution File: gl3-9.ppt in Solutions Manual or on Solutions Disk

UNIT 2 ■ WORKING WITH PRESENTATIONS

      d. Press Ctrl+Enter (or click the I-beam pointer on "Click to add subtitle").

      e. Key the subtitle **A Good 4 U Seminar**

  3. Add a new slide with the Bulleted List layout by following these steps:

      a. Press Ctrl+Enter (or click <u>N</u>ew Slide on the Common Tasks toolbar, select Bulleted List, and click OK).

      b. Key **Basic Food Groups** as the title.

      c. Key the following bulleted text:

- **Fats, oils, and sweets**
- **Milk, yogurt, and cheese**
- **Meat, poultry, fish, eggs, beans, and nuts**
- **Vegetables**
- **Fruit**
- **Rice, bread, and pasta**

  4. Add a third slide with the Bulleted List layout.

  5. Key **Elements of a Healthy Diet** as the title of the slide.

  6. Key the following bulleted text:

- **Variety - Choose from all basic food groups**
- **Moderation - Match calories to your needs**
- **Low Fat - Fewer than 30% of calories**
- **Vegetarians - Choose protein complements**

  7. Check spelling and style in the presentation.

  8. Review the changes made by the style checker to slides 1 and 3. Restore the uppercase "G" and "S" in the slide 1 subtitle.

  9. Save the presentation as *[your initials]***3-9.ppt**.

 10. Create headers and footers for Notes and Handouts. Include the date and your name at the top of the page and the page number and filename at the bottom.

 11. Print the presentation as handouts, 3 slides per page, black and white, framed.

 12. Save and close the presentation.

EXERCISE 3-10

Demote and promote bullets.

  1. Open the file **Pyramid1.ppt** and display the fourth slide.

  2. Demote the second bullet in the left column by following these steps:

Exercise 3-10:
Objective 3
Required File: Pyramid1.ppt
Solution File: gl3-10.ppt in Solutions Manual or on Solutions Disk

NOTE
Presentations in the Skills Review and Lesson Applications are quite similar. This approach reflects the real-world situation in which a PowerPoint user creates a presentation and "tweaks" its design and content, as requested by management or clients. Students are able to see a presentation with a variety of "looks."

LESSON 3 ■ STARTING WITH A BLANK PRESENTATION

      a. Click the I-beam pointer anywhere in the second bullet ("Use sparingly").

      b. Click ⬛ on the Formatting toolbar.

3. In the left column, demote the two bulleted items that include the text "2 to 3 servings."

4. Demote the first bullet in the right column using the Tab key by following these steps:

      a. Position the insertion point between the bullet and the first word in the first item ("Vegetables").

      b. Press Tab.

5. Click the Undo button ⬛ to restore the size and position of "Vegetables."

6. Demote the second, fourth, and sixth bullets in the right column (which all end in "servings").

7. Use ⬛ to demote the last bullet in the right column ("6 to 11 servings") another level.

8. Promote the last bullet by positioning the insertion point between the bullet and the number "6" and pressing Shift + Tab.

9. Check spelling in the presentation.

10. Save the presentation as *[your initials]*__3-10.ppt__.

11. Create headers and footers for Notes and Handouts. Include the date and your name at the top of the page and the page number and filename at the bottom.

12. Print the presentation as handouts, 6 slides per page, black and white, framed.

13. Save and close the presentation.

EXERCISE 3-11

Change design templates and color schemes.

1. Open the file **Pyramid2.ppt**.

2. Apply a new design template by following these steps:

      a. Choose Apply Design from the Format menu (or click Apply Design on the Common Tasks toolbar).

      b. In the Apply Design dialog box, double-click **Notebook.pot**.

      c. Scroll to slide 2 to see the design of a bulleted list slide.

3. Change the color scheme by following these steps:

Exercise 3-11:
Objective 5
Required File: Pyramid2.ppt
Solution File: gl3-11.ppt in Solutions Manual or on Solutions Disk.

UNIT 2 ■ WORKING WITH PRESENTATIONS

   a. Choose Slide Color Scheme from the Format menu (or from the shortcut menu).
   b. In the Color Scheme dialog box, click the fourth choice.
   c. Click Preview and drag the Color Scheme dialog box out of the way to see the effect on the slide. (Note: This change in color scheme is most evident on bulleted list slides, where the background color changes to white.)
   d. Click Apply to All.
   e. Switch to Slide Sorter view and click the Black and White View button on the Standard toolbar to see how the slide will print in black and white. Click the button again to display the presentation in color.

4. Click to undo the color change and then click to reapply the color change.
5. Check spelling and style in the presentation.
6. Save the presentation as *[your initials]*3-11.ppt.
7. Create headers and footers for Notes and Handouts. Include the date and your name at the top of the page and the page number and filename at the bottom.
8. Print the presentation as handouts, 6 slides per page, black and white, framed.
9. Save and close the presentation.

EXERCISE 3-12

Change slide layout, change bullet levels, and add speaker's notes to a presentation.

1. Open the file Pyramid2.ppt and display slide 3.
2. Change the layout of slide 3 by following these steps:
   a. Click Slide Layout on the Common Tasks toolbar.
   b. Select 2 Column Text and click Apply.
   c. Cut the last two bulleted items ("Eat moderately" and "Limit fats") from column 1 and paste them to column 2 (or drag and drop the items to column 2).
3. On slide 3, convert the text following the hyphens to second level bullets by following these steps:
   a. In the first bulleted item in column 1, select and delete the hyphen before "from." With the insertion point to the left of "from," press Enter to create a new bullet.
   b. Demote the new bullet one level.

Exercise 3-12:
Objectives 3, 4, 6
Required File: Pyramid2.ppt
Solution File: gl3-12.ppt in Solutions Manual or on Solutions Disk.

94

LESSON 3 ■ STARTING WITH A BLANK PRESENTATION

    c. Delete the remaining hyphens on slide 3 and change the text following the hyphens to second level bullets. (The bulleted text in slides 3 and 4 should now follow the same style.)

4. Switch to Notes Page view.

5. Change the Zoom setting to 100%.

6. Under slide 1, activate the notes text box and key the following text:

Remind staff about Good 4 U's mission to serve healthy food.

New menu items that balance food proportions according to FDA guidelines will be introduced next month.

7. Scroll to the second slide and key the following note text:

The USDA has classified foods into five basic groups.

8. Scroll to the third slide and key the following note text:

At Good 4 U, we promote the elements of a healthy diet.

9. Scroll to the last slide and key the note text:

A good diet consists of foods from each of the five main groups, and may contain a little fat, oil, and sweetener. The number of servings from each group is important.

10. Check spelling and style in the presentation.

11. Save the presentation as *[your initials]***3-12.ppt.**

12. Edit headers and footers for Notes and Handouts. Include the date and your name at the top of the page and the page number and filename at the bottom.

13. Print the presentation as notes pages, black and white, framed.

14. Save and close the presentation.

95

UNIT 2 ■ WORKING WITH PRESENTATIONS

Lesson Applications

EXERCISE 3-13

Create a title slide, add slides, apply a design template, and change the color scheme.

1. Start a blank presentation.
2. Create a title slide with the title **First in Food Safety** and the subtitle **Good 4 U Employee Training**
3. Use the Bulleted List layout to create three new slides, as shown in Figure 3-13.

FIGURE 3-13

Slide 2
- Our Food Safety Programs
  - Food handler training
  - Management inspections
  - Safety supervisors on-site
  - Reports to USDA

Slide 3
- Safe Food Handling Practices
  - Wear gloves, hair nets, and beard nets
  - Wash hands before and after handling food
  - Wear clean uniforms
  - No smoking

Slide 4
- Food Procurement
  - Know your suppliers
  - Prefer local growers
  - Prefer organic food
  - Insist on freshness
  - Insist on cleanliness
  - Test for pesticides

4. Change the layout of slide 4 to 2 Column Text.
5. Cut the last three bullets in column 1 and paste them into column 2.

Assessment Resources:
- Solutions Manual
- Test Bank with Software
- Portfolio Builder
- Alternative Assessment Guide
- Certification Procedures

Lesson Applications:
Provide independent practice for students. Objectives are indicated for each Exercise.

Exercise 3-13:
Objectives 1, 2, 4, 5
Required File: None
Solution File: gl3-13.ppt in Solutions Manual or on Solutions Disk.

LESSON 3 ■ STARTING WITH A BLANK PRESENTATION

6. Apply the design template **high voltage.pot** to the presentation.
7. Change the color scheme to the second one in the first row (with the white background).
8. Check spelling and style in the presentation. (Ignore the possible inconsistencies reported in the Style Checker Summary dialog box.)
9. On slide 1, restore the uppercase "E" and "T" in "Employee Training."
10. Save the presentation as *[your initials]***3-13.ppt**.
11. Create headers and footers for Notes and Handouts. Include the date and your name at the top of the page and the page number and filename at the bottom.
12. Print the presentation as handouts, 6 slides per page, black and white, framed.
13. Save and close the presentation.

EXERCISE 3-14

Change slide layouts, demote bullets, add slides, and change the color scheme.

1. Open the file **Safety1.ppt**.
2. In slide 4, cut the bulleted items in column 2 and paste them at the bottom of column 1.
3. Change the layout of slide 4 to Bulleted List.
4. Choose the first standard color scheme (with the black background) for this template.
5. Edit text in slide 4 and demote bullets as shown in Figure 3-14.

FIGURE 3-14

NOTE
Advise students to review a presentation after they style-check and spell-check. The style checker may make an unwanted change.

Exercise 3-14:
Objectives 1–5
Required File: Safety1.ppt, Safety2.ppt
Solution File: gl3-14.ppt in Solutions Manual or on Solutions Disk.

The completed presentation for this Exercise may be used in a student's portfolio.

97

UNIT 2 ■ **WORKING WITH PRESENTATIONS**

6. Add a new slide 5 using the text shown in Figure 3-15.

FIGURE 3-15

```
• Training inspections
   - Scheduled
   - Cooperative
• Internal evaluation inspections
• USDA inspections
```

7. Open the file **Safety2.ppt**. Arrange both presentations on the screen in Slide Sorter view.
8. Copy slide 2 ("Should We Be Safe?") from **Safety2.ppt** to the slide 2 position in **Safety1.ppt**.
9. Close **Safety2.ppt**.
10. Check spelling in the presentation and save it as *[your initials]***3-14.ppt**.
11. Create headers and footers for Notes and Handouts. Include the date and your name at the top of the page and the page number and filename at the bottom.
12. Print the presentation as handouts, 6 slides per page, black and white, framed.
13. Save and close the presentation.

EXERCISE 3-15

Create a title slide, add slides, demote bullets, apply a design template, and change the color scheme.

1. Key the presentation shown in Figure 3-16 (on the next page).
2. Apply the design template to **Meadow.pot**.
3. Change the color scheme to the Standard scheme with the white background.
4. Change the slide 6 title so it appears on one line.
5. Reverse the positions of slides 2 and 3.
6. Check spelling in the presentation.

Exercise 3-15:
Objectives 1–3, 5
Required File: None
Solution File: gl3-15.ppt in Solutions Manual or on Solutions Disk

The completed presentation for this Exercise may be used in a student's portfolio.

FIGURE 3-16

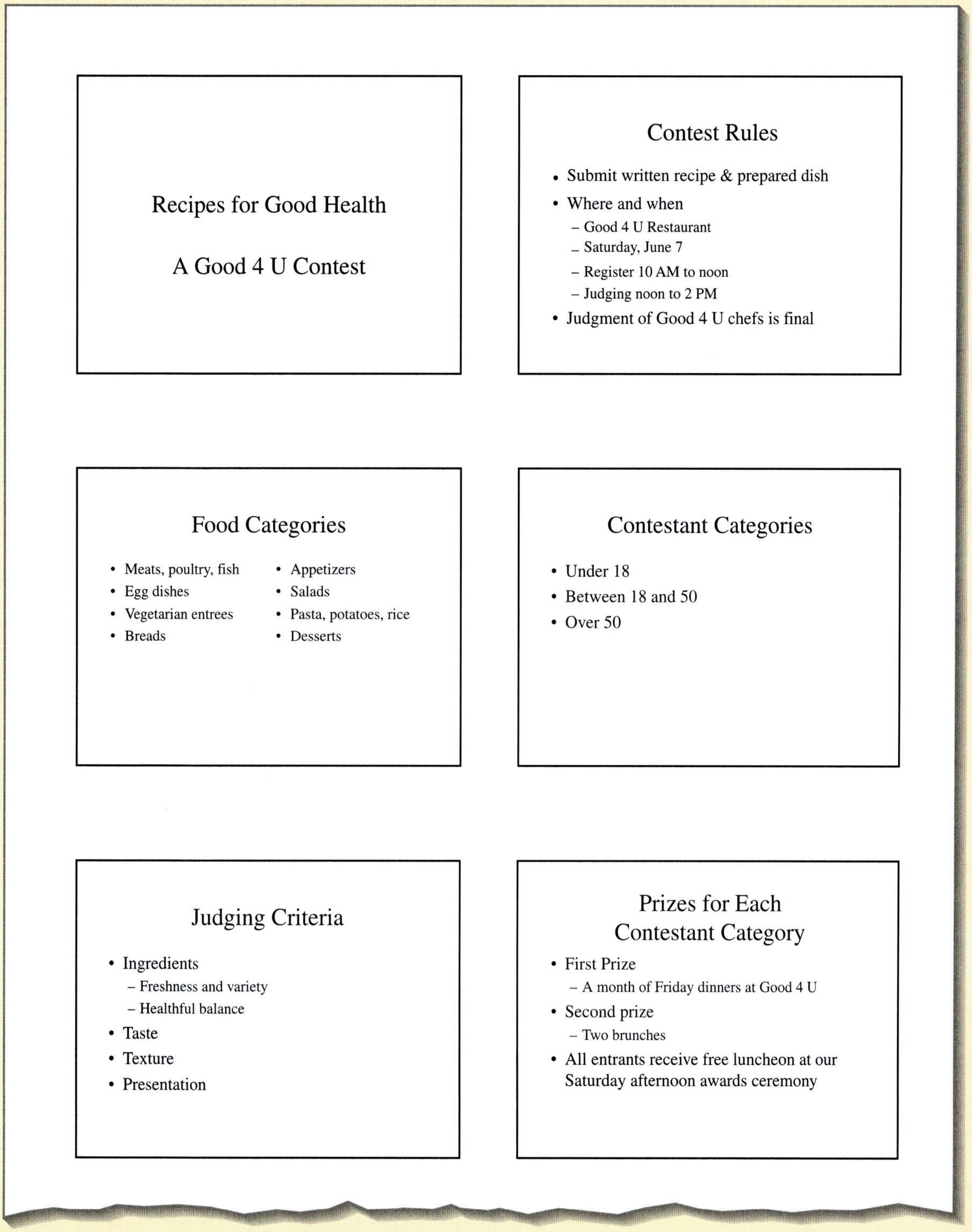

Recipes for Good Health

A Good 4 U Contest

Contest Rules

- Submit written recipe & prepared dish
- Where and when
  - Good 4 U Restaurant
  - Saturday, June 7
  - Register 10 AM to noon
  - Judging noon to 2 PM
- Judgment of Good 4 U chefs is final

Food Categories

- Meats, poultry, fish
- Egg dishes
- Vegetarian entrees
- Breads
- Appetizers
- Salads
- Pasta, potatoes, rice
- Desserts

Contestant Categories

- Under 18
- Between 18 and 50
- Over 50

Judging Criteria

- Ingredients
  - Freshness and variety
  - Healthful balance
- Taste
- Texture
- Presentation

Prizes for Each Contestant Category

- First Prize
  - A month of Friday dinners at Good 4 U
- Second prize
  - Two brunches
- All entrants receive free luncheon at our Saturday afternoon awards ceremony

7. Save the presentation as *[your initials]*__3-15.ppt__.

8. Create headers and footers for Notes and Handouts. Include the date and your name at the top of the page and the page number and filename at the bottom.

9. View the presentation in Black and White view.

10. Print the presentation as handouts, 6 slides per page, black and white, framed.

11. Save and close the presentation.

EXERCISE 3-16

Add a new slide, choose a slide layout, demote bullets, change design templates, and add speaker's notes.

1. Open the file **Recipe1.ppt**.
2. Apply the **Ribbons.pot** design template to the presentation.
3. Add a new slide after the title slide as shown in Figure 3-17.

FIGURE 3-17

4. Change slide 3 ("Food Categories") to the 2 Column Text layout. Move the last four bulleted items from column 1 to column 2.

5. Create the last slide of the presentation as shown in Figure 3-18.

Exercise 3-16:
Objectives 1–6
Required File: Recipe1.ppt
Solution File: gl3-16.ppt in Solutions Manual or on Solutions Disk

The completed presentation for this Exercise may be used in a student's portfolio.

FIGURE 3-18

6. Key the following subtitle for slide 1:

   Rules, Judging, and Prizes

7. Key the following speaker's notes for slide 1:

   Local businesses are sponsoring this contest.

8. Key the following speaker's notes for slide 2:

   Three volunteer taste testers will be "drafted" from the list of entrants.

9. Check spelling in the presentation.
10. Save the presentation as *[your initials]***3-16.ppt.**
11. Create headers and footers for Notes and Handouts. Include the date and your name at the top of the page and the page number and filename at the bottom.
12. Print slides 1 and 2 as notes pages, black and white, framed
13. Print the entire presentation as handouts, 6 slides per page, black and white, framed.
14. Save and close the presentation.

LESSON 4

Using Outline View

OBJECTIVES

After completing this lesson, you will be able to:
1. Start a presentation in Outline view.
2. Add a new slide in Outline view.
3. Promote and demote outline entries.
4. Expand a slide.
5. Create a summary slide.
6. Move bulleted items in Outline view.
7. Move slides in Outline view.
8. Import a Word outline into PowerPoint.

 Estimated Time: 1½ hours

Outlining helps you organize and create a presentation by focusing on the presentation's content and flow rather than its appearance. Working in PowerPoint's Outline view, you can create the text content of all slides and change slide order. You can even create an outline in Word and insert it into PowerPoint. PowerPoint then automatically creates a presentation from the Word outline.

Objective 1

LESSON 4 ■ **USING OUTLINE VIEW**

Starting a Presentation in Outline View

You can develop a new presentation entirely in Outline view. As soon as you choose the first slide layout, just switch to Outline view.

EXERCISE 4-1 Start a New Blank Presentation in Outline View

1. Start a new blank presentation and choose Title Slide as the first slide layout.
2. Apply the design template **Blush.pot** and change the slide color scheme to the fourth standard color.

NOTE

3. Click the Outline View button ▤ or choose Outline from the View menu. Notice that the blank title slide is represented as an icon and numbered slide 1. The Outlining toolbar appears at the left and the slide miniature is displayed on the right.
4. Click the black rectangle next to the slide icon in the upper left corner of the screen to activate slide 1. The rectangle changes to an insertion point.

> **NOTE:** The default is for the slide miniature to be displayed in Outline view. If the slide miniature does not appear in Outline view, you can display it by choosing Slide Miniature from the View menu.

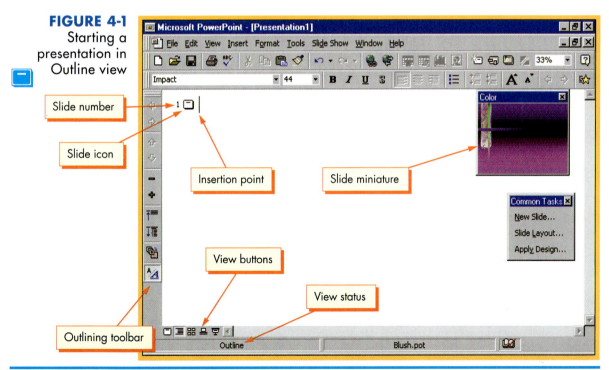

FIGURE 4-1
Starting a presentation in Outline view

The Outline View button may look different on screens with resolution higher than 640 x 480.

Use PowerPoint Classroom Presentation #4 to display screens from the lesson, including this one, in a slide-show format.

103

UNIT 2 ■ WORKING WITH PRESENTATIONS

5. Key **Promotional Posters** as the slide title. The title appears in the slide miniature as you type.

6. Press Enter. A new slide icon for slide 2 appears.

7. Press Tab. The new line is now a bullet on the first slide.

8. Key **Good 4 U Public Relations Training** as the subtitle.

Objective 2

Adding a New Slide in Outline View

After the title slide, when you insert a slide in Outline view, it is automatically formatted in the Bulleted List layout. You can insert a new slide in several ways, including the following:

- Click New Slide on the Common Tasks toolbar or 🖼 on the Standard toolbar.
- Press Enter at the end of a title line.

NOTE
- Press Ctrl+Enter at the end of a bulleted or subtitle line.

Pressing Enter at the end of a bulleted item or subtitle line inserts another bullet or subtitle line.

EXERCISE 4-2 Add New Slides in Outline View

1. While still in Outline view, place the insertion point after the text "Training," if necessary, and press Ctrl+Enter. A second slide icon appears. Notice that the slide miniature is now blank, since a new blank slide is now active.

FIGURE 4-2
Creating an outline

2. Key **Poster Purpose** as the title and press Enter. A third slide icon appears.

3. Press Tab. The third slide is demoted to a bullet for the second slide.

4. Key **Inform customers** and press Enter. The text for the bulleted item appears on the slide miniature and a second bullet appears.

5. Press Ctrl+Enter. Space for the blank bullet remains and another slide icon appears.

NOTE
You may want to emphasize how Enter and Ctrl+Enter work in outlining—Enter inserts an item at the same level as the previous item; Ctrl+Enter either moves to a blank item or inserts a new slide.

In PowerPoint Classroom Presentation #4.

104

LESSON 4 ■ USING OUTLINE VIEW

6. Using the <u>N</u>ew Slide button on the Common Tasks toolbar, insert three more blank slides. There should now be six slides in your presentation.
7. Press `Backspace` three times to delete these new slides.

✓ Objective 3
Promoting and Demoting Outline Entries

You can demote slide titles and promote or demote bulleted items three ways:
- Click Promote ⬅ and Demote ➡ on the Outlining toolbar.
- Press `Tab` to demote an entry or `Shift`+`Tab` to promote an entry.
- Select an item and drag it left to demote it or right to promote it.

In Outline view, you can also join or split slides by demoting or promoting entries. When a title is demoted, it becomes a bulleted item on the previous slide. When a first-level bullet is promoted, it becomes a new slide.

TABLE 4-1 **Outlining Toolbar Buttons**

BUTTON	NAME	ACTION
⬅	Promote	Raises item one level
➡	Demote	Lowers item one level
⬆	Move Up	Moves selection up one line
⬇	Move Down	Moves selection down one line
−	Collapse	Shows titles only for selected slides
+	Expand	Shows details for selected slides
▤	Collapse All	Displays titles only for entire outline
▥	Expand All	Displays details for entire outline
▦	Summary Slide	Creates a new slide from titles of selected slides
ᴬ	Show Formatting	Turns character formatting on and off

NOTE: At the end of this lesson, the Command Summary lists keyboard shortcuts for Outlining toolbar buttons.

✓**Objective 3 Assignment:**
Exercise 4-11 (Skills Review) can be assigned after completing Objective 3.

NOTE
Review the buttons on the Outlining toolbar with students. Make sure they understand the difference between promoting/demoting and moving.

105

UNIT 2 ■ WORKING WITH PRESENTATIONS

EXERCISE 4-3 Promote and Demote Using the Toolbar and Keyboard

1. Click the blank line just below "Inform customers" to position the insertion point (when you click this line, the bullet appears). Key **Promote our image** and press Enter to start a new bullet.

2. Key the following bulleted items:
   - **Design suggestions**
   - **Keep it simple**
   - **Readability**

   Notice that the slide miniature now shows a title and five bulleted items.

3. Position the insertion point anywhere in "Design suggestions" and click the Promote button on the Outlining toolbar (or press Shift+Tab). The bullet becomes a new slide containing the next two bullets.

 NOTE: In Outline view, you can click anywhere in an entry or select the entry before demoting or promoting with Tab or Shift+Tab. In Slide view, the insertion point must be positioned between the bullet and the text.

4. Click the Demote button to rejoin the two slides.

5. Position the pointer over the slide 2 icon. Notice that the pointer changes to a four-headed arrow.

6. Click the slide 2 icon. The entire slide and all its bullets are selected.

7. Position the pointer over the first bullet character on slide 2. Observe that the pointer again changes to a four-headed arrow.

8. Click the bullet. The rest of the slide contents are deselected and only the single bulleted item is selected.

9. Click the pointer anywhere in "Keep it simple" and press Tab to demote it to a level 2 bullet under "Design suggestions." The slide miniature now shows it as a level 2 bullet.

10. Click the "Design suggestions" bullet. Notice that this bullet and its sub-bullet are selected.

11. Promote "Keep it simple" to a level 1 bullet.

12. Promote "Design suggestions" to a new slide. Slide 3 should now be "Design suggestions" and contain two bulleted items, "Keep it simple" and "Readability."

NOTE
In step 1, point out that there is no visible bullet (only blank space) until the line is clicked.

LESSON 4 ■ USING OUTLINE VIEW

EXERCISE 4-4 Promote and Demote by Dragging

1. Move the arrow pointer over the slide icon for "Design suggestions" until it becomes a four-headed arrow.

2. Click the slide icon. The slide title for slide 3 and its bulleted items are selected.

3. Drag the icon right. The pointer becomes a two-headed arrow and a vertical line appears.

FIGURE 4-3
Demoting by dragging

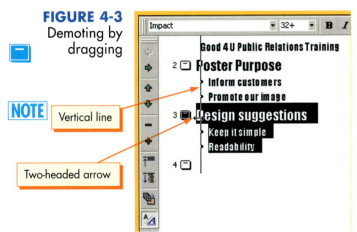

4. Drag until the vertical line aligns with the bullets and then release. The title is demoted to a first-level bullet and its bullets are demoted to second-level bullets.

5. Position the pointer over the "Design suggestions" bullet, drag the selected material further right, and release. The items are demoted another level.

6. Drag the selected material back to the left until the vertical line aligns with the left edge of the slide icons and release. The material is promoted to its original level.

NOTE: If you drag selected material up or down instead of left or right, the four-headed arrow changes shape, indicating you may be changing the order of the lines or dragging the material to a different slide.

✏ Objective 4

Expanding a Slide

As you create a presentation in Outline view, you may want to expand items on a slide into a series of individual slides. The Expand Slide feature creates one new slide for each item or paragraph on the current slide. You can use Expand Slide in Outline, Slide Sorter, and Slide views.

NOTE
In step 1, stress that the four-headed arrow indicates you can move a selection. This pointer changes to a two-headed arrow when you begin dragging. In step 3, when dragging the selection, students should drag the slide icon.

In PowerPoint Classroom Presentation #4.

NOTE
In step 5, remind students to move the pointer over the first-level bullet until they see the four-headed arrow and then begin dragging.

✏ **Objective 4 Assignment:**
Exercise 4-12 (Skills Review) can be assigned after completing Objective 4.

107

UNIT 2 ■ **WORKING WITH PRESENTATIONS**

EXERCISE 4-5 Break a Slide into Several Separate Slides

FIGURE 4-4
Expanding a slide

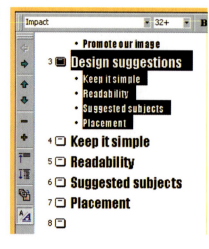

1. Key the following bulleted items after "Readability":

   - **Suggested subjects**
   - **Placement**

2. With the insertion point located anywhere in the text of slide 3, choose E<u>x</u>pand Slide from the <u>T</u>ools menu. Notice that the original slide remains unchanged and each of its first level bullets is now the title of a new slide.

3. Select slide 5, "Readability," press Ctrl + Enter, and key the following bulleted items:

   - **Large, simple titles**
   - **Limited number of text items**
   - **Color and graphics**
   - **Limited number of high-contrast colors**
   - **Graphics with sports or health theme**

4. Select slide 6, "Suggested subjects," press Ctrl + Enter, and key the following bulleted items:

   - **Menu items**
   - **Price specials**
   - **Nutritional highlights**
   - **Special events**

5. On slide 7, "Placement," key the following bulleted items:

   - **Post in high traffic areas**
   - **Consider target audience**
   - **Remove promptly when dated**

6. Delete slide 4, "Keep it simple."

7. Delete any blank slides after slide 6, "Placement."

In PowerPoint Classroom Presentation #4.

108

LESSON 4 ■ USING OUTLINE VIEW

Objective 5
Creating a Summary Slide

Just as you can expand a slide into individual slides, you can also create summary slides based on the titles of existing slides. You can use summary slides to frame the contents of a presentation, either as an outline at the beginning or as a wrap-up at the end. You can also use summary slides to create hyperlinks, which is covered in Lesson 15: "Creating Slide Show Effects."

The Summary Slide button ▦ on the Outlining toolbar creates a new slide from the titles of selected slides. The summary slide creates a bulleted list from the titles of the selected slides, inserting the new slide in front of the first selected slide.

EXERCISE 4-6　Create a Summary Slide

1. Click within the slide 2 title, "Poster Purpose." Using the I-beam pointer, drag to the bottom of the outline to select slides 2-6.
2. Click the Summary Slide button ▦ on the Outlining toolbar. A summary slide is inserted in front of the "Poster Purpose" slide. Notice that the bulleted items on the summary slide are the titles of all the selected slides.
3. Change the default title of the summary slide to **Effective Posters**.
4. If necessary, delete the blank line at the end of the summary slide.

Objective 6
Moving Bulleted Items in Outline View

In Outline view, you can move selected bulleted items within slides or between slides several different ways:

- Click Move Up ▲ or Move Down ▼ on the Outlining toolbar.
- Drag selected bullets up or down.
- Cut and paste.

You can use ▲ and ▼ without selecting an item first. Only the item that contains the insertion point is moved.

109

UNIT 2 ■ WORKING WITH PRESENTATIONS

EXERCISE 4-7 Move Bulleted Items

1. Delete the four bulleted items under slide 4, "Design suggestions." These items are now redundant with the expanded slides.

2. Demote the title of slide 5 by placing the insertion point anywhere in the title text, "Readability," and clicking . The "Readability" slide and its bulleted items are now joined to slide 4.

3. On slide 4, select "Color and graphics" by clicking its bullet or dragging the I-beam pointer across the text.

4. Click the Move Up button on the Outlining toolbar. The selected bullet moves up one level.

5. Click again until "Color and graphics" is the first bullet on the "Design suggestions" slide.

> **TIP:** Use Undo to restore the previous positioning

6. Select the last bullet on the "Design suggestions" slide ("Graphics with sports or health theme").

7. Click until the selected bullet is under "Color and graphics."

FIGURE 4-5
Moving an element by dragging

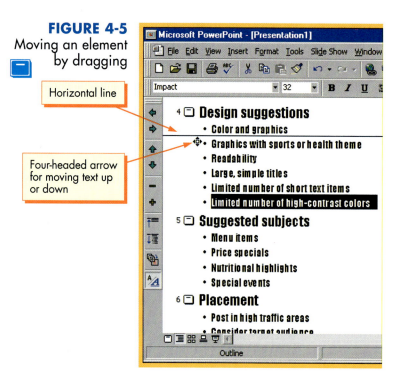

8. Select the "Limited number of high-contrast colors" bullet. Drag the bullet character up. Continue to drag up, positioning the horizontal line under "Color and graphics," and then release. Notice the shape of the four-headed arrow as you drag up.

> **NOTE:** You can select more than one bullet or slide and drag the selection to a new position. First, drag the I-beam pointer over the text to select it. Next, move the pointer over the selection and use the white arrow pointer to drag it to a new position. An insertion point guides your placement rather than a horizontal line.

In PowerPoint Classroom Presentation #4.

110

LESSON 4 ■ **USING OUTLINE VIEW**

NOTE

9. Select the first two bullets after "Color and graphics" (drag the I-beam over the text from "Limited" through "health theme") and click ▶. Both items are demoted.

10. Demote "Large, simple titles" and "Limited number of short text items" under "Readability."

11. Select the "Special events" bullet on slide 5 and click ✂ to cut the item.

12. Position the insertion point to the left of the "M" in "Menu items" and click the Paste button 📋. The "Special events" bullet is moved before "Menu items."

13. Demote "Price specials" and "Nutritional highlights" under "Menu items."

Objective 7
Moving Slides in Outline View

In Outline view, you can move entire slides in the same way you move bulleted items. When you select a slide icon, you select the contents of the entire slide. You can then use ▲ and ▼, cut and paste, or drag and drop.

You can also change the outline display to see only slide icons and titles by clicking the Collapse All button 🗎. This feature helps you see the big picture of your outline and also makes moving slides easier and safer. For example, when dragging collapsed slides, there's no danger of dropping a slide in the middle of another slide.

EXERCISE **4-8** **Move Slides in Outline View**

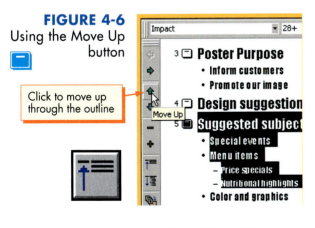

FIGURE 4-6
Using the Move Up button

1. Click the "Suggested subjects" slide icon to select the entire slide.

2. Click ▲ several times until "Suggested subjects" becomes slide 4. The slide moves up through each line of the current slide 4. The slide number changes when "Suggested subjects" appears above "Design Suggestions."

3. Click the Collapse All button 🗎 to display only titles for the outline. Scroll up, if necessary, to see all six slides.

4. Select slide 4, if necessary, and drag it after slide 5. When all slides are collapsed, dragging a slide places it above or below all the text in another collapsed slide.

NOTE
Have students practice dragging a bullet (or a slide in Exercise 4-8) to a different position in the outline. Items remain selected when you drop them. Undo will reverse a sequence of position changes.

Objective 7 Assignment:
Exercise 4-13 (Skills Review) and Exercises 4-15 through 4-17 (Lesson Applications) can be assigned after completing Objective 7.

In PowerPoint Classroom Presentation #4.

111

UNIT 2 ■ WORKING WITH PRESENTATIONS

 NOTE: When you select (or move) a collapsed slide, you select (or move) all its hidden text.

5. Click the Expand button ✚ to display the hidden text of the "Suggested subjects" slide.
6. Click the Collapse button ▬ to display only the slide title.
7. Click in the word "Suggested" to deselect the slide.
8. Click ⬆ to move the slide up. Notice that the slide does not have to be selected to be moved up.

 TIP: It's easier to move slides in a long outline when only the slide titles are showing.

9. Click the Expand All button to display the entire outline.
10. Click the Show Formatting button to turn off the display of formatting. It is often easier to read the text of an outline when you turn off the formatting applied by the template. Notice that more of the text is displayed on the screen. Note also that this does not affect the formatting of the text in Slide view.
11. Change the summary list (slide 2) to reflect the changes you made to the outline. (See revised slide 2 in Figure 4-7.)

FIGURE 4-7
Unformatted outline with revised summary slide

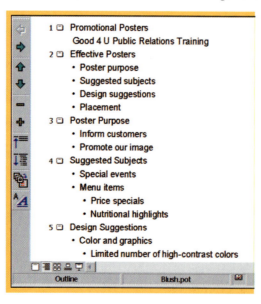

12. Check spelling and styles in the presentation. (Use the style checker defaults to change all titles to title case and all body text to sentence case. After running the style checker, change the case of the slide 1 subtitle back to title case.)
13. Save the presentation as *[your initials]*__4-8.ppt__.
14. Create headers and footers for Notes and Handouts. Include the date and your name at the top of the page and the page number and filename at the bottom.
15. Activate slide 1 and view the presentation in Slide Show view or Slide view.
16. Print the presentation outline. (In the Print dialog box, choose Outline View from the Print *what* drop-down list.) Print the presentation again as handouts, 6 slides per page, black and white, framed.

In PowerPoint Classroom Presentation #4.

Point out that headers and footers applied to notes and handouts appears on outlines, too.

112

LESSON 4 ■ USING OUTLINE VIEW

17. Save and close the presentation.

✓ Objective 8
Importing a Word Outline into PowerPoint

You can insert an outline created in another application (such as Microsoft Word or another word processor) into a new blank presentation or an existing one. PowerPoint will use your outline formatting (tab characters, indents, or heading styles) to create slide titles and bullets.

EXERCISE 4-9 Insert a Word Outline into PowerPoint

You move an outline into PowerPoint using the Slides from Outline command on the Insert menu.

NOTE

1. Open Microsoft Word.

    NOTE: You can use another word processor.

2. Key the material shown in Figure 4-8. (Press `Tab` once or twice where indicated to create indents.)

FIGURE 4-8

```
Poster Ideas

        [Tab]Good 4 U Public Relations Training

In Our Restaurant

        [Tab]Menu items

        [Tab]Contests

        [Tab]Ingredient profiles

        [Tab][Tab]Exotic ingredients

        [Tab][Tab]Organic ingredients
```

continues

✓ Objective 8 Assignment:
Exercises 4-14 (Skills Review) and 4-18 (Lesson Applications) can be assigned after completing Objective 8.

NOTE
In Exercise 4-9, students create an outline in Word and import it into PowerPoint. The lesson asks them to use tabs to create the outlining levels. You may want to have them use styles. For example, styles like Heading 1, Heading 2, and Heading 3 translate into slide titles, bullets, and sub-bullets.

113

UNIT 2 ■ **WORKING WITH PRESENTATIONS**

continued

```
Vendor Profiles
        [Tab]Local organic farmers
        [Tab]Herb farms
        [Tab]Fisheries
Special Event Announcements
        [Tab]New Health Marathon
        [Tab][Tab]Pasta party
        [Tab][Tab]Awards dinner
        [Tab]July 4th Celebration
        [Tab][Tab]In-line skating race
        [Tab][Tab]Bike race
```

3. Save the outline as *[your initials]***4-9.doc**.
4. Print the outline and close the document.
5. Open a blank PowerPoint presentation, cancel the New Slide dialog box, and switch to Outline view.
6. Choose Slides from Outline on the Insert menu. The Insert Outline dialog box appears.
7. Navigate to the folder where you store your files. Choose *[your initials]***4-9.doc** from the list of files or key the filename in the File name text box.
8. Click Insert. PowerPoint interprets the structure of your outline, which you created using tab characters, and creates new slides from the first-level headings and bullets from the second-level headings.
9. Apply the **Meadow.pot** design template to the presentation.
10. Switch to Slide view to see the presentation. All slides appear in Bulleted List style.
11. Change the first slide to the Title Slide layout.

NOTE
In step 7, show students how to browse to locate the necessary file, if necessary.

LESSON 4 ■ USING OUTLINE VIEW

EXERCISE 4-10 **Insert a Slide from Another Presentation**

In addition to adding a whole series of slides by importing a Word outline, you can add an individual slide or slides from another PowerPoint presentation. Instead of opening one presentation and copying and pasting the slide to the other presentation, you can use the Slides from Files command on the Insert menu.

1. Switch to Slide Sorter view and select slide 4. You'll insert two slides after this slide from another presentation.

 NOTE: When inserting slides, first select the slide you want to insert another slide after.

2. Choose Slides from Files on the Insert menu. The Slide Finder dialog box opens.
3. Navigate to the folder where you store your files. Choose *[your initials]* **4-8.ppt** from the list of files or key the filename in the File name text box.

TIP: If you insert slides from a particular presentation often, use the Slide Finder to locate it and click Add to Favorites. Then your presentation file will appear on the List of Favorites tab of the Slide Finder. You can click Remove when you no longer need it there.

4. In the Slide Finder dialog box, click Display to display miniatures of the presentation slides.
5. Using the horizontal scroll bar below the slide miniatures, display slides 4 through 6. (See Figure 4-9 on the next page.)
6. Click slides 5 ("Design Suggestions") and 6 ("Placement") to select them. Click Insert and then click Close. PowerPoint inserts the selected slides into your presentation.
7. Change the slide color scheme of the entire presentation to the first standard color.
8. Check spelling in the presentation.
9. Save the presentation as *[your initials]***4-10.ppt**.
10. Create headers and footers for Notes and Handouts. Include the date and your name at the top of the page and the page number and filename at the bottom.

UNIT 2 ■ **WORKING WITH PRESENTATIONS**

FIGURE 4-9
Inserting slides from another presentation file

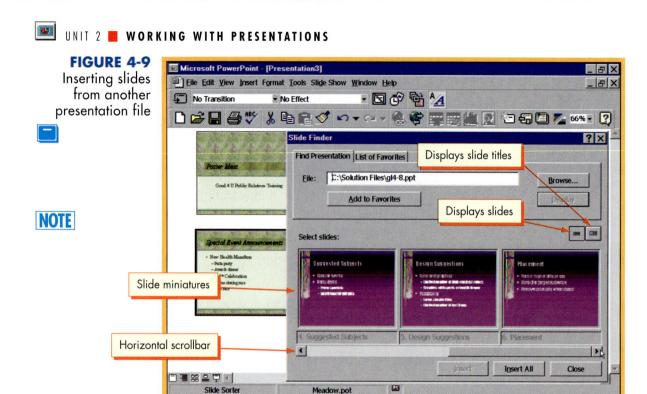

NOTE

NOTE: You can use the two buttons in the Slide Finder dialog box, just above the slide miniatures, to change the display. The left button displays slide miniatures; the right button displays a list of slide titles with one slightly larger miniature of the selected slide.

11. Print the presentation as handouts, 6 slides per page, black and white, framed.

12. Save and close the presentation.

In PowerPoint Classroom Presentation #4.

NOTE
Point out the pair of buttons in the Slide Finder dialog box, just above the slides, that allow you display either slide miniatures or slide titles. By default, PowerPoint displays slide miniatures.

116

LESSON 4 ■ **USING OUTLINE VIEW**

COMMAND SUMMARY
NOTE

FEATURE	BUTTON	MENU	KEYBOARD
Outline View		View, Outline	
Promote			Alt + Shift + ← or Shift + Tab
Demote			Alt + Shift + → or Tab
Move Up			Alt + Shift + ↑
Move Down			Alt + Shift + ↓
Collapse All			Alt + Shift + 1
Expand			Alt + Shift + +
Collapse			Alt + Shift + −
Expand All			Alt + Shift + A
Show Formatting (on/off)			/ on numeric keypad
Insert outline		Insert, Slides from Outline	
Insert slides		Insert, Slides from Files	

USING HELP

NOTE

In this lesson, you learned to insert an outline with the Insert, Slides from Outline command. You can also export PowerPoint presentations as Microsoft Word outlines.

Use Help to learn how to export PowerPoint outlines to Word:

1. Choose Contents and Index from the Help menu.
2. On the Index tab, key **outlines** in box 1.
3. Double-click "exporting to Microsoft Word."
4. Review the procedure and then close Help.

NOTE
Point out that the Command Summary lists a variety of ways to accomplish a particular task. Students can decide which method they prefer to use.

NOTE
Encourage students to follow the steps in "Using Help." Software companies are increasingly using their online Help programs—rather than printed documentation—to train users and assist in answering user questions.

UNIT 2 ■ WORKING WITH PRESENTATIONS

TEST BANK

Concepts Review

TRUE/FALSE QUESTIONS

Each of the following statements is either true or false. Indicate your choice by circling **T** or **F**.

(T) F **1.** The Outline command is on the View menu.

(T) F **2.** You can use Ctrl+Enter both to activate the next slide placeholder and to insert a new slide.

(T) F **3.** The Demote button on the Outlining toolbar has the same effect as the Demote button on the Formatting toolbar.

T (F) **4.** You can show just the slide titles on your outline by clicking the Expand button.

(T) F **5.** You can drag and drop bulleted items from one slide to another.

(T) F **6.** You can use the Move Up button to change the positions of slides in your outline.

T (F) **7.** Once you create a slide, you cannot split it into two slides.

(T) F **8.** You use the Insert menu to insert an outline created in another application into PowerPoint.

SHORT ANSWER QUESTIONS

Write the correct answer in the space provided.

1. Which key do you press to insert another bullet at the same level?
   Enter

2. What happens when you demote the title of slide 3 in a presentation?
   It becomes a bulleted item and slides 2 and 3 merge

3. If a slide has 5 first-level bullets, what happens when you promote the third bullet?
   Slide is split (forming 2 slides with 2 bullets each)

4. A slide has several bullets. If you select the title with the four-headed arrow in Outline view and press Tab, what happens?
   The title and bullets are demoted and joined to the previous slide

---

CLOSE

Concepts Review: Allows students to check their understanding.

TEST BANK Consider using the Test Bank to provide an additional review of lesson concepts.

118

LESSON 4 ■ USING OUTLINE VIEW

5. Which two toolbars contain Demote and Promote buttons?
   Outlining and Formatting

6. Besides using the Move Up and Move Down buttons or the drag-and-drop method, how else can you move items in an outline?
   Cut and Paste, or Alt+Shift+Up Arrow and Alt+Shift+Down Arrow

7. How can you turn character formatting on and off in Outline view?
   Show Formatting button or Forward slash / on numeric keypad

8. Which dialog box do you use to insert slides from another presentation?
   Slide Finder

CRITICAL THINKING

Answer these questions on a separate page. There are no right or wrong answers. Support your answers with examples from your own experience, if possible.

1. Do you prefer creating slides in Slide view or Outline view? Why?
2. When would you want to create your outline in PowerPoint? In Word? What are the advantages of developing an outline in Word?
3. Which method of promoting and demoting do you prefer? Why?

Skills Review

EXERCISE 4-11

Start a blank presentation in Outline view, add slides, and demote outline entries.

1. Start a blank presentation.
2. Choose Title Slide as the layout for the first slide.
3. Apply the design template **Notebook.pot**.
4. Switch to Outline view.
5. Key **Good 4 U Restaurant** as the slide title and press [Enter].
6. Press [Tab]. Key **Advertising campaign**
7. Add a new slide by following these steps:
   a. Press [Ctrl]+[Enter].
   b. Key **Types of Media**

Critical Thinking Questions:
Answers will vary based on students' preferences, observations, experiences, and research.

Skills Review:
Provides guided practice for students. Objectives are indicated for each Exercise.

Exercise 4-11:
Objectives 1–3
Required File: None
Solution File: gl4-11.ppt in Solutions Manual or on Solutions Disk

119

UNIT 2 ■ WORKING WITH PRESENTATIONS

   c. Press [Enter] and press [Tab].
   d. Key the following bulleted items:
    • **Print**
    • **Newspapers**
    • **Magazines**
    • **Broadcast**
    • **Radio**
    • **Television**

 8. Add a new slide, key the title **Target Markets** and the following bulleted items:
   • **Health-conscious adults**
   • **Active sports enthusiasts**
   • **Business professionals**

 9. Add a new slide, key the title **Special Campaigns** and the following bulleted items:
   • **Good Health marathon**
   • **July 4th celebration**

 10. On slide 2, demote the bullets "Newspapers" and "Magazines" to sub-bullets under "Print" by following these steps:
   a. Position the insertion point anywhere in the "Newspapers" bulleted item.
   b. Click the Demote button [→].
   c. Position the insertion point anywhere in the "Magazines" bulleted item and click [→].

 11. Using the I-beam, select the bulleted text "Radio" and "Television." Click [→] to demote the text as sub-bullets under "Broadcast."

 12. Check spelling in the presentation.

 13. Save the presentation as *[your initials]***4-11.ppt**.

 14. Create headers and footers for Notes and Handouts. Include the date and your name at the top of the page and the page number and filename at the bottom.

 15. View the presentation in Slide Show view.

 16. Print the presentation outline. (Choose Outline View from the Print dialog box's Print w̲hat drop-down list.)

 17. Save and close the presentation.

LESSON 4 ■ USING OUTLINE VIEW

EXERCISE 4-12

Add slides, promote and demote bulleted items, and expand a slide.

1. Open the file **Media1.ppt** and switch to Outline view.
2. Key three new slides as shown in Figure 4-10.

FIGURE 4-10

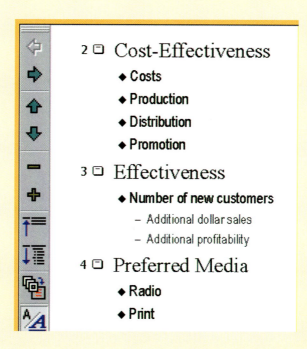

3. Join slides 2 and 3 by following these steps:
   a. Position the insertion point in the slide 3 title. (Do not select the slide.)
   b. Press [Tab] (or click [→]).
4. Promote the last two bullets in slide 2 ("Additional dollar sales" and "Additional profitability") by following these steps:
   a. Click the first bullet with the four-headed arrow pointer to select it.
   b. Drag the selection to the left until the vertical line aligns with the previous bullet and then release.
   c. Repeat steps a and b for the last bullet.
5. Demote the last three bullets by following these steps:
   a. Position the insertion point in "Number of new customers."
   b. Drag the I-beam pointer down until the three lines are selected.
   c. Press [Tab].

⊟Exercise 4-12:
Objectives 2–4
Required File: Media1.ppt
Solution File: gl4-12.ppt in Solutions Manual or on Solutions Disk

121

UNIT 2 ■ WORKING WITH PRESENTATIONS

6. Demote the "Production" bullet by dragging it to the right one level.
7. Demote the "Distribution" bullet using the Demote button.
8. Demote the "Promotion" bullet using the keyboard (Alt+Shift+→).
9. Expand slide 3 by following these steps:
   a. Position the insertion point anywhere in slide 3.
   b. Choose Expand Slide from the Tools menu.
10. Key the following bulleted items in slide 4:
    - **Reaches large audience**
    - **Can be targeted to a specific market**
11. Key the following bulleted items in slide 5:
    - **Highly cost-effective**
    - **Proven results**
12. Delete slide 3.
13. Check spelling in the presentation.
14. Save the presentation as *[your initials]***4-12.ppt**.
15. Create headers and footers for Notes and Handouts. Include the date and your name at the top of the page and the page number and filename at the bottom.
16. View the presentation in Slide view. Print the presentation outline and print handouts (6 slides per page).
17. Save and close the presentation.

EXERCISE 4-13

Move bullets and slides in Outline view and create a summary slide.

1. Open the file **Media2.ppt**, apply the design template **Portrait Notebook.pot**, and switch to Outline view.
2. Click [A] to turn off formatting.
3. Move the "Newspapers" bullet from slide 3 to the end of slide 5 by following these steps:
   a. Position the insertion point in the bullet or select the bullet.
   b. Click [↓] (or press Alt+Shift+↓) until the bullet is positioned below "Magazines."
4. Move the "Electronic" bullet from slide 4 to the end of slide 3 (below "Print").

Exercise 4-13:
Objectives 5–7
Required File: Media2.ppt
Solution File: gl4-13.ppt in Solutions Manual or on Solutions Disk.

LESSON 4 ■ USING OUTLINE VIEW

5. Drag and drop the "Fliers" bullet on slide 5 to a new position on the slide by following these steps:

   a. Position the pointer over the "Fliers" bullet until the four-headed arrow appears.

   b. Drag the bullet up until the pointer becomes a small, four-headed arrow.

   c. Position the horizontal line just under the slide title, "Print Media," and then release.

6. Select the "Evaluate costs" bullet on slide 2 and its sub-bullets and move them above the "Evaluate effectiveness" bullet.

7. Click [icon] (or press [Alt]+[Shift]+[1]) to display only slide titles.

8. Move slide 4 ("Electronic Media") after slide 5.

9. Move slide 2 ("Return on Investment") to the end of the presentation.

10. Click [icon] to display all details.

11. Create a summary slide by following these steps:

    a. Position the insertion point anywhere in the slide 2 title, "Media Categories." Drag to the bottom of the outline to select slides 2 through 5.

    b. Click the Summary Slide button [icon] on the Outlining toolbar.

    c. Change the title of slide 2, "Summary Slide," to **Discussion Topics**

    d. If necessary, remove the extra bullet at the end of slide 2.

12. Click [icon] to turn the formatting display back on.

13. Check spelling in the presentation.

14. Save the presentation as *[your initials]*4-13.ppt.

15. Create headers and footers for Notes and Handouts. Include the date and your name at the top of the page and the page number and filename at the bottom.

16. Review the presentation in Slide view. Print the presentation outline and print handouts (6 slides per page).

17. Save and close the presentation.

EXERCISE 4-14

Create an outline in Word and import it into PowerPoint.

1. Create the outline shown in Figure 4-11 (on the next page) using Microsoft Word or another word processor, pressing [Tab] where indicated.

2. Save the file as *[your initials]*4-14.doc.

3. Print and close the document.

Exercise 4-14:
Objective 8
Required File: None
Solution Files: gl4-14.ppt and gl4-14.doc in Solutions Manual or on Solutions Disk.

NOTE
Consider showing students how to use styles (Heading 1, Heading 2, and Heading 3) instead of tabs to create a document that will translate into slide titles, bullets, and sub-bullets.

123

UNIT 2 ■ **WORKING WITH PRESENTATIONS**

FIGURE 4-11

```
Introducing Our Honey Candies
        [Tab]Good 4 U's New Healthy Treat
Exciting Flavors
        [Tab]Exotic honey-licorice
        [Tab]Scintillating honey-cinnamon
        [Tab]Fabulous honey-fruit flavors
        [Tab][Tab]Tangy lemon
        [Tab][Tab]Robust orange
        [Tab][Tab]Apple cider
Candy Types
        [Tab]Soft-filled sweetness
        [Tab]Dramatic stick
        [Tab]Discrete drops
Availability
        [Tab]At our restaurant
        [Tab]By phone or mail order
        [Tab]In attractive gift packs
```

   4. Open a blank presentation in PowerPoint, cancel the New Slide dialog box, and switch to Outline view.
   5. Insert the Word outline into PowerPoint by following these steps:
      a. Choose Slides from Out*l*ine from the *I*nsert menu.
      b. Locate the file *[your initials]***4-14.doc** and click In*s*ert.
   6. Switch to Slide view and change the first slide to Title Slide layout. Check that your presentation has a total of 4 slides.
   7. Apply the design template **Pulse.pot**.
   8. Check spelling in the presentation.

124

LESSON 4 ■ **USING OUTLINE VIEW**

9. Save the presentation as *[your initials]***4-14.ppt.**
10. Create headers and footers for Notes and Handouts. Include the date and your name at the top of the page and the page number and filename at the bottom.
11. Print the presentation as handouts, 6 slides per page, black and white, framed.
12. Save and close the presentation.

UNIT 2 ■ **WORKING WITH PRESENTATIONS**

Lesson Applications

EXERCISE 4-15

Start a new presentation in Outline view, add slides, promote and demote heads, and move bullets and slides.

1. Start a presentation in Outline view with Title Slide as the first layout.
2. Key the two slides as shown in Figure 4-12.

FIGURE 4-12

3. Make "Food Services" and the following bullets a separate slide.
4. Make "Merchandise" and the following bullets a separate slide.
5. Add the following bullets to the "Our Products" slide:
   - **Merchandise**
   - **Food services**
6. Reverse the order of the bullets on the "Merchandise" slide ("Caps," "T-shirts," "Honey and confections").
7. Collapse the outline and move the "Merchandise" slide before the "Food Services" slide.
8. Apply the **Zesty.pot** design template and change the slide color scheme to the second option in the second row of standard colors.

Assessment Resources:
- Solutions Manual
- Test Bank with Software
- Portfolio Builder
- Alternative Assessment Guide
- Certification Procedures
- Mid-Term and Final Exams

Lesson Applications:
Provide independent practice for students. Objectives are indicated for each Exercise.

Mid-Term Exam:
If your class is on a semester schedule, you can now assign Mid-Term 1 from the Mid-Term and Final Exams booklet.

Exercise 4-15:
Objectives 1–3, 6–7
Required File: None
Solution File: gl4-15.doc in Solutions Manual or on Solutions Disk.

LESSON 4 ■ USING OUTLINE VIEW

NOTE

9. Check spelling in the presentation. Make sure all slide 1 text is title case, all slide titles are title case, and all bulleted text is sentence case.

10. Save the presentation as *[your initials]***4-15.ppt.**

11. Create headers and footers for Notes and Handouts. Include the date and your name at the top of the page and the page number and filename at the bottom.

12. Print the presentation as handouts, 6 slides per page, black and white, framed.

13. Save and close the presentation.

EXERCISE 4-16

Move bullets in Outline view, promote outline items, and expand a slides to create new ones.

1. Open the file **MktTrng.ppt** and switch to Outline view.
2. Select and delete slide 2, "Elements of Marketing."
3. Revise the bullets in the new slide 2, "Marketing Is People," as follows:
   - **Respect**
     - Co-workers
     - Customers
     - Yourself
   - **Expect the best from**
     - Co-workers
     - Customers
     - Yourself
4. Expand slide 3 ("What Are We Marketing?") into three additional slides using the Expand Slide feature.
5. Under the new slide 4, "Our food," key the following bulleted items:
   - **Eat in**
   - **Take out**
   - **Delivered and catered**
6. Under slide 5, "Our merchandise," key the following bulleted items:
   - **Food products**
   - **Apparel and accessories**
7. Move the three bulleted items under slide 7, "Marketing Our Staff," positioning them under slide 6, "Our service."
8. Delete slide 7.

NOTE
Without using the style checker, students are instructed to make sure the case of their slides is consistent. They should check that the title slide text (both title and subtitle) is title case, all other slide titles are title case, and bulleted text is sentence case (unless it contains a proper name). You might ask students to check the case of their presentation text from this point forward (instead of using the style checker and having to undo its changes or modify the checker's defaults).

Exercise 4-16:
Objectives 3, 4, 5–7
Required File: MktTrng.ppt
Solution File: gl4-16.doc in Solutions Manual or on Solutions Disk.

127

UNIT 2 ■ WORKING WITH PRESENTATIONS

9. View the presentation in Slide view. Change slide 2 to a two-column layout, moving the second bullet and its sub-bullets to the right column placeholder.
10. Check spelling in the presentation. Edit the titles on slides 4 through 6 so they appear in title case (example, "Our Food").
11. Save the presentation as *[your initials]***4-16.ppt.**
12. Create headers and footers for Notes and Handouts. Include the date and your name at the top of the page and the page number and filename at the bottom.
13. Print the presentation outline and print handouts (6 slides per page).
14. Save and close the presentation.

EXERCISE 4-17

Move bulleted items in Outline view, move slides, and promote and demote bullet items.

1. Open the file **Honeys1.ppt**.
2. Working in Outline view, move bullets and slides as shown in Figure 4-13.

FIGURE 4-13

2 ▢ New Product Lines
- Honey candies
- Products Made with honey
  - Iced teas and fruit-ades
  - Breads
  - Desserts
- Jarred Honeys

3 ▢ Gift Sales Services
- Delivery
- Extra charges vary with services
- Express delivery required for perishables

4 ▢ Dining sales techniques
- Mention honeys among ingredients
- Offer honey breads for dessert
- Serve honey samplers with tea and coffee

Exercise 4-17:
Objectives 3, 6, 7
Required File: Honeys1.ppt
Solution File: gl4-17.ppt in Solutions Manual or on Solutions Disk

The completed presentation for this Exercise may be used in a student's portfolio.

LESSON 4 ■ USING OUTLINE VIEW

3. On slide 3, move and add text as follows:

   Gift Sales Services
   - **Gift wrapping**
   - **Protective packaging**
   - **Gift certificates**
   - **Delivery**
     - **Extra charges vary with services**
     - **Express delivery required for perishables**

4. Apply the design template **Blush.pot**.

5. Check spelling in the presentation and review the presentation in Slide view. (Leave the spelling of "fruit-ades" unchanged.)

6. Save the presentation as *[your initials]***4-17.ppt**.

7. Create headers and footers for Notes and Handouts. Include the date and your name at the top of the page and the page number and filename at the bottom.

8. Print the presentation as handouts, 6 slides per page, black and white, framed.

9. Save and close the presentation.

EXERCISE 4-18

Insert a word-processed outline into a presentation, move bullets and slides, and insert a slide from another presentation.

1. Open the file **Honeys2.ppt**, apply the design template **Ribbons.pot**, and switch to Outline view.

2. Using a word processor (like Microsoft Word), open the file **Hnyprod.rtf**.

3. Modify the outline by moving the text for the "Breads and Desserts with Honey" slide before the "Jarred Honeys" slide.

4. Save the word-processed outline as *[your initials]***4-18.doc** and close it.

5. Position the insertion point at the end of slide 2 in **Honeys2.ppt** (after "Jarred honeys") and insert the word-processed outline *[your initials]* **4-18.doc**. ("Honey Beverages" becomes slide 3, "Bread and Desserts with Honey" becomes slide 4, and "Jarred Honeys" becomes slide 5.)

6. Add a new slide after slide 5 with the title **Good 4 U Honey Promotion** and the following bullets:
   - **Honey-tasting contest**
   - **Bread and honey samples at take-out counter**
   - **Complimentary honey candies after meals**

Exercise 4-18:
Objectives 2, 3, 6–8
Required Files: Honeys2.ppt, Hnyprod.rtf
Solution Files: gl4-18.ppt and gl4-18.doc in Solutions Manual or on Solutions Disk

The completed presentation for this Exercise may be used in a student's portfolio.

129

7. Change slide 3 ("Honey Beverages") to two-column layout, moving the second bullet and its sub-bullets to the right column placeholder. Delete any blank lines in Outline view, if necessary.

8. In slide 7, move "Offer honey breads for dessert" after "Serve honey samplers…."

9. Position the insertion point at the end of slide 7 (after "dessert") and insert slide 3 from the file **Honeys1.ppt**. The slide "Gift Sales Services" becomes new slide 8.

10. Check spelling in the presentation. (Leave the spelling of "Fruit-ades" unchanged.)

11. Save the presentation as *[your initials]***4-18.ppt.**

12. Create headers and footers for Notes and Handouts. Include the date and your name at the top of the page and the page number and filename at the bottom.

13. Review the presentation in Slide view and fix unattractive line breaks. In slide 3, "(no caffeine)" should appear on a separate line. In slide 6, "at take-out counter" should appear on a separate line.

14. Print the presentation outline and print handouts (6 slides per page).

15. Save and close the presentation.

Working with Text

LESSON 5

OBJECTIVES

After completing this lesson, you will be able to:
1. Apply text attributes to selected text.
2. Apply text attributes to a text placeholder.
3. Control fonts in a presentation.
4. Work with bullets.
5. Change text alignment.
6. Change the size and position of a text placeholder.
7. Make text attribute changes to a master slide.

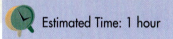

Estimated Time: 1 hour

By varying text appearance you can add interest to a PowerPoint presentation. You can change text appearance as you key it or change selected text, a selected placeholder, or an entire presentation.

Objective 1
Applying Text Attributes to Selected Text

You can change the appearance of selected text in your presentation by applying text attributes. For example, you can change the font face (such as Times New Roman or Arial) and font size (measured in points), and apply a text style (such as bold or italic) and effect (such as underline or shadow). You use the Formatting toolbar or the Font dialog box to change selected text.

PREPARE
Point out to students that the learning objectives show what they will learn in the lesson. Each heading in the lesson correlates to a learning objective.
Required Files
Heart1.ppt

TEACH
Teaching Resources:
• PowerPoint Classroom Presentations
• School-to-Work Strategies Manual
• Internet Manual
• Spanish Glossary
• Methodology Video
• Certification Procedures

Objective 1 Assignment:
Exercise 5-17 (Skills Review) can be assigned after completing Objective 1.

UNIT 2 ■ WORKING WITH PRESENTATIONS

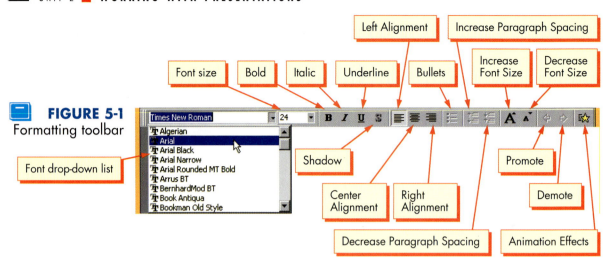

FIGURE 5-1
Formatting toolbar

EXERCISE 5-1 Change Text Attributes with the Toolbar

1. Open the file **Heart1.ppt**.

FIGURE 5-2
Font Size drop-down list

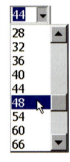

NOTE

2. Click the title placeholder of the first slide to activate it and key **Heart**

3. Select the word you just keyed. Click the down arrow next to the Font box on the Formatting toolbar to open the drop-down list and choose Arial. As you can see, text formatting in PowerPoint is similar to text formatting in a word processor.

4. With "Heart" still selected, click the down arrow next to the Font Size box. Scroll down the drop-down list and choose 48. The text size increases to 48 points.

5. Click the Decrease Font Size button . The font size decreases by one size. Notice the Font Size box now shows 44.

6. Click the Increase Font Size button twice. The font size increases by two sizes to 54 points.

7. Position the insertion point to the right of "Heart" and press [Spacebar]. Click the Bold button and then the Italic button to turn these attributes on. Key **Smart!** The word appears as bold italic. Notice that this word is also 54-point Arial, like the previous word.

 TIP: You can choose attributes and then key text, or you can select existing text and then change its attributes.

Use PowerPoint Classroom Presentation #5 to display screens from this lesson in a slide-show format.

NOTE
In steps 3 and 4, make sure students know how to open, choose from and scroll in a drop-down list.

LESSON 5 ■ **WORKING WITH TEXT**

NOTE

8. Select the word "Heart." On the Drawing toolbar, locate the Font Color button. Click its down arrow to open the font color submenu.

9. Position your pointer on the gray bar at the top of the font color submenu and drag it to the right side of the screen. Many of PowerPoint's submenus can be converted to floating toolbars in this manner. Unlike menus, floating toolbars stay open and available until you close them.

FIGURE 5-3
Font Color submenu

10. Click the red box on the Font Color floating toolbar. The selected text becomes light blue. You don't see the color you select until you deselect the text.

11. Click in the word "Smart" to deselect "Heart." "Heart" is now red.

12. Close the Font Color toolbar by clicking its Close button.

EXERCISE 5-2 Change Text Attributes with the Font Dialog Box

NOTE

1. Select the words "Good 4 U" in the subtitle.

2. Right-click the selected text to display the shortcut menu. Choose Font to open the Font dialog box. This dialog box is similar to the one in your word processor.

3. Set the Font to Arial, set the Font Style to Bold Italic, set the Size to 40, and check Underline. Notice the additional options available in this dialog box.

FIGURE 5-4
Font dialog box

NOTE

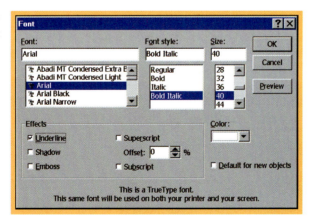

NOTE
Step 8 introduces the Drawing toolbar, which is discussed in greater detail in later lessons.

In PowerPoint Classroom Presentation #5.

NOTE
Remind students they can also choose Font from the Format menu to open the Font dialog box.

NOTE
Point out that almost all Font dialog box options are available on the Formatting toolbar. Students may find the dialog box more convenient when applying several attributes. Note that some effects (superscript and subscript, for instance) do not appear on the toolbar.

133

UNIT 2 ■ WORKING WITH PRESENTATIONS

4. Click Preview and drag the Font dialog box to the side so you can see the selected text under it.

5. Drag the dialog box back to the center of the screen (so you can see the OK button). Click OK to accept the formatting and close the dialog box.

6. With the text still selected, click the Underline button [U] on the Formatting toolbar to deselect this attribute. Deselect the text, which is now 40-point Arial bold italic.

7. Position the insertion point after "Good 4 U" and press [Enter] to create a two-line subtitle.

8. Create headers and footers for Notes and Handouts. Include the date and your name at the top of the page and the page number and filename at the bottom.

9. Save the presentation as *[your initials]***5-2.ppt** and print the title slide only as handouts, 2 slides per page, black and white, framed.

 NOTE: You can change text attributes in Slide view or Outline view using either the toolbars or the Font dialog box.

EXERCISE 5-3 Change the Case of Selected Text

If you find that you keyed text in uppercase and want to change it, you don't have to rekey it. Using the Change Case command on the Format menu, you can change any text to Sentence case, lowercase, UPPERCASE, or Title Case. You can also cycle through uppercase, lowercase, and title cases by selecting text and pressing [Shift]+[F3].

1. Move to slide 3 and select the title "Walk to good health." Notice that only the first word is capitalized.

2. Choose Change Case from the Format menu. The Change Case dialog box appears.

FIGURE 5-5
Change Case dialog box

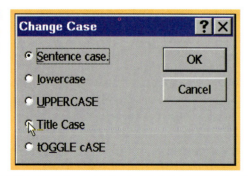

3. Choose Title Case and click OK. Now every word except "to" is capitalized.

4. With the title still selected, press [Shift]+[F3]. The case changes from title case to uppercase. Press [Shift]+[F3] again to change the text to lowercase. Press it a third time to change the text back to title case.

In PowerPoint Classroom Presentation #5.

LESSON 5 ■ **WORKING WITH TEXT**

5. Select the first bulleted item by dragging the I-beam across all its words. This text was keyed with [CapsLock] turned on.

6. Open the Change Case dialog box again, choose tOGGLE cASE, and click OK. This option reverses the current case, changing uppercase letters to lowercase and lowercase letters to uppercase.

7. Select the two bullets under "Walking" ("reduces…" and "lowers…"). Open the Change Case dialog box, choose <u>S</u>entence case, if necessary, and click OK.

[NOTE] **NOTE:** The style checker can automatically change bulleted items to sentence case and titles to title case. However, it may also change proper names to lowercase, so be sure to review your work after you use the style checker.

Objective 2
Applying Attributes to Text Placeholders

You can change the formatting for all text in a placeholder or text box at one time. To do this, you select the text box or text placeholder instead of the text inside it.

For instance, after keying text, you might want to make all the text in a bullet placeholder smaller. First you select the placeholder and then click the Decrease Font Size button. You use the same formatting tools for a selected text box as you use for selected text.

You can select placeholders and text boxes several ways:

- Click the border of an active placeholder with the arrow pointer.
- Press [Esc] while a placeholder is active.
- Press [Tab] to select the next placeholder on a slide.
- Press [Esc] to deselect a placeholder or other object.

EXERCISE 5-4 Select Text Placeholders

1. Move to slide 2 and click anywhere in the title text to make the text box active. Notice the border is made of tiny diagonal lines and small white squares.

[NOTE] 2. Point to any place on the border between two small squares. When you see the four-headed arrow pointer, click the border. Notice that the insertion point is no longer active and the border's appearance has changed slightly—it is now made of small dots instead of diagonal lines.

[NOTE]
The style checker can also change case, but it is still best to create text as you intend it to appear.

[NOTE]
Point out the difference between the border of the placeholder when it is selected versus merely active. The difference is subtle.

UNIT 2 ■ WORKING WITH PRESENTATIONS

FIGURE 5-6
Selected placeholder

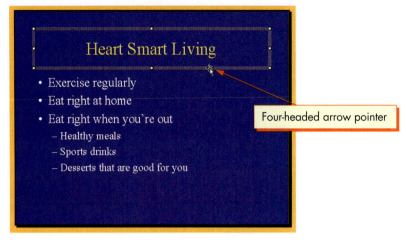

3. Press Tab. The bullet text box is selected.

> **NOTE:** Tab cycles through all objects on a slide, not just text boxes. If a slide contains a graphic object, Tab selects that as well.

4. Press Esc to deselect the bullet text box.

EXERCISE 5-5 Apply Text Attributes to Selected Placeholders

1. Move to slide 4 in Slide view.
2. Hold down Shift and click the title text box. This is another way to select a text box, providing the text box is not already active (containing the insertion point). If the text box is active, this method selects text instead of the text box.
3. Click the Decrease Font Size button . The title font is decreased to 40 points.
4. Click to undo the action.
5. Press Tab to select the bullet text box. Notice the 28+ in the Font Size box. This indicates there is more than one font size in the text box and that 28 point is the smallest size.
6. Click in the first bullet. Notice that its font size is 32 point. Click the first sub-bullet below it, which is 28 point. Notice that when you click text inside a placeholder, its border is no longer selected.
7. Press Esc to select the placeholder border.
8. Click the Increase Font Size button . The Font Size box now displays 32+, indicating the smallest text size in the placeholder is 32 points.

In PowerPoint Classroom Presentation #5.

136

LESSON 5 ■ **WORKING WITH TEXT**

9. With the bullet text border still selected, click [A↑] twice so 24+ appears in the Font Size box.

TIP: Another way to increase or decrease font size is to press Ctrl + Shift + > or Ctrl + Shift + <.

10. Click the arrow on [A▼] and choose yellow, making all bullet text on this slide yellow.

Objective 3
Controlling Presentation Fonts
NOTE

After you finish a presentation, you may decide that a different font will look better. You can change the font in the entire presentation easily and quickly with the Replace Font command.

If the fonts you chose for your presentation aren't available on another computer, you can embed the fonts in the presentation when you save it. This ensures that your presentation displays correctly on the other computer.

EXERCISE 5-6 Replace Fonts in a Presentation

1. Display slide 1. The slide contains the fonts Arial and Times New Roman. The rest of the presentation is in Times New Roman.

2. Choose Replace Fonts from the Format menu to display the Replace Font dialog box.

3. Open the Replace drop-down list and choose Arial. (This list contains the fonts currently used in the presentation.)

FIGURE 5-7
Replace Font dialog box

4. Open the With drop-down list to display the available fonts, choose Impact, and click Replace.

5. Drag the dialog box out of the way to see the change on slide 1. The Arial font used in the title and subtitle is replaced with Impact.

NOTE
Fonts have a powerful effect on the appearance of a presentation. You may want to have the students experiment with different fonts, and then discuss which fonts would be appropriate for certain kinds of presentations.

In PowerPoint Classroom Presentation #5.

137

6. Choose Times New Roman from the Replace list and choose Arial from the With list. Click Replace and close the dialog box. Notice the change in the last line of the subtitle and on the other slides, which are now in Arial instead of Times New Roman.

EXERCISE 5-7 Embed Fonts in a Presentation

NOTE

You can save, or embed, any TrueType font included with Windows or PowerPoint in a presentation. By embedding TrueType fonts, you make sure presentations look exactly the way you designed them.

1. Click to open the Font drop-down list on the Formatting toolbar. Notice that the fonts Arial and Impact are TrueType fonts, as indicated by the logo **T** to the left of the fonts. Notice that most of the fonts available on your computer are TrueType fonts.

2. Press [Esc] to close the drop-down list. Choose File, Save As from the menu to display the Save As dialog box.

3. Check the option Embed TrueType.

4. Save the presentation as *[your initials]***5-7.ppt**. The presentation is now saved with the TrueType fonts Arial and Impact.

5. Change the footer to reflect the current filename, and print handouts, 6 slides per page, black and white, framed. Save the presentation.

TIP: If you are concerned about file size and disk space, don't embed TrueType fonts unless it's necessary. Embedded fonts increase the size of your presentation files.

Objective 4
Working with Bullets

Although PowerPoint automatically places bullets in front of body text, you may decide that some slides would look better without the bullets. You can remove bullets, add new ones, and change the shape and color of bullets.

EXERCISE 5-8 Turn Bullets On and Off

1. Display slide 2. Click within the bulleted text to activate the text box. Press [Esc] to select the text box border.

NOTE
There are approximately 150 more TrueType fonts on the Office 97 CD in the Valupack\MSFonts folder. Open the file _preview.gif in the same folder to see samples of each font.

Objective 4 Assignment:
Exercise 5-18 (Skills Review) can be assigned after completing Objective 4.

LESSON 5 ■ **WORKING WITH TEXT**

2. Click the Bullets button ≡ on the Formatting toolbar. This turns bullets off for the entire text box and moves the text to the left.

3. Click ≡ again to reapply the bullets.

4. Click within the first bulleted item, "Exercise regularly," and click ≡ to turn off the bullet.

5. Click ≡ again to reapply the bullet.

EXERCISE **5-9** **Change the Color and Shape of a Bullet**

You use the Bullet dialog box to change the color and shape of a bullet. To change the bullet shape, you can choose a character from another font. Fonts that contain potential bullet characters include Symbol, Wingdings, and Monotype Sorts.

NOTE

1. With the bullet text box on slide 2 activated, right-click the text box border to display the shortcut menu and choose Bullet.

2. In the Bullet dialog box, open the Bullets from drop-down list and choose the Symbol font.

FIGURE 5-8
Bullet dialog box

NOTE

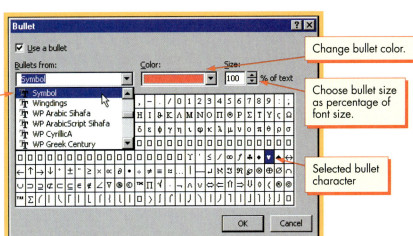

3. Click the heart character in the grid. The heart is enlarged for easy viewing.

4. Open the Color drop-down box and choose red.

NOTE: Choose the Automatic option if you want the bullet to be the color scheme font color.

5. Click OK. The bullets on the slide change to red hearts. Notice that the default size of the heart is somewhat large in proportion to the text.

NOTE
Right-clicking the text box border selects the border and displays the shortcut menu. It's important for the text box to be selected so students can practice changing all bullets on the slide. If the insertion point is in a line of bulleted text, only that bullet changes.

In PowerPoint Classroom Presentation #5.

NOTE
Using the Bullet dialog box, encourage students to look at the characters of other fonts, such as Wingdings and Monotype Sorts. Some of the more interesting characters are difficult to see on the screen. Have students experiment with different shapes, colors, and sizes.

139

UNIT 2 ■ WORKING WITH PRESENTATIONS

6. With the text box still selected, choose Bullet from the Format menu.
7. Change the Size to 90 percent and click OK. The bullets are slightly smaller.
8. Select the last three lines of bulleted text (beginning with "Healthy meals") and open the Bullet dialog box.
9. Choose the right-pointing arrow (→) in the sixth row and click OK. The sub-bullets on this slide are now red arrows.

Objective 5
Changing Text Alignment

Bullets, titles, and subtitles are all considered to be paragraphs in PowerPoint. Just as in a word processor, when you press Enter, a new paragraph begins. You can align paragraphs with the left or right margin or center them between margins. You can also justify long paragraphs so both margins are squared off.

EXERCISE 5-10 Change Text Alignment

1. Move to slide 5 and turn bullets off for the two lines of bulleted text.
2. Position the insertion point in "Earn Good 4 U discounts."
3. Choose Alignment from the Format menu and choose Right from the submenu. The paragraph aligns to the right.

 NOTE: Notice the keyboard shortcuts listed on the Alignment submenu for aligning paragraphs.

4. Click the Left Alignment button on the Formatting toolbar. The paragraph aligns to the left.

5. Select the text box border and click the Center Alignment button. Both paragraphs are centered horizontally within the text box.

 NOTE: You can apply alignment attributes to an entire text box just as you applied text formatting.

Objective 6
Changing Size and Position of Text Placeholders

There are times when you will want to change the way text is positioned on a slide. For example, you may want to make a text box narrower or wider to con-

NOTE
Students do not practice using the justify alignment option in this Exercise, but you may want to explain or demonstrate its use.

140

LESSON 5 ■ **WORKING WITH TEXT**

trol how text wraps to a new line or you may want to move all the text up or down on a slide.

You can change the size and position of text placeholders several different ways:

- Drag a *resize handle* to change the size and shape of a text placeholder. Resize handles are the eight small boxes along the border of a selected placeholder.
- Drag the text box border to move the text to a new position.
- Change text box size and position settings using the Format AutoShape dialog box.

EXERCISE 5-11 Change the Size and Shape of a Text Box by Dragging the Resize Handles

1. Display slide 5, if necessary, and select the bullet text box. Notice the small white boxes around the border. These are the resize handles.
2. Position the pointer over the bottom center resize handle. The pointer changes to a double-headed arrow ↕.
3. Drag the bottom border of the selected text box up until it is just below "Eat right on us." As you drag, a dotted line shows the changing shape of the box and the pointer turns into a thin cross. When you release the mouse, notice that the position of the text on the slide did not change.

FIGURE 5-9
Resizing a text box

In PowerPoint Classroom Presentation #5.

141

UNIT 2 ■ WORKING WITH PRESENTATIONS

4. Position the pointer over one of the lower corner resize handles.

5. Drag the corner handle toward the center of the text. Notice that using a corner resize handle changes both the height and width of the box and the position of the text is adjusted accordingly.

6. Click to restore the text box to its previous size, with the bottom border just under "Eat right on us."

EXERCISE 5-12 Move a Text Box by Dragging its Border

1. Select the text box of slide 5, if necessary.

NOTE

2. Position the pointer over the text box border. The pointer changes to the four-headed arrow pointer ✥.

3. Drag the text box down until it is vertically centered on the slide.

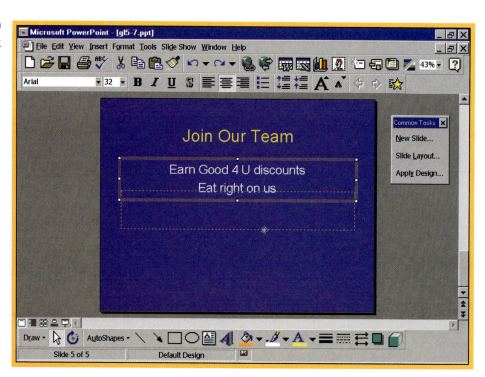

FIGURE 5-10
Moving a text box

4. Deselect the text box. The text is now centered on the slide.

NOTE
Make sure students understand that to move the placeholder by dragging they place the pointer over the border, not the resize handle.

In PowerPoint Classroom Presentation #5.

142

LESSON 5 ■ WORKING WITH TEXT

EXERCISE 5-13 Use the Format AutoShape Dialog Box

The Format AutoShape dialog box offers, among other things, a way to change the size and placement of text boxes using exact measurements. *Autoshape* is a term that refers to rectangles, circles, and many irregular shapes in PowerPoint that can contain text, as well as shapes you can use for drawing.

1. Move to slide 2 and select the bullet text box.

2. Right-click the text box border and choose Format AutoShape from the shortcut menu. Notice the different tabs in the Format AutoShape dialog box that you can use to change the look of your text box. (You can also open this dialog box by choosing AutoShape from the Format menu when a text box is selected.)

FIGURE 5-11
Format AutoShape dialog box, Position tab

NOTE

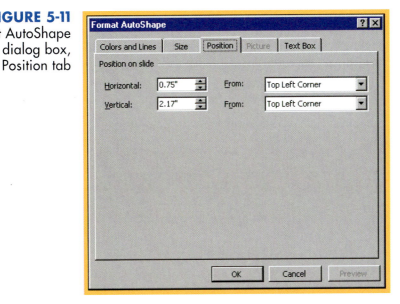

3. Click the Position tab, if necessary, and key **2** in the Horizontal text box. This places the text box two inches from the top left corner of the slide.

4. Click the Preview button and drag the dialog box to see the new position of the text. Notice that the text box moved to the left and its border now extends beyond the right edge of the slide.

5. Click the Size tab. Key **4** in the Height box and **6** in the Width box, making the text box 4 inches tall and 6 inches wide.

6. Click OK. The text box is now sized appropriately for the text inside it and is attractively positioned on the slide.

7. Save the presentation as *[your initials]* **5-13.ppt**.

NOTE
You may want to point out that one advantage of using the Format AutoShape dialog box to resize placeholders is that it allows you to precisely position and resize placeholder boxes. This can be useful when you are trying to achieve uniformity among several slides.

143

UNIT 2 ■ **WORKING WITH PRESENTATIONS**

8. Change the footer to reflect the current filename and print only slide 2 as a handout, 2 slides per page, black and white, framed.

✓Objective 7
Using Master Slides to Format Text

A *master slide* contains formatted text placeholders and background items that are designed to appear on all slides in a presentation. Changes that you make on a master slide appear on all slides in the presentation that are based on that master. There are two masters that you can use for slides:

- Title master, which includes text placeholders for the title and subtitle of the title slide
- Slide master, which includes text placeholders for the title and bullet text

In general, the slide master and the title master contain the same design elements (such as background color, graphic, and text formatting). However, the title master is arranged differently to accommodate title and subtitle text. The slide master is often less elaborate, leaving room for bulleted text and other information. You can change the formatting and design of the masters and thus set the tone for the entire presentation.

EXERCISE 5-14 Change Font Attributes on the Slide and Title Masters

There are two ways to display the slide and title masters:

- Use the View menu.
- Use Shift + the Slide View button 🗖.

1. Display slide 4. Notice that this is the only slide with yellow bullet text. You'll use the masters to change all bullet text to this color and to make some additional changes.

NOTE

2. To display the slide master, choose Master from the View menu and then choose Slide Master (or hold down Shift and click the Slide View button 🗖). Dotted placeholders indicate the position for title text, bulleted text, and footer information. You can change the size, shape, position, and text attributes for any of these text placeholders. (See Figure 5-12 on the next page.)

3. Position the pointer over the dotted border of the bullet text placeholder until a four-headed arrow appears and click to select the placeholder. When you select a placeholder on a master slide, you format it the same way as you format a slide text box.

NOTE
When you press Shift + click the Slide View button to display masters, the slide master appears *unless* you were viewing slide 1, in which case the title master appears. Make sure students practice switching between the title and slide master using either the vertical scroll bar or the Page Up and Page Down keys. Stress the importance of checking the status bar to make sure they're viewing the correct master before they make changes. Additionally, stress the importance of working with both masters to produce consistently formatted presentations.

✓**Objective 1 Assignment:**
Exercise 5-20 (Skills Review) and Exercises 5-21 through 5-24 (Lesson Applications) can be assigned after completing Objective 7.

144

LESSON 5 ■ **WORKING WITH TEXT**

FIGURE 5-12
Slide master

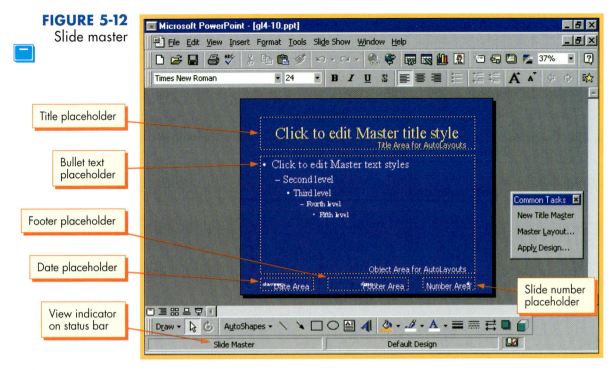

NOTE: An easy way to tell if you're viewing the slide master or title master is to check the indicator on the left side of the status bar.

4. Change the font color for the bullet text placeholder to yellow using the Font Color button on the Drawing toolbar.

5. Click within the first level bullet. Format the bullet character as a red heart that is 90% of the font size.

6. Select the title placeholder and change its font to 40 point. Add a text shadow to the title by clicking the Shadow button on the Formatting toolbar.

7. Press `PgDn` or use the vertical scroll bar to display the title master.

TIP: You can switch between the title and slide master by pressing `PgDn` and `PgUp`, using the vertical scroll bar, or using the View menu.

8. Review the elements on the title master. Some of the changes you made to the slide master are reflected on the title master (the font color is yellow and the title is 40 point). PowerPoint does this automatically to make sure your presentation is consistently formatted.

In PowerPoint Classroom Presentation #5.

UNIT 2 ■ **WORKING WITH PRESENTATIONS**

FIGURE 5-13
Title master

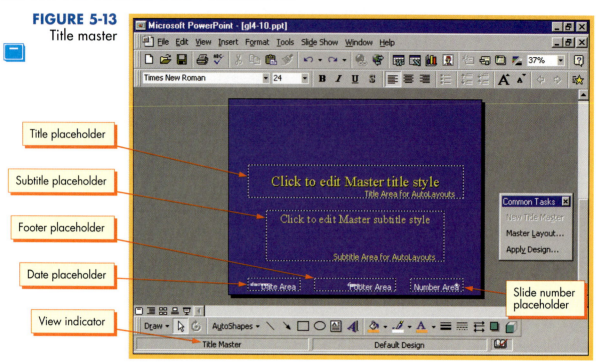

> **NOTE:** Unless you start a new presentation with a title slide, the presentation will not include a title master. To create one, display the slide master and choose Insert, New Title Master or press Ctrl+M.

9. Select the title placeholder and change the font to Arial Black.

10. To return to Slide view, click the Slide View button ▭ or choose Slide from the View menu. Scroll through the presentation and notice that most of the changes you made to the masters are reflected in the presentation. However, the formatting you applied to individual slides earlier in the lesson is overriding the master slide formatting. You correct this in the next exercise.

EXERCISE 5-15 Reapply the Slide Layout

As you've seen, changing a master does not override changes you make to individual slides. When you format individual slides and then format a slide master, you can reapply the slide layout to the individual slides to apply the master slide formatting. This ensures the entire presentation is formatted consistently.

1. Display slide 1. Click Slide Layout on the Common Tasks toolbar to open the Slide Layout dialog box. With the Title Slide layout selected, click

---

In PowerPoint Classroom Presentation #5.

NOTE
When you make changes to a master slide, all slides based on that master reflect the changes. However, if you change fonts, colors, or bullets on individual slides, those changes override master slide changes. To make the slide master take effect on these slides, you must reapply the slide layout, which students do in Exercise 5-15.

NOTE
Remind students of other methods of opening the Slide Layout dialog box.

146

LESSON 5 ■ **WORKING WITH TEXT**

Reapply. The title formatting applied earlier is now replaced by the title master formatting.

2. Display slide 2. This slide had its text box sized and positioned and its sub-bullets changed to arrows earlier in the lesson.

3. Reapply the bulleted list layout to slide 2. The arrow bullets change back to hyphens and the text box size and position changes back to the default.

4. Display slide 4 and reapply the bulleted list layout. The bullet text size is increased to 32 point, like the other bulleted list slides.

5. Display slide 5 and press F4 or choose Repeat Slide Layout from the Edit menu. The bulleted list layout is reapplied.

  TIP: The Repeat command repeats the last action you performed on the current slide or object. You can also use the Repeat command for text formatting and editing.

EXERCISE 5-16 Add Slide Numbers to a Slide

When the master slides are displayed, you can see placeholders for the date, footer, and slide number. You can format these placeholders the same way you format bullet text and title text placeholders.

1. Choose Header and Footer from the View menu and click the Slide tab, if necessary. Apply slide numbers to all slides except the title slide.

2. Scroll through the slide to see the slide numbers on slides 2 through 5. Notice that the font is relatively small and the font color does not match the rest of the slide color scheme.

3. Display the slide master.

 4. Select the number placeholder in the bottom right corner of the screen. Increase the zoom to 75% or more so you can see the characters <#> more clearly. Position the insertion point before these characters. Key **Slide** and press Spacebar.

5. Select the number placeholder (click its border). Change the font color to yellow and the font size to 20 point.

FIGURE 5-14
Formatting the number placeholder

NOTE
Explain that the Repeat command only repeats the last action. When using it for formatting, for example, if you select a text box, click the Italic button, click the Bold button, select another text box, and press F4, PowerPoint applies the Bold attribute only. However, if you apply multiple attributes in a dialog box, the Repeat command repeats the dialog box selections.

NOTE
Zoom settings vary based on the monitors and resolution used in the classroom. Point out that the "Fit" zoom setting is the best for overall viewing.

In PowerPoint Classroom Presentation #5.

UNIT 2 ■ **WORKING WITH PRESENTATIONS**

6. Reduce the zoom, if necessary, to make all three placeholders visible (date, footer, and number). Select and delete the date and footer placeholders.

7. Center-align the text in the number placeholder and drag the placeholder to the bottom center of the slide.

8. Return to Slide view, change the zoom to Fit, and display slide 2. Notice the size, color, and position of the slide number, as well as the word "Slide" before the number. View the rest of the presentation.

FIGURE 5-15
Slide with formatted and repositioned slide number

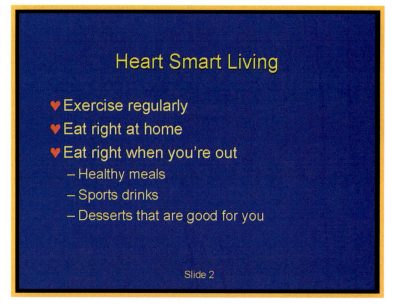

9. Save the presentation as *[your initials]***5-16.ppt**.

10. Change the handout footer to reflect the current filename and print the presentation as handouts, 6 slides per page, black and white, framed.

 NOTE: When you open the Header and Footer dialog box, notice on the Slide tab that the changes you made to the slide master are reflected in the Preview box.

11. Save and close the presentation.

In PowerPoint Classroom Presentation #5.

LESSON 5 ■ **WORKING WITH TEXT**

COMMAND SUMMARY

> **NOTE**

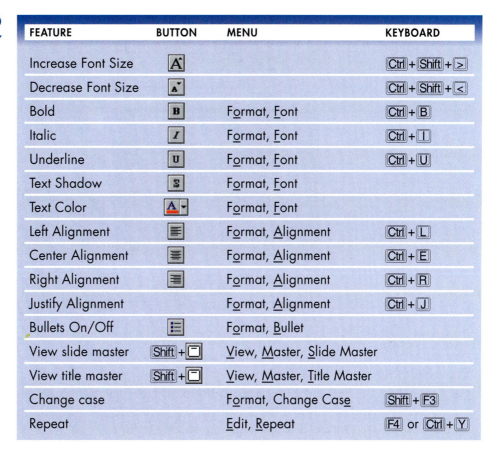

FEATURE	BUTTON	MENU	KEYBOARD
Increase Font Size	A▲		Ctrl + Shift + >
Decrease Font Size	A▼		Ctrl + Shift + <
Bold	B	Format, Font	Ctrl + B
Italic	I	Format, Font	Ctrl + I
Underline	U	Format, Font	Ctrl + U
Text Shadow	S	Format, Font	
Text Color	A▼	Format, Font	
Left Alignment	≡	Format, Alignment	Ctrl + L
Center Alignment	≡	Format, Alignment	Ctrl + E
Right Alignment	≡	Format, Alignment	Ctrl + R
Justify Alignment		Format, Alignment	Ctrl + J
Bullets On/Off	≡	Format, Bullet	
View slide master	Shift + ☐	View, Master, Slide Master	
View title master	Shift + ☐	View, Master, Title Master	
Change case		Format, Change Case	Shift + F3
Repeat		Edit, Repeat	F4 or Ctrl + Y

USING HELP

> **NOTE**

Working with the slide and title masters helps you create consistent and professional looking presentations. In later lessons you learn how to place art on a slide master so it appears throughout your presentation.

Use Help to learn more about master slides:

1. Choose Contents and Index from the Help menu and display the Index tab.
2. Key **slide master** in the text box and click Display.
3. Display the topic "The slide master." PowerPoint displays an overview screen about slide and title masters.

> **NOTE**
> Point out that the Command Summary lists a variety of ways to accomplish a particular task. Students can decide which method they prefer to use.

> **NOTE**
> Encourage students to follow the steps in "Using Help." Software companies are increasingly using online Help programs—rather than printed documentation—to train users and assist in answering user questions.

149

UNIT 2 ■ **WORKING WITH PRESENTATIONS**

FIGURE 5-16
Slide master Help screen

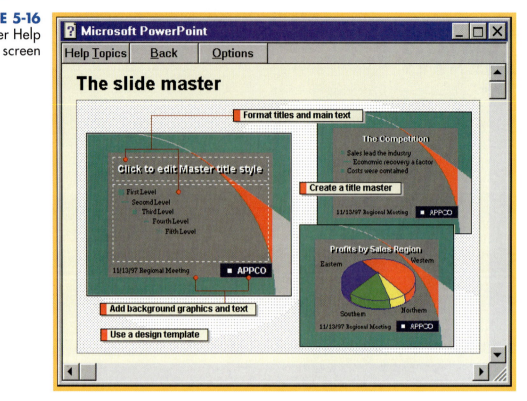

4. Click to display the topics on the Help screen, including the topic "Create a title master."
5. Close Help when you finish.

In PowerPoint Classroom Presentation #5.

150

LESSON 5 ■ WORKING WITH TEXT

TEST BANK

Concepts Review

TRUE/FALSE QUESTIONS

Each of the following statements is either true or false. Indicate your choice by circling **T** or **F**.

T F   1. You can change selected text from uppercase to lowercase using the Shift+F3 keyboard shortcut.

T F   2. You can apply text attributes before you key text.

T **F**   3. Sentence case capitalizes the initial letter of important words in a paragraph.

T F   4. To search for and replace one font with another throughout a presentation, use the Replace Fonts dialog box.

T **F**   5. Changes on the slide master override changes you make to individual slides.

T F   6. The button can turn bullets on or off.

T F   7. You can delete placeholders on a master slide.

T **F**   8. You can drag a sizing handle to reposition a placeholder.

SHORT ANSWER QUESTIONS

Write the correct answer in the space provided.

1. What must you do before you can change an attribute for existing text?
   Select the text

2. Which dialog box do you use to change the color of text?
   Font dialog box

3. Which toolbar buttons change font size?
   Font Size, Increase Font Size, Decrease Font Size

4. What is the quickest way to add a shadow to text?
   Select the text and click the Shadow button on the Formatting toolbar

5. Which commands do you need to choose to change bullet color?
   Format, Bullet, Color

Concepts Review: Allows students to check their understanding.

TEST BANK Consider using the Test Bank to provide an additional review of lesson concepts.

151

UNIT 2 ■ WORKING WITH PRESENTATIONS

6. How can you display the slide master without using the <u>V</u>iew menu?
   Press Shift and click the Slide View button

7. Which dialog box do you use to change the size of a placeholder using exact measurements?
   Format AutoShape, Size tab

8. What does the button ▤ do to selected text?
   Centers it

CRITICAL THINKING

Answer these questions on a separate page. There are no right or wrong answers. Support your answers with examples from your own experience, if possible.

1. Explain how font faces can affect a presentation. Can you use too many fonts in a presentation? Explain your answer.

2. Adding different bullet shapes can add interest and emphasis to a presentation. How do you think a presentation would look if every slide included different bullets? If all the bullets were the same?

Skills Review

EXERCISE 5-17

Apply text attributes to selected text.

1. Open the file **Walk1.ppt**.
2. Change font size of the presentation title by following these steps:
   a. On slide 1, select the text "Power Walking" by dragging the I-beam pointer across the text.
   b. Choose 44 from the Font Size drop-down list on the Formatting toolbar.
3. Increase the font size of the title on slide 3 by following these steps:
   a. Select the title text of slide 3.
   b. Click the Increase Font Size button A˄ until 44 appears in the Font Size box.
4. Decrease the font size of the title on slide 4 to 44 points by using the Decrease Font Size button A˅.

Critical Thinking Questions:
Answers will vary based on students' preferences, observations, experiences, and research.

Skills Review:
Provides guided practice for students. Objectives are indicated for each Exercise.

Exercise 5-17:
Objective 1
Required File: Walk1.ppt
Solution File: gl5-17.ppt in Solutions Manual or on Solutions Disk

LESSON 5 ■ **WORKING WITH TEXT**

5. Decrease the font size of the title on slide 5 to 44 points using the Font dialog box by following these steps:
   a. Select the title text.
   b. Choose Font from the Format menu.
   c. Choose 44 from the Size list and click OK.

6. Change the case of the text on slide 5 by following these steps:
   a. Select the last bulleted item by dragging the I-beam pointer across the text.
   b. Choose Change Case from the Format menu.
   c. Click tOGGLE cASE and click OK.

7. Change the font size of the title of slide 6 to 44 point.

8. Working in either Outline or Slide view, underline the title text in slide 1 by selecting the text and clicking the Underline button [U] on the Formatting toolbar. Do the same for the remaining slide titles.

9. Check spelling in the presentation. (Ignore the misspelling of "approx.")

10. Save the presentation as *[your initials]***5-17.ppt.**

11. Create headers and footers for Notes and Handouts. Include the date and your name at the top of the page and the page number and filename at the bottom.

12. Print the presentation as handouts, 6 slides per page, black and white, framed.

13. Save and close the presentation.

EXERCISE 5-18

Apply text attributes to text placeholders and selected text, and work with bullets.

1. Open the file **Walk2.ppt**.
2. Change the color of the title on slide 1 by following these steps:
   a. Press [Tab] until the title text box is selected or click the title text and then click its border.
   b. Choose Font from the Format menu.
   c. Click the down arrow to open the Color palette, choose black, and click OK.
3. Press [Tab] to select the subtitle placeholder and change the subtitle to red.
4. Change the title on slide 2 to black and shadowed by following these steps:
   a. Move to slide 2 and click the title.

Exercise 5-18:
Objectives 1, 2, 4
Required File: Walk2.ppt
Solution File: gl5-18.ppt in Solutions Manual or on Solutions Disk

153

UNIT 2 ■ WORKING WITH PRESENTATIONS

   b. Click the slant-line border to select the title text box.

   c. Click the arrow on the Font Color button on the Drawing toolbar and choose black.

   d. Click the Shadow button on the Formatting toolbar.

5. Change the titles of slides 3 and 4 to black and shadowed.

6. Decrease the font size of the bullet placeholder on slide 2 by one font size.

7. Change the bullets for slide 2 by following these steps:

   a. Select the bullet placeholder, if necessary.

   b. Choose Bullet from the Format menu

   c. Choose Wingdings from the Bullets from drop-down list.

   d. Choose the check mark symbol, which is on the last row, fourth from the right.

   e. Click OK.

8. Remove bullets from selected text on slide 2 by following these steps:

   a. Select the two second-level bulleted items under "When."

   b. Click the Bullets button on the Formatting toolbar.

   c. Remove bullets from the two items under "Where."

9. Change the bullets for slides 3 and 4 using the same bullet style as slide 2.

10. On slide 2, add and format a word by following these steps:

    a. Change the fourth bullet to read **Free refreshments afterward**

    b. Select the word "Free."

    c. Click the Bold button.

11. Check spelling in the presentation. (Ignore the misspelling of "approx.")

12. Save the presentation as *[your initials]***5-18.ppt.**

13. Create headers and footers for Notes and Handouts. Include the date and your name at the top of the page and the page number and filename at the bottom.

14. Print the presentation as handouts, 6 slides per page, black and white, framed.

15. Save and close the presentation.

EXERCISE 5-19

Apply text attributes, change text alignment, and change size and position of text boxes.

   1. Open the file **Walk2.ppt**

Exercise 5-19:
Objectives 2, 5, 6
Required File: Walk2.ppt
Solution File: gl5-19.ppt in Solutions Manual or on Solutions Disk.

154

LESSON 5 ■ **WORKING WITH TEXT**

2. Change the size of the title slide text box by following these steps:
   a. Display slide 1.
   b. Select the subtitle text box.
   c. Position the pointer over the bottom right corner resize handle on the border.
   d. When you see the double-headed arrow, drag the resize handle toward the center of the text, changing both the height and width of the text box until it is just large enough to fit the text.

3. Move the subtitle text box to a new position by following these steps:
   a. Select the text box border, if necessary.
   b. Position the pointer on the top border between two sizing handles.
   c. Using the four-headed arrow pointer, drag the text box to the center of the slide.

4. Display slide 2 and change the alignment of the title by following these steps:
   a. Place the insertion point anywhere in the title.
   b. Click the Center Alignment button 🗐 on the Formatting toolbar.

5. Center-align the titles of slides 3 and 4.

6. Resize the bullet text box in slide 3 to fit the text and center the text box below the title. Do the same for the bullet text box on slide 4.

7. Check spelling in the presentation. (Ignore the misspelling of "approx.")

8. Save the presentation as *[your initials]***5-19.ppt**.

9. Create headers and footers for Notes and Handouts. Include the date and your name at the top of the page and the page number and filename at the bottom.

10. Print the presentation as handouts, 6 slides per page, black and white, framed.

11. Save and close the presentation.

EXERCISE 5-20

Work with the presentation masters.

1. Open the file **Power1.ppt**.
2. Apply formatting to the slide and title masters by following these steps:
   a. Display the slide master by pressing [Shift] and then clicking the Slide View button 🔲. If the title master is displayed, drag the scroll bar up to display the slide master (or press [PgUp]).

Exercise 5-20:
Objectives 2, 4, 5, 7
Required File: Power1.ppt
Solution File: gl5-20.ppt in Solutions Manual or on Solutions Disk.

UNIT 2 ■ WORKING WITH PRESENTATIONS

NOTE

    b. Select the title placeholder by clicking its dashed border. Change the font to 44-point Arial italic shadowed.

    c. Display the title master. Select the subtitle placeholder and increase its text size to 36 point.

3. Click to display slide 1. Delete the line space between the two lines of text in the subtitle (press [Backspace] before "August"). View the slide titles throughout the presentation.

4. Change the font, attributes, and bullets on the slide master by following these steps:

    a. Display the slide master by choosing <u>M</u>aster from the <u>V</u>iew menu and then choosing <u>S</u>lide Master.

    b. Select the bullet text placeholder.

    c. Change the font to Arial italic.

    d. Select the level 1 bullet. Choose <u>B</u>ullet from the F<u>o</u>rmat menu, choose one of the star symbols on the second row of the Monotype Sorts fonts, and click OK.

5. Format the slide number placeholder on the slide master by following these steps:

    a. Select the slide number placeholder in the lower right corner of the slide master.

    b. Set the Zoom to 75%.

    c. Change the font size to 20-point italic.

    d. Position the insertion point in front of the <#> symbols.

    e. Key **Slide** and press [Spacebar].

    f. Choose Fit from the Zoom list to return to normal size.

6. Return to Slide view. Using the Header and Footer dialog box, apply slide numbers to all slides except the title slide.

7. Check spelling in the presentation.

8. Save the presentation as *[your initials]*__5-20.ppt__.

9. Create headers and footers for Notes and Handouts. Include the date and your name at the top of the page and the page number and filename at the bottom.

10. Print the presentation as handouts, 6 slides per page, black and white, framed.

11. Save and close the presentation.

NOTE
Reinforce that title formatting applied on the slide master is automatically applied to the title placeholder on the title master.

LESSON 5 ■ WORKING WITH TEXT

Lesson Applications

EXERCISE 5-21

Apply text attributes to selected text and placeholders, work with bullets, and make changes to the slide master.

1. Open the file **Walk3.ppt**.
2. On the slide master, center-align the title placeholder and make it bold.
3. Change the first-level bullet to the diamond shape (second character in the fourth row) in the Monotype Sorts grid. Set the bullet to 90% of the text size.
4. On slide 1, change the color of the date text to light orange. Edit the date to the current month and year.
5. Move to slide 4 and change the title to simply "Concession Products" on one line.
6. Change the layout of slide 4 to two-column.
7. Delete the bulleted item "Good 4 U meals" and rearrange the text as shown in Figure 5-17:

FIGURE 5-17

8. On slide 4, increase the font size of each column by one increment (making the first-level bullets 32 point and the second-level bullets 28 point).

Assessment Resources:
- Solutions Manual
- Test Bank with Software
- Portfolio Builder
- Alternative Assessment Guide
- Certification Procedures

Lesson Applications:
Provide independent practice for students. Objectives are indicated for each Exercise.

Exercise 5-21:
Objectives 1, 2, 4, 5, 7
Required File: Walk3.ppt
Solution File: gl5-21.ppt in Solutions Manual or on Solutions Disk.

UNIT 2 ■ WORKING WITH PRESENTATIONS

9. Check spelling in the presentation.
10. Save the presentation as *[your initials]*5-21.ppt.
11. Create headers and footers for Notes and Handouts. Include the date and your name at the top of the page and the page number and filename at the bottom.
12. Print the presentation as handouts, 6 slides per page, black and white, framed.
13. Save and close the presentation.

EXERCISE 5-22

Apply text attributes to selected text and text placeholders, work with bullets and the slide master, and replace fonts.

1. Open the file **Recycle1.ppt**.
2. Edit slide 1 so the title reads **Recycling Program**, and the subtitle reads **Good 4 U Management Training**. Change the font color of the subtitle to white.
3. In slide 2, make the words "waste," "costs," and "landfill overloads" bold.
4. In slide 3, increase the font size of the title to 48 points.
5. Use the slide master to change the titles of all slides to bold.
6. Use the slide master to change all first-level bullets to stars (★) sized as 90% of text. Change the second-level bullets to check marks (✓) sized as 80% of text. (Choose from the Monotype Sorts font.)
7. Change the second-level bulleted text to italic.
8. Add the following speaker notes to slide 2:

   Discuss how waste reduction is cost-effective.

9. Add the following speaker notes to slide 3:

   Mention our targeted percentages for the coming year.

10. Use the Replace Fonts command to replace Arial with Times New Roman in the presentation.
11. Check spelling in the presentation. (Ignore the spellings of "carters," "recyclables," and "recyclers.")
12. Save the presentation as *[your initials]*5-22.ppt.
13. Create headers and footers for Notes and Handouts. Include the date and your name at the top of the page and the page number and filename at the bottom.

Exercise 5-22:
Objectives 1–4, 7
Required File: Recycle1.ppt
Solution File: gl5-22.ppt in Solutions Manual or on Solutions Disk.

LESSON 5 ■ **WORKING WITH TEXT**

14. Print the presentation as handouts, 6 slides per page, black and white, framed. Print speaker notes for slides 2 and 3, black and white.
15. Save and close the presentation.

EXERCISE 5-23

Apply text attributes to selected text and text placeholders, work with bullets and the slide master, align text, and resize and reposition text boxes.

1. Create a new presentation consisting of the text shown in Figure 5-18.

FIGURE 5-18

```
Slide 1    Power Walking Event
           Good 4 U - August 1998

           Agenda
           • Increase recognition of Good 4 U Restaurant
Slide 2    • Attract target clientele (fitness, health, and sports participants)
           • Interest a wider clientele

           Overview
           • Advertise Power Walking for Healthy Hearts
           • Organize Power Walking seminars and walks
Slide 3    • Interest Other Sponsors
           • Make Power Walking an Annual Event
           • Schedule "paths for every pace"

           Participants
           • Local sports figures
Slide 4    • Good 4 U staff
           • Park personnel
           • Community members
```

Exercise 5-23:
Objectives 1, 2, 4–7
Required File: None
Solution File: gl5-23.ppt in Solutions Manual or on Solutions Disk.

The completed presentation for this Exercise may be used in a student's portfolio.

159

UNIT 2 ■ WORKING WITH PRESENTATIONS

2. Apply the **Zesty.pot** design template and change the slide color scheme to pale yellow.

3. In slide 3, change the case of the bullet text box to sentence case.

4. Use the slide master to change all bullets to red hearts sized at 90% of text.

5. Use the slide master to change all text to Arial with the bold text attribute. Left-align the titles for all slides.

6. In slide 1, center the text in the title placeholder.

7. In slide 3, change the font color of the words "healthy hearts" to red and make the words italic.

8. Start the text *"healthy hearts"* on a new line by pressing Enter before the text. Center the new line and remove its bullet.

9. In slide 4, resize the bullet text box to fit the text and center it on the slide.

10. Check spelling in the presentation.

11. Save the presentation as *[your initials]*5-23.ppt.

12. Create headers and footers for Notes and Handouts. Include the date and your name at the top of the page and the page number and filename at the bottom.

13. Print the presentation as handouts, 6 slides per page, black and white, framed.

14. Save and close the presentation.

EXERCISE 5-24

Apply text attributes to text and text placeholders, work with bullets and the slide master, change alignment, resize and reposition placeholders, and embed the presentation font in the file.

1. Open the file **Walk4.ppt**.

2. Apply the **Contemporary Portrait.pot** design template and change the slide color scheme to the fifth standard color option (white with blue accents).

3. Resize the subtitle placeholder on slide 1 so "Good 4 U Promotional Training" fits on one line. Center the subtitle placeholder horizontally on the slide.

4. Use the slide master to check that the title and bullet text placeholders are formatted as Arial Black. Check the title master placeholders as well.

Exercise 5-24:
Objectives 1–7
Required File: Walk4.ppt
Solution File: gl5-24.ppt in Solutions Manual or on Solutions Disk

The completed presentation for this Exercise may be used in a student's portfolio.

5. At the end of the presentation, insert two new slides using the Bulleted List layout as shown in Figure 5-19.

FIGURE 5-19

```
Annual Event
• Establish volunteer committees
• Schedule year-round support events
    - Training
    - Practice walks
    - Advertising

Paths for Every Pace
• Beginner
• Intermediate
• Experienced
```

6. Reapply the bullet text slide layout to slide 2.
7. Edit the first bullet on slide 2 to read **Increase Good 4 U name recognition**
8. Insert line breaks (Shift+Enter) before the parentheses in the second and third bullets on slide 2 and remove the bold from the text in parentheses.
9. Edit the second bullet on slide 3 to read **Organize power walking seminars**
10. On slide 4, reapply bullets to the text in the bullet text box.
11. On slide 5, reapply the bullets to the lines that begin "Training walks" and "Good 4 U sports drinks."
12. Edit the bullets on slide 5 to read as follows:
    - **Lectures in Good 4 U banquet room**
        - **Conducted by local marathon winners**
    - **Training walks in Central Park**
        - **Free Good 4 U sports drinks and bananas**
13. Use the slide master to change the second-level bullets to check marks (✓) using the Monotype Sorts font.
14. On the slide master, format the slide number placeholder as 20-point Arial italic and add the word **Slide** before <#>. Center-align the text in

UNIT 2 ■ WORKING WITH PRESENTATIONS

   the number placeholder and make the placeholder narrower to fit the text.

15. Delete the footer and date placeholders on the slide master and move the slide number placeholder to the bottom center of the slide.

16. Resize and reposition the text placeholders in slides 4 and 8, centering them on the slides.

17. Check spelling in the presentation.

18. Save the presentation as *[your initials]***5-24.ppt** so the TrueType font (Arial Black) is embedded in the file.

19. Add slide numbers to all but the title slide. Create headers and footers for Notes and Handouts. Include the date and your name at the top of the page and the page number and filename at the bottom.

20. Print the presentation as handouts, 6 slides per page, black and white, framed.

21. Save and close the presentation.

UNIT 2 ■ APPLICATIONS

Unit 2 Applications

APPLICATION 2-1

Starting with a blank presentation, create a presentation, apply a design template, choose slide layouts, insert slides, change slide layouts, change text attributes, work with the slide master, and resize placeholders.

1. Begin a blank presentation. Choose the Title Slide layout for the first slide and apply the template **Pulse.pot**.
2. Working in either Outline view or Slide view, key the presentation shown in Figure U2-1. Use the Bulleted List layout for slides 2 through 4.

FIGURE U2-1

Slide 1
```
Power Walk and Breakfast
    Good 4 U Promotional Strategy
```

Slide 2
```
Objectives
•   Encourage morning power walkers to breakfast at G4U
•   Make G4U a social center for power walkers
```

Slide 3
```
Strategies
•   Guided walks
•   Seminars
•   G4U merchandise
•   Advertising
```

Slide 4
```
Cost/Benefits Analysis
•   Costs
    -   Walk guides' salaries
    -   Seminar leaders' salaries
    -   Merchandise costs
    -   Advertising costs
•   Benefits
    -   Increase breakfasts served
    -   Increase repeat business
    -   Merchandise sales
    -   Increase general sales
```

Assessment Resources:
- Solutions Manual
- Test Bank with Software
- Portfolio Builder
- Alternative Assessment Guide
- Certification Procedures
- Projects Manual

Unit Applications:
Provide independent practice of the skills acquired from each lesson in the Unit.

Project:
After students complete Unit 2, you can assign Project #2 from the Projects Manual.

Unit Application 2-1:
Required File: None
Solution File: glu2-1.ppt in Solutions Manual or on Solutions disk

163

3. Change the slide color scheme to brown, which is the second option on the second row of standard colors.

4. Create a Good 4 U "logo" by formatting those words in the slide 1 subtitle: Format "Good 4 U" as bold, format "4 U" as italic, and increase the font size of the "4" to 40 points.

5. Replace all instances of "G4U" with the logo you just created using copy and paste.

6. Using the slide master, change the title and bulleted text placeholders to Arial. (This automatically changes the font of the title master, as well.)

7. On slide 3, resize the bullet text box to fit the text and then center the text box horizontally below the title.

8. Change the slide 4 layout to two-column and move the "Benefits" bullet and all its second-level bullets into the right column.

9. Turn off the bullets for "Costs" and "Benefits" and center-align these items. For the second-level bullets on this slide, change the hyphen to a solid dot from the Symbol font, sized as 90% of the text.

10. Resize the two text boxes on slide 4 so every item under "Costs" and "Benefits" appears on a single line with no word wrapping. Reposition the text boxes on the slide, centering them attractively under the title. (It's okay if the text boxes overlap or extend off the slide, as long as the text does not.)

11. Check spelling in the presentation.

12. Save the presentation as *[your initials]***u2-1.ppt**.

13. Create headers and footers for Notes and Handouts. Include the date and your name at the top of the page and the page number and filename at the bottom.

14. Print the presentation as handouts, 6 slides per page, black and white, framed.

15. Save and close the presentation.

APPLICATION 2-2

Expand a slide in Outline view, apply a design template, work with the slide and title masters, change bullets, apply text attributes to selected text and placeholders, and resize and position placeholders.

1. Open the file **Seafood1.ppt** and apply the template **Whirlpool.pot**.

2. Switch to Outline view. Select slide 2 and use the Expand Slide command to create a six-slide presentation.

Unit Application 2-2:
Required File: Seafood1.ppt
Solution File: glu2-2.ppt in Solutions Manual or on Solutions disk

The completed presentation for this Application may be used in a student's portfolio.

3. On slide 2, delete the second- and third-level bullets so the slide contains only four bulleted items (which are the titles of slides 3 through 6).
4. View the presentation in Slide view.
5. Use the slide master to change the title and text placeholders to Times New Roman, bold, shadowed.
6. Display the title master. Check that the title font is Times New Roman, bold, shadowed. Remove the bold from the subtitle placeholder.
7. On slide 1, format "Good 4 U" as a logo so "Good 4 U" is bold and shadowed, "4 U" is italic, and "4" is two font sizes larger than its surrounding text.
8. On slide 2, change the bullets to light purple ship wheels ☸ (Wingdings, third row) sized as 150% of text. (Use the light purple that is identified as Follow Fills Scheme Color when you point to it.)
9. On slide 3, change the bullets to light purple starfish ☆ (Monotype Sorts, second row) sized as 150% of text.
10. On slide 4, change the bullets to light purple yin-yangs ☯ (Wingdings, fourth symbol in third row) sized as 125% of text.
11. On slide 5, change the bullets to light purple wavy lines ♒ (Wingdings, third row) sized as 125% of text.
12. On slide 6, change the first-level bullets to light purple ship wheels sized as 150% of text. Remove the bullets for the second-level text and reduce this text by one font size.
13. Using the slide master and the Format Autoshape dialog box, size the bulleted text placeholder to 4 inches wide and position it 3 inches from the top corner of the slide. Check the bulleted text position on each slide.
14. Check spelling in the presentation.
15. Save the presentation as *[your initials]***u2-2.ppt**.
16. Create headers and footers for Notes and Handouts. Include the date and your name at the top of the page and the page number and filename at the bottom.
17. Print the presentation as handouts, 6 slides per page, black and white, framed.
18. Save and close the presentation.

UNIT 2 ■ WORKING WITH PRESENTATIONS

APPLICATION 2-3

Insert an outline from a word-processing document into PowerPoint, create a summary slide, apply a design template, change a slide layout, apply text attributes, and add speaker notes.

1. Open a blank PowerPoint presentation, cancel the New Slide dialog box, and switch to Outline view.

2. Insert the word-processed outline from the file **Walk5.rtf** into the presentation.

3. Change slide 1 to Title Slide layout.

4. Apply the template **Dads Tie.pot** to the presentation.

5. On slide 2, promote the level 3 bullets under "Healthy diet" to level 2 bullets.

6. Move slide 5 above slide 4.

7. While still in Outline view, create a summary slide of slides 2 through 5. Change the summary slide title to **Topics of Discussion**

8. Use the slide master to format all slide titles as Arial, bold, and shadowed. Change first-level bullets to boxed check marks ☑ (Wingdings font, last row) that are black and sized as 90% of text.

9. On slide 1, format "Good 4 U" as a logo so "Good 4 U" is bold and shadowed, "4 U" is italic, and "4" is two font sizes larger than its surrounding text.

10. Format the bulleted text on slides 2 and 3 as sentence case. (Use the Change Case dialog box.)

11. Add the following speaker note to slide 1:

    Read first paragraph from mayor's press release on power walk event.

12. Check spelling in the presentation.

13. Save the presentation as *[your initials]***u2-3.ppt**.

14. Create headers and footers for Notes and Handouts. Include the date and your name at the top of the page and the page number and filename at the bottom.

15. Print the presentation as handouts, 6 slides per page, black and white, framed. Print the first slide only as a notes page.

16. Save and close the presentation.

Unit Application 2-3:
Required File: Walk5.rtf
Solution File: glu2-3.ppt in Solutions Manual or on Solutions disk

The completed presentation for this Application may be used in a student's portfolio.

UNIT 2 ■ APPLICATIONS

APPLICATION 2-4

Write presentation text, format bullets, apply a design template and color scheme, change fonts, apply text attributes, create a summary slide, reposition placeholders, and change alignment.

1. Open the file **Patch1.ppt**, which contains the beginning of a presentation about a New York City community gardening project supported by Good 4 U.

2. Imagine that Good 4 U is coming to your town to set up a community gardening project. Change "New York City" in slides 1 and 2 to your city or town.

3. On slide 3, add three to five bullets describing how Good 4 U will support the community gardening effort.

4. On slide 4, add at least two bullets describing crop categories, and use sub-bullets to list specific crops. Use the two-column layout.

5. Add a fifth slide titled **How Pea-Patching Helps Good 4 U** and include at least two reasons.

6. In Outline view, create a summary slide of slides 2 through 5. Move the summary slide to the end of the presentation. Change its name to **Summary** and adjust the bulleted text to sentence case (without changing "Good 4 U").

7. Apply the design template **Motivating a Team – Dale Carnegie Training.pot** from the folder Microsoft Office\Templates\Presentations. Change the color scheme to one of the Standard choices that prints well in Black and White view.

8. Change the bullets on all the slides to a symbol appropriate to the theme of the presentation. Use a smaller, less obtrusive symbol for second-level bullets. Make sure they are the same color as the first-level bullets.

9. Use the Good 4 U logo (as created in Application 2-2, step 7) to replace the "Good 4 U" throughout the presentation.

10. Where needed, adjust the font size of title text and bullet text to create an attractive presentation.

11. If necessary, use line breaks to improve the appearance of long lines and resize and reposition text boxes to create balance.

12. Check spelling in the presentation.

13. Save the presentation as *[your initials]***u2-4.ppt**.

14. Add slide numbers to all slides except the title slide. Position the numbers at the bottom right corner of the slide and increase the font size to 20 point.

Unit Application 2-4:
Required File: Patch1.ppt
Solution File: glu2-4.ppt in Solutions Manual or on Solutions disk

The completed presentation for this Application may be used in a student's portfolio.

NOTE In this Application, students are asked to write some of their own slide content. Consequently, students' solution files will vary. A sample file is shown in the Solutions Manual and on the Solutions disk.

NOTE Make sure students know how to choose a template from the Presentations folder. Alternatively, you may want to specify another template. In addition, remind students how to use the Black and White View button on the Standard toolbar to see how a color scheme prints in black and white (assuming that the printers in your classroom print in black and white).

167

15. Create headers and footers for Notes and Handouts. Include the date and your name at the top of the page and the page number and filename at the bottom.
16. Print the presentation as handouts, 6 slides per page, black and white, framed.
17. Save and close the presentation.

UNIT 3

Customizing a Presentation

LESSON 6 Working with PowerPoint Objects
LESSON 7 Working with Lines, Fills, and Colors
LESSON 8 Manipulating PowerPoint Objects

LESSON 6

Working with PowerPoint Objects

OBJECTIVES

After completing this lesson, you will be able to:
1. Use clip art.
2. Format and crop clip art.
3. Use WordArt for special effects.
4. Add text boxes.
5. Rotate text.
6. Work with basic drawing tools.
7. Use basic AutoShapes.
8. Place text in an AutoShape.

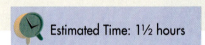

Estimated Time: 1½ hours

An effective slide presentation uses more than text alone. While text carries most of the information, you can use several types of objects to emphasize your message and draw attention to the presentation. For example, you can add chart objects, free-floating text objects, and clip art objects to a presentation.

You can resize, move, shade, color, and frame objects. In this lesson, you concentrate on manipulating clip art and objects created with the drawing tools.

PREPARE

Each heading in the lesson correlates to a learning objective.

Required Files
Open1.ppt   Sailing4.wmf*
*Available on Microsoft Office CD-ROM. See "Adding Additional Clip Art," page xiv, for file location and instructions.

TEACH

Teaching Resources:
- PowerPoint Classroom Presentations
- School-to-Work Strategies Manual
- Internet Manual
- Spanish Glossary
- Methodology Video
- Certification Procedures

LESSON 6 ■ **WORKING WITH POWERPOINT OBJECTS**

Objective 1
Using Clip Art

Included with PowerPoint are expertly drawn pictures known as *clip art*. These pictures are contained in the Microsoft Clip Gallery. You can insert clip art into your presentation in one of two ways:

- Click the Insert Clip Art button.
- Choose Clip Art from the Insert menu.

If your slide uses a layout that includes a *clip art placeholder*, just double-click the placeholder to insert clip art. Note that you are not limited to PowerPoint clip art. You can use many different graphic formats with PowerPoint.

FIGURE 6-1
Microsoft Clip Gallery dialog box

Clip art keywords

NOTE

EXERCISE | **6-1** | **Use the Clip Art Find Function**

One way to find appropriate clip art images for your presentations is to use keywords.

1. Open the file **Open1.ppt**.

NOTE

2. Click the Insert Clip Art button on the Standard toolbar. The Microsoft Clip Gallery 3.0 dialog box displays a list of categories and a thumbnail sketch of pictures within the category (see Figure 6-1 on the next page). Notice there are also tabs for pictures, sounds, and videos.

Use PowerPoint Classroom Presentation #6 to display screens from the lesson, including this one, in a slide-show format.

NOTE
When PowerPoint is first installed, clip art images that come with the program must be added to the Microsoft Clip Gallery. Additional clip art used in this book (located on the Microsoft Office CD ROM) should also be installed. To add clip art, see "Adding Additional Clip Art" at the beginning of this text.

NOTE
You may want to review the options in the Microsoft Clip Gallery dialog box. Click the Help button in the dialog box for detailed information on using and organizing clip art.

171

UNIT 3 ■ CUSTOMIZING A PRESENTATION

    NOTE: If you see the Additional Clips dialog box when you click [icon], click OK. This dialog box alerts you to additional clip art available on the Microsoft Office CD-ROM.

3. Click **F**ind. The Find Clip dialog box appears. You can use this dialog box to locate a picture that matches a subject you key in the **K**eywords text box.

4. Key **success** in the **K**eywords text box and click **F**ind Now. All clip art images whose description includes the word "success" are displayed.

5. Click each image and observe the description at the bottom of the dialog box. Most keywords associated with clip art images relate to business goals. You can use the Find command to choose an image that enhances the theme of your presentation.

6. Click Cl**o**se to close the Clip Gallery dialog box.

EXERCISE 6-2 Insert Clip Art

 The Microsoft Clip Gallery shows you *thumbnails* of available clip art—miniaturized versions of the actual images. A thumbnail is usually larger and more detailed after you insert it in a slide.

1. Open the **I**nsert menu and choose **P**icture, **C**lip Art to reopen the Microsoft Clip Gallery dialog box.

2. Scroll down the Categories list on the left side of the dialog box and select the Transportation category. Thumbnails of the images in the Transportation category are displayed.

3. Scroll through the images, if necessary, and select the sailboat with the red and yellow sail. Notice the clip art keywords at the bottom of the dialog box.

4. Click **I**nsert. The image is inserted in slide 1 and the Picture toolbar appears.

 TIP: You can also double-click a picture's thumbnail to insert the picture.

EXERCISE 6-3 Change the Size and Position of a Clip Art Object

You can easily resize clip art, move it to another position on the slide, or move it to another slide. Resizing and moving clip art is similar to resizing and moving

NOTE
The Additional Clips dialog box opens each time you want to insert clip art, unless you check Don't remind me again in the dialog box.

NOTE
You might want to discuss the AutoClipArt feature, in which PowerPoint suggests clip art for a slide based on the slide content. For example, if a slide title is "Strategies," choose AutoClipArt from the Tools menu, and then click View ClipArt. PowerPoint will display all clip art images with the word "strategy" in their descriptions.

NOTE
Point out the Magnify option in the Microsoft Clip Gallery dialog box. When this box is checked, the selected image appears larger and its filename (excluding the extension) is displayed.

NOTE
If the Picture toolbar does not appear when the picture is selected, you can use the View menu or the shortcut menu to display it.

LESSON 6 ■ **WORKING WITH POWERPOINT OBJECTS**

NOTE

a text box. First, you select the clip art by clicking it. Once selected, clip art images display the same small square resize handles you see on a selected text box.

You can make the object larger or smaller by dragging its handles. Drag a corner handle to size the clip art proportionally. *Proportional sizing* means the relationship between the height and width of the object is maintained. Dragging the side handles changes the original proportions of the clip art, creating a tall, thin image or a short, fat one.

1. On slide 1, click the sailboat picture to select it, if necessary.

   NOTE: You may need to drag the Picture toolbar away from the slide area.

2. Position the pointer inside the object. A four-headed arrow pointer appears.

NOTE

3. Place the pointer on the top center handle. The pointer changes to a double-headed arrow.

4. Drag the handle up. The object becomes taller, changing the look of the image.

5. Click .

FIGURE 6-2
Dragging to resize clip art proportionally

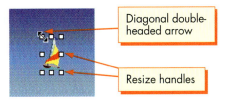

6. With the sailboat still selected, place the pointer on a corner handle. The pointer changes to a diagonal double-headed arrow. Use a corner handle to resize the clip art proportionally.

7. Drag the corner handle diagonally away from the center of the sailboat until the picture is about twice its original size.

8. Click .

9. Click Format Picture on the Picture toolbar. The Format Picture dialog box appears.

   NOTE: You can also display the Format Picture dialog box by right-clicking the sailboat and choosing Format Picture from the shortcut menu.

10. Click the Size tab, if necessary.

11. Click Lock aspect ratio, if necessary. This locks the *aspect ratio*, which means that if the height or width of the image is changed, the corresponding dimension is automatically adjusted.

12. Under Size and rotate, set the Height to 1.75" and click OK. Because the Lock aspect ratio is in effect, both the height and width resized proportionately.

13. Position the pointer inside the object. A four-headed arrow appears.

NOTE
You may want to let students experiment by dragging any resize handle and observing the result. You can have the students click Undo or delete the sailboat and insert it again.

NOTE
Remind students to be aware of the changing shape of the pointer throughout this lesson.

In PowerPoint Classroom Presentation #6.

173

14. Drag the sailboat to the bottom of the slide. As you are dragging, a dotted line shows the position the image will occupy.

FIGURE 6-3
Dragging to move clip art

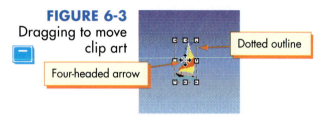

NOTE: Whenever you drag to move an object or text, make sure you are not dragging a resize handle by mistake. You must see the four-headed arrow pointer and not the two-headed arrow.

15. Position the sailboat attractively on the left side of the horizon. You can also use the arrow keys to adjust the position of the selected sailboat.

FIGURE 6-4
Repositioned and resized clip art

Objective 2
Format and Crop Clip Art

You can use the Picture toolbar to control various aspects of an image's appearance, such as brightness, contrast, and color. The toolbar also contains a tool that you can use to trim parts of a clip art image, just as you might do with a page from a magazine using a pair of scissors. This is called *cropping* the image.

In the next exercises, you work with the sailboat image on a new slide where you change its appearance and crop it.

EXERCISE 6-4 Change Clip Art Settings

1. Insert two new slides after slide 1, using the Blank layout.

In PowerPoint Classroom Presentation #6.

LESSON 6 ■ **WORKING WITH POWERPOINT OBJECTS**

2. On slide 3, use [icon] to insert the sailboat clip art.

3. Right-click the sailboat and choose Format P<u>i</u>cture from the shortcut menu. Click the Size tab, if necessary.

4. Under Size and rotate, set the H<u>e</u>ight to 4". (Be sure Lock <u>a</u>spect ratio is selected or the sailboat's proportions will be distorted.)

5. Click OK to resize the sailboat.

6. Position the sailboat on the water on the left side of the horizon.

7. With the sailboat selected, click the More Brightness button [icon] on the Picture toolbar four times. Notice that some of the details of the image become noticeably brighter.

8. Click the Less Brightness button [icon] twice to reduce the brightness.

FIGURE 6-5
Picture toolbar

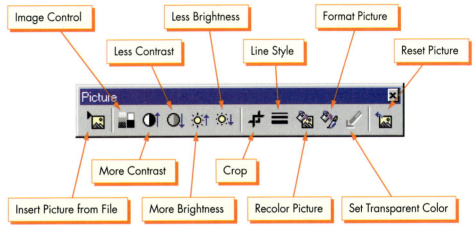

EXERCISE 6-5 Crop a Clip Art Object

1. Select the sailboat on slide 3, if necessary.

2. Click Crop [icon] on the Picture toolbar. The pointer changes to a cropping tool [icon].

3. Position the cropping tool on the bottom center handle and drag the handle up until the bottom edge of the dotted clip art border is above the blue waves. (See Figure 6-6 on the next page.)

4. Position the pointer in the center of the image and drag it down until the bottom edge of the sailboat is level with the water's edge.

5. Click anywhere outside the image to deactivate the cropping tool (or you can click [icon] on the Picture toolbar).

In PowerPoint Classroom Presentation #6.

175

UNIT 3 ■ **CUSTOMIZING A PRESENTATION**

FIGURE 6-6
Sailboat after cropping

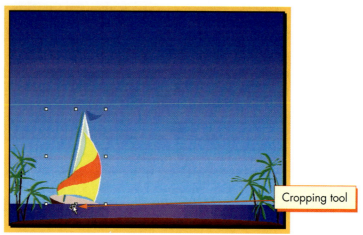

✓ Objective 3
Using WordArt For Special Effects

WordArt can create special effects with text that are not possible with normal text formatting tools. You can stretch or curve text, and add special shading effects, dramatic 3-D effects, and much more. And because they are drawn objects, you can use drawing tools to modify and enhance WordArt text.

As you learned in previous lessons, you can change the text formatting for an entire presentation by changing the text on the slide master. Similarly, you can use the slide master to add drawing objects and clip art to every slide in a presentation. Any clip art image or WordArt text object you add to the slide master automatically appears on every slide in the presentation in the same location on the slide.

EXERCISE 6-6 Add WordArt Text Objects to the Slide Master

In this exercise you create a WordArt object and copy it to the slide master.

1. Display slide 1.

2. Click the Insert WordArt tool [A] on the Drawing toolbar. The WordArt Gallery dialog box appears. See Figure 6-7 on the next page.

3. Choose the first style in the third row of the WordArt Gallery (the yellow-orange color) and click OK. The Edit WordArt Text dialog box appears.

In PowerPoint Classroom Presentation #6.

✓ **Objective 3 Assignment:**
Exercise 6-19 (Skills Review) can be assigned after completing Objective 3.

176

LESSON 6 ■ **WORKING WITH POWERPOINT OBJECTS**

FIGURE 6-7
WordArt Gallery dialog box

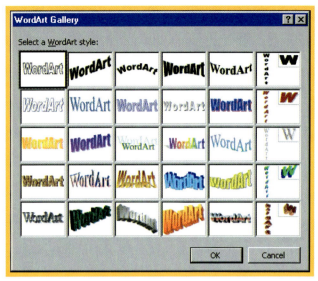

NOTE

4. Key **Good 4 U** and click OK. The WordArt text object is added to the slide. Notice that the object is selected and the WordArt toolbar appears.

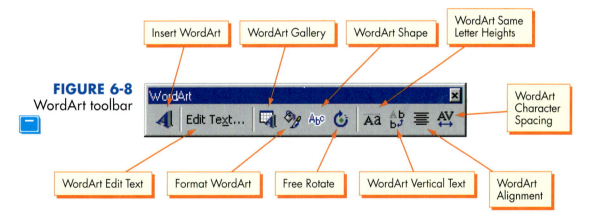

FIGURE 6-8
WordArt toolbar

5. Use a corner resize handle to enlarge the WordArt object proportionally, making it a size appropriate for a slide title.

6. Drag the object to the top of the slide so you can see how the object should look as a slide title. (You move WordArt objects the same way you move a clip art image—point to the center of the WordArt object and use the four-headed arrow to drag it.)

7. With the WordArt object selected, click the WordArt Shape button on the WordArt toolbar. A menu of text shapes appears. See Figure 6-9 on the next page.

8. Choose the Wave 1 shape, which is the fifth shape in the third row. The WordArt object changes to the selected shape. With the WordArt object now formatted, you cut and paste it into the slide master.

In PowerPoint Classroom Presentation #6.

NOTE
If the WordArt toolbar does not appear, you can use the View menu or the shortcut menu to display it.

177

UNIT 3 ■ CUSTOMIZING A PRESENTATION

FIGURE 6-9
WordArt Shape menu

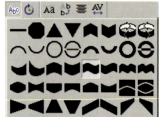

NOTE

9. Right-click the WordArt object and choose Cut from the shortcut menu. The WordArt object is cut from the slide and copied onto the Clipboard.
10. Choose Master from the View menu and then choose Slide Master. The slide master appears.
11. Right-click above the title placeholder and choose Paste. The WordArt object is pasted into the slide master.
12. Adjust the position of the WordArt object in the title placeholder, centering it to appear as a title.
13. Return to Slide view. Scroll through the presentation. Notice that the WordArt object appears on every slide in the same location as a slide title.

FIGURE 6-10
WordArt text object as slide title

NOTE: Text added to a presentation as a WordArt object is not checked by the spelling checker. PowerPoint treats it as an object, not text. Make sure you type and proofread WordArt text objects carefully.

Objective 4
Working with Floating Text Boxes

Until now, you worked with text placeholders that automatically appear when you insert a new slide. Sometimes you'll want to put text outside the text placeholders or create freeform text boxes on a blank slide.

You can add text boxes to a slide by clicking the Text Box button 📄 on the Drawing toolbar, then dragging the pointer to define the width of the text box. You can also just click the pointer and the text box adjusts its width to the size of your text. You can change the size and position of text boxes the same way you change text placeholders.

In PowerPoint Classroom Presentation #6.

NOTE
In step 9, students may have trouble displaying the correct shortcut menu if they right-click when the regular arrow pointer is visible. This deselects the WordArt object. To avoid this, they should right-click the object when they see the four-headed arrow pointer.

LESSON 6 ■ **WORKING WITH POWERPOINT OBJECTS**

EXERCISE 6-7 Create a Floating Text Object

1. Display slide 1.
2. Click the Text Box button 📄 on the Drawing toolbar. Note the new shape of the pointer ↧. The cross shows you where the text will appear when you start typing. You can define the size of the text box by dragging or you can simply begin typing.

FIGURE 6-11
Creating a floating text box

3. Place the pointer below the "G" in "Good 4 U" and click. A small text box containing an insertion point appears.
4. Key **Here we grow again!** Notice how the text box gets wider as you key text.

NOTE: If you accidentally drag as you click the text tool pointer, PowerPoint will think you want to restrict the width of the text box and the text you key will wrap within a tall and narrow text box. If this happens, click 🔄▼ and try again.

5. Click the text box border to select it. You select the text box the same way you select a text placeholder. Change the text to red, 32-point Arial bold, shadowed.

TIP: To start another line in a text box, press Enter and continue keying. The box expands to accommodate the new line.

EXERCISE 6-8 Create a Fixed-Width Floating Text Box

When you drag the pointer to define the width of a text box before keying the text, the box retains that width and the text wraps within the box.

1. To create another text box, click 📄. Position the pointer under the text box you created above, aligning it with the "w" in "we." Click and hold down the left mouse button. The pointer now has a cross shape.

2. Drag diagonally to create a rectangle that is about as large as the title. Dragging to draw a text box automatically turns on word wrapping. Unlike the text box you created in the previous exercise, the text in this box will wrap from one line to the next.

In PowerPoint Classroom Presentation #6.

NOTE
If the insertion point is active, you can also select a text box border by pressing the ESC key; if the insertion point is not active, you can select a text box border by pressing the Tab key.

NOTE
In step 2, the height of the text box is not important, as the height of the box adjusts to the text. Students must drag the pointer to see a rectangle shape.

UNIT 3 ■ CUSTOMIZING A PRESENTATION

3. In the text box, key **Welcomes you to our new restaurant in beautiful Miami Beach**. The height of the box expands to fit the text.

4. Click the text box border to select it. Format the text as white, 40-point Times New Roman bold. Don't worry if your text box overlaps the other text box or the edges of the template design. You change that in the next steps.

5. With the text border selected, drag the center sizing handle to the right to make the text box wider. Make the text box wide enough so all the text wraps to three lines.

6. Drag the text box border to position it at the right side of the slide as shown in Figure 6-12.

FIGURE 6-12
Fixed-width text box

Objective 5
Rotating Text

NOTE

You can rotate objects you create in PowerPoint using the Free Rotate tool on the Drawing toolbar or by changing the Rotation setting in the Format AutoShape dialog box. You can rotate text boxes, AutoShapes, free form drawings, and in some cases, clip art. You can also control rotation of text boxes and placeholders using the Format Text Box and Format AutoShape dialog boxes.

EXERCISE 6-9 Rotate a Text Object

1. On slide 1, click "Here we grow again!"
2. Drag the text box toward the left side of the slide.

In PowerPoint Classroom Presentation #6.

Objective 5 Assignment:
Exercises 6-20 (Skills Review) and 6-25 (Lesson Applications) can be assigned after completing Objective 5.

NOTE
You can rotate any placeholder text, including titles and blocks of bulleted text. Clip art can be rotated when it is ungrouped (which is covered in Lesson 8). After an object is rotated, part of it may extend beyond the edge of the slide.

LESSON 6 ■ **WORKING WITH POWERPOINT OBJECTS**

3. Click the Free Rotate button on the Drawing toolbar. A circling arrow pointer appears at the top of the pointer and four round green handles appear on the text border.

4. Place the tip of the pointer over the lower left green handle. Press and hold the mouse button. Notice that the circling arrow pointer changes to four circling arrows. Drag the rotating handle down, using Figure 6-13 as a guide. The dotted lines show the position of the rotation as you drag.

FIGURE 6-13
Rotating text

NOTE: If you hold down the Shift key as you drag the green handle, you can rotate an object in precise 15-degree increments.

5. Click again or click anywhere outside the selected object to deselect the tool.

EXERCISE | **6-10** | **Change Rotation Settings in the Format Text Box Dialog Box**

1. Select the "Here we grow again!" text box, if necessary.

2. Right-click the text box border and choose Format Text Box from the shortcut menu.

3. Click the Size tab in the Format Text Box dialog box, if necessary.

4. Key **30** in the Rotation text box to rotate the text 30 degrees clockwise. Click Preview to see the results. (Drag the dialog box to one side to see the slide, if necessary.)

5. With the dialog box still open, key **–30** in the Rotation text box. Negative numbers rotate an object in a counter-clockwise direction.

6. Click OK. The text box is now on an exact 30-degree angle.

7. Move the rotated text down so it does not overlap the title and is angled attractively on the left side of the slide.

In PowerPoint Classroom Presentation #6.

181

UNIT 3 ■ CUSTOMIZING A PRESENTATION

Working with Basic Drawing Tools

☑ **Objective 6**

In addition to ready-made clip art, PowerPoint provides you with a variety of drawing tools that you can use to create your own drawings. In this lesson, you learn basic drawing skills. In later lessons, you learn how to enhance simple drawings and create more complex drawings.

TABLE 6-1 Drawing Toolbar

NOTE

BUTTON/NAME	PURPOSE
Draw ▾	Open the Draw menu, which contains tools for aligning, grouping, rotating, flipping, and other manipulations for drawn objects.
Select Object	Select an object. This tool is automatically in effect when no other tool is in use.
Free Rotate	Rotate an object. Any object can be rotated 360 degrees.
AutoShapes ▾	Open the AutoShapes menu, which contains predefined shapes that you can manage the same way as other objects.
Line	Draw a straight line.
Arrow	Draw an arrow.
Rectangle	Draw a rectangle or square.
Oval	Draw an oval or circle.
Text Box	Draw a text box.
Insert WordArt	Insert a Microsoft WordArt object.
Fill Color	Fill an object with colors, patterns, or textures.
Line Color	Change the color of an object's outline.
Font Color	Change the color of selected text.
Line Style	Choose a line style and thickness for the outline of a selected object.
Dash Style	Apply dotted or dashed line styles to an object.
Arrow Style	Apply arrowheads to selected lines.
Shadow	Apply shadow effects to an object. This is not the same as the Shadow tool on the Formatting toolbar, which works only on text.
3-D	Apply 3-D effects to an object.

☑ **Objective 6 Assignment:**
Exercise 6-21 (Skills Review) can be assigned after completing Objective 6.

NOTE
You may want to review with students the appearance and purpose of the tools on the Drawing toolbar.

LESSON 6 ■ **WORKING WITH POWERPOINT OBJECTS**

EXERCISE 6-11 Draw Simple Lines and Shapes

In this exercise you draw a rectangle, an oval, and a line.

1. Display slide 2. Click the Rectangle ▣ tool on the Drawing toolbar. The mouse pointer changes to a cross.
2. Move the pointer to the left side of the slide below the title.
3. Click and hold down the mouse button. Drag diagonally down and to the right. Release the mouse button. A turquoise rectangle with a white outline appears. (You learn how to change colors and line styles in the next lesson.) See Figure 6-14 for the approximate size and placement of the completed rectangle.

FIGURE 6-14
Drawn objects

 NOTE: If you don't like the shape of an object after you draw it, delete it and start again. To delete an object, select it and press Delete.

4. Click the Oval ◯ tool.
5. Move the pointer below the first "o" in the title.
6. Click and hold down the mouse button. Drag diagonally down and to the right. Release the mouse button. See Figure 6-14 for the approximate size and placement of the completed oval.

7. Click the Line ╲ tool.
8. Position the pointer on the left edge of the slide, just above the palm trees, for the beginning point of the line.
9. Click and hold down the mouse button. Drag the line diagonally down to the water's edge. Release the mouse button.

In PowerPoint Classroom Presentation #6.

183

UNIT 3 ■ CUSTOMIZING A PRESENTATION

10. To add another line, click ▧ again. Draw a second line using Figure 6-14 as a guide.

TIP: You can draw multiple lines by double-clicking ▧. Double-clicking keeps the tool activated, so you can draw as many lines as you want. When you finish drawing, click ▧ again to deactivate it. This method also works with other drawing tools, including AutoShapes.

EXERCISE 6-12 Create Squares and Circles

PowerPoint provides you with an easy method for creating a perfect square or a perfectly round circle. Simply hold down [Shift] as you draw. When you hold down the [Shift] key, you can draw a *constrained* object. This means you control the drawing or movement of the object in precise increments or proportions. When you constrain a rectangle as you draw it, the rectangle becomes a square. A constrained oval becomes a circle. Many objects can be constrained to 15-degree increments.

1. Still working on slide 2, click anywhere on the rectangle to select it. (Notice the resize handles.) Press [Delete] to delete the object.
2. Click Rectangle ▢.
3. Position the pointer below and to the left of the "G" in the slide's title.
4. Press and hold down [Shift] and drag diagonally down and to the right. Release the mouse button first and then [Shift]. See Figure 6-15 for the approximate size and placement of the completed square.

FIGURE 6-15
A square and a circle

NOTE: Your square may look like a rectangle on your monitor if your monitor's horizontal size and vertical size are not perfectly synchronized. Your square will print correctly even it is distorted on the screen. To check the size, open the Format Object dialog box and click the Size tab. The height and width should have the same measurement.

5. Delete the oval.

NOTE
In step 4, make sure students understand they must release the mouse before releasing Shift.

In PowerPoint Classroom Presentation #6.

184

LESSON 6 ■ **WORKING WITH POWERPOINT OBJECTS**

   6. Click Oval.

   7. Position the pointer below the second "o" in the title.

   8. While pressing Shift, drag diagonally down and to the right to create a circle that is centered below the title.

EXERCISE 6-13 Draw Constrained Lines

You can use Shift to add constrained lines to your presentation, which are lines that are exactly vertical, horizontal, or at a 15-degree angle.

   1. Still working on slide 2, delete the two lines you drew previously by selecting them and pressing Delete.

   2. Click. Position the pointer at the bottom center edge of the circle.

   3. Hold down Shift and drag straight down to the horizon. (As you drag, notice that the line remains straight if you move the mouse right or left.) Release the mouse button and then release Shift.

   4. Click. Move the pointer to the bottom edge of the square, near the right corner.

   5. Hold down Shift and drag down to the horizon. Without releasing the mouse button, move the mouse to the right, toward the end point of the first line. Notice that the line jumps in 15-degree increments as you move left and right, up and down.

   6. When the two lines join, release the mouse button and then release Shift. See Figure 6-16 for the approximate placement of these lines. (If your diagonal line jumps past the end point of the first line, delete it and try again, adjusting the starting point of the line to a slightly different location on the bottom of the square.)

FIGURE 6-16
Drawing constrained lines

NOTE
In step 6, tell students it may take several tries to get the two lines to join precisely. If drawing constrained lines is problematic, have students draw the lines without holding down the Shift key.

In PowerPoint Classroom Presentation #6.

185

UNIT 3 ■ CUSTOMIZING A PRESENTATION

EXERCISE 6-14 Resize Drawn Objects

Like clip art or text objects, you can resize drawn objects randomly (without maintaining the original proportions) or proportionally. To resize a drawn object proportionally, hold down [Shift] as you drag a corner resize handle. Pressing [Shift] constrains the proportions when resizing, just as it constrains proportions when you draw circles or squares.

1. Still working on slide 2, select the circle.
2. Place the pointer on the lower left corner handle. The pointer changes to a double-headed arrow.
3. To resize the circle proportionally, hold down [Shift] and drag the handle down and to the right to make the circle larger.
4. Click [↶▾].
5. Drag the same handle without holding down [Shift]. The circle becomes an oval.
6. Right-click the oval and choose Format AutoShape from the shortcut menu. Click the Size tab, if necessary.
7. Under Size and rotate, key **1.5** in the Height text box and **1.5** in the Width text box and then click Preview to view the results. The object is once again a circle, because it has the same height and width. (Remember, you can move the dialog box out of the way by dragging its title bar.)
8. Click Cancel to close the dialog box without resizing the object and then click [↶▾] to restore the circle to its original state.

> **NOTE:** To make the object shrink or grow from the center rather than the side, hold down [Ctrl] while dragging the handle. To retain the object's proportion, hold down [Shift] and [Ctrl] while dragging the handle.

✓ Objective 7

Using Basic AutoShapes

PowerPoint provides an assortment of predefined shapes called AutoShapes. You can use AutoShapes to draw perfectly shaped arrows, stars, flow chart objects, callouts, and other shapes with minimal effort.

You resize these shapes the same way you resize other objects. Some shapes include an additional yellow diamond handle to reshape the object after it is drawn.

✓ Objective 7 Assignment:
Exercise 6-23 (Skills Review) can be assigned after completing Objective 7.

LESSON 6 ■ **WORKING WITH POWERPOINT OBJECTS**

EXERCISE 6-15 Create AutoShapes

FIGURE 6-17
Making the
AutoShape menu
float

NOTE

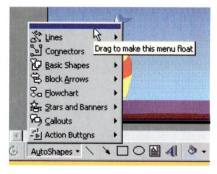

1. Display slide 3.
2. Click the AutoShapes button on the Drawing toolbar to display the AutoShapes menu.
3. Position the pointer over the thin gray bar at the top of the AutoShapes menu. Its color changes to blue and a ScreenTip appears.
4. Drag the AutoShape menu to the upper left corner of the screen. The menu changes to a toolbar that remains on your screen until you close it. You can change its position by dragging its blue bar or close it by clicking the Close button ☒ in the upper left corner of the toolbar.
5. Click the Callouts button 🗩 on the AutoShapes toolbar.
6. Click the Round Rectangular Callout button 🗩, which is the second button in the first row.
7. Position the cross pointer to correspond with the upper left corner of the callout shown in Figure 6-18.
8. Drag the cross pointer diagonally down and to the right.
9. Using the callout's border and resize handles, resize and reposition it to make it look like Figure 6-18.

FIGURE 6-18
Creating an
AutoShape

 NOTE: Like other graphic objects, a selected Auto-Shape object is surrounded by eight resize handles. Some objects also have a small yellow diamond *adjustment handle*. You use this handle to change angles, roundness, and points of the object.

10. Place the pointer on the adjustment handle. The pointer changes to a small arrowhead.
11. Drag the adjustment handle so it nearly touches the edge of the sail on the sailboat. You add text to the AutoShape later in the lesson.

NOTE
Encourage students to explore the various shapes available within each AutoShape category. You may want to explain how the Action Buttons category is used to create hyperlinks in a presentation.

187

UNIT 3 ■ CUSTOMIZING A PRESENTATION

EXERCISE 6-16   Create a Constrained AutoShape

Just as you made a constrained circle and a constrained square, you can use Shift to create a symmetrical AutoShape.

1. Display slide 2. Click Stars and Banners on the AutoShapes toolbar to display a submenu.
2. Click the 16-Point Star, which is the second button in the second row of the submenu.
3. Position the pointer to the right of the circle.
4. Hold down Shift and drag down. When the star's size is similar to the circle and the square, release the mouse and then release Shift.
5. Drag the star so it is level with the circle and square, if necessary.
6. Draw another diagonal line from the star to the horizon, connecting to the end points of the other two lines. See Figure 6-19 for the placement of these objects.
7. Close the AutoShapes toolbar.

FIGURE 6-19
Constrained AutoShape

NOTE: To resize an AutoShape proportionally, hold down Shift as you drag a corner handle. To make the object shrink or grow from the center rather than the side, hold down Ctrl while dragging the handle. To retain the object's proportions, press and hold Shift and Ctrl while dragging the handle.

✍ **Objective 8**

Placing Text in a Graphic Object

Frequently, the purpose of drawing an object in a presentation is to place text in it. The object serves as an attention-getting background for the text. You can key the text directly into the object or you can cut and paste it from other locations.

In the remaining exercises, you add text to the drawn objects on slides 2 and 3.

In PowerPoint Classroom Presentation #6.

✍ **Objective 8 Assignment:**
Exercise 6-22 (Skills Review) and Exercises 6-24 and 6-26 (Lesson Applications) can be assigned after completing Objective 8.

LESSON 6 ■ WORKING WITH POWERPOINT OBJECTS

EXERCISE 6-17 Place Text in a Graphic Object

1. Display slide 3 and select the callout object.
2. Key **Grand Opening** and press Enter. Key **July 1998!**. Because the callout object was selected, the text appears inside it.
3. Select the text and format it as dark blue, 28-point Arial bold. Resize the callout to fit the text, if necessary.
4. Display slide 2 and select the square object.
5. Key **FUN** and format the text as dark blue, 28-point Arial shadowed.
6. Select the circle object, key **In the**, and format the text as dark blue, 24-point Arial shadowed.
7. Select the star object, key **SUN**, and format the text as dark blue, 36-point Arial shadowed.

EXERCISE 6-18 Edit Text in a Rotated Object

1. Still working on slide 2, select the square.
2. Open the Format AutoShape dialog box and click Size, if necessary.
3. In the Rotation text box, key **–17** to rotate the object 17 degrees counterclockwise. Click OK. The object and the text are rotated.
4. Select the star and open the Format AutoShape dialog box again.
5. In the Rotation text box, key **17** to rotate the object 17 degrees clockwise and click OK.
6. With the star still selected, move the pointer over the text "SUN" until an I-beam appears.

FIGURE 6-20
Edited text in a rotated object

7. Click the I-beam to place an insertion point. The object and text rotate to a horizontal position for easy text editing.
8. Revise the text to **Sun!**
9. Deselect the star to return it to its rotated angle.

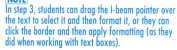
In step 3, students can drag the I-beam pointer over the text to select it and then format it, or they can click the border and then apply formatting (as they did when working with text boxes).

In PowerPoint Classroom Presentation #6.

UNIT 3 ■ CUSTOMIZING A PRESENTATION

10. Check spelling in the presentation.
11. Save the presentation as *[your initials]*6-18.ppt.
12. Create a handout header with the date and your name and a handout footer with the page number and the filename.
13. Print the presentation as handouts, 3 slides per page, black and white, framed.
14. Save and close the presentation.

COMMAND SUMMARY

FEATURE	BUTTON	MENU	KEYBOARD
Insert Clip Art		Insert, Picture, Clip Art	
Format Picture		Format, Picture	
Insert WordArt		Insert, Picture, WordArt	
Text Box		Insert, Text Box	
Free Rotate		Format, AutoShape	
AutoShapes	AutoShapes	Insert, Picture, AutoShapes	

USING HELP

There are many ways to enhance a presentation by importing graphics or creating your own objects. In addition to using clip art, this lesson introduced you to the many tools on the Drawing toolbar.

Using Help to learn more about drawing objects:

1. Open the Help Index by choosing Contents and Index from the Help menu and clicking the Index tab.
2. Key **drawing** in the text box.
3. Under "drawing objects," double-click the topic "AutoShapes" and double-click "Ways to draw."
4. In the Help window, click a topic to examine it, such as "Create Shapes."
5. Close Help when you finish.

NOTE
Point out that the Command Summary lists a variety of ways to accomplish a particular task. Students can decide which method they prefer to use.

NOTE
Encourage students to follow the steps in "Using Help." Software companies are increasingly using their online Help programs—rather than printed documentation—to train users and assist in answering user questions.

LESSON 6 ■ **WORKING WITH POWERPOINT OBJECTS**

FIGURE 6-21
Drawing Help window

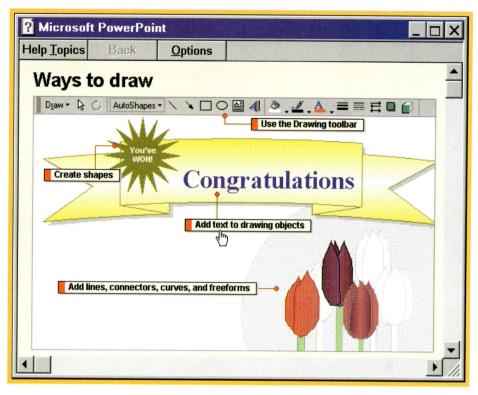

In PowerPoint Classroom Presentation #6.

191

UNIT 3 ■ CUSTOMIZING A PRESENTATION

TEST BANK

Concepts Review

TRUE/FALSE QUESTIONS

Each of the following statements is either true or false. Indicate your choice by circling **T** or **F**.

T **(F)** 1. Every AutoShape includes an adjustment handle.

T **(F)** 2. When you want to change the height of an object, but not the width, press [Shift] while dragging a sizing handle.

(T) F 3. Anything placed on a PowerPoint slide is considered to be an object.

T **(F)** 4. You can type text only in an existing placeholder.

T **(F)** 5. Only text objects can be rotated.

(T) F 6. You can use AutoShape tools to draw arrows and stars.

(T) F 7. Use [Shift] with ▢ to create a square.

(T) F 8. To move a text box, the pointer must remain on the border and not touch a resize handle.

SHORT ANSWER QUESTIONS

Write the correct answer in the space provided.

1. How do you draw a perfect circle?
   Use Shift key and Oval button

2. What is the shape and color of the handle you point to when rotating an object?
   Green circle

3. What kind of handle is the yellow diamond?
   Adjustment handle

4. What do you use to create floating text?
   Text box

5. Where do you view clip art?
   Microsoft Clip Gallery

Concepts Review: Allows students to check their understanding.

TEST BANK Consider using the Test Bank to provide an additional review of lesson concepts.

LESSON 6 ■ **WORKING WITH POWERPOINT OBJECTS**

6. Which button on which toolbar do you use to change the angle of text or a drawn object?

   Free Rotate button on the Drawing toolbar

7. Where do you place the pointer when sizing objects?

   On a resize handle

8. Which key do you hold to size an object proportionally?

   Shift key

CRITICAL THINKING

Answer these questions on a separate page. There are no right or wrong answers. Support your answers with examples from your own experience, if possible.

1. Select three pieces of clip art from the Microsoft Clip Gallery and explain the type of presentation in which you might use it.
2. Comparing random and proportional sizing, which objects are better proportionally sized? When would you want to use a distorted object?

Skills Review

EXERCISE 6-19

Insert and size clip art and create WordArt text objects.

1. Open the file **Train4.ppt**.
2. Replace the title in slide 1 with a WordArt text object by following these steps:
   a. Delete the title placeholder.
   b. Click the Insert WordArt button on the Drawing toolbar.
   c. Select the first WordArt style in the last column and click OK.
   d. Key **Franchise Training** and click OK.
3. Change the formatting of a WordArt text object by following these steps:
   a. Select the WordArt object, if necessary.
   b. Click the Edit Text button on the WordArt toolbar (or double-click the WordArt object).
   c. Change the font to 60-point Arial Black, bold. Click OK.

Critical Thinking Questions:
Answers will vary based on students' preferences, observations, experiences, and research.

Skills Review:
Provides guided practice for students. Objectives are indicated for each Exercise.

Exercise 6-19:
Objectives 1–3
Required Files: Train4.ppt and clip art file 1stplace.wmf (see page xiv for clip art file location and instructions)
Solution File: gl6-19.ppt in Solutions Manual or on Solutions Disk

4. Change the size and position of the WordArt object by following these steps:

    a. Click the WordArt object to select it, if necessary.

    b. Drag a corner handle slightly toward the center to reduce the size of the image.

    c. Point to the center of the WordArt object. Using the four-headed arrow, drag the object to position it attractively on the slide.

    TIP: To resize WordArt proportionately, you must hold down the Shift key even if you're dragging a corner handle.

5. Add clip art to the slide master by following these steps:

    a. Switch to the slide master by pressing Shift while clicking ▫. Use the vertical scroll bar to move from the title master to the slide master.

    b. Click the Insert Clip Art button 🖼 on the Standard toolbar and click Find to open the Find Clip dialog box.

    c. In the Keywords text box, key **Awards** and click Find Now.

    d. Choose the black and white first place ribbon image and click Insert.

6. Resize and reposition the clip art by following these steps:

    a. Still working on the slide master, click the ribbon image to select it, if necessary

    b. Drag a corner handle away from the center of the image to make the ribbon slightly larger. (Remember, a corner handle sizes clip art proportionally.).

    c. Using the four-headed arrow, drag the ribbon to the lower right corner of the slide.

7. Insert the same clip art image on the title master, making it a little larger than on the slide master.

    TIP: Copy the image on the slide master, paste it on the title master, and then resize it.

8. Return to Slide view and review all slides, making sure the clip art does not interfere with text.

9. Save the presentation as *[your initials]***6-19.ppt**.

10. Create a handout header with the date and your name, and a handout footer with the page number and the filename.

11. Print as handouts, 6 slides per page, black and white, framed.

12. Save and close the presentation.

LESSON 6 ■ **WORKING WITH POWERPOINT OBJECTS**

EXERCISE 6-20

Insert, size, and move clip art and text objects.

1. Open the file **Train1.ppt**.
2. Insert clip art in a clip art placeholder by following these steps:
   a. Move to slide 2 and double-click the clip art placeholder to open the Microsoft Clip Gallery.
   b. Find all the coffee-related images by clicking Find, keying **Coffee** in the Keywords text box, and clicking Find Now.
   c. Select the image of the coffee cup that has the keyword "Coffee." (The clip art keywords are displayed at the bottom of the Clip Gallery dialog box.) Click Insert.
3. Make the coffee cup slightly smaller and position it attractively on the left side of the slide.

[NOTE]

4. Move to slide 4. Insert a picture of a computer or computer disk from the Business category of the Microsoft Clip Gallery. Resize the image appropriately and position it attractively on the left side of the slide.
5. Move to slide 6. Insert the seafood dinner image in the clip art placeholder. (Use Find to find images with the "Seafood" keyword.) Resize the seafood clip art proportionally so it doesn't overlap the text on the slide.
6. Create a floating text box by following these steps:
   a. Move to slide 2. Click the Text Box button 📄 on the Drawing toolbar.
   b. Place the pointer at the bottom left of the slide, below the clip art, and click. (Be careful not to drag the mouse when you click.)
   c. Key **Ask for our list of wholesale appliance dealers**.
   d. Click the border to select the text box, then change the font to 20-point Arial bold italic.
   e. With the text box still selected, drag it by its border, not by a resize handle, until it is positioned at the bottom center of the slide.
7. Draw a fixed width text box by following these steps:
   a. Move to slide 4. Click 📄 and drag the pointer below the clip art to create a 3-inch wide rectangle.
   b. Key **Our computer guru, Charles Warden, can help you set up your system**.
   c. Change the font to 20-point Arial bold italic.
   d. Resize and reposition the text box attractively below the clip art.

Exercise 6-20:
Objectives 1, 2, 4, 5
Required Files: Train1.ppt and clip art files soup.wmf and meal2.wmf (see page xiv for clip art file locations and instructions)
Solution File: gl6-20.ppt in Solutions Manual or on Solutions Disk

[NOTE]
In step 4, students are asked to choose a clip art image. You may want to specify an image. The solution file uses Disk.wmf from the MS Office CD-ROM. See page xiv for file locations.

195

UNIT 3 ■ CUSTOMIZING A PRESENTATION

8. Move to slide 6. Add a text box to the bottom of the slide with the text **Please submit menu suggestions to Michelle Jenkins**. The text should appear all on one line. Format the text as 20-point Arial bold italic. Center the text box at the bottom of the slide.

9. Check spelling in the presentation

10. Save the presentation as *[your initials]***6-20.ppt**.

11. Create a handout header with the date and your name and a handout footer with the page number and the filename.

12. Print as handouts, 6 slides per page, black and white, framed.

13. Save and close the presentation.

EXERCISE 6-21

Use drawing tools to create simple and constrained shapes and to rotate text.

1. Open the file **Train2.ppt**. Move to slide 3.

2. Use the drawing tools to create the shapes shown in Figure 6-22. First, create the short wide rectangle that appears on top of the circle by following these steps:
   a. Click ▢.
   b. Position the cross pointer at the bottom left of the slide.
   c. Drag the pointer diagonally down and to the right, creating a short wide rectangle like the one shown in the figure. Release the mouse button.

FIGURE 6-22

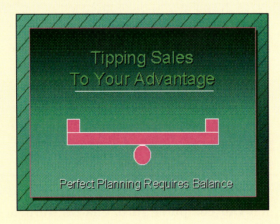

3. Precisely size and position the rectangle by following these steps:
   a. Right-click the rectangle, then choose Format Aut<u>o</u>Shape from the shortcut menu.

🖫**Exercise 6-21:**
Objectives 5, 6
Required File: Train2.ppt
Solution File: gl6-21.ppt in Solutions Manual or on Solutions Disk.

LESSON 6 ■ **WORKING WITH POWERPOINT OBJECTS**

    b. Click the Size tab, if necessary. Key **0.5** in the H<u>e</u>ight text box and **6** in the Wi<u>d</u>th text box.

    c. Click the Position tab. Key **2.0** in the <u>H</u>orizontal text box and **4.5** in the <u>V</u>ertical text box. Click OK.

4. Create the circle shown in Figure 6-22 by following these steps:

    a. Click .

    b. Position the pointer at the bottom center of the new rectangle.

    c. Hold down [Shift] and drag diagonally down and to the right to create a small circle. Release the mouse button first and then [Shift].

    d. Move the circle, if necessary, so it touches the bottom edge of the rectangle and is centered under the rectangle.

> **TIP:** You can fine-tune a selected object's position by pressing the Arrow keys on your keyboard.

5. Draw two small squares, one sitting on each end of the rectangle. Use the Format AutoShape dialog box to make the squares exactly 0.5 inch wide and 0.5 inch high. Position the squares so they appear balanced, using Figure 6-22 as a guide for placement. (You can copy and paste the first rectangle once you size it.)

6. Create a floating text box centered at the bottom of the slide containing the text **Perfect Planning Requires Balance**. Format the text as 32-point Arial shadowed.

7. Create a horizontal line on slide 3 by following these steps:

    a. Click ▨.

    b. Position the pointer below the word "To" in the title.

    c. Hold down [Shift] and drag to the right to underline the title. Release the mouse button first and then [Shift].

    d. Adjust the position of the line, if necessary, by dragging with the four-headed arrow or using the Arrow keys.

8. Move to slide 4 and create a small floating text box in the upper left corner, keying the text **1998**. Format the text as 36-point Arial bold.

9. Rotate the text box you created in step 8 above by following these steps:

    a. Right-click the text box border and choose Format Text B<u>o</u>x from the shortcut menu. Click the Size tab, if necessary.

    b. Key **–25** in the Ro<u>t</u>ation text box and click OK.

    c. Reposition the text box appropriately, if necessary.

10. Check spelling in the presentation.

11. Save the presentation as *[your initials]***6-21.ppt**.

UNIT 3 ■ CUSTOMIZING A PRESENTATION

12. Create a handout header with the date and your name and a handout footer with the page number and the filename.

13. Print as handouts, 6 slides per page, black and white, framed.

14. Save and close the presentation.

EXERCISE 6-22

Insert clip art, create AutoShapes, and add text to an AutoShape.

1. Open the file **Train3.ppt**.

2. Create a left arrow AutoShape by following these steps:

   a. Move to slide 3 and click AutoShapes on the Drawing toolbar.

   b. Choose Block Arrows on the AutoShapes menu and choose the Left Arrow (the second button in the first row).

   c. Position the cross pointer just above the purple bar at the far right of the graph and click.

3. Rotate the arrow by following these steps:

   a. Click the Free Rotate button.

   b. Place the pointer over the upper right corner rotate handle.

   c. Drag the handle up until the arrow points down at about a 30-degree angle. Reposition the arrow so it points to the top of the purple bar, as shown in Figure 6-23.

4. Draw a square text box in the space to the right of the graph. Key **Los Angeles division sales expected to double in 4th quarter**. Change the font to 20-point Arial.

5. Adjust the position, size, and rotation of the arrow and text box so they appear as shown in Figure 6-23.

FIGURE 6-23

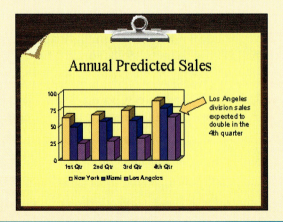

Exercise 6-22:
Objectives 1, 7, 8
Required File: Train3.ppt
Solution File: gl6-22.ppt in Solutions Manual or on Solutions Disk.

198

LESSON 6 ■ **WORKING WITH POWERPOINT OBJECTS**

6. On slide 4, key the following bulleted items in the existing text box:
   ✗ **Our mission is to provide good healthy food and good healthy fun.**
   ✗ **Our franchise training is designed to help you meet these goals.**

NOTE

7. On slide 4, insert an appropriate picture from the Sports & Leisure category in the clip art placeholder. Size the picture to balance the text.

8. On slide 5, use the 5-Point Star AutoShape (from the <u>S</u>tars and Banners submenu) to draw a constrained star in the upper right corner. Make the star approximately 2 inches wide.

9. Place text in the star by following these steps.
   a. Select the star.
   b. Key **Star**, press Enter, and key **Team**. Make the text bold.
   c. Adjust the size of the star so all the text fits inside it.

10. Check spelling in the presentation.
11. Save the presentation as *[your initials]***6-22.ppt**.
12. Create a handout header with the date and your name and a handout footer with the page number and the filename.
13. Print as handouts, 6 slides per page, black and white, framed.
14. Save and close the presentation.

NOTE
In step 7, students are asked to choose a clip art image. You may want to specify an image. The solution file uses Dancers2.wmf from the MS Office CD-ROM. See page xiv for file locations.

ASSESS

Assessment Resources:
• Solutions Manual
• Test Bank with Software
• Portfolio Builder
• Alternative Assessment Guide
• Certification Procedures

Lesson Applications:
Provide independent practice for students. Objectives are indicated for each Exercise.

UNIT 3 ■ CUSTOMIZING A PRESENTATION

Lesson Applications

EXERCISE 6-23

Insert, move, and size clip art.

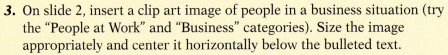

1. Open the file **Mktg.ppt**.
2. On slide 1, insert the jigsaw clip art image that you can find using the keyword "Strategy." If you find more than one image that fits this description, choose the jigsaw with the angled effect. Size and position the image so it is centered below the slide's subtitle.
3. On slide 2, insert a clip art image of people in a business situation (try the "People at Work" and "Business" categories). Size the image appropriately and center it horizontally below the bulleted text.
4. On slide 3, draw a small constrained diamond AutoShape (from the Basic Shapes category) that is approximately 1.5 inches wide and centered below the slide text. Draw a horizontal line, approximately 3 inches long, across the center of the diamond.
5. On slide 4, insert the Business Crowd clip art that you can find using the keyword "Crowd." Size and position the image so it is centered below the slide text and crop one person from each side of the crowd.
6. On slide 5, insert a clip art image of money or coins. Size and position the image appropriately in the lower left corner of the slide.
7. In Slide Sorter view, move slide 5 before slide 4.
8. Check spelling in the presentation.
9. Save the presentation as *[your initials]***6-23.ppt**.
10. Create a handout header with the date and your name and a handout footer with the page number and the filename.
11. Print as handouts, 6 slides per page, black and white, framed.
12. Save and close the presentation.

EXERCISE 6-24

Work with AutoShapes containing text and add clip art to the slide master.

1. Open the file **Cook1.ppt**.
2. Rotate the "Good *4 U*" text on slide 1 so it slants upward in the lower right corner. Increase the text by one font size. Adjust the text position, if necessary.

Exercise 6-23:
Objectives 1, 2, 7
Required Files: Mktg.ppt and clip art files puzzle.wmf and people1.wmf (see page xiv for clip art file locations and instructions)
Solution File: gl6-23.ppt in Solutions Manual or on Solutions Disk.

NOTE
In steps 3 and 6, students are asked to make their own clip art choices. You may want to specify images. The solution file uses agree.wmf and coins3.wmf from the MS Office CD-ROM. See page xiv for file locations.

Exercise 6-24:
Objectives 1, 5, 7, 8
Required File: Cook1.ppt
Solution File: gl6-24.ppt in Solutions Manual or on Solutions Disk.

 The completed presentation for this Exercise may be used in a student's portfolio.

LESSON 6 ■ WORKING WITH POWERPOINT OBJECTS

3. Draw a rounded rectangular callout AutoShape to the right of the carrots. Key the text **Look what's cooking!** in the callout. Make the text bold and change its color to black. Adjust the size of the callout to fit the text and drag the adjustment handle so it is pointing to the carrots.

4. Insert a new slide after slide 1 using the Bulleted List layout.

5. On slide 2, key **Good *4 U* Menu** in the title placeholder. Increase the size of the "*4*" to 48 points.

6. Key the following items in the bullet placeholder:
    - **Good *4 U* Veggie Burger**
    - **Simply Good Shrimp Salad**
    - **Good Fruit Combo**
    - **Andre's Lemon Dill Chicken**

7. Insert a new slide after slide 2 using the Bulleted List layout.

8. In the new slide, key **Franchise Recognition Program** in the title placeholder and then key the following bulleted text:
    - **Use the finest quality ingredients**
    - **Recognize creativity**
    - **Encourage safety in all areas of operation**
    - **Create a healthy and fun atmosphere for guests and staff**

9. Insert a new slide after slide 3 using the Title Only layout.

10. Key **Promoting Excellence** in the title placeholder.

11. Below the title, draw a large, 16-Point Star AutoShape, placing it in the center of the slide. Key the following two lines of text in the star:

    The Good *4 U*
    Seal of Approval

12. Format the text as 32-point Times New Roman bold with a text shadow. Change the size of the "*4*" to 40 points. Rotate the star so the text slants upward.

13. On the slide master, insert an image of fruit or a fruit basket (use the keyword "Fruit"). Move the image to the lower right corner and adjust its size appropriately (making it no larger than 2 inches high or wide).

14. Check spelling in the presentation.

15. Save the presentation as *[your initials]***6-24.ppt**.

16. Create a handout header with the date and your name and a handout footer with the page number and the filename.

17. Print as handouts, 6 slides per page, black and white, framed.

18. Save and close the presentation.

NOTE
In step 13, students are asked to make their own clip art choice. You may want to specify an image. The solution file uses Frtbskt1.wmf from the MS Office CD-ROM. See page xiv for file location.

201

UNIT 3 ■ CUSTOMIZING A PRESENTATION

EXERCISE 6-25

Insert, move, size, and rotate text, and add clip art to the slide master.

1. Open the file **Hiring.ppt**.
2. On the slide master, add the Plum clip art, which you can find using the keyword "Plum." Reduce the size of the plum by 50% and position it in the lower right corner of the slide, inside the colored box border.
3. Still working on the slide master, change the title text color to the same shade of green as the first-level bullets. Change the font to Arial Black.
4. Copy the plum from the slide master and paste it to the title master. Adjust the plum's position on the title master.
5. On the title master, center-align the title text and change the font of the subtitle to Arial Black. Switch to Slide view.
6. On slide 1, create in the upper left corner a floating text box with the text **Good 4 U**. Change the font to 28-point Arial Black and shadowed. Italicize "4 U" and change the size of the "4" to 32 points.
7. Rotate the "Good *4 U*" text approximately 30 degrees and reposition it in the upper left corner.
8. Move the text box containing "New Employee Orientation" down toward the middle of the slide.
9. In the subtitle placeholder, key **New Hires**, followed by a hyphen and today's date. Center the text below "New Employee Orientation."
10. On slide 2, start the text "Company Vision" as a new bullet line. Delete the "&" from the second bullet.
11. Insert a Bulleted List slide after slide 3 with the title **Who's Who** and the following bulleted items:
    - **Julie Wolfe and Gus Irvinelli are the co-owners of the restaurant**
    - **Michele Jenkins is the head chef**
    - **Roy Olafsen is the marketing manager**
12. On slide 5, key the following bulleted text:
    - **Good *4 U* is growing rapidly with our new franchising philosophy**
    - **Our healthy living message has worldwide appeal**
    - **We are relying on you, our new employees, to help us grow**
13. On slide 5, move the bullet text box down and to the right. Rotate the title text box into the upper left corner at a 30-degree angle and adjust its position, if necessary. Remember that you can fine-tune the rotated text position by selecting the text box, then pressing the Arrow keys on your keyboard. Reposition the bullet text box, if necessary.

Exercise 6-25:
Objectives 1, 3, 4, 5
Required Files: Hiring.ppt and clip art file plum.wmf (see page xiv for clip art file location and instructions)
Solution File: gl6-25.ppt in Solutions Manual or on Solutions Disk.

The completed presentation for this Exercise may be used in a student's portfolio.

LESSON 6 ■ **WORKING WITH POWERPOINT OBJECTS**

14. Check spelling in the presentation.
15. Save the presentation as *[your initials]***6-25.ppt**.
16. Create a handout header with the date and your name and a handout footer with the page number and the filename.
17. Print as handouts, 6 slides per page, black and white, framed.
18. Save and close the presentation.

EXERCISE 6-26

Use the drawing tools.

1. Open the file **Fund1.ppt**.
2. On slide 1, create the shapes shown in Figure 6-24. First, draw an oval and center it below the title. Then, draw a thin wide rectangle over the oval. Lastly, draw two vertical lines placed where the oval and rectangle intersect.

FIGURE 6-24

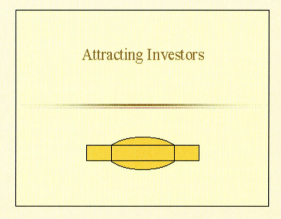

3. Key **Good 4 U** in the rectangle. (Remember to select the rectangle first.) Change the font to 32-point Times New Roman bold. Italicize "4 U" and change the size of the "4" to 40 points. Change the text color to dark red.
4. Still working on slide 1, delete the title placeholder and replace it with a WordArt text object. Choose the third style in the fourth row, the style in which the color is shaded gold and the words slant together at the top. Key the text **Attracting Investors**. Choose 54-point Arial Black for the WordArt font. Change the WordArt shape to Inflate Bottom (the third shape in the fourth row). Increase the WordArt object slightly and position it attractively at the top of the slide.

Exercise 6-26:
Objectives 2, 6–8
Required File: Fund1.ppt
Solution File: gl6-26.ppt in Solutions Manual or on Solutions Disk.

The completed presentation for this Exercise may be used in a student's portfolio.

203

UNIT 3 ■ CUSTOMIZING A PRESENTATION

5. On slide 2, change the title to **Objectives** and key the following bulleted text:
   - **Obtain investors to establish Good *4 U* as a franchise**
   - **Revisit the current business plan**
   - **Hire a marketing consulting firm**
6. In the first bullet, start "Good" on a new unbulleted line.
7. Draw an AutoShape Cube (from the Basic Shapes category) that is approximately 1.25 inches tall and 3 inches wide below the bulleted list. Key the following two lines in the cube:

   **Investors are our
   building blocks**
8. Format the cube's text as 28-point Arial. Use the adjusting handle to reduce the thickness of the cube, then adjust its overall width and height, if necessary, so the text fits inside.
9. On slide 3, key the following bulleted text:
   - **Organic fruit**
   - **Fresh veggies**
   - **Free-range chicken**
   - **Fish from our well-managed fish farm**
10. Resize the text box so it appears centered between the two pictures and increase the brightness of the two clip art images slightly.
11. On slide 4, key the text shown in Figure 6-25.

FIGURE 6-25

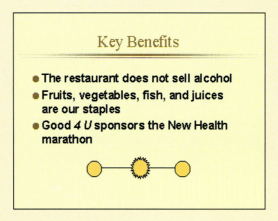

12. As shown in Figure 6-25, draw a horizontal line across the bottom of the slide below the bulleted text. Draw a small circle and position it at the left end of the horizontal line. Copy the circle, paste it, and move the copy to the right end of the line.

13. Draw a 24-Point Star AutoShape and position it in the center of the line.
14. On slide 5, key the text shown in Figure 6-26.

FIGURE 6-26

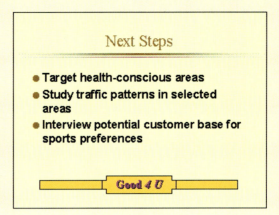

15. As shown in Figure 6-26, draw a long thin rectangle across the bottom of the slide. Draw an elongated Cross AutoShape (from the Basic Shapes category). Place the shape over the center of the rectangle.
16. Key **Good 4 U** in the cross. Change the font to 32-point Times New Roman bold and shadowed. Change the text color to dark red.
17. Use the slide master to make slide titles bold.
18. Check spelling in the presentation.
19. Save the presentation as *[your initials]*__6-26.ppt__.
20. Create a handout header with the date and your name and a handout footer with the page number and the filename.
21. Print as handouts, 6 slides per page, black and white, framed.
22. Save and close the presentation.

LESSON 7
Working with Lines, Fills, and Colors

OBJECTIVES

After completing this lesson, you will be able to:
1. Change the line color and style of objects.
2. Change the fill color of objects.
3. Work with fill patterns, shading, and textures.
4. Use the Format Painter tool to copy line, fill, and text formatting.
5. Add fill and shading effects to slide master objects.
6. Change the colors of a clip art object.
7. Change a presentation color scheme.
8. Change black and white settings for better printing.

 Estimated Time: 1½ hours

In Lesson 6, you learned how to create shapes and add clip art to your presentation. In that lesson, every shape in your presentation had the same color. This lesson shows you how to enhance your presentation by applying color, patterns, shading, and line styles to shapes you draw, text placeholders, and clip art.

Objective 1
Changing the Line Color and Style of Objects

To emphasize or separate text, clip art, or other objects from the rest of your slide, you can create a border using a variety of color and line options.

Each heading in the lesson correlates to a learning objective.

Required Files
Train2.ppt   Train5.ppt   gldngate.wmf*
*Available on Microsoft Office CD-ROM. See "Adding Additional Clip Art," page xiv, for file location and instructions.

Teaching Resources:
- PowerPoint Classroom Presentations
- School-to-Work Strategies Manual
- Internet Manual
- Spanish Glossary
- Methodology Video
- Certification Procedures

LESSON 7 ■ **WORKING WITH LINES, FILLS, AND COLORS**

| EXERCISE | 7-1 | **Add a Border to a Text Placeholder and Change Its Line Style** |

You can add a border to a text placeholder in one of two ways:
- Click the Line Style button ≡ on the Drawing toolbar.
- Choose Colors and Li<u>n</u>es from the F<u>o</u>rmat menu.

FIGURE 7-1
Line styles

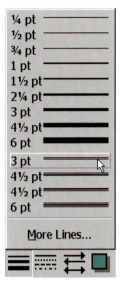

1. Open the file **Train5.ppt**.
2. On slide 1, click anywhere on the title text to activate the placeholder, and then click the placeholder border to select it.
3. Click the Line Style button ≡ on the Drawing toolbar. The line style menu appears.
4. Click to select the 3 pt double lines. Double lines now frame the title text.
5. Deselect the text box to view the change and change the zoom to 100% to see the double lines clearly. The line color is the default color. (You change line color later in this lesson.)
6. Select the text box again and apply the first 4½ pt double-line style to the title text border.
7. Restore the zoom to the Fit setting.
8. Move to slide 3 and select the star object.
9. Apply the 6 pt single-line style. A thicker border now surrounds the object.
10. With the star still selected, click the Dash Style button ≡ on the Drawing toolbar.
11. Apply the Round Dot style, which is the second style item on the menu. Changing a line or object border to a dash style can produce a dramatic effect.

FIGURE 7-2
Dash styles

| EXERCISE | 7-2 | **Change the Line Color of an Object's Border** |

You can change the color of a border in one of two ways:
- Click the Line Color button on the Drawing toolbar.
- Choose Colors and Li<u>n</u>es from the F<u>o</u>rmat menu.

NOTE
When you choose Colors and Li<u>n</u>es from the Format menu, you open the Format AutoShape dialog box (Colors and Lines tab). The Format AutoShape dialog box offers several options in one location, an especially helpful feature if you're making many style changes to one object.

Use PowerPoint Classroom Presentation #7 to display screens from the lesson, including this one, in a slide-show format.

NOTE
Make sure students understand the difference between the Line Style and Dash Style buttons.

207

UNIT 3 ■ CUSTOMIZING A PRESENTATION

NOTE

1. On slide 3, select the star, if necessary.
2. Click the arrow on the Line Color button ![icon] on the Drawing toolbar to display the line color choices. The gray bar at the top of the menu indicates it can be floated.

FIGURE 7-3
Line colors

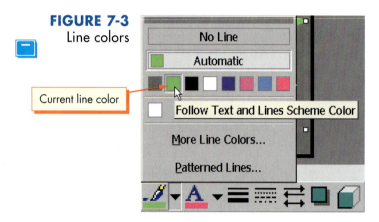

3. Move the mouse pointer over each color sample without clicking and notice the ScreenTips. These tips identify the automatic colors for the PowerPoint objects that make up a presentation.
4. Select the dark red color on the right. The ScreenTip indicates this color is used as an accent color (and as a followed hyperlink if you're working on Web pages).

EXERCISE 7-3 Add Arrowheads to Straight Lines

You can add an arrowhead to a straight line one of two ways:
- Click the Arrow Style button ![icon] on the Drawing toolbar.
- Choose Colors and Lines from the Format menu (or choose Format AutoShape from the shortcut menu).

1. Move to slide 4.
2. Using the Line button ![icon], draw a straight diagonal line that slants down from the right, pointing toward the tallest bar on the graph.

FIGURE 7-4
Arrowhead styles

3. With the line still selected, use ![icon] to make the line thicker. Select the 3 pt single-line style. (You can increase the zoom to see the change more clearly.)
4. Click the Arrow Style button ![icon].
5. Select the large left-pointing arrow, which is Arrow Style 6. The arrow points away from the graph.

NOTE: The placement of the arrow is determined by where you started drawing the line. The left arrowhead appears at the beginning of the line and the right arrowhead appears at the end of the line.

NOTE
Remind students how to use a button that contains an arrow, such as the Line Color button. They must click the arrow to display the color choices. If they click the button and not the arrow, they apply the current (or most recently applied) color.

In PowerPoint Classroom Presentation #7.

208

LESSON 7 ■ WORKING WITH LINES, FILLS, AND COLORS

FIGURE 7-5
Adjusting the arrow

6. Click again. Select the large right-pointing arrow, which is Arrow Style 5.
7. Adjust the length and angle of the arrow by dragging its tail with the two-headed arrow.
8. Right-click the arrow and choose Format AutoShape from the shortcut menu.
9. Click the Colors and Lines tab, if necessary. This dialog box contains many options, making it easy to change several properties of an object at once.

FIGURE 7-6
Format AutoShape dialog box, Colors and Lines tab

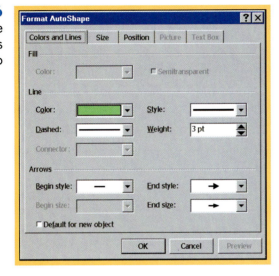

10. Open the Line Color drop-down list. The first line of color samples represents the colors for the current presentation.
11. Point to the gray color sample on the first line, which the ScreenTip identifies as the color scheme's background color.
12. Click the gray background color to select it.
13. Click the Preview button and drag the dialog box out of the way to see the new color of the arrow. The arrow fades into the background.
14. Change the color to dark pink, the Accent scheme color. Preview the change.
15. Click OK to accept the color and close the Format AutoShape dialog box.

 NOTE: You use the same technique to change the color of a line as you use to change the color of an object border.

✓Objective 2

Changing the Fill Color of Objects

When you draw an object on a slide, the color of the object is determined by the presentation's color scheme. You can choose a new fill color for an object. You can also change the fill color of a text placeholder or any other PowerPoint object.

In PowerPoint Classroom Presentation #7.

✓**Objective 2 Assignment:**
Exercise 7-21 (Skills Review) can be assigned after completing Objective 2.

209

UNIT 3 ■ CUSTOMIZING A PRESENTATION

NOTE You change the fill color using one of two options:
- The Fill Color button  on the Drawing toolbar
- The Format AutoShape dialog box

EXERCISE 7-4   Change the Fill Color of an Object

1. Move to slide 3 and right-click the star. Choose Format AutoShape to open the Format Autoshape dialog box.

FIGURE 7-7
Changing an object's fill color

NOTE

NOTE

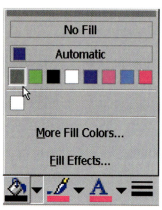

2. Click the Fill Color arrow to open the fill color drop-down menu. Choose the Black sample that follows the shadow scheme color and click OK.

3. With the star still selected, click the arrow next to the Fill Color button . Click the gray sample, the background scheme color.

4. Click ≡ and choose the 4½ pt line style to make the dotted border on the star thinner.

EXERCISE 7-5   Remove Fill Colors and Lines from Objects

1. Move to slide 5 and select the large triangle AutoShape.
2. Click the 🖌 arrow and choose No Fill. The color disappears, but the line remains.
3. With the triangle still selected, use 🖌 to choose No Line. The triangle's border disappears. Although it looks like the object disappeared, it is still there.
4. Select the circle. Remove the line from the circle so it appears as a blue dot.

✏️ **Objective 3**

Adding Patterns, Shading, and Textures

To add more interest to the objects in your slide, you can add special effects such as fill patterns, shading, and textures. PowerPoint provides many pat-

---

NOTE
Students will be using the Fill Color and Line Color buttons extensively throughout this text. Make sure they can distinguish between these buttons.

In PowerPoint Classroom Presentation #7.

NOTE
You may want to have students float the menus for the Fill Color and Line Color buttons.

NOTE
In step 3, remind students to click the Fill Color arrow, not the button itself, to display the fill color choices.

✏️ **Objective 3 Assignment:**
Exercises 7-22 (Skills Review) and 7-25 (Lesson Applications) can be assigned after completing Objective 3.

210

LESSON 7 ■ **WORKING WITH LINES, FILLS, AND COLORS**

NOTE terns, including textures that resemble wood and marble surfaces. You can further customize your slides using picture files created in other programs as images for object fill effects.

EXERCISE 7-6 Apply a Shaded Fill to an Object

In PowerPoint, applying a shaded fill means adding a *gradient fill* to an object, in which one color fades to another color. A gradient fill can use one or two colors or preset color combinations that are built into PowerPoint. You can also lighten or darken these colors and specify the direction of the gradient fill, such as horizontally or diagonally.

1. Move to slide 5 if necessary. Click the text in the invisible triangle so its border is visible. Click the border to select the entire object, just as you would select a text box.

    NOTE: If you just click the text, you will be in Edit mode. To select the entire object and all the text inside it, click its border.

2. Click and choose Fill Effects at the bottom of the menu. The Fill Effects dialog box appears.

3. Click the Gradient tab, if necessary.

4. In the Colors options box, click Preset. The Preset colors list box appears, containing specially created gradient fills. Select some of these preset colors and then view the display in the Variants box.

FIGURE 7-8
Fill Effects
dialog box

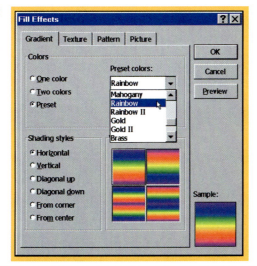

5. Choose Rainbow from the Preset colors list box.

6. In the Shading styles option box, choose From corner.

7. Under Variants, click the option in the lower left corner. Click the Preview button and drag the dialog box out of the way so you can see the effect.

8. Click OK to accept the shading and close the dialog box.

NOTE
Point out that patterns, like other fills, should be used appropriately. Patterns, shading, and textures can add interest, but they can also be distracting.

 In PowerPoint Classroom Presentation #7.

211

UNIT 3 ■ CUSTOMIZING A PRESENTATION

9. Deselect the triangle. Because you changed the shading of the triangle, the text is not legible. Select the text in the triangle, change the font color to white, and apply a text shadow.

10. Select the triangle, use ▤ to apply a ¼ pt border to the triangle, and change the line color to black.

EXERCISE 7-7 Shade a Circle to Add Dimension

1. Still working on slide 5, select the circle on top of the triangle.
2. Use 🪣▾ to open the Fill Effects dialog box and display the Gradient tab.
3. Choose the One Color option, if necessary.
4. Move the Dark/Light slider to the right of center until the color samples shade from purple to white.
5. In the Shading styles option box, choose From center.
6. Choose the right Variants option, which contains a light color in the center.
7. Click OK. The circle now appears to be a sphere.

FIGURE 7-9
Using gradient fills

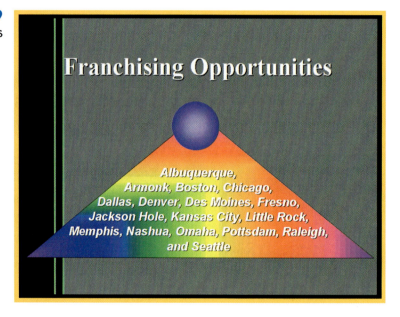

EXERCISE 7-8 Add a Shaded Fill to a Text Placeholder

1. Move to slide 2 and select the bulleted text placeholder.

In PowerPoint Classroom Presentation #7.

212

LESSON 7 ■ **WORKING WITH LINES, FILLS, AND COLORS**

2. Choose Colors and Lines from the Format menu to open the Format AutoShape dialog box. Click the Colors and Lines tab, if necessary.
3. Click the Fill Color arrow and choose Fill Effects.
4. In the Fill Effects dialog box, choose the Two colors option.
5. Choose black for Color 1 and gray for Color 2.
6. Choose the Horizontal shade style and the upper right variant (which is darkest at the bottom).
7. Click OK to accept the shading. Click OK again to close the Format AutoShape dialog box.
8. Deselect the bulleted text to observe the shading.
9. Move to slide 6. Apply the same shading to the text placeholder you applied on slide 2.

EXERCISE 7-9 Add a Fill Pattern to an Object

1. On slide 6, right-click the first blue diamond and choose Format AutoShape from the shortcut menu.
2. In the Format AutoShape dialog box, choose No Line from the Line Color drop-down list.
3. Choose Fill Effects from the Fill Color drop-down list box.

FIGURE 7-10
Adding a pattern fill to an object

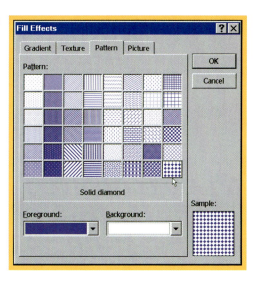

4. Click the Pattern tab.
5. Choose the solid diamond Pattern, which is the last pattern in the last row.
6. Change the Background color to black and click OK.
7. Click Preview to view the changes. The change is very slight.
8. Reopen the Fill Effects dialog box and change the Foreground color to pink. Click OK and preview the change.
9. Click OK to close the Format AutoShape dialog box.

In PowerPoint Classroom Presentation #7.

213

UNIT 3 ■ CUSTOMIZING A PRESENTATION

EXERCISE 7-10 Add a Textured Fill to an Object

Besides gradient color shading and patterns, you can also apply textured fill effects such as marble and wood grain.

1. On slide 6, right-click the second blue diamond and open the Format AutoShape dialog box. Click the Colors and Lines tab, if necessary.
2. Choose black for the Line Color.
3. Choose Fill Effects from the Fill Color drop-down list and click the Texture tab.
4. Choose Granite, the last option in the second row.

FIGURE 7-11
Texture tab in the Fill Effects dialog box

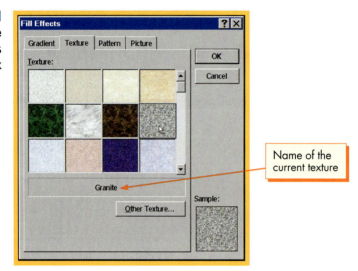

5. Click OK to accept the texture and close the Fill Effects dialog box.
6. Click OK to close the Format AutoShape dialog box.

Objective 4

Using the Format Painter Tool

If you use Word or Excel, you're probably familiar with the *Format Painter* tool. This tool makes it easy to copy the formatting from one object to another object.

> **NOTE:** Because the Format Painter copies all formatting, you may inadvertently copy unwanted formatting or lose formatting you want. For example, if you copy the formatting from a drawn object to a text placeholder, you may copy the colors and borders but lose word wrapping and centering. The Undo command comes in handy in such cases.

In PowerPoint Classroom Presentation #7.

214

LESSON 7 ■ WORKING WITH LINES, FILLS, AND COLORS

EXERCISE **7-11** **Copy Formatting from One Object to Another Object**

1. On slide 6, select the checkerboard diamond.
2. Click the Format Painter tool 🖌 on the Standard toolbar. The checkerboard formatting is picked up by the Format Painter and the mouse pointer has a paintbrush attached to it.
3. Select the body text next to the diamond. The text now appears in a tiny size with a checkerboard background. Click ↶▼.
4. Select the second diamond with the granite fill and double-click 🖌 to copy the formatting to more than one object.
5. Click the top diamond and then click the bottom diamond. All diamonds now have the granite fill. Notice that the Format Painter button is still turned on.
6. Click 🖌 again or press Esc to restore the normal mouse pointer.

NOTE: Just as you can copy objects from one slide to another, you can copy formatting from one slide to another using Format Painter.

Objective 5

Adding Fill and Shading Effects to Master Slides and Backgrounds

In previous lessons you learned how to change a presentation by changing text formatting and adding graphic elements to master slides. You can also change fill and line colors on master slides and remove unwanted elements that are included in the templates you use.

In addition, you can change background shading effects for an entire presentation. You don't need to be on a master slide to make background changes.

EXERCISE **7-12** **Apply a Fill Effect to a Master Slide Object**

1. Switch to the slide master. (Remember, press Shift while clicking 🗖 and use the scroll bar, if necessary, to display the slide master.)
2. Right-click the black rectangle on the left slide and choose Format AutoShape.
3. Click the Colors and Lines tab, if necessary, and choose Fill Effects from the Fill Color drop-down menu.

215

UNIT 3 ■ CUSTOMIZING A PRESENTATION

4. Click the Gradient tab, if necessary, and choose Two colors.
5. Choose Black for color 1 and Gray for color 2.
6. Choose the Horizontal shading option and the lower-right variant (the one with the darkest color in the middle). Click OK and click OK again to close the Format AutoShape dialog box.
7. With the shaded rectangle still selected, click the Format Painter button and switch to the title master using the vertical scroll bar.
8. Click the black rectangle on the title master to copy the shading effect.

EXERCISE 7-13 Change the Color of a Master Slide Object

1. Working on the title master, deselect the rectangle, if necessary.
2. Select the left green vertical line and press Delete to delete it.

   NOTE: Selecting a line that's on top of another object can be tricky. Place the four-headed arrow pointer directly on top of the line and click. If you see just two sizing handles, the line is selected.

3. Select the remaining green line and change its line color to the pink sample that follows the accent scheme color.

FIGURE 7-12
Title master with fill effects and line color changes

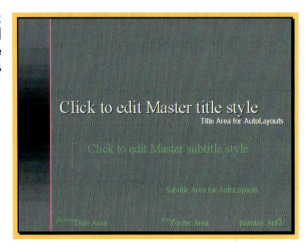

4. Switch to the slide master and make the same line changes so it matches the title master.
5. Switch to Slide view and scroll through the slides to observe your changes.

In PowerPoint Classroom Presentation #7.

216

LESSON 7 ■ WORKING WITH LINES, FILLS, AND COLORS

EXERCISE 7-14 **Change a Presentation's Background Effect**

One way to change a presentation's overall appearance quickly and easily is to change background effects and background colors using the Background command on the Format menu. You can change background effects for an entire presentation or for just one slide.

1. Working on any slide in Slide view, choose Ba*c*kground from the *F*ormat menu. The Background dialog box opens.

FIGURE 7-13
Background dialog box

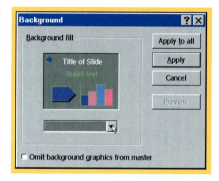

2. Click the sample color box's down arrow and choose *F*ill Effects.

3. Click the Texture Tab, choose Granite, and click OK. Click *A*pply to apply the granite texture to the background of the current slide.

4. Move to another slide to verify that its background has not changed.

5. With any slide displayed, reopen the Background dialog box.

6. Open the Fill Effects dialog box and click the Gradient tab.

7. Choose the two color option, with black as color 1 and gray as color 2.

8. Choose the horizontal shading style, if necessary, and the first variant, with the darkest color at the top of the sample.

9. Click OK and then click Apply *t*o all. Scroll through the presentation to verify that the shaded background appears on all slides.

EXERCISE 7-15 **Remove Master Slide Graphics from a Slide**

Sometimes the master slide graphics interfere with the design of one or more slides in your presentation. You can use the Background dialog box to eliminate master slide graphics on individual slides.

1. Move to slide 5, "Franchising Opportunities." Notice that the master slide graphics on the left interfere with this slide's design.

2. Open the Background dialog box.

3. Check the box in the lower left corner of the dialog box labeled "Omit background graphics from master."

In PowerPoint Classroom Presentation #7.

217

UNIT 3 ■ CUSTOMIZING A PRESENTATION

4. Click <u>A</u>pply. The rectangle and vertical line are deleted from the slide.

 NOTE: If you click Apply <u>t</u>o all by mistake, you delete the master slide graphics from all slides. In that case, click Undo and try again.

5. Scroll through the presentation to verify that all other slides still display the master graphic elements.

☑ Objective 6
Changing the Colors of a Clip Art Object

If you find a piece of clip art you like but the colors are not right for your presentation, you can recolor it. You can change the colors of any Clip Gallery picture supplied with Microsoft Office. You can also recolor other graphic formats, including 256 color bitmaps. It is best to use simple drawings when recoloring.

You recolor clip art using the Recolor Picture dialog box, which can be displayed one of two ways:

- Click the Recolor Picture button on the Picture toolbar.
- Choose Format P<u>i</u>cture from the shortcut menu and click R<u>e</u>color on the Picture tab.

EXERCISE 7-16 Recolor a Clip Art Object

1. Move to slide 2 ("Required Restaurant Equipment") and select the knife and fork picture.
2. Click the Recolor Picture button on the Picture toolbar to open the Recolor Picture dialog box. Each color in the clip art object appears as an <u>O</u>riginal color. These colors include lines, backgrounds, and fills that make up the clip art object.

 NOTE: The Picture toolbar appears when a picture is selected. If the toolbar is not displayed, choose <u>T</u>oolbars from the <u>V</u>iew menu and click Picture.

3. In the Change box, choose <u>F</u>ills, if necessary.
4. Click the <u>N</u>ew drop-down list for the second color (black) and choose pink. The knife and fork are now pink.

☑ **Objective 6 Assignment:**
Exercises 7-23 (Skills Review) and 7-27 (Lesson Applications) can be assigned after completing Objective 6.

LESSON 7 ■ **WORKING WITH LINES, FILLS, AND COLORS**

5. Change the first color (white) to black and click OK. The picture is recolored to match the color scheme of your presentation.

6. Move to slide 1 and insert the Golden Gate Bridge clip art image that you can find using the keywords Golden Gate.

7. Use [icon] to crop the bottom of the picture so no blue water shows. Reposition the picture at the bottom left so the left side of the picture aligns with the pink vertical line on the slide.

8. Click [icon] to open the Recolor Picture dialog box. Notice that this picture contains many colors.

9. Select the Colors option in the Change box, if necessary.

10. Drag the scroll bar to the bottom of the list of colors. The last color you see should be white. Above the white are three shades of orange and two shades of gray.

FIGURE 7-14
Recolor Picture dialog box

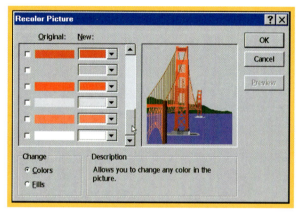

11. Change the two darker shades of orange to the dark pink, which is the last color of the color sample box. Change the lighter orange to the lighter pink in the color sample box.

12. Click Preview to view the changes. Move the dialog box out of the way, if necessary.

13. Click OK to accept the colors.

Objective 7

Changing a Presentation Color Scheme

In Lesson 3, you learned how to apply a design template to a presentation and how to modify the standard color scheme for the chosen template. Although most PowerPoint templates have different color schemes, these choices may not be suitable for your needs. If this is the case, you can change one or more colors in a scheme or create an entirely new color scheme.

In PowerPoint Classroom Presentation #7.

219

UNIT 3 ■ CUSTOMIZING A PRESENTATION

EXERCISE | **7-17** | **Make Custom Color Changes to a Color Scheme**

1. Choose Slide Color Scheme from the Format menu to open the Color Scheme dialog box.
2. Click the Custom tab. The Color Scheme dialog box displays eight standard colors for the current color scheme.

FIGURE 7-15
Color Scheme dialog box, Custom tab

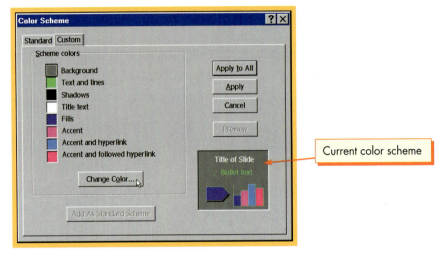

3. In the Scheme colors box, select the gray color next to Background, if necessary, and click Change Color. The Background Color dialog box appears with a honeycomb of colors you can choose from. Note that the original gray color is selected (it has a white outline).
4. Click the next darker shade of gray, above and slightly to the right of the original color. The sample box in the lower right corner displays the new color and current color.

FIGURE 7-16
Background Color dialog box

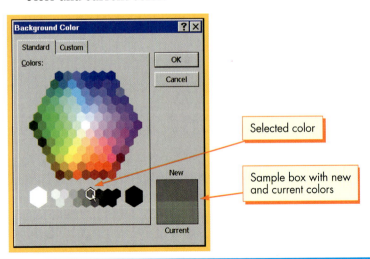

In PowerPoint Classroom Presentation #7.

220

LESSON 7 ■ **WORKING WITH LINES, FILLS, AND COLORS**

5. Click OK to accept the new background color.

6. In the Color Scheme dialog box, double-click the green Text and Lines color. The Text & Line Color dialog box opens.

7. Select the slightly darker shade of green, above and to the left of the original color. Click OK.

8. Click Apply to All to apply these subtle changes to the color scheme.

9. Scroll through all slides to view the changes.

EXERCISE 7-18 Create a New Color Scheme

1. Open the Slide Color Scheme dialog box.

2. Double-click the gray Background color to open the Background Color dialog box.

NOTE

3. Choose a medium blue and click OK.

4. Click Preview to see the color change. If you don't like the color, change it to a different shade of blue.

5. Click Add As Standard Scheme. Click the Standard tab. Notice that the new scheme appears as one of the choices.

6. Click Apply to All and click OK. Scroll through the presentation to observe the dramatic changes.

EXERCISE 7-19 Copy a Color Scheme Between Presentations

You use the Format Painter tool to copy the color scheme from a slide in one presentation to another slide or slides in another presentation.

1. Open the file **Train2.ppt**. Choose Arrange All from the Window menu and change both presentations to Slide Sorter view.

2. Click within the **Train2.ppt** window to activate it, if necessary, and press Ctrl+A to select all slides in the presentation.

3. Select one of the slides in **Train5.ppt**. Click the Format Painter button to pick up the slide's color scheme.

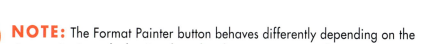

NOTE: The Format Painter button behaves differently depending on the view you're in and what is selected in the presentation. When you're in Slide Sorter view, the Format Painter picks up a selected slide's color scheme.

NOTE
You can choose a custom color—one that is not part of the standard color scheme—by clicking the More Colors option that is available in different dialog boxes and color menus. Colors that are not part of the standard color scheme do not change when you change a presentation's color scheme or apply a new template. Likewise, clip art colors do not change unless you recolor the pictures with standard colors.

UNIT 3 ■ CUSTOMIZING A PRESENTATION

4. Click one of the selected slides in **Train2.ppt**. The color scheme is applied to all slides in the presentation.

5. Close **Train2.ppt** without saving. Maximize **Train5.ppt**.

Objective 8
Changing Black and White Settings

In many cases, slides look great in color, but the text becomes difficult or impossible to read when you print your presentation in black and white. To remedy this, you can adjust the black and white settings for your presentation—for an entire slide, a master slide, or individual objects on any slide or master slide. By changing the black and white settings, you can control the black and white version of your presentation without affecting the color version.

EXERCISE 7-20   Change Black and White Settings for Printing

1. With the presentation still in Slide Sorter view, click the Black and White View button on the Standard toolbar. The slides appear in black and white. Notice that you can't read the body text on slides 2 and 6.

2. Double-click slide 2 to display it in Slide view.

3. Right-click a blank part of the slide where there is no graphic or text object. Point to Black and White on the shortcut menu. A series of black and white options appears on a submenu.

> **NOTE:** The Black and White command is available only on the shortcut menu and only when slides are displayed in black and white mode.

4. Choose Light Grayscale from the submenu. The entire slide turns to gray, but this doesn't improve the appearance.

5. Click to undo the change.

6. Right-click the bulleted text box border, point to Black and White, and choose Grayscale from the submenu. Deselect the text box to view the effect. This is an improvement, but you can make the text still more legible by choosing a different black and white setting.

7. Right-click the bulleted text box border and reopen the Black and White submenu. This time choose the Inverse Grayscale setting. Now the text is easy to read.

Objective 8 Assignment:
Exercise 7-24 (Skills Review) and Exercises 7-26 and 7-28 (Lesson Applications) can be assigned after completing Objective 8.

LESSON 7 ■ **WORKING WITH LINES, FILLS, AND COLORS**

FIGURE 7-17
Changing black and white settings

NOTE: You can also make black and white setting changes to master slide text placeholders. That way, the necessary changes will apply to all text placeholders in a presentation. You can then change individual text boxes as needed.

8. Move to slide 3. Change the star's black and white setting to Bla_c_k with White Fill. Apply the same setting to the triangle on slide 5.
9. Change the shaded text box on slide 6 to _I_nverse Grayscale.
10. While still in black and white mode, view the presentation in Slide Sorter view.
11. Change back to Slide view. Move to slide 1 and click to switch back to color mode.
12. Save the presentation as *[your initials]***7-20.ppt**.
13. Create a handout header with the date and your name and a handout footer with the page number and filename.
14. Print the presentation as handouts, 6 slides per page, black and white, framed.
15. Save and close the presentation.

NOTE
Depending on where you right-click, the Black and White submenu may appear to the left or to the right of the shortcut menu.

In PowerPoint Classroom Presentation #7.

223

UNIT 3 ■ CUSTOMIZING A PRESENTATION

COMMAND SUMMARY
NOTE

FEATURE	BUTTON	MENU	KEYBOARD
Borders		Format, Colors and Lines	
Border colors		Format, Colors and Lines	
Arrowheads		Format, Colors and Lines	
Fills		Format, Colors and Lines	

USING HELP

NOTE

After working with lines, fills, and colors to enhance a presentation, it's important to check how the presentation will print in black and white and make necessary adjustments.

Using Help to learn more about black and white print options:

1. Open the Help Index by choosing Contents and Index from the Help menu and clicking the Index tab.
2. Key **black** in the text box.
3. Double-click the index entry "black and white." Double-click the topic "Change how an object will look when printed in black and white."
4. Review the Help window and click ▶ for more information about black and white default options.
5. Close Help when you finish.

NOTE
The Command Summary lists a variety of ways to accomplish a particular task. Students can decide which method they prefer. In addition to the commands listed, reinforce the shortcut menu method for opening the Format AutoShape dialog box. Students can then display the Colors and Lines tab and choose line and fill options from one location.

NOTE
Encourage students to follow the steps in "Using Help." Software companies are increasingly using their online Help programs—rather than printed documentation—to train users and assist in answering user questions.

LESSON 7 ■ **WORKING WITH LINES, FILLS, AND COLORS**

TEST BANK

Concepts Review

TRUE/FALSE QUESTIONS

Each of the following statements is either true or false. Indicate your choice by circling **T** or **F**.

(T) F 1. You can use the Format Painter tool to copy formatting from one slide to another.

T **(F)** 2. Format Painter doesn't copy text formatting.

(T) F 3. Light grayscale is a black and white print option.

(T) F 4. When you draw an object, it appears in a color that the template chooses.

T **(F)** 5. Using the Apply button in the Color Scheme dialog box applies the color scheme to all slides in a presentation.

T **(F)** 6. Only one color can be used as a gradient fill.

T **(F)** 7. When changing the color scheme, you change only the text color.

(T) F 8. Wood and marble patterns are examples of textured fills.

SHORT ANSWER QUESTIONS

Write the correct answer in the space provided.

1. What dialog box do you use to change the colors in an AutoShape?
   Format AutoShape

2. How do you check to see if a slide will print well in black and white?
   Click the Black and White View button

3. Where do you find the command that you use to change black and white settings?
   Shortcut menu in Black and White view

4. Which toolbar button do you use to choose textured backgrounds?
   Fill Color

5. What do you use to view a color scheme before you commit to it?
   Preview button

Concepts Review:
Allows students to check their understanding.

TEST BANK
Consider using the Test Bank to provide an additional review of lesson concepts.

CLOSE

225

UNIT 3 ■ CUSTOMIZING A PRESENTATION

6. Which toolbar button do you use to add a border?
   Line Style

7. Which button on which toolbar do you use to change the colors in clip art?
   Recolor Picture on the Picture toolbar

8. Which button can you use to copy fills and colors to another object?
   Format Painter

CRITICAL THINKING

Answer these questions on a separate page. There are no right or wrong answers. Support your answers with examples from your own experience, if possible.

1. Think of the way you used shading to add dimension to a simple circle. What other objects could you change using shading to add dimension?

2. Which objects in a presentation are most suited to borders? What types of border styles and colors work best against what types of backgrounds?

Skills Review

EXERCISE 7-21

Create borders, change line colors and styles, and change fill colors.

1. Open the file **Fund1.ppt**. Apply the **Serene.pot** design template.
2. On slide 1, move the title placeholder down, positioning it just above the horizontal line.
3. On slide 2, change the title to **Objectives** and key the following bulleted text:
   - **Complete the business plan**
   - **Complete the marketing plan**
   - **Locate interested investors**
   - **Investigate other funding options**
4. Create a text border by following these steps:
   a. Click the placeholder border on slide 2.
   b. Click the Line Style button ≣ on the Drawing toolbar.
   c. Choose the 3 pt line style.
   d. Resize the placeholder to frame the text. Reposition the text box in the center of the slide.

Critical Thinking Questions:
Answers will vary based on students' preferences, observations, experiences, and research.

Skills Review:
Provides guided practice for students. Objectives are indicated for each Exercise.

Exercise 7-21:
Objectives 1, 2
Required File: Fund1.ppt
Solution File: gl7-21.ppt in Solutions Manual or on Solutions Disk

226

LESSON 7 ■ **WORKING WITH LINES, FILLS, AND COLORS**

5. On slide 3, key the following bulleted text:
   - **Low-fat menus**
   - **Non-alcoholic beverages**
   - **Vegetarian meals**
   - **Fresh-baked breads**
6. Apply a 3 pt line border to the text box on slide 3, then size and position it appropriately as you did with slide 2.
7. Change the border color and property of an object by following these steps:
   a. On slide 2, select the bulleted text border.
   b. Click the arrow on the Line Color button.
   c. Choose the dark green sample that follows the shadows color.
   d. On slide 3, select the bulleted text border.
   e. Click the Dash Style button and choose the Round Dot style.
   f. Increase the dotted border to 6 pt.
8. Add an arrowhead to a straight line by following these steps:
   a. On slide 3, use the Line tool to draw a line that begins at the top of "fat" and ends below the "c" in "Specialties."
   b. Using, change the thickness to 6 pt.
   c. Click the Arrow Style button and choose Arrow Style 6, which is the large left-pointing arrow. (The arrowhead should be pointing down.)
9. On slide 4, key the following bulleted text:
   - **Quick return of invested funds**
   - **Name recognition**
   - **"Healthy" image**
10. Add a 4½ pt double-line border to the text placeholder. Resize and reposition the placeholder in the center of the slide.
11. Change the fill color of an object by following these steps:
    a. At the bottom center of slide 4, draw a 5-point star AutoShape. Make it exactly 1.25 inches wide and 1.19 inches high. Adjust its position, if necessary.
    b. Click the arrow next to the Fill Color button and choose dark green (the shadows scheme color).
    c. Set the line color to No Line.
12. Copy the star on slide 4 and paste it to slide 1. Enlarge to by 50% and change the fill color to one of the lighter colors in the color scheme. Add a 1 pt black border to the star.
13. Delete slide 5.

227

UNIT 3 ■ CUSTOMIZING A PRESENTATION

14. Check spelling in the presentation.
15. Save the presentation as *[your initials]*__7-21.ppt__.
16. Create a handout header with the date and your name and a handout footer with the page number and filename.

NOTE

17. Print as handouts, 6 slides per page, black and white, framed.
18. Save and close the presentation.

EXERCISE 7-22

Change fill colors and shading of objects.

1. Open the file **Cook2.ppt**.
2. Remove fill color and lines from an object by following these steps:
   a. Move to slide 2 and select the diamond.
   b. Use the Fill Color button to choose No Fill.
   c. With the diamond selected, use the Line Color button to choose No Line.
   d. Move to slide 4 and remove the line from the circle.
3. Apply a shaded fill to an object by following these steps:
   a. Move to slide 2 and select the invisible diamond by placing the insertion point in the diamond text and clicking. Click the border.
   b. Click the Fill Color arrow and choose Fill Effects.
   c. Click the Gradient tab, if necessary.
   d. Choose Two colors (blue and white).
   e. Choose the Horizontal shade style and the bottom left Variants option (with white in the middle).
   f. Click the Preview button, drag the dialog box out of the way so you can view the results, and click OK.
4. Shade a circle to add dimension by following these steps:
   a. Move to slide 4 and select the circle.
   b. Click the Fill Color arrow, choose Fill Effects, and click the Gradient tab, if necessary.
   c. Click the One Color option and choose blue, if necessary.
   d. Move the Dark/Light slider all the way to the right.
   e. Choose the From center shade style and the right Variants option (which is white in the center).
   f. Click OK.

NOTE
From this lesson forward, remind students to check their presentations in Black and White view, before printing, to make sure that text is legible. Encourage students to experiment with the Black and White menu settings.

Exercise 7-22:
Objectives 2, 3
Required File: Cook2.ppt
Solution File: gl7-22.ppt in Solutions Manual or on Solutions Disk

LESSON 7 ■ **WORKING WITH LINES, FILLS, AND COLORS**

5. Add a shaded fill to a text placeholder by following these steps:
   a. Move to slide 3 and select the two bulleted text placeholders by pressing down the [Shift] key and clicking the two placeholders.
   b. Choose Colors and Lines from the Format menu.
   c. Choose Fill Effects from the Fill Color drop-down list box.
   d. Click the Two colors option.
   e. Choose green for Color 1 and white for Color 2.
   f. Choose the Horizontal shade style and the upper right variant (with the darkest color on the top). Click OK.
   g. Click Preview to view the changes and then click OK
6. Change the bulleted text on slide 3 to Arial bold. Use the slide master and title master to make all titles Arial bold.
7. Check spelling in the presentation.
8. Save the presentation as *[your initials]***7-22.ppt**.
9. Create a handout header with the date and your name and a handout footer with the page number and filename.
10. Print as handouts, 6 slides per page, black and white, framed.
11. Save and close the presentation.

EXERCISE 7-23

Copy formatting using Format Painter, recolor a clip art object, and change background shading.

1. Open the file **Miami1.ppt**.
2. Copy formatting from one object to another object by following these steps:
   a. Move to slide 3 and select the center star on the bottom of the slide.
   b. Double-click the Format Painter button.
   c. Click the left star and then click the right star.
   d. Click again or press [Esc] to turn off Format Painter.
3. Move to slide 1. Insert a palm tree clip art image that you can find using the keyword "palm." Choose the single palm tree silhouette that has the description "Palm Tree Silhouette."
4. Reduce the size of the picture to about 2 inches tall and place it to the left of the subtitle.
5. Recolor the clip art object by following these steps:

Exercise 7-23:
Objectives 4–6
Required Files: Miami1.ppt and clip art file palmtre2.wmf (see page xiv for clip art file locations and instructions)
Solution File: gl7-23.ppt in Solutions Manual or on Solutions Disk.

229

UNIT 3 ■ CUSTOMIZING A PRESENTATION

      a. With the picture selected, click the Recolor Picture button on the Picture toolbar.

> **NOTE:** If the Picture toolbar is not displayed, choose View, Toolbars, Picture.

      b. Choose the Colors option in the Change option box.

      c. Choose More Colors and select a dark gray from the honeycomb of colors. Click OK and then click OK again.

6. Change the background for the entire presentation by following these steps:

      a. Working on any slide, choose Background from the Format menu.

      b. Click the color sample arrow and choose Fill Effects.

      c. Choose the Two colors option, keeping the medium brown that follows the background scheme color for color 1 and choosing pink for color 2.

      d. Choose the top right variant that has the darkest color at the bottom and click OK.

      e. Click Apply to all.

7. On the slide master, change the title text size to 60 point and change its color to the medium brown that follows the background scheme color. Make the bullet text bold.

8. On slide 1, select the title and click **A** repeatedly until the font size box reads "106+". Change the text color to turquoise, following the Accent Scheme color.

9. Change the background for slide 1 only by reversing the variant so the shading is dark at the top and light at the bottom.

10. Check spelling in the presentation.

11. Save the presentation as *[your initials]***7-23.ppt**.

12. Create a handout header with the date and your name and a handout footer with the page number and filename.

13. Print as handouts, 6 slides per page, black and white, framed.

14. Save and close the presentation.

EXERCISE 7-24

Add fill effects to slide master objects, change color scheme, use Format Painter, and change black and white settings.

1. Open the file **Open2.ppt**. Apply the **Fireball.pot** design template.

Exercise 7-24:
Objectives 1–8
Required File: Open2.ppt
Solution File: gl7-24.ppt in Solutions Manual or on Solutions Disk.

LESSON 7 ■ **WORKING WITH LINES, FILLS, AND COLORS**

2. Remove graphic elements from the slide master by following these steps:
   a. Display the slide master.
   b. Point to the graphic between the title placeholder and text placeholder and click to select it.
   c. Press Delete. Leave the graphic on the title master.

3. Create a custom color scheme by following these steps:
   a. With the slide master still displayed, choose Slide Color Scheme from the Format menu.
   b. Click the Custom tab.
   c. Double-click the Background scheme color (black) and click the Standard tab, if necessary.
   d. Choose dark blue in the upper right corner of the Standard colors.
   e. Click OK and click Apply to All.

4. Add an AutoShape object to the slide master and change its fill effects by following these steps:
   a. Use ▢ to draw a thin rectangle between the title placeholder and the text placeholder. It should be approximately the same width as the placeholders and about 0.25 inches high.
   b. Click ✎▾ and select No Line.
   c. Using 🖌▾, display the Gradient tab of the Fill Color dialog box. Click Preset and choose Early Sunset from the Preset colors drop-down list.
   d. Choose the Vertical shading style and the upper left variant. Click OK.

5. Select the thin rectangle and click the Draw button on the Drawing toolbar. Choose Change AutoShape, Basic Shapes, and change the shape to a rounded rectangle. Drag the adjustment handle to the right as far as it goes to create rounder corners.

6. Display slide 2 and add a gradient fill to the bulleted text box. Use the Two colors option and the current colors (orange and dark blue). Use the vertical shading style with the lower-right variant (with orange in the center). Click OK.

7. Make the bulleted text bold with a text shadow.

8. Resize and reposition the text box on slide 2, centering it on the slide.

9. Apply the same fill and text effects to the text boxes on slides 3 and 4 using the Format Painter tool. Resize and reposition the text boxes appropriately.

10. Change black and white settings by following these steps:
    a. Move to slide 2 and select the bulleted text box.
    b. Click 🅱.

231

  c. Right-click the border of the bulleted text box. Choose Black and <u>W</u>hite from the shortcut menu and then choose Bla<u>c</u>k with White Fill from the submenu.

  d. Use Format Painter to apply the same black and white setting to the text boxes on slides 3 and 4.

  e. Return to color mode by clicking ▨.

11. Check spelling in the presentation.

12. Save the presentation as *[your initials]***7-24.ppt**.

13. Create a handout header with the date and your name and a handout footer with the page number and filename.

14. Print as handouts, 6 slides per page, black and white, framed.

15. Save and close the presentation.

Assessment Resources:
- Solutions Manual
- Test Bank with Software
- Portfolio Builder
- Alternative Assessment Guide
- Certification Procedures

LESSON 7 ■ **WORKING WITH LINES, FILLS, AND COLORS**

Lesson Applications

EXERCISE 7-25

Change the line colors, line styles, and fill colors of objects.

1. Open the file **Franch1.ppt**. Apply the "Facilitating a Meeting" design template found in the Presentations folder.

2. Change the template's color scheme to the sample with the yellow background and red accent color in the Color Scheme dialog box.

3. On the slide master, select and delete the large diamond object. Do not remove the diamond from the title master.

4. Delete the Dollar sign clip art image on slide 2. Replace it with the work group clip art image that you can find using the keywords "work group." Size and position the new image so it occupies the same position on the slide as the old image.

5. On slide 3, draw a diagonal line slanting down and to the left, pointing to the tallest column on the graph.

6. Make the line 3 points wide and add an arrowhead. Change the arrow color to black.

7. Add a floating text box at the tail of the arrow with the text **Estimating over $89,000** on two lines. Change the font to 20-point Arial bold.

8. Add a 3-point black border to the text box. Adjust the position and size of the arrow and text box, if necessary.

9. On slide 4, remove the bullets from the placeholder and key **10% discount off the lunch menu, Monday through Thursday**

10. Change the font to 36-point bold. Right-align the text, then resize the text box so the text wraps to four lines. If necessary, change the text color to purple. Reposition the text box so it is centered with the clip art.

11. Change the text box fill to a 2-color gradient. Choose the yellow that follows the background scheme color for color 1 and the pale yellow that follows the accent and followed hyperlink scheme color for color 2. Choose the horizontal shading style that has the darkest color at the top.

12. Change the text box border to a bold pattern of red diagonal lines by doing the following: Click ≡, choose More Lines, click the Line Color arrow, and choose Patterned Lines. Choose the third pattern in the bottom row (with large left-slanting diagonal lines). For the pattern background color, choose the red that follows the text scheme color and

---

Lesson Applications:
Provide independent practice for students. Objectives are indicated for each Exercise.

Exercise 7-25:
Objectives 1–3
Required Files: Franch1.ppt and clip art file writegrp.wmf (see page xiv for clip art file locations and instructions)
Solution File: gl7-25.ppt in Solutions Manual or on Solutions Disk.

NOTE
Make sure students know how to switch between the Presentation Designs folder and the Presentations folder to locate the templates used in this lesson.

233

UNIT 3 ■ CUSTOMIZING A PRESENTATION

for the foreground, choose the yellow that follows the background scheme color. Change the line weight to 8 point.

13. On slide 5, add a thin double-line border around the text box and change its color to red. Resize the text box to fit the text and center it on the slide.

14. Change the black and white setting for the text box on slide 4 to grayscale. Review all the slides in Black and White view and make any other necessary adjustments.

15. Check spelling in the presentation.

16. Save the presentation as *[your initials]***7-25.ppt**.

17. Create a handout header with the date and your name and a handout footer with the page number and filename.

18. Print as handouts, 6 slides per page, black and white, framed.

19. Save and close the presentation.

EXERCISE 7-26

Work with shading and fills.

1. Open the file **Hiring.ppt**. Apply the Contemporary Portrait design template in the Presentation Designs folder.

2. On slide 1, draw a 16-point star below the title. Make the star 3.5 inches high and 5 inches wide. Position the star where a subtitle would ordinarily be placed.

3. Apply a two-color gradient fill to the star, choosing orange for color 1 and yellow for color 2. Choose the F<u>r</u>om center shading style and the variant that has the lightest color in the center. Remove the border from the star.

4. Add the text **Good 4 U** to the inside of the star. Format the text as black, 44-point Times New Roman bold with the "4 U" in italic and the "4" two font sizes larger. Rotate the star 15 degrees.

5. Insert a new slide after slide 3 using the Bulleted List layout.

6. Key **Who's Who** as the title of the new slide. Remove the bullets and key the following text:

   Julie Wolfe, Co-Owner

   Gus Irvinelli, Co-Owner

   Michelle Jenkins, Head Chef

   Roy Olafsen, Marketing Manager

7. On slide 5 ("Summary"), key the following bulleted text:

Exercise 7-26:
Objectives 1–4, 8
Required File: Hiring.ppt
Solution File: gl7-26.ppt in Solutions Manual or on Solutions Disk.

The completed presentation for this Exercise may be used in a student's portfolio.

LESSON 7 ■ WORKING WITH LINES, FILLS, AND COLORS

- Six-month probation period
- Annual salary increases
- Quarterly stock purchase options
- Annual profit sharing

8. Draw a 16-point star that is 1.75 inches high and 3.25 inches wide. Using Format Painter, copy the formatting of the star on slide 1 to this new star. Position the star in the bottom right corner of the slide.

9. Key **Substantial** in the star and change its text formatting to 24-point Arial bold, if necessary.

10. Rotate the star 15 degrees. Draw a 4½-point black line with an arrowhead pointing from the star to the text "Annual profit sharing."

11. Adjust the presentation's black and white settings as needed so all text is legible in a black and white printout.

12. Check spelling in the presentation.

13. Save the presentation as *[your initials]***7-26.ppt**.

14. Create a handout header with the date and your name and a handout footer with the page number and filename.

15. Print as handouts, 6 slides per page, black and white, framed.

16. Save and close the presentation.

EXERCISE 7-27

Apply textured fills, copy formatting, and recolor clip art.

1. Open the file **Train1.ppt**. Apply the design template **Notebook.pot** found in the Presentation Designs folder.

2. Change the title master's title and subtitle to dark brown. Make the title text bold.

3. On slide 1, draw a diamond AutoShape below the subtitle. Make the diamond slightly wider than the subtitle and 0.5 inch high.

4. Apply the Oak wood grain texture (found in the last row of textures) to the triangle.

5. Use Format Painter to copy the formatting of the bulleted text placeholder on slide 3 to the one on slide 4 (to apply the check mark bullets to slide 4).

6. On slide 4, draw the right arrow AutoShape (on the Block Arrows menu). Make the arrow 1.5 inches wide and 0.75 inches high. Use Format Painter to fill the arrow with the wood grain texture from the diamond on slide 1. Position the arrow so it points to the first bullet that begins with the word "Pentium."

Exercise 7-27:
Objectives 3, 4, 6
Required Files: Train1.ppt and clip art file wheat.wmf (see page xiv for clip art file locations and instructions)
Solution File: gl7-27.ppt in Solutions Manual or on Solutions Disk.

The completed presentation for this Exercise may be used in a student's portfolio.

235

UNIT 3 ■ CUSTOMIZING A PRESENTATION

7. Still working on slide 4, edit the text of the first bullet to read "Pentium computer (network server)." Edit the second bullet so it starts with "Two" instead of "2."

8. Move both the arrow and the bulleted text box to the left about 1 inch and make the text box wide enough to fit the first bullet on one line. Delete the line break from the last bullet line so the text appears on one line.

9. Delete slide 5 ("Annual Sales Per Division").

10. On slide 2, in the clip art placeholder, insert a clip art image that is appropriate to the slide content. Size the image as needed.

11. On slide 3, replace the clip art with another image that is appropriate to the slide content. Size the image as needed.

12. On slide 5 ("Sample Menu"), insert the stylized grain clip art image that you can find using the keyword "Grain." Resize it to 2.5 inches tall.

13. Increase the menu text on slide 5 by one font size and position the clip art and text box so they're balanced.

14. Recolor the grain image on slide 5 by opening the Recolor Picture dialog box, choosing Fills in the Change option box, and changing both brown samples to the dark red that follows the accent scheme color.

15. Check spelling in the presentation.

16. Save the presentation as *[your initials]***7-27.ppt**.

17. Create a handout header with the date and your name and a handout footer with the page number and filename.

18. Print as handouts, 6 slides per page, black and white, framed.

19. Save and close the presentation.

EXERCISE 7-28

Change the presentation color scheme; work with line colors, patterns, and fills; change black and white settings.

1. Open the file **Mktg.ppt**. Apply the design template **Flyer (Standard).pot** found in the Presentations folder.

2. Change the color scheme to the second sample on the top row of the Color Scheme dialog box.

3. Change the background color for the presentation to the medium blue that follows the accent and hyperlink color scheme.

4. Change the background for slide 1 only to a one-color horizontal gradient, using the medium blue color. Adjust the shading slider so it shades to a light blue. Choose the first shading variant on the second row (with the lightest shade in the center).

NOTE
In steps 10 and 11, students are asked to make their own clip art choices. You may want to specify images. The solution file uses chef2.cgm and ceo.wmf from the MS Office CD-ROM. See page xiv for file locations.

Exercise 7-28:
Objectives 1–3, 5, 7, 8
Required File: Mktg.ppt
Solution File: gl7-28.ppt in Solutions Manual or on Solutions Disk.

The completed presentation for this Exercise may be used in a student's portfolio.

NOTE
Make sure students know how to switch between the Presentation Designs folder and the Presentations folder to locate the templates used in this lesson.

5. On the title master, move the graphic object and the subtitle down about .5 inch.
6. On the slide master, reduce the first level bullet text size to 28 point and change the bullet color to light green.
7. Add a text shadow to the slide master's title text placeholder
8. Apply a horizontal one-color gradient fill to the bulleted text placeholder, shading to light blue. Use the variant with the lightest color at the top.
9. On slide 1, change the subtitle font to 44-point Times New Roman bold. Italicize "4 U" and make the "4" two font sizes larger. Center-align the subtitle text.
10. Delete the title placeholder. Create a WordArt text object, using the second sample in the third row (purple text that slants up). Key **Marketing Strategy** in the Edit WordArt Text dialog box and change the font to 48-point bold. Insert the WordArt object and move it to the title position at the top of the slide. Drag the object's yellow adjustment handle up as far as it will go, to eliminate the slant. Resize the object to 1.25 inches high and 8.75 inches wide.
11. Change the WordArt's fill color to the dark blue that follows the title text scheme color.
12. Apply a 2.25-point light blue outline to the WordArt object.
13. Adjust the bulleted text box size for each slide in the presentation.
14. Check the presentation's black and white settings, adjusting them if necessary to ensure a legible black and white printout.
15. Check spelling in the presentation.
16. Save the presentation as *[your initials]***7-28.ppt**.
17. Create a handout header with the date and your name and a handout footer with the page number and filename.
18. Print as handouts, 6 slides per page, black and white, framed.
19. Save and close the presentation.

LESSON 8
Manipulating PowerPoint Objects

OBJECTIVES After completing this lesson, you will be able to:
1. Select multiple objects.
2. Align, flip, and distribute objects.
3. Group and ungroup objects
4. Work with layers of objects.
5. Apply object shadows and 3-D effects.
6. Use the duplicate command.
7. Work with advanced clip art editing.

 Estimated Time: 1½ hours

In earlier lessons, you learned how to add clip art, text objects, and drawings to a presentation. This lesson shows you how to move or change a group of objects, layer objects, and align objects. These are techniques to help you create more effective presentations.

Objective 1
Selecting Multiple Objects

When you want to treat several objects on a slide the same way, such as making them all the same color, you can select all the objects at the same time using multiple selection techniques. There are two basic ways to select multiple objects:

238

PREPARE
Each heading in the lesson correlates to a learning objective.
Required Files
Mktg2.ppt   circarro.wmf*
*Available on Microsoft Office CD-ROM. See "Adding Additional Clip Art," page xiv, for file location and instructions.

TEACH
Teaching Resources:
• PowerPoint Classroom Presentations
• School-to-Work Strategies Manual
• Internet Manual
• Spanish Glossary
• Methodology Video
• Certification Procedures

LESSON 8 ■ **MANIPULATING POWERPOINT OBJECTS**

- Select one object, then hold down [Shift] and click another object.
- Draw a selection rectangle around the objects you want to select.

You can also select all the objects on a slide by choosing Select All from the Edit menu or by pressing [Ctrl]+[A].

EXERCISE 8-1 Select Multiple Objects

1. Open the file **Mktg2.ppt**.
2. On slide 1, click the long thin horizontal arrow at the top of the screen. Notice its sizing handles.
3. Hold down [Shift] and click the vertical arrow on the right side of the slide. Notice that there are sizing handles around both objects, indicating they are both selected.
4. With the two arrows selected, use [icon] to set the fill color to yellow. Both selected arrows turn yellow.
5. With the two yellow arrows selected, press [Shift] and click the bottom and left arrows. Now all four long thin arrows are selected.

FIGURE 8-1
Multiple selected objects

6. With all the arrows selected, change the fill to a two-color vertical gradient. Choose dark red, following the background scheme color, for Color 1, and choose orange, following the fills color scheme, for Color 2. Use the upper left variant (with red on the left and orange on the right).

EXERCISE 8-2 Remove an Item from a Group of Selected Objects

Sometimes you will want to change the composition of a group of selected items as you work. One way is to deselect all the objects by clicking a blank

Use PowerPoint Classroom Presentation #8 to display screens from the lesson, including this one, in a slide-show format.

239

UNIT 3 ■ CUSTOMIZING A PRESENTATION

part of the slide. Another way is to hold down Shift and click the selected item to deselect it, leaving the remaining items in the group selected.

1. To deselect the arrow at the top of the slide and leave the other three selected, hold Shift and click the top arrow. The remaining three arrows are still selected.

2. Hold Shift and deselect the bottom arrow. The bottom arrow is deselected, leaving the two side arrows selected.

3. Change the shading style of the two side arrows to horizontal, using the upper left variant.

4. Deselect all the arrows by clicking a blank area of the slide, then select the arrow at the bottom of the slide. Change its gradient fill to the one with the orange on the left side.

EXERCISE 8-3 Select Objects Using the Selection Rectangle

1. Move to slide 2.
2. Position the pointer in the lower-left corner of the slide.

FIGURE 8-2
Selection rectangle

NOTE

3. Drag the mouse pointer diagonally to the right and up until you see a dotted box surrounding all four orange arrows. (It's okay if the box overlaps the slide text.) This dotted box is called a *selection rectangle*. Only objects completely enclosed in the selection rectangle are selected.

4. Release the mouse button. Resize handles surround each arrow.

5. If one of the arrows does not have a set of resizing handles, draw a new selection rectangle.

 NOTE: Sometimes it is easier to add the missing object to the selection using the Shift + click method rather than drawing a new selection rectangle.

In PowerPoint Classroom Presentation #8.

NOTE
When you draw a selection rectangle, all the objects you want to select should be well within the rectangle. To select all objects on a slide using the selection rectangle, draw the rectangle so it covers the entire screen.

240

LESSON 8 ■ **MANIPULATING POWERPOINT OBJECTS**

6. Change the fill of the selected arrows to a vertical gradient, using the same red and orange as on the arrows on slide 1. Choose the variant that has red on the right side.

✓Objective 2
Aligning, Flipping, and Distributing Objects

PowerPoint has a number of tools that you can use to re-orient objects on a slide. You can rotate and flip them, creating mirror images of the original. Objects can be aligned together, either vertically or horizontally. You can also distribute multiple objects, spacing them evenly across the slide either horizontally or vertically.

EXERCISE 8-4 Align Objects Horizontally and Vertically

1. Still working on slide 2, select the four arrows, if necessary. Notice that the arrows are not positioned evenly on the slide.
2. To display the Align or Distribute floating toolbar, click D<u>r</u>aw on the Drawing toolbar and point to <u>A</u>lign or Distribute. Point to the gray title bar of this submenu and drag it to a convenient place on the screen, out of the way of the selected arrows.

 NOTE: If the Drawing toolbar is not in view, choose <u>T</u>oolbars from the <u>V</u>iew menu and then choose Drawing.

TABLE 8-1 **Alignment Options**

[NOTE]

CHOOSE BUTTON	TO DO THIS
Align Left	Vertically align the left edges of objects
Align Center	Vertically align the centers of objects
Align Right	Vertically align the right edges of objects
Align Top	Horizontally align the top edges of objects
Align Middle	Horizontally align the center points of objects
Align Bottom	Horizontally align the bottom edges of objects
Distribute Horizontally	Space objects evenly in a horizontal direction
Distribute Vertically	Space objects evenly in a vertical direction
Relative to Slide	A toggle button. When turned on, align or space objects relative to slide. When turned off, align objects relative to each other.

✓**Objective 2 Assignment:**
Exercise 8-19 (Skills Review) can be assigned after completing Objective 2.

[NOTE]
Review Table 8-1 in class. Sometimes the concepts of Centers and Middles can be confusing.

241

UNIT 3 ■ CUSTOMIZING A PRESENTATION

3. Notice that the first three buttons on the toolbar control vertical alignment and the next three buttons control horizontal alignment.

4. Check the Align or Distribute toolbar to be sure that Relative to Slide is not selected. If it is, click it to turn off that option.

NOTE: When working with the Align or Distribute commands, be sure you pay attention to the Relative to Slide button. If it's selected, all alignment actions will be relative to the slide, not the selected objects.

5. Click the Align Top button [图]. The objects line up with the top arrow.

6. Deselect the arrows, then drag the arrow furthest to the right up about 1 inch and drag the arrow furthest to the left down 1 inch.

NOTE

TIP: To help you position objects, you can choose Ruler from the View menu to display a horizontal and vertical ruler.

7. Select all four arrows, then click the Align Bottom button [图]. The objects align horizontally again, but this time they align with the bottom arrow.

8. Click [图] to return the arrows to their previous positions.

9. Click the Align Left button [图]. The objects align vertically, aligning with the arrow furthest to the left, but one arrow is hidden because it is underneath another arrow.

10. Click [图] and then click the Align Right button [图]. The objects are arranged vertically, aligning with the arrow furthest to the right.

EXERCISE 8-5 Distribute Objects Horizontally and Vertically

1. Still working on slide 2, select the four arrows, if necessary.

2. Click the Distribute Vertically button [图]. The arrows are now evenly spaced, but overlap.

3. Deselect the arrows, then drag the top arrow up about 0.5 inch.

4. Reselect the four arrows and click [图] again. Now the arrows are spaced further apart.

5. With the arrows still selected, click the Distribute Horizontally button [图]. Nothing happens because all the arrows are in the same relative horizontal position.

NOTE

6. Deselect the arrows, then drag the bottom arrow about 3 inches to the left.

7. Reselect the arrows, then click [图] again. Now the arrows are evenly spaced horizontally, but they are not aligned.

8. Click [图].

NOTE
You may want to show students how to display the rulers (View menu, Ruler) to give them a sense of the slide's dimensions and to help them position objects. Rulers are discussed in the next lesson.

NOTE
Remind students how to use the Format AutoShape dialog box (Position tab) to change the horizontal or vertical position of an object relative to the top left corner.

LESSON 8 ■ **MANIPULATING POWERPOINT OBJECTS**

EXERCISE 8-6 Align Objects Relative to the Slide

The Relative to Slide button makes it easy to center an object horizontally or vertically on a slide. For example, you can center a text box perfectly. You can also use the Relative to Slide setting to distribute objects evenly across a slide from edge to edge.

1. Still working on slide 2, select the bulleted text box.
2. Click the Relative to Slide button on the Align or Distribute toolbar to turn on that option.

3. Click the Align Center button . The text box is centered horizontally on the slide.

FIGURE 8-3
Objects horizontally aligned and distributed

4. Click the Align Middle button . The text box is now also centered vertically on the slide.
5. With Relative to Slide still turned on, select all four arrows at the bottom of the screen.
6. Click Distribute Horizontally . Now the arrows are evenly spaced across the entire width of the slide.

EXERCISE 8-7 Flip Objects on a Slide

Use the rotate or flip tools on a single object or a group of objects. Some of the things you can rotate or flip are drawn objects, text boxes, and WordArt.

1. To display the Rotate or Flip toolbar, click Draw on the Drawing toolbar, point to Rotate or Flip, and drag the submenu's title bar to float the toolbar.

2. Select the four arrows at the bottom of slide 2, if necessary. Click the Rotate Right button . The arrows point down.
3. Click the Flip Vertical button . The arrows are flipped vertically and now point up. If the arrows extend past the bottom edge of the slide, use Align Bottom or the Up arrow key on your keyboard to move the arrows up.

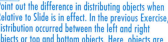

Point out the difference in distributing objects when Relative to Slide is in effect. In the previous Exercise, distribution occurred between the left and right objects or top and bottom objects. Here, objects are distributed evenly between the slide's edges.

In PowerPoint Classroom Presentation #8.

UNIT 3 ■ CUSTOMIZING A PRESENTATION

4. Select the WordArt title, "Objectives."
5. Click the Rotate Left button to place the WordArt on its side.
6. If necessary, click Relative to Slide button to turn it on. Click Align Middle, and then click Align Left. The WordArt is now centered vertically and aligned with the left edge of the slide.
7. With the WordArt still selected, use the right arrow key on your keyboard to move the WordArt to the left so it's centered between the left edge of the slide and the text box.

FIGURE 8-4
Rotated and flipped objects

Objective 3
Grouping and Ungrouping Objects

You can use grouping to "glue" two or more objects together so they behave as one object. If you then move one member of a group, all the other members move with it. Grouping assures that objects meant to stay together don't accidentally get moved individually or deleted. When you need to work on an individual member of a group, you can ungroup the objects, make your changes, then regroup them.

EXERCISE 8-8 Group Objects

1. Still working on slide 2, delete the arrow furthest to the left, then select the three remaining arrows at the bottom of the slide. Notice the three sets of resize handles.
2. Choose Group from the Draw menu. Now there is only one set of resize handles, indicating that all three arrows are grouped as a single object.

In PowerPoint Classroom Presentation #8.

244

LESSON 8 ■ **MANIPULATING POWERPOINT OBJECTS**

FIGURE 8-5
Objects after grouping

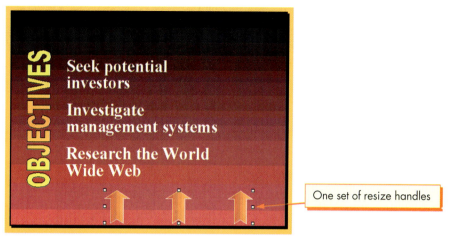

3. *Deselect the object. Drag the left arrow up just below the text of the last bullet. All the arrows move up.*
4. *Click Rotate Left, then decrease the zoom setting so you can see all three arrows. The three arrows rotate as one unit.*
5. *Use Align Middle to center the arrows vertically (relative to the slide), then use Align Right to right-align them.*
6. *With the group of arrows still selected, use the left arrow key to move the arrows so they are centered between the right edge of the slide and the text box.*
7. *Increase the zoom setting to Fit.*

EXERCISE 8-9 Ungroup Objects

You can ungroup objects to change their relative position or to change the formatting of individual members of the group.

1. *Still working on slide 2, right-click the group of arrows and choose Grouping from the shortcut menu. Choose Ungroup from the submenu. Individual resize handles are displayed for each object.*
2. *To make sure the selected arrows are spaced vertically, turn on Relative to Slide, if necessary, and click Distribute Vertically.*
3. *Deselect the arrows (they are ungrouped now) and use the Format Painter tool to copy the shading form the WordArt object to the middle arrow. (The remaining arrows should keep their orange-to-red shading.)*
4. *Select all the arrows again. Choose Regroup from the Draw menu to group the objects again.*

In PowerPoint Classroom Presentation #8.

245

UNIT 3 ■ CUSTOMIZING A PRESENTATION

5. With the arrows still selected, use the Size tab in the Format Object dialog box to change the height of the grouped object to 4 inches. Then distribute the group again vertically relative to the slide. As you can see, grouped objects behave as a single object in many ways.

FIGURE 8-6
Completed slide 2

6. Close both floating toolbars.

Objective 4
Working with Layers of Objects

Although objects appear to be drawn on one surface, each of a slide's objects actually exists as a separate layer. Imagine that the objects are drawn on individual sheets of transparent plastic stacked on top of one another. When you rearrange the sheets, different objects appear on the top, sometimes hiding parts of the objects beneath them. The most recently drawn object is added to the top of the stack.

Within a stack of objects, you can move an individual object backward and forward in the following ways:

- Move an object to the bottom of the stack.
- Move an object down one layer in the stack.
- Bring an object to the top of the stack.
- Bring an object forward one layer in the stack.

EXERCISE 8-10 Create Overlapping Objects

1. Move to slide 3. Draw a large rectangle that covers the text box below the title. The rectangle fill hides the text box.

In PowerPoint Classroom Presentation #8.

Objective 4 Assignment:
Exercises 8-20 (Skills Review) and 8-23 (Lesson Applications) can be assigned after completing Objective 4.

246

LESSON 8 ■ **MANIPULATING POWERPOINT OBJECTS**

NOTE

2. Click D<u>r</u>aw on the Drawing toolbar, choose O<u>r</u>der, and float the Order submenu.

3. Click the Send to Back button on the Order toolbar. The rectangle moves behind the text and the text is once again visible.

4. With the rectangle selected, use the D<u>r</u>aw menu to change the AutoShape to a notched right arrow (on the Block <u>A</u>rrows menu, second shape in the fifth row). Resize the shape and move its adjustment handle so it looks like the arrow in Figure 8-7.

FIGURE 8-7
Overlapping text and object

NOTE

NOTE: To manipulate an object that is located behind several other objects, you must send the top objects to the back one at a time until the desired object is on top.

Objective 5

Applying Object Shadows and 3-D Effects

You can add interest and depth to an object by applying shadows and 3-D effects. You apply these effects using the Shadow button and 3-D button on the Drawing toolbar. Each button displays a menu of 20 shadow and 3-D effects and each effect can be individually customized.

EXERCISE 8-11 Apply a Shadow Effect

FIGURE 8-8
Shadow menu

NOTE

1. Move to slide 1 and select the quad-arrow object under the subtitle.

2. Click the Shadow button on the Drawing toolbar to display a menu of shadow effects.

3. Choose Shadow Style 1, which is the first style in the first row. A strong black shadow appears.

NOTE
When objects are close together, it may be difficult to select a specific object. Explain that you may have to move or send an object back so the object resize handles are distinct.

NOTE
In PowerPoint Classroom Presentation #8.

NOTE
Make sure students understand that an object completely hidden behind another object cannot be selected until the topmost object is sent backward or to the bottom of the stack.

NOTE
This is the first time the Shadow button on the Drawing toolbar is used. Make sure students do not confuse this with the Shadow button on the Formatting toolbar.

247

UNIT 3 ■ CUSTOMIZING A PRESENTATION

4. Click ■ again and choose Shadow Style 3. This shadow style is even more dramatic. Each style orients the position and the depth of the shadow in a different way. Try several other shadow styles.

5. Change back to Shadow Style 1.

 NOTE: Some of the shadow styles may change the shadow standard color from black to gray. You learn how to change the shadow color in the next exercise.

EXERCISE 8-12 Customize a Shadow

1. Select the quad-arrow object, if necessary.
2. Click ■ and choose <u>S</u>hadow Settings. The Shadow Settings toolbar is displayed. You use the buttons on this toolbar to control the angle and color of the shadow.

3. Click the Nudge Shadow Up button ■ four times. Notice that each time you click the button, the shadow moves up slightly.
4. Click the Nudge Shadow Left button ■ twice. The shadow gradually moves to the left each time you click the button.
5. Click the arrow on the Shadow Color button ■▼ and choose another shadow color.
6. Click ↶▼ to change the shadow back to black.
7. Click the arrow next to ■▼ again and click <u>S</u>emitransparent Shadow. The shadow color is lightened.

FIGURE 8-9
Object with shadow effects applied

8. Close the Shadow Settings toolbar.

In PowerPoint Classroom Presentation #8.

248

LESSON 8 ■ **MANIPULATING POWERPOINT OBJECTS**

EXERCISE 8-13 Choose a 3-D Effect

1. Still working on slide 1, select the WordArt title, "Marketing Strategy."
2. Click the 3-D button on the Drawing toolbar to display a menu of 3-D effects.

FIGURE 8-10
3-D menu

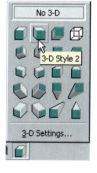

3. Choose 3-D Style 2. A dramatic 3-D effect is applied to the object.
4. Click again and choose 3-D Style 18. Notice that some 3-D styles rotate the object and create depth. Try other styles and note the differences. Like shadows, use these effects sparingly.
5. Reapply 3-D Style 2.

EXERCISE 8-14 Customize a 3-D Effect

1. With the WordArt on slide 1 still selected, click and choose 3-D Settings. You use the 3-D Settings toolbar to change the color, angle of rotation depth, and other features of the 3-D effect. These tools are fun to play with. Try them on all types of objects, not just WordArt.

FIGURE 8-11
3-D Settings toolbar

2. Click the Tilt Up button twice. The angle of the object is shifted up, decreasing its depth.
3. Click 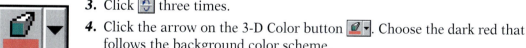 three times.
4. Click the arrow on the 3-D Color button 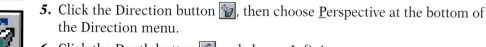. Choose the dark red that follows the background color scheme.
5. Click the Direction button, then choose Perspective at the bottom of the Direction menu.
6. Click the Depth button and choose Infinity.
7. Close the 3-D Settings toolbar.
8. Change the black and white settings for the 3-D WordArt title to inverse grayscale.
9. Drag the quad arrow on top of the "Good 4 U" subtitle.

In PowerPoint Classroom Presentation #8.

NOTE
Point out that shadow and 3-D effects can be quite similar, depending on the object.

NOTE
You may want to have students experiment with the various buttons on the 3-D Settings toolbar. Remind them to use Undo to reverse their actions after they try each effect.

249

UNIT 3 ■ CUSTOMIZING A PRESENTATION

10. Right-click the quad arrow and choose O<u>r</u>der from the shortcut menu. Choose Send to Bac<u>k</u>, placing the quad arrow behind the text.

FIGURE 8-12
3-D and shadow effects on slide 1

11. Select both the subtitle text and the quad arrow, and center them horizontally relative to the slide.

12. Move the quad arrow and subtitle text down on the slide about 1 inch. Adjust the position of the WordArt title, if necessary.

✓ Objective 6
Using the Duplicate Command

The Duplicate command is an ideal tool for creating evenly spaced objects, either in a straight row or at an angle. Duplicated objects can overlap one another or be spaced apart.

To duplicate objects, choose Dupl<u>i</u>cate from the <u>E</u>dit menu or press [Ctrl]+[D].

EXERCISE 8-15 Use the Duplicate Command

1. Move to slide 4. Draw a small notched right arrow to the left of "Determine methods." Using the Format Painter, copy the formatting from the WordArt "Evaluating Results" to the notched right arrow.

2. Align the middles of the arrow and the text box relative to each other. (Select both objects, turn off Relative to <u>S</u>lide, if necessary, and click the Align Middle button on the Align or Distribute toolbar.)

3. Group the text box and the notched arrow.

4. Choose Dupl<u>i</u>cate from the <u>E</u>dit menu or press [Ctrl]+[D]. A copy appears slightly offset from the original.

NOTE

5. Being careful not to deselect the copy, use the four-headed arrow pointer to drag it down and to the right about 0.5 inch. (You can also use the arrow keys on your keyboard.)

In PowerPoint Classroom Presentation #8.

✓ **Objective 6 Assignment:**
Exercises 8-21 (Skills Review) and 8-24 (Lesson Applications) can be assigned after completing Objective 6.

NOTE
In step 5, when students position the duplicate object, they should be careful not to deselect it. If they do, the Duplicate command will not copy the object with the specified spacing. In that case, they need to begin again.

250

LESSON 8 ■ **MANIPULATING POWERPOINT OBJECTS**

> **NOTE:** The Duplicate command works only if the duplicate copy remains selected. As soon as it is deselected, the command is no longer in effect. If that happens, delete the duplicate and start again.

6. Press `Ctrl`+`D`. A second copy appears, which is offset the same amount as the first copy.

7. Press `Ctrl`+`D` again. You should now have four copies on the slide.

FIGURE 8-13
Creating duplicates

8. Change the text in the duplicated text boxes as shown in Figure 8-13.

9. Select all the text boxes and arrows (everything on the slide except the WordArt title).

10. Group the selection and center it horizontally relative to the slide.

Objective 7
Advanced Clip Art Editing

NOTE   In Lesson 6, you learned how to crop a clip art image, and in Lesson 7, you learned how to recolor an image. Many clip art images can be ungrouped, so you can treat individual parts of the image like ordinary PowerPoint objects. Once clip art is ungrouped, or disassembled, you can delete an individual part of the image or change the color of just one part.

EXERCISE **8-16** **Disassemble a Clip Art Image**

NOTE
1. Move to slide 5. Insert the clip art image with the four circling arrows that you can find using the keywords "Harmony Teamwork." Change its height and width to 2.5 inches and move it below the text on the slide.

2. Ungroup the clip art image using Ungroup on the Draw menu (or on the shortcut menu). A dialog box opens, asking if you want to convert the object to a PowerPoint drawing. When you convert a clip art picture to a PowerPoint drawing, you can manipulate its components as if they are AutoShapes or freeform objects.

In PowerPoint Classroom Presentation #8.

Objective 7 Assignment:
Exercise 8-22 (Skills Review) and Exercises 8-25 and 8-26 (Lesson Applications) can be assigned after completing Objective 7.

NOTE
Point out that many complex clip art pictures must be ungrouped repeatedly before their smallest elements can be selected.

NOTE
Remind students how to size clip art proportionally using the Format Picture dialog box.

251

UNIT 3 ■ CUSTOMIZING A PRESENTATION

3. Click Yes. The circling arrows now appear as separate objects with their own resize handles.
4. Deselect the objects.

EXERCISE 8-17 Formatting Parts of a Clip Art Image

1. Select the purple arrow in the upper half of the circle.
2. Change it to a one-color, turquoise, horizontal shade, using the upper left variant.

FIGURE 8-14
Clip art image after making changes

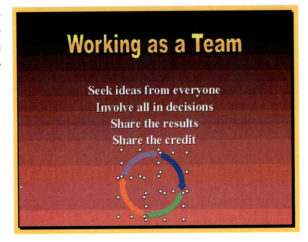

3. Select the blue arrow in upper half of the circle. Change it to a one-color, orange, horizontal shade, using the upper left variant.
4. Use Format Painter to change the fill of the remaining arrows in the circle, alternating the colors turquoise and orange.

EXERCISE 8-18 Regroup and Rotate a Clip Art Image

1. Draw a selection box around the entire circle of arrows to select all the objects.

2. Group the clip art image parts.
3. With the object still selected, click on the Drawing toolbar and rotate the image clockwise until the turquoise arrows appear at the top and bottom of the circle.

   NOTE: If you rotate multiple objects that are not grouped, the objects rotate independently of one another.

4. In the middle of the circle, add a floating text box with the text **Good 4 U** in 28-point Times New Roman bold. Make the "4" two fonts sizes larger than the rest of the text.

In PowerPoint Classroom Presentation #8.

NOTE
At step 2, stress to students that once they ungroup clip art to convert it to a PowerPoint drawing, they must then group the picture before it can be rotated.

252

LESSON 8 ■ **MANIPULATING POWERPOINT OBJECTS**

5. Center the text box inside the circle.
6. Draw a selection box around both the circle and text box and group them into a single object. Center the grouped object horizontally on the slide.

FIGURE 8-15
Completed clip art image

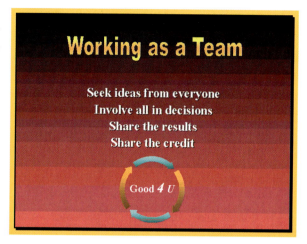

7. Close the floating toolbars that you opened during this lesson. Let the Common Tasks toolbar remain open. (If it is closed, use the <u>V</u>iew menu to reopen it.)
8. Check spelling in the presentation.
9. Move to slide 1 and switch to Black and White view. Change the black and white setting of the quad arrow object to black with white fill.
10. Scroll through the presentation and check the black and white settings for the balance of the presentation. Make any necessary changes.
11. Save the presentation as *[your initials]***8-18.ppt**.
12. Create a handout header with the date and your name and a handout footer with the page number and filename.
13. Print the presentation as handouts, 6 slides per page, black and white, framed.
14. Save and close the presentation.

COMMAND SUMMARY

NOTE

FEATURE	BUTTON	MENU	KEYBOARD
Select all objects		<u>E</u>dit, Select A<u>l</u>l	Ctrl + A
Group objects		<u>D</u>raw, <u>G</u>roup	Ctrl + Shift + G
Ungroup objects		<u>D</u>raw, <u>U</u>ngroup	Ctrl + Shift + H
Duplicate		<u>E</u>dit, Dup<u>l</u>icate	Ctrl + D

In PowerPoint Classroom Presentation #8.

NOTE
Point out that the Command Summary lists a variety of ways to accomplish a particular task. Students can decide which method they prefer to use.

253

UNIT 3 ■ CUSTOMIZING A PRESENTATION

USING HELP

NOTE PowerPoint provides extensive help for all facets of working with objects. If you're unsure about such features as aligning, distributing, or grouping objects, use Help for clarification.

Explore Help Contents for topics on manipulating objects:

1. Open Help Contents by choosing Contents and Index from the Help menu and clicking the Contents tab.
2. Double-click the topic "Drawing and Working with Objects."
3. Double-click the topic "Arranging, Aligning, and Positioning Objects."
4. Double-click "Ways to arrange objects."

FIGURE 8-16
Help screen for arranging objects

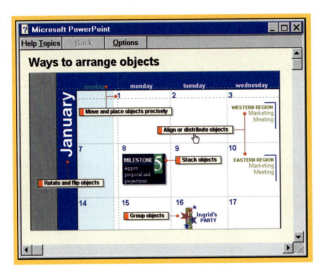

5. Point to and click the topics in the Help window.
6. Close Help when you finish.

NOTE
Encourage students to follow the steps in "Using Help." Software companies are increasingly using their online Help programs—rather than printed documentation—to train users and assist in answering user questions.

In PowerPoint Classroom Presentation #8.

LESSON 8 ■ **MANIPULATING POWERPOINT OBJECTS**

TEST BANK

Concepts Review

TRUE/FALSE QUESTIONS

Each of the following statements is either true or false. Indicate your choice by circling **T** or **F**.

T **(F)** 1. You cannot use selection rectangles to select multiple objects.

(T) F 2. The Bring Forward command brings objects forward one layer at a time.

(T) F 3. If you continually click the Rotate Left button, the object eventually returns to its original position.

T **(F)** 4. To select multiple objects, press Ctrl while clicking each object.

T **(F)** 5. You cannot create a series of evenly spaced objects on a diagonal using the Duplicate command.

(T) F 6. There are 20 different 3-D effects that you can apply to an object.

T **(F)** 7. You cannot change the color of shadows.

(T) F 8. The keyboard command to select all objects on a slide is Ctrl+A.

SHORT ANSWER QUESTIONS

Write the correct answer in the space provided.

1. On what layer does the most recently drawn object appear?
   Top

2. What appears when you drag the mouse to select multiple objects?
   Selection rectangle

3. Which tool do you use to flip an object left to right?
   Flip Horizontal

4. To select multiple objects with the mouse, which key do you press while clicking?
   Shift

5. Which command separates combined objects?
   Draw, Ungroup

Concepts Review:
Allows students to check their understanding.

TEST BANK
Consider using the Test Bank to provide an additional review of lesson concepts.

255

UNIT 3 ■ CUSTOMIZING A PRESENTATION

6. Which align option do you select to horizontally align the bottom edges of multiple objects?
   Align Bottom

7. Which command do you use to place an object at the top of a stack?
   Draw, Order, Bring to Front

8. What do you need to do to a clip art image before you can remove an unwanted element?
   Disassemble or Ungroup it

CRITICAL THINKING

Answer these questions on a separate page. There are no right or wrong answers. Support your answers with examples from your own experience, if possible.

1. In this lesson you learned how to work with layers of objects. Which objects might you place on top of each other? When would you find it useful to overlap them?

2. Think of the way you used the Duplicate command to add evenly spaced objects to your slide. In what other ways could you use this feature? Which objects would you duplicate?

Skills Review

EXERCISE 8-19

Select multiple objects, and align, flip, and distribute objects.

1. Open the file **Cook3.ppt**.
2. Select multiple objects by following these steps:
   a. On slide 1, click one of the small green diamonds below the subtitle.
   b. Press and hold [Shift] while clicking the remaining two diamonds.
   c. With all diamonds selected, change the fill color to black.
3. Align and distribute the selected diamonds by following these steps:
   a. Click D<u>r</u>aw on the Drawing toolbar and point to <u>A</u>lign or Distribute.
   b. Float the Align or Distribute submenu by dragging its gray title bar.

Critical Thinking Questions:
Answers will vary based on students' preferences, observations, experiences, and research.

Skills Review:
Provides guided practice for students. Objectives are indicated for each Exercise.

Exercise 8-19:
Objectives 1, 2
Required File: Cook3.ppt
Solution File: gl8-19.ppt in Solutions Manual or on Solutions Disk

256

LESSON 8 ■ **MANIPULATING POWERPOINT OBJECTS**

   c. If necessary, turn off the Relative to Slide option by clicking it on the Align or Distribute toolbar.

   d. Click the Align Top button.

   e. Click the Distribute Horizontally button.

4. Use a selection rectangle to select multiple objects by following these steps:

   a. Move the pointer to the upper right corner of slide 1.

   b. Drag the pointer diagonally down and to the left, drawing a dotted box large enough to surround the cluster of red squares in the upper right corner. (Don't include the single red square on the left side of the slide.)

   c. To add the last red square to the group, press and hold Shift while clicking the square on the left side of the slide.

   d. Change the fill color of the selected squares to black.

5. Align and distribute objects relative to the slide by following these steps:

   a. Click Relative to Slide on the Align or Distribute toolbar to turn it on.

   b. Reselect all the black squares, if necessary.

   c. Click the Align Top button.

   d. Click Distribute Horizontally. You should have a series of evenly spaced, black squares along the top edge of the slide. If not, click several times and try again.

6. With all the black squares still selected, copy and paste them. Drag the pasted group of selected squares down and to the right to form a checkerboard pattern.

7. Deselect the squares. Copy just one square and paste it on the left end of the second row to complete the checkerboard pattern.

8. Use the selection rectangle method to select all the squares in both rows. Copy and paste them, and move the pasted copy to the bottom of the slide.

9. Copy and paste the checkerboard pattern to the top and bottom edge of the slide master so all slides in the presentation have the checkerboard pattern. (You don't need to copy the checkerboard pattern to the title master.)

10. Flip and rotate an object by following these steps:

    a. Move to slide 3. Select the red at the bottom of the graph.

    b. Click Draw on the Drawing toolbar and drag the Rotate or Flip submenu's gray title bar to float the Rotate or Flip toolbar.

    c. Click the Flip Horizontal button to make the arrow point to the right.

    d. Click the Rotate Left button to make the arrow point up.

    e. Position the arrow on the right side of the chart between the chart and its legend. Use Figure 8-17 on the next page as a guide.

257

UNIT 3 ■ CUSTOMIZING A PRESENTATION

FIGURE 8-17

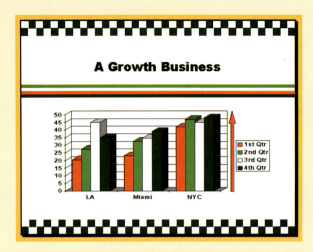

11. Review the black and white settings of your presentation making adjustments where needed.
12. Close all floating toolbars except the Common Tasks toolbar.
13. Check spelling in the presentation.
14. Save the presentation as *[your initials]*__8-19.ppt__.
15. Create a handout header with the date and your name and a handout footer with the page number and filename.
16. Print as handouts, 6 slides per page, black and white, framed.
17. Save and close the presentation.

EXERCISE 8-20

Work with layers of objects and center objects relative to the slide.

1. Open the file **Miami2.ppt**.
2. Draw a constrained Sun AutoShape (found in the sixth row of the Basic Shapes menu). Position the sun on top of the subtitle text. Size the sun to 2 inches high and wide.
3. Change the sun's fill to a two-color, horizontal gradient fill, using the peach color that follows the accent and hyperlink scheme color and the pale yellow that follows the text and lines scheme color. Choose the variant with the darkest color in the middle. Remove the outline from the sun.
4. Display the subtitle text in front of the sun by following these steps:
   a. Click Order on the Draw menu, then drag the submenu's gray title bar to display the Order toolbar.
   b. With the sun selected, click the Send to Back button.

Exercise 8-20:
Objectives 2, 4
Required File: Miami2.ppt
Solution File: gl8-20.ppt in Solutions Manual or on Solutions Disk

LESSON 8 ■ **MANIPULATING POWERPOINT OBJECTS**

5. Copy the sun from slide 1 and paste it on slide 2. Reduce its size proportionally to 1.5 inches wide. Move the sun so it covers the uppercase "G" in the title and send it to the back. Reposition the sun, if necessary, so the "G" is centered inside it. (Hint: Use the arrow keys on your keyboard to fine-tune the sun's position.)

6. Insert a new slide after slide 2 using the Bulleted List layout, with the title **What We Offer** and the following bulleted items:
   - **Beach-front setting**
   - **Patio juice bar**
   - **Boardwalk**
   - **Same great menu**

 NOTE: If you have difficulty seeing the insertion point when keying text, switch to Black and White view.

7. Resize the text placeholder, making it large enough for the text to fit.
8. Center the text box relative to the slide by following these steps:
   a. If necessary, display the Align or Distribute toolbar.
   b. Select the bulleted text box.
   c. Turn on the Relative to Slide option, if necessary.
   d. Click the Align Center button, then click the Align Middle button .
9. Copy the sun from slide 2 and paste it on slide 3. Move it so it covers the "W" in "We," then send it to the back. Adjust its position so the "W" appears centered in the sun.
10. Close all toolbars except the Common Tasks toolbar.
11. Check the presentation's black and white settings and, if necessary, make adjustments so it prints well in black and white. (Hint: The sun will print better in light grayscale.)
12. Check spelling in the presentation.
13. Save the presentation as *[your initials]***8-20.ppt**.
14. Create a handout header with the date and your name and a handout footer with the page number and filename.
15. Print as handouts, 6 slides per page, black and white, framed.
16. Save and close the presentation.

EXERCISE 8-21

Align, group, and duplicate objects; and apply shadow and 3-D effects.

1. Open the file **Media3.ppt**.

Exercise 8-21:
Objectives 1–6
Required File: Media3.ppt
Solution File: gl8-21.ppt in Solutions Manual or on Solutions Disk.

259

2. Move to slide 2, then duplicate the arrow four times by following these steps:

   a. Select the arrow, then press Ctrl+D (or choose Duplicate from the Edit menu).

   b. Being careful not to deselect the duplicated arrow, drag or use the arrow keys to position it as shown in Figure 8-18.

FIGURE 8-18

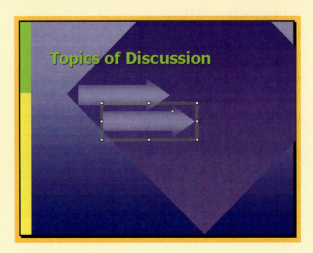

   c. Press Ctrl+D twice more so there are four arrows on the slide.

3. Key the following text inside the arrows:

   Arrow 1: **Quality**

   Arrow 2: **Frequency**

   Arrow 3: **Effectiveness**

   Arrow 4: **Cost**

4. Apply a 3-D effect to the arrows by following these steps:

   a. Select all four arrows.

   b. Click the 3-D button on the Drawing toolbar, then choose 3-D Style 2 from the submenu.

   c. Click 3-D again and click 3-D Settings.

   d. On the 3-D Settings toolbar, click the Direction button, and choose Perspective.

   e. Click the Depth button and choose 72 pt.

5. Change the order of the arrows to reveal the hidden part of the arrowheads, by following these steps:

   a. If necessary, deselect all the arrows then select just the third one, which contains the text "Effectiveness."

LESSON 8 ■ MANIPULATING POWERPOINT OBJECTS

     b. Choose O_r_der on the D_r_aw menu, then float the Order menu.

     c. Click the Bring to Front button 🗇.

     d. Click the arrow with the text "Frequency" and click 🗇 again.

     e. Click the arrow with the text "Quality" and click 🗇 again.

6. Group the four arrows by following these steps:

     a. Select all four arrows.

     b. Choose _G_roup from the D_r_aw menu.

7. Move the group of arrows down and to the left so the tails of the arrows extend slightly to the left of the diamond.

8. On slide 4, select the four green dots. Align their tops and distribute them evenly among themselves. Group the four green dots.

9. Still working on slide 4, select the title text box and the green dots. Align their middles so the green dots appear to be part of the title.

10. Apply a shadow effect to the title text and the green dots by following these steps:

     a. If necessary, select both the green dots and the title text box.

     b. Click the Shadow button 🔲.

     c. Choose Shadow Style 6 (the second style on the second row).

11. Change the shadow color by following these steps:

     a. With the title and green dots still selected, click 🔲 once again.

     b. Click _S_hadow Settings at the bottom of the Shadow menu to display the Shadow Settings toolbar.

     c. Click the arrow next to Shadow Color 🔲▾ and choose navy blue, following the background color scheme.

12. Place the text box on slide 4 (which contains the 3 lines of text) so it's framed appropriately within the diamond.

13. Check the slides in Black and White view and make necessary adjustments.

14. Close all floating toolbars that you opened for this exercise. Leave the Common Tasks toolbar open.

15. Check spelling in the presentation.

16. Save the presentation as *[your initials]***8-21.ppt**.

17. Create a handout header with the date and your name and a handout footer with the page number and filename.

18. Print as handouts, 6 slides per page, black and white, framed.

19. Save and close the presentation.

261

UNIT 3 ■ CUSTOMIZING A PRESENTATION

EXERCISE 8-22

Duplicate objects and disassemble clip art images.

1. Open the file **Open3.ppt**.
2. On the slide master, insert the beach umbrella clip art image that you can find by using the keyword "Tropics." Move the image to the lower right corner and make it about twice its original size.
3. Edit the clip art image by following these steps:
   a. Select the clip art image, if necessary, and choose Ungroup from the Draw menu.
   b. Click Yes in the dialog box that asks if you want to convert the object.
   c. Without deselecting any of the parts, regroup the clip art image.
   d. With the picture regrouped, display the Rotate or Flip toolbar and flip the image horizontally so the umbrella points in the opposite direction.
   e. Copy the beach umbrella image to the title master.
4. On slide 1, draw a constrained Sun AutoShape (on the sixth row of the Basic Shapes menu) that is four inches wide. Change the sun's fill to a two-color gradient, shading from the center, using yellow and pale beige. Choose the variant with the yellow in the center. Remove the lines.
5. Center the sun over the title and subtitle and send it to the back.
6. On slide 2, create a floating text box with the text **A health-conscious restaurant**. Format the text as 28-point Arial bold.
7. Still working on slide 2, draw a 0.75 inch constrained Sun AutoShape. Place the sun to the left of the text box. Don't change the sun's fill or outline—it should be yellow with a dark brown outline. Use Figure 8-19 on the next page as a guide for the sun and the text box.
8. Align the middles of the sun and the text box, then group them.
9. Copy the group to the Clipboard, then paste it three times, allowing the copies to remain where they are pasted.
10. Drag one copy of the sun, positioning it approximately two inches from the bottom edge of the slide, roughly aligned with the first copy.
11. Select all the sun/text combinations and distribute them vertically relative to each other. If the spacing doesn't look correct, move the bottom line up or down a small amount, then vertically redistribute them. Then left align the sun/text combinations.
12. Edit lines 2 through 4 as shown in Figure 8-19.

Exercise 8-22:
Objectives 1–4, 6, 7
Required Files: Open3.ppt and clip art file
sandtoys.wmf (see page xiv for clip art file locations and instructions)
Solution File: gl8-22.ppt in Solutions Manual or on Solutions Disk.

FIGURE 8-19

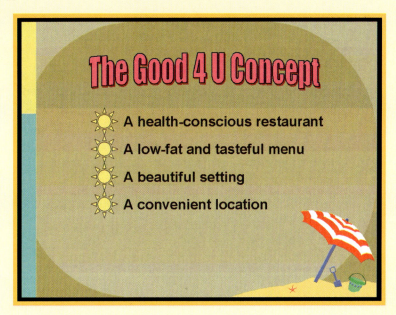

13. Group all four lines, then adjust the group's position on the slide, if necessary.
14. Copy the grouped text and paste it on slide 3. Ungroup the copied text and delete the last line. Edit the three remaining lines to show the following text:

    Line 1: **Beach front**

    Line 2: **Patio juice bar**

    Line 3: **Boardwalk**
15. Move the three lines so they are centered under the title.
16. Copy the sun AutoShape from slide 1 and paste it on slide 4. Center the text and sun relative to the slide and send the sun to the back. If necessary, adjust the text position so it appears centered on top of the sun.
17. Check the slides in Black and White view and make necessary adjustments.
18. Check spelling in the presentation.
19. Save the presentation as *[your initials]***8-22.ppt**.
20. Create a handout header with the date and your name and a handout footer with the page number and filename.
21. Print as handouts, 6 slides per page, black and white, framed.
22. Save and close the presentation.

UNIT 3 ■ CUSTOMIZING A PRESENTATION

Lesson Applications

EXERCISE 8-23

Select, align, and layer multiple objects, and group and ungroup objects.

1. Open the file **Franch2.ppt**.
2. On the title master, select all the tiny diamonds. Align their tops relative to each other. Then distribute them evenly relative to themselves. Group the diamonds and center the group horizontally relative to the slide.
3. Copy the group of diamonds and paste them on the slide master. Position the diamonds just below the horizontal group of stripes and wavy lines.
4. Still working on the slide master, change the first level bullet to the small diamond from the Symbol font. Make it 75% of the font size.
5. On the title master, ungroup the group of diamonds, then select one random diamond near the center of the group and change its color to light blue. Regroup the diamonds, including the light blue diamond. Change the black and white setting for the group of diamonds to inverse grayscale.
6. Change the presentation's background to a two-color, horizontal gradient fill, using shading that is black at the top and the dark blue that follows the background scheme color on the bottom.
7. On slide 1, position the large diamond over the subtitle and send it to the back. Center the diamond and the subtitle vertically relative to each other, then center both objects horizontally relative to the slide. Move both objects down so they're centered between the row of diamonds and the bottom of the slide.
8. On slide 2, adjust the bullet text box size to fit the text, then horizontally center the text box on the slide.
9. On slide 3, reduce the width of the bullet text box to 6.75 inches, reduce the font size to 28 points, and center the text box horizontally on the slide. Make the same changes to the text box on slide 4.
10. On slide 5, change the color of the diamond to the lavender that follows the accent and hyperlink scheme color and apply a text shadow. Group the text box and the diamond and center them horizontally on the slide. Center the group between the row of diamonds and the bottom of the slide.
11. Check the presentation's black and white settings and make adjustments if necessary.
12. Close all floating toolbars that you may have opened.

Assessment Resources:
- Solutions Manual
- Test Bank with Software
- Portfolio Builder
- Alternative Assessment Guide
- Certification Procedures

Lesson Applications:
Provide independent practice for students. Objectives are indicated for each Exercise.

Exercise 8-23:
Objectives 1–4
Required File: Franch2.ppt
Solution File: gl8-23.ppt in Solutions Manual or on Solutions Disk.

LESSON 8 ■ MANIPULATING POWERPOINT OBJECTS

13. Check spelling in the presentation.
14. Save the presentation as *[your initials]*__8-23.ppt__.
15. Create a handout header with the date and your name and a handout footer with the page number and filename.
16. Print as handouts, 6 slides per page, black and white, framed.
17. Save and close the presentation.

EXERCISE 8-24

Work with slide master objects, layers, shadows, and 3-D effects.

1. Open the file **Hiring2.ppt**.
2. Delete all graphic elements on the slide master as well as the title master. Only the text placeholders should remain.
3. On the title master, draw a 0.25 inch circle, creating a small dot in the center of the slide. Make the dot dark pink, the color that follows the accent and hyperlink scheme color. Remove the outline from the dot, and give it a shadow using Style 8.
4. Copy the dot you just created and duplicate it fifteen times, so you have a total of 16 dots. Select all the dots, then align their tops relative to each other. Distribute the dots horizontally relative to the slide. You should now have a line of evenly spaced dots across the middle of the title master.
5. Group the dots.
6. Select the title placeholder, the group of dots, and the subtitle placeholder, and distribute them vertically relative to each other (not to the slide). This spaces the line of dots evenly between the two placeholders.
7. Copy the group of dots and paste it to the slide master, between the title placeholder and the bullet text placeholder.
8. Move the bullet text placeholder down 0.5 inch to add some extra space for the dots.
9. Change the bullet shape for all the bullets in the placeholder to the fifth arrow in the bottom row of the Monotype Sorts bullets. Change their color to bright green.
10. With the bullet text placeholder selected, apply shadow Style 14 to the entire placeholder.
11. Change the slide master's title text to the custom purple on the second row of text colors. Change the font to Arial Black and apply Shadow Style 14 to the text.

Exercise 8-24:
Objectives 1–3, 5–7
Required File: Hiring2.ppt
Solution File: gl8-24.ppt in Solutions Manual or on Solutions Disk.

The completed presentation for this Exercise may be used in a student's portfolio.

265

UNIT 3 ■ CUSTOMIZING A PRESENTATION

12. On slide 1, delete the title and title placeholder. Above the row of dots, create a WordArt title with the words "New Employee Orientation." Use the fifth WordArt style on the second row (the dark blue one). Make the font 54-point Impact and change its fill color to the custom purple color on the second row of samples. Change the WordArt shadow to Shadow Style 8 and change the shadow color to black. (Hint: Shadow color is on the Shadow Settings toolbar.)

13. Draw a rounded rectangle where the subtitle would appear. Make the rectangle 1 inch high and 3.5 inches wide. Apply a black, one-color horizontal gradient fill with the darkest color at the top. Adjust the shading intensity so the bottom is the same shade as the top of the slide's background. Remove the line around the rectangle.

14. Inside the rectangle, key **Good 4 U** in bright green, 44-point Times New Roman bold. Make the "4 U" italicized and make the "4" two font sizes bigger.

15. Apply the second 3-D style to the rectangle, change its direction to Perspective, change its depth to 72 pt., and change its color to purple.

16. On slide 2, reapply the Bulleted Text AutoLayout so the text shading takes effect. Change the second bullet to read **Company Vision**. Resize the bullet text box so it just fits the text, then center the text box vertically and horizontally on the slide.

17. On slide 3, reapply the Bulleted Text AutoLayout. Resize the text box to 6 inches wide and center it horizontally on the slide.

18. On slide 4, reapply the Bulleted Text AutoLayout, then key the following text in the bulleted text placeholder:

    ➡ **Reinforce our message of healthy living**

    ➡ **Describe our new franchising philosophy**

    ➡ **Encourage fresh ideas from new employees**

19. Make the text box 5.5 inches wide and center it horizontally on the slide.

20. Check the presentation's black and white settings and make adjustments where necessary.

21. Check spelling in the presentation.

22. Save the presentation as *[your initials]***8-24.ppt**.

23. Create a handout header with the date and your name and a handout footer with the page number and filename.

24. Print as handouts, 6 slides per page, black and white, framed.

25. Save and close the presentation.

LESSON 8 ■ MANIPULATING POWERPOINT OBJECTS

EXERCISE 8-25

Group and ungroup objects, align and distribute objects, work with layers, and edit clip art.

1. Open the file **Cook4.ppt**.
2. Apply the **Contemporary Portrait.pot** design template to the presentation. Change the template's color scheme to the first sample in the second row of the standard color scheme dialog box. Customize the color scheme by changing the title text color to black. Apply the new scheme to all slides.
3. Reapply the AutoLayouts for each slide in the presentation so the colors for the new scheme take effect.
4. On slide 1, center-align the subtitle inside its text box, then resize the text box size to fit the text. Center the subtitle text horizontally relative to the slide.
5. Select the carrot clip art image on slide 1, then zoom to 150%. Disassemble (ungroup) the carrot, then select just the orange part and ungroup it again. Change the fill color of the light part of the carrot to a brighter shade of orange. Change the fill color of the brown part of the carrot to dark orange.
6. Select the stem part of the carrot and increase its line thickness to 1½ points. Restore the zoom to Fit, select the entire carrot, and group all its parts.
7. Increase the carrot's size proportionately, making it 3 inches tall, and rotate it to the right 60 degrees. Position the carrot underneath the text "What's Cooking?"
8. Make the apple slightly smaller and move it from the upper right corner to the middle of the carrot, hiding part of it.
9. Insert the grapes clip art image that you can find using the keywords "Fruits Grapes." Choose the image with the large, light lavender grapes. Make the grapes image twice its original size and move it to the left of the apple.
10. Select the carrot and bring it forward one step so it is on a layer between the apple and the grapes. Adjust the position of the three images to look like the example in Figure 8-20 (on the next page).
11. Group the three images. Copy the group to the slide master (not the title master). Position the image in the lower right corner and decrease its size proportionately, making it 75% of the original size.
12. On slide 2, adjust the size of the bullet text box to fit the text and center it horizontally and vertically relative to the slide.

Exercise 8-25:
Objectives 1–4, 7
Required Files: Cook4.ppt and clip art file grapes6.wmf (see page xiv for clip art file locations and instructions)
Solution File: gl8-25.ppt in Solutions Manual or on Solutions Disk.

The completed presentation for this Exercise may be used in a student's portfolio.

267

UNIT 3 ■ CUSTOMIZING A PRESENTATION

FIGURE 8-20

13. On slide 4, reduce the bullet text by one font size and adjust the size of the text box to fit the text. Delete the clip art placeholder (the coffee cup should remain).
14. Make the coffee cup 2.5 inches high and wide, then select both the text box and the coffee cup and align their middles relative to each other. Move both objects down slightly and distribute them horizontally relative to the slide to improve their spacing.
15. Check spelling in the presentation.
16. Save the presentation as *[your initials]*8-25.ppt.
17. Create a handout header with the date and your name and a handout footer with the page number and filename.
18. Print as handouts, 6 slides per page, black and white, framed.
19. Save and close the presentation.

EXERCISE 8-26

Align and layer objects, edit clip art, and apply 3-D effects.

1. Open the file **Franch3.ppt**.
2. Customize the presentation's color scheme by changing the gray accent and followed hyperlink color to a lighter shade of gray (choose the

Exercise 8-26:
Objectives 1–5, 7
Required File: Franch3.ppt
Solution File: gl8-26.ppt in Solutions Manual or on Solutions Disk.

The completed presentation for this Exercise may be used in a student's portfolio.

LESSON 8 ■ MANIPULATING POWERPOINT OBJECTS

shade to the left of the existing shade on the standard shades honeycomb).

3. Delete the black and white machinery image on the title master and replace it with an appropriate image from the Sports & Leisure category. Make the image approximately the same size as the deleted machinery image.

4. Replace the machinery image on the slide master with another image from the Sports & Leisure category. Size the image to fit in the upper left corner.

5. On slide 1, delete the "Good 4 U" title and its placeholder. In its place, create a WordArt image using the first choice in the first row of the WordArt Gallery. Key **Good 4 U** and format it as 60-point Arial Black. Position the WordArt appropriately and make it approximately 1 inch wider (don't change its height).

6. Apply the 3-D Style 4 (wire frame) to the WordArt. Using the Direction button on the 3-D Settings toolbar, turn on the perspective option and change the direction to the second choice in the bottom row (which places the perspective vanishing point directly behind and slightly above the WordArt image).

7. On slide 2, resize the text box to fit the text and center the text box horizontally and vertically on the slide.

8. Draw a constrained diamond AutoShape on slide 2. Make the shape 4.5 inches wide. Change the fill color to the lightest shade of gray (the one you customized earlier). Remove the lines. Position the diamond on top of the text and send it to the back.

9. Select both the diamond and the text box and align their middles and centers relative to each other. Move both objects down on the slide about 0.5 inch.

10. Copy the diamond and paste it to slide 3. Position the diamond on top of the clip art image, then send it to the back. Select the clip art image and display the Picture toolbar, if necessary. Use the Image Control button to choose Grayscale. Click the More Contrast button three times to sharpen the image slightly. Align the centers and middles of the clip art and diamond relative to each other, then move them slightly to the left.

11. Still working on slide 3, adjust the text box size to fit the text, then adjust its vertical position so it is in balance with the graphic images. Your completed slide should look like Figure 8-21 (on the next page).

12. Format slide 5 in the same style as slide 3, then format slide 4 in the same style as slide 2.

13. Check the slides in Black and White view and make necessary adjustments.

NOTE
In steps 3 and 4, students make their own clip art selections for the title and slide masters. You may want to direct them to choose an object for the title master and a person for the slide master or you may want to have them choose specific images. The solution file uses sailing.wmf and sprint.wmf from the MS Office CD-ROM. See page xiv for file locations.

269

UNIT 3 ■ CUSTOMIZING A PRESENTATION

FIGURE 8-21

14. Check spelling in the presentation.
15. Save the presentation as *[your initials]***8-26.ppt**.
16. Create a handout header with the date and your name and a handout footer with the page number and filename.
17. Print as handouts, 6 slides per page, black and white, framed.
18. Save and close the presentation.

Unit 3 Applications

APPLICATION 3-1

Work with clip art; use drawing tools; add gradient fills, patterns, and object shadows; group and order objects; and duplicate objects.

1. Start a new blank presentation and apply the template Facilitating a Meeting found in the Presentations folder. Change the color scheme to the one with the dark blue background. Delete all the graphic elements, including the large diamond, on both the slide and title masters.

2. Change the presentation background to a pattern using the diagonal pattern sample in the bottom row, third from the left. The foreground should be the dark blue that follows the background scheme and the background should be dark purple (the accent and followed hyperlink color). Apply the pattern to all slides.

3. On the title master, draw a rectangle 5.75 inches high and 8.23 inches wide. Apply a diagonal down gradient fill to it, using the same dark blue and purple that you used for the pattern background in step 2. Choose the variant with the lightest color in the middle.

4. Apply an object shadow to the rectangle using Shadow Style 14. Using the Shadow Settings toolbar, make the shadow color dark blue.

5. Draw a constrained 5-point star in the center of the rectangle. Make it dark purple with no outline. Resize the star proportionally so it is almost as high as the rectangle.

6. Center the rectangle and star vertically and horizontally relative to the slide. Group the star and rectangle, then send the objects to the back so the text placeholders are visible. Adjust the size of the title placeholder so it fits inside the rectangle, then horizontally center both the title placeholder and the subtitle placeholder relative to the slide. Change the rectangle and star's black and white setting to inverse gray scale.

7. Still working on the title master, center-align the text within the text placeholders and apply a dark blue object shadow to the text using shadow style 6. (Select both placeholders and use the Shadow button on the Drawing toolbar).

8. Copy the rectangle and star you drew on the title master, paste it to the slide master, and send it to the back. Adjust the text placeholders' size and position so they fit inside the rectangle, then apply the same object shadow and shadow color to the text placeholders that you used on the title master.

9. Create a title slide and three bulleted text slides using the text shown in Figure U3-1.

Assessment Resources:
- Solutions Manual
- Test Bank with Software
- Portfolio Builder
- Alternative Assessment Guide
- Certification Procedures
- Projects Manual
- Mid-Term and Final Exams

Unit Applications:
Provide independent practice of the skills acquired from each lesson in the Unit.

Project:
After students complete Unit 3, you can assign Project #3 from the Projects Manual.

Final Exam:
If your class is on a semester schedule, you can now assign Final Exam 1 from the Mid-Term and Final Exams booklet.

Unit Application 3-1:
Required Files: clip art files dancers.wmf and couple3.wmf (see page xiv for clip art file locations and instructions)
Solution File: glu3-1.ppt in Solutions Manual or on Solutions disk

UNIT 3 ■ CUSTOMIZING A PRESENTATION

FIGURE U3-1

10. On slide 2, center-align the title and bullet text. Remove the bullets.
11. Draw an AutoShape using the Up Ribbon shape (on the Stars and Banners submenu, the first shape in the third line). Make the shape large enough to cover the slide's body text and as wide as the text box. Apply a dark blue and dark purple vertical gradient fill to the ribbon with the lightest color in the middle. Remove the ribbon's outline, then send it to the back so you can see the text. Drag the top adjusting handle to the left until the center part of the ribbon is wide enough to frame the text, then adjust the height of the ribbon. See Figure U3-2 for the finished result.

FIGURE U3-2
Slide 2

UNIT 3 ■ APPLICATIONS

12. On slide 3, center-align the title. Adjust the bulleted text box size to fit the text and center the text box horizontally and vertically relative to the slide.

13. Still working on slide 3, insert the black and white clip art image of two ballroom dancers that you can find using the keyword "dancers" (or the filename Dancers.wmf). Resize the dancers proportionally to 1.5 inches tall, then recolor the image so the black part becomes dark blue and the white part becomes dark purple.

14. Move the dancers to just inside the bottom left corner of the rectangle. Duplicate the dancers 4 times, arranging the copies across the bottom of the rectangle. Align them horizontally relative to each other, then group them and center-align the group relative to the width of the slide.

15. On slide 4, center-align all the text and remove the bullets. Insert the clip art image showing a couple in formal attire that you can find using the keyword "couples" (or the filename Couple3.wmf). Place the image below the text and adjust the brightness down several levels so the image blends better with the background.

16. Review the presentation in Black and White view and make any necessary changes.

17. Check spelling in the presentation.

18. Save the presentation as *[your initials]***u3-1.ppt**.

19. Create a handout header with the date and your name and a handout footer with the page number and filename.

20. Print as handouts, 6 slides per page, black and white, framed.

21. Save and close the presentation.

APPLICATION 3-2

Create and format WordArt objects; group and ungroup objects; insert and recolor clip art; and align, rotate, and flip objects.

1. Start a new blank presentation and apply the template **Dads Tie.pot** found in the Presentation Designs folder. Resize the horizontal striped graphic on the title master to 0.25 inch high, making it a thin horizontal line. Ungroup the graphic twice, then change the color of four randomly selected stripes to bright red. (You will need to choose More Fill Colors.)

2. Regroup the horizontal stripe graphic, then copy it and paste it to the slide master. Don't change the copied position—instead, resize the bullet text placeholder so it starts just below the horizontal stripe.

Unit Application 3-2:
Required File: clip art file pencil1.wmf (see page xiv for clip art file location and instructions)
Solution File: glu3-2.ppt in Solutions Manual or on Solutions disk

273

UNIT 3 ■ CUSTOMIZING A PRESENTATION

3. Delete the vertical striped graphic on the slide master, then horizontally center the title and bullet text placeholders relative to the slide. Change the color of the text placeholder bullets to bright red and change the font to dark blue Arial Black (using the blue that follows the title text scheme color).

4. Create a title slide and two bulleted text slides, as shown in Figure U3-3. Do not key the title text—you'll create WordArt titles in step 5.

FIGURE U3-3

Slide 1
```
Good 4 U
        Restaurant Franchise Opportunities
```

Slide 2
```
Advantages
    ■ Fast-growing market
    ■ Excellent income potential
    ■ Expert training and support
```

Slide 3
```
Objectives
    ■ Help people achieve a healthy lifestyle
    ■ Help you grow a healthy business
```

5. Delete the title text placeholders on each slide, then Create WordArt titles using the title text in Figure U3-3. Choose the fourth WordArt style in the third row (which has multicolor characters and a shadow).

6. Using the Format WordArt dialog box, check the Lock aspect ratio box and then proportionally size each WordArt title to 1.3 inches high. Set the vertical position to 0.8 inches. Center each title horizontally on the slide.

NOTE: The first title appears larger than the others because it has no descending letters (such as "g" and "j" that extend below the text baseline).

7. On the title slide, change the WordArt fill to a vertical 2-color gradient fill using the bright blue that follows the fills scheme color and the dark blue that follows the title text scheme color. Choose the variant with the lighter color in the middle. Outline the WordArt with the dark blue color. Change the WordArt shadow to Shadow Style 4.

8. Using the Format Painter, copy the WordArt formatting to the titles on slides 2 and 3.
9. Resize and reposition bullet text boxes as needed to create a pleasing composition. On slide 1, center-align the subtitle text.
10. On slide 1, insert the horizontal pencil clip art image that you can find using the keyword "pencil". Resize the pencil to 0.1 inch high and 1.5 inches wide.
11. Move the pencil below the subtitle, then ungroup it. Make the body of the pencil red, then regroup it.
12. Rotate the pencil 15 degrees counterclockwise, so the point is lower than the eraser. Copy and paste the pencil, then flip the copy horizontally. Align the middles and centers of the two pencils relative to each other, then group them and center them below the subtitle.
13. Center the subtitle placeholder horizontally, if necessary.
14. Check spelling in the presentation.
15. Save the presentation as *[your initials]***u3-2.ppt**.
16. Create a handout header with the date and your name and a handout footer with the page number and filename.
17. Print as handouts, 6 slides per page, black and white, framed.
18. Save and close the presentation.

APPLICATION 3-3

Recolor and crop clip art, apply fills, align objects, group objects, apply and format object shadows, work with Word Art.

1. Start a blank presentation and apply the template Flyer (standard).pot found in the Presentations folder. Change the slide color scheme to the one with the yellow background.
2. On the title master, delete the diamonds and the orange rectangle behind them, but don't delete the brown horizontal lines. Change the title text and subtitle text font to Arial, then change the subtitle text to the brown color that follows the accent scheme color. Apply a text shadow to the subtitle text.
3. Change the slide master graphics and text formatting to match the title master. Change the first level bullet to the solid round bullet from the Symbol font and change its color to maroon, following the title text scheme color.
4. Insert three runner images of your choice on the title master. You can find the runners using the keyword "run." Make each runner 2 inches tall and place them close together. Align them and space them evenly

Unit Application 3-3:
Required Files: clip art files laward.wmf and firewks.wmf (see page xiv for clip art file locations and instructions)
Solution File: glu3-3.ppt in Solutions Manual or on Solutions disk

The completed presentation for this Application may be used in a student's portfolio.

NOTE
In step 4, students are asked to choose three clip art images of runners. You may want to have them choose specific images. The solution file uses jogger3.wmf, jogger4.wmf, and jogger5.wmf from the MS Office CD-ROM. See page xiv for file locations.

275

relative to each other. They should overlap slightly. Group the three runners, then position them attractively on top of the two horizontal lines, centered horizontally. Copy the runners and paste them on the slide master (on top of the horizontal lines and extending into the bulleted text box).

5. Create a title slide and 3 bulleted text slides using the text shown in Figure U3-4.

FIGURE U3-4

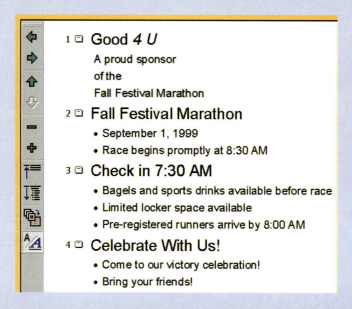

6. On slide 1, increase the title text font to 60 pt and move the text box up slightly. Center-align the subtitle text and move its text box down slightly.

7. On slide 2, center-align the bullet text and remove the bullets. Change the bullet text box to a rounded rectangle. (Hint: Select the text box and use Change AutoShape command on the Draw menu.)

8. Apply a brown outline to the rounded rectangle. It should have the same pale yellow fill color as the background. Apply Shadow Style 2 and change the shadow color to brown. Nudge the shadow up and to the right a little for more dimension. Resize the text box to frame the text and position it attractively on the slide.

9. Apply similar text box formatting to the bulleted text on slide 3 but keep the text left-aligned and keep the bullets. Adjust the width of the text box so "8:00" wraps to the next line.

10. On slide 4, remove the bullets, center-align the text, and apply the same text box formatting as above.

11. Insert a new slide after slide 4 using the blank layout. Remove the master slide elements from slide 5 only.

UNIT 3 ■ APPLICATIONS

12. On slide 5, insert the blue ribbon image with the white center you can find using the keyword "medals" (or the filename Laward.wmf). Make the image 5.75 inches high and 5.25 inches wide. Recolor the image using pale yellow for the center. Make the circular border maroon and brown and keep the ribbon blue.

13. Create a WordArt image using the fifth sample in the first row of styles. Make the font 40-pt Times New Roman bold and key the following text on three lines:

    Award Ceremony
    6 PM
    Central Park

14. Change the WordArt shape to Button (Curve), which is the fourth choice in the second row. Change both the fill and outline colors to brown.

15. Position the WordArt inside the medal's border. Resize the WordArt by using its sizing handles to make it rounder so it fits attractively inside the medal.

16. Group the WordArt text and the medal. Move the objects down until the blue ribbon almost touches the bottom of the slide.

17. Still working on slide 5, insert the fireworks clip art image that you can find with the keywords "Fireworks Celebration" (or the filename Firewks.wmf). Crop the image to remove the gray waterfront objects, leaving only the fireworks. Resize the cropped picture proportionally so it is the full width of the slide, then move it to the top of the slide and send it to the back.

18. Check spelling in the presentation.

19. Save the presentation as *[your initials]***u3-3.ppt**.

20. Create a handout header with the date and your name and a handout footer with the page number and filename.

21. Print as handouts, 6 slides per page, black and white, framed.

22. Save and close the presentation.

APPLICATION 3-4

Work with Word Art; apply and format 3-D effects; and ungroup, group, and recolor clip art.

1. Open the file **Staff.ppt**.
2. On the title master, move the title placeholder and subtitle placeholder up approximately 0.5 inch. Insert the clip art image of a lecturer that you can find using the keywords "Meeting Communication" (or the filename lecture.wmf). Resize the image proportionally so it is 1.5

Unit Application 3-4:
Required Files: Staff.ppt and clip art images lecture.wmf and meeting.wmf (see page xiv for clip art file locations and instructions)
Solution File: glu3-4.ppt in Solutions Manual or on Solutions disk

The completed presentation for this Application may be used in a student's portfolio.

inches high, then center it horizontally approximately 1 inch from the bottom edge of the slide.

3. Ungroup the clip art image and change the fill color of the instructor to dark blue, the right person to light blue, the left person to light green, and the blackboard to light gray.

4. Group the blue person and the green person, then copy them and move the copy to the lower left corner of the slide. Resize the copy proportionally, making it 0.4 inch high, then change its fill color to dark blue.

5. Make 15 additional copies of the dark blue people, then align their tops relative to themselves and distribute them evenly across the bottom of the slide. Group the dark blue people and position them just above the bottom of the slide. Regroup the lecturer, the blackboard, and the two people from the original clipart image. Use Figure U3-5 as a guide.

FIGURE U3-5

6. Copy the group of dark blue people and paste it on the slide master in the same position.

7. On the slide master, insert the clip art image that you can find using the key words "Leadership Information" (or the filename meeting.wmf). Resize the image proportionally so it is 1.75 inches high at the bottom of the bulleted text placeholder.

8. Ungroup the clip art image on the slide master and delete the lecturer and blackboard. Change the fill color of the desk to dark blue. Change the green people to light green (ungrouping the image again where necessary) and the blue people to light blue. Regroup the image.

UNIT 3 ■ APPLICATIONS

9. On slide 1, delete the title placeholder. Key **Staff Training Schedules** as the subtitle. Format the text as 36 point-Arial bold shadowed.

10. Still working on slide 1, create a WordArt title using the text **Good 4 U** and the fourth choice in the second row of styles (the style with the gray and white horizontal gradient fill). Format the text as 60 point Arial Black bold.

11. Increase the width of the WordArt to 7 inches and position it above the subtitle.

12. Apply a 3-D effect to the WordArt using 3-D Style 20. Change the perspective color to dark purple, following the background scheme color. Position the WordArt title so the 3-D effect touches the top edge of the slide and is centered horizontally, as shown in Figure U3-5. Adjust the position of the subtitle, if necessary, to create a pleasing arrangement.

13. Create three new slides using the 2-column text layout. Key the text shown in figure U3-6, but don't key the titles. Right-align the text in the right text boxes and remove the bullets on all three slides. Resize and arrange the text boxes attractively on each slide. Be sure to align the tops of the text boxes.

FIGURE U3-6

Slide 2
```
Training Videos
      Managers            8:30 AM
      Servers            10:15 AM
      Greeters            1:00 PM
      Kitchen staff       3:15 PM
```

Slide 3
```
On-the-job Training
      Managers            7:30 PM
      Servers             5:30 PM
      Greeters            8:15 PM
      Kitchen staff       4:30 PM
```

Slide 4
```
Food Services Training
      Managers        January 17
      Servers         January 18
      Greeters        January 19
      Kitchen staff   January 20
```

279

14. Create WordArt titles for slides 2, 3, and 4 using the fourth WordArt style in the second row (the same one you used for the title slide). Format the text as 60-point Arial Black bold. Apply the Can Up WordArt shape (the third shape in the third row). Apply 3-D Style 20 and make the 3-D effect dark purple. Change the perspective depth from infinity to 288 point.

TIP: To make your job easier, create the first WordArt title, copy and paste it to the two other slides, and then edit its text by double-clicking the WordArt image.

15. If the first and last characters of the WordArt titles appear chopped off, edit the WordArt text by adding a space before the first character and after the last character.
16. Check the black and white settings for the presentation making changes where necessary.
17. Check spelling in the presentation.
18. Save the presentation as *[your initials]***u3-4.ppt**.
19. Create a handout header with the date and your name and a handout footer with the page number and filename.
20. Print as handouts, 6 slides per page, black and white, framed.
21. Save and close the presentation.

LESSON 9
Advanced Text Manipulation

OBJECTIVES After completing this lesson, you will be able to:
1. Control paragraph indents using the ruler.
2. Set tab stops and create a tabbed table.
3. Change line spacing and paragraph spacing.
4. Change text box margins and word wrap options.
5. Work with page setup options.
6. Customize handout masters and notes masters.

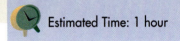

Estimated Time: 1 hour

In earlier lessons, you learned how to add text to a slide and change text attributes such as color, font, font style, and font size. In this lesson, you learn how to change the indent settings, set tab stops and line spacing, and manipulate text in other ways.

✓ Objective 1
Working with Indents

Each text placeholder has a ruler that you can use to change paragraph indents and tab settings. These settings affect all text in a placeholder. To apply different settings to some of the text, you put that text in a separate placeholder.

PREPARE
Point out to students that the learning objectives show what they will learn in the lesson. Each heading in the lesson correlates to a learning objective.
Required Files
Picnic1.ppt

TEACH
Teaching Resources:
• PowerPoint Classroom Presentation
• School-to-Work Strategies Manual
• Internet Manual
• Spanish Glossary
• Methodology Video
• Certification Procedures

✓ **Objective 1 Assignment:**
Exercise 9-15 (Skills Review) can be assigned after completing Objective 1.

LESSON 9 ■ ADVANCED TEXT MANIPULATION

FIGURE 9-1
Paragraph indents

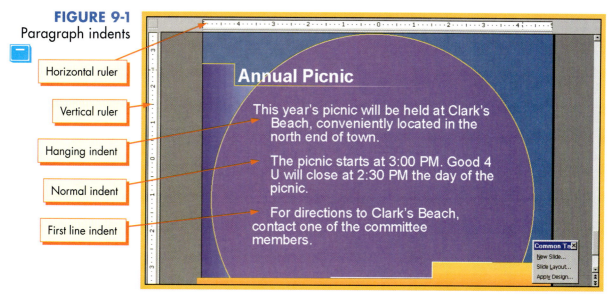

EXERCISE 9-1 Change Paragraph Indents

1. Open the file **Picnic1.ppt** and move to slide 2.
2. Choose Ruler from the View menu. The vertical and horizontal rulers appear.

    NOTE: Ruler is a toggle command. Choose it once to display the rulers, choose it again to hide them.

3. Move to slide 2 and select the bullet text box. Remove the bullets by clicking 📋. The paragraphs now have *hanging indents*.

NOTE

4. Click anywhere within the placeholder as if you were planning to edit some text. Notice the *indent markers* that appear on the ruler. Also notice that the white portion of the ruler indicates the width of the text placeholder.

   NOTE: You must have an insertion point somewhere inside a text box to change settings on the ruler. The appearance of the ruler reflects whether the entire placeholder is selected or the insertion point is active within the placeholder.

NOTE

5. Point to the *first-line indent* marker (the top triangle) and drag it right to the 1-inch mark on the ruler. The first line of each paragraph is now indented. Notice that each paragraph in the placeholder is indented the

 Use PowerPoint Classroom Presentation #9 to display screens from the lesson, including this one, in a slide-show format.

NOTE In step 4, have students practice clicking inside the placeholder and on the placeholder's border to see how the ruler's appearance changes.

NOTE In step 5, students not familiar with indent markers may experience trouble dragging them. Stress the importance of pointing precisely to the desired marker before dragging. Review the three parts: the top indent marker, the bottom indent marker, and the bottom rectangle, which moves both markers.

283

UNIT 4 ■ CUSTOMIZING—BEYOND THE BASICS

same way. To create different indents for different paragraphs, you must put them in separate text boxes.

FIGURE 9-2
Indent markers

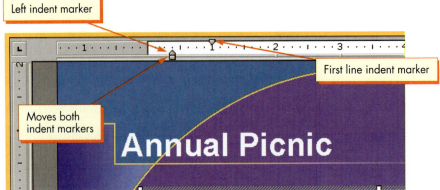

NOTE: If a text placeholder contains more than one bullet level, you see more than one set of indent markers on the ruler.

6. Drag the small rectangle (below the bottom triangle) to the zero mark on the ruler (the left edge of the white portion.). Notice that both triangles move when you drag the rectangle.

7. Drag the *left indent* marker (bottom triangle) to the right until it aligns with the first-line indent marker (the top triangle). Now all the lines of the paragraphs are indented the same amount.

8. Drag the small rectangle to the zero mark on the ruler once again. Now there are no indents set for this text box.

EXERCISE 9-2 Change Bullet Spacing

Sometimes you may want to change the distance between the bullets and text in a text placeholder. You can easily do this by dragging the bottom indent marker left to decrease the space and right to increase the space.

1. Move to slide 3. Click within the left bulleted text box (containing "Veggie burgers"). Notice the position of the indent markers.

2. Point to the left indent marker (the bottom triangle, not the small rectangle) and drag it right to the 1-inch mark on the ruler. The text is now indented 1 inch, but the bullet remains in its original position. Drag the left indent marker left to the 0.5-inch mark.

3. Click within the right bulleted text placeholder and drag the left indent marker right to the 0.5-inch mark.

In PowerPoint Classroom Presentation #9.

NOTE
When using bulleted text, the bottom indent marker moves the text located to the right of the bullet. In a paragraph that is not bulleted, the bottom indent marker moves all lines of text in the paragraph except the first line. The bullet and the first line of an unbulleted paragraph are moved by the top indent marker.

LESSON 9 ■ ADVANCED TEXT MANIPULATION

EXERCISE 9-3 Apply Indent Settings to the Slide Master

You can also change indent settings on the slide master. Slide master changes are automatically reflected on individual slides. However, formatting that you apply to individual slides before you change the master are not changed by the master slide. To make master slide changes take effect on those slides, reapply the slide layout.

1. Display the slide master.
2. Click inside the bullet text placeholder. Notice that there are five sets of indent markers, one for each bullet level.

FIGURE 9-3
Changing indents on the slide master

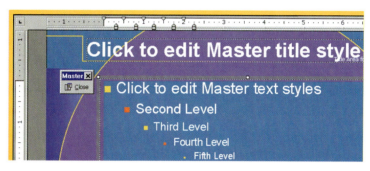

NOTE

3. Drag the left indent marker (the bottom triangle) for the first indent level to the left 1/16-inch (between the two ruler marks), making the bullet spacing slightly smaller.
4. Switch to Slide view and move to slide 2. Slide 2 had its bullets removed previously.

NOTE

5. Choose Slide Layout from the Common Tasks toolbar, then choose Reapply. Bullets appear on the slide, set to reflect master slide settings. Click to return to no bullets.

NOTE

6. Move to slide 3. The bullets were manually changed here, so the master slide changes did not take effect.
7. Move to slide 4. Since no changes were made to this slide, the master changes were applied automatically.

☑ Objective 2

Working with Tabs

You can set tabs to create simple tables in PowerPoint. You set tabs the same way you set tabs in Word. By default, tabs are left-aligned and set at 1-inch intervals. To set your own tabs, click the Tab Type button to choose the alignment, then click the ruler at the location where you want the tab. You learn to create more elaborate tables in Lesson 13.

In PowerPoint Classroom Presentation #9.

NOTE
Point out that a bulleted text placeholder can have as many as five sets of indent markers, one for each bullet level defined on the slide master.

NOTE
Step 5: The Reapply button appears only when the layout selected matches the existing layout of the current slide. To see this, move to any slide and choose Slide Layout. Notice the Reapply button. Click a different slide layout. The button caption changes to Apply. Click the original layout. The caption returns to Reapply.

NOTE
Step 6: Explain to students that master slide changes never override changes made manually to individual slides. Reapplying a slide layout always sets a slide's formatting to match the master's formatting.

☑ **Objective 2 Assignment:**
Exercise 9-16 (Skills Review) can be assigned after completing Objective 2.

285

UNIT 4 ■ CUSTOMIZING—BEYOND THE BASICS

EXERCISE 9-4 Set Tabs in a Text Box

1. Insert a new slide after slide 2 using the Title Only layout.
2. Key the title **Picnic Committee Award Winners**.
3. Draw a text box approximately 7" wide, positioning the upper-left corner about 1.5 inches below the word "Picnic."
4. Key the following, pressing where indicated:
   Darren Haley Tab **Sports Program** Tab **4798** Tab **112.76**
   Select the text box and change the font to 20-point Arial. Turn off the bullet, if necessary.
5. Make the text box wider, if necessary, to make all text appear on one line.
6. Click anywhere within the text box to activate the text box ruler.
7. Click the Tab Type button at the left end of the ruler. Each time you click the button, a different tab type icon appears, allowing you to cycle through the four tab type choices.

TABLE 9-1 Types of Tabs

CHOOSE	TO DO THIS
L	Left-align text at the tab setting
⊥	Center the text at the tab setting
⌐	Right-align text at the tab setting
⊥.	Align decimal points at the tab setting

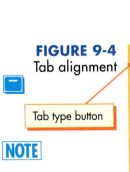

FIGURE 9-4 Tab alignment

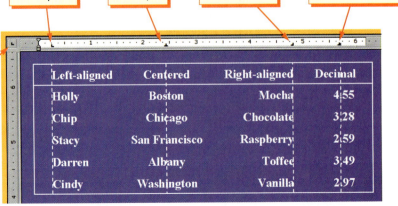

Left-aligned tab stop — Centered tab stop — Right-aligned tab stop — Decimal-aligned tab stop

Tab type button

NOTE To draw a text box, click the text box icon on the Drawing toolbar, then click at the starting position and drag a box to the desired width. Do not be concerned about the length. The box grows lengthwise as text lines are added.

NOTE Step 4: Because tabs are set at the default setting when students key this line, some text may appear not to be tabbed. Tell students not to press the Tab key twice. If they do, the completed table will be incorrect. (They can delete the extra tab to correct this.)

In PowerPoint Classroom Presentation #9.

NOTE When making a tabbed table, it is better to work with a text box instead of a bulleted text placeholder. That way, the indent markers will not interfere with the tabs. To use tabs with a bulleted text placeholder, you must key text before pressing the Tab key. When you press Tab at the beginning of a line, the line is demoted one bullet level.

LESSON 9 ■ ADVANCED TEXT MANIPULATION

8. Click until the center-aligned tab icon appears. Click the ruler at the 3-inch position. The text "Sports Program" moves so it is centered under the tab marker.

NOTE

9. Set a left-aligned tab marker at the 4.75-inch position and a decimal-aligned tab marker at the 6.375-inch mark (the third tick mark after 6 inches). Notice that the numbers you key move to align with the tabs.

 TIP: Increase the zoom, if necessary, for an enlarged view of the ruler.

EXERCISE 9-5   Create a Tabbed Table

1. Working in the text box you created on slide 3, position the insertion point at the end of the line, then press Enter to start a new line.
2. Key the balance of the table, shown in Figure 9-5, pressing Tab between columns and pressing Enter at the end of each line.

FIGURE 9-5
Creating a tabbed table

Darren Haley	Sports Program	4798	112.76
Chip Francis	Activities	4823	107.50
Holly Berber	Music	4799	72.06
Stacy Marvel	Site Planning	4862	67.45
Cindy Washington	Food	4812	55.94

NOTE: Once you set tabs for a table, you can change or remove them. To change the position of a tab marker, simply drag it to a new position on the ruler. To remove a tab marker, drag it down, off the ruler.

3. Click inside the text box, if necessary, to activate the ruler. Drag the center-aligned tab marker from the 3-inch position on the ruler to 3.25 inches. The entire column moves to the right.
4. Drag the center-aligned marker down and off the ruler to remove it. The table re-aligns in an unattractive way.
5. Click to restore the table's appearance.

NOTE
If students have trouble locating the tab positions on the ruler, they can change the zoom to a larger setting. The enlarged ruler will enable students to see the tick marks more easily.

In PowerPoint Classroom Presentation #9.

287

UNIT 4 ■ CUSTOMIZING—BEYOND THE BASICS

6. Select the entire text box by clicking its border and add a 1 pt white border (the default border setting).

7. Center the text box horizontally on the slide.

EXERCISE 9-6 Create Column Headings for a Tabbed Table

Because tab and indent settings in PowerPoint affect all text in a placeholder, you may need to put column headings in a separate text box to align them attractively with your table columns.

1. Still working on slide 3, create a second text box above the table, making it the same width as the table. Remove the bullet, if necessary. You fine-tune the size and position later.

2. Key the following in the text box:
   Name [Tab] **Responsibility** [Tab] **Extension** [Tab] **Points**

3. Change the font to 20-point Arial and adjust the vertical position of the text box, if necessary, so it does not overlap the table.

4. Set the following tabs in the heading text box:

   Center-aligned   3.25 inch mark
   Center-aligned   5.00 inch mark
   Right-aligned   6.75 inch mark

5. Add a 1 pt white border to the heading text box.

6. Adjust the position of the heading text box so its bottom border touches the top border of the table. Both text boxes should be left-aligned in relation to each other.

> **TIP:** You can fine-tune the placement of a selected object, such as a text box, by holding down [Ctrl] while pressing the arrow keys. This method moves the object in small increments.

7. Adjust the tab marker positions in the heading text box, if necessary, so the headings align above the table columns as shown in Figure 9-6 (on the next page).

NOTE

8. To make the heading text box exactly 7 inches wide, right-click it, choose Format Text B_o_x from the shortcut menu, click the Size tab, and set the width to **7**. Click OK.

9. Using the same method, make the table text box exactly 7 inches wide.

10. Select both text boxes and center them on the slide.

NOTE
Let students know they can set the width for both text boxes simultaneously if they are both selected before opening the Format AutoShape dialog box. Additionally, if a space character is inserted at the end of a line in the table, text may wrap to the next line. If this happens, have students delete spaces at the end of a line.

LESSON 9 ■ **ADVANCED TEXT MANIPULATION**

FIGURE 9-6
Completed table with column headings

Objective 3

Controlling Line Spacing

You can control line spacing by adding more space between the lines in a paragraph or by adding more space between paragraphs. Line spacing can be set in points or line units.

EXERCISE | **9-7** | **Change Line Spacing within Paragraphs**

Changing the space between lines of text or between paragraphs allows you to make your text layout easier to read and enhance the overall design of your slide. To change spacing between lines within a paragraph, you can:

- Choose Line Spacing from the Format menu.
- Click the Increase Paragraph Spacing button or the Decrease Paragraph Spacing button on the Formatting toolbar. These buttons increase or decrease the space between lines within a paragraph by increments of 0.1 line.

NOTE

1. Move to slide 2. Click within the first paragraph in the text box.
2. Choose Line Spacing from the Format menu. The Line Spacing dialog box appears.

In PowerPoint Classroom Presentation #9.

NOTE
The naming of the Increase and Decrease Paragraph spacing buttons may be confusing. These buttons increase or decrease the spacing within a paragraph; not the spacing between paragraphs.

289

FIGURE 9-7
Line Spacing dialog box

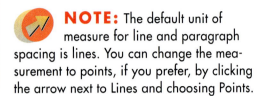

3. In the Line Spacing option box, key **1.3** or click the up arrow until 1.3 appears. Click Preview to view the changes. The line spacing of the first paragraph has increased. Click OK to accept the changes.

   NOTE: The default unit of measure for line and paragraph spacing is lines. You can change the measurement to points, if you prefer, by clicking the arrow next to Lines and choosing Points.

4. Usually you will want to change the line spacing for an entire text placeholder. Select the placeholder, re-open the Line Spacing dialog box, and change the line spacing to 1 line. Click OK. The text is now easier to read and more attractively placed.

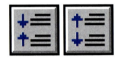

5. With the text box still selected, click [icon] twice. The line spacing decreases.
6. Click [icon] once to increase the line spacing.

EXERCISE 9-8 Change Spacing between Paragraphs

You have seen how you can change line spacing in text placeholders. You can also change the amount of space before or after a paragraph using options in the Line Spacing dialog box.

1. Still working on slide 2, click within the second paragraph and open the Line Spacing dialog box.
2. Under Before Paragraph, change the line setting to 2 lines.
3. Click Preview to view the changes. Click OK. The text will look better if the spacing between all paragraphs is uniform.
4. Select the entire text box and open the Line Spacing dialog box. Change the Before paragraph spacing to 1 line and the After paragraph spacing to 0. (The Line spacing should remain at 0.9 lines). Click OK. The text is now evenly spaced in the text placeholder.
5. Decrease all the text in the text placeholder by one font size.

Objective 4
Working with Text Box Settings

You can change the position of text within its text box or AutoShape. For example, you can place text in the upper left corner or vertically centered relative

In PowerPoint Classroom Presentation #9.

Objective 4 Assignment:
Exercise 9-20 (Lesson Applications) can be assigned after completing Objective 4.

LESSON 9 ■ ADVANCED TEXT MANIPULATION

to its text box. You can also change the box margins, the text box size, and word wrap options. These options are found on the Text Box tab of the Format AutoShape dialog box.

TABLE 9-2   **Text Box Options**

CHOOSE	EFFECT
Text anchor point	Specify the position where text begins in an object.
Internal margin	Adjust the distance from the text to the Left, Right, Top, or Bottom margins.
Word-wrap text in autoshape	Make text wrap to fit within an object.
Resize autoshape to fit text	Make an object adjust to the size of text.
Rotate text within autoshape by 90°	Turn the text sideways inside the autoshape.

EXERCISE 9-9   Change the Text Anchor Position

NOTE

The text anchor point is the position from which text begins within a placeholder or AutoShape. For example, in a bulleted list placeholder, the text begins at the top of the placeholder. When you key text in an AutoShape, it begins at the center. This point remains fixed when text shrinks and grows during editing. You can change the anchor point to Top, Middle, Bottom, Top Centered, Middle Centered, or Bottom Centered.

FIGURE 9-8
Examples of text anchoring

1. Move to slide 5. Select the bulleted text box containing the committee member names.
2. Apply a dark purple fill and remove the bullets. Notice that the text is positioned in the upper left corner of the box.
3. Right-click the text box border, choose Format AutoShape from the shortcut menu, and click the Text Box tab. Drag the dialog box to the right so you can see the text box.

NOTE
You may want to discuss with students the difference between center aligning text and centering the anchor point in a text box. In this example, center-aligning the text would result in an uneven left margin. After step 5 in this Exercise, the text in this text box is left aligned but its anchor point is set to Middle Centered.

 In PowerPoint Classroom Presentation #9.

291

4. Open the Text anchor point list box, choose Bottom, and click Preview. The text moves to the bottom of the box.

5. Choose Middle Centered and click Preview again. The text is now centered vertically and horizontally in the text box. Click OK.

FIGURE 9-9
Changing the text anchor position

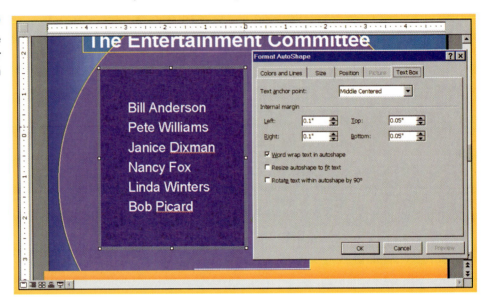

6. Change the text box AutoShape to a rounded rectangle. (Click Draw on the Drawing toolbar and choose Change AutoShape, Basic Shapes.)

EXERCISE 9-10 Resize the Text Box to Fit

When you choose the Resize autoshape to fit text option, the text box automatically shrinks or grows as you add or delete text and when you change the font size.

1. With the committee members text box still selected, re-open the Format AutoShape dialog box and choose the Text Box tab. Drag the dialog box to the right so you can see the text box.

2. Check the Resize autoshape to fit text check box and click Preview. The text box shrinks in height, but not in width.

3. Clear the Word wrap text in autoshape check box and click Preview again. Now the text box shrinks in width. Word wrap changes the way the Resize option works.

4. Click OK to apply the text box settings.

5. Increase the committee members text one font size. Notice that the text box grows.

In PowerPoint Classroom Presentation #9.

LESSON 9 ■ ADVANCED TEXT MANIPULATION

EXERCISE 9-11 Change Text Box Margins

Use the Internal margin option to change the space between the text and the edge of the text box.

1. With the committee members text box still selected, re-open the Text Box tab of the Format AutoShape dialog box.
2. Under Internal margin, set the Left box to **0.5** and click Preview. The left margin becomes wider.
3. Set the Right margin to **0.5** inch and the Top and Bottom margins to **0.3** inches. Click OK. The text box size increases to accommodate the wider margins.
4. Reduce the text by one font size. The text box again shrinks to fit the new text size.

EXERCISE 9-12 Use Text Box Options to Format an AutoShape

When you key text in an AutoShape, the text is automatically anchored at the middle center position, word wrap is turned off, and resize AutoShape is turned off. You can change these settings so your text fits into the AutoShape.

1. Insert a new slide after slide 5 using the blank autolayout.
2. Draw a Diamond AutoShape in the center of the slide, approximately 1 inch wide and 1 inch tall.
3. Fill the diamond with a two-color gradient, choosing dark purple (Shadows Scheme Color) for color 1 and light purple (Accent Scheme Color) for color 2. Choose the From center option and the variant with the lighter center. Remove the diamond's outline.
4. With the AutoShape selected, key **See you at the beach!** The text extends outside the diamond's border.
5. Change the text font to 48-point Arial bold.
6. Open the Format AutoShape dialog box and click the Text Box tab. Check the Resize AutoShape to fit text check box. Click OK. The text fits inside the diamond, but the diamond is too large for the slide.
7. Resize the diamond by dragging the left-center sizing handle toward the center of the slide. The text automatically word wraps even though the word wrap option was not chosen.
8. Adjust the width of the diamond so the text wraps to three lines.
9. Position the diamond in the center of the slide.

293

UNIT 4 ■ CUSTOMIZING—BEYOND THE BASICS

FIGURE 9-10
Text word wrapped inside an AutoShape

10. Save the presentation as *[your initials]*9-12.ppt.
11. Add the date and your name to the handout header and the filename to the handout footer.
12. Adjust the black and white settings, if necessary.
13. Print as handouts, 6 slides per page, black and white, framed.

Objective 5

Working with Page Setup Options

You can display and print your presentation in different ways: as an on-screen show using your computer's monitor, as overhead transparencies, as 35mm slides, or as color or black and white printouts. Your printouts can be in landscape or portrait orientation. PowerPoint has built-in page size settings for each method. You use the Page Setup dialog box to choose page size settings.

NOTE: You can change the page size of your presentation at any time, but it's generally best to start with the correct one. Changing to a page size with different proportions can distort the graphics in your presentation.

EXERCISE 9-13 Change Page Setup Options

So far, you've worked with slides that are sized for an on-screen presentation in landscape orientation. In this exercise, you change the page setup to a paper

In PowerPoint Classroom Presentation #9.

Objective 5 Assignment:
Exercises 9-18 (Skills Review) and 9-19 (Lesson Applications) can be assigned after completing Objective 5.

LESSON 9 ■ ADVANCED TEXT MANIPULATION

NOTE

presentation in portrait orientation. This sort of paper presentation might be placed in a binder and distributed at a meeting when no computer is available.

1. Apply the Contemporary Portrait template to the presentation.
2. Choose Page Setup from the File menu. In the Page Setup dialog box, notice that the current presentation is sized for an on-screen presentation in landscape orientation. Notice that notes and handouts use portrait orientation.
3. Open the Slides sized for drop-down list and notice the options. Choose Letter Paper.

FIGURE 9-11
Changing page setup options

NOTE

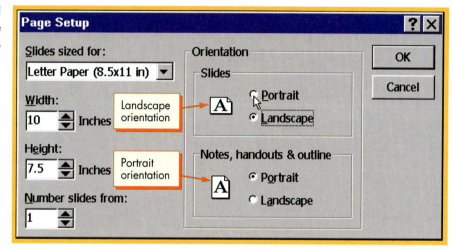

4. Under Slides, click Portrait and click OK. The slide proportions change to the new orientation.
5. Scroll through the presentation and notice the distortion in some of the graphics.
6. Make the following changes to fix the layout:
   - On slide 1, widen the subtitle text box and center it horizontally.
   - On slide 2, make the text box 5.25 inches wide and center it horizontally.
   - On slide 3, make the font size in the table boxes one size smaller, make both text boxes wider, and adjust the tabs to make the text align correctly. Adjust the paragraph spacing in both text boxes to make the table more attractive.
   - On slide 4, resize the clip art, making it smaller and more proportional, and adjust its position.
   - On slides 5 and 6, remove the fill from the text boxes.
7. View the presentation in Slide Sorter view.

NOTE
Make sure students understand the difference between landscape and portrait orientation.

 In PowerPoint Classroom Presentation #9.

NOTE
Point out that you can use the Page Setup dialog box to change the orientation of notes, handouts, and outlines from portrait to landscape.

295

UNIT 4 ■ CUSTOMIZING—BEYOND THE BASICS

NOTE

8. Print slide 3 of the presentation. You print the entire presentation as handouts in the next exercise.

Objective 6

Customizing Handout and Notes Masters

Just as the slide master controls the appearance of the slides in your presentation, the notes master and handout master control the overall look and formatting of notes and handouts. You can customize these masters using the same techniques you used with slide and title masters.

EXERCISE 9-14   Work with the Handout and Notes Masters

1. Open the View menu and choose Master, Notes Master to display the notes master. Notice the portrait orientation of the slide. You can select any text placeholder on the notes master and move or format it. You can also insert an object on the page.

2. Open the View menu and choose Master, Handout Master to display the handout master. You should also see the Handout Master toolbar. (If the toolbar is not displayed, choose it from the View menu, Toolbars submenu.)

3. Click the first button on the Handout Master toolbar , which shows how handouts will print with 2 slides per page. Notice the portrait orientation of the slides, which are represented by dotted outlines.

4. Click the button that shows the positioning of 3 slides per page , then click the button that shows a 6 slide per page handout .

FIGURE 9-12
Viewing the handout master

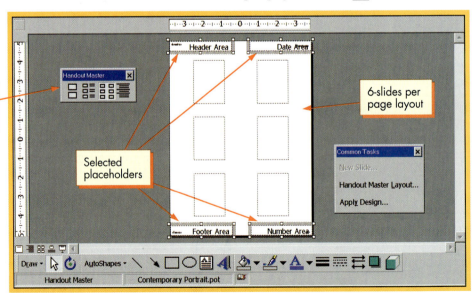

NOTE
If printing is not a problem in your classroom, you might have students print all slides in the presentation, not just slide 3.

Objective 6 Assignment:
Exercises 9-17 (Skills Review) and 9-21 (Lesson Applications) can be assigned after completing Objective 6.

In PowerPoint Classroom Presentation #9.

LESSON 9 ■ ADVANCED TEXT MANIPULATION

5. Select all four text placeholders on the handout (Header, Date, Footer, Number). Change the formatting to Arial bold italic.

 NOTE: Although you can work with the text placeholders on the note or handout master, you cannot alter the position of the slides on the page.

6. Select only the Date placeholder and delete it. Select the Header placeholder. Center-align the text in the placeholder and center the placeholder horizontally on the page.

 TIP: To restore a deleted handout placeholder, you can click Handout Master Layout on the Common Tasks toolbar and check the item you want to restore.

[NOTE]

7. With the Header placeholder selected, increase the zoom to 75%. Under the Header placeholder, draw a floating text box with the text **Annual Picnic Presentation**. Change the text box font to 12-point Arial bold italic and center the text box under the Header placeholder.
8. Save the presentation as *[your initials]***9-14.ppt**.
9. Use the View menu to update the handout footer with the new filename.
10. Print the presentation as handouts, 6 slides per page, black and white, framed.
11. Switch back to slide 1 in Slide view. Save and close the presentation.

COMMAND SUMMARY
[NOTE]

FEATURE	BUTTON	MENU	KEYBOARD
Increase paragraph spacing		Format, Line Spacing	
Decrease paragraph spacing		Format, Line Spacing	
Notes master	Shift +	View, Master, Notes Master	
Handout master	Shift +	View, Master, Handout Master	

[NOTE]
You may want to point out that students can apply a background color or color scheme to the handout or notes master. Right-click a blank area on the handout or notes master and notice the options on the shortcut menu.

[NOTE]
Point out that the Command Summary lists a variety of ways to accomplish a particular task. Students can decide which method they prefer to use.

UNIT 4 ■ CUSTOMIZING—BEYOND THE BASICS

TEST BANK

Concepts Review

TRUE/FALSE QUESTIONS

Each of the following statements is either true or false. Indicate your choice by circling **T** or **F**.

(T) F 1. You can use many different tab settings in one text placeholder.

(T) F 2. The word wrap option adjusts text to fit inside an object or placeholder.

T (F) 3. Text aligns to the left of a left tab setting.

T (F) 4. The Increase Paragraph Spacing button increases only the space between paragraphs.

(T) F 5. Top, Middle, and Bottom Centered are text anchor point options.

(T) F 6. You can remove a tab marker by dragging it off the ruler.

T (F) 7. The top indent marker moves all lines of text in a text block.

(T) F 8. Unless you change page setup options, slides print in landscape orientation and handouts print in portrait orientation.

SHORT ANSWER QUESTIONS

Write the correct answer in the space provided.

1. What do you call the position where text is attached to a placeholder?
   Text anchor point

2. Which kind of tab do you use to align rows of dollars and cents?
   Decimal tab

3. Which indent marker do you use to change the distance between bullets and text?
   Left indent marker (bottom triangle)

4. In which dialog box do you find the option to automatically adjust an object's size to accommodate text?
   Format AutoShape dialog box, Text Box tab

5. Where do you change indents, set tab stops, and move tab stops?
   On the ruler

Concepts Review:
Allows students to check their understanding.

TEST BANK
Consider using the Test Bank to provide an additional review of lesson concepts.

LESSON 9 ■ ADVANCED TEXT MANIPULATION

6. Which function does ▦ perform?
   Increases line spacing within selected paragraphs

7. Assuming that the word wrap and resize autoshape to fit text options were applied, which settings do you change to modify the amount of space between text and the edge of an object?
   Internal margin settings on Text Box tab, Format AutoShape dialog box

8. Which menu do you open to turn on the ruler?
   View menu

CRITICAL THINKING

Answer these questions on a separate page. There are no right or wrong answers. Support your answers with examples from your own experience, if possible.

1. Think of ways you might use the indent markers. When would you want lines in a block to indent at different points?

2. Comparing the difference between the different types of tab stops, when would you use centered tabs? Left-aligned tabs? Right-aligned tabs?

Skills Review

EXERCISE 9-15

Work with bullets and indents.

1. Open the file **Award.ppt**.

2. Move to slide 2. If the ruler is not in view, choose <u>R</u>uler from the <u>V</u>iew menu.

3. Create first-line indents by following these steps:
   a. Remove the bullets from the bulleted text box.
   b. Click within the text box to activate the ruler.
   c. Drag the first line indent marker (top triangle) right to the 1-inch mark on the ruler.
   d. Drag the small rectangle left to the zero point on the ruler.

4. Move to slide 3 and change the bullet spacing by following these steps:
   a. Click within the bulleted text box.

Critical Thinking Questions:
Answers will vary based on students' preferences, observations, experiences, and research.

Skills Review:
Provides guided practice for students. Objectives are indicated for each Exercise.

Exercise 9-15:
Objective 1
Required File: Award.ppt
Solution File: gl9-15.ppt in Solutions Manual or on Solutions Disk

299

UNIT 4 ■ CUSTOMIZING—BEYOND THE BASICS

    b. Drag the bottom indent marker right to the 0.75-inch position on the ruler.

5. On the slide master, change the first-level bullet to a star of your choice from the Monotype Sorts font. Make the star dark blue and 100% of font size.

6. Move to slide 4 and change the bulleted text indent to 0.75 inches. Move the entire placeholder down 0.5 inch on the slide.

7. Move to slide 5 and format the text boxes to have no bullets and no indents by following these steps:

    a. Select both text boxes and remove the bullets.

    b. Make the text in both text boxes one size smaller.

    c. Click within the left text box and drag the left indent marker (bottom triangle) to the zero point. Do the same to the right text box.

8. Underline the following on slide 5: "Employee," "Hobbies," "Years of Service," and "Position."

9. Save the presentation as *[your initials]***9-15.ppt**.

10. Add the date and your name to the handout header and the filename to the handout footer.

11. Adjust the black and white settings, if necessary.

12. Print as handouts, 6 slides per page, black and white, framed.

13. Save and close the presentation.

EXERCISE 9-16

Set tabs and create tabbed tables.

1. Open the file **Marath.ppt**.

2. Move to slide 2 and add tabs to the table by following these steps:

    a. Display the ruler if necessary, then click anywhere within the table to activate the ruler.

    b. Click 📐 until it displays a right tab.

    c. Click the ruler at the 4-inch mark.

    d. Drag the tab marker to the 5-inch mark on the ruler.

    e. Add another right tab at the 6-inch mark on the ruler.

3. Insert a new slide after slide 2 using the Title Only layout. Key **Station Assignments** in the title placeholder.

4. Create a tabbed table by following these steps:

Exercise 9-16:
Objectives 1, 2
Required File: Marath.ppt
Solution File: gl9-16.ppt in Solutions Manual or on Solutions Disk

LESSON 9 ■ ADVANCED TEXT MANIPULATION

   a. Draw a text box approximately 2 inches below the top of the slide and the same width as the title text.

   b. Key the following table heading:
   Description Tab **Class** Tab **Station**

   c. Draw a second text box the same width as the title directly below the table heading.

   d. Key the following, pressing Tab between each column.

Under 18	A	10
18-39	B	30
40-54	C	40
55 and Over	D	20

5. Format the table by following these steps:

   a. Select both text box objects and align their left edges.

   b. Change the heading text to 36-point Arial bold. Change the text color to pink and apply a text shadow.

   c. In the heading text box, set a center tab at 4 inches and a right tab at 7 inches.

    TIP: You may need to make the heading text box wider to set the 7-inch tab stop.

   d. Change the table text size to 32-point Arial.

   e. In the table text box, set a left tab at 4 inches and a right tab at 6.25 inches.

6. Indent the table text 0.25 inches by following these steps:

   a. Click within the body of the table (not the heading).

   b. Drag the small rectangle on the ruler to the 0.25-inch position. Both triangles should be aligned on top of the rectangle.

   c. Adjust the text table tab markers slightly to fine-tune the alignment of the columns under the heading.

7. Group the table and the table heading, then position the group so it is attractively placed on the slide.

8. Save the presentation as *[your initials]***9-16.ppt**.

9. Add the date and your name to the handout header and the filename to the handout footer.

10. Check the black and white settings and adjust if necessary.

11. Print as handouts, 6 slides per page, black and white, framed.

12. Save and close the presentation.

NOTE
In step 5d, you may want to remind students to press Tab only once between columns. Tell them that columns will align properly after tabs are set on the ruler.

301

UNIT 4 ■ CUSTOMIZING—BEYOND THE BASICS

EXERCISE 9-17

Change line spacing and paragraph spacing and customize the handout master.

1. Open the file **Lunch.ppt**.
2. Change line spacing within paragraphs by following these steps:
    a. Move to slide 2 and click within the descriptive paragraph below the bold heading "Stuffed Spinach Bread."
    b. Choose Line Spacing from the Format menu.
    c. Change the line spacing setting to 1.1 lines and click OK.

NOTE

    d. Change the line spacing for each description for the remaining three appetizers to 1.1 lines. (Use the Repeat command.)
3. Change spacing between paragraphs by following these steps:
    a. Move to slide 3 and click within the paragraph that begins "Cool crisp salad."
    b. Open the Line Spacing dialog box. Under Before Paragraph, change the setting to 0.1 lines. Click OK.
    c. Change the paragraph spacing for each remaining side dish description (the text that isn't bold) to match.
    d. Click within the bold text "Old Fashioned Cornbread."
    e. Change the Before Paragraph setting to 0.5 lines.
    f. Change the Before Paragraph settings for each remaining bold side dish name to match.
4. Reduce the line spacing for all the text in both placeholders on the Side Dish Specials slide following these steps:
    a. Select both text placeholders.
    b. Click the Decrease Paragraph button ![icon] once.
5. Move to slide 4 and select both placeholders.
6. Change the line spacing to 0.9 lines.
7. For each bold heading (the lunch special names), change the before paragraph space to 1 line and the after paragraph space to 0 lines.

NOTE

8. For each paragraph that isn't bold (the descriptions), change the before and after paragraph spacing to 0 lines.
9. Customize the handout master by following these steps:
    a. Choose View, Master, Handout Master.
    b. Delete the Number placeholder.
    c. Position the insertion point after the text "<footer>" in the Footer placeholder. (Increase the zoom to work with the placeholder text.)

Exercise 9-17:
Objectives 3, 6
Required File: Lunch.ppt
Solution File: gl9-17.ppt in Solutions Manual or on Solutions Disk.

NOTE
Step 2d: Remind students how to use the Repeat command (click within the paragraph and press either F4 or press Ctrl+Y).

NOTE
Step 8: You may want to explain to students that when you set the before paragraph spacing for the first paragraph in a text box, the results will not show on the slide.

LESSON 9 ■ ADVANCED TEXT MANIPULATION

    d. Key a comma, a space, and the text **Presentation on Lunch Specials**.

    e. Center the Footer placeholder horizontally, center-align the text within the placeholder, and make the text bold.

10. Save the presentation as *[your initials]***9-17.ppt**.

11. Add the date and your name to the handout header and the filename to the handout footer. Clear the Page number check box, if necessary.

12. Switch to Slide view and adjust the black and white settings, if necessary.

13. Print as handouts, 6 slides per page, black and white, framed.

14. Save and close the presentation.

EXERCISE 9-18

Change text anchor attributes and change page setup options.

1. Open the file **Update1.ppt**. Change the color scheme to the second standard choice (with the white background).

2. Change the presentation to a letter paper presentation in portrait orientation by following these steps:

    a. Choose Page Setup from the File menu.

    b. Open the Slides sized for drop-down list and choose Letter Paper.

    c. Under Slides, click Portrait and click OK.

3. Change the text alignment and text anchor properties of the title slide subtitle by following these steps:

    a. On slide 1, select the subtitle text box and left-align the subtitle text.

    b. Open the Format AutoShape dialog box and click the Text Box tab.

    c. Choose Middle Centered in the Text anchor point list box.

    d. Preview the change and without closing the dialog box, click the Position tab.

    e. Set the vertical position at 6 inches from the top left corner.

    f. Preview the change and click OK.

4. On slide 2, remove the bullet and hanging indent. Then change the text box resize option using these steps:

    a. Select the text box and open the Format AutoShape dialog box.

    b. Click the Text Box tab.

    c. Check the Resize autoshape to fit text check box. If necessary, check the Word wrap text in autoshape check box. Click OK.

5. Using the right center resize handle, make the text box about 1 inch narrower. Increase the text box font by one size. Center the text box

Exercise 9-18:
Objectives 1, 3–5
Required File: Update1.ppt
Solution File: gl9-18.ppt in Solutions Manual or on Solutions Disk.

horizontally and position it 4 inches from the top of the slide. With the text box selected, click [icon] twice to increase its paragraph spacing.

6. Fit text into an AutoShape by following these steps:

   a. Move to slide 3 and right-click anywhere on the slide title.

   b. Choose Format AutoShape from the shortcut menu and click the Text Box tab.

   c. Set the Resize AutoShape to fit text option and click OK.

   d. Change the font size of the title text to 48 point.

7. On slide 3, change the vertical position of the bulleted text box to 6 inches from the top of the slide.

8. On slide 4, resize the bulleted text placeholder to fit the text and move the text box down one inch. (Tip: Add 1 inch to the vertical position setting on the Position tab.)

9. On slide 5, remove the first level bullet and the hanging indent. Change the Before paragraph spacing of the second level hyphen bullets to 0.5 lines. Move the text box to 3.6 inches from the top of the slide.

10. On slide 6, make the bulleted text box 4.5 inches wide and set the Format AutoShape option so the text box resizes to fit the text. Set the Before Paragraph setting for the text box to 0.5 lines.

11. Move the text box to the lower right corner of the slide.

12. Save the presentation as *[your initials]***9-18.ppt**.

13. Add the date and your name to the handout header and the filename to the handout footer.

14. Change the black and white settings on individual slides and on the slide masters, as necessary.

15. Print as handouts, 6 slides per page, black and white, framed.

16. Save and close the presentation.

LESSON 9 ■ ADVANCED TEXT MANIPULATION

Lesson Applications

EXERCISE 9-19

Work with indents, tab stops, and page setup options.

1. Open the file **Inventry.ppt**.
2. Working on the slide master, change the size of the bulleted text box to 4.5 inches high by 8.5 inches wide. Center the text box horizontally relative to the slide. Increase the slide title text by one font size and make it bold.
3. Still working on the slide master, increase the space between the bullet and text for the first level bullet to 0.5 inches. Change the first level bullet to the solid dot found in the Monotype Sorts font.
4. On slide 2, make the bulleted text box 6 inches wide. Remove the bullets and the hanging indent. Center the text box under the title and move it down 0.5 inches.
5. On slide 3, make the text box 7.5 inches wide and reposition the text box so the bullets are aligned under the first character in the title.
6. On slide 4, remove the second level bullets. Italicize the second level text and make it one font size smaller. Move the bullet text box to the right so the bullets align with the first character in the title text.
7. On slide 5, remove the bullets from the table and insert a left-aligned tab at the 3-inch mark on the ruler. Increase the table text by one font size and center the table horizontally and vertically relative to the slide.
8. On slide 6, move the bulleted text box down 0.5 inches and right 0.5 inches.
9. Save the presentation as *[your initials]***9-19a.ppt**.
10. Add the date and your name to the handout header and the filename to the handout footer.
11. Adjust the black and white settings if necessary.
12. Print as handouts, 6 slides per page, black and white, framed.
13. Change the page setup options to resize the slides for letter paper and portrait orientation.
14. Adjust the size and position of the text boxes on slides 2 through 6 as needed, centering them horizontally and vertically on the slide. Delete the dot graphics from the title and slide masters.
15. Save the presentation as *[your initials]***9-19b.ppt**.
16. Update the handout footer with the new filename, then print handouts, 6 slides per page, black and white, framed.
17. Save and close the presentation.

ASSESS

Assessment Resources:
• Solutions Manual
• Test Bank with Software
• Portfolio Builder
• Alternative Assessment Guide
• Certification Procedures

Lesson Applications:
Provide independent practice for students. Objectives are indicated for each Exercise.

Exercise 9-19:
Objectives 1, 2, 5
Required File: Inventry.ppt
Solution Files: gl9-19a.ppt and gl9-19b.ppt in Solutions Manual or on Solutions Disk.

305

UNIT 4 ■ CUSTOMIZING—BEYOND THE BASICS

EXERCISE 9-20

Work with line spacing and text anchor options

1. Open the file **Newyr2.ppt**.

2. On slide 2, remove all the bullets and hanging indents from both text boxes. Center-align the text in the left box, change its font size to 40 points, and change its text color to gold (the title text scheme color). Format the text in the right text box as 20-point Arial bold.

3. Size and position the left text box so it is 8 inches wide, 2.75 inches from the top of the slide, and 1 inch from the left edge of the slide. Change the font size of the line that begins "Festivities begin" to 32 points. Change the before paragraph spacing in the text box to 0 lines.

4. Resize the directions text box so its text wraps on three lines. Center the text box horizontally and position it 5.75 inches from the top of the slide.

5. Insert a new slide after slide 2 using the Title Only layout. Key **Evening Menu** in the title placeholder. Draw a 3-inch circle below the title and to the left. Using Figure 9-13 as a guide, key the "Appetizers" text in the circle.

FIGURE 9-13
Slide 3

6. Make the word "Appetizers" bold, shadowed, and burgundy (the accent scheme color). Make the rest of the text 18-point, bold, shadowed, and dark pink (the fills scheme color).

7. Using the Format AutoShape dialog box, remove the outline and fill the circle with a 2-color gradient using cream (the text and lines scheme color) and gold. Choose the <u>F</u>rom corner shading style and the first variant, with the darkest color in the lower right. Using the Size tab,

Exercise 9-20:
Objectives 1, 3, 4
Required File: Newyr2.ppt
Solution File: gl9-20.ppt in Solutions Manual or on Solutions Disk.

The completed presentation for this Exercise may be used in a student's portfolio.

LESSON 9 ■ ADVANCED TEXT MANIPULATION

change the size of the circle to 2.75 inches high and 3 inches wide. Change the text anchor point to middle centered.

8. Copy the ball and paste it three times. Use Figure 9-13 as a guide for positioning the balls in an overlapping fashion. Edit the text in the 3 copied balls as shown in the figure.

9. Change the shading of the Main Course ball so it shades from cream to light pink (a custom colors). The Side Dishes ball should shade from cream to bright blue and the Desserts ball from cream to bright green.

10. On slide 4, remove all the bullets and hanging indents. Make all the first level text bold and pink. Make the second-level text bold.

NOTE

11. Change the AutoShape to a rounded rectangle with a dark gray fill. Apply object shadow style 6 to the rectangle and change the shadow color to dark pink.

12. Change the text box margins of the rectangle shape to 0.3 inches all around and make the width 7.5 inches. Change the text anchor point to Middle Centered and set the "Resize autoshape to fit text" option. Change the line spacing for the second level paragraphs to 0.8 lines.

13. Center the rectangle horizontally relative to the slide and move it down slightly.

14. Adjust the black and white settings if necessary.

15. Save the presentation as *[your initials]***9-20.ppt**.

16. Add the date and your name to the handout header and the filename to the handout footer.

17. Print as handouts, 6 slides per page, black and white, framed.

18. Save and close the presentation.

EXERCISE 9-21

Create a tabbed table, change line spacing, change box margins and anchor point settings, and customize the handout master.

1. Start a new blank presentation using the Contemporary Portrait template. Choose the color scheme with the black background.

2. Display the title master. Open the Clip Gallery and use the Find feature to display all baseball pictures. Choose the player with the wide stance swinging the bat (filename basebal2.wmf).

3. Resize the player to 2.75 inches high and move him to the left of the subtitle text box. Copy and paste the ball player in the lower right corner of the slide master.

4. On slide 1, key a two-line title using **Good 4 U** and **Softball Schedule**.

NOTE
Students should be careful to apply the shadow to the rectangle, not the text within the rectangle. To prevent this, the rectangle should be active (with the insertion point in it), not selected, before applying the shadow.

Exercise 9-21:
Objectives 1–4, 6
Required File: clip art file basebal2.wmf (see page xiv for clip art file locations and instructions)
Solution File: gl9-21.ppt in Solutions Manual or on Solutions Disk.

The completed presentation for this Exercise may be used in a student's portfolio.

307

UNIT 4 ■ CUSTOMIZING—BEYOND THE BASICS

5. Key **Spring/Summer 1999** for the subtitle.

6. Using the Title Only layout, create slide 2 as shown in Figure 9-14. Key the table and its heading all in one text box. Use 24-point Arial for all the table text and make the heading bold. Set appropriate tabs. Set the line spacing for the heading at 1.5 lines and line spacing for the body of the table at 1 line. Set the before paragraph spacing to 0.2 lines for the whole table. Disable the word wrap option for the text box and enable the "Resize autoshape to fit text "option. Add a 2¼-point border to the text box and draw a 3-point line under the heading.

FIGURE 9-14
Slide 2

7. Using the 2 Column Text layout, create slide 3 as shown in Figure 9-15 (on the next page). Remove all bullets, center the text in each text box, and make the first line of each text box bold and red. Apply a one-color gold horizontal gradient fill to both text boxes using the darkest setting, with the darkest color at the bottom. Disable the word wrap text box option and enable the "Resize AutoShape to fit text" option. Make all internal margins 0.4 inches. Position the text boxes as shown.

8. Using the Title Only layout, create slide 4 as shown in Figure 9-16 (on the next page). Draw a rounded rectangular callout AutoShape, flip it horizontally, and drag the adjustment diamond to the baseball player's head. Add a 3-point cream outline. Disable the word wrap text box option and enable the "Resize AutoShape to fit text" option.

9. Adjust the black and white settings if necessary.

10. Save the presentation as *[your initials]***9-21.ppt**.

11. Add the date and your name to the handout header and the filename to the handout footer.

LESSON 9 ■ ADVANCED TEXT MANIPULATION

FIGURE 9-15
Slide 3

FIGURE 9-16
Slide 4

12. Display the handout master and format all the text placeholders as 14-point Arial bold.
13. Print as handouts, 6 slides per page, black and white, framed.
14. Save and close the presentation.

309

LESSON 10
Advanced Drawing Techniques

OBJECTIVES

After completing this lesson, you will be able to:
1. Use guides to position and measure objects.
2. Use zoom for precise object placement.
3. Explore the Snap and Nudge features.
4. Draw using the Freeform tool.
5. Edit points on a freeform drawing.
6. Draw using the curve tool.

 Estimated Time: 1½ hours

PowerPoint has some powerful tools you can use to control the position of objects to give your presentations a professional look. In Lessons 5 and 6, you learned how to control the size and position of objects by keying measurements in dialog boxes. In this lesson, you use the guides, nudge, and snap features to measure and place objects. You also work with advanced drawing tools to create curves and freeform objects.

Objective 1
Using Guides to Position and Measure Objects

You can display dotted horizontal and vertical lines on your slides to help you position text and drawing objects. You can hide these lines, called *guides,* when you don't need them and display them again when you do need them. Guides

PREPARE
Each heading in the lesson correlates to a learning objective.
Required Files
AdCamp.ppt   car.wmf*
*Available on Microsoft Office CD-ROM. See "Adding Additional Clip Art," page xiv, for file location and instructions.

TEACH
Teaching Resources:
- PowerPoint Classroom Presentations
- School-to-Work Strategies Manual
- Internet Manual
- Spanish Glossary
- Methodology Video
- Certification Procedures

Objective 1 Assignment:
Exercise 10-12 (Skills Review) can be assigned after completing Objective 1.

LESSON 10 ■ **ADVANCED DRAWING TECHNIQUES**

do not print or appear in a slide show. When you display guides for the first time, you see one horizontal and one vertical line, each centered on the slide.

TABLE 10-1 **Working with Guides**

WHILE DRAGGING A GUIDE, PRESS	TO DO THIS
Shift	Measure the distance from the guide's starting position to its new position
Ctrl	Add a new guide
Shift + Ctrl	Add a new guide at a measured distance from an existing guide

EXERCISE 10-1 Work with Guides

1. Open the file **AdCamp.ppt** and move to slide 3 ("Newspaper Advertising").
2. To display guides, choose <u>G</u>uides from the <u>V</u>iew menu. Notice that <u>G</u>uides is a toggle command.

   NOTE: To see the guides more clearly, click to display the slide in black and white.

3. To prepare to move a guide, position the mouse pointer so it touches the vertical guide near the bottom of the slide, below the newspaper clip art object. Make sure you are clear of the clip art.

FIGURE 10-1
Working with guides in Black and White view

NOTE
In this Exercise, if students are having difficulty precisely positioning guides, you may want to tell them to turn on Snap to Grid, found on the D<u>r</u>aw menu. Snap to Grid is discussed later in this lesson.

Use PowerPoint Classroom Presentation #10 to display screens from the lesson, including this one, in a slide-show format.

311

UNIT 4 ■ CUSTOMIZING—BEYOND THE BASICS

> **NOTE:** When you drag the guide, make sure you see the white arrow pointer. If you drag the I-beam or four-headed arrow by mistake, you will move or resize an object instead of moving the guide.

4. Press and hold the mouse button. The measurement "0.00" appears over the pointer, indicating the guide is in the center of the slide.

FIGURE 10-2
Vertical guide moved 1.25 inches to the left

5. While pressing the mouse button, move to the left until the measurement 1.25 appears, then release the mouse. The horizontal guide moves to the left, 1.25 inches from the center of the slide. Release the mouse button.

6. To add a second vertical guide to the slide, point to the first guide and press and hold the [Ctrl] key while dragging the guide to the right. The plus sign below the indicator shows that you are adding a guide. Drag the guide 1.25 inches to the right of center. Notice that as you drag the guide, the indicator shows "0.00" as it passes the center of the slide, then increases as you drag to the right.

FIGURE 10-3
Adding a second vertical guide

7. Release the mouse button and then the [Ctrl] key.

8. Enlarge the newspaper picture proportionally so it fills the space between the guides (making the picture 2.5 inches wide and centered horizontally).

9. Remove the right vertical guide by dragging it to the right, off the edge of the slide.

> **NOTE:** You can add as many horizontal and vertical guides as you like. When you no longer need them, simply drag them off the slide. You can remove all but one set of guides that way. You can hide the remaining set of guides, but you cannot remove them.

10. Hide the guides by choosing <u>G</u>uides from the <u>V</u>iew menu. You can also press [Ctrl]+[G] to turn guides on or off.

EXERCISE 10-2 Make Measurements Using Guides

You can measure the distance from a guide to an object on a slide by dragging the guide while pressing the [Shift] key.

In PowerPoint Classroom Presentation #10.

312

LESSON 10 ■ **ADVANCED DRAWING TECHNIQUES**

NOTE

1. Move to slide 5 ("Direct Mail") and display the guides.

2. Drag the horizontal guide to the bottom of the screen. Because there is only one horizontal guide displayed, it will not be removed by moving it to the edge of the slide.

NOTE

3. While pointing to the horizontal guide (at the bottom edge of the screen), press and hold both [Shift] and the mouse button. Notice the measurement "0.00."

4. While holding [Shift], drag the guide up to the top edge of the postcard. Release the mouse and [Shift]. The distance from the bottom edge of the slide to the top of the postcard is 2.25 inches.

5. Without using [Shift], point to the horizontal guide and hold down the mouse button. The measurement indicates the horizontal guide is 1.5 inches below the center of the slide. Release the mouse button.

6. Using the techniques presented in steps 2, 3, and 4 above, move the vertical guide 2 inches in from the right edge of the slide. Align the right edge of the mailbox with the guide.

FIGURE 10-4
Measuring and positioning with guides

7. Position the post card 2 inches from the left edge of the slide.

8. Select the postcard, stamp, and mailbox. Use the Distribute <u>H</u>orizontally command to space the selected objects evenly.

9. Center the three objects vertically relative to each other.

Objective 2
Using Zoom

In previous lessons, you changed the zoom to view different parts of a slide. Zoom can be useful when you need to place objects precisely or view objects in fine detail for editing.

NOTE
One vertical guide and one horizontal guide are automatically positioned at the center of a slide when you create a new presentation. If you move the guides while editing or add additional guides and then save the presentation, the new positions are saved with the presentation. If you have two separate presentations open at the same time, you can set different guides for each. However, all the slides contained in one presentation have the same guide settings.

NOTE
You may want to allow some extra time for students to practice with the guides. Remember that when you simply drag a guide, it indicates the distance the guide moves from the center of the slide. When you press the Ctrl key while dragging, you add a new guide, and when you press the Shift key while dragging, you measure the distance from a guide's starting point to its ending point.

In PowerPoint Classroom Presentation #10.

313

UNIT 4 ■ CUSTOMIZING—BEYOND THE BASICS

EXERCISE 10-3 Use Zoom

NOTE

1. Move to slide 4 and select the radio.
2. Click the Zoom arrow to open the Zoom drop-down list and choose 200%. The radio is magnified in the center of the screen.

 NOTE: The zoomed window displays the center of the slide if no object is selected.

3. Ungroup the radio and click a blank part of the screen to deselect the radio parts. Click the radio handle to select the radio case and change its fill color to blue.
4. Regroup the radio parts and change the zoom to Fit (the option at the bottom of the Zoom drop-down list).

 NOTE: You can also zoom to values not on the Zoom drop-down list. To do this, select the value in the Zoom text box, key another value, and press Enter.

✏ Objective 3
Exploring the Snap and Nudge Features

The Snap and Nudge options offer more ways to align objects. You can set Snap so when you place an object close to another object, it "snaps" to the object as if it was magnetic, making the edges of the two objects touch. You can also set Snap so an object aligns with an imaginary grid. The grid consists of invisible horizontal and vertical lines covering your slide and is fixed at 12 points to the inch. When you turn on the grid, your objects automatically snap to the closest grid line. Sometimes Snap may be just what you need; at other times, it can keep you from precisely placing or drawing objects. You can use Nudge to move an object in very small increments, one tiny step at a time.

EXERCISE 10-4 Use the Snap to Grid Option

Like guides, the Snap to Grid option is a toggle. You click the option once to turn it on and click again to turn it off.

1. With slide 4 displayed, click D<u>r</u>aw on the Drawing toolbar, point to <u>S</u>nap, and click To <u>G</u>rid to turn the option on, if necessary. (If the To <u>G</u>rid

NOTE
The zoom settings suggested in this Exercise may not be correct for the screen resolution of the computers in your classroom. You may want to experiment with zoom settings before starting the class to determine the settings that work best.

✏ **Objective 3 Assignment:**
Exercise 10-13 (Skills Review) can be assigned after completing Objective 3.

LESSON 10 ■ ADVANCED DRAWING TECHNIQUES

button appears to be pushed in, Snap to Grid is already in effect and clicking it will turn off the option.)

2. If necessary, turn off Snap to Shape and hide the guides if they are showing.

3. Insert the clip art of the red sports car from the transportation category. (You can use the keywords "sports car" to locate the picture.) Size the picture proportionally so it is the same width as the radio.

 NOTE: You can use the Size tab on the Format Object and Format Picture dialog boxes to check the width of both the radio and the car to make them precisely the same width.

4. Position the car above the radio, but not touching it.

5. Select the radio and increase the zoom to 150%. Scroll down, if necessary, until both the car and the radio appear on the screen.

6. Drag the car so the bottoms of the tires exactly touch the top of the radio's handle. Notice how the car jumps from one position to the next. This is because Snap to Grid is turned on.

TIP: To temporarily disable the Snap to Grid option or guides, press Alt while dragging an object.

7. Use the Draw menu to turn off Snap to Grid. Drag the car up and down. Notice that you can drag the car smoothly and more precisely.

EXERCISE 10-5 Use the Nudge Option

The Nudge option gives you yet another way to precisely position an object.

1. With the car selected, change the zoom to 300%.

2. Click Draw on the Drawing toolbar and point to Nudge. Point to the bar at the top of the Nudge menu and drag it to create a floating toolbar. Position the floating toolbar at a convenient place on your screen. (See Figure 10-5 on the next page.)

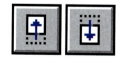

3. With the car selected, click the Nudge Up button a few times, then click the Nudge Down button until the car tires are once again precisely placed on top of the radio.

NOTE: You can also nudge a selected object with the Up, Down, Left, and Right arrow keys on your keyboard.

NOTE
You may want to discuss the Snap to Shape feature, which helps to place two objects so they exactly touch each other. This feature usually works best with regularly shaped objects such as circles, squares, or text boxes.

315

UNIT 4 ■ CUSTOMIZING—BEYOND THE BASICS

FIGURE 10-5
Using the Nudge option to precisely position an object

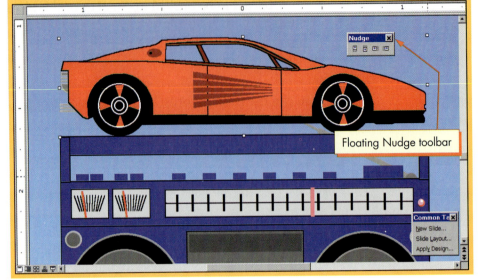

4. Change the zoom setting to Fit and then reactivate the Snap to Grid option.
5. Select both the car and the radio, center them horizontally relative to the slide, and group them.
6. Close the Nudge toolbar.

✓ Objective 4
Using the Freeform Tool

Using the Freeform tool you can draw irregular straight-sided or curved shapes. You can draw either closed objects (the end points meet) or open objects (the end points don't meet). Keep the following points in mind when you draw with the Freeform tool:

- To draw connected straight lines, click at the starting point, then click at the end point of each line segment where you want a new side to start.
- To draw curved lines, drag the pointer. As you drag, the pointer changes to a pencil shape.
- You can use both straight lines and curved lines in a freeform object.
- To complete a drawing, double-click at the end point or press Esc.

In the following exercises, you experiment with freeform drawing on a blank slide. Once you perfect your technique, you copy and paste your drawing to the appropriate slide.

In PowerPoint Classroom Presentation #10.

✓ **Objective 4 Assignment:**
Exercises 10-16 and 10-17 (Lesson Applications) can be assigned after completing Objective 4.

LESSON 10 ■ **ADVANCED DRAWING TECHNIQUES**

EXERCISE **10-6** Practice Drawing with the Freeform Tool

 1. Move to slide 7, which is a blank slide. Display the rulers, if necessary.

2. Click A<u>u</u>toShapes on the Drawing toolbar, point to <u>L</u>ines, and make the Lines submenu into a floating toolbar.

FIGURE 10-6
Freeform tool on the Lines toolbar

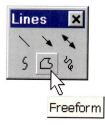

3. To practice drawing, you'll make an ice cream cone shape. Don't worry if your drawing is not perfect. You can delete it and try again until you get the feel of it. Click the Freeform tool on the Lines floating toolbar.

4. Position the crosshair pointer near the center of the slide and click the left mouse button once to anchor the starting point.

FIGURE 10-7
Practice with the Freeform tool

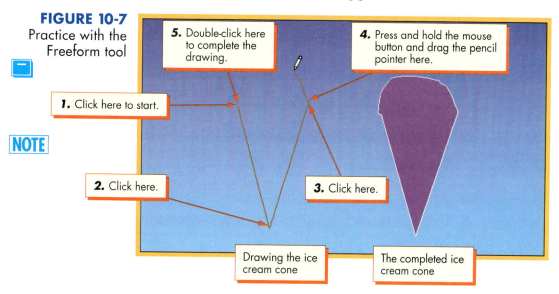

5. Click a second point diagonally down and to the right and a third point diagonally up and to the right of the second point. (See Figure 10-7.)

6. To draw the curved part of the ice cream cone, press and hold the mouse button at the third point, then drag a curved shape using Figure 10-7 as a guide. Notice that when you start dragging, the pointer changes to a pencil.

7. Make the curved shape touch the starting point. If necessary, double-click at the starting point to complete the drawing and deactivate the Freeform tool. The completed cone is filled with pink and outlined in white.

NOTE
Encourage students to spend some time experimenting with the Freeform tool at the end of Exercise 10-6 before going on to the next Exercise. Remind them that they can delete their drawings and try again until they feel comfortable using the tool.

In PowerPoint Classroom Presentation #10.

NOTE
When drawing a freeform shape, a fill is automatically applied if the freeform is a closed figure (the start point and the end point meet). If a drawing does not result in a closed figure, it is not filled by default. However, you can apply a fill manually to an open figure.

NOTE
If a freeform drawing is closed (the endpoint touches the starting point) it will not be necessary to double-click to deactivate the drawing tool. It will happen automatically. Many times a student will draw a shape that doesn't quite close. It is always necessary to double-click or press [ESC] to end a freeform object when the endpoints do not meet.

317

UNIT 4 ■ CUSTOMIZING—BEYOND THE BASICS

 NOTE: You can also press Esc to complete a drawing and deactivate the Freeform tool.

EXERCISE 10-7 Create a Freeform Object with Curved Lines

1. Delete the ice cream cone and any other practice drawings you created on slide 7.
2. Click . Hold down the mouse. The pointer changes to a pencil shape. Draw a small irregular-shaped round object, making sure you complete the object by joining the end point to the starting point.
3. Once you feel comfortable drawing curved objects, draw a cloud shape similar to the shape in Figure 10-8, making it about 2 inches long.

FIGURE 10-8
Freeform cloud shape

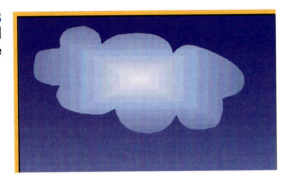

 NOTE: Don't worry if your drawing doesn't look like the figure, just do your best to make something similar. Drawing curved shapes takes some practice.

4. Change the cloud size to 1.75 inches wide and 0.75 inches high using the Format AutoShape dialog box.
5. Change the cloud's fill to the Daybreak gradient preset, choosing the From center option with the lightest color in the center.
6. Remove the cloud's outline.
7. Switch to Black and White view and change the cloud's black and white setting to Bla**c**k with White Fill. Switch back to Normal view.

TIP: Sometimes gradient fills do not print correctly in black and white. If this happens, you can change the object's black and white setting to Black with White Fill, Black, or White.

8. Copy the cloud and paste it on slide 2. Drag the cloud to the upper left corner, copy it again, and paste it three times.
9. Arrange the clouds in the upper right corner using Figure 10-9 as a guide.

NOTE

In PowerPoint Classroom Presentation #10.

NOTE
You might have students vary one cloud shape from another, rotate a cloud, or overlap clouds.

318

LESSON 10 ■ ADVANCED DRAWING TECHNIQUES

FIGURE 10-9
Slide 2 with clouds

EXERCISE 10-8 Draw a Freeform Object with Straight Lines

1. Delete the drawing objects on slide 7.
2. Click and draw a freeform arrow using Figure 10-10 as a guide. Don't worry if your arrow is not perfect. You learn how to edit a freeform drawing in the next exercise. Remember, to draw straight lines, click at the end point for each side of the drawing; do not drag the pointer.

TIP: You can modify a freeform object while drawing by pressing Backspace or Delete twice to undo the last end point.

FIGURE 10-10
Drawing a freeform arrow

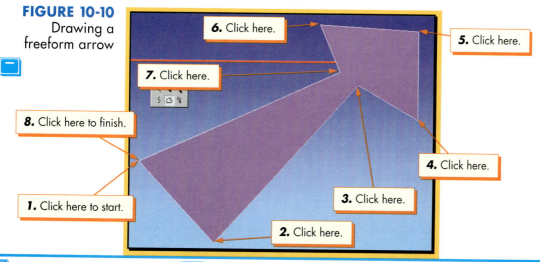

In PowerPoint Classroom Presentation #10.

NOTE
Stress that when drawing freeform objects with straight lines, you don't hold down the mouse button as in dragging. Instead, you move the pointer and click.

319

UNIT 4 ■ CUSTOMIZING—BEYOND THE BASICS

Editing a Freeform Drawing

Objective 5

After you draw a freeform object, you may want to modify its shape. You make such changes by using a reshaping handle called a *vertex*. You can add, delete, and move vertexes.

TABLE 10-2 **Working with Vertexes (Edit Points)**

NOTE

TO MAKE THIS HAPPEN	DO THIS	POINTER SHAPE
Move a vertex	Drag it to a new position.	✥
Add a new vertex	Point to a place on a line between two vertexes, then press Ctrl while clicking the line.	┽
Delete a vertex	Press Ctrl while clicking the vertex.	X

EXERCISE 10-9 Edit a Straight Line Freeform Object

1. On slide 7, right-click the freeform arrow you just drew and choose <u>E</u>dit Points from the shortcut menu. A series of small black squares—vertexes—appears at each of the line segment endpoints. When you point to a vertex, the pointer changes to a four-headed arrow that you can use to alter the object's shape.

    NOTE: You can also choose <u>E</u>dit Points from the D<u>r</u>aw menu.

2. Place the pointer on the bottom-most vertex at the bottom of the arrow. Drag the vertex to the right about 0.5 inches.

3. Place the pointer on the bottom right point of the top of the arrow. Drag the vertex slightly to the left to change the shape of the arrowhead.

4. To add a new vertex, place the pointer on the middle of the line forming the base of the arrow. Notice the crosshair pointer shape. Press and hold the Ctrl key and click. A new vertex appears. Drag the vertex out and away from the arrow to change its shape.

5. To delete a vertex, place the pointer on the new vertex. Press and hold the Ctrl key. Notice the pointer shape is now an "X." While holding the Ctrl key, make sure the "X" pointer is visible and click. The vertex is removed and the drawing changes shape.

Objective 5 Assignment:
Exercises 10-14 (Skills Review) and 10-18 (Lesson Applications) can be assigned after completing Objective 5.

NOTE
PowerPoint provides extensive methods for drawing and editing drawing objects that extend beyond the scope of this course. You may want to show students how to use the Scribble tool and how to work with the edit points on curved freeform objects. For example, you can set vertexes as straight, smooth, or corner points. (Right-click a vertex and notice the options on the shortcut menu.)

LESSON 10 ■ **ADVANCED DRAWING TECHNIQUES**

6. Add another vertex at the base of the arrow and drag it toward the center of the drawing.

FIGURE 10-11
The arrow after editing

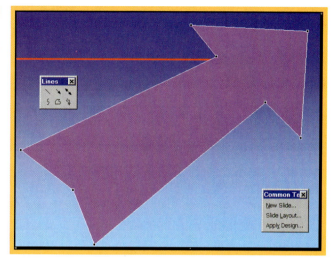

7. Continue editing points until your drawing looks similar to the one in Figure 10-11.

8. Once the arrow is the shape you like, change the fill to a two-color gradient using light blue for color 1 and medium blue for color 2. Choose the diagonal down shade and the first variant with the darker blue in the lower left corner. Remove the arrow's outline.

9. Copy and paste the arrow to slide 6 ("Yellow Pages"). Send the arrow to the back and add a text shadow to the bulleted text.

10. Change the black and white settings for the arrow to light grayscale.

11. Delete the arrow on slide 7, leaving a blank slide for more drawing.

✓ Objective 6
Using the Curve Tool

The Curve tool makes it easy to create smooth curved lines, but it works best with uncomplicated shapes. To use the Curve tool, select it from the Lines toolbar. Click on the slide where you want the curve to start, then click wherever you want the curve to change shape or direction. To complete a curve drawing, double-click its endpoint or press Esc.

EXERCISE 10-10 Use the Curve Tool

1. Move to slide 7 and delete any practice drawings on the slide.

In PowerPoint Classroom Presentation #10.

✓ **Objective 6 Assignment:**
Exercise 10-15 (Lesson Applications) can be assigned after completing Objective 6.

321

UNIT 4 ■ CUSTOMIZING—BEYOND THE BASICS

2. Select the Curve tool on the Lines toolbar, then click a starting point anywhere on the slide. Move the crosshair diagonally down and click again. Notice the straight diagonal line that appears.

3. Move the crosshair diagonally up and click again. Notice that the line changed into a curve.

4. Make several more clicks in any position to get a feel for how this tool works.

5. End the curved drawing by double-clicking.

NOTE: If you see only resize handles but no line after completing the drawing, use [icon] to apply a line color to the selected line.

6. Practice drawing curves like the one in Figure 10-12. Keep your best attempt and delete the others.

FIGURE 10-12
Curve tool drawing

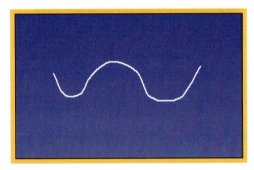

7. Display the curve drawing edit points. Notice that a vertex appears along the curve every place you click.

8. Practice adding, deleting, and dragging some vertexes to change the curve's shape. Practice drawing and editing with the Curve tool until you feel comfortable using it.

EXERCISE 10-11 Create a Finished Curve Tool Drawing

1. Move to slide 5 and draw and edit a curved line using , connecting the postcard, stamp, and mailbox. Use Figure 10-13 as a guide.

FIGURE 10-13
Curve drawing on slide 5

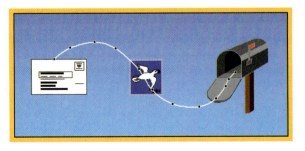

2. Select the curve by clicking it (without displaying the edit points). Change its color to red and make its line thickness 3 points. Add a solid arrowhead at the right end of the line.

3. Bring the postage stamp to the front so the red line is behind it.

In PowerPoint Classroom Presentation #10.

322

LESSON 10 ■ **ADVANCED DRAWING TECHNIQUES**

FIGURE 10-14
Completed curve drawing

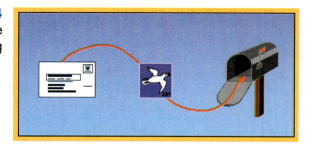

4. Group the postcard, stamp, mailbox, and curved line. Center the group horizontally on the slide.
5. Delete practice slide 7.
6. Adjust the black and white settings as needed
7. Save the presentation as *[your initials]***10-11.ppt**.
8. Add the date and your name to the handout header and the filename to the handout footer.
9. Print as handouts, 6 slides per page, black and white, framed.
10. Save and close the presentation.

COMMAND SUMMARY

NOTE

FEATURE	BUTTON	MENU	KEYBOARD
Display guides		View, Guides	
Nudge up	🔼	Draw, Nudge, Up	↑
Nudge down	🔽	Draw, Nudge, Down	↓
Nudge left	◀	Draw, Nudge, Left	←
Nudge right	▶	Draw, Nudge, Right	→

In PowerPoint Classroom Presentation #10.

NOTE
Point out that the Command Summary lists a variety of ways to accomplish a particular task. Unless the Nudge toolbar is displayed, the easiest method for moving an object incrementally is to use the Arrow keys. Holding down the Ctrl key while using the Arrow keys provides even more control.

UNIT 4 ■ CUSTOMIZING—BEYOND THE BASICS

TEST BANK

Concepts Review

TRUE/FALSE QUESTIONS

Each of the following statements is either true or false. Indicate your choice by circling **T** or **F**.

(T) F 1. Pressing ↑ is the keyboard equivalent of Nudge Up.

(T) F 2. You can use the Freeform tool to draw both straight and curved lines.

(T) F 3. If a specific percentage is not listed in the Zoom drop-down list box, you can key it in the box.

T (F) 4. You can edit points on objects drawn with the Freeform tool but not on objects drawn with the Curve tool.

T (F) 5. Press Alt while dragging a guide to measure the distance from the guide to another point on the slide.

(T) F 6. You can have more than one vertical guide on the screen at once.

T (F) 7. You can use the View menu to display an object's edit points.

(T) F 8. The Curve tool is available from the AutoShape menu, Line submenu.

SHORT ANSWER QUESTIONS

Write the correct answer in the space provided.

1. What key can you press to temporarily turn off the Snap to Grid feature?
   Alt key

2. Which menu do you open to turn the Snap to Grid option on or off?
   Draw menu on the Drawing toolbar

3. What shape is the pointer when you delete a vertex?
   x

4. How do you delete a point from a freeform drawing?
   Press Ctrl while clicking the vertex

5. How do you display and hide guides?
   Choose Guides from the View menu or shortcut menu

Concepts Review:
Allows students to check their understanding.

TEST BANK
Consider using the Test Bank to provide an additional review of lesson concepts.

LESSON 10 ■ ADVANCED DRAWING TECHNIQUES

6. How do you display a second horizontal guide?

   Press Ctrl and drag the guide

7. If you have three horizontal guides displayed, how do you remove just one of them?

   Drag it off the screen

8. What shape is the mouse pointer when you are drawing a rounded freeform object?

   Pencil

CRITICAL THINKING

Answer these questions on a separate page. There are no right or wrong answers. Support your answers with examples from your own experience, if possible.

1. PowerPoint gives you many ways to control the size and position of objects on a slide. In what situations do you think guides are the best tool to use?
2. Which drawing tool do you think you'd use most often in presentations? How would you use it? Which tool do you feel most comfortable with and which would you like more practice with?

Skills Review

EXERCISE 10-12

Position guides and align objects with guides.

1. Open the file **SpEvent.ppt** and display the slide master.
2. Display the guides by choosing <u>G</u>uides from the <u>V</u>iew menu.
3. Position the vertical guide 2 inches from the left edge of the slide master by following these steps:
   a. Point to the vertical guide near the bottom of the slide where the guide is not on top of any object.
   b. Drag the guide to the left edge of the slide.
   c. Hold down the Shift key and drag the guide to the right until you see 2.00 on the guide indicator.

Critical Thinking Questions:
Answers will vary based on students' preferences, observations, experiences, and research.

Skills Review:
Provides guided practice for students. Objectives are indicated for each Exercise.

Exercise 10-12:
Objective 1
Required File: SpEvent.ppt
Solution File: gl10-12.ppt in Solutions Manual or on Solutions Disk

325

UNIT 4 ■ CUSTOMIZING—BEYOND THE BASICS

4. Add a second vertical guide 1 inch from the right edge of the slide by following these steps:

   a. Point to the vertical guide making sure you see the arrow pointer.

   b. Press and hold the [Ctrl] key, then drag the guide to the right edge of the slide.

   c. Working with the right guide, press the [Shift] key and drag the guide to the left until you see 1.00 on the guide indicator.

5. Resize both the title placeholder and the bullet text placeholder so their left edges align with the left guide and their right edges align with the right guide.

6. Position the horizontal guide 0.5 inches from the top of the slide master. Add a second horizontal guide 1.5 inches below the first by following these steps:

   a. Point to the horizontal guide being sure to see an arrow pointer.

   b. While pressing and holding both the [Ctrl] and [Shift] keys, drag the guide until you see 1.50 on the indicator.

7. Move the bullet text placeholder so its top edge aligns with the second horizontal guide, then move the title placeholder so its top edge aligns with the top guide.

8. Move the top horizontal guide so it is 2.75 inches from the top of the slide.

9. Add a vertical guide 0.75 inch from the left edge of the slide.

10. Draw a triangle approximately 1 inch high and 0.75 inches wide. Use the Format AutoShape dialog box to adjust the size to exactly these measurements.

11. Align the triangle's top and left points with the left vertical guide and the top horizontal guide, as shown in Figure 10-15.

FIGURE 10-15
Placement of guides and triangles

326

LESSON 10 ■ ADVANCED DRAWING TECHNIQUES

12. Apply a one-color blue (title text color) gradient fill to the triangle, choosing the darkest setting, shading it from the center using the variant with the dark shade in the center.

13. Duplicate the triangle (Ctrl+D) and drag the copy directly below the first triangle so its top point aligns with the second horizontal line (and overlaps the first triangle slightly). See Figure 10-15 for placement.

14. Duplicate the triangle 4 more times to create a vertical line of 6 triangles.

15. Remove the bullets from the bullet text placeholder.

16. Group the triangles and copy them to the title master.

17. View each slide and adjust the black and white settings, if necessary.

18. Save the presentation as *[your initials]***10-12.ppt**.

19. Add the date and your name to the handout header and the filename to the handout footer.

20. Print as handouts, 6 slides per page, black and white, framed.

21. Save and close the presentation.

EXERCISE 10-13

Use the zoom and snap options.

1. Open the file **FoodGrp.ppt**.

2. Hide the guides if they are showing, turn off the Snap to Grid option, and turn on Snap to Shape following these steps:
   a. Click Draw on the Drawing toolbar.
   b. Point to Snap.
   c. On the Snap submenu, click To Grid, if necessary, to turn it off.
   d. Reopen the Snap submenu and turn on the Snap to Shape option.

3. Near the bottom left corner of the title slide, draw a small square. Use the Size tab of the Format AutoShape dialog box to make the square exactly 0.42 inches high and 0.42 inches wide.

4. If necessary, make the fill color of the square dark red, following the fills scheme color.

5. Copy and paste the square, then change the copy's color to reddish brown, the accent scheme color.

6. Drag the copy to the right of the first square. It should snap to the edge of the square perfectly. Zoom to a large size to check its position, then zoom back to a size convenient for working.

7. Make another copy of the square, this time making it bright orange, the title text scheme color. Position it next to the second square.

Exercise 10-13:
Objectives 2, 3
Required File: FoodGrp.ppt
Solution File: gl10-13.ppt in Solutions Manual or on Solutions Disk

327

UNIT 4 ■ CUSTOMIZING—BEYOND THE BASICS

8. Make a dark yellow square and position it next to the orange square.
9. Copy the middle two squares and paste them to the right of the dark yellow square, creating a row of 6 aligned squares.
10. Group the squares, then copy the group and position it to the right of the original squares.
11. Copy and paste the group of squares two more times, positioning them to make a strip that is as wide as the slide.
12. Turn Snap to Shape off, then turn on Snap to Grid so you can precisely size the strip of squares to the width of the slide.
13. Group all the squares, then adjust the position and width of the strip so it is exactly the width of the slide.
14. Cut the strip of squares and paste it on the title master. Position it between the title placeholder and the subtitle placeholder.
15. Copy the strip of squares to the slide master and move it to the bottom edge.
16. Using the Colors and Lines tab of the Format Object dialog box, change the colors to semitransparent (on the slide master only).
17. View the presentation in Slide Show view and check it in Black and White view, making adjustments if necessary.
18. Save the presentation as *[your initials]***10-13.ppt**.
19. Add the date and your name to the handout header and the filename to the handout footer.
20. Print as handouts, 6 slides per page, black and white, framed.
21. Save and close the presentation.

EXERCISE 10-14

Draw a freeform shape.

1. Open the file **Strategy.ppt**.
2. Change the slide color scheme to the one with the green background.
3. Insert a blank slide for practice drawings.
4. Create a floating Lines toolbar following these steps:
   a. Click AutoShapes on the Drawing toolbar.
   b. Point to Lines, then point to the gray bar at the top of the Lines menu and drag it away from the AutoShapes menu.
5. Draw a freeform object in the shape of a mountain by following these steps:
   a. On the practice slide, click .

Exercise 10-14:
Objectives 2, 4, 5
Required File: Strategy.ppt
Solution File: gl10-14.ppt in Solutions Manual or on Solutions Disk

LESSON 10 ■ ADVANCED DRAWING TECHNIQUES

b. Holding down the mouse button as you drag, draw a large irregular mountain shape on the slide. Close up the shape by making the end points meet, as shown in Figure 10-16.

FIGURE 10-16
Mountain shape

NOTE

6. Apply a two-color horizontal gradient fill to the mountain using medium green (the background scheme color) and dark green (the shadows scheme color). Choose the lower right shade variant (with the light color in the middle). Remove the mountain's outline.

7. Modify the shape by following these steps:

    a. To display the drawing's vertexes, right-click the mountain and choose Edit Points from the shortcut menu.

    b. Increase the zoom to view the vertexes more clearly.

    c. To delete a vertex, press and hold Ctrl, and point to a vertex. When you see the x-shape pointer, click.

    d. To add a new vertex, press and hold Ctrl while clicking the mountain's outline at a point between two vertexes.

8. Change the mountain's black and white setting to light grayscale.

9. Size the mountain to 7.5 inches high and 7.5 inches wide at the base using the Format AutoShape dialog box.

10. Copy and paste the mountain. Resize the copy so it becomes a smaller version of the original mountain. Move the copy to the right about 1 inch. Group the mountains.

11. Copy and paste the mountains to the title master and the slide master. On each master slide, send the mountains back one step at a time until the

NOTE
Students should draw the mountain by combining curved and straight lines: Draw the hump as a curved shape by holding down the mouse, then release the mouse to draw a straight line for the base, connecting to the starting point.

329

UNIT 4 ■ CUSTOMIZING—BEYOND THE BASICS

title placeholder, subtitle placeholder, and bullet text placeholder are all visible.

12. Delete the practice slide, view the presentation, and check its black and white settings.

13. Save the presentation as *[your initials]***10-14.ppt**.

14. Add the date and your name to the handout header and the filename to the handout footer.

15. Print as handouts, 6 slides per page, black and white, framed.

16. Save and close the presentation.

EXERCISE 10-15

Draw a curved line, using guides for precision.

1. Open the file **MiamiFun.ppt**.
2. Insert a new blank practice slide and display the guides, if necessary.
3. Set three vertical guides to the left of the center guide, spaced 1.5 inches from each other. Set up three more guides with the same spacing to the right of the center guide, making a total of 7 vertical guides.
4. Move the horizontal guide 0.25 inches below the top edge of the shaded rectangle at the bottom of the slide. Set a second guide 0.5 inches above that guide. Refer to Figure 10-17 for guide placement.

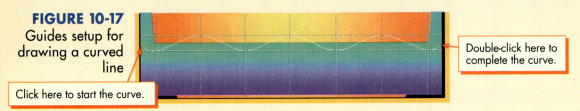

FIGURE 10-17 Guides setup for drawing a curved line

Click here to start the curve.

Double-click here to complete the curve.

5. Draw a curved line following these steps:
    a. Display the Lines floating toolbar and click [5].
    b. Click the Curve tool crosshair on the left top edge of the shaded rectangle being careful to click just inside the edge of the slide.
    c. Click again at the intersection of the leftmost vertical guide and the bottom horizontal guide.
    d. Click at the intersection of the second vertical guide and the top horizontal guide.
    e. Continue across the slide, clicking in a pattern to create the curve shown in Figure 10-17.

Exercise 10-15:
Objectives 1, 5, 6
Required File: MiamiFun.ppt
Solution File: gl10-15.ppt in Solutions Manual or on Solutions Disk.

LESSON 10 ■ **ADVANCED DRAWING TECHNIQUES**

  - **f.** Double-click just inside the right edge of the slide to complete the curve. Be careful when making the final point to click inside the edge of the slide.
  - **g.** If necessary, display the curve's edit points and adjust their placement.
6. Right-click the curve and choose Format AutoShape from the shortcut menu.
7. Click the Colors and Lines tab and set the line weight to 54 pt. For the line color, choose Patterned lines. Make the foreground color light green and the background blue. Choose the diamond pattern in the lower right corner of the pattern samples.
8. Format the patterned line's black and white setting as light grayscale.

9. Display the line's edit points and drag each edit point out and off the slide so the end of the corner edges of the line are outside the slide.
10. Copy the patterned line and paste it on the title master and again on the slide master. Adjust the line's position so it covers the top edge of the shaded rectangle.
11. Delete the practice slide.
12. View the presentation in Slide Show view and check its black and white settings.
13. Save the presentation as *[your initials]***10-15.ppt**.
14. Add the date and your name to the handout header and the filename to the handout footer.
15. Print as handouts, 6 slides per page, black and white, framed.
16. Save and close the presentation.

NOTE
Remind students that it's okay if a graphic object extends past the edges of the slide. In this case, the curve extends beyond the left and right edges.

UNIT 4 ■ CUSTOMIZING—BEYOND THE BASICS

Lesson Applications

EXERCISE 10-16

Draw a straight-sided freeform object using guides.

1. Open the file **Summary.ppt**.
2. Delete the graphic shape on the title master and also on the slide master. Delete the black horizontal line on the title master.
3. Set a horizontal guide at 0.25 inches from the top of the slide. Set a second guide 2 inches below the first one. Set five more horizontal guides, starting 1 inch below the second guide and spaced 1 inch apart.
4. Move the vertical guide 0.5 inches from the left edge of the slide, then set 5 more guides spaced 1 inch apart, starting 1 inch to the right of the first guide. Place one more vertical guide 0.5 inches from the right edge of the slide.

FIGURE 10-18
Guides for drawing straight-sided freeform object

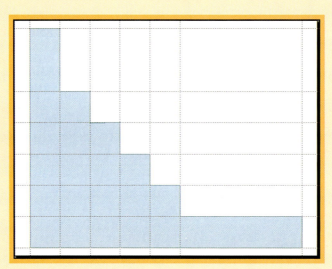

5. Add a blank practice slide and draw the shape shown in Figure 10-18 using the Freeform tool.
6. Reposition and resize the freeform shape so its edges extend to the edges of the slide. Hide the guides.
7. Apply a 3 pt orange outline and a two-color horizontal gradient fill using light blue and pale yellow. Choose the upper left variant with blue on the top and yellow on the bottom.
8. Change the background for all slides to a horizontal two-color gradient fill using the same blue and yellow, but choosing the variant that is blue in the middle and yellow on the outside.

Assessment Resources:
- Solutions Manual
- Test Bank with Software
- Portfolio Builder
- Alternative Assessment Guide
- Certification Procedures

Lesson Applications:
Provide independent practice for students. Objectives are indicated for each Exercise.

Exercise 10-16:
Objectives 1, 4
Required File: Summary.ppt
Solution File: gl10-16.ppt in Solutions Manual or on Solutions Disk.

LESSON 10 ■ ADVANCED DRAWING TECHNIQUES

9. Copy the freeform shape to the slide master and to the title master. Adjust its position if necessary.
10. Delete the practice slide.
11. On slide 1, right-align the title and subtitle text and adjust the text box positions if they overlap the freeform object.
12. On slide 4, create the following information as a tabbed table. Use 28-point Arial bold text. Use right-aligned tabs for the "Leased" and "Bought" columns.

	Leased	Bought
Kitchen	15,450	25,350
Dining	14,400	18,650
Office	10,500	25,500
Other	15,250	16,300

13. Add 0.5 inch paragraph spacing between the column headings and the numbers. There should be no extra paragraph spacing before or after the text below the headings. Place the table attractively below the slide title, to the right of the freeform object.
14. Move and resize the bulleted text boxes on slides 2 and 3 if they overlap the freeform object.
15. View the presentation in Slide Show view and check the black and white settings.
16. Save the presentation as *[your initials]***10-16.ppt**.
17. Add the date and your name to the handout header and the filename to the handout footer.
18. Print as handouts, 6 slides per page, black and white, framed.
19. Save and close the presentation.

EXERCISE 10-17

Draw with a variety of drawing tools.

1. Open the file **MParty.ppt**.
2. Add a new slide for practice drawing.
3. On the practice slide, create a confetti collage by drawing irregular shapes and vertical lines using the Freeform tool. (You can also try drawing lines with the Scribble tool.) Color the shapes in various colors from the color scheme. Use Figure 10-19 (on the next page) as a guide.
4. Select all the items you drew and group them. Copy the group, then flip it horizontally and vertically.
5. Ungroup all the confetti items and randomly move and recolor some of them.

Exercise 10-17:
Objectives 1, 4
Required File: MParty.ppt
Solution File: gl10-17.ppt in Solutions Manual or on Solutions Disk.

The completed presentation for this Exercise may be used in a student's portfolio.

UNIT 4 ■ CUSTOMIZING—BEYOND THE BASICS

FIGURE 10-19
Confetti

6. When you are satisfied with the composition of your confetti, group it and size it so it extends from the top to the bottom of the slide and is approximately 1.5 inches wide.

7. Copy the confetti to the slide master and the title master, then delete the practice slide.

8. On the title master, move the text placeholders to the right to make a nice composition with the confetti. Center both text placeholders relative to each other. Add a 3-point outline to the subtitle placeholder using a complementary color. Make the placeholder's internal margins 0.5 inches wide on all sides and change its text box settings to word wrap and automatic resizing.

9. On the slide master, set two vertical guides, one 3 inches to the left of center and the other 4.5 inches to the right of center. Reduce the width of both the title placeholder and the bullet text placeholders so they fit between the guides. For the bullet text placeholder, change its text box settings to word wrap and resize to fit. Set its text box margins to 0.25 inches all around and give the placeholder a 3-point outline. For the title placeholder, increase the font size to 48 point.

10. Move to the title slide in Slide view. Change the title text font to 66 point and change the first line of the subtitle text to 44 point. Move both text boxes up on the page until they appear centered vertically.

11. Adjust the length of the bullet text boxes on slides 2 and 3 if necessary.

12. Check the presentation in Slide Show view and check its black and white settings.

13. Save the presentation as *[your initials]***10-17.ppt**.

14. Add the date and your name to the handout header and the filename to the handout footer.

15. Print as handouts, 6 slides per page, black and white, framed.

16. Save and close the presentation.

EXERCISE 10-18

Draw decorative freeform shapes.

1. Open the file **Samples.ppt**. Apply the **Blush.pot** template.

2. On both the slide master and the title master, ungroup the graphic elements, then remove the pink horizontal stripe, the yellow vertical stripe, and the multi-color rectangle shape. Make sure the shaded background remains intact.

Exercise 10-18:
Objectives 1–5
Required File: Recipe1.ppt
Solution File: gl10-18.ppt in Solutions Manual or on Solutions Disk.

 The completed presentation for this Exercise may be used in a student's portfolio.

334

3. Change the font for all title and slide master text placeholders to Arial Black. Change the second level bulleted text to Arial with no bullet and no hanging indent. Reduce the size of all bulleted text by one font size.

4. Add a blank slide to use for drawing practice. Using the Freeform tool, draw a long thin irregular shape like the one shown in Figure 10-20.

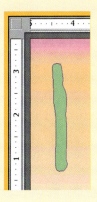

FIGURE 10-20
Draw this long thin shape

5. Resize the drawing to 2.5 inches high and 0.4 inches wide. Apply a one-color gradient fill, shading from very dark green at the top to bright green at the bottom. Remove the outline.

6. Position the shape about 1 inch from the left edge of the slide with the top of the shape slightly overlapping the top of the slide.

7. Copy and paste the shape. Resize the copy to 5.5 inches high by 0.4 inches wide. Change the gradient fill to green at the top and white at the bottom.

8. Position the copy so its top slightly overlaps the original drawing's bottom. Increase the zoom to make sure the objects overlap smoothly. It's okay if the copy extends beyond the slide's bottom edge.

9. Make a copy of the longer object and rotate it 90 degrees to the left. Apply a two-color vertical gradient fill choosing the pink that follows the accent and hyperlink scheme color and the peach that follows the shadows scheme color. Choose the variant that has pink on the left and peach on the right.

10. Use a guide to position the new object 0.5 inch from the top edge of the slide. Resize the object to extend from the left edge to the right edge of the slide.

11. Group the two green objects, then bring the green group to the front. Use a guide to position it 0.5 inch from the left edge of the slide.

12. Group all the objects you drew, then copy the group and paste it to the slide master. Adjust the position of the graphic. Bring the title placeholder one level in front of the graphic.

13. Copy the drawing to the title master. Ungroup it, then reposition the pink object so it is centered vertically on the slide. Regroup the drawn objects.

14. Delete the practice slide, and save the presentation as *[your initials]* **10-18.ppt**.

15. Add the date and your name to the handout header and the filename to the handout footer.

16. Print as handouts, 6 slides per page, black and white, framed.

17. Save and close the presentation.

UNIT 4 ■ CUSTOMIZING—BEYOND THE BASICS

Unit 4 Applications

APPLICATION 4-1

Work with bullets, indents, and tabs; change paragraph spacing; and customize a handout master.

1. Open the file **JobFair.ppt**. Change the color scheme to the third scheme in the second row of color schemes (the one with the white background and red, blue, green, and gray bars) and apply a white marble textured background to all slides in the presentation.

2. On the slide master, increase all text in the title placeholder and bullet placeholder by one size and make all text bold.

3. Change the color of the Good 4 U logo from green to red and apply Shadow Style 6 to the object. Change the shadow color to semi-transparent gray and nudge the shadow down and to the right to make it more dramatic.

4. Insert a title master by choosing New Title Master on the Common Tasks toolbar. (A title master is not always automatically available.)

5. On the title master, increase the title text to 60-point bold and the subtitle text to 48-point bold. Move both text placeholders to the top half of the slide.

6. Resize the red logo proportionally to 8 inches wide. Center the logo horizontally on the bottom half of the title master and nudge its shadow down and to the right enough to give it more depth.

7. On slide 1, key the title **Great Jobs 4 U** and the subtitle **at**.

8. On slide 2, change the bullet to the slightly larger round bullet from the Symbol font, make it red, and decrease the bullet spacing to 0.25 inches from the text.

9. Still working on slide 2, change the before paragraph spacing to 0.5 lines. Make the text box just wide enough for the text in the first bullet and center the text box horizontally on the slide.

10. Insert a new slide after slide 2 using the Title Only layout. Key the title **Salary Ranges** and create a tabbed table using the following text:

    Wait staff [Tab] $ [Tab] 8.00 [Tab] plus tips

    Assistant chefs [Tab] $ [Tab] 12.50 [Tab] to start

    Experienced chefs [Tab] $ [Tab] 17.50 [Tab] and up

11. Format the table text as 32-point bold, insert appropriate tab stops, and size and position the text box appropriately.

Assessment Resources:
- Solutions Manual
- Test Bank with Software
- Portfolio Builder
- Alternative Assessment Guide
- Certification Procedures
- Projects Manual

Unit Applications: Provide independent practice of the skills acquired from each lesson in the Unit.

Project: After students complete Unit 4, you can assign Project #4 from the Projects Manual.

Unit Application 4-1: Required File: JobFair.ppt Solution File: glu4-1.ppt in Solutions Manual or on Solutions disk

UNIT 4 ■ APPLICATIONS

12. On slide 4, change the slide layout to Title Slide. Arrange the title and subtitle text so they are closer together and positioned attractively above the Good 4 U logo.

13. Using the Replace Font command, change Times New Roman to Tahoma throughout the presentation. (Use Arial if you don't have Tahoma.)

14. Review the presentation, making adjustments to text size and text box placement as needed to make an attractive presentation.

15. Change the black and white setting for each slide to light grayscale.

16. Customize the handout master by deleting the page number placeholder and adding the text **Job Fair Presentation** to the footer placeholder (after "<footer>"). Center the footer placeholder horizontally, center align the footer text, and increase the font one size.

17. Save the presentation as *[your initials]***u4-1.ppt**.

18. Create a handout header with the date and your name and a handout footer with the filename. Clear the page number check box, if necessary.

19. Print as handouts, 6 slides per page, black and white, framed.

20. Save and close the presentation.

APPLICATION 4-2

Change page setup options and use drawing tools to create a menu.

1. Start a new blank presentation. Set the page orientation to Portrait with slides sized for Letter Paper.

2. Apply the "Facilitating a Meeting" template from the Presentations folder. Change to the second color scheme and remove the large diamond graphic from both the slide master and title master.

3. Insert a new slide using the Title Only layout. On slide 1, key **July 4th Brunch Menu** for the title and decrease the font size to 24-point Tahoma. The text should have a shadow and be left-aligned.

4. Draw an oval 1 inch high and 2 inches wide. Key **Starters** in the oval. Format the text as 24-point Tahoma with a text shadow and purple text color. Change the oval's fill color to white with a purple outline. Apply Shadow Style 6 to the oval. Nudge the shadow down and to the right to make it a little bigger and make the shadow purple.

5. Copy and paste the oval. Format the copy as follows:
   - Resize to 1.5 inches high and 3.75 inches wide.
   - Set text box margins to 0.0 inches all around, turn on word wrap, and set the text box anchor to Middle.

Unit Application 4-2:
Required File: None
Solution File: glu4-2.ppt in Solutions Manual or on Solutions disk

The completed presentation for this Application may be used in a student's portfolio.

337

UNIT 4 ■ CUSTOMIZING—BEYOND THE BASICS

- Change the font to 12-point Tahoma, black text color, no shadow.
- Left-align the text and set a 2.25-inch decimal tab.
- Make sure line spacing is set at 1 line and spacing before and after paragraphs is set to 0.

6. Change the text "Starters" in the second oval to **Red, White, and Blue**. After "blue," insert a tab and key **3.50**. Press Enter and key **Raspberries and blueberries with a lightly sweetened vanilla yogurt topping**

7. Change the text "Red, White, and Blue" to 14 point, shadowed, and purple.

FIGURE U4-1
Slide 1

8. Copy and paste the oval three times and change the text in each oval to match the Starter menu items shown in Figure U4-1. Arrange the ovals in an overlapping pattern at the top of the screen using the figure as a guide.

9. Select all the ovals and copy them to the bottom half of the slide. Change all the purple text to dark blue (a custom color) and change the outline and shadow color of the copied ovals to dark blue as well.

10. In the copied ovals, key the Bread menu items shown in Figure U4-1.

11. In Slide Sorter view, copy the slide to make a new slide 2.

FIGURE U4-2
Slide 2

12. On slide 2, omit the background graphics from the master. Copy the purple and yellow vertical bars from the slide master and paste them on slide 2. Position the bars on slide 2 on the right side of the slide creating a mirror image of slide 1. Right-align the title on slide 2.

13. Select all the ovals on slide 2, group them, flip them horizontally, and ungroup them. This completes the mirror image of slide 1.

14. Key the Main Dish and Beverage menu items as shown in Figure U4-2.

UNIT 4 ■ APPLICATIONS

15. Check spelling in the presentation.
16. Check black and white settings and make changes, if necessary.
17. Insert your name in the footer using the following format: *[your name]*, **Manager**

 NOTE: Your name appears only on the slide 1 because you turned off master graphic elements on slide 2.

18. Save the presentation as *[your initials]***u4-2.ppt**.
19. Print both pages of the presentation as full-size slides.
20. Save and close the presentation.

APPLICATION 4-3

Use drawing tools, work with the snap to grid feature, change line and paragraph spacing, and change bullets and indents.

1. Open the file **Owners.ppt**. Change the slide color scheme to the first choice in the bottom row of color scheme samples.
2. Insert a new blank slide to use for practice drawing.
3. On the new slide, use the Rectangle tool to draw a 0.5 inch square. Apply the purple fill color that follows the accent and hyperlink scheme color. Remove the outline from the square.
4. Turn off snap to grid and hide guides, if necessary. Using the Freeform tool, draw an irregular shape that is square overall. Make it as large as is convenient for you. In the next two steps, you resize and position the shape within the square. See Figure U4-3 as a guide to the freeform shape.

FIGURE U4-3
Freeform shape within a square

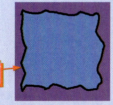

Freeform shape

5. When you get a shape you like, size it to 0.45 inch high by 0.45 inch wide. If necessary, change the fill color of the object to medium blue, following the fills scheme color. Keep the outline black.
6. Drag the irregular shape inside the square, center the objects relative to each other, and group them.
7. Turn snap to grid back on and move the grouped object to the left edge of the slide, roughly centered vertically. Zoom in on the grouped square object.
8. Using the Duplicate command, along with snap to grid and zoom, create a continuous horizontal line composed of copies of the grouped square object. Group the entire line of objects and size it to the width of the slide, if necessary.

Unit Application 4-3:
Required File: Owners.ppt and clip art file Handshk1.wmf (see page xiv for clip art file locations and instructions)
Solution File: glu4-3.ppt in Solutions Manual or on Solutions disk

The completed presentation for this Application may be used in a student's portfolio.

339

UNIT 4 ■ CUSTOMIZING—BEYOND THE BASICS

9. Copy the group of squares and paste it onto the title master, positioned directly below the title placeholder.
10. On the slide master, move the bullet text placeholder down 0.5 inch and paste the group of squares directly below the title placeholder.
11. On the slide master, change the first level bullet to a solid square from the Monotype Sorts font, sized as 85% of the text. Increase the indent of the bulleted text to 0.5 inch.
12. Change the presentation background to a two-color horizontal gradient using blue and green. Choose the variant with blue on top and green on the bottom.
13. Delete your practice slide.
14. Insert a new slide after slide 4 using the Bulleted Text layout. Key the title **The Time is Now** and the following bulleted items:
    - **Talk to other owners**
    - **Review franchise packet materials**
    - **Review financing information**
    - **Submit application**
15. Increase the before paragraph spacing of the bulleted text to 0.5 lines. Size the text box to fit the text and position it attractively on the slide.
16. Insert the clip art image of the two shaking hands, using the keyword "handshake." Size the image to the size of the bulleted text box, position it over the text box, and format it as a watermark. (Hint: Watermark is an image control option.)
17. Send the clip art to the back. Align the clip art object and the text box relative to each other.
18. On slide 3, change the line spacing to 1.2 and increase the before paragraph spacing to 0.5. Make the text box 3.5 inches high and 6 inches wide and position it attractively on the slide.
19. Go through the remaining slides and make size and placement adjustments as needed.
20. View the presentation in Slide Show view and check its black and white settings.
21. Check spelling in the presentation.
22. Save the presentation as *[your initials]***u4-3.ppt**.
23. Add the date and your name to the handout header and the filename to the handout footer.
24. Format the handout master placeholders as bold.
25. Print handouts, 6 slides per page, black and white, framed.
26. Save and close the presentation.

UNIT 5

Advanced Topics

LESSON 11 Creating a Chart
LESSON 12 Creating a Table
LESSON 13 Creating Flowcharts and Organization Charts
LESSON 14 Animation and Slide Show Effects
LESSON 15 Using the Internet

Creating a Chart

OBJECTIVES

After completing this lesson, you will be able to:
1. Insert a chart.
2. Change sample data.
3. View a new chart.
4. Edit a chart.
5. Format a chart.
6. Add shapes and text objects to a chart.
7. Create a pie chart.

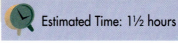
Estimated Time: 1½ hours

NOTE

Charts are diagrams that display numbers in pictorial format. Charts can help you understand the significance of numeric information more easily than viewing the same information as a table or list of numbers.

Objective 1
Inserting a Chart

When you create a new slide, the New Slide dialog box offers three slide Auto-Layouts that include a *chart placeholder*, which is the dotted box that shows the position of the chart on the slide. Two of the layouts include both chart and text placeholders; the third is for chart-only slides.

Point out to students that the learning objectives show what they will learn in the lesson. Each heading in the lesson correlates to a learning objective.

Required Files
Finan1.ppt

Teaching Resources:
- PowerPoint Classroom Presentations
- School-to-Work Strategies Manual
- Internet Manual
- Spanish Glossary
- Methodology Video
- Certification Procedures

NOTE
This lesson provides a basic introduction to charts. You may want to explore some of the advanced chart features with students, such as 3-D charts, line charts, combination charts, and importing Excel data.

LESSON 11 ■ **CREATING A CHART**

EXERCISE 11-1 Choose a Chart Slide Layout

1. Open the file **Finan1.ppt**.
2. Click [icon]. In the New Slide dialog box, notice the three chart options in the second row.

FIGURE 11-1
Chart layout

3. Choose Chart, which is the last layout on the second row, and click OK. A new slide with the chart placeholder appears.
4. Key **Special Events Forecast** in the title placeholder.
5. Double-click the chart icon in the chart placeholder. By activating the chart icon, you open Microsoft Graph within PowerPoint. A sample chart and sample data appear, along with a new toolbar at the top of the screen with chart-related buttons.

Objective 2
Changing Sample Data

When you open Microsoft Graph, a sample datasheet appears, making it easier for you to understand how to enter your own numbers. As you enter data, you can monitor the results on the sample chart. You key new information by overwriting the sample data or by deleting it and keying your own data.

EXERCISE 11-2 Make Changes to Sample Data

The datasheet contains rows and columns of cells. You enter each number or label in a separate cell the same way that you would enter information in Excel. The datasheet also contains gray column heads and row heads that indicate the row numbers and column letters.

1. If necessary, drag the datasheet by its title bar to the upper left corner of the slide so you can see the sample chart. You can also use zoom and the scroll bars to adjust the screen so you can see everything and you can resize the datasheet to make it larger or smaller.

NOTE: When working in Microsoft Graph, be sure to click your mouse pointer only in the datasheet or within the sample chart. If you click anywhere else, Microsoft Graph closes and you return to Slide view. If that happens, double-click the chart displayed on the slide to return to Microsoft Graph.

Use PowerPoint Classroom Presentation #11 to display screens from the lesson, including this one, in a slide-show format.

You may want to tell students that the terms "chart" and "graph" are sometimes used interchangeably, although in this lesson chart is used consistently.

When you begin Exercise 11-2, stress that students are actually working in the Microsoft Graph program. Point out the different toolbars and menu items.

Make sure students understand what happens when they click outside the chart. If they click off the chart (for example, the gray area of the slide), the data sheet and Chart menu disappear and the Slide view is redisplayed.

343

UNIT 5 ■ ADVANCED FEATURES

FIGURE 11-2
Creating a chart

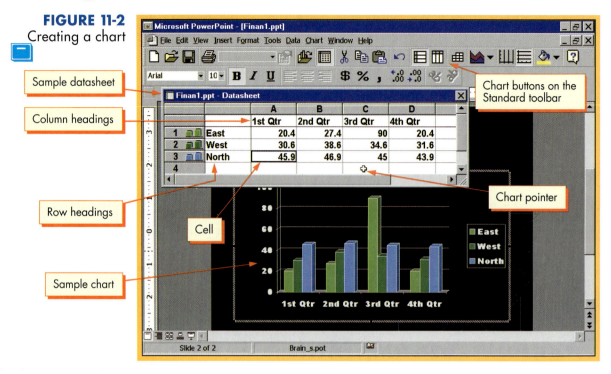

2. On the datasheet, click the word "East." A heavy black border surrounds the cell that contains "East." Notice that the mouse pointer is a white cross when working on the datasheet.

3. Move around the datasheet by clicking on individual cells, then try pressing Enter, Tab, Shift+Enter, Shift+Tab, and the arrow keys to get the feel of how to navigate in a datasheet.

4. Click cell A3 (the cell in column A, row 2 that contains the value 45.9).

5. Key **90** and press Enter. Notice that the blue bar for the first quarter becomes taller automatically.

6. Click [↶] to restore the blue bar to its original height.

NOTE: Although you can perform multiple undo actions elsewhere in PowerPoint and in other Microsoft Office programs, you get only one chance to undo an action when editing a chart. Be careful when making changes!

TABLE 11-1 | **Chart-Related Buttons on the Standard Toolbar**

BUTTON/NAME	FUNCTION
Chart Objects	Select an element of the chart.
Format	Format the selected chart item.
Import File	Import data from a spreadsheet or text file.

continues

In PowerPoint Classroom Presentation #11.

NOTE
You may need to tell students who are not familiar with Excel or other spreadsheet programs that entering data in a cell is a two-part process: they must key the data and then move to another cell. If the insertion point remains in the cell, the chart does not reflect the change. Students can press Tab, an Arrow key, or Enter to complete the entering process.

NOTE
Stress the difference between PowerPoint and Microsoft Graph regarding undo.

LESSON 11 **CREATING A CHART**

TABLE 11-1 Chart-Related Buttons on the Standard Toolbar *continued*

BUTTON/NAME	FUNCTION
View Datasheet	Display or hide the datasheet window.
By Row	Display chart data by rows.
By Column	Display chart data by columns.
Data Table	Display the values for each data series in a grid below the chart.
Chart Type	Change the chart type for the active chart or a selected data series.
Category Axis Gridlines	Show or hide category axis gridlines.
Value Axis Gridlines	Show or hide value axis gridlines.
Legend	Add or remove a chart legend
Drawing	Show or hide the Drawing toolbar.
Fill Color	Change the fill color or fill effect of the selected chart object.

EXERCISE 11-3 Delete Sample Data

1. Click cell A1, the 1st quarter cell for the West region.
2. Press Delete to delete the contents of cell A1. The first column in the chart is also deleted.
3. Drag the pointer from cell A2 to cell D2 to select the four numbers in row 2.
4. Press Delete. All the dark green chart columns for the West region are deleted along with their data.
5. Click the gray box in the upper left corner of the datasheet. The entire datasheet is selected.
6. Press Delete. The datasheet is now blank and ready for you to key new data. Notice that the chart disappears.

FIGURE 11-3
Editing the datasheet

Click here to select the entire datasheet.

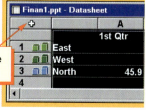

In PowerPoint Classroom Presentation #11.

345

UNIT 5 ■ ADVANCED FEATURES

EXERCISE 11-4 Key New Chart Data

The Microsoft Graph datasheet looks just like an Excel spreadsheet with one exception: There is an unnumbered row above row 1 and an unlettered column to the left of column A. This is where you key chart labels that appear below columns or in a legend.

NOTE: If you key labels in other rows or columns or leave gaps between columns or rows as you enter data, your chart will not display correctly.

1. Click the first cell in the upper left corner. All the cells in the datasheet are deselected. Now you can enter new data.

2. Key the numbers and labels shown in Figure 11-4. Be sure to put the labels in the top row and leftmost column. Notice how the chart grows as you key data.

3. Click the cell with the label "Los Angeles." Notice that the label is truncated.

4. Move the pointer to the right edge of the gray box at the top of the column containing Los Angeles (see Figure 11-4 for exact placement).

5. Drag the double-headed arrow pointer to the right to make the first column wide enough to display the entire label. (The chart will display properly even when datasheet columns are too narrow.)

FIGURE 11-4
Datasheet with new data

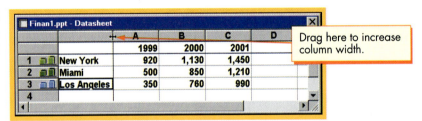

✓ Objective 3
Viewing the New Chart

Once you finish entering data, you can hide the datasheet by clicking its close button ⊠ or by clicking the View Datasheet button 🔳 on the Standard toolbar. To redisplay the datasheet, click 🔳 again (or choose <u>D</u>atasheet from the <u>V</u>iew menu).

To return to Slide view, simply click anywhere outside the datasheet and outside the chart area.

In PowerPoint Classroom Presentation #11.

✓ **Objective 3 Assignment:**
Exercise 11-19 (Skills Review) can be assigned after completing Objective 3.

346

LESSON 11 ■ **CREATING A CHART**

EXERCISE | **11-5** | **Hide the Datasheet and Return to Slide View**

1. Click the View Datasheet button 🔲 on the Standard toolbar to hide the datasheet.
2. Click 🔲 again to display the datasheet.
3. Click in the gray desktop area outside the slide to return to Slide view and close Microsoft Graph. The PowerPoint menu and toolbars reappear.

Objective 4
Editing a Chart

Once you create a chart, you can easily edit its data, colors, and other features. If Microsoft Graph is closed, double-click the chart in Slide view to edit it.

EXERCISE | **11-6** | **Edit an Existing Chart**

NOTE

1. In Slide view, on slide 2, double-click the chart to reactivate Microsoft Graph. If necessary, display the datasheet by clicking 🔲.
2. Key **1,450** in cell C3 to change the Los Angeles data for the year 2001.
3. Key **2002** in the first row of column D and press Enter. Notice that a space for new columns appears on the chart.
4. Delete the entry you just keyed. Notice that the space reserved for the new columns remains on the chart.
5. Right-click the column D head (the gray box at the top of the data column with "D" in it) to select the column and open the shortcut menu. Choose Cle<u>a</u>r Contents. Column D is no longer displayed on the chart and the extra space is removed.

EXERCISE | **11-7** | **Switching Rows and Columns**

NOTE

When you key data for a new chart, Microsoft Graph interprets each row of data as a *data series*. On a column chart, each data series is usually displayed in a distinct color. For example, using the current chart, the New York row is one data series and is displayed in light green. Miami is a second data series, displayed in dark green, and Los Angeles is a third, displayed in blue.

Sometimes it's hard to predict if it's best to arrange your data in rows or columns. Fortunately, you can enter it either way and switch back and forth.

NOTE
Point out that to students that they can resize the datasheet window just as they'd resize any window: position the pointer on a corner or side edge of the datasheet window and drag the double-headed arrow.

NOTE
Although many people consider bar charts to be either horizontal or vertical, PowerPoint uses "column chart" for vertical bars and "bar chart" for horizontal bars to distinguish the different orientations.

347

UNIT 5 ■ ADVANCED FEATURES

1. Close the datasheet, which is now complete.
2. Click the By Column button on the Standard toolbar. The chart columns are now grouped by city instead of by year. The city names are displayed below each group of columns.
3. Click the By Row button to group the chart columns by year again.
4. Click again and return to Slide view.
5. Omit the background graphics from slide 2 (choose Ba**c**kground from the F**o**rmat menu, click the check box, and click **A**pply). Your chart should look like the one shown in Figure 11-5.
6. Save the presentation as *[your initials]***11-7.ppt**.
7. Add the date and your name to the handout header and add the filename to the handout footer. Print handouts, 2 slides per page, framed.

FIGURE 11-5
Chart with new data

⚐ Objective 5

Formatting a Chart

You can apply a wide variety of format options to charts. The default chart type is a 3-D column chart, but other types include bar, area, line, pie, and surface. You can change the colors, patterns, fonts, and number formats of a chart. You can also modify the position and style of the legend.

EXERCISE 11-8 Work with Colors, Patterns, and Line Formatting

You can change the colors of individual columns in the chart or an entire

In PowerPoint Classroom Presentation #11.

NOTE
Review the parts of the chart pointed out in this figure. These parts reference some of the tools listed in Table 11-1 (value axis, category axis, gridlines, legend). Students become more familiar with these parts later in the lesson.

⚐ **Objective 5 Assignment:**
Exercises 11-20 (Skills Review) and 11-23 (Lesson Applications) can be assigned after completing Objective 5.

348

LESSON 11 ■ **CREATING A CHART**

group of columns. You can even change the background color to achieve a special effect. Other special fill effects including textures and gradient fills can be used the same way you use them for other PowerPoint objects. You can also change the outline style of columns, bars, and other chart elements.

1. If necessary, move to slide 2 in Slide view.
2. Double-click the chart to open Microsoft Graph. Hide the datasheet.
3. Point to one of the light green columns and notice the ScreenTip that appears, identifying the data series. All parts of the chart have ScreenTips to help you select the object you want to work on.
4. Click a light green column. All the light green columns are selected.
5. Click the arrow next to the Fill Color button on the Standard toolbar to display the color menu. Float the menu by dragging its title bar.

FIGURE 11-6
Fill Color floating menu

6. Move the pointer across the second row from the bottom, which contains the currently selected color. ScreenTips identify some of the colors as "Standard Colors," which means they follow the presentation color scheme. It's usually best to use the standard colors.
7. Click the gold box (the fifth color in the second row from the bottom). The selected columns in the chart become gold.
8. Click Fill Effects on the floating menu. Click the Pattern tab, if necessary. Change the background color to red, the first color in the bottom row.
9. Choose the wide upward diagonal pattern in the third column in the last row and click OK. The columns are now gold with diagonal red stripes.
10. Select the dark green columns and re-open the Fill Effects dialog box. Change the background to bright green and choose the wide horizontal stripes pattern in the fourth column in the bottom row. Click OK.
11. Double-click a blue column to open the Format Data Series dialog box. This is another place you can change the fill color or fill effect in a chart.
12. Click the Patterns tab and click Fill Effects. Change the fill pattern to wide vertical stripes, using dark blue as the background color. Click OK.
13. Still working on the Patterns tab of the Format Data Series dialog box, notice the border options on the left side of the dialog box.
14. Click the Border Color down arrow to change the column's border to dark blue. Click OK. With a dark background, the columns look better with a dark border.
15. Using the Format Data Series dialog box, change the border of the green columns to dark green and the border of the red and yellow columns to red. Close Microsoft Graph.

In PowerPoint Classroom Presentation #11.

Remind students they can also open the Format Data Series dialog box by right-clicking the column and choosing Format Data Series from the shortcut menu.

349

UNIT 5 ■ ADVANCED FEATURES

EXERCISE 11-9 Explore Parts of a Chart

 NOTE

Charts contain many different elements that you can format. PowerPoint provides several different tools to help you navigate around the chart and select the part of the chart you want to work on.

1. Double-click the chart to open Microsoft Graph.
2. Move the pointer over the words "New York." The ScreenTip identifies this part of the chart as the "Category Axis."
3. Using the tip of the pointer, point to a horizontal white line (gridline) within the chart. The ScreenTip identifies this as "Value Axis Major Gridlines."
4. Move the pointer around other parts of the chart and try to find the Plot area, Chart area, and Legend.

FIGURE 11-7
Chart Object drop-down list

5. On the Standard toolbar, click the down arrow to open the Chart Objects drop-down list. A list of the various chart elements is displayed.
6. Choose Floor from the list to select the chart floor. For formatting, it can be easier to select the chart's smaller elements this way instead of clicking with the pointer.
7. Click the Fill Color button arrow and choose Black. The chart's floor color is now black.

EXERCISE 11-10 Format the Value Axis

In PowerPoint you can alter the appearance of your chart's axes by changing text color, size, font, and number formatting. You can also change scale and tick mark settings. The *scale* indicates the values that are displayed on the value axis and the intervals between those values. *Tick marks* are small measurement marks, similar to those found on a ruler, that can cross the value axis and the category axis.

NOTE

1. Point to one of the numbers on the left side of the chart. Double-click when you see the "Value Axis" ScreenTip to open the Format Axis dialog box.

> **NOTE:** You can also open the format axis dialog box by selecting the axis and clicking the Format button 🗉 on the Standard Toolbar or choosing Selected Axis from the Format menu.

2. Click the Font tab and choose Arial, 14 point.

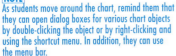

LESSON 11 ■ **CREATING A CHART**

3. Click the Number tab. In the Category box, choose Currency.
4. Click the Scale tab. Clear the Auto checkboxes for Mi*n*imum, Ma*x*imum, M*a*jor Unit, and M*i*nor Unit. Instead of using these default values, you set your own scale values in the next two steps.
5. In the Ma*x*imum field, key **1500** to set the largest number on the value axis.
6. In the M*a*jor Unit field, key **500** to set the intervals between the numbers on the value axis.
7. Click OK. The chart now shows fewer horizontal gridlines and each value is formatted with a dollar sign, a comma separating thousands, and a decimal point.

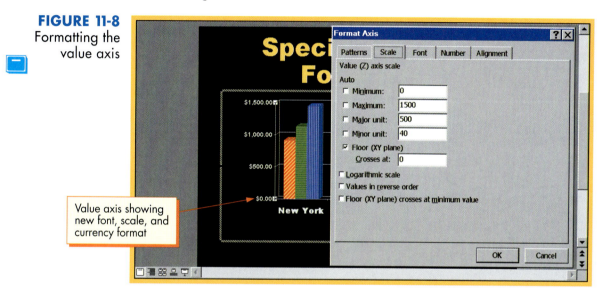

FIGURE 11-8
Formatting the value axis

Value axis showing new font, scale, and currency format

8. Select the value axis, if necessary, by clicking one of the numbers.
9. Using the Formatting toolbar, click the Italic button to change the value axis labels to italic.
10. Click the Font Size arrow and choose 16.
11. Click the Decrease Decimal button twice to remove decimal places from the numbers.

 NOTE: Using the Formatting toolbar to change text and number formatting is sometimes more convenient than using a dialog box.

EXERCISE 11-11 Format the Category Axis

1. Right click "New York" and choose F*o*rmat Axis from the shortcut menu.

In PowerPoint Classroom Presentation #11.

351

UNIT 5 ■ ADVANCED FEATURES

 2. In the Format Axis dialog box, click the Font tab, and choose Arial, 16 point. Click OK to close the dialog box.

 3. With the Category axis still selected, click *I* on the Formatting toolbar to make the category axis labels italic.

EXERCISE 11-12 Insert Axis Titles

1. Move the mouse pointer near the edge of the chart until you see the "Chart Area" ScreenTip. Right-click the Chart Area and choose Chart Options from the shortcut menu.

2. In the Chart Options dialog box, click the Titles tab. In the Category (X) axis text box, key **Special Events**

FIGURE 11-9
Rotating the axis title

3. In the Value (Z) axis text box, key **(thousands)** and click OK. The new titles appear on the slide.

4. Right-click "(thousands)" and choose Format Axis Title from the shortcut menu.

5. Click the Alignment tab. Under Orientation, drag the red diamond up to 90 degrees to change the text to a vertical orientation.

6. Click the Font tab, change the font to 14-point Arial, Bold Italic, and click OK.

7. Click the Category axis title ("Special Events") to select it. Use the Formatting toolbar to change the font to Arial.

EXERCISE 11-13 Make Changes to the Legend

You can customize the appearance of the chart *legend*, which is the box that shows the colors and patterns assigned to the data series or categories. You can change the style and appearance of the border, set background colors and patterns, and change the size and style of the fonts. You can also control the placement and overall size of the legend.

1. Right-click the legend box and choose Format Legend from the shortcut menu. The Format Legend dialog box appears with many of the same features of other formatting dialog boxes.

2. Click the Font tab and change the font to 16-point Arial, Bold Italic.

3. Click the Patterns tab and change the border to None.

NOTE
In the Format Axis dialog box, point out the Auto scale option in the lower left corner. Auto scale sizes text automatically if you change the overall dimensions of a chart.

NOTE
In step 3, you may want to mention that simple text formatting, such as making text bold or italic, can also be applied to a selected chart text object using the Formatting toolbar or keyboard shortcuts. For example, with the legend or an axis selected, you can press Ctrl+I to make the text italic.

 In PowerPoint Classroom Presentation #11.

352

LESSON 11 ■ **CREATING A CHART**

4. Click the Placement tab and choose Top. Click OK. The legend appears above the chart in the new font and without a surrounding border. Note that selection handles still surround the legend.

5. Using a right or left handle, resize the legend box to make it wider so there is more space between the legend items.

6. Point to the center of the legend. Using the arrow pointer, drag the legend down so it is below the top grid line and centered above the middle blue column. Adjust the width of the legend, if it overlap2 any columns.

FIGURE 11-10
Completed chart

☑**Objective 6**

Adding Shapes and Text Objects

You can add many interesting effects to your chart. For example, you can add objects that help you make a particular point or highlight one aspect of the data. You can also annotate your charts with text—an especially useful option when your presentation contains a series of related but different charts.

EXERCISE | **11-14** | **Use the Drawing Toolbar in the Chart Window**

1. Activate Microsoft Graph, display the Drawing toolbar by clicking the Drawing button on the Standard toolbar, and hide the datasheet.

2. Click the Text Box button, then click just above the top gridline on the chart, above the New York group of columns. Key **LA may top NY in 2001** in the floating text box.

In PowerPoint Classroom Presentation #11.

☑**Objective 6 Assignment:**
Exercises 11-21 (Skills Review) and 11-24 (Lesson Applications) can be assigned after completing Objective 6.

UNIT 5 ■ ADVANCED FEATURES

3. With the text box selected, use the Formatting toolbar to change the text to 16-point Arial bold italic.

FIGURE 11-11
Chart with arrow and floating text

NOTE

4. Use AutoShapes to draw a small right arrow. Make it red and rotate it, as shown in Figure 11-11. Arrange the arrow and floating text box to match the figure.

 NOTE: You can also draw and add text in Slide view.

5. In Slide view, change the slide 2 title to **Sales Forecast**.

6. Click the chart once to select it. Notice that it has sizing handles. Reposition and resize the chart appropriately for the slide. You can drag the chart and its handles just as you do any other object in Slide view.

7. Change the black and white settings for the chart (not the entire slide) to inverse grayscale. Save the presentation as *[your initials]***11-14.ppt**.

8. Update the handout footer to show the new filename.

9. Print handouts, 2 slides per page, black and white, framed.

Objective 7
Creating a Pie Chart

Pie charts are a simple, yet highly effective presentation tool that show numeric data as a percentage of a total. Each value in the total is displayed as a "slice" of the pie. The bigger the slice, the larger its percentage.

EXERCISE 11-15 Create a Pie Chart

In this exercise, you create a pie chart to display the breakdown of the restaurant's sales by category.

1. Insert a new slide after slide 2 using the Title Only layout.

2. Key the title **1998 Sales Categories**. Change the font size to 44-point. Deselect the placeholder.

3. Click the Insert Chart button  on the Standard toolbar. The sample chart and datasheet appear.

4. Click the arrow on the Chart Type button on the Standard toolbar. The Chart Type drop-down list appears.

In PowerPoint Classroom Presentation #11.

NOTE
In step 4, students may need a reminder about how to work with AutoShapes and how to rotate an object when using Free Rotate.

Objective 7 Assignment:
Exercises 11-22 (Skills Review) and 11-25 (Lesson Applications) can be assigned after completing Objective 7.

LESSON 11 ■ CREATING A CHART

FIGURE 11-12
Chart Type
drop-down list

5. Choose Pie Chart, the first option in the fifth row. A pie chart replaces the column chart, displaying sample data.

 NOTE: By default, only the first row of data in the datasheet is plotted in a pie chart.

6. On the datasheet, click the gray box in the upper left corner to select all the sample data and then delete it.
7. Key the data shown in Figure 11-13.

FIGURE 11-13
Datasheet for
a pie chart

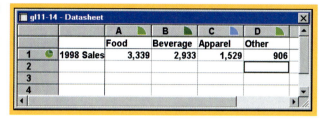

8. Close the datasheet to view the chart.

EXERCISE 11-16 Add Pie Slice Labels

You can add labels to the chart's data series and edit those labels individually.

1. Right-click one of the pie slices and choose F*o*rmat Data Series from the shortcut menu.
2. Click the Data Labels tab, choose Show label *a*nd percent, and click OK. Data labels appear next to the slices. The percentages represent a slice's percentage of the total. Notice that with the addition of data labels, the legend is no longer needed and the pie is now very small.

NOTE: Depending on the pie chart, sometimes parts of the data labels may be hidden by the edges of the chart placeholder. In this case, you need to resize the pie using the plot area resize handles.

3. Click a data label (watch for the ScreenTip "1998" Data Labels before clicking). All the data labels are selected. Change the font for the labels to 16-point Arial bold italic. The pie becomes a little larger.
4. Select the legend box and delete it. The pie becomes even larger.
5. Click the data label "Other 10%" once to select all labels. Click the label again to select only that label. You can now edit this label.

In PowerPoint Classroom Presentation #11.

355

UNIT 5 ■ ADVANCED FEATURES

FIGURE 11-14
Pie chart with data labels

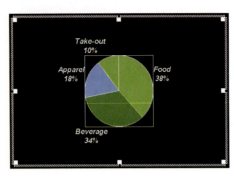

6. Click within the selected label's text to display an insertion point. Delete the word "Other" (but not 10%), and key in its place **Take-out**

7. Click anywhere within the chart to deselect the label.

EXERCISE 11-17 Format the Pie Plot Area

1. Move the mouse pointer over a corner of the pie chart frame until the "Plot Area" ScreenTip appears, then right-click and choose F_ormat Plot Area from the shortcut menu. The Format Plot Area dialog box opens. This dialog box has only one tab.

2. Under Border, click _None and click OK. The pie border is removed.

3. With the pie's plot area still selected, drag its lower right corner down to make the pie as big as possible without hiding the "Beverage" label. Drag the upper left corner up as far as you can without losing the "Take-out" label. Deselect the plot area by clicking outside of it.

 NOTE: You cannot drag the plot area to center it. However, if you resize the plot area from opposing corners, you can center it within the chart area.

EXERCISE 11-18 Add Finishing Touches

You can enhance the appearance of your pie chart with additional effects, such as changing the color of a slice or *exploding* a slice (dragging it out from the center of the pie) for emphasis.

1. Click the center of the pie once to select all the slices. Notice that each slice has one selection handle.

2. Click the Food slice. Six resize handles appear around the selected slice.

3. Use [icon] to change the color of the Food slice to the blue that is the sixth color in the Standard Colors row. Change the Apparel slice to gold and the Take-out slide to red. Note that you can use F_ill Effects to apply gradient fills, patterns, or textures to individual slices as well.

4. Place the pointer in the middle of the Apparel slice and drag it slightly away from the center of the pie. This is called exploding a slice.

In PowerPoint Classroom Presentation #11.

NOTE
You may want to demonstrate how to explode an entire pie (have all slices separated from each other): select the entire pie and drag any slide away from the center.

LESSON 11 ■ CREATING A CHART

5. Return to Slide view. Create a floating text box below the pie with the text **Apparel includes revenue from trademark licensing**. Format the text as 20-point Arial Black and center the text box horizontally.

> **NOTE:** Although you can also insert floating text boxes in the active chart, it is sometimes easier to do this in Slide view because you are not restricted by the size of the chart area.

6. Omit the background graphics from the master slide on slide 3.

FIGURE 11-15
Pie chart with exploded slice and floating text box

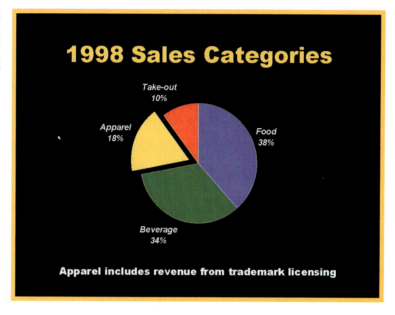

7. Save the presentation as *[your initials]***11-18.ppt**.
8. Update the handout footer to the new filename.
9. Print as handouts, 3 slides per page, black and white, framed.
10. Save and close the presentation.

COMMAND SUMMARY

FEATURE	BUTTON	MENU	KEYBOARD
Insert Chart		Insert, Chart	
Change Chart Type		Chart, Chart Type	
Insert or remove a legend		Chart, Chart Options, Legend	
View Datasheet		View, Datasheet	
By Row		Data, Series In Rows	
By Column		Data, Series in Columns	

In PowerPoint Classroom Presentation #11.

NOTE
Point out that the Command Summary lists a variety of ways to accomplish a particular task. Students can decide which method they prefer.

UNIT 5 ■ ADVANCED FEATURES

TEST BANK

Concepts Review

TRUE/FALSE QUESTIONS

Each of the following statements is either true or false. Indicate your choice by circling **T** or **F**.

(T) F 1. PowerPoint offers three different AutoLayout choices for slides with charts.

T **(F)** 2. The sample datasheet for a new chart is always blank.

T **(F)** 3. You cannot see the chart while you are working on the datasheet.

(T) F 4. You can change the colors and patterns of columns in a column chart to whatever you find appealing.

(T) F 5. All numeric data in a chart must be entered into the chart's datasheet.

T **(F)** 6. Every chart must include a legend box.

T **(F)** 7. The scale on the value axis is set by PowerPoint and cannot be changed.

(T) F 8. You can change the number formatting for chart values using the Formatting toolbar in Microsoft Graph.

SHORT ANSWER QUESTIONS

Write the correct answer in the space provided.

1. What do you do if you don't want to use the sample data in the datasheet?
   Key new data

2. How do you change the grouping of the data series on a chart from columns to rows?
   Use By Row button

3. While working on a chart, how do you display the datasheet if it is not visible?
   Click View Datasheet button

4. What type of number formatting do you apply to values to display dollar signs?
   Currency

Concepts Review:
Allows students to check their understanding.

TEST BANK
Consider using the Test Bank to provide an additional review of lesson concepts.

LESSON 11 ■ **CREATING A CHART**

5. In Microsoft Graph, what item on the Standard toolbar can you use to select different parts of a chart?
   Chart Objects drop-down list

6. Which button can you click to change the color of a selected pie slice?
   Fill Color button

7. How can you change the font size for chart labels without opening a dialog box?
   Select label, then click Font Size box on Formatting toolbar

8. What are the small measurement marks called that intersect a value or category axis?
   Tick marks

CRITICAL THINKING

Answer these questions on a separate page. There are no right or wrong answers. Support your answers with examples from your own experience, if possible.

1. How do you decide if a chart is needed in your presentation? Do you think a presentation can have too many charts? Explain your answer.

2. Imagine you are trying to explain to someone how you spend your waking hours during a typical day. Can you think of a chart that would break down your activities into different categories and show how much time you spend on each during the day? Describe the chart's appearance and the values that you would include.

Skills Review

EXERCISE 11-19

Create a new presentation that includes a simple column chart.

1. Start a new presentation and apply the Contemporary Portrait template found in the Presentation Designs folder. On the slide master, change the title text placeholder font to Arial.

2. On slide 1, key **Financial Summary** as the title and **Good 4 U** as the subtitle. Increase the subtitle text size to 40 point and the "4" to 44 point.

Critical Thinking Questions:
Answers will vary based on students' preferences, observations, experiences, and research.

Skills Review:
Provides guided practice for students. Objectives are indicated for each Exercise.

Exercise 11-19:
Objectives 1–3
Required File: None
Solution File: gl11-19.ppt in Solutions Manual or on Solutions Disk

NOTE
By changing the slide title font on the slide master, the default chart font changes. This step is here to make sure the chart that students create has appropriately sized labels so they don't need to change font sizes in this early Exercise.

359

UNIT 5 ADVANCED FEATURES

3. Insert a new slide using the Bulleted List layout. Key the title **Highlights** and the following bulleted items:

    Earnings consistently on target

    Minimal seasonal fluctuations

    Steady increase from previous year

4. Insert a new slide using the Chart layout. Key **1999 Quarterly Earnings** for the title.

5. Create a chart by following these steps:

    a. Double-click in the chart placeholder on slide 3.

    b. Click the upper left gray box on the datasheet to select all the existing data and press Delete.

    c. Key the data shown in Figure 11-16.

FIGURE 11-16
Datasheet

		A 1st Qtr	B 2nd Qtr	C 3rd Qtr	D 4th Qtr
1	New York	1,888	2,008	2,116	1,543
2	Los Angeles	1,743	1,799	1,844	1,849
3	Miami	1,634	1,439	1,783	1,469
4					

6. View the new chart by following these steps:

    a. Click the View Datasheet button to hide the datasheet.

    b. Click in the gray area outside the slide to return to Slide view.

7. Click the chart once in Slide view to select it, then adjust the chart size by dragging the left middle sizing handle to the right 0.5 inch and dragging the top middle sizing handle down 0.5 inch.

8. Check the chart's black and white settings and make changes if necessary.

9. Save the presentation as *[your initials]***11-19.ppt**.

10. Add the date and your name to the handout header and the filename to the handout footer.

11. Print as handouts, 6 slides per page, black and white, framed.

12. Save and close the presentation.

EXERCISE 11-20

Edit and format an existing chart.

1. Open the file **Finan2.ppt**.

2. Edit the chart on slide 4 by following these steps:

NOTE
In these Exercises, you might ask students to print the chart slides full size in addition to printing handouts for the presentation.

Exercise 11-20:
Objectives 4–5
Required File: Finan2.ppt
Solution File: gl11-20.ppt in Solutions Manual or on Solutions Disk

LESSON 11 ■ **CREATING A CHART**

    a. Double-click the chart to open Microsoft Graph.

    b. On the datasheet, click cell A2 containing the value "-2%."

    c. Key **2%** in the selected cell to overwrite the current value. Press Enter.

    d. Click View Datasheet 🗐 to hide the datasheet.

3. Change the fill of columns to patterns by following these steps:

    a. With Microsoft Graph still open, click one of the dark blue columns to select the Gross Margin data series.

    b. Click the Fill Color 🎨▾ button arrow on the Standard toolbar and float the toolbar by dragging its gray title bar.

    c. Choose F̲ill Effects and click the Pattern tab.

    d. Change the foreground color to the lavender found to the left of the white sample on the third row from the bottom.

    e. Choose the wide upward diagonal pattern (third sample in the bottom row) and click OK.

    f. Use the same steps to change the fill pattern of the light blue columns to the wide downward diagonal pattern (in the second row from the bottom). Change its foreground color to white. Close the Fill Color Floating menu.

4. Change the outline color of a series of columns by following these steps:

    a. Right-click one of the columns in the Gross Margin series and choose F̲ormat Data Series from the shortcut menu.

    b. On the Patterns tab, click the C̲olor arrow in the Border option group.

    c. Choose the dark blue-gray color in the Standard Colors row. Click OK.

5. Change the outline color of the columns in the Operating Margin series to the same dark blue/gray color.

6. Change the font for the Category axis labels by following these steps:

    a. Click the category axis label "1997" to select the category axis.

    b. On the Formatting toolbar, choose Arial and click the Italic button.

7. Format the value axis by following these steps:

    a. Right-click a number on the value axis and choose F̲ormat Axis from the shortcut menu.

    b Click the Scale.

    c. Key **25%** in Max̲imum text box, then key **5%** in the Ma̲jor unit text box.

    d. Click the Font tab and choose Arial and Bold Italic. Click OK.

8. Format the legend by following these steps:

    a. Right-click the legend and choose F̲ormat Legend from the shortcut menu.

UNIT 5 ■ ADVANCED FEATURES

   b. Click the Placement tab and choose <u>B</u>ottom.
   c. Click the Pattern tab, choose <u>N</u>one for Border, and click OK.
   d. Increase the width of the legend slightly by dragging its resize handles.
   e. Use the Formatting toolbar to change the legend font to Arial bold italic.
9. Adjust the presentation's black and white settings, if necessary.
10. Save the presentation as *[your initials]***11-20.ppt**.
11. Add the date and your name to the handout header and the filename to the handout footer.
12. Print as handouts, 6 slides per page, black and white, framed.
13. Save and close the presentation.

EXERCISE 11-21

Add shapes and text to an existing chart.

1. Open the file **Finan3.ppt**.
2. Move to slide 4 and double-click the chart to open Microsoft Graph. Hide the datasheet.
3. Change the color of the columns to medium blue.
4. Add special text formatting to the category axis by following these steps:
   a. Double-click the category axis to open the Format Axis dialog box.
   b. Click the Font tab and choose Arial, Bold, and 14 point. Change the text color to red.
   c. Click the Alignment tab. Drag the red diamond up to the 30 degree setting. Click OK.
5. Change the value axis formatting by following these steps.
   a. Click the value axis to select it, then use the Formatting toolbar to choose 14 point and bold.
   b. With the value axis still selected, click the Currency Style button $ to add dollar signs.
   c. Click the Decrease Decimals button twice to eliminate the decimal places.
6. Add a value axis title by following these steps:
   a. Move the pointer near the edge of the chart border until you see the Chart Area ScreenTip.
   b. Right-click, then choose Chart <u>O</u>ptions from the shortcut menu.
   c. On the Titles tab, key **(thousands)** in the Value (Z) axis text box. Click OK.

🖫Exercise 11-21:
Objective 6
Required File: Finan3.ppt
Solution File: gl11-21.ppt in Solutions Manual or on Solutions Disk.

LESSON 11 ■ CREATING A CHART

7. Format the value axis title by following these steps:
   a. Right-click "(thousands)" and choose F<u>o</u>rmatAxis Title from the shortcut menu.
   b. On the Alignment tab, move the red diamond to the 90 degree position.
   c. On the Font tab, choose Bold Italic and 14 point.

NOTE

8. Add drawing objects to the chart by following these steps:
   a. Click the Drawing button on the Standard toolbar to display the Drawing toolbar.
   b. Click , then click the pointer at the top of the chart above the May column and key **New Health Marathon**
   c. Change the text size to 16 point.
   d. Click . Position the pointer at the end of "Marathon" and drag it toward the top of the November column.
   e. Increase the arrow's weight to 2¼ point.

9. Adjust the presentation's black and white settings, if necessary.
10. Save the presentation as *[your initials]***11-21.ppt**.
11. Add the date and your name to the handout header and the filename to the handout footer.
12. Print as handouts, 6 slides per page, black and white, framed.
13. Save and close the presentation.

EXERCISE 11-22

Create and format a pie chart.

1. Open the file **Apparel1.ppt**.
2. Insert a new slide after slide 4 using the Chart layout. Key the title **1999 Apparel Sales**
3. Create a pie chart by following these steps:
   a. Double-click the chart placeholder and enter the chart data shown in Figure 11-17.
   b. Click the arrow on the Chart Type button and choose Pie Chart.

FIGURE 11-17
Datasheet for pie chart

NOTE
In step 8, students should make sure the data sheet is not activated. If it is, the Text Box button may be disabled.

Exercise 11-22:
Objective 7
Required File:Apparel1.ppt
Solution File: gl11-22.ppt in Solutions Manual or on Solutions Disk.

363

4. Format a pie slice by following these steps:
   a. Hide the datasheet.
   b. Click the black pie slice (Elbow pads) once to select the entire pie.
   c. Click the black slice again to select the individual slice.
   d. Click ![icon] and choose gold in the second row from the bottom.
5. Delete the pie's legend.
6. Add data labels by following these steps:
   a. Move the pointer along the outside edge of the pie until the Plot Area ScreenTip appears, then right-click and choose Chart Options from the shortcut menu.
   b. Click the Data Labels tab, choose Show labels and percent, and click OK.
7. Resize the pie by following these steps:
   a. Select the Plot Area (left click), if necessary.
   b. Drag the upper left resize handle away from the center of the pie, making the pie as large as possible without hiding "Elbow Pads."
   c. Drag the lower right corner away from the center in the same manner.
8. Format the plot area by following these steps:
   a. Right-click the pie's plot area and choose Format Plot Area from the shortcut menu.
   b. Click None for Border and click OK.
9. Explode a pie slice by following these steps:
   a. Select the pink "Visors" slice.
   b. Drag the slice away from the center of the pie.
10. Change the font for the data labels by following these steps:
    a. Click any data label to select all labels.
    b. Change the font to Arial.
    c. Click the "Visors" label to select that individual label.
    d. Change the font to 20 points to make it larger than the other labels.
11. Adjust the position of the chart placeholder in Slide view, if necessary.
12. Adjust the presentation's black and white settings, if necessary.
13. Save the presentation as *[your initials]* **11-22.ppt**.
14. Add the date and your name to the handout header and the filename to the handout footer.
15. Print as handouts, 6 slides per page, black and white, framed.
16. Save and close the presentation.

LESSON 11 ■ CREATING A CHART

Lesson Applications

EXERCISE 11-23

Create a presentation containing a column chart and format the chart.

1. Start a new presentation and apply the **Fireball.pot** template.
2. On the title slide, key the title **Three Years of Phenomenal Sales** and the subtitle **Good 4 U**. Increase the subtitle text to 48 point and the "4" to two sizes larger.
3. Create a bulleted text slide with the title **Highlights** and the following bulleted text:
   - **New York revenue still increasing**
   - **Miami and Los Angeles meeting goals**
   - **Revenues reach 120% of budget**
4. Insert a new slide after slide 2 using the Chart layout. Key the title **1997-1999 Sales**
5. Create a column chart using the data shown in Figure 11-18.

FIGURE 11-18
Data for chart

		A	B	C	D
		1997	1998	1999	
1	New York	4,101	5,398	6,988	
2	Miami	2,045	2,996	3,847	
3	Los Angeles	1,197	1,800	2,834	
4					

6. Change the value axis scale settings to have a maximum of 8,000 and a major unit of 2,000.
7. Change the font for the value axis, category axis, and legend to 16-point Tahoma bold. (Use Arial if your computer doesn't have Tahoma.)
8. Apply a one-color horizontal gradient fill to each column, shading from the column's original color at the top to black at the bottom. Make the outline for each column black.
9. Change the floor color of the chart to black.
10. Move the legend to the bottom and remove its border.
11. In Slide view, drag the chart until it is centered.
12. Change the black and white settings for the chart to inverse grayscale.
13. Save the presentation as *[your initials]***11-23.ppt**.
14. Add the date and your name to the handout header and the filename to the handout footer.

Assessment Resources:
- Solutions Manual
- Test Bank with Software
- Portfolio Builder
- Alternative Assessment Guide
- Certification Procedures

Lesson Applications:
Provide independent practice for students. Objectives are indicated for each Exercise.

Exercise 11-23:
Objectives 1–5
Required File: None
Solution File: gl11-23.ppt in Solutions Manual or on Solutions Disk.

365

UNIT 5 ■ ADVANCED FEATURES

15. Print as handouts, 6 slides per page, black and white, framed.
16. Save and close the presentation.

EXERCISE 11-24

Create a presentation that contains a chart; format the chart text, legend, and category and value axes; and add an AutoShape.

1. Open the file **Earnings.ppt** and apply the Presentation Guidelines template from the Presentations folder. Change the slide color scheme to the second choice on the first line (the light blue background).
2. On the slide master and title master, delete the large diamond shape.
3. Insert a new slide between slides 2 and 3 using the Chart layout and the title **Gross Income**
4. Create a column chart on the new slide using the following data:

	1997	1998	1999
New York	229.6	302.2	428.5
Miami	86.2	99.7	150.3
San Francisco	43.9	72.0	129.8
Los Angeles	98.7	101.4	162.7

5. Reduce the font size of the value and category axes to 16 point.
6. Change the number format of the value axis to currency with no decimal places and change the scale settings so the values are displayed at intervals of 100.
7. Add a value axis title with the text **(thousands)** and rotate it 90 degrees. Format the text as 14-point Tahoma italic.
8. Move the legend to the top of the chart and remove its border. Resize the legend to be as wide as the chart and adjust its position if necessary.
9. In Slide view, adjust the chart's position relative to the slide, if needed.
10. Draw an AutoShape arrow from the text "New York" to the purple arrow in the 1999 data series, rotating the arrow to make it point diagonally. Key **Impressive!** in the AutoShape. Change the text color to white, Arial bold. Use a font size appropriate for the arrow size.
11. Adjust the presentation's black and white settings, if necessary.
12. Save the presentation as *[your initials]***11-24.ppt**.
13. Add the date and your name to the handout header and the filename to the handout footer.
14. Print as handouts, 6 slides per page, black and white, framed.
15. Save and close the presentation.

Exercise 11-24:
Objectives 1–6
Required File: Earnings.ppt
Solution File: gl11-24.ppt in Solutions Manual or on Solutions Disk.

The completed presentation for this Exercise may be used in a student's portfolio.

LESSON 11 ■ CREATING A CHART

EXERCISE 11-25

Create a presentation with a pie chart using a customized template.

1. Open the file **Expense1.ppt**. Apply the **Fireball.pot** template.
2. Create a custom color scheme by changing the current background scheme color to medium blue (use the color that is third from the right in the top row of the Standard color honeycomb).
3. On the title master, ungroup the fireball graphic and delete all graphic objects except the horizontal bar.
4. On the slide master, delete the fireball graphic. Move the title placeholder up 0.25 inch and move the bullet text placeholder down 0.25 inch. Center-align the title placeholder text.
5. Change the font to Arial for all text on both the title and slide masters.
6. Near the top of the title master, draw a constrained five-point star that is 0.75 inch high. Apply a two-color vertical gradient fill using orange and blue with orange on the left side. Remove the star's outline.
7. Move the star to the left end of the horizontal bar and use the Duplicate command to make a string of stars across the bar, leaving some space between the stars.
8. Group the stars and the horizontal line, center the group horizontally, and copy the group to the slide master between the two text placeholders.
9. Insert a new slide after slide **1** using the Chart layout. Key the title **Expense Breakdown**
10. Create a pie chart on the new slide 2 using the following data:

	Food	Payroll	Depreciation	Lease
1998 Expenses	2,190	1,813	577	1,737

11. Resize the pie as large as it can be and still fit inside the chart border.
12. Remove the pie's plot area border. Change the pie slices outline to black.
13. Add data labels to the chart, shown as percentages only, formatted as 22-point Arial bold. Select each percentage and drag it onto the pie slice.
14. Increase the legend font to 22 point and remove its border.
15. In Slide view, adjust the position of the pie chart as needed. Resize and center the bulleted text placeholders throughout the presentation.
16. Adjust the presentation's black and white settings, and save as *[your initials]***11-25.ppt**.
17. Add the date and your name to the handout header and the filename to the handout footer.
18. Print as handouts, 6 slides per page, black and white, framed.
19. Save and close the presentation.

Exercise 11-25:
Objectives 1–5, 7
Required File: Expense1.ppt
Solution File: gl11-25.ppt in Solutions Manual or on Solutions Disk.

The completed presentation for this Exercise may be used in a student's portfolio.

NOTE
In step 12, you may want to remind students to use the Pattern tab on the Format Data Series to change the pie slice outline color.

367

LESSON 12
Creating a Table

OBJECTIVES After completing this lesson, you will be able to:
1. Create a Word table.
2. Key text in a table.
3. Use the Word Tables and Borders toolbar.
4. Work with column alignment.
5. Recolor a Word table.
6. Edit a table.

Estimated Time: 1 hour

An easy way to convey data on a slide is to present it in the form of a table. A *table* displays data in rows and columns. The data can take the form of either numbers or text.

PowerPoint uses both Word and Excel to create slides with tables. This lesson focuses on Word, which provides greater flexibility in design, content, and formatting.

Objective 1
Creating a Word Table

There are two easy ways to insert a blank Word table in a presentation:
- Click the Insert Microsoft Word Table button 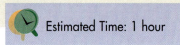 on the Standard toolbar.
- Use the Table AutoLayout.

 Point out to students that the learning objectives show what they will learn in the lesson. Each heading in the lesson correlates to a learning objective.

Required Files
Manage1.ppt

 Teaching Resources:
- PowerPoint Classroom Presentations
- School-to-Work Strategies Manual
- Internet Manual
- Spanish Glossary
- Methodology Video
- Certification Procedures

LESSON 12 ■ CREATING A TABLE

EXERCISE 12-1 Starting a Table

NOTE
When you add a new table to a slide, you must define the structure of the table before you can enter data.

1. Open the file **Manage1.ppt**. Insert a new slide after slide 3 using the Table layout in the first row.

FIGURE 12-1 Table layout

2. Add the title **Employment Levels, 1998**

NOTE

3. Double-click the table icon to insert the new table. The Insert Word Table dialog box appears.

4. Change the Number of columns to **4** and the Number of rows to **4**. Click OK. A blank Word table with 4 rows and 4 columns appears on the slide and Word is activated. Notice the Word toolbars and menu bar.

TIP: A quick way to add another row to an existing table is to move the pointer to the lower right corner of the screen and press Tab. Word automatically installs a new, blank row, with the pointer positioned in the first column of that row.

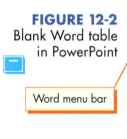

FIGURE 12-2 Blank Word table in PowerPoint

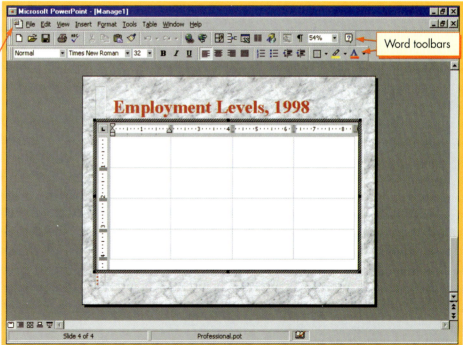

NOTE

NOTE
Although the emphasis in this lesson is on building and formatting Word tables, make sure students understand that they can also insert Excel worksheets in slides. Explain that they have more formatting and style options with tables when they are created as Word tables rather than as Excel worksheets.

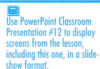
Use PowerPoint Classroom Presentation #12 to display screens from the lesson, including this one, in a slide-show format.

NOTE
Reinforce the concept that working with the Word table activates Word. Point out the appearance of the Word toolbars and menu bar.

NOTE
Figures 12-2 and 12-3 may have a different appearance if the Show/Hide ¶ button on the Word Standard toolbar is turned on.

369

UNIT 5 ■ ADVANCED FEATURES

Keying Text in the Table

Objective 2

NOTE

You enter data in a new table just as you would in a spreadsheet. Each data item, label, heading, or number is entered in a *cell*, which is the box formed by the intersection of a row and a column.

EXERCISE 12-2   Key Table Text

1. Click a cell in the second row. Notice that the blinking insertion point indicates the active cell.

2. Press [Tab] to move to the next cell. This is a keyboard method for moving around the table. Many people find it more convenient when entering data in tables.

3. Press [Shift]+[Tab] to move to the preceding cell; press [↑] or [↓] to move up and down in the table. Press [Enter] to go to the next line within the cell, which may affect the height of the row. If you press [Enter] by accident, remove the unwanted line by pressing [Backspace].

    NOTE: You can click the Show/Hide ¶ button ¶ on the Word Standard toolbar to hide paragraph marks just as you would when working with a Word document.

4. Key the table data shown in Figure 12-3.

FIGURE 12-3
Data in a Word table

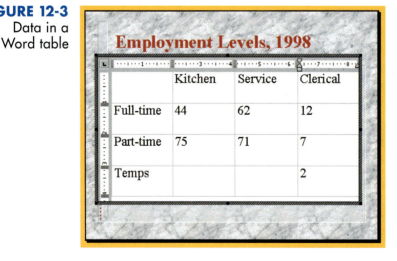

5. Click outside the table to return to Slide view. Notice that the table appears rather plain in this state. In subsequent exercises you improve its appearance.

NOTE
Make sure students understand what a cell is in a table.

In PowerPoint Classroom Presentation #12.

LESSON 12 ■ CREATING A TABLE

EXERCISE **12-3** Select Cells, Columns, and the Entire Table

 You can select portions of a table in a number of different ways. Once a portion of a table or an entire table is selected, you can apply formatting.

1. Double-click the table to reactivate the Word table.

FIGURE 12-4
Selecting a cell

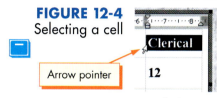

2. To select a single cell, move the pointer over the left side of the "Clerical" cell until the pointer changes to a white arrow and click. The "Clerical" cell is selected. Notice that only part of the cell is highlighted, which is the portion of the cell containing the data.

3. Click any cell to deselect the "Clerical" cell.

4. To select an individual column, move the pointer over the top edge of the "Service" cell until the I-beam changes to a small black down arrow, which is the column selection pointer.

FIGURE 12-5
Selecting a column

5. With the column selection pointer displayed, click the mouse button. The "Service" column is selected.

6. Click any cell to deselect the "Service" column.

7. To select all the cells, position the pointer in the upper left cell, then drag the mouse across all cells in the table.

 TIP: You can also select all cells in a table by choosing Select Table from the Table menu.

8. Use the Formatting toolbar to set the font to 36-pt Times New Roman bold.
9. Click outside the table to see how it looks in Slide view.

Objective 3
Using the Word Tables and Borders Toolbar

Once you create a Word table and key the data, you can use the Tables and Borders toolbar in Word to greatly enhance the appearance of your table. You can use it to center the text, make your columns all the same size, add fill color to one or more cells, or change the borders of the table.

Activate the Tables and Borders toolbar by clicking the Tables and Borders button on the Word Standard toolbar.

EXERCISE **12-4** Change Text Position in a Table Row

1. Double-click the table to reactivate it.

NOTE
Describe some of the ways to select cells. Students can drag the I-beam over a cell or group of cells. To select the entire table, they can use the Table menu or the Alt key + 5 on the numeric keypad (Num Lock must be turned off).

In PowerPoint Classroom Presentation #12.

371

UNIT 5 ■ ADVANCED FEATURES

2. Click the Tables and Borders button  on the Word Standard toolbar. The Tables and Borders toolbar is displayed.

FIGURE 12-6
Word Tables and Borders toolbar

NOTE

3. Move the pointer across the buttons on the Tables and Borders toolbar and observe the ScreenTips for the various buttons. You can use these buttons to control many aspects of a table's formatting.

NOTE

4. Move the pointer into the table. Notice that the pointer is in the shape of a pencil. Press `Esc` to restore the regular mouse pointer.

5. Select all the table cells by choosing Select T_a_ble from the T_a_ble menu.

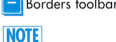

6. Click the Center Vertically button 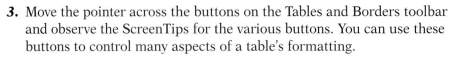 on the Tables and Borders toolbar. The table data is now centered vertically.

7. Click within the table to deselect the data.

> **NOTE:** You can exercise more control over vertical centering in cell contents by setting the _B_efore spacing value on the Indents and Spacing tab of the Paragraph dialog box. This dialog box is accessed with the command F_o_rmat, _P_aragraph.

EXERCISE 12-5 Change Column Sizes and Distribute Columns

You can set column sizes individually or in groups of columns.

FIGURE 12-7
Resizing a column

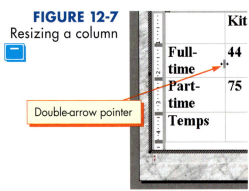

Double-arrow pointer

1. Move the mouse pointer to the right gridline of the first column until the pointer changes to a double arrow.

2. Hold down the mouse button and drag the column border to the right, setting the new column width to 2½ inches, using the ruler at the top of the table as your guide. Notice that the adjacent column shrinks in size to compensate for the expansion of the first column.

> **TIP:** You can use the same technique to change the row heights by positioning the pointer on the bottom border of a row.

3. Select the three columns furthest to the right by positioning the pointer in the "Kitchen" cell and dragging through "2," the last cell. Note that you

In PowerPoint Classroom Presentation #12.

NOTE
Point out to students that some of the ScreenTip names for the Tables and Borders toolbar buttons are dynamic. That is, the name changes to show the option currently in effect, such as the Borders button.

NOTE
The pencil pointer is used to draw a table or apply direct changes to the existing table. This feature is beyond the scope of this Lesson. You may want to show students how to use it. When they see this pointer, pressing [Esc] restores the regular arrow or I-beam pointer.

LESSON 12 ■ CREATING A TABLE

must select entire columns, otherwise only the selected portions of the columns will have their widths changed.

4. Click the Distribute Columns Evenly button on the Tables and Borders toolbar. The three columns are now all the same width.

> **NOTE:** Many of the commands available on the Tables and Borders toolbar are also available on the table's shortcut menu, which you can display by right-clicking a selection.

5. Deselect the selected columns. Notice that the right border of the table lies very close to the table placeholder. The placeholder should be slightly larger than the table, otherwise the table's outside borders may not show.

6. Drag the right middle resize handle on the table placeholder slightly to the right so the table border is better displayed.

EXERCISE 12-6 Add Fill Color to a Cell

You can change the color of one or more cells in your table.

1. Select the cells in the left column.
2. Click the arrow on the Shading Color button on the Word Tables and Borders toolbar. A color menu is displayed.
3. Choose Teal, which is the second color in the second row from the bottom. The shade is applied to the cells.
4. Change the shade of the remaining cells in row 1 to Teal.
5. Select the remaining unshaded cells and change their shade to Gray-35%, which is the last color in the second row on the menu.
6. Click one of the teal-shaded cells to observe the new shading.

> **NOTE:** You can change a cell's font color by selecting the cell and clicking the Font Color button on the Word Formatting toolbar.

EXERCISE 12-7 Add Colored Borders to the Table

You can apply color to the gridlines and borders in a table just as you can to a chart. You can also control the style of the lines.

1. Select all the cells in the table by choosing Select Table from the Table menu.

373

UNIT 5 ■ ADVANCED FEATURES

2. Click the Border Color button [icon] on the Tables and Borders toolbar and choose dark red. When borders and gridlines are applied to the table, they will be dark red.

3. Click the Line Weight arrow [3 pt] on the Tables and Borders toolbar and choose 3 pt.

4. With all the cells still selected, click the arrow next to the Border button [icon] on the Tables and Borders toolbar. A drop-down menu is displayed. Notice that this menu can be floated, if necessary.

5. Choose All Borders [icon]. Gridlines and an outside border are now applied to the table. Notice that the Border button and its ScreenTip now reflect the current border style.

6. Return to Slide view.

NOTE

TIP: If one side of the table does not show the applied border in Slide view, you may need to increase the size of the table placeholder.

FIGURE 12-8
Table with fill color, borders, and gridlines

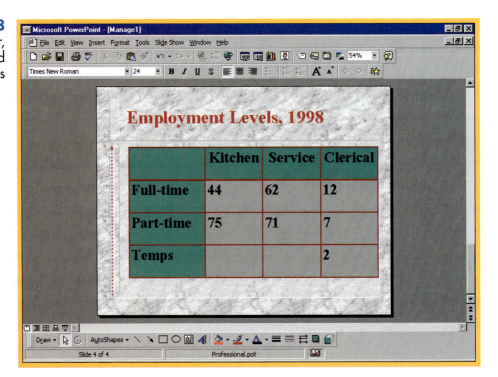

Objective 4
Working with Column Alignment

You can usually improve the appearance of a table by aligning the contents. This is especially true when the table contains numbers. You can also align

NOTE
You may want to explain to students that the borders do not always display in Slide view if the edges are not visible when they are applied in the Word table.

In PowerPoint Classroom Presentation #12.

Objective 4 Assignment:
Exercise 12-12 (Skills Review) can be assigned after completing Objective 4.

374

LESSON 12 ■ CREATING A TABLE

column and row headings. Generally, numbers should be decimal-aligned. (You can use decimal-alignment whether the numbers contain decimals or not.)

EXERCISE 12-8 Align Numbers and Column Headings

1. Double-click the table to reactivate it.
2. Select the column headings in row 1 ("Kitchen," "Service," and "Clerical").
3. Click the Center button on the Word Formatting toolbar. The headings are now horizontally centered in their cells.
4. Select the cells with numbers.
5. Position the pointer over the Tab Type button just to the left of the horizontal ruler. (See Figure 12-9.) The ScreenTip shows the current tab type.
6. Click the Tab Type button until it is set to Decimal Tab.
7. Click the horizontal ruler at 3½ inches. A decimal tab is inserted in the ruler and the selected numbers are all decimal aligned.
8. Click on different number cells in the three columns and notice that the decimal tab is automatically set in the correct position for each column. Note that the tabs can also be set for columns individually.

FIGURE 12-9
Decimal-aligning numbers

9. To see the effect of decimal alignment, change the Full-time Kitchen number to **44.0** and the Part-time Kitchen number to **75.00**. Notice that the numbers are aligned with their decimals.
10. Restore the Kitchen numbers to their original values.

NOTE: You can only use decimal tabs on left-aligned columns. If a column is center aligned, the decimal tabs do not work.

EXERCISE 12-9 Change Cell Indents

Cell indents can be used to position text and numbers within a cell, using the indent markers on the ruler.

1. Select the first column. Click the Align Right button on the Word Formatting toolbar to right align the column labels.

In PowerPoint Classroom Presentation #12.

375

2. Position the pointer over the right indent marker. Notice the ScreenTip that appears over the marker.

3. Drag the right indent marker slightly (1 or 2 tick marks on the ruler) to the left. The text no longer touches the edge of the cells.

FIGURE 12-10
Changing cell indents

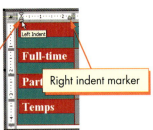

4. With the cells in column 1 still selected, click the Align Left button on the Word Formatting toolbar to left align the column labels.

5. Position the pointer over the left indent marker and drag it 0.25 inch to the right. Note that the left indent marker is the square marker. (The two markers above it are First Line Indent and Hanging Indent markers.)

6. If your column labels wrap to two lines, move the right indent marker back to where it was.

✏ Objective 5
Recoloring a Word Table

Although you can change the colors and shadings of a table while you are working in Word, it is sometimes easier to do so after you return to PowerPoint. You can then modify the table colors to match the presentation scheme for a more consistent look.

EXERCISE 12-10 Recolor a Word Table

1. In Slide view, click the table once to select it. (Double-clicking the table activates the Word table.)

2. Right-click the table, choose Format Object from the shortcut menu, and click the Picture tab in the Format Object dialog box.

3. Click Recolor. The Recolor Picture dialog box is displayed. Notice that all the colors of the table are represented under Original.

 TIP: When a color appears more than once in the Recolor Picture dialog box, you can find its location in the table by changing it to a contrasting color and observing which portion of the preview changes.

4. Click Fills. Four color samples now appear.

5. Change the teal to gray and the gray to white.

6. Click OK, then click OK again to close the Format Object dialog box. The fill colors are now gray and white.

NOTE Make sure students can locate and identify the different indent markers on the ruler.

In PowerPoint Classroom Presentation #12.

Objective 5 Assignment: Exercise 12-13 (Skills Review) and Exercises 12-15 and 12-16 (Lesson Applications) can be assigned after completing Objective 5.

NOTE Explain to students that color is typically applied to a table in two stages. First you apply color to individual elements in a table in Word. Then in Slide view, the colors are customized to fit the presentation color scheme. You cannot change the color of a table in Slide view unless color was first applied in Word.

NOTE Remind students to right-click to display the shortcut menu for commonly used commands. When you right-click an activated Word table, the shortcut menu displays table-related Word commands (such as Delete rows and Table AutoFormat). When you right-click the table object in PowerPoint, the menu displays PowerPoint commands such as Cut, Paste, and Format Object).

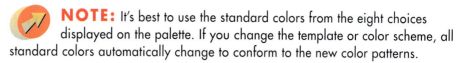

NOTE: It's best to use the standard colors from the eight choices displayed on the palette. If you change the template or color scheme, all standard colors automatically change to conform to the new color patterns.

7. Click the table once to select it and center the table horizontally relative to the slide (D<u>r</u>aw, <u>A</u>lign or Distribute, Align <u>C</u>enter).

Objective 6
Making Changes to a Table

To edit table text, simply reactivate the Word table. If you decide to change the presentation color scheme, you may want to change the table colors to match the presentation's color scheme.

EXERCISE 12-11 Change Table Text and the Presentation Template

To edit the text of a table, you simply activate the Word table.

1. Double-click the table. When you activate the Word table, the colors temporarily revert to the original colors you chose when you first created the table. The colors change back to the PowerPoint colors when you finish editing and return to PowerPoint.

2. In the "Part-time" row, key the following new values:

    82   87   8

3. Return to Slide view and insert a new slide after slide 4 using the Title Only layout (not the Table layout).

4. On the new slide, key the title **Projected Employment, 1999**

5. Copy the table on slide 4 and paste it to the new slide.

6. Double-click the slide 5 table. Again, notice that the colors temporarily revert to the original colors when the table was first created.

7. In the "Full-time" row, key the following new values:

    50   71   13

8. In the "Part-time" row, key the following new values:

    80   75   9

9. Return to Slide view. If the table borders are not entirely displayed, double-click the table and resize the table placeholder.

10. Apply the Facilitating a Meeting design template, which is found in the Presentations folder.

Objective 6 Assignment:
Exercises 12-14 (Skills Review) and 12-17 (Lesson Applications) can be assigned after completing Objective 6.

377

UNIT 5 ■ ADVANCED FEATURES

NOTE

11. Change the color scheme to yellow, using the second color scheme on the bottom row. Notice that the colors of the table are automatically changed to match the colors in the presentation. This is because you used standard colors when recoloring the table.

12. For both tables, change the dark red border to pale yellow by right-clicking the table, choosing Format Object from the shortcut menu, and clicking the Picture tab, if necessary. Click Recolor and then click Fills. The pale yellow is the last color on the menu.

13. Save the presentation as *[your initials]***12-11.ppt**.

14. Add the date and your name to the handout header and the filename to the handout footer.

15. Print as handouts, 6 slides per page, black and white, framed.

16. Save and close the presentation.

FIGURE 12-11
Edited table in a new template

COMMAND SUMMARY

FEATURE	BUTTON	MENU	KEYBOARD
Select table		Table, Select Table	Alt + 5 (numeric keypad, Num Lock off)

NOTE
Remind students that if they apply a color or a template and find it objectionable, they can use Undo.

In PowerPoint Classroom Presentation #12.

378

LESSON 12 ■ CREATING A TABLE

TEST BANK

Concepts Review

TRUE/FALSE QUESTIONS

Each of the following statements is either true or false. Indicate your choice by circling **T** or **F**.

T **(F)** 1. You can expand the width of a column in a table, but only one at a time.

(T) F 2. When you define the size of a table (the number of rows and columns), you must include the headings in your count.

(T) F 3. Gridlines can be any color you want.

T **(F)** 4. Borders and gridlines are available in only one thickness.

(T) F 5. The colors in a table should be consistent with the rest of the presentation.

T **(F)** 6. A Word table can be recolored only in Word.

(T) F 7. Numbers can be decimal-aligned within an individual cell.

(T) F 8. The Table layout includes a placeholder for a Word table.

SHORT ANSWER QUESTIONS

Write the correct answer in the space provided.

1. What do you call a box that contains text or numbers in a table?
   Cell

2. To create a table with one row of headings and five rows of data, how many rows would you specify when defining the size of the table?
   Six

3. What dialog box do you use to recolor a table?
   Format Object

4. What menu command selects all the data in a table?
   Table, Select Table

5. How do you move from one cell to another in a table?
   Mouse, arrow keys, or Tab key

CLOSE

Concepts Review:
Allows students to check their understanding.

TEST BANK
Consider using the Test Bank to provide an additional review of lesson concepts.

379

UNIT 5 ■ ADVANCED FEATURES

6. How do you center values in a table using a toolbar?
   Use the Center button on the Word Formatting toolbar

7. Which button, on which toolbar, can make columns all the same width?
   Distribute Columns Evenly on Word Tables and Borders toolbar

8. How do you activate a table to edit it?
   Double-click it

CRITICAL THINKING

Answer these questions on a separate page. There are no right or wrong answers. Support your answers with examples from your own experience, if possible.

1. How would you decide if a table or a chart is a better presentation tool for a particular set of data? Which criteria should govern the use of one form over the other?

2. If you are adding a table slide to a lengthy presentation that includes a variety of slide types, what should you do to ensure the table slide is visually consistent with the rest of the slides?

Skills Review

EXERCISE 12-12

Create a table and change column alignment.

1. Open the file **Manage2.ppt**. Apply the design template **Notebook.pot**. Change the title text color in both the Title and Slide Masters to dark brown (the second color on the color menu). Change the subtitle and bullet text color to black.

2. Insert a new slide after slide 3 using the Table layout, with the title **Capital Equipment, 1998**

3. Create a table on slide 4 with 3 columns and 5 rows by following these steps:
   a. Double-click the table placeholder.
   b. In the Word Table dialog box, key **3** for the number of columns, **5** for the number of rows, and click OK.
   c. Key the data shown in Figure 12-12 in the table. To move from cell to cell, use Tab, the arrow keys, or click with the mouse.

Critical Thinking Questions:
Answers will vary based on students' preferences, observations, experiences, and research.

Skills Review:
Provides guided practice for students. Objectives are indicated for each Exercise.

Exercise 12-12:
Objectives 1, 2, 4
Required File: Manage2.ppt
Solution File: gl12-12.ppt in Solutions Manual or on Solutions Disk

FIGURE 12-12

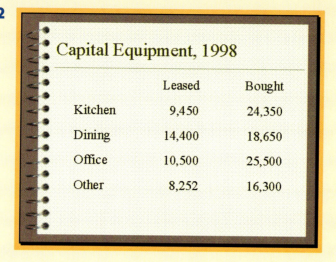

4. Change label alignment by following these steps:
   a. Select the first column by positioning the pointer at the top of the column and clicking the small black selection arrow.
   b. Drag the left indent marker on the ruler to the right to the 0.5-inch mark.
   c. Drag across the cells with the words "Leased" and "Bought" to select both cells.
   d. Click the Center button ≡ on the Word Formatting toolbar.

5. Change the number alignment by following these steps:
   a. Select all the cells with numbers by clicking the first number and dragging across all of them.
   b. Click the Align Right button ≡ on the Word Formatting toolbar to right-align the numbers
   c. Drag the right indent marker on the ruler to the left approximately 0.75 inch, until the numbers appear aligned underneath the column headings.

6. Click outside the table to return to PowerPoint Slide view.

7. Click the table once to select it, then use the Align or Distribute command (on the Draw menu, Drawing toolbar) to center-align the table horizontally relative to the slide.

8. Save the presentation as *[your initials]***12-12.ppt**.

9. Add the date and your name to the handout header and the filename to the handout footer.

10. Print as handouts, 6 slides per page, black and white, framed.

11. Save and close the presentation.

UNIT 5 ■ ADVANCED FEATURES

EXERCISE 12-13

Apply formatting to an existing table using the Word Tables and Borders toolbar and recolor the table.

1. Open the file **Reserve1.ppt**.
2. Apply the design template **Contemporary Portrait.pot**.
3. Display slide 5, titled "Reservation Requests." Double-click the table text to activate the Word table.
4. Display the Tables and Borders toolbar by clicking the Tables and Borders button on the Word Standard toolbar.
5. Change the font of all the table text by following these steps:
   a. If necessary, press Esc to deactivate the pencil pointer.
   b. Select all the cells in the table by dragging the I-beam pointer from the upper left corner cell to the lower right corner cell.
   c. Use the buttons on the Word Formatting toolbar to change the font to Arial bold.
6. Change the font color of the labels by following these steps:
   a. Select the labels in the first column.
   b. Click the arrow next to the Font Color button on the Word Formatting toolbar.
   c. Choose dark red.
   d. Change the labels in the first row to dark red. (Tip: You can use the Repeat command.)
7. Add borders and gridlines to the table by following these steps:
   a. Select all the cells in the table and click the arrow on the Line Weight button on the Borders and Tables toolbar.
   b. Choose 3 pt from the drop-down menu.
   c. Click the Border Color button and choose dark red.
   d. Click the arrow on the Border button and choose All Borders.
8. Change the width of the first column by following these steps:
   a. Click any cell to deselect all the cells.
   b. Move the mouse pointer to the right border of the first column until a double arrow appears.
   c. Hold down the mouse button and drag the column to the right to the 2.25-inch mark on the table ruler.
9. Make the second, third, and fourth columns the same size by following these steps:

Exercise 12-13:
Objectives 3, 5
Required File: Reserve1.ppt
Solution File: gl12-13.ppt in Solutions Manual or on Solutions Disk

382

LESSON 12 ■ CREATING A TABLE

   a. Select the second, third, and fourth columns by first selecting the second column using the column selection arrow. Then press Shift and select the third and fourth columns using the column selection arrows.

   b. Click the Distribute Columns Evenly button 🔲 on the Tables and Borders toolbar.

10. Select all the cells with numbers, then adjust the right indent marker on the ruler so the numbers appear centered in the cells.

11. Center the table text and numbers vertically by following these steps:

    a. Select all the cells in the table by choosing Select Table from the Table menu.

    b. Click the Center Vertically button 🔲 on the Tables and Borders toolbar.

12. Change the shading of the row and column headings by following these steps:

    a. Select the cells in the first column.

    b. Click the arrow on the Shading Color button 🔲 on the Tables and Borders toolbar and choose Gray-25% (the third color in the second row).

    c. Repeat the shading for the three remaining unshaded cells in the first row.

13. Return to Slide view and center the table on the slide.

14. Move to slide 4 and resize the title placeholder so it fits on one line.

15. Save the presentation as *[your initials]***12-13.ppt**.

16. Add the date and your name to the handout header and the filename to the handout footer.

17. Print as handouts, 6 slides per page, black and white, framed.

18. Save and close the presentation.

EXERCISE 12-14

Edit data in an existing table, format the table, work with alignment, and recolor the table.

1. Open the file **Menu2.ppt**.

2. Display slide 4, double-click the table, select all the text, and change the font to 24-point Arial bold.

3. Edit the numbers in the table as follows:

	1997	1998	1999
Meat	15	14	12
Vegetarian	9	10	12

4. Reduce the width of the last column (1999) by dragging its right border to the 6-inch mark on the ruler. (Hint: If you can't see the last column's right border, make the table placeholder a little wider.) Move the right border of the first column to the 2-inch mark.

Exercise 12-14:
Objectives 3–6
Required File: Menu2.ppt
Solution File: gl12-14.ppt in Solutions Manual or on Solutions Disk.

383

5. Select the three columns with numbers and make them the same size using the Distribute Columns Evenly button ⊞.
6. Make each row approximately 0.75 inch high by dragging each row's bottom border. Use the Distribute Rows Evenly button ⊟ to make all the rows exactly the same height.

TIP: You can hold down [Alt] as you drag to see the exact row height on the ruler. Additionally, you can select all rows and drag one row's bottom border to make all rows the same height.

7. Adjust the size of the placeholder so it is slightly larger than the table.
8. Using a 2¼ pt line, add a dark blue inside and outside border to the table.
9. Center the column headings and decimal-align the numbers, setting the decimal tab so the numbers appear to be centered below the headings. (Don't center the row headings.)
10. Center all text vertically in each row.
11. Apply turquoise shading to the cells in the first row and the first column, and yellow shading to the cells containing numbers. Make the numbers red (keep the heading font black).
12. Return to Slide view and position the table attractively on the slide.
13. Recolor the table in Slide view by following these steps:
    a. Right-click the table, choose Format Object from the shortcut menu, and click the Picture tab, if necessary.
    b. Click Recolor, then change both black samples to green.
    c. Change the navy blue to orange.
    d. Change the turquoise to light blue.
    e. Change the red to medium blue.
    f. Change the bright yellow to pale yellow. Click OK in both dialog boxes.
14. Change the line spacing for the slide 4 title text box to 1 line.
15. Check the black and white settings.
16. Save the presentation as *[your initials]* **12-14.ppt**.
17. Add the date and your name to the handout header and the filename to the handout footer.
18. Print as handouts, 6 slides per page, black and white, framed.
19. Save and close the presentation.

NOTE
Color is applied in two stages in this exercise: first in Word and then in Slide view, where the colors are customized to fit the presentation color scheme.

Assessment Resources:
- Solutions Manual
- Test Bank with Software
- Portfolio Builder
- Alternative Assessment Guide
- Certification Procedures

LESSON 12 ■ CREATING A TABLE

Lesson Applications

EXERCISE 12-15

Create a presentation with a table slide, change alignment, apply formatting to the table, and recolor it.

1. Create a new presentation using the design template **Blush.pot**. Insert a Title slide with the title **Advertising Analysis** and the subtitle **Print Advertising**. Change the slide color scheme to the purple option. Ungroup the graphics on both the title and slide masters and delete the multicolored, rectangular graphic element.

2. Insert a Bulleted List slide with the title **Print Advertising, 1999** and the following three bulleted items:
   - **Campaigns use a variety of print media**
   - **Each medium targets a specific market segment**
   - **Every campaign must meet specific sales objectives**

3. Insert another slide, using the Bulleted List layout, with the title **Coupon Redemption** and the following bulleted items:
   - **Effective measure of return on investment**
   - **Used for promotional purposes in a variety of print media**

4. Insert a new slide after slide 3, using the Table layout, with the title **Coupons Redeemed, 1999**

5. Create a table with 4 columns and 4 rows, using the data shown in Figure 12-13.

FIGURE 12-13

Coupons Redeemed, 1999

Newspaper Magazine	Coupons Redeemed	Average Check	Cost of One Ad
NY Times	414	$31.50	$6,800
NY Magazine	476	$25.00	$2,850
NY Runner	1,063	$23.50	$975

Lesson Applications:
Provide independent practice for students. Objectives are indicated for each Exercise.

Mid-Term Exam:
If your class is on a semester schedule, you can now assign Mid-Term Exam 2 from the Mid-Term and Final Exams booklet.

Exercise 12-15:
Objectives 1–5
Required File: None
Solution File: gl12-15.ppt in Solutions Manual or on Solutions Disk.

385

UNIT 5 ■ ADVANCED FEATURES

6. Change the font for all cells to 28-point Impact.
7. Vertically center the text in all rows and center the column headings in columns 2 through 4. (Don't center the numbers or the row headings.)
8. Right-align all the numbers and set a right indent for the number cells so the numbers appear centered under their headings.
9. Adjust the width of column 1 so "NY Magazine" fits on one line and adjust the width of the last column so the entire table is 8 inches wide. Select the second, third, and fourth columns and evenly distribute them.
10. Make the border color green and add a thick bottom border to the cells in row 1 and a thick right border to the cells in the first column.
11. In Slide view, open the Format Object dialog box and use the Recolor button on the Picture tab to change the colors in the table. Change the color text and numbers to match the title text color and change the borders to white.
12. Adjust the black and white settings for the table to inverse grayscale.
13. Review the presentation. Change the bulleted text placeholder on the slide master to 8 inches wide with 0.5 line spacing before paragraphs.
14. Save the presentation as *[your initials]***12-15.ppt**.
15. Add the date and your name to the handout header and the filename to the handout footer.
16. Print as handouts, 6 slides per page, black and white, framed.
17. Save and close the presentation.

EXERCISE 12-16

Edit and format a presentation including a table slide, applying formatting and changing colors to match a presentation scheme.

1. Open the file **Advert3.ppt**. Change the background of the entire presentation to a two-color gradient fill, using medium blue and dark blue and choosing the From title shading style with the darkest color in the center.
2. Customize the slide color scheme as follows: Change the title text from bright yellow to a darker shade, using the honeycomb sample to the right of the original color. Change the accent color to bright red, and change the accent and hyperlink color to hot pink.
3. On the slide master, make the title placeholder bold.
4. Delete the last two slides in the presentation. After slide 1, insert a Table slide with the title **Advertising Analysis**

Exercise 12-16:
Objectives 1–5
Required File: Advert3.ppt
Solution File: gl12-16.ppt in Solutions Manual or on Solutions Disk.

The completed presentation for this Exercise may be used in a student's portfolio.

LESSON 12 ■ CREATING A TABLE

NOTE

5. Create a table with 3 columns and 5 rows using the following data:

	New Customers	Total Revenue
Newspaper	28%	30%
Radio	10%	5%
Mailers	12%	18%
Yellow Pages	6%	12%

6. Change the table text to 28-point Arial bold.

7. Center all the text vertically. Center the headings for columns 2 and 3 and indent the first column 0.25 inch.

8. Make the table 8 inches wide by adjusting the column widths. Column 1 should be wide enough so "Yellow Pages" fits on one line and columns 2 and 3 should be equal width.

9. Decimal-align the numbers so they appear centered under their column headings.

10. Make the first row yellow and the remaining cells turquoise. Change the column heading font to green and add a red, 3 pt outside border.

11. In Slide view, open the Format Object dialog box and recolor the table as follows: Change the yellow to medium blue, change the turquoise to dark blue, change the green to gold, and make the second black text color white.

12. Center the table horizontally on the slide and position it 2.25 inches from the top of the slide. Make sure the red border appears on all sides of the table.

13. Adjust the black and white settings for the table to inverse grayscale.

14. On slide 1, change "Student's Name" in the subtitle to your name.

15. Save the presentation as *[your initials]***12-16.ppt**.

16. Add the date and your name to the handout header and the filename to the handout footer.

17. Print as handouts, 6 slides per page, black and white, framed.

18. Save and close the presentation.

EXERCISE 12-17

Edit and format a presentation including a table slide, add data, change alignment, and change table colors.

1. Open the file **Market1.ppt**.

2. Apply the design template **Angles.pot**. Ungroup the graphic elements on the slide master and apply a one-color, moderately dark red gradient

---

NOTE
In step 5, resize the table in the table editing window.

Exercise 12-17:
Objectives 1–6
Required File: Market1.ppt
Solution File: gl12-17.ppt in Solutions Manual or on Solutions Disk.

The completed presentation for this Exercise may be used in a student's portfolio.

387

to each object. Use the vertical shading style with the variant that has the lightest color on the left. (Hint: Use the Format Painter to speed up the process.) Be careful not to change the fill of the text placeholder. Apply the same fill effects to the title master.

3. Customize the slide color scheme as follows: Change the green accent and hyperlink color to dark red, change the title text color to pale yellow, and change the accent color to a less bright shade of blue.

4. Insert a new slide after slide 3 using the Table layout with the title **Marketing Expenses, 1998**. Create a table with 3 columns and 5 rows using the following data:

	Budgeted Amount	**Percent of Budget**
Advertising	$295,000	50.4%
Direct Mail	$95,000	16.2%
Sports Events	$140,000	24.0%
Promotions	$55,000	9.4%

5. Change the font size of the table text to 28 points.

6. Adjust the table placeholder so it is slightly larger than the actual table, then drag the right column border of the third column to the 7.5-inch mark, reducing the overall width of the table. Make the second and third columns the same size.

7. Align the column labels and number appropriately. Be sure the right edges of all numbers are aligned.

8. Center all the table text vertically

9. With the Word table still active, change the colors of the numbers and make the labels a different color. Add a 3 pt inside and outside border, using a third color.

10. In Slide view, recolor the table, making the labels pale yellow, the number white, and the borders black.

11. Insert another slide after slide 4 using the Table layout, titled **Marketing Budget, 1999** and using the following table data. Format the second table the same as the first one. (Hint: Copy the first table to the new slide.)

	Budgeted Amount	**Percent of Budget**
Advertising	$306,800	49.8%
Direct Mail	$98,800	16.0%
Sports Events	$150,000	24.5%
Promotions	$60,000	9.7%

12. On a new slide, create a pie chart using the percentages for the 1999 budget. Use a pie chart type of your choice and format it attractively to go with the rest of the presentation.
13. Check the black and white settings of the slides and make necessary adjustments.
14. Save the presentation as *[your initials]***12-17.ppt**.
15. Add the date and your name to the handout header and the filename to the handout footer.
16. Print as handouts, 6 slides per page, black and white, framed.
17. Save and close the presentation.

LESSON 13
Creating Flowcharts and Organization Charts

OBJECTIVES

After completing this lesson, you will be able to:
1. Draw flowchart AutoShapes.
2. Connect flowchart shapes using connectors.
3. Insert an organization chart.
4. Add placeholder boxes.
5. Rearrange boxes and apply chart formatting.

 Estimated Time: 1 hour

Flowcharts are diagrams used to show a sequence of events. Flowcharts are usually associated with computer programs, but they can be useful in other situations, such as showing instructions for planting a tree or processing a retail sale.

NOTE

Organization charts—or "org" charts, for short—are diagrams that are typically used by businesses or work groups to show who reports to whom, and who is responsible for what function or task. Org charts can also be useful for describing other types of relationships, such as a family tree. Using PowerPoint you can incorporate org charts and flowcharts into your presentations.

Objective 1
Drawing Flowchart AutoShapes

PowerPoint provides special AutoShapes that are designed for flowcharts. You can format and position these shapes as you would any AutoShape.

PREPARE
Point out to students that the learning objectives show what they will learn in the lesson. Each heading in the lesson correlates to a learning objective.
Required Files
Org1.ppt

TEACH
Teaching Resources:
• PowerPoint Classroom Presentations
• School-to-Work Strategies Manual
• Internet Manual
• Spanish Glossary
• Methodology Video
• Certification Procedures

NOTE
This lesson assumes that Microsoft Organization Chart 2.0 is installed on your computers. If it is not, see "Installation Requirements" at the beginning of this text for instructions on how to install this component.

LESSON 13 ■ CREATING FLOWCHARTS AND ORGANIZATION CHARTS

EXERCISE 13-1 **Draw Flowchart AutoShapes**

1. Open the file **Org1.ppt**. Insert a Title Only slide after slide 2 with the title **New Purchasing Procedure**.

2. Choose Flowchart from the AutoShapes menu. Float the Flowchart submenu.

3. Choose the second shape in the first row (called "Flowchart: Alternate Process"). In the upper left corner of the slide, draw a rectangle approximately 1 inch high by 2.5 inches wide.

4. Key **Get Purchase Pre-Approval** in the rectangle. Select the rectangle and format the text as black 18-point Arial bold. Change the AutoShape border color to black to match the font color.

5. Using the Text Box tab in the Format AutoShape dialog box, turn on the word wrap option, turn off the resize autoshape option, change the text anchor point to Middle Centered, and change the internal margins to 0.05 inch all around.

6. Adjust the AutoShape size so the text wraps to two lines, if necessary.

7. Make five additional copies of the AutoShape (six boxes total) and arrange the shapes in two columns as shown in Figure 13-1. Change the text in each AutoShape to match the text in the figure.

FIGURE 13-1
Flowchart AutoShapes

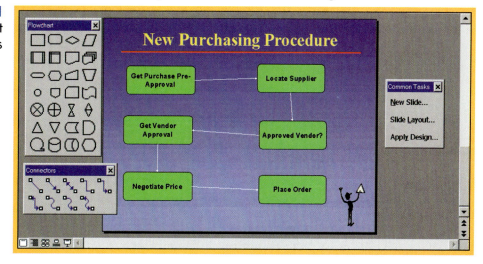

✓ Objective 2
Connecting Flowchart AutoShapes

You use *connector lines* to link the shapes in a flowchart. Connector lines have endpoints that automatically attach to a shape's *connection sites*—the small blue handles that appear when you work with connector lines.

NOTE
You may want to explain to students that flowchart shapes found on the Flowchart menu are derived from computer programming flowchart techniques.

NOTE
Point out to students that duplicating or copying existing shapes is the fastest way to achieve balance and symmetry in flowcharts.

Use PowerPoint Classroom Presentation #13 to display screens from the lesson, including this one, in a slide-show format.

✓ Objective 2 Assignment:
Exercises 13-14 (Skills Review) and 13-18 (Lesson Applications) can be assigned after completing Objective 2.

391

UNIT 5 ■ ADVANCED FEATURES

Connector lines are usually used with Flowchart AutoShapes, but they can also be used with most other AutoShapes. When you rearrange AutoShapes on a slide, the connector lines stay attached and adjust to the new position of the AutoShapes they connect.

EXERCISE 13-2 Add Straight Arrow Connectors

1. Choose Co**n**nectors from the A**u**toShapes menu and float the Connectors submenu.

FIGURE 13-2
Connection sites and pointer

2. Choose the second connector in the top row (Straight Arrow Connector) and move the pointer over one of the green AutoShapes. Notice the blue connection sites that appear and the change in pointer shape.

3. Click the pointer on the right connection site of the first AutoShape ("Get Purchase Pre-Approval") and move the pointer to the right. Notice the dashed line that appears.

4. Move the pointer to the second box ("Locate Supplier") and click its left connection site to connect the two boxes. Notice that the endpoints of the selected connector are red.

5. Select the first box and change its position slightly. Notice that the two boxes stay connected when you move one.

6. Draw a second connector from the "Locate Supplier" box to the "Approved Vendor?" box. Using the same method, draw the other connectors shown in Figure 13-1 (shown earlier).

EXERCISE 13-3 Change Flowchart AutoShapes

You can change flowchart AutoShapes just as you change other AutoShapes. In flowcharts, the diamond shape is traditionally used to signify a decision-making point, where a "Yes" takes one path and a "No" takes another path.

1. Select the "Approved Vendor?" box, then choose **C**hange AutoShape from the **D**raw menu. Choose **F**lowchart and then choose the diamond in the first row (Flowchart: Decision).

2. Drag one of the diamond's side resize handles to make it slightly wider. Notice the connection lines adjust and stay connected.

3. Change the last box in the right column ("Place Order") to the first shape in the third row of Flowchart shapes (Terminator). Reduce the height of this AutoShape to approximately 0.5 inch.

In PowerPoint Classroom Presentation #13.

392

LESSON 13 ■ CREATING FLOWCHARTS AND ORGANIZATION CHARTS

4. Create a small floating text box with the text **Yes**. Format it with no border, no fill, and make the text 16-point Arial bold, center-aligned, and black. Change all its internal margins to 0.00 inch. Position the text box below the diamond shape.

5. Draw a straight connector (the first connector on the Connectors menu) from the diamond to the top of the "Yes" box.

6. Choose the Elbow Arrow Connector (fifth Connector on the menu) and draw a connector from the bottom of the "Yes" box to the top of the "Negotiate Price" box. Notice that the connector automatically bends as necessary to make a neat path between the two shapes.

7. Create a small text box above the connector between "Get Vendor Approval" and "Approved Vendor." Key **No** in the text box and format it the same as the "Yes" text box.

8. Select the connector between "Get Vendor Approval" and "Approved Vendor." Drag its right endpoint away from the diamond shape and reconnect it to the left side of the "No" box.

9. Draw a straight connector from the "Approved Vendor?" diamond to the right side of the "No" box.

EXERCISE 13-4 Align Flowchart Elements and Apply Finishing Touches

Sometimes it's preferable to have the flowchart connectors point at odd angles, but other times you'll want them aligned horizontally or vertically.

1. Float the Align or Distribute submenu (from the Draw menu).

2. Select the three shapes in the right column and the "yes" box. Using the Align or Distribute commands, align their centers relative to each other.

3. Select the three shapes in the left column and align their centers relative to each other. Now all the vertical connectors are straight.

4. Select the top two shapes and align their middles relative to each other. Align the middles of the bottom two shapes.

5. Select the "No" box along with the two middle shapes and align their middles. Now all the connectors are straight and neat.

NOTE

6. If necessary, select the bottom two shapes and move them down to create more room within the flowchart.

7. Select the first box ("Get Purchase Pre-Approval") and change it to the Right Arrow on the Block Arrows AutoShape menu. Move the arrow's adjustment handle up to fit the text. Change the arrow fill color to pink

8. Change the fill color of the diamond to red and the last box ("Place Order") to yellow.

NOTE
Point out that the elbow connector has a yellow adjustment handle just like many other AutoShapes. By dragging the handle up or down, you can control where it bends. You may want to instruct students to click the elbow arrow connector (which starts below "Yes") and drag the yellow handle up slightly. Students may need to then adjust the position of the "Yes" box and any other connector that goes out of alignment.

393

9. Select all the elements of the flow chart and group them.
10. Center the flow chart horizontally relative to the slide and adjust its vertical position if necessary.
11. Save the presentation as *[your initials]***13-4.ppt**.

FIGURE 13-3
Completed flowchart

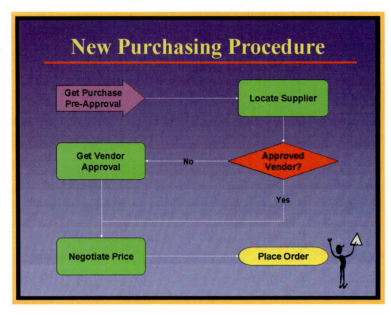

Objective 3
Inserting an Organization Chart

The easiest way to insert an org chart in a presentation is to add a new slide with the Organization Chart layout. Org charts are created and edited in a separate program called Microsoft Organization Chart, which you activate within PowerPoint.

EXERCISE 13-5 Start the Org Chart Application

When you start a new org chart, you begin with a default chart template containing four boxes. A *chart box* is the most basic structural unit in an org chart. This rectangular box contains space for one or more lines of information, such as a name and a title. Each chart box is positioned on a *level* in the chart, which indicates its position in the hierarchy of the organization. The top box in an org chart is level 1.

FIGURE 13-4
Organization Chart layout

1. Insert a new slide between slides 2 and 3 using the Organization Chart layout. Key the title **New Management Structure**.

In PowerPoint Classroom Presentation #13.

394

LESSON 13 ■ CREATING FLOWCHARTS AND ORGANIZATION CHARTS

2. Double-click the org chart placeholder. The Microsoft Organization Chart editing screen appears, displaying the four-box org chart. This editing screen has its own menus and toolbar. The level 1 box at the top overlaps the boxes below.

FIGURE 13-5
Blank org chart

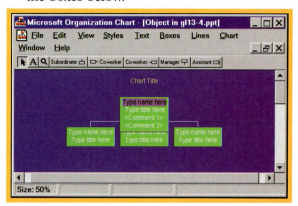

3. Click next to the level 1 box, which is the box on top. The "<Comment 1>" and "<Comment 2>" lines disappear and the overlap is eliminated.

4. Click inside the level 1 box. The text in the box is selected.

5. Click inside the level 1 box again. The two Comment lines reappear. Each box can have as many as four lines for an individual's name, title, and two lines of comments.

6. Click the left level 2 box. The text is highlighted.

7. Click in the box again. The two Comment lines appear.

TABLE 13-1 Organization Chart Toolbar

BUTTON (NAME)	FUNCTION
(Select)	Select and drag objects
A (Enter Text)	Create background (floating) text object
66% (Zoom)	Reduce chart so it fits in window or magnify part of chart
Subordinate	Add subordinate box (or boxes) to a box
:Co-worker	Add co-worker box (or boxes) to left of a box
Co-worker:	Add co-worker box (or boxes) to right of a box
Manager:	Add manager box to a box
Assistant:	Add assistant box (or boxes) to a box

NOTE

EXERCISE 13-6 Enter Text in the Placeholder Boxes

1. Click the level 1 box. The contents of the box are selected.

2. Key **President** and press Enter. The name is entered and the title line is now selected. Key **CEO**.

In PowerPoint Classroom Presentation #13.

NOTE
Review the buttons and icons on the Microsoft Organization Chart toolbar with students. It will be helpful for students to associate the icon with the type of org chart box, particularly when they begin adding boxes to the text.

UNIT 5 ■ ADVANCED FEATURES

3. Click the left level 2 box. Although the fields specify "Name" and "Title," you can enter any text.
4. Key **Operations** and press Enter. The title line is selected.
5. Press Delete and click the center level 2 box. (Notice that the title line in the left box is removed from the box.)
6. Key **Sales & Marketing** in the center level 2 box, press Enter, and delete the title.
7. Click the right level 2 box, key **Administration**, and delete the title. Click outside the box.

NOTE: The Organization Chart editing screen provides space for a chart title at the top of the chart. You can ignore or delete this space, as your PowerPoint slide provides its own title.

Objective 4
Adding Placeholder Boxes

NOTE You can add new boxes and levels to an existing org chart by adding subordinate, assistant, or co-worker boxes.

EXERCISE 13-7 Insert Subordinate Boxes

NOTE

1. Click the Subordinate button. The pointer changes from an arrow to a tiny subordinate box icon.

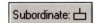

2. Click the Administration box on level 2. A blank box appears under the Administration box. Next, you insert multiple subordinate boxes at one time.
3. Click the Subordinate button twice. The status bar now reads "Create: 2."
4. Click the Operations box. Two boxes appear under Operations.
5. Click the Subordinate button three times, then click the Sales & Marketing box. Three boxes appear under Sales & Marketing. The screen scrolls left to accommodate the increased number of boxes.
6. Maximize or resize the window to see the entire chart.

FIGURE 13-6
Org chart with subordinate boxes added

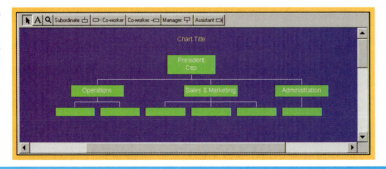

NOTE
Explain to students that it is often easier to lay out the structure of the chart before filling in the boxes. The structure determines the size of the boxes, which in turn determines how much text will fit in the boxes.

NOTE
You might want to introduce keyboard shortcuts for adding boxes. For example, you can select a box and press the F2 key to add a subordinate. Keyboard shortcuts are listed in the Command Summary at the end of this lesson.

In PowerPoint Classroom Presentation #13.

396

LESSON 13 ■ CREATING FLOWCHARTS AND ORGANIZATION CHARTS

EXERCISE 13-8 Add Assistant and Co-worker Boxes

You may add assistant boxes to the org chart for positions that provide administrative assistance or other support. You may also add boxes for additional people reporting to the same manager—that is, co-worker boxes.

1. Click the Assistant button on the toolbar.

2. Click the level 1 box, President CEO. An assistant box is added just below the President CEO box.

3. Click the Right Co-worker button three times, and then click the blank subordinate box under the Administration box. Three co-worker boxes are added to the right of the existing box for a total of four boxes now reporting to Administration.

EXERCISE 13-9 Key Text in Boxes

Once you set up the structure of your org chart, you can add all the names and titles to the boxes.

NOTE

1. Click the level 1 box , select the word "President," and key **Julie Wolfe**. Press [Enter] and key **Gus Irvinelli**, overwriting "CEO." Key **Co-owners** in the Comment 1 field.

2. Key **Troy Scott** as the name in the assistant box. Press [Enter] and key **Administrative Assistant** as the title.

3. In the two boxes under Operations, key the following employees:

Kitchen	**Purchasing**
Eric Dennis	Jessie Smith
Assistant Chef	Purchasing Mgr

   TIP: You can press [Ctrl] + an Arrow key to move from box to box in an org chart. For example, [Ctrl] + Right or Left Arrow move to a different box on the same level; [Ctrl] + Up or Down Arrow move to a new level.

4. In the three boxes under Sales & Marketing, key the following employees:

Events	**Merchandise**	**Marketing**
Ian Mahoney	Lila Nelson	Evan Johnson
Sales Mgr	Sales Mgr	Marketing Mgr

5. In the four boxes under Administration, key the following employees (leaving the last box blank):

NOTE
When keying information in a box, pressing Enter activates the next field. You can also click a field to activate it.

UNIT 5 ■ ADVANCED FEATURES

MIS	Billing & Acctg	Human Resources
Chuck Warden	Sarah Conners	Chris Davis
MIS Mgr	Accounting Mgr	HR Mgr

6. Expand the text in the second level boxes as follows:

Operations	Sales & Marketing	Administration
Michele Jenkins	Roy Olafsen	Michael Peters
Head Chef	Marketing Mgr	Administration Mgr

EXERCISE 13-10 Delete Boxes

If you have more boxes than necessary, you can delete them at any time. You can also adjust the chart size within the window to see the entire chart.

1. Use the horizontal scroll bar to display the right, empty box under Administration.

2. Click the box and press **Delete**. The box is deleted and the remaining level 3 boxes shift to the right. Even with the box deleted, it's still impossible to see the entire chart at this level of magnification.

3. Maximize the Organization Chart window, if necessary, and choose View, Size to Window from the menu. The chart size is reduced so it fits within the window. Although it's difficult to read the chart content, you can see the overall structure of the chart.

4. Save your changes to the org chart by choosing File, Update from the menu.

FIGURE 13-7
Entire org chart sized to fit in the window

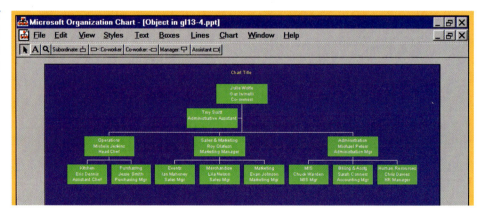

✓ Objective 5

Rearranging and Formatting Boxes

Organizations change frequently in many companies. You may need to promote, demote, or move org chart boxes as the reporting structure changes.

In PowerPoint Classroom Presentation #13.

✓ **Objective 5 Assignment:**
Exercises 13-15 and 13-16 (Skills Review) and Exercise 13-17 (Lesson Applications) can be assigned after completing Objective 5.

398

LESSON 13 ■ CREATING FLOWCHARTS AND ORGANIZATION CHARTS

Once your chart is complete, you can change the color of the chart boxes, text, lines, and background; add shadows to the boxes; change the font; and alter the style of the connecting lines.

EXERCISE 13-11 Promote and Demote Boxes

1. Switch back to 50% of Actual view by pressing `F10`.
2. Position the pointer over the bottom edge of the Events box.
3. Click and hold down the mouse button. The box is highlighted.
4. Drag the box over Merchandise (Lila Nelson). Observe the pointer carefully as you move the box across and slightly down—the pointer alternates between an arrow and a small subordinate box icon. Release the mouse when the button is the subordinate box icon, making Ian Mahoney report to Lila Nelson. (If you release the mouse button when the arrow is displayed, Ian Mahoney becomes a co-worker of Lila Nelson.)

FIGURE 13-8
Dragging to demote a box

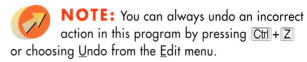

NOTE: You can always undo an incorrect action in this program by pressing `Ctrl`+`Z` or choosing Undo from the Edit menu.

5. Edit Lila Nelson's box, changing the name to **Merchandise & Events**.
6. Edit Ian Mahoney's box, deleting "Events" and changing the comment to **Sales Associate**.
7. Click the MIS box (located under Administration) to select it, then choose Edit, Cut from the menu or press `Ctrl`+`X` to cut the box.
8. Click the co-owners box on level 1 and choose Edit, Paste Boxes from the menu or press `Ctrl`+`V`. The MIS box is now positioned at the right end of level 2, reporting directly to the restaurant co-owners.
9. Cut the Purchasing box (Jesse Smith) under Operations and paste it to report to Administration.

EXERCISE 13-12 Change Box Style and Arrangement

Depending on the size of your org chart, you may find it useful to rearrange the grouping style of multiple boxes under a manager. For example, you can stack the boxes vertically instead of horizontally.

In PowerPoint Classroom Presentation #13.

399

UNIT 5 ■ ADVANCED FEATURES

1. Add another subordinate box to Administration by clicking the Subordinate button and clicking the Administration Mgr box.

2. In the new box, key **Payroll & Benefits** as the name, **John Larson** as the title, and **Payroll Mgr** as Comment 1. Four boxes now report to Administration.

NOTE

3. Use the arrow pointer to draw a selection rectangle around the four boxes that report to Administration. When you release the mouse button, all four boxes in the subgroup are selected.

FIGURE 13-9
Style options

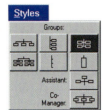

4. Choose Styles from the menu and choose the third option in the first row, which stacks the four boxes in two vertical columns.

5. Select the boxes reporting to Sales & Marketing. Choose Styles from the menu and choose the second option in the first row. The boxes in this subgroup are now stacked in a single vertical column.

TIP: You can also select multiple boxes by holding down the Shift key and clicking the desired box. This technique is a good way to select nonadjacent boxes.

6. Use the File menu to update the chart.

EXERCISE 13-13 Use Fill Colors, Fonts, and Shadows

NOTE

1. To select all boxes in the chart, press Ctrl + A.

2. Choose Text, Fonts from the menu, change the font to 18-point Arial bold, and click OK. The boxes enlarge to accommodate the text size.

3. With all boxes selected, choose Boxes, Shadow, and the third shadow style in the second column. Deselect the boxes to view the shadow.

NOTE

4. Use the View menu to size the chart to fit the window. Select all the boxes except the co-owners, choose Boxes, Color from the menu, and choose medium blue. With the boxes selected, choose Boxes, Border Color, and change the border color to red.

NOTE: You can change the color and style of the connecting lines by selecting one or more lines and choosing Lines from the menu.

5. Select the four level 2 boxes and make them dark blue.

6. Select the co-owners box. Choose Text, Color, and change the text color to yellow. Change the box color to red and font size to 24 point.

NOTE
The technique in step 3 is the same as drawing a selection rectangle to select objects in Slide view. For students who are not comfortable with this technique, you might want to introduce the keyboard command Ctrl+G to select a group (select the first box in the group and use the command to select the remaining boxes). Alternatively, students can use the Shift key, as explained in the Tip.

In PowerPoint Classroom Presentation #13.

NOTE
In step 1, remind students of the other ways to select all boxes (the Edit, Select command and the selection rectangle technique).

NOTE
Org charts cannot be recolored in PowerPoint. Students must return to Microsoft Organization Chart to do this.

400

LESSON 13 ■ CREATING FLOWCHARTS AND ORGANIZATION CHARTS

7. Update the chart and choose File, Close to return to PowerPoint.
8. In Slide view, resize the org chart proportionately to make it fill the entire slide and center it horizontally relative to the slide.

FIGURE 13-10
Completed org chart

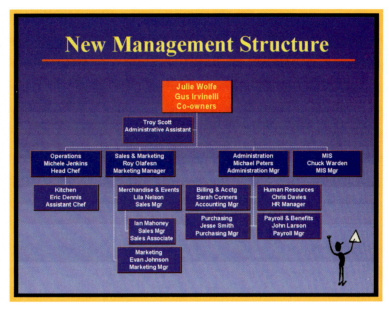

9. Change the black and white setting for the flowchart to black with white fill and save the presentation as *[your initials]***13-13.ppt**.
10. Add the date and your name to the handout header and the filename to the handout footer.
11. Print as handouts, 6 slides per page, black and white, framed.
12. Save and close the presentation.

COMMAND SUMMARY

NOTE

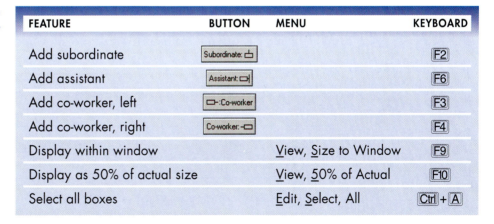

In PowerPoint Classroom Presentation #13.

NOTE
The Command Summary includes keyboard shortcuts for working on an org chart. Students can decide which method they prefer to use.

401

UNIT 5 ■ ADVANCED FEATURES

TEST BANK

Concepts Review

TRUE/FALSE QUESTIONS

Each of the following statements is either true or false. Indicate your choice by circling **T** or **F**.

T **(F)** 1. Flowcharts are always created in MS Organization Chart.

(T) F 2. You use the Organization Chart layout to insert an org chart.

(T) F 3. You can use any shape in a flowchart.

T **(F)** 4. You can move within an org chart using [Shift] + Arrow keys.

(T) F 5. If you add too many boxes to an org chart, you can always delete the extra boxes.

(T) F 6. You can change the color of the boxes in an org chart.

(T) F 7. An org chart is treated as a resizable object on the slide.

T **(F)** 8. You can use a shape's connection sites to resize the shape.

SHORT ANSWER QUESTIONS

Write the correct answer in the space provided.

1. How do you display the connection sites of a shape?
   Click a connector tool and position it over the shape

2. What term refers to the top box in an org chart?
   Level 1

3. Which shape is often used in a flowchart to show a decision point?
   Diamond

4. How do you access the Connectors submenu?
   On the Drawing toolbar, choose AutoShapes, Connectors

5. How do you see an entire chart if its structure exceeds the window size?
   Use View, Size to Window

6. If you have six people reporting to one manager, how do you change the six boxes so they are stacked vertically instead of lined up horizontally?
   Use Styles menu

Concepts Review: Allows students to check their understanding.

TEST BANK Consider using the Test Bank to provide an additional review of lesson concepts.

LESSON 13 ■ CREATING FLOWCHARTS AND ORGANIZATION CHARTS

7. Besides dragging, how can you rearrange boxes in an org chart?

Cut and Paste

8. What type of flowchart connector has a right-angle bend?

Elbow connector

CRITICAL THINKING

Answer these questions on a separate page. There are no right or wrong answers. Support your answers with examples from your own experience, if possible.

1. Think of a task that you had to explain or a job you had to describe to someone and try drawing it in a flowchart.
2. Org charts are by nature rather detail-oriented. Based on what you learned about designing presentations, how can you ensure that an org chart follows the rule of simplicity?

Skills Review

EXERCISE 13-14

Create a simple flowchart.

1. Open the file **Proc1.ppt**.
2. On slide 3 ("Procedures"), draw a Right Arrow AutoShape from the Block Arrows submenu. Key **Listen to grievance** in the arrow. Format the text as 18-point Arial bold, shadowed. Change the arrow color to dark pink, remove its outline, and apply Shadow Style 6.
3. Change the text box properties for the arrow to word wrap with 0.00 internal margins and set the text anchor point to Middle Centered.
4. Adjust the height, width, and adjusting handle for the arrow to make the text wrap to two lines and fit attractively inside the arrow.
5. Draw a flowchart AutoShape by following these steps:
    a. Click AutoShapes on the Drawing toolbar, choose Flowchart, and float the menu.
    b. Click the Decision AutoShape (diamond) and draw the shape to the right of the arrow. Key **Employee talked to Mgr?** in the shape.
    c. Format the diamond as bright green and the text as black 18-point Arial bold.
    d. Apply the same text box and shadow options used for the arrow.

Critical Thinking Questions:
Answers will vary based on students' preferences, observations, experiences, and research.

Skills Review:
Provides guided practice for students. Objectives are indicated for each Exercise.

Exercise 13-14:
Objectives 1, 2
Required File: Proc1.ppt
Solution File: gl13-14.ppt in Solutions Manual or on Solutions Disk

403

UNIT 5 ■ ADVANCED FEATURES

6. Draw a connector line between the two shapes using these steps:

   a. Choose Co**n**nectors from the A**u**toShapes menu and float the Connectors submenu.

   b. Click the Straight Arrow connector and move the pointer on top of the pink arrow to display the blue connector sites.

   c. Click the connector site at the tip of the arrow.

   d. Move the pointer to the green diamond and click the connector site on the left side of the diamond.

   NOTE
   e. To change the connector color, select the connector, if necessary, click the Line Color drop-down arrow, and choose gray (background scheme color). Increase the line thickness of the connector to 4½ pt.

FIGURE 13-11
Completed flowchart

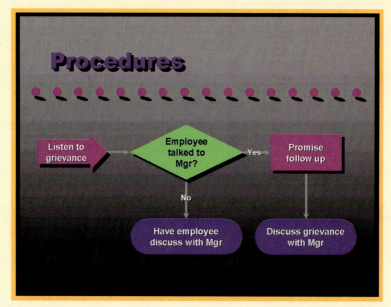

7. Add the remaining three AutoShapes shown in Figure 13-11, coloring and formatting them as shown. Key the text shown inside each AutoShape. Don't worry about aligning them yet.

8. Insert connectors between the shapes as shown in the figure.

9. Insert a text box between the diamond and square with the text **Yes**. Format the text as 16-point white, bold, and shadowed. Remove the fill and border. Size the text box appropriately and adjust its position so it rests on top of the connector.

10. Create a similar text box with the text **No**. Position it as shown.

11. Align flowchart AutoShapes by following these steps:

    a. Select the arrow, diamond, and square in the first row of shapes.

    b. Using the Align and Distribute commands, distribute them horizontally relative to the slide.

NOTE
Heavy connector lines sometimes appear to extend into the AutoShape. To correct that, select a connector and send it to the back.

LESSON 13 ■ CREATING FLOWCHARTS AND ORGANIZATION CHARTS

   c. Select the three shapes in the first row again, if necessary, and add the "Yes" box to the selection.

   d. Align the middles of the selected objects relative to themselves (not to the slide).

   e. Select the green diamond, the purple rounded rectangle below it, and the "No " text box. Align their centers relative to themselves.

   f. Align the remaining shapes similarly.

12. Group all the shapes and text boxes in the flowchart, then center the group horizontally relative to the slide. Adjust its vertical position if necessary.

13. Save the presentation as *[your initials]***13-14.ppt**.

14. Add the date and your name to the handout header and the filename to the handout footer.

15. Print as handouts, 6 slides per page, black and white, framed.

16. Save and close the presentation.

EXERCISE 13-15

Create a presentation that includes a simple org chart and delete unnecessary boxes.

1. Open the file **Kitch1.ppt**. Insert a new slide after slide 3 using the Organization Chart layout, with the title **Operations**.

2. Double-click the org chart placeholder and add text to the chart by following these steps:

   a. In the level 1 box, key **Michele Jenkins** as the name, press Enter, and key **Head Chef & Operations Mgr** as the title.

   b. Click the left box on level 2 and key **Eric Dennis** as the name and **Asst Chef & Kitchen Mgr** as the title.

   c. Press Ctrl+← to activate the middle box on level 2. Key **Claudia Pell** as the name and **Maitre d' & Service Mgr** as the title.

3. Click the right box on level 2 to select it and press Delete to remove it.

4. Change the color of the org chart boxes by following these steps:

   a. Draw a selection rectangle around all three boxes. (If you miss a box, hold down Shift and click the box to add it to the selection.)

   b. Choose Color from the Boxes menu, chose the cream color, and click OK.

5. Change the font of the org chart boxes by following these steps:

   a. Select the text "Michele Jenkins" in the top box.

   b. Choose Font from the Text menu. Choose Arial Black, italic, and 18 point. Click OK.

Exercise 13-15:
Objectives 3, 5
Required File: Kitch1.ppt
Solution File: gl13-15.ppt in Solutions Manual or on Solutions Disk

405

UNIT 5 ■ ADVANCED FEATURES

6. Return to Slide view by choosing File, Close and Return, and clicking Yes at the prompt to update the chart.

7. Make the org chart smaller by dragging one of its corner resize handles. Position the org chart attractively on the slide.

8. Check the black and white settings and save the presentation as *[your initials]***13-15.ppt**.

9. Add the date and your name to the handout header and the filename to the handout footer.

10. Print as handouts, 6 slides per page, black and white, framed.

11. Save and close the presentation.

EXERCISE 13-16

Add, promote, demote, and rearrange boxes in an existing org chart.

1. Open the file **Kitch2.ppt**. Move to slide 3 and double-click the org chart to activate it.

2. Add 3 subordinate boxes to the G. Robinson level 2 box by following these steps:
   a. Click the Subordinate button three times.
   b. Click the G. Robinson box.
   c. In the left box, key **Pastry** as the name and **G. Gordon** as the title.
   d. In the middle box, key **Cooks** as the name, **L. Tilson** as the title, **S. Mason** as Comment 1, and **J. Fulman** as Comment 2.
   e. In the right box, key **Banquets** as the name and **T. Domina** as the title.

3. Promote the level 3 Banquets box to level 2 by following these steps:
   a. Click outside the Banquets box to deselect it.
   b. Position the pointer over the Banquets box, hold down the mouse button, and drag the box over the level 1 box, "Kitchen."
   c. When the pointer changes to a subordinate box icon, release the mouse button.

4. Change the organizational style of the boxes under G. Robinson by following these steps:
   a. Select the two boxes under G. Robinson.
   b. Choose Styles from the menu and choose the second option, in which the boxes are stacked vertically.
   c. Do the same for the two boxes under Facilities & Maint.

5. Change the color of the level 1 box (Kitchen) to yellow.

Exercise 13-16:
Objectives 4, 5
Required File: Kitch2.ppt
Solution File: gl13-16.ppt in Solutions Manual or on Solutions Disk

LESSON 13 ■ **CREATING FLOWCHARTS AND ORGANIZATION CHARTS**

6. Return to Slide view, move the slide title closer to the top of the slide, and resize the org chart appropriately on the slide.

7. Check the black and white settings and save the presentation as *[your initials]***13-16.ppt**.

8. Add the date and your name to the handout header and the filename to the handout footer.

9. Print as handouts, 6 slides per page, black and white, framed.

10. Save and close the presentation.

Assessment Resources:
- Solutions Manual
- Test Bank with Software
- Portfolio Builder
- Alternative Assessment Guide
- Certification Procedures

407

UNIT 5 ■ ADVANCED FEATURES

Lesson Applications

EXERCISE 13-17

Create a flowchart and construct a menu using an org chart.

1. Open the file **Newyr3.ppt**. Insert a new slide 2 using the Title Only layout and key the title **New Year's Eve Reservations**.

2. In the upper left corner, below the title, draw a Pentagon AutoShape (Block Arrows, the third item in the fifth row). Make it about 0.75 inch high and 2 inches wide. Make its text anchor point Middle Centered.

3. In the pentagon shape, key **Call friends**. Make the text white 24-point Arial bold, shadowed. Adjust the size of the AutoShape to fit the text. Apply a blue fill and a black border.

4. To the right of the pentagon, insert a clip art image of a telephone (use the keyword "phone"). Size the phone to approximately 1 inch square and color it white with a black outline using the picture recolor method. (Don't ungroup the picture.)

5. Draw a curved arrow connector from the point of the pentagon to the left side of the phone. With the connector selected, change the line thickness to 4½ pt and change the line style to Round Dot.

FIGURE 13-12
Completed flowchart

6. Using Figure 13-12 as a guide, insert the AutoShapes shown and key the appropriate text inside each shape. Format the text and the text box

Lesson Applications:
Provide independent practice for students. Objectives are indicated for each Exercise.

Exercise 13-17:
Objectives 1–5
Required File: Newyr3.ppt and clip art file phonesym.wmf (see page xiv for clip art file locations and instructions)
Solution File: gl13-17.ppt in Solutions Manual or on Solutions Disk.

NOTE
This is a fairly challenging Lesson Application in which students create both a flowchart and an org chart. It may take some extra time for your students to complete.

The completed presentation for this Exercise may be used in a student's portfolio.

408

LESSON 13 ■ CREATING FLOWCHARTS AND ORGANIZATION CHARTS

options to match the blue pentagon and color the shapes to match the figure (or choose other colors you like).

7. Copy the telephone and position it as shown in the figure. Add the connectors, formatting them like the first connector you drew.

8. Create the "Yes" and "No" text boxes using no fill, no border, and white 16-point Arial bold text. Position the text boxes as shown in the figure.

9. Insert a new slide after slide 2 using the Chart layout. Delete the title placeholder, then double-click the org chart placeholder.

10. Add an additional level 2 box, for a total of 4.

11. Arrange the level 2 boxes using the third style in the first row. Make each second level box a different bright color.

12. Add 2 subordinate boxes below each level 2 box. Apply the second style in the third row (which arranges text as a list) to each subordinate box.

13. Key the text shown in Figure 13-13.

FIGURE 13-13
Completed org chart

14. Format the first level text as 36-point Times New Roman bold and change the box color to black.

15. Format the text in the second level boxes as black, 24-point Times New Roman italic.

16. Make the third level text 16-point Arial bold italic.

17. Select the line connecting the first level to the second level and change its color to black. (Only the lines from the second to the third level should be visible now.)

18. Update the chart and return to slide view. Enlarge the chart so it fills the slide, then center it on the slide.

UNIT 5 ■ ADVANCED FEATURES

19. Check the presentation's black and white settings, then save the presentation as *[your initials]***13-17.ppt**.

20. Add the date and your name to the handout header and the filename to the handout footer.

21. Print as handouts, 6 slides per page, black and white, framed.

22. Save and close the presentation.

EXERCISE 13-18

Create a simple org chart using AutoShapes and connector lines.

1. Start a new presentation using the **Zesty.pot** design template. Apply the last standard color scheme.

2. On the slide master, change the title text to purple with a text shadow. Reduce the text by one size.

3. Reduce the bulleted text on the slide master by one size. Change the placeholder's internal margins to 0.25 inch all around, turn on the resize autoshape to fit option, and change the text anchor point to Middle. Apply a two-color horizontal gradient fill, shading from red at the top to purple at the bottom. Change the text and bullet color to white.

4. Still working on the bulleted text placeholder on the slide master, change its AutoShape to a rounded rectangle and apply 3-D Style 2.

5. Apply the same formatting to the subtitle placeholder on the title master.

6. On slide 1, key a two-line title with **Good 4 U** on the first line and **Organization Structure** on the second line. Key **Administration Management** as the subtitle.

7. Insert a new slide 2 using the Bulleted Text layout. Key **Administration Management** for the title and the following two bullets:

   Michael Peters, Administration Manager
   Responsible for business management of the restaurant

8. Insert a new slide 3 using the Title Only layout. Key **Administration Org Chart** for the title.

9. Draw a rounded rectangle 1.25 inches high by 2.75 inches wide. Position it near the top of the white part of the slide, horizontally centered. Format it with the same fill and 3-D effect as the text placeholder on the slide master. Key **Michael Peters** as the first line of the AutoShape and **Administration** as the second line. Format the text as white 20-point Arial Black with a text shadow.

10. Make a copy of the AutoShape. Resize the copy to 1 inch high and 2 inches wide. Make three copies of the resized shape, then arrange all

Exercise 13-18:
Objective 2
Required File: None
Solution File: gl13-18.ppt in Solutions Manual or on Solutions Disk.

The completed presentation for this Exercise may be used in a student's portfolio.

four copies in a horizontal row below the original AutoShape. Align their bottoms relative to each other and distribute them horizontally relative to the slide.

11. Reduce the text size of the copied shapes to 18 point and key the following names and responsibilities in the shapes:

| **Jessie Smith** | **Sara Conners** | **Chris Davies** | **John Larson** |
| **Purchasing** | **Billing** | **Personnel** | **Payroll** |

12. Draw an elbow connector from the bottom of the Michael Peters box to the top of the Jessie Smith box. Change the connector line to purple with 3-point line weight. Draw similarly formatted elbow connectors to each of the other boxes in the second row.

13. If necessary, re-align and redistribute the boxes so all the lines are perfectly aligned.

14. Group the org chart you just created and position it attractively on the slide.

15. Change the black and white settings for the org chart and all other 3-D boxes in the presentation to inverse grayscale.

16. Save the presentation as *[your initials]***13-18.ppt**.

17. Add the date and your name to the handout header and the filename to the handout footer.

18. Print as handouts, 6 slides per page, black and white, framed.

19. Save and close the presentation.

411

LESSON 14
Animation and Slide Show Effects

OBJECTIVES

After completing this lesson, you will be able to:
1. Create transition effects.
2. Use text animations.
3. Create object animations.
4. Create chart animations.
5. Add animation effects to a template design.
6. Add hyperlinks.
7. Set slide timings.

 Estimated Time: 1 hour

Slide presentations can incorporate a variety of visual and audio effects. For example, you can control the transitions between slides and slide elements to emphasize your material. Presentations can include animated graphics, video clips, and audio clips that catch your audience's attention. Finally, you can rehearse and time your slide show to produce a polished presentation.

Objective 1
Creating Transition Effects

A *transition effect* determines the way a slide appears and disappears during a slide show. For example, a slide can appear like vertical blinds or a checkerboard or it can dissolve from the previous slide. You can control the speed of

PREPARE Point out to students that the learning objectives show what they will learn in the lesson. Each heading in the lesson correlates to a learning objective.

Required Files
Animate.ppt

TEACH Teaching Resources:
- PowerPoint Classroom Presentations
- School-to-Work Strategies Manual
- Internet Manual
- Spanish Glossary
- Methodology Video
- Certification Procedures

LESSON 14 ■ ANIMATION AND SLIDE SHOW EFFECTS

these transition effects and enhance them with a sound effect. You can also set the time to advance to the next slide or choose to advance manually using the mouse.

To set transitions between slides, use the Slide Transition dialog box, which you can open two ways:

NOTE

- Choose Slide Transition from the Slide Show menu or shortcut menu.
- In Slide Sorter view, use the Slide Transition button on the Slide Sorter toolbar.

EXERCISE 14-1 Create a Transition Effect

1. Open the file **Animate.ppt**. Display slide 2.
2. Choose Slide Transition from the Slide Show menu. The Slide Transition dialog box opens.

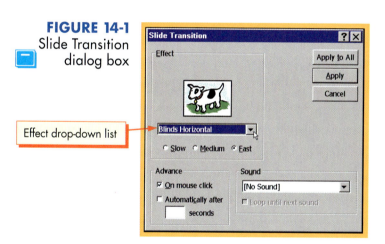

FIGURE 14-1
Slide Transition dialog box

Effect drop-down list

3. Choose any effect from the Effect drop-down list. The picture of the dog changes to a picture of a key and demonstrates the effect. Sample a few other effects and then choose the Blinds Horizontal effect. Click Apply.
4. Click the Slide Show button to display the effect. Press Esc to return to Slide view.
5. Switch to Slide Sorter view. Notice that the Slide Sorter toolbar replaces the Formatting toolbar.

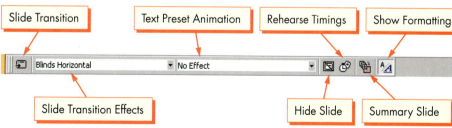

FIGURE 14-2
Slide Sorter toolbar

6. Click slide 2, if necessary, then click the Slide Transition button on the Slide Sorter toolbar.

NOTE
Encourage students to explore different effects throughout the lesson, but warn them of overuse in a final presentation. Special effects can be distracting; too many different effects may look unprofessional; some effects may be inappropriate for some audiences.

Use PowerPoint Classroom Presentation #14 to display screens from the lesson, including this one, in a slide-show format.

413

UNIT 5 ■ ADVANCED FEATURES

7. In the Slide Transition dialog box, change the effect to Checkerboard Across. Observe the effect on the dog picture.

8. Click <u>S</u>low to control the speed of the transition. Under Advance, choose <u>O</u>n mouse click, if necessary. This default option means you advance slides in the slide show by clicking the mouse button.

NOTE

9. Choose Typewriter from the So<u>u</u>nd drop-down list and click <u>A</u>pply to apply the effect to this slide only. The typewriter sound will be played when the slide show moves from slide 1 to slide 2.

10. Click the Transition icon under slide 2 to see a demonstration of the effect.

11. Select slide 1 and switch to Slide Show view to see your transition operate in a slide show. After slide 1 displays (which you'll notice contains a preset transition effect for the WordArt object), click the left mouse button to display slide 2. The slide appears through a slow checkerboard pattern accompanied by a typewriter sound.

12. Press Esc or right-click and choose End Show from the shortcut menu.

> **TIP:** Avoid using too many different transitions in a presentation so your audience can concentrate on your message, not on your special effects.

EXERCISE 14-2 Choose a Global Transition

NOTE

You can apply the same transition to any number of selected slides

1. Switch to Slide Sorter view, if necessary. Choose Select A<u>l</u>l from the <u>E</u>dit menu (or press Ctrl+A) to select all slides in the presentation.

2. Choose Cover Left-Down from the Slide Transition Effects drop-down list (which is now blank) on the Slide Sorter toolbar. All slides now have a transition icon under them.

3. Click the Slide Transition button to open the Slide Transition dialog box. Notice that Cover Left-Down is the selected effect.

4. Click <u>F</u>ast, choose Slide Projector from the So<u>u</u>nd drop-down list and click Apply <u>t</u>o All.

5. Click the Slide Transition icon under each slide to preview the transition effect, which is now the same for all slides.

EXERCISE 14-3 Hide a Slide

NOTE

You can create a short presentation from a long one by hiding selected slides. You might also hide slides that contain optional or sensitive information. The

---

NOTE
In step 9, point out the difference between the Apply and Apply to All buttons. It's important that students don't click Apply to All in this step.

NOTE
Starting with a "global" transition will add uniformity to a presentation. Students can change the transition effect on selected slides for exceptional purposes.

NOTE
A single presentation can be tailored for different audiences using the Hide Slide feature. Students can produce alternative slides and then show either one or the other, depending on the audience. Target audiences can be identified on the notes page.

414

LESSON 14 ■ ANIMATION AND SLIDE SHOW EFFECTS

easiest way to hide slides is to click the Hide Slide button on the Slide Sorter toolbar or choose Hide Slide from the shortcut menu.

 NOTE: Hidden slides appear in Slide view but not in Slide Show view.

1. Click between slides to deselect all slides, if necessary.

FIGURE 14-3
Slide 3 marked as hidden

2. Right-click slide 3 to select it and choose Hide Slide from the shortcut menu. The slide number below the slide is marked by a box and a diagonal line.

 TIP: Hide Slide is a toggle command. Choose it to hide a slide and choose it again to display the slide.

3. Select slide 1 and switch to Slide Show view. Slide 1 appears with the Cover Left-Down effect and the slide projector sound.

NOTE

4. Click the left mouse button (or press PgDn) to display slide 2. Click again. Slide 4, "Where We're Going," appears. Slide 3, "Financial History," was skipped.

5. Continue viewing more of the slide show or press Esc.

Objective 2
Creating Text Animations

You can focus attention on individual text elements by using a build effect. To *build* is to add elements to a slide, one at a time. For instance, you can add single paragraphs or bullets to a slide. You can also *animate* elements on a slide, which means to add special visual or sound effects to an object on a slide. You can dim the elements that were previously added, so the audience will pay more attention to the new element. Build elements can also include sound effects.

You can apply text build effects in the following ways:

- Use the Text Preset Animation drop-down list on the Slide Sorter toolbar.
- Choose Custo**m** Animation from the Sli**d**e Show menu.

EXERCISE 14-4 Apply a Text Build

You can apply a text build to an individual slide or to a group of selected slides.

1. Select slide 4 in Slide Sorter view.

NOTE
You might want to point out to students that they can suppress printing a hidden slide in their handouts by using the Print hidden slide option in the Print dialog box.

NOTE
In step 2, right-clicking a slide in Slide Sorter view sometimes brings up an abbreviated shortcut menu that does not contain the Hide Slide command. If that happens, click another slide, then try right-clicking the slide you want to hide again.

In PowerPoint Classroom Presentation #14.

NOTE
Remind students they can advance a slide show element by clicking or by pressing Page Down. Additionally, you might ask students to press the F1 key during a slide show to display a list of keyboard and mouse controls.

415

UNIT 5 ■ ADVANCED FEATURES

2. Open the Text Preset Animation drop-down list on the Slide Sorter toolbar and choose Dissolve. (You have to scroll to locate this effect.)

3. Select slide 1, change to Slide Show view, and click through the slides until slide 4 appears ("Where We're Going"). The slide title appears, but not the bullets.

4. Click once. The first bullet dissolves onto the slide.

5. Click again to display the second bullet. Click again to display the last bullet, and end the slide show.

6. In Slide Sorter view, select slides 2, 5, and 7. (Press [Shift] and click to add a slide to a selection.) You'll apply the same build effect to all three slides.

NOTE: PowerPoint applies text build effects only to text objects. If you include a slide with no text object in your selection, text build effects do not apply to that slide.

7. Choose Appear from the Text Preset Animation drop-down list. Note that you cannot add sound from the Slide Sorter toolbar (but you can add it using the shortcut menu).

8. View the new text build on slides 2, 5, and 7 in Slide Show view.

TIP: If you want most slides in your presentation to have the same text build effect, apply the effect to all slides and then modify the exceptions.

EXERCISE 14-5   Animate a Text Build

1. Select slide 4, if necessary, switch to Slide view, and select the text placeholder.

FIGURE 14-4
Custom Animation dialog box

2. Choose Custom Animation from the Slide Show menu (or from the shortcut menu). In the Custom Animation dialog box, click the Effects tab. The Dissolve effect is already set from the text build you applied from the toolbar.

3. Under Introduce text, choose By Letter from the drop-down list. This setting displays each letter one at a time.

NOTE
In step 2, point out the options that are automatically selected under the Effects tab of the Custom Animation dialog box when you select a specific object on a slide for animation.

In PowerPoint Classroom Presentation #14.

416

LESSON 14 ■ **ANIMATION AND SLIDE SHOW EFFECTS**

4. Under <u>E</u>ntry animation and sound, change Dissolve to Wipe Left.
5. Choose Typewriter from the Sound drop-down list.
6. Choose light brown (shadows scheme color) from the <u>A</u>fter animation drop-down list to dim a line of text before the next text build appears. Click OK.

TIP: When you choose to dim text after animation, you should select a color on the color palette that makes the dimmed object readable, but less conspicuous on the slide's background.

7. Switch to Slide Show view. Click the left mouse button to see the first paragraph appear one letter at a time from the left. Each letter is accompanied by a typewriter sound.
8. Click again. The first paragraph changes to brown as the next paragraph wipes on from the left.
9. End the slide show.

TIP: In Slide view, you can click the Animation Effects button on the Formatting toolbar to display a toolbar with frequently used animation effects. Once you become more familiar with using these effects, this toolbar can help you apply settings to slide objects quickly.

Objective 3
Creating Object Animations

In a slide show, you can have objects transition one at a time on the screen just as you did with text. Any object, including WordArt, tables, clip art, and AutoShapes can be animated.

EXERCISE 14-6 **Create and Animate an Object Build**

1. Double-click slide 4 to display it in Slide view.
2. Select the ruler graphic at the bottom of the slide. Choose Custo<u>m</u> Animation from the Sli<u>d</u>e Show menu.
3. In the Custom Animation dialog box, click the Effects tab, if necessary.
4. Under <u>E</u>ntry animation and sound, choose Fly From Left for the animation effect and Whoosh for the sound effect. Click OK.
5. Select the ruler graphic at the right of the screen. Apply the Fly From Bottom effect with the Whoosh sound effect. Notice the three items now in the Animation <u>o</u>rder list box.

NOTE
Discuss the color choices for dimming text items. Which colors work with which backgrounds?

NOTE
Have students display the Animation Effects toolbar and point out the various buttons (select a slide object first, especially a text object, to see the full range of buttons). This toolbar is useful to students once they become more familiar with the use of animation effects.

NOTE
Point out to students that they have more sound and text animation options available when individually applied to slides with the Custom Animation dialog box.

417

UNIT 5 ■ ADVANCED FEATURES

FIGURE 14-5
Changing the animation order of objects

6. Select Text 2, the first item in the Animation order list box, and click the down arrow button to move the text box to the third position. Select Group 3 (the right ruler) and move it down to the second position, if necessary. Click OK.
7. Switch to Slide Show view to see the objects build on slide 4. End the slide show.

NOTE: When adding sound effects for transitions or builds, you can choose Other Sound from the Sound drop-down list to apply other sound files available on your computer. Sound files have a .wav extension. To preview a sound file, right-click its filename and choose Play.

Objective 4
Creating Chart Animations

If your presentation includes charts, you can add animation effects to it. Bars, columns, pie slices, data points, and other chart elements can all be given the same visual and sound effects as other elements of a presentation.

EXERCISE 14-7 Add Animation Effects to a Chart

1. On slide 6, right-click the chart and open the Custom Animation dialog box. Click the Chart Effects tab, if necessary.
2. Under Introduce chart elements, choose By Series from the drop-down list.
3. Clear the Animate grid and legend check box.
4. Under Entry animation and sound, choose Wipe Up and apply the Cash Register sound.
5. Click the Timing tab. Under Start animation, click Automatically, **0** seconds after previous event. This makes the chart columns appear automatically one after the other without a mouse click. Click OK.
6. View the slide in Slide Show view then end the slide show.

Objective 5
Adding Animation Effects to a Template

Just as you can animate text, objects, and charts, you can also animate elements of a template. Be aware that some template designs are more appropri-

---

In PowerPoint Classroom Presentation #14.

NOTE Encourage students to use other .wav files that may be available on their computers. Look in folders such as Win 95\Media or MS Office\Sounds for appropriate files, or load additional files from the Valupack folder on the Microsoft Office CD ROM. Refer to "Appendix G: Multimedia and Pack and Go," for more information about adding audio and video files to a presentation.

NOTE In step 3, point out that the grid and legend are included in the animation by default.

NOTE Remind students that if they are applying animation effects to a template design in the slide master, the effects appear on every slide in the presentation. They should apply such effects sparingly.

LESSON 14 ■ **ANIMATION AND SLIDE SHOW EFFECTS**

ate than others. Make sure animation effects add to the presentation without distracting the viewer from the message.

EXERCISE 14-8 Animate a Template Design

1. Display the slide master. Just below the left edge of the title placeholder, draw a tiny circle and color it dark red. Use the Format AutoShape dialog box to make the circle 0.1 inches high by 0.1 inches wide.
2. Right-click the circle and open the Custom Animation dialog box
3. Apply the Appear effect and choose chime sound.
4. Click the Timing tab. Under Start animation, choose Automatically **0** seconds. Click OK.
5. Use the Duplicate command to create a row of 20 red dots across the slide just below the title, distributing the dots evenly and aligning them in a straight row.
6. Right-click one dot, then open the Custom Animation dialog box. Notice the long list of ovals in the Animation order list box. The animation was copied to each dot. Click Preview, then click OK.

NOTE: When you apply animation effects to both a master slide and an actual slide you cannot control which animation group will appear first. Some experimentation may be necessary to get objects displayed in the order that you want.

7. Display the complete slide show starting with slide 1 to see the effect of your slide master animation.

✏ Objective 6
Adding Hyperlinks

You can insert an object on a slide that, when clicked, displays an additional slide. This object, which can be a button, special text, or other object, is called a *hyperlink*. Hyperlinks are especially useful when your presentation includes a summary slide.

NOTE: You can create hyperlinks to another PowerPoint presentation, an Excel file, any other document, and even to the Internet during a slide show. To do this, use the Action Settings dialog box.

NOTE
Once students are familiar with basic slide show operation, you might show them how to use the pen pointer for highlighting during a show. Using the shortcut menu, you can switch from the arrow to the pen pointer and choose a pen color as well.

✏ **Objective 6 Assignment:**
Exercise 14-12 (Skills Review) can be assigned after completing Objective 6.

419

UNIT 5 ■ ADVANCED FEATURES

EXERCISE 14-9 Add Hyperlinks to a Summary Slide

1. In Slide Sorter view, select slides 2 through 7.
2. Click the Summary Slide button on the Slide Sorter toolbar. The summary slide appears in the slide 2 position.
3. Double-click the summary slide to display it in Slide view. Change the title to **Good 4 U in a Nutshell**.
4. Choose Action Buttons on the Slide Show menu (or from the AutoShapes menu). The Action Buttons submenu is displayed. Notice that you can float this menu. Choose the Forward or Next button ▷. The pointer changes to a cross.

FIGURE 14-6
Action buttons

5. Using the cross pointer, draw a small box on top of the first bullet. The Actions Settings dialog box appears. Click the Mouse Click tab, if necessary.

   NOTE: If you just click instead of drawing a shape, you create a very large action button which you can later resize.

FIGURE 14-7
Hyperlink to Slide dialog box

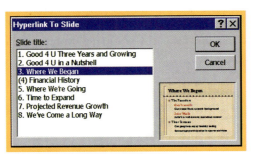

6. Open the Hyperlink to: drop-down list and choose Slide. The Hyperlink to Slide dialog box appears, containing a list of slide titles for all slides in the presentation.
7. Choose slide 3 ("Where We Began") and click OK. Click OK again to close the Action Settings dialog box.
8. Drag the yellow resize handle to the right to add a three-dimensional effect to the button. Adjust the button's size, if necessary. Change the fill color to the same brown as the bullet. See Figure 14-8.
9. Switch to Slide Show view and click the Action button to see the presentation jump to slide 3. End the slide show.
10. Copy the first Action button and paste the copy over the second bullet.
11. With the second Action button selected, choose Hyperlink from the shortcut menu and choose Edit Hyperlink.
12. In the Hyperlink to: drop-down list, choose Slide, then choose the slide title that matches the second bullet. Click OK and click OK again.

NOTE
Students who are familiar with creating a summary slide in Outline view may find creating one in Slide Sorter view an interesting and more visual alternative.

 In PowerPoint Classroom Presentation #14.

LESSON 14 ■ **ANIMATION AND SLIDE SHOW EFFECTS**

13. Repeat the previous three steps for each of the remaining bullets on the summary slide.

FIGURE 14-8
Completed summary slide with action buttons

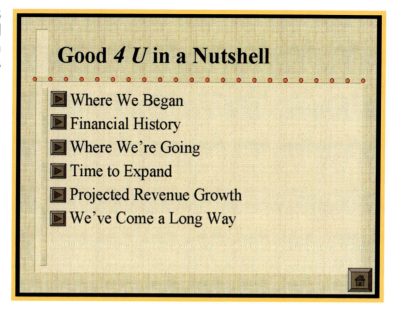

14. Align and distribute the hyperlink buttons so they make a straight row.

15. Display the slide master and add a Home action button to the lower right corner of the slide, as shown in Figure 14-8. Set the hyperlink for the button to slide 2 ("Good 4 U in a Nutshell").

16. Display slide 2 in Slide Show view. Try each action button on slide 2, and return to the summary slide by clicking the Home button.

✓ Objective 7

Timing Slides

NOTE   Instead of advancing slides manually during a presentation, you can set timings that advance slides automatically without clicking the mouse. This type of slide show is best used in a self-running presentation at a kiosk.

EXERCISE 14-10   Set Timings as Part of a Slide Transition

To set slide timings, enter them directly into the Slide Transition dialog box.

1. In Slide Sorter view, select slide 1 and click ▣ on the Slide Sorter toolbar.

In PowerPoint Classroom Presentation #14.

✓ **Objective 7 Assignment:**
Exercises 14-11 (Skills Review) and Exercises 14-13 and 14-14 (Lesson Applications) can be assigned after completing Objective 7.

NOTE
Point out that slide timings are usually not intended for use on slides with action buttons.

421

UNIT 5 ■ ADVANCED FEATURES

2. In the Slide Transition dialog box, key **3** in the text box to Advance Automatically after 3 seconds. Note that because On mouse click remains selected, you can still advance the slide with a mouse click.

3. Click Apply. The timing :03 appears under the slide.

4. Select the remaining slides and click .

5. Set the automatic timing to **6** seconds and click Apply. The timing :06 appears under the rest of the slides.

6. Choose Set Up Show from the Slide Show menu to open the Set Up Show dialog box. This dialog box allows you to display specific slides in a slide show and set advance options.

7. Under Advance slides, click Using timings and click OK.

NOTE: If you set timings, slides do not automatically advance *unless* you activate the Using timings option in the Set Up Show dialog box.

8. Choose Slide Show on the View menu. The slide show begins and advances automatically using the timings you set. The animations appear onscreen at evenly spaced intervals within the slide timings you set.

9. View the slide show to the end of the presentation.

NOTE: For a self-running presentation accompanied by recorded speech, click Rehearse Timings on the Slide Sorter toolbar to "talk through" a presentation. Your talk is automatically timed and the slide timings are set accordingly. If proper audio equipment is connected to the computer, you can record the voice narration.

10. Save the presentation as *[your initials]***14-10.ppt**.

11. Add the date and your name to the handout header and the file name to the handout footer.

12. Print as handouts, 6 slides per page, black and white, framed.

13. Save and close the presentation.

COMMAND SUMMARY

FEATURE	BUTTON	MENU	KEYBOARD
Slide Transition		Tools, Slide Transition	
Hide Slide		Tools, Hide Slide	

NOTE
Point out the options in the Set Up Show dialog box, including the Loop continuously option, which can be used when setting up a presentation at a demonstration table.

NOTE
Stress the importance of setting the Using timings option in the Set Up Show dialog box to ensure that slides display automatically during a slide show.

422

LESSON 14 ■ ANIMATION AND SLIDE SHOW EFFECTS

Concepts Review

TEST BANK

TRUE/FALSE QUESTIONS

Each of the following statements is either true or false. Indicate your choice by circling **T** or **F**.

(T) F *1.* A dissolve is a transition effect.

T **(F)** *2.* Only one kind of slide transition can be used in a presentation.

(T) F *3.* You can preview a transition before applying it to a slide.

(T) F *4.* You can change the speed of a slide transition.

T **(F)** *5.* Text builds cannot include sound effects.

(T) F *6.* You can set different timings for each slide in a slide show.

(T) F *7.* Text builds are set in the Custom Animation dialog box.

(T) F *8.* A special effect that accompanies a slide is called a transition.

SHORT ANSWER QUESTIONS

Write the correct answer in the space provided.

1. What do you call an object, that when clicked, displays another slide?
   Hyperlink

2. What do you do first to apply the same transition to an entire slide show?
   Select all slides

3. Which toolbar contains drop-down lists for slide transitions and text builds?
   Slide Sorter toolbar

4. How do you display the submenu of action buttons?
   Choose Action Buttons from Slide Show menu

5. What is the purpose of the 🔲 button?
   Hide a slide or display a hidden slide

6. When working in Slide Sorter view, what can you click to preview the transition effects you applied to a slide?
   Transition icon

Concepts Review: Allows students to check their understanding.

TEST BANK Consider using the Test Bank to provide an additional review of lesson concepts.

423

UNIT 5 ■ ADVANCED FEATURES

7. Which dialog box lets you change the animation order of slide objects?
   Custom Animation

8. How do you set an animation effect to start without a mouse click?
   Custom Animation dialog box, Timing tab, Automatically option

CRITICAL THINKING

Answer these questions on a separate page. There are no right or wrong answers. Support your answers with examples from your own experience, if possible.

1. Which transition effects do you like best and which ones do you think should be used in a business presentation?
2. Adding sound effects, text builds, and slide transitions to a slide show allows for a great deal of variety. How can you avoid clutter?

Skills Review

EXERCISE 14-11

Create transition effects, text builds, and an object animation; set slide timings.

1. Open the file **Hiring3.ppt**.
2. Create transition effects for slides by following these steps:
   a. Working in Slide Sorter view, right-click slide 1 and choose Slide Transition from the shortcut menu.
   b. Choose Box Out from the Effect drop-down list.
   c. Chose Slow for the speed and click Apply.
   d. Select slides 2 and 3 and click the Slide Transition button 🔲 on the Slide Sorter toolbar.
   e. Choose Checkerboard Down, Medium, and click Apply.
3. Create text builds for slides 2 and 3 by following these steps:
   a. Display slide 2 in Slide view. Select the bulleted text box, then right-click its border.
   b. Choose Custom Animation from the shortcut menu and click the Effects tab.
   c. Choose Fly from Top from the Entry animation and sound drop-down list.

Critical Thinking Questions:
Answers will vary based on students' preferences, observations, experiences, and research.

Skills Review:
Provides guided practice for students. Objectives are indicated for each Exercise.

🔲**Exercise 14-11:**
Objectives 1–3, 7
Required File: Hiring3.ppt
Solution File: gl14-11.ppt in Solutions Manual or on Solutions Disk

424

LESSON 14 ■ ANIMATION AND SLIDE SHOW EFFECTS

    d. Choose the Whoosh sound and choose dark gold (the fills color scheme) from the <u>A</u>fter animation drop-down list.

    e. Apply the same text build effects to slide 3.

4. Animate a clip art drawing following these steps:

    a. On slide 1, right-click the clip art object and choose Custo<u>m</u> Animation from the shortcut menu.

    b. Choose the Dissolve effect from the Effects tab.

    c. Click the Timing tab and choose A<u>u</u>tomatically, 0 seconds. Click OK.

5. View the slide show beginning with slide 1. Click the left mouse button to change slides and to view the text builds.

6. Apply slide transitions and slide timings to all slides by following these steps:

    a. In Slide Sorter view, select all slides and click 🗔.

    b. In the Slide Transition dialog box, key **3** in the Advance text box to advance slides automatically after 3 seconds. Click Apply <u>t</u>o All.

    c. Choose <u>S</u>et Up Show from the Sli<u>d</u>e Show menu. Under Advance slides, make sure <u>U</u>sing timings is selected. Click OK.

7. Run the slide show to review your transitions and timings.

8. Save the presentation as *[your initials]***14-11.ppt.**

9. Add the date and your name to the handout header and the filename to the handout footer.

10. Print as handouts, 3 slides per page, black and white, framed.

11. Save and close the presentation.

EXERCISE 14-12

Add animation effects to a template design and a chart and create a hyperlink.

1. Open the file **BevSales.ppt** and switch to Slide Sorter view.

2. Hide slide 5 (the chart slide) by selecting the slide and clicking the Hide Slide button 🗔 on the Slide Sorter toolbar.

3. On slide 4, set up a hyperlink to slide 5 by following these steps:

    a. Display slide 4 in Slide view and choose Action Butt<u>o</u>ns from the Sli<u>d</u>e Show menu.

    b. Choose the Forward or Next button ▷ on the Action Buttons submenu.

    c. Position the cross pointer in the lower left corner of the slide and draw the button so it is sized slightly larger than a bullet.

NOTE
When presentations are three slides long, students are asked to print handouts 3 slides per page. You might have them use the lined area of the printout to detail the builds and transitions. You might ask students to print 3 slides per page for all presentations for this purpose.

Exercise 14-12:
Objectives 4–6
Required File: BevSales.ppt
Solution File: gl14-12.ppt in Solutions Manual or on Solutions Disk

425

UNIT 5 ■ ADVANCED FEATURES

    d. When the Actions Settings dialog box opens, click the Mouse Click tab, if necessary. Open the <u>H</u>yperlink to: drop-down list and choose Slide.

    e. In the Hyperlink To Slide dialog box, choose "(5) Beverage Sales" and click OK. Click OK to close the Action Settings dialog box.

    f. Resize the action button, if necessary, and change its fill and outline color to gray.

4. Apply animation settings to the chart on slide 5 by following these steps:

    a. Select the chart. Open the Custom Animation dialog box and click the Chart Effects tab, if necessary.

    b. Under <u>I</u>ntroduce chart elements, choose By Category and deselect the Ani<u>m</u>ate grid and legend check box.

    c. Under <u>E</u>ntry animation and sound, choose Wipe Up and click OK.

5. Apply animation effects to the template design by following these steps:

    a. Display the slide master. Select the dotted arrow line below the title.

    b. Open the Custom Animation dialog box.

    c. Choose Stretch From Left as the entry animation.

    d. On the Timing tab, set the line to start automatically (at 0 seconds).

    e. Click OK. Apply the same effect to the dotted line in the title master.

6. In Slide Sorter view, select all slides (press Ctrl + A) and apply the Wipe Down slide transition.

7. Run the slide show from slide 1, clicking to display the slides and effects. After displaying slide 4, click the Action button to display slide 5, then end the slide show.

8. Save the presentation as *[your initials]***14-12.ppt.**

9. Add the date and your name to the handout header and the filename to the handout footer.

10. Print as handouts, 6 slides per page, black and white, framed.

11. Save and close the presentation.

NOTE
You could ask students to print a second copy of the presentation using the Print hidden slide option in the Print dialog box to suppress printing the hidden slide.

Assessment Resources:
- Solutions Manual
- Test Bank with Software
- Portfolio Builder
- Alternative Assessment Guide
- Certification Procedures

LESSON 14 ■ ANIMATION AND SLIDE SHOW EFFECTS

Lesson Applications

EXERCISE 14-13

Create slide transitions, text and object builds, and a hyperlink object; add slide timings.

1. Open the file **Events3.ppt**. Apply the **Fireball.pot** template. Customize the color scheme by changing the black background to the darkest blue available. Change the presentation background to a one-color horizontal gradient fill, shading from dark blue to black with black at the bottom.

2. On the slide master, delete the fireball graphic, including the horizontal line attached to it. In its place, draw a long thin right-pointing block arrow AutoShape. Use the arrow's adjustment handle to make a smaller arrowhead. Apply a vertical gradient fill to the arrow, using the Late Sunset preset. Choose the variant with the lightest color on the right. Remove the outline from the arrow.

3. Apply the Fly From Left animation effect to the arrow, using the Whoosh sound. Make the arrow appear automatically in zero seconds.

4. Replace the fireball graphic on the title master with a copy of the arrow you created on the slide master.

5. Insert a new slide after slide 3 using the Text & Clip Art layout titled **Promotional Ideas**. Key the following bullets:

   - **Think globally**
     - Multicultural themes
     - Environmental events
     - Health events
     - Sports events
   - **Brainstorm with staff**

6. Insert the World Globe (Western Hemisphere) clip art that you can find using the keyword "globe." Size the globe to the height of the bulleted text box. Recolor the map to fit the presentation color scheme. Apply the Dissolve animation effect to the globe, making it appear automatically.

7. Hide slide 3. Create a 0.5-inch square action button on slide 2 that hyperlinks to slide 3, using the Information button 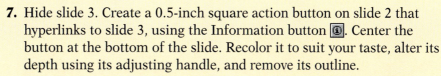. Center the button at the bottom of the slide. Recolor it to suit your taste, alter its depth using its adjusting handle, and remove its outline.

8. Create a similarly formatted action button on slide 3, but use the Return button style . (This button should hyperlink to slide 2.) Test both action buttons.

Lesson Applications:
Provide independent practice for students. Objectives are indicated for each Exercise.

Exercise 14-13:
Objectives 1–3, 5–7
Required Files: Events3.ppt and clip art file globewst.wmf (see page xiv for clip art file locations and instructions)
Solution File: gl14-13.ppt in Solutions Manual or on Solutions Disk.

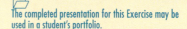
The completed presentation for this Exercise may be used in a student's portfolio.

UNIT 5 ■ ADVANCED FEATURES

9. Apply the slide transition effect Split Vertical Out to all slides, at medium speed, with the Whoosh sound.

10. To the bulleted text on slides 4 and 5 only, apply the text build Split Vertical Out, dimming to gold after the build.

11. Set up the presentation to advance slide 1 automatically after 3 seconds and to advance the rest of the slides after 6 seconds.

12. View the presentation using these timings. After all slide 2 text is displayed, click the action button to display slide 3. Continue with the automatic settings.

13. Save the presentation as *[your initials]***14-13.ppt.**

14. Add the date and your name to the handout header and the filename to the handout footer.

NOTE 15. Print as handouts, 6 slides per page, black and white, framed.

16. Save and close the presentation.

EXERCISE 14-14

Create slide transitions, text and object builds, and animate a chart.

1. Open the file **Contest.ppt**. Change the color scheme to the sample with the blue background, then change the background fill effect to a one-color blue horizontal gradient fill, moderately dark, with the lightest color in the middle. On the slide master and title master, change all the text to Arial bold, shadowed.

2. On slide 1, ungroup the target clip art image and ungroup the three darts. Create the following object builds for the darts:
First dart: Fly From Top, laser
Second dart: Fly From Top-Right, laser
Third dart: Fly From Right, laser

3. Re-open the Custom Animation dialog box and set the timing for each dart so it appears automatically, zero seconds after the previous event. Preview the animation. If the darts do not appear in clockwise order, adjust the order in the Animation order list box.

4. Copy one of the darts and paste it on the slide master. Rotate the dart so it is horizontal, pointing to the right. Reduce the size of the dart by 50%. Move the dart to the right edge of the slide, vertically positioned between the title placeholder and the bullet text placeholder.

5. Animate the dart on the slide master with these settings:
Fly from left, Laser sound, Hide after animation, and start animation automatically zero seconds after previous event.

NOTE
You could ask students to print a second copy of the presentation using the Print hidden slide option in the Print dialog box to suppress printing the hidden slide.

Exercise 14-14:
Objectives 1–5
Required Files: Contest.ppt
Solution File: gl14-14.ppt in Solutions Manual or on Solutions Disk.

The completed presentation for this Exercise may be used in a student's portfolio.

6. Apply the dissolve effect to the crowd image on slide 3 and make it appear automatically.

7. On slide 4, apply the dissolve effect to each clip art image. Make all three images appear automatically, with the plate of spaghetti first, the chili pepper second, and the pie third.

8. On slide 6, animate the pie chart by category and apply the dissolve effect. Do not animate the legend.

9. To slides 2 through 6, apply the Wipe Down slide transition at medium speed with no sound. Make the bulleted text fly from the top and dim to black after building.

10. Adjust the animation order for each slide where necessary so the clip art animations appear before the text animations.

11. Run the slide show to view the animations. Make any corrections, then check the black and white settings.

12. Save the presentation as *[your initials]***14-14.ppt.**

13. Add the date and your name to the handout header and the filename to the handout footer.

14. Print as handouts, 6 slides per page, black and white, framed.

15. Save and close the presentation.

LESSON 15
Using the Internet

OBJECTIVES

After completing this lesson, you will be able to:
1. Create hyperlinks to Internet sites.
2. Use Internet hyperlinks in a presentation.
3. Browse the Web.
4. Create a presentation to publish on the Internet.

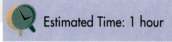

Estimated Time: 1 hour

The World Wide Web was created by placing a series of hypertext documents on many computers around the world and connecting them through a network called the Internet. A *hypertext document*, or Web Page, is a text document that can contain pictures, sounds, movies, and most importantly, hyperlinks that connect you to other hypertext documents.

Objective 1
Creating Hyperlinks to Internet Sites

In the previous lesson, you learned how to use hyperlinks to branch to another slide or file. You can also use hyperlinks to connect to a location on the Internet. During a presentation, you can use Internet hyperlinks to jump to a specific Web site related to the presentation topic.

To link to a Web site, you need to know the site's "address" or *URL* (Uniform Resource Locator). A URL is a combination of characters that are understood by

---

PREPARE

Point out to students that the learning objectives show what they will learn in the lesson. Each heading in the lesson correlates to a learning objective.

Required Files
Walk5.ppt   Juice.ppt

TEACH

Teaching Resources:
- PowerPoint Classroom Presentations
- School-to-Work Strategies Manual
- Internet Manual
- Spanish Glossary
- Methodology Video
- Certification Procedures

LESSON 15 ■ USING THE INTERNET

the Internet and identify a Web site's location on the Internet. For example, the Web address for Microsoft is **http://www.microsoft.com**. The prefix **http://** (which stands for Hypertext Transport Protocol) is used for all Web addresses.

You can create Internet hyperlinks in one of two ways:

- Define specific text as an Internet hyperlink using the Insert Hyperlink button on the Standard toolbar.
- Convert text to an Internet hyperlink using the Action Settings dialog box.

NOTE: You cannot link to the Web without an Internet connection. Your computer must be equipped with a modem and have the proper software installed. You need an Internet service provider, such as Microsoft Network, and a browser, such as Microsoft Internet Explorer or Netscape Navigator.

EXERCISE 15-1 Insert an Internet Hyperlink

1. Open the file **Walk5.ppt**. Display slide 6.
2. Select the text "5-day weather forecast."

3. Click the Insert Hyperlink button on the Standard toolbar. In the Insert Hyperlink dialog box, notice that you can create two different types of hyperlinks: one to connect to an Internet location and the other to connect to another slide in the presentation.

FIGURE 15-1
Insert Hyperlink dialog box

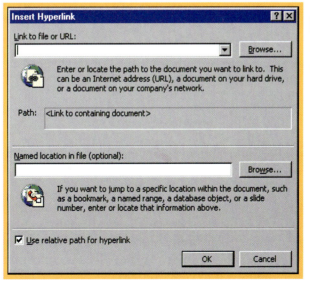

TIP: The keyboard shortcut Ctrl+K is another way to open this dialog box.

Use PowerPoint Classroom Presentation #15 to display screens from the lesson, including this one, in a slide-show format.

431

UNIT 5 ■ ADVANCED FEATURES

NOTE

4. In the Link to file or URL text box, key **http://www.weather.com**. This is the address for the Weather Channel's Web site.

5. Click OK and deselect the text. The text is formatted as hypertext—it is underlined and appears in the hypertext scheme color used in this template (purple).

6. View the slide in Slide Show view.

NOTE

7. Position the pointer over the hypertext without clicking it. The pointer changes to a hand and a ScreenTip shows the address for the hyperlink.

EXERCISE 15-2 Create an Internet Hyperlink Using the Action Settings

1. Display slide 4 in Slide view and select the text "*The New York Times*" in the last bullet point.

2. Choose Action Settings from the Slide Show menu. The Action Settings dialog box appears.

3. On the Mouse Click tab, click the Hyperlink to option and choose URL from the drop-down list. The Hyperlink to URL dialog box appears.

FIGURE 15-2
Hyperlink to URL dialog box

4. Key **http//:www.nytimes.com** and click OK. Click OK again to close the Action Settings dialog box. The selected text is now a hyperlink to the New York Times Web site.

5. Click 🖥 and position the pointer over the hypertext. The URL for the hypertext is displayed as a ScreenTip.

6. Return to Slide view.

Objective 2
Using an Internet Hyperlink

NOTE

Once you set up an Internet hyperlink, you can activate it when you run the presentation in a slide show. Like any other hyperlink, clicking an Internet hyperlink branches the presentation. PowerPoint uses the default browser software on your computer to display the Web site information. A *browser* is software that allows you to view Web pages.

NOTE
The prefix http:// is not required with some browsers. Additionally, remind students to check Web addresses carefully when they type them, using the exact syntax.

NOTE
Web pages and addresses change. You may want to test the addresses used in this lesson to make sure the instructions are still valid.

Use PowerPoint Classroom Presentation #15 to display screens from the lesson, including this one, in a slide-show format.

NOTE
The following Exercise assumes students can connect to the Internet, using either Microsoft's Internet service or another service provider. Instruct students on how to connect and disconnect from the Internet.

LESSON 15 ■ USING THE INTERNET

EXERCISE 15-3 Use an Internet Hyperlink

1. Display slide 6 in Slide Show view.
2. Click the <u>5-day weather forecast</u> hyperlink. The presentation jumps to the Weather Channel home page on the Web if your Internet connection is already activated. If it is not, you may be asked to sign in. If you receive an error message, ask your instructor how to proceed.
3. Scroll to the bottom of the Web page
4. Click the hyperlink <u>Back to the top</u> to go to the top of the page (or scroll back to the top).

NOTE
5. Scroll to the "Enter a city" text box and key **New York**. Click the "go city" button.
6. View the information for the current weather conditions in New York.

NOTE
7. Close the Close button of your browser window to close the browser and disconnect from the Internet.

NOTE
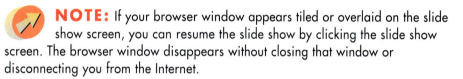

NOTE: If your browser window appears tiled or overlaid on the slide show screen, you can resume the slide show by clicking the slide show screen. The browser window disappears without closing that window or disconnecting you from the Internet.

8. Position the pointer over the hyperlink again. Notice the hyperlink color changed to dark maroon. Once a hyperlink is activated in a session, it changes color. (You can still click it to revisit the location.)
9. Return to Slide view.

Objective 3
Browsing the Web

You don't need a hyperlink to browse the Web. If the Microsoft Internet Explorer is activated on your computer, you can connect to the Web easily using the Web toolbar. PowerPoint also provides direct links to specific Microsoft Web sites. Once connected to the Web, you can use it to browse, research, get online support, or download a file.

EXERCISE 15-4 Browse the Web to Download a File

In this Exercise, you connect to the Web to download a clip art file from a Microsoft Web site.

NOTE
Step 5: You might suggest that students check the weather for other cities or click on other hyperlinks on the Web site.

NOTE
Step 7: You may want students to remain connected to the Internet at this point in the lesson.

NOTE
The browser may appear tiled when it first appears on the screen. Tell students to click the maximize button in the browser window.

433

UNIT 5 ■ ADVANCED FEATURES

1. Click the Web Toolbar button on the Standard toolbar. PowerPoint displays the Web toolbar.
2. Click <u>G</u>o on the Web toolbar and choose <u>O</u>pen. The Open Internet Address dialog box appears. You use this dialog box when you want to go to a specific Web address.

FIGURE 15-3
Open Internet Address dialog box

3. Click Cancel to close the dialog box.
4. Open the <u>H</u>elp menu and choose Microsoft on the <u>W</u>eb. The submenu lists direct links to Microsoft Web support sites as well as some general sites like <u>B</u>est of the Web and Search the <u>W</u>eb.

5. Close the menu without choosing a menu option.
6. Display slide 1 and click to open the Microsoft Clip Gallery. Click the Internet button at the bottom right corner of the dialog box to connect you to the Microsoft Web address http://microsoft.com/clipgallerylive automatically.
7. Click OK if you see the prompt shown in Figure 15-4.

FIGURE 15-4
Connecting to the Web to download clip art

 NOTE: If your Internet connection is not active, you may be asked to sign in. If you receive an error message, ask your instructor how to proceed.

8. When the Microsoft Clip Gallery Live Web page appears, review the end-user information at the left of the screen. If it's okay with your instructor, click Accept.
9. At the left side of the page, open the category drop-down list and choose Sports & Leisure. Click Go to browse the sports clip art files.
10. Scroll the clip art displayed. This page shows just 12 of the 81 pictures available in this category.

NOTE
Step 1: Review with students the buttons on the Web toolbar. These buttons are similar to those used in most browsers.

In PowerPoint Classroom Presentation #15.

NOTE
Step 4: Point out that the Search the Web button appears in a variety of places, such as the Web Toolbar, the Open dialog box, and the Insert File dialog box.

NOTE
This Exercise assumes that Microsoft Internet Explorer is connecting to an Internet service provider. The Web address for the Microsoft Clip Gallery Live Web site is provided if you need to direct students to another browser.

LESSON 15 ■ **USING THE INTERNET**

NOTE

11. Scroll down to the bottom of the screen and click the Next arrow to display the next screen of clip art, pictures 13 through 24. Locate the file PEOP002015_x5.WMF (shown in Figure 15-5).

FIGURE 15-5
Clip art to download

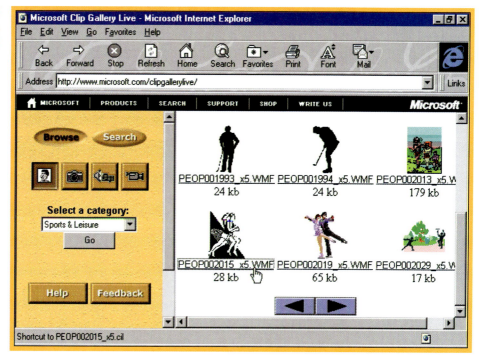

NOTE

12. When you're asked what you want to do with the file, choose Open it. Click OK. The file is automatically downloaded into the Microsoft Clip Gallery on your computer in the Sports & Leisure category. You can also find it in the Downloaded Clip category.

13. Insert the new clip art file into slide 1 and close your Internet connection.

14. Resize the clip art and position it in between the title and subtitle placeholders, moving the placeholders so the clip art fits attractively between them. Copy the image to the slide master, resized and positioned in the lower left corner of the slide.

15. Apply the Box In transition effect between all slides, with Fly From Left text builds.

16. Save the presentation as *[your initials]***15-4.ppt**.

17. Add the date and your name to the handout header and the filename to the handout footer.

18. Print as handouts, 6 slides per page, black and white, framed.

19. Save and close the presentation. Click 🌐 to hide the Web toolbar.

NOTE
Encourage students to browse through the clip art files. You may want to have them download a different file that appears in on a later page in the clip art collection. You may also want to point out the Search feature and the icons for pictures, audio, and video clips. If the computers in your classroom are equipped with sound cards and speakers, you can direct students to browse the audio and video files.

In PowerPoint Classroom Presentation #15.

NOTE
Netscape Navigator does not automatically load clip art to the Microsoft Clip Gallery.

435

UNIT 5 ■ ADVANCED FEATURES

Creating a Presentation to Publish on the Internet
Objective 4

Documents on the Web are formatted in *Hypertext Markup Language (HTML)*. You can create your own Web page by converting an existing presentation or by creating a new presentation using HTML format. You can then share your Web page with others by publishing it on the Web.

NOTE

There are two ways to create a Web presentation. If you're starting a new presentation, use the AutoContent Wizard, which will get you started with an attractive, Web-oriented template that contains Action buttons typically found on a Web page. If you have an existing presentation you'd like to convert to a Web page, use the Save As HTML command on the File menu.

EXERCISE 15-5 Create a Web Presentation with the AutoContent Wizard

NOTE

1. Choose New on the File menu, click the Presentations tab, and double-click the AutoContent Wizard icon. Choose Sales/Marketing for the presentation type and select the Marketing Plan option.

2. For Output options, choose Internet, kiosk. This option adds Action buttons to the presentation.

NOTE

3. On the Presentation options screen, select Copyright notice on each page, if necessary, and key **Copyright** *[your name]*. This text appears on each screen of your Web presentation. Note that information on the Web is available to everyone on the Internet. If your presentation contains information that you don't want to have used or copied elsewhere, either with or without your permission, you must include a copyright notice.

4. Select Date last updated, if necessary, and include your e-mail address if you have one. Web sites often include this information to show the timeliness of the information and how to contact the Web site author.

5. Click Finish. The presentation appears in Outline view so you can insert your own content. View the presentation in Slide Show view. Web site Action buttons advance the presentation from slide to slide and return the presentation to the beginning. Examine the last slide, which allows you to apply action settings to icons.

6. End the slide show. To publish a presentation on a Web site, you save it in HTML format which you'll do for a similar presentation in the next exercise.

7. Close the presentation without saving.

NOTE
Point out that Web presentations can include the full range of animation and sound effects, however, the person accessing the site must have the PowerPoint Animation Player, which is a free Internet browser extension that shows presentations with the fullest fidelity and animation effects available.

NOTE
Although most students are well past the need for the AutoContent Wizard by now, point out that one of the advantages of using it initially is that it demonstrates how a Web presentation might be structured.

NOTE
Remind students that information placed on the Web is available to everyone on the Internet. Adding a copyright notice to a Web page does not necessarily prevent unauthorized dissemination of material on the page.

LESSON 15 ■ USING THE INTERNET

EXERCISE 15-6 **Convert an Existing Presentation to HTML Format**

PowerPoint provides a wizard to help you prepare an existing presentation for publication on the Web. It helps you choose a graphic format, create navigation buttons and an index page, and more.

1. Open the file **Juice.ppt**. This file is a completed version of the one you created but did not save in the previous exercise.

2. Review the slide content and save the file as a regular presentation file with the name *[your initials]***15-6.ppt**.

3. Choose Save as HTML from the File menu. Close the Office Assistant if it appears. The first screen of the wizard appears.

4. Click Next and choose New layout, if necessary. The settings you choose for a presentation that is converted to HTML format can be saved and applied to other presentations.

5. Click Next and choose Standard as the page style layout, if necessary. Standard page layouts look good in all browsers that display graphics. Browser frame page layouts require browsers that support HTML frames, such as Microsoft Internet Explorer or Netscape Navigator.

FIGURE 15-6
Page style layout options in the Save as HTML Wizard

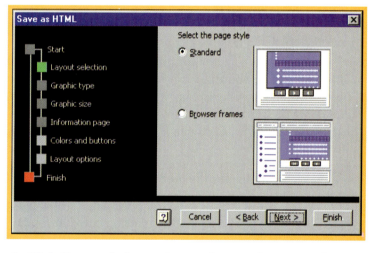

NOTE

6. Click Next and choose GIF as the Graphic Type, if necessary. All graphic elements in a presentation, such as the clip art and the template design elements, are converted to graphic image files in the HTML format. GIF files produce good, all-round images.

TIP: Keep in mind that a Web screen with many image files takes longer to load. Your Web audience will become impatient if the time it takes to draw a screen seems excessive. Choose the number and complexity of graphic images for your Web pages carefully.

In PowerPoint Classroom Presentation #15.

NOTE
JPEG files allow more control over the image resolution, but the file sizes increase as the resolution is increased so it takes longer to draw the screen.

437

UNIT 5 ■ ADVANCED FEATURES

NOTE

7. Click Next and choose a monitor resolution of 640 by 480, if necessary. Change the width of graphics to full width.

8. Click Next and enter your email address, if you have one, or a company Web site address in the home page text box. This information is placed on the information page that is first displayed when your presentation is accessed on the Web.

9. Click Next and choose Use browser colors, if necessary.

10. Click Next and choose the smaller, rectangular button style.

11. Click Next and choose the option that places the navigation buttons on the right side of the slide.

12. Click Next and key the location where you save your files. (Include the drive, such as A:\, or the drive and folder, such as A:\lesson files.)

13. Click Next, and then click Finish. At the prompt to save the settings for use with another HTML presentation, click Don't Save.

14. Click OK when the message has been successfully saved. The presentation was converted to HTML format and PowerPoint created a file folder with the name *[your initials]*15-6 that contains all the files necessary for the presentation to be published on the Web.

EXERCISE 15-7 View a Presentation in HTML Format

It's a good idea to view a presentation you converted to HTML format in a browser before you upload it to the Web. Presentations can appear quite different when viewed via a browser. A presentation converted to HTML format can only be viewed via a browser. To view the presentation, use the Go button on the Web toolbar and open the Index.htm file, which is the first page in your Web presentation.

1. Click [icon] to display the Web toolbar, if necessary.

2. Click the Go button on the Web toolbar and click Open.

NOTE

3. Click Browse and locate the folder created in the last exercise. Click Open.

4. Choose All Files (*.*) from the Files of type drop-down list to see all the files contained in the folder. Notice also the file Index.htm. This is the first page of the Web presentation and every Web site must have a file of this name as its first screen.

> **TIP:** PowerPoint automatically creates the Index file for you when it converts your presentation to HTML format, but you may want to "dress up" the appearance of the Index screen as it appears in the browser. To do this, you can open the Index file in Word, format it attractively, and then save it with the same filename (Index.htm) with the other HTML files in the presentation.

NOTE
Step 7: Have students choose a resolution that suits their monitors. Many Office 97 users are using 800 x 600 resolution.

NOTE
Step 3: Remind students that they are looking for a file folder, not just a filename. A typical Web presentation has many files in the HTML file folder.

LESSON 15 ■ USING THE INTERNET

FIGURE 15-7
HTML files created for a Web presentation

Index file

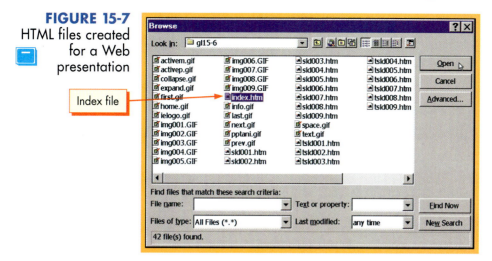

5. Select the file **index.htm** and click Open. Click OK. The browser loads the index file and displays it as it will appear when it is accessed on the Web. Scroll down the screen and notice that the title of each slide in the presentation appears as hyperlinked text.

FIGURE 15-8
Index page as it appears in the browser

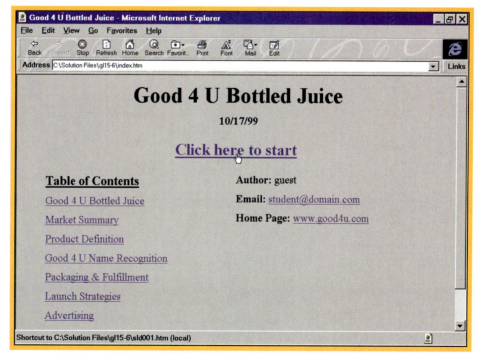

6. Click Click here to start to display the first slide in the presentation. Slide 1 appears. Notice that you can use navigation buttons on the right side of the screen to move through the presentation.

In PowerPoint Classroom Presentation #15.

NOTE
Students may be surprised at the look of their presentations when viewed in the browser, especially the index, or "information" page. Point out that they may use other software, such as Microsoft Word, to change the appearance of the index file (as described in the Tip on the previous page).

439

UNIT 5 ■ ADVANCED FEATURES

FIGURE 15-9
Slide 1 of Web presentation

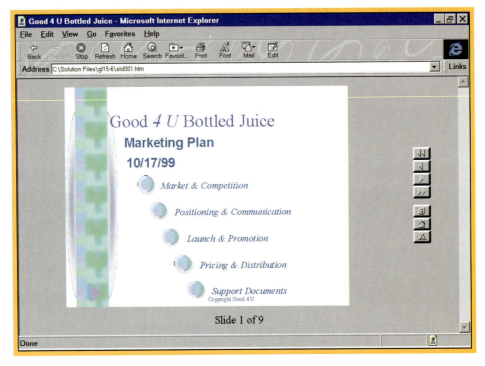

7. View the Web presentation. If you want to print one or more pages, you can choose Print from the File menu of your browser's menu bar.

 NOTE: If you need to modify the Web presentation, you will need to make the change in the original PowerPoint presentation and use the Save as HTML command again.

8. Close the browser and close the presentation without saving.

Publishing Your Presentation on the Web

Once you create a Web presentation and convert it to HTML format, you're ready to publish it on the Word Wide Web. To place a presentation on the Web, you upload it to an Internet site. This means you copy the presentation files (for example, the contents to the *[your initials]*15-6 file folder) to the server of an Internet service provider.

You first need to contact your local Internet service provider to find out the specific requirements. Your Web page will be assigned a unique address and the service provider may charge a fee for the space you use on its server. Ask your instructor for additional details.

In PowerPoint Classroom Presentation #15.

440

LESSON 15 ■ USING THE INTERNET

COMMAND SUMMARY

FEATURE	BUTTON	MENU	KEYBOARD
Insert Hyperlink	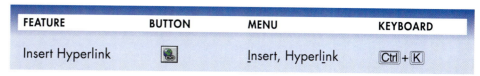	Insert, Hyperlink	Ctrl + K

USING HELP

NOTE PowerPoint provides an abundance of Help topics related to using the Web, publishing on the Web, and Microsoft Web support.

Use Help to learn more about creating Web pages:

1. Display Help Contents (Help, Contents and Index, Contents tab).
2. Double-click "Working with Online and Internet Documents."
3. Double-click the topic "Working with documents on intranets and the Internet." Review the comprehensive list of topics.
4. Display the topic "About creating a Web page." Explore the topics displayed on the Help screen.

FIGURE 15-10
Help screen about creating a Web page

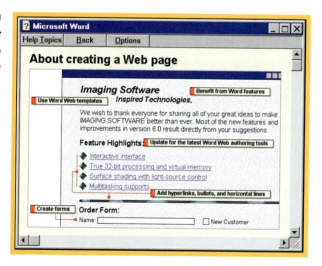

5. Click Help Topics and explore other topics that interest you.
6. Close Help when you finish.

 NOTE: You can run a Web tutorial from Internet Explorer by opening the Help menu, choosing Microsoft on the Web, and then clicking Web Tutorial.

NOTE
Encourage students to follow the steps in Using Help. Extensive help about the Internet and the Web is provided by PowerPoint's Help system and by Microsoft's online Help system.

In PowerPoint Classroom Presentation #15.

441

UNIT 5 ■ ADVANCED FEATURES

Unit 5 Applications

APPLICATION 5-1

Add a table, a chart, and a flowchart to a presentation and apply transition effects.

1. Open the file **HdCount.ppt**. Apply the **Notebook.pot** design template.
2. Insert a new slide after slide 3 using the Table layout with the title **Current Breakdown**. Create a table using the data shown in Figure U5-1.

FIGURE U5-1

	F/T Kitchen	P/T Kitchen	F/T Service	P/T Service
Weekdays	15	13	23	13
Weekends	10	15	11	22

3. Change the table text font to 26 point and adjust the column widths so they're just wide enough to fit the text. Make sure columns 2 through 5 are distributed evenly.
4. Apply the shading Gray-50% to the cells containing the labels "Weekdays" and "Weekends." Shade the cells that contain values Gray-25%. Shade the cells in row 1 blue. Add 1 point gridlines and borders.
5. Center all data horizontally and vertically.
6. Return to Slide view. Re-color the table using colors from the template's color scheme. Position or resize the table as needed.
7. Insert a new slide after slide 4 using the Chart layout with the title **Past, Current, Projected**. Create a column chart using the data shown in Figure U5-2.

FIGURE U5-2

	1996	1997	1998	1999
Full-time	41	40	48	38
Part-time	30	35	46	61

Assessment Resources:
- Solutions Manual
- Test Bank with Software
- Portfolio Builder
- Alternative Assessment Guide
- Certification Procedures
- Projects Manual
- Mid-Term and Final Exams

Unit Applications:
Provide independent practice of the skills acquired from each lesson in the Unit.

Project:
After students complete Unit 5, you can assign Project #5 from the Projects Manual.

Final Exam:
If your class is on a semester schedule, you can now assign Final Exam 2 from the Mid-Term and Final Exams booklet.

Unit Application 5-1:
Required File: HdCount.ppt
Solution File: glu5-1.ppt in Solutions Manual or on Solutions disk

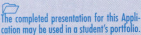
The completed presentation for this Application may be used in a student's portfolio.

UNIT 5 ■ APPLICATIONS

8. Change the data series to two different colored patterns, using the colors from the template's color scheme. Move the legend to the bottom, make it slightly wider, center it, and delete its border. Make other adjustments to the chart if you want to.

9. In Slide view, draw a text box or AutoShape at the top of the chart with the text **Projecting 61 P/T, 38 F/T**. Draw an arrow from the text box (or shape) to the top of the 1999 columns. Format the text object and the arrow as you like.

10. Insert a new slide after slide 5 using the Title Only layout with the title **Plan for Increasing P/T Headcount**. Reduce the title font to fit the text on one line.

11. On new slide 6, create a flowchart showing the following 5 steps, placing the text for each step in a different shape (exclude the word "Step" and the number). Arrange the shapes in clockwise order and draw arrows from the first shape to the second, from the second to the third, and so on.

    Step 1: **Advertise P/T positions**

    Step 2: **T. Scott to schedule interviews**

    Step 3: **M. Peters to interview and hire applicants**

    Step 4: **J. Farla to train**

    Step 5: **L. Klein to assign schedules**

12. Format the shapes, text, and arrows as you like.

13. Apply the slide transition effect Random Bars Vertical to all slides.

14. View the slide show and check the black and white settings.

15. Save the presentation as *[your initials]***u5-1.ppt**.

16. Add the date and your name to the handout header and the filename to the handout footer.

NOTE

17. Print as handouts, 6 slides per page, black and white, framed.

18. Save and close the presentation.

APPLICATION 5-2

Create transition effects, object animations, and hyperlinks to other slides in a presentation.

1. Open the file **News.ppt**. Apply the Contemporary Portrait design template. Change the color scheme to the one with the black background.

2. On the title master, delete the graphic element. Draw a lightening bolt AutoShape (Basic Shapes) under the title, sized at 1.75 inches high and 8.25 inches wide. Apply the preset Fire fill, shading from the center

NOTE
For all completed Applications, you might ask students to note their slide show effects on their presentation printouts.

Unit Application 5-2:
Required File: News.ppt
Solution File: glu5-2.ppt in Solutions Manual or on Solutions disk

The completed presentation for this Application may be used in a student's portfolio.

443

with the darkest color in the center. Remove the outline. Position the shape between the title and subtitle placeholders.

3. Apply the following animation effects to the lightening bolt: Fly From Top, laser sound, start automatically.

4. On the slide master, delete the graphic element. Resize the bulleted text placeholder to 3.75 inches high, keeping its position in relation to the title placeholder. Copy the lightening bolt from the title master to the slide master. Resize it to 75% of its original size and place it at the bottom right of the slide. Rotate it to increase its angle and make it point directly into the bottom right corner.

5. In Slide Sorter view, create a summary slide for slides 2 through 4. Change the title of the new summary slide (now slide 2) to **What's Happening**

6. On slide 2, indent the bulleted text to 1 inch from the bullet and increase the paragraph spacing to 1.5 lines. Draw action buttons over the bullets, using the Forward or Next button ▷. Each button should be a hyperlink to the slide that matches the bulleted text title.

7. Format the action buttons using the same fill as the lightening bolt. Size the buttons as desired, aligned and spaced appropriately.

8. On slide 5 ("Franchisee Annual Meeting"), omit the background graphic from the master. (Hint: Use the Background dialog box.) Draw a large sun AutoShape using the same fill applied to the action buttons. Redistribute the bulleted text as shown in Figure U5-3, creating AutoShapes or text boxes. Use curved arrow connectors to connect the sun to the text objects. Experiment with placement and line and color styles until you have the design you want.

FIGURE U5-3
Slide 5

UNIT 5 ■ APPLICATIONS

9. Apply these animation effects to the sun: Zoom In, whoosh sound, start automatically. The sun should appear first, followed by the text objects and lines using the dissolve effect. (You may want to group the connectors and lines into one object so they dissolve together with one mouse click.)
10. View the slide show, making necessary adjustments.
11. Check the black and white settings and save the presentation as [your initials]**u5-2.ppt**.
12. Add the date and your name to the handout header and the filename to the handout footer.
13. Print as handouts, 6 slides per page, black and white, framed.
14. Save and close the presentation.

APPLICATION 5-3

Create an Internet hyperlink in a presentation, browse the Web and download a file, apply transition effects and object animations, and convert the presentation to HTML format.

1. Start a new presentation. On the title slide, key the title **Good 4 U** using the standard logo format. For the subtitle, key **Company News**.
2. Insert four bulleted text slides using the text in Figure U5-4.

FIGURE U5-4

Slide 2

What's Happening

- San Francisco opening in June
- New York renovations in progress
- Franchisee annual meeting

Slide 3

San Francisco Opening

- Interiors nearing completion
- Furniture and décor being installed
- Grand opening press releases in progress

continues

Unit Application 5-3:
Required File: None
Solution File: glu5-3.ppt in Solutions Manual or on Solutions disk

The completed presentation for this Application may be used in a student's portfolio.

445

UNIT 5 ■ ADVANCED FEATURES

continued

Slide 4

New York Renovations

- Main dining room completed
- Landscaping and redesign of rear outdoor patio ready for Memorial Day

Slide 5

Franchisee Annual Meeting

- Miami Country Club, April 3-4
- Morning meetings, afternoon recreation
- Golf, tennis, volleyball
- If rain: Banquet Room at Good *4 U*
- Current forecast:

3. Turn off the bullet for the line that begins "If rain" and center the line.

4. Apply the Ocean preset fill effect to the background, using the From title shading style with the variant that is blue on the outside.

5. Change the font of all text to Arial bold red. Add a shadow to all slide titles. Draw a dotted 4½ pt black arrow below the title on both the slide and title masters.

6. Change the bullets to dark blue stars sized at 125%. Increase the indent between the bullet and the text.

7. Use the Search the Web button to connect to the Web site **http//:www.microsoft.com/clipgallerylive/**. Under the category Food & Dining, locate the file FOOD001784_x5.WMF and download it to the Microsoft Clip Gallery in PowerPoint. Insert the downloaded clip art in slide 1. Ungroup it and place the coffee cup between the title and subtitle on slide 1. Use the same image or one of the other images on the remaining slides (do not use the bottle). If you use the same image on all slides, alter the color, placement, size, and so on.

8. On slide 5, convert the text "Current forecast" in the last bullet to an Internet hyperlink using the URL **http://www.weather.com**. Run the slide show for the slide and test the connection. Add the current Miami

NOTE
For step 7, you may want to specify another clip art image to download. If students can't download, you may want to direct them to an existing image in the Microsoft Clip Gallery.

UNIT 5 ■ APPLICATIONS

forecast for five days from now at the end of the bullet (for example: Hot, sunny, high 92). Change the color of the hyperlink text to yellow.

9. Apply transition effects and object animations to the presentation. View the slide show and adjust the effects, if needed.

10. Save the presentation as *[your initials]***u5-3.ppt**.

11. Add the date and your name to the handout header and the filename to the handout footer.

12. Print as handouts, 6 slides per page, black and white, framed

13. Convert the presentation to HTML format for a Web presentation. Use the standard page layout, a GIF graphic type, and 640 by 480 screen resolution. To the information page, add your e-mail address or the address **student@domain.com**. Use the browser colors and a large square button style with the buttons placed on the right side of the slides.

14. View the presentation in the browser. Print the information page and slide 1.

15. Close the browser and close the presentation.

APPLICATION 5-4

Write a presentation with at least five slides, including a table slide and an org chart slide, and apply slide show effects.

1. In a new presentation, create an organization chart containing at least three levels and six boxes. Use the chart to show a business, school, family, or anything that has a structure. Format the org chart attractively.

2. Create a presentation around this slide, including a title slide, at least two bulleted text slides (one of which uses a clip art and text layout), and a slide containing an attractively formatted table. Organize the slides in appropriate order.

3. Apply a template of your choice and customize it by changing colors, fonts, spacing, alignment, and other features.

4. Include at least one AutoShape or floating text box in the presentation. Add another drawing object, such as a freeform shape, if desired.

5. Make sure the color scheme of all slide objects matches the template colors.

6. Add slide show effects, including slide transitions, text builds, and object builds. Apply slide timings, then run the slide show with your timings.

Unit Application 5-4:
Required File: None
Solution File: sample glu5-4.ppt in Solutions Manual or on Solutions disk

The completed presentation for this Application may be used in a student's portfolio.

NOTE
In this Application, students are asked to write a presentation. Consequently, students' solution files will vary. A sample file appears in the Solutions Manual and on the Solutions disk.

7. Save the presentation as *[your initials]***u5-4.ppt**.
8. Add the date and your name to the handout header and the filename to the handout footer.
9. Print as handouts, 6 slides per page, black and white, framed.
10. Save and close the presentation.

Portfolio Builder

List of Files Produced in the Portfolio Builder

Filename	Document
*[Your initials]*Res1.doc	Resumé created using a Word Resumé Template
*[Your initials]*Res2.doc	Resumé created using the Word Resumé Wizard
*[Your initials]*Prospects.doc	List of prospective employers
*[Your initials]*DocList.doc	List of presentations to include in your Portfolio
*[Your initials]*CvrLtr.doc	Cover letter
*[Your initials]*AppInfo.doc	Information for use in filling out Employment Applications
10-15 additional presentations	The presentations listed in your Presentation List.

Optional Documents

Thank you letter

Contact Reference Sheet

Contact Reference Card

Portfolio Builder

OBJECTIVES By using this Portfolio Builder, you will learn how to:
1. Build a resumé.
2. Identify prospective employers.
3. Build a portfolio.
4. Target your resumé and portfolio.
5. Write a cover letter.
6. Fill out an employment application.
7. Prepare for a job interview.
8. Follow up an interview.

Finding a job is difficult—especially today in the midst of downsizing. The number of applicants often exceeds the availability of jobs. So you need to distinguish yourself from other people interested in the same job. You need to show a prospective employer what you can do.

This *Portfolio Builder* helps you build a resumé that will tell prospective employers about your work background. It also assists you in building a "representational portfolio"—a collection of your best work that you can show as evidence of your skills. The documents in your portfolio will be geared to specific employers. Finally, the *Portfolio Builder* leads you though the job-search process: including contacting prospective employers, filling out an employment application, and following up after interviews.

PORTFOLIO BUILDER

FIGURE P-1
The job-search process

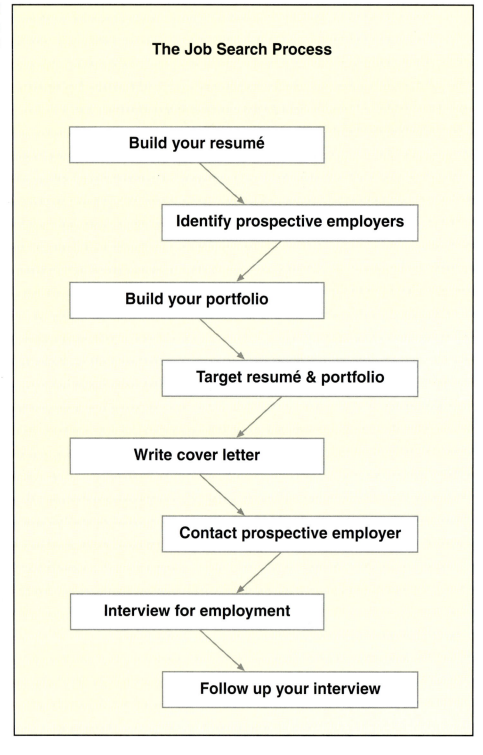

PORTFOLIO BUILDER

The *Portfolio Builder* will be helpful to you if you're planning to search for immediate employment. It is also a useful final project because it requires you to demonstrate skills you have gained from this course. Even if you're not looking for a job, it will help prepare you for an eventual job search.

Building a Resumé

A resumé is a representation of you on paper. It provides a first impression of you to a potential employer.

Building a resumé is an exercise in self-discovery. To create one, you must review your experience, identify your skills, and focus on a goal. Once you have created a resumé that states your strengths and objectives, you can begin the process of marketing yourself to prospective employers.

Although a good resumé will not guarantee a job, it is a primary tool in the job-search process.

There are three types of resumés:

- The *chronological* resumé is the traditional type of resumé. It lists your work history, starting with your most recent job. It includes a brief description of the position and your accomplishments. This is a "where you've been" type of resumé.

- The *functional* resumé highlights your skills or areas of expertise. It is a "what you can do" type of resumé.

- The *combination* resumé highlights your skill areas *and* lists the jobs you have held.

The following six pages illustrate these three kinds of resumés.

P-5

Chronological Résumé Description

Contact Information: Your name, address, and telephone number should appear at the top of the resumé. Spell out your address (do not abbreviate "Street" or "Avenue"). Include your ZIP code. Use a telephone number where you can be reached during the day or where a message can be left. Include other forms of contact, such as an e-mail address or fax number, if available. Don't use your current employer's telephone or fax number.

Job Objective: Your job objective represents the specific field or job title that you are pursuing. If you're targeting a specific job, tailor your objective to that position. Include the job type, the industry, and the geographical area in your objective (example: "Marketing position with a computer software vendor in the Chicago area"). To keep your options open, write a broader objective.

Work Experience: Describe the jobs that you have held, beginning with your most recent position. List the years of employment, company names and locations, and specific job titles. Include current and past jobs, part-time work, self-employment, volunteer work, and internships, as appropriate. The job description should focus on quantified achievements and specific skills.

Education: List the schools and training programs that you have attended. List your most recent education—school, degree or program, and date completed. Omit information about your high school if you have a college degree. Include any additional information, such as continuing education, seminars, or special course work that is related to your objective. This section can appear before **Work Experience** if you're a recent graduate, or if your education or training is your most important qualifying factor.

Additional Information: Your resumé can contain additional information that may be relevant to the job you are pursuing. For example, a section on computer proficiency can be included. You can also include **Activities**, **Professional Organizations**, or **Honors/Awards** as separate sections.

References: References are often not included on a resumé, but are provided separately if requested. Line up your references in advance, and list them on a sheet of paper. Include the name, address, telephone number, and title (if appropriate). You can ask a previous employer for a letter of recommendation, which you can then photocopy.

FIGURE P-2 Chronological resumé*

12 Juniper Drive
Any Town, State 00000
(000) 000-0000
E-mail: dmartin@xxx.xxx

Donald Martin

Objective

Seeking position as microcomputer salesperson in dynamic retail environment.

Work Experience

1996–1998   Electronics Depot   Any Town, State
Sales Associate
- Specialized in sales of computer hardware and software in busy retail outlet.
- Selected Salesperson of the Year for Midwest region.
- Established customer training program for computer sales that produced $80,000 in its first year.

1994–1996   Video Time   Any Town, State
Assistant Manager
- Managed video-rental store during most heavily-trafficked hours (evenings and weekends). Effectively handled as many as 250 customer contacts per day.
- Trained and supervised five sales assistants.
- Started "Old Time Cinema Club" that boosted sales of backlist videos by 50%.

1993–1994   Fairway Department Store   Any Town, State
Sales Assistant
- Assisted customers in busy Electronics Department.
- Handled more than $2,000 per day in cash sales.
- Completed sales training program.

Education

1997   Fargo Technical College   Any Town, State
- A.A., Microcomputer Systems Technology
- G.P.A. 3.93

Software/Hardware Training

- Proficiency in all Microsoft Office applications and PageMaker on both the PC and Macintosh computer.
- Can perform diagnostics on PCs and peripheral equipment, and can install/upgrade PC components such as network cards, memory chips, disk drives, and modems.

References

Available upon request.

*Created using a modified version of Word's Contemporary resumé style.

PORTFOLIO BUILDER

Functional Resumé Description

Contact Information: Your name, address, and telephone number should appear at the top of the resumé. Spell out your address (do not abbreviate "Street" or "Avenue"). Include your ZIP code. Use a telephone number where you can be reached during the day or where a message can be left. Include other forms of contact, such as an e-mail address or fax number, if available. Don't use your current employer's telephone or fax number.

Job Objective: Your job objective represents the specific field or job title that you are pursuing. If you're targeting a specific job, tailor your objective to that position. Include the job type, industry, and geographical area in your objective (example: "Marketing position with a computer software vendor in the Chicago area"). To keep your options open, write a broader objective.

Functional Sections: In a functional resumé, these sections provide the bulk of the information about you. Include two to four sections that describe a particular area of expertise or involvement. These areas should be directly related to the position you are pursuing. (In this resumé, the functional sections appear with the headings **Casework**, **Document Drafting**, and **Computer Skills**.) As an alternative to creating job-specific sections, create functional sections with the headings **Qualifications** and **Accomplishments**. Under these headings, list concise action statements that will catch the attention of a prospective employer.

Work Experience: A functional resumé lists your job history by date, company name and location, and title, beginning with the most recent position. Job descriptions are not included, as the resumé focuses on qualifications and skills, not work history.

Education: List the schools and training programs that you have attended. List your most recent education—school, degree or program, and date completed. Omit information about your high school if you have a college degree. Include any additional information, such as continuing education, seminars, or special course work that is related to your objective. This section can appear immediately below your **Objective** if you're a recent graduate, or if your education or training is your most important qualifying factor.

Additional Information: Your resumé can contain additional information that may be relevant to the job you are pursuing. For example, you can include sections with the following headings: **Activities**, **Professional Organizations**, **Honors/Awards**. The heading **References** may be listed at the bottom, followed by the text "Available on request" (see Chronological Resumé for more information).

FIGURE P-3 Functional resumé*

8809 Orange Terrace
Any Town, State 00000
Telephone (000) 000-0000
Fax (000) 000-0000

Lesley Brown

Objective	Paralegal position in computer or patent law
Casework	- Researched state and federal computer and patent laws. Wrote briefs for attorneys. - Prepared preliminary arguments and pleadings in computer law. - Obtained affidavits.
Document Drafting	- Drafted contracts under the supervision of an attorney. - Prepared tax returns, incorporations, patent filings, and trust agreements. - Prepared reports and schematic diagrams. - Assisted computer law specialists in preparing hardware and software patents, contracts, applications, shareholder agreements, and packaging agreements.
Computer Skills	- Word-processing software (Word for Windows and WordPerfect). - Advanced use of database software (Access) and spreadsheet software (Excel). - Researched on-line databases using Internet search engines.
Employment	1995–Present Collimore & Hapke, Attorneys-at-Law Any Town, State **Legal Assistant**
Education	1998 York State Technical College Any Town, State **Associate Degree, Paralegal Technology**
Activities	Legal Eagles Public Library Volunteer coordinator of weekly youth discussion group that teaches basic law principles.

*Created using a modified version of Word's Professional resumé style.

PORTFOLIO BUILDER

Combination Resumé Description

Contact Information: Your name, address, and telephone number should appear at the top of the resumé. Spell out your address (do not abbreviate "Street" or "Avenue"). Include your ZIP code. Use a telephone number where you can be reached during the day or where a message can be left. Include other forms of contact, such as an e-mail address or fax number, if available. Don't use your current employer's telephone or fax number.

Job Objective: Your job objective represents the specific field or job title that you are pursuing. If you're targeting a specific job, tailor your objective to that position. Include the job type, the industry, and the geographical area in your objective (example: "Marketing position with a computer software vendor in the Chicago area"). To keep your options open, write a broader objective.

Functional Sections: Include two or three sections that describe a particular area of expertise or involvement, or that summarize your qualifications and accomplishments. Use concise statements that are easy to read.

Work Experience: As in the chronological resumé, list and describe the jobs that you have held, beginning with your most recent position. Include the years of employment, the company names and locations, and the specific job titles. You can include current and past jobs, part-time work, self-employment, volunteer work, internships, and so on, as appropriate. The job description should focus on quantified achievements and specific skills. Be careful not to repeat the same information here that you have listed in the Functional Sections.

Education: List the schools and training programs that you have attended. List your most recent education—school, degree or program, and date completed. Omit information about your high school if you have a college degree. Include any additional information that might be relevant, such as continuing education, seminars, or special course work. This section can appear above **Work Experience** if you're a recent graduate, or if your education or training is your most important qualifying factor.

Additional Information: Your resumé can contain additional information that may be relevant to the job you are pursuing. For example, you can include sections with the following headings: **Activities**, **Professional Organizations**, **Honors/Awards**. The heading **References** may be listed at the bottom, followed by the text "Available on request" (see Chronological Resumé for more information).

FIGURE P-4 *Combination resumé**

ANNA LUPONE
1002 LOOKOUT POINT
ANY TOWN, STATE 00000
TELEPHONE (000) 000-0000
E-MAIL 00000@AOL.COM

OBJECTIVE

Corporate Word Processing Administrative Assistant

SUMMARY OF QUALIFICATIONS

- ◊ Four years experience in administrative/clerical support positions.
- ◊ Easily establish rapport with managers, staff, and customers.
- ◊ Proficient at analyzing statistics and market trends to develop accurate forecasts and effective sales presentations.
- ◊ Excellent problem-solving, project management, decision-making, and time management skills.
- ◊ Proven ability to prioritize and complete multiple tasks, independently and with little supervision.
- ◊ Bilingual: English/Spanish.

COMPUTER SKILLS

Operating Systems:	DOS and Microsoft Windows 95
Word Processing:	Word for Windows, WordPerfect
Graphics:	PageMaker, PowerPoint
Database and Spreadsheets:	Access, Excel, Lotus 1-2-3
Keyboard Speed:	85 wpm

PROFESSIONAL EXPERIENCE

1994–Present   COCA COLA COMPANY   Atlanta, Georgia
Administrative Assistant
- ◊ Analyze sales volume and profit.
- ◊ Finalize and package forecasting reports for annual sales of $100 million.
- ◊ Monitor monthly spending and reconciliation for $8 million budget.
- ◊ Manage $200,000 in advertising and promotional materials.

EDUCATION

1998   Blake Business Institute   Any Town, State
A.S., Administrative Office Technology
- ◊ Dean's List, 4.0 GPA

REFERENCES

Available on request.

*Created using a modified version of Word's Elegant resumé style.

Choosing a Resumé Format

What type of resumé is right for you? Consider the following:

TABLE P-1 Choosing a Resumé Type

RESUMÉ TYPE	PREFERABLE IF:
Chronological	You have a history of steady work that reflects growth, and you are looking for a job in the same field or a related field.
Functional	You are new to the workforce, have gaps in your work history, or are changing careers.
Combination	You have some work history that is worth showcasing *and* want to highlight your marketable skills.

Be aware that the chronological resumé is the most traditional and conservative type of resumé. It is also the easiest to prepare. The functional and combination resumés, which use more innovative approaches, require greater thought, planning, and creativity.

Tips on Resumé Writing

When preparing your resumé, give yourself plenty of time, and keep in mind the following basics:

Content

- Everything in your resumé should support your job objective. Omit anything that doesn't.
- Be clear about what your skills are, both in your own mind and on paper. Your resumé should answer the question, "Why should I hire you?"
- Your resumé should convey the impression that you're focused. It should be targeted to a specific occupation or career field.
- Don't shortchange yourself. Emphasize any accomplishments, awards, and recognition you've received that supports your job objective.
- Mention promotions, raises, and bonuses, if appropriate, to prove your track record.
- Don't misrepresent yourself. Lying or exaggerating can only hurt—not help—you.

PORTFOLIO BUILDER

- Stress the positive—never include negative information about yourself. Your resumé should reflect what you *can* do, not what you can't.

Writing Style

- Strive for crisp, concise writing. Use short, easy-to-understand sentences.
- Use action words and phrases in your job and skill descriptions. For example, begin each description with words such as "Analyzed," "Administered," "Developed," "Initiated," "Organized," and so on.
- Use buzzwords and terminology that relate to the job you are pursuing.
- Proofread your resumé thoroughly for typographical, grammatical, or punctuation errors.

Appearance

- Your resumé should look professional. It should have an attractive layout, an easy-to-read format, and enough "white space" so that it is not too text-heavy.
- Use a good-quality printer to print your resumé. Avoid sending out photocopies, if possible.
- Limit your resumé to one page, unless you have substantial work experience that is relevant to your current job objective.

Getting Help

- Attend resumé and career workshops offered at your school or in your community.
- Read books about resumé writing to learn how to identify your skills, document your experience, and deal with special problems. Review resumé samples in such books.
- Ask someone whose judgment you trust to read your resumé before you send it out.

Resumé Templates and the Resumé Wizard

Word provides three resumé templates and a Resumé Wizard to help you create a resumé.

 NOTE: This Portfolio Builder assumes that you're using Word as your word-processing application. If you aren't, check your word processor for help on preparing resumés.

P-13

PORTFOLIO BUILDER

Before using a resumé template or the Resumé Wizard, check the New dialog box to see if they are available. (The templates may have to be installed separately. Refer to "Installation Requirements" on page xiii for instructions on adding components.)

NOTE: Use the Resumé Wizard or resumé templates as a basis upon which to build your resumé. Modify the layout and formatting of the resumé to make it unique. Remember, you don't want your resumé to look exactly like everyone else's.

EXERCISE P-1 Use a Resumé Template

The resumé templates allow you to create a chronological resumé based on one of three styles: Elegant, Contemporary, and Professional.

1. Choose New from the File menu, choose the Other Documents tab, and then double-click one of the resumé template icons.

NOTE: To preview the template before choosing it, click the resumé template icon, and then view it in the Preview box.

FIGURE P-5
Resumé templates in the New dialog box

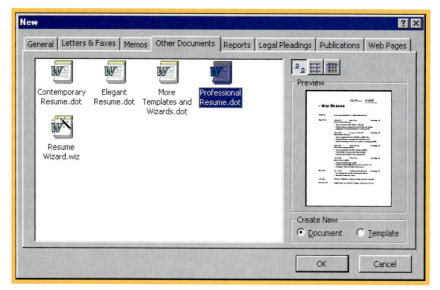

2. Replace all of the placeholder text in the document with your own information.

3. Make any formatting modifications. Save the document as *[your initials]***Res1.doc** and print it.

PORTFOLIO BUILDER

EXERCISE P-2 Use the Resumé Wizard

The Resumé Wizard guides you through the steps needed to create a chronological or functional resumé using one of the three resumé styles.

1. Choose New from the File menu, choose the Other Documents tab, and then double-click the Resumé Wizard icon. Click Next to start.

2. In the next dialog box, choose a resumé style. Click Next to display the next dialog box.

FIGURE P-6
Choosing a resumé style

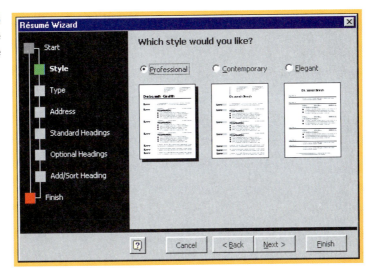

3. Choose the resumé type, and then click Next.
4. Enter your name and mailing address, and then click Next.

FIGURE P-7
Choosing headings for your resumé

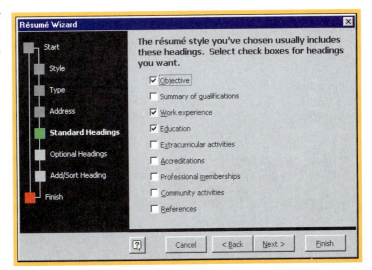

P-15

PORTFOLIO BUILDER

5. Choose the resumé headings you want, and then click Next.
6. Choose any additional headings you desire, and then click Next.
7. Key any additional headings you want to add to the resumé, and then click Next.
8. Reorder any of the resumé headings you've chosen, and then click Next.
9. Click Finish to view the resumé.
10. At the Office Assistant prompt, choose an option or click Cancel.

> **TIP:** You can click the Office Assistant option to create a quick cover letter at this point. The letter will contain sample text for you to replace with your own information. See the section "Writing a Cover Letter" in this Portfolio Builder to learn about cover-letter basics.

11. Replace the placeholder text in the resumé with your own information.
12. Make any modifications. Save the document as *[your initials]***Res2.doc**.

Identifying Prospective Employers

Now that you've prepared a resumé, it's time to think about who will view it. Your next step is to identify the companies in your area—and the people within those companies—who may be hiring people with your skills.

Always try to identify the manager in each company or organization who heads up the division, department, or group in which you hope to work. Avoid applying through a Human Resources staff member, if at all possible. In the Human Resources Department, it's easy to become just another applicant who receives no special attention.

Help Wanted Ads

Help-wanted ads can represent a useful way to research the hiring trends of a local company. Help-wanted ads are, however, less useful as a source of real employment opportunities. They should never be used as the primary focus of your job search. In fact, some experts believe that only 10 percent of all available jobs are listed in the newspaper.

Use the back issues of your local newspapers to find out whether a company has been hiring recently, what kinds of jobs have recently been advertised, and if a particular contact person was listed in the ad.

Networking

Talk to people who are in a position to provide information about job leads and the hiring process at particular companies. They can be friends, relatives, acquaintances—anyone who can put you in touch with a job contact. Try to identify the people within a company who have the power to hire you. Get the correct spelling of each person's name, official correct job title, department, company, and, if possible, a telephone number.

Company Research

An easy way to begin your company research is with the *Yellow Pages*. Use it to locate businesses in the field in which you're interested. (You may need to use the "Business-to-Business" section for some types of businesses.)

The business section of your local library contains reference books that can give you even more information about local companies. Some of the best sources are:

- *Standard & Poor's Register of Corporations, Directors, and Executives.* McGraw-Hill. (Volume 2 lists companies by location.)
- *The National Directory of Addresses and Phone Numbers.* Gale Research, Inc.
- *Million Dollar Directory.* Dun & Bradstreet.
- *Job Seeker's Guide to Private and Public Companies.* Gale Research, Inc.
- *Job Opportunities for Business and Liberal Arts Graduates.* Peterson's Guides, Inc.
- *Job Opportunities for Engineering, Science, and Computer Graduates.* Peterson's Guides, Inc.

Some of these sources are also available in easy-to-use software versions that allow you to search for particular companies based on specific criteria. Your local librarian can often provide help in locating information about specific companies as well.

Using the Internet

Many sources of company and career information are available on the Internet. Many companies operate their own Web site or home page, and some even list their job openings there. If a prospective employer is a large company, search the Internet based on the company's name. Often, promotional materials from the company (and available in a local public library) will indicate its Internet or Web site address.

PORTFOLIO BUILDER

Microsoft Network, America Online, CompuServe, and Prodigy offer many career-oriented services as well. Search for such general keywords as "career," "employment," or "job." A targeted search using more specific keywords may produce results that prove more immediately useful to your job search.

You can also use your Internet browser to search for locations with appropriate keywords. For example, one recent search showed 600,000 matches for the keyword "career." Obviously, the more targeted your search of the Internet, the more useful it may be.

Specialized employment search engines on the Internet may prove useful. Because these services list jobs from across the nation (and around the world), they may be less useful for a local job search. A list of places to look for jobs on the Internet follows (remember that Internet options change rapidly, so this list may need to be updated and new options may be available):

- E-Span Employment Database
  Search by keyword and company name.
  http://www.espan.com

- On-Line Career Center
  Search by keyword.
  http://www.occ.com

- The Monster Board
  Search by location and job discipline.
  http://www.monster.com

- CareerPath
  Searches classified ads in U.S. newspapers by category.
  http://www.careeerpath.com

EXERCISE P-3 Identify Prospective Employers

1. Identify at least five prospective employers. They may be located anywhere, but should represent the type of company for which you could imagine working.

2. For each prospective employer, obtain the name of a job contact. (This person would typically be a manager of the department, division, or group in which you would like to work.)

3. Key the list of prospective employers in a worksheet. Include the contact's name, department, company name, address, city, state, ZIP code, telephone number, and fax number. Save the worksheet as *[your initials]***Prospects.xls** and then print it. You'll use this list throughout this *Portfolio Builder*.

PORTFOLIO BUILDER

Building Your Portfolio

Your resumé *describes* your experience and your skills. Your portfolio *demonstrates* your skills. It represents the best work that you can do. It also should be work with which a prospective employer can identify—that is, presentations that the employer will understand.

The first step in building your portfolio is to decide what types of presentations belong in it. Use the following checklist as a starting point to create a list of possible presentations for your portfolio.

TABLE P-2 **Possible Presentations for Portfolio**

PRESENTATION	COMMENTS
Recommending a strategy	Locate information about a past strategy that was adopted. Include charts and graphics.
Product/Services overview	Use company brochures. Include charts and graphics.
Progress report	Obtain information from annual reports available at public library. Include charts and graphics.
Corporate home page	Create a Web home page for a company. Include hyperlinks.
Business plan	Obtain information from annual reports available at the public library. Include charts and graphics. Perhaps an organization chart or flowchart is required.
Company meeting	Perhaps the agenda of the last shareholders' meeting was published in an annual report or company press release.
Organization overview	Identify a company's management structure (names, titles, departments). Include an organization chart.
Financial overview	Obtain information from annual reports available at the public library. Include charts and graphics.
Marketing plan	Research the local papers, magazines that cover businesses similar to the business you are targeting, and other sources that may be recommended by a reference librarian. Include charts and graphics.

NOTE: All of the above presentation templates are available through the AutoContent Wizard. If any of these templates are not installed on your computer, refer to "Installation Requirements" at the beginning of this textbook for information on how to add a component or locate files on the CD-ROM. You can also go the Microsoft Office Web site (www.microsoft.com) and download templates and wizards.

PORTFOLIO BUILDER

EXERCISE P-4 Develop a List of Presentations for the Portfolio

1. Develop a list of up to 15 presentations for inclusion in your portfolio. Use Table P-2 as a checklist, but also consider presentations that you may have prepared in other courses related to your field of work. If you have work experience, list actual presentations that you created. Use the following headings for your presentation list (see Figure P-8 on the next page):

   Number   **Type of Presentation**   **Description**

2. Save the list as *[your initials]***DocList.doc** and print it.

3. Finalize your presentation list by reviewing it with someone who is familiar with your job search area. Adjust the list as needed. Save and print it.

EXERCISE P-5 Build Your Portfolio

It isn't necessary to begin every presentation from scratch. In fact, it may not even be a good idea. Use material from your other courses, key material from brochures and newsletters that you might receive from a professional association, or recreate sample documents from people in positions similar to the one in which you are interested.

1. Create each of the presentations listed in your presentation list.

2. Adjust every presentation to give it as professional an appearance as possible. Focus on formatting. Demonstrate the skills that you learned in this course.

3. Consult the appropriate style reference for your profession to check that your formatting is acceptable.

4. Spell-check, save, and print your presentations.

5. Ask someone familiar with your future profession to review your presentations (preferably in a slide-show format) and then modify them as necessary.

PORTFOLIO BUILDER

FIGURE P-8 Sample presentation list for student seeking marketing position with a high tecnology company

No.	Type of Presentation	Description
1.	Resumé	Cover some of the details from your resumé.
2.	Progress report	Report on the progress of a marketing campaign for the company's most-recently introduced product.
3.	Business plan	Outline the company's business plan, possibly in relation to a new product or service.
4.	Financial overview	Describe the company's performance over the last three years. Use a column chart.
5.	Organizational overview	Describe the organizational structure of the company. Include an organizational chart.
6.	Company meeting	Present the agenda of the annual shareholder's meeting as published in the latest annual report.
7.	Technical report	Describe a technical aspect of the company. Use technical terms and include a flowchart.
8.	Corporate home page	Develop a Web home page for the company.
9.	Strategy recommendation	Recommend a strategy that the company recently adopted.
10.	Selling a product	Use the sales brochure about the company's products or services.

PORTFOLIO BUILDER

Targeting Your Resumé and Portfolio

So far you've created a resumé and a portfolio of documents that reflect something about you. Now it's time to *target* a specific company and tailor your portfolio, including your resumé, to that company.

EXERCISE P-6 Target Your Resumé to an Employer

1. From your list of five prospective employers, choose one as your target. Review the information you've gathered about the company. If you feel you don't have enough information, collect additional material. Ultimately, you should be very familiar with the company—and the position—you've targeted.
2. Review Table P-3.

TABLE P-3 Targeting Your Resumé

TARGETING SUGGESTIONS

Objectives

- ☐ Change the job type to one that more closely resembles a job type available at the targeted company.
- ☐ Change the description of the industry or geographical area to one that more closely resembles those for the target company.

Chronological Resumé

- ☐ Reorder the bullets under a previous job in "Work experience" to emphasize skills that apply to the targeted position.
- ☐ Reorder or modify "Additional information" areas to emphasize skills that apply to the targeted position.

Functional Resumé

- ☐ Reorder or modify the "Functional sections" to emphasize skills that apply to the targeted position.
- ☐ Reorder or modify "Additional information" areas to emphasize skills that apply to the targeted position.

continues

TABLE P-3   **Targeting Your Resumé** *(continued)*

☞ TARGETING SUGGESTIONS
Combination Resumé
☐ Reorder or modify the "Functional sections" to emphasize skills that apply to the targeted position.
☐ Reorder the bullets under a previous job in "Work experience" to emphasize skills that apply to the targeted position.
☐ Reorder or modify "Additional information" areas to emphasize skills that apply to the targeted position.

3. Based on the checklist shown in Table P-3, modify your resumé to increase its appeal to your targeted company.

> **NOTE:** Modifying a resumé does not mean fabricating work experience. You can, however, increase your appeal to a specific employer by highlighting certain skills. You can also minimize potential problem areas through the design and format selected for your resumé (for example, by deciding to use a functional resumé rather than a chronological one).

4. Spell-check and save your resumé.

5. Print the final copy of your resumé on appropriate paper stock.

Choosing Paper

The most commonly used resumé papers are 20-pound bond or 50-pound offset (both weigh the same) in a linen (textured) or laid (flat) finish. A 24-pound paper is thicker, has more texture, and is usually more expensive than 20-pound bond or 50-pound offset papers. You might consider using 24-pound Nekoosa, Classic Linen, or Becket Cambric for higher-level positions.

Let your resumé speak for itself. Don't go overboard in selecting a paper that will make your resumé stand out. Such a strategy could backfire. Don't use colored stock, for example. Neutral stock in different shades of white, gray, or beige is recommended.

If you're uncertain about paper choices, visit a stationery store, an office supplies store, a printer, or a local copy shop. Buy enough paper to use for your resumés, cover letters, and follow-up letters. Your envelopes should match the stationery. Your portfolio presentations shouldn't be printed on the same stock as your resumé, however.

PORTFOLIO BUILDER

EXERCISE P-7 Target Your Portfolio to an Employer

The job contact at your targeted company is likely to respond more favorably to your portfolio if you take the time to tailor it to the company. It shows that you made an effort to learn about your prospective employer. It may also provide more conversational opportunities in a job interview.

1. Review Table P-4.

TABLE P-4	**Targeting Your Portfolio**
	TARGETING SUGGESTIONS
☐	Use the targeted company's name in presentation titles and its address where appropriate.
☐	Modify the contents of presentations so that they apply specifically to the targeted company.
☐	Do not change a report from one of your classes (other than to make any corrections your instructor may have recommended). It's a good idea to let the targeted company know that the report was submitted as a class assignment, especially if it relates to your chosen field.

2. Based on the checklist shown in Table P-4, modify the presentations in your portfolio to increase their appeal to the targeted company.

3. Spell-check and save the portfolio presentations.

4. Print the final copies of your portfolio presentations (in color, if possible). Use standard printer paper.

NOTE: It would be better to show your presentation in a slide-show format, with transition effects, but this may not always be possible. Use PowerPoint's Pack and Go feature to allow your presentation to be shown, even if your prospective employer doesn't have PowerPoint. You can also put your presentation on a clean disk with an attractive label (indicating your name, address, and telephone number) and leave it with your prospective employer.

Writing a Cover Letter

It's been said that sending a resumé without a cover letter is like giving a gift without a card. It's incomplete and confusing, and it only decreases the value of the resumé that you've spent so much time preparing and fine-tuning.

PORTFOLIO BUILDER

The Cover Letter Recipient A cover letter should be addressed to the job contact at a targeted company—never to Human Resources or Personnel.

First Paragraph The first paragraph should explain what job you are applying for and why you are interested in it. Be as specific as you can. Describe how you heard about the job opening. If someone told you about the company or the job opening, mention the person's name (but make sure to get his or her permission first). Describe why the work of the department or company holds particular interest for you, but don't go overboard with superlatives or hype.

Second Paragraph Describe your credentials in the second paragraph. Don't repeat your resume. Focus, instead, on the skills, experiences, or accomplishments that are most likely to appear relevant to the employer. If you're responding to an ad, incorporate language from the ad. If you've previously read a job description or had a discussion with the employer, try to use the language the employer used in describing the position. Mention two or three key credentials.

Third Paragraph Use the third paragraph to describe what you can do for the company. You need to show that you understand the employer's needs and that you have something to offer. In this paragraph (or as a separate paragraph), you should request a personal meeting. You could then indicate the time when it's easiest to reach you, whether the employer can contact you at work, and if you'll be following up with a phone call.

General Tips

- Your cover letter should be printed on the same paper as your resume and should be printed in the same way.
- Do not use the letterhead of your current employer.
- Use the same typeface for both your cover letter and your resume.
- Use the standard business letter format.
- Don't send your portfolio with your resume and cover letter. The portfolio is generally shown in an interview, but printed copies of a presentation (in color, if possible) can be sent to a prospective employer who expresses an interest in viewing it.

P-25

PORTFOLIO BUILDER

FIGURE P-9 Sample cover letter

Donald Martin
12 Juniper Drive
Any Town, State 00000
(000) 000-0000

January 22, 1998

Ward T. Cleaver, Manager
The Computer Warehouse, Inc.
6 Old King's Highway
Any Town, State 00000

Dear Mr. Cleaver:

I am seeking a position as a microcomputer salesperson, and read in the *Any Town News* that The Computer Warehouse was opening a new store on Old King's Highway. I have visited The Computer Warehouse in Lincoln and was impressed with the variety of hardware and software carried by the store. The store's focus on customer service was also exceptional, both through its "Trouble-Free Technical Support" program and its wide range of software training courses.

As my enclosed resumé indicates, I specialized in the sales of computer hardware and software at the Electronics Depot on Main Street. Although the sale of computers and software constitutes only a small portion of the overall sales of the Electronics Depot, computer and software sales increased by 42 percent in the past year. Part of this increase was due to the Customer Training Program that I developed. In its first year, the program produced revenues of $80,000.

Opening a new store and training a new sales staff is a difficult prospect. With my proven background in sales and customer training, I feel I would be an asset to your sales staff and would welcome the opportunity to meet with you personally to discuss your staff needs. I will contact you in the next week to schedule an appointment at your convenience. Thank you for your consideration.

Sincerely,

Donald Martin

Enclosure

PORTFOLIO BUILDER

EXERCISE P-8 Write a Cover Letter

Using your word-processor application, write a cover letter to accompany your resumé.

1. Using the standard business letter style (if necessary, check the *Gregg Reference Manual*), write a cover letter for your resumé. Use the three-paragraph format described earlier.

2. Ask someone familiar with your resumé and with jobs in your chosen field to review your letter. Make any necessary modifications.

3. Spell-check the cover letter and save it as *[your initials]***CvrLtr.doc**.

4. Print your cover letter using the same stationery as your resumé.

5. Print an envelope for your cover letter and resumé. If possible, use the same stationery for the envelope, cover letter, and resumé.

NOTE: Some people believe that you should use a large envelope so you don't have to fold your resumé. Others recommend a standard business envelope.

TIP: You can use Word's Letter Wizard to write a cover letter for your resumé. Choose New from the File menu, choose the Letters & Faxes tab, and double-click the Letter Wizard icon. Follow the steps to create the letter. Remember to choose the page design that matches your resumé, specify whether you're using preprinted letterhead, include "Mr." or "Ms." in the recipient's name area, and include an enclosure notation. After creating the letter, you can add, remove, or change letter elements by choosing Letter Wizard from the Tools menu.

Filling Out an Employment Application

Some companies require that every applicant, at every level, fill out an employment application. Other companies don't even use one. Generally, however, companies do use some form of an employment application. Whether you need to fill out such a form will depend on the company's internal personnel policies.

Often applicants are asked to fill out an employment application when they arrive at the company for an interview. To minimize stress in an already stressful situation, prepare for the employment application beforehand by creating a reference sheet that contains any information that might be included in the

PORTFOLIO BUILDER

application and isn't found on your resumé. (Of course, you should refer to your resumé in filling out your employment application. Make sure to bring an extra copy for reference.)

Tips for Employment Applications

- Be as specific as possible when describing the position that you are seeking.
- Be careful when listing a required salary. A salary that is too high may eliminate you for some acceptable jobs, while a figure that is too low might weaken your negotiating position. Sometimes it is better to leave this line blank.
- Be prepared to list dates (month and year) for the schools you have attended. Some applications may also ask for your grade-point average and your class rank.
- Be prepared to list the following information for your previous employers: address, telephone number, name and title of supervisor, start date and end date (month and year), and a description of your duties.
- If some questions are not applicable to the job you are seeking, it is usually acceptable to write "Not Applicable" next to the question.

EXERCISE P-9 Create a Reference Sheet for an Employment Application

1. Review the "Tips for Employment Applications." Note any information that isn't covered by your resumé.
2. Key all information that you will need to fill out an employment application. Use any format that makes sense to you.
3. Save the file and print it.

Employment Interviews

Once you have contacted a potential employer and scheduled an appointment to meet, you'll need to prepare yourself to make a good impression in person. No matter how good your resumé or credentials may be, only the interview can, ultimately, land you the job.

PORTFOLIO BUILDER

The more interviews you go on, the better your interviewing skills will be.

 NOTE: If possible, avoid scheduling an interview on a Monday, which is often the most hectic day in a business environment.

Preparing Yourself

- Confirm your appointment the day before, and make sure you arrive at the interview on time.
- Become as familiar with the company as possible. Read articles about the company, if they are available, or talk to people who are, or have been, employed by the company. It's always flattering to a prospective employer when an applicant appears knowledgeable about the company in an interview.
- Approach the interview with a clear mental picture of your capabilities and your job objective. Review your resumé immediately before meeting the prospective employer. Think positively.

Presenting Yourself

- Come to the interview equipped with copies of your resumé, your references, and any recommendation letters you have gathered. Have your portfolio on hand, as well as a notepad and a pen.
- Look your best. Your attire and grooming are critical to making a good impression. Dress neatly and professionally, in a manner that is appropriate to the company you are visiting. If necessary, get help in selecting an interview outfit from someone who dresses well.
- Be yourself. Act as relaxed as you possibly can, sit in a comfortable position, and focus on the interviewer.
- Ask questions. Learn what you can about the job, the company, to whom (or to how many people) you'd report, and so on. If no job is available, or the job opening is not appropriate for you, ask for recommendations about other people in the company that you might contact.
- At the end of the interview, if you want the job, express your interest in it, and be ready to explain why the company should hire you.

PORTFOLIO BUILDER

Frequently Asked Interview Questions

The following are frequently asked interview questions. You may want to rehearse your answers before the interview. Never offer negative or unnecessary information to an interview question.

- Can you tell me about yourself?
- Why should I hire you?
- What are your major strengths? Weaknesses?
- What are your short-term goals? Long-term goals?
- Why do you want to leave your present job? (if employed)
- Why did you leave your previous job?
- What do you enjoy most (or least) about your current (or previous) job?
- Why do you want to work here?
- What salary do you expect to receive?

Following Up the Interview

To be successful in the interview process, you should take two important follow-up steps:

- Send a "thank you" letter.
- Keep track of your contacts.

"Thank You" Letters

Always send a "thank you" letter within 24 hours after you've interviewed with someone. It creates a positive impression, shows that you have good follow-up skills and good social skills, and reminds the person of your meeting.

The letter should be short and friendly, thanking the person for his or her time and for any information he or she may have provided. You may want to mention something that reminds the person of who you are, in case many people have interviewed for the position.

Even if you know that the interview will not lead to a specific job offer, a "thank you" letter demonstrates your professionalism.

FIGURE P-10 Sample "thank you" letter #1

Dear Ms. Jones:

Thank you for the opportunity of interviewing for the sales position. I enjoyed meeting you and appreciate the information that you shared with me.

I am very interested in the position and believe I could quickly become a productive member of your sales team.

Thanks again for the interview, and I look forward to hearing from you.

Sincerely,

FIGURE P-11 Sample "thank you" letter #2

Dear Ms. Jones:

Thank you for the interview and the information you gave me yesterday. I really appreciate your recommendation that I meet with John Doe in the Marketing Department.

I have scheduled an interview with Mr. Doe and look forward to meeting him. If this contact eventually leads to a job offer, I will be most grateful.

Thanks again for your time and help.

Sincerely,

Keeping Track of Contacts

Be organized in your job search. Keep track of everyone who has received your resumé by creating a contact log.

PORTFOLIO BUILDER

FIGURE P-12
Sample format for contact log

Date Sent	Contact Name	Company	Telephone	Comments

In addition, develop a system for organizing your contacts so that you can follow up with telephone calls as appropriate. You can use a computer application of your choice or simple index cards to create the system.

If you use index cards, enter all pertinent reference information for each contact on the card. Place the cards in a box, and then sort them in the order that you want to contact the individuals. You can use tabs as date markers.

FIGURE P-13
Sample format for contact reference card

Company: _____

Contact Person: _____

Position:_____ Department:_____

Address:_____

Phone: _____ Fax:_____

Notes: _____

_____

_____

_____

P-32

Appendices

- **A** Windows Tutorial
- **B** Using the Mouse
- **C** Using Menus and Dialog Boxes
- **D** PowerPoint Toolbars
- **E** File Management
- **F** Proofreader's Marks
- **G** Multimedia and Pack and Go

APPENDIX A

Windows Tutorial

If you're unfamiliar with Windows, we suggest that you review this Windows tutorial.

If you've never used Windows before, you may need additional help with some basic Windows actions. At appropriate points in this Tutorial, a Note will guide you to one of the two Appendixes covering basic Windows actions (Appendix B: "Using the Mouse," and Appendix C: "Using Menus and Dialog Boxes").

Starting Windows

Individual computers may be set up differently. In most cases, however, when you turn on your computer, Windows will load and the Windows desktop will appear.

The desktop contains *icons*, or symbols representing windows. If you double-click an icon, the window represented by that icon opens. Two icons are especially important:

- My Computer
  Opens a window that contains icons representing each input and output device on your printer or in your network.

- Recycle Bin
  Opens a window listing files you have deleted. Until you empty the Recycle Bin, these files can be undeleted.

TIP: If you don't know how to use the mouse to point, click, double-click, or drag and drop, see Appendix B: "Using the Mouse."

Using the Start Menu

The Start button on the taskbar at the bottom of the desktop is probably the most important button in Windows. Clicking displays the Start menu from which you can perform any Windows task.

APPENDIX A ■ WINDOWS TUTORIAL

 NOTE: If Microsoft Office is installed on your computer, additional options may appear on your Start menu.

1. Turn on the computer. Windows will load, and the Windows desktop will appear.

NOTE: When you start Windows, you may be prompted to log on to Windows or, if your computer is attached to a network, to log on to the network. If you are asked to key a user name and a password, ask your instructor for help.

2. Click *Start* on the Windows taskbar. The Start menu appears.

 TIP: If you don't know how to choose a command from a menu, see Appendix C: "Using Menus and Dialog Boxes."

FIGURE A-1
Windows desktop

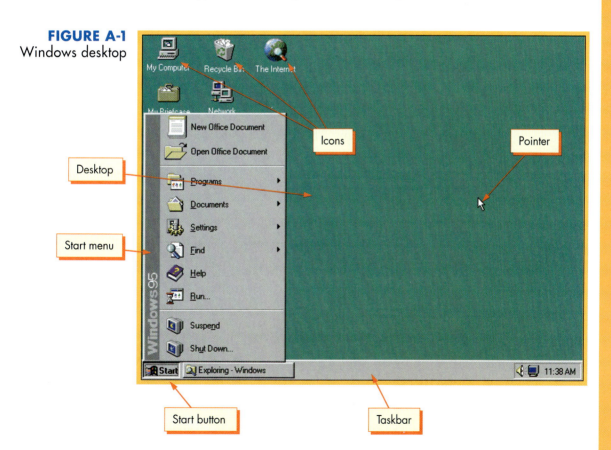

A-3

APPENDICES

TABLE A-1 Start Menu

COMMAND	USE
Programs	Displays a list of programs you can start.
Documents	Displays a list of documents that you've opened previously.
Settings	Displays a list of system components for which you can change settings.
Find	Helps you find a folder or a file.
Help	Starts Help. You can then use Help to find out how to perform a task in Windows.
Run	Starts a program or opens a folder when you type an command.
Shut Down	Shuts down or restarts your computer, or logs you off (if you are on a network).

Using the Programs Command

The Programs command is the easiest way to open a program.

1. Click **Start**.
2. Point to Programs. The Programs submenu appears, listing the programs present on your computer. Every computer will have a different list of programs.

FIGURE A-2
Programs submenu

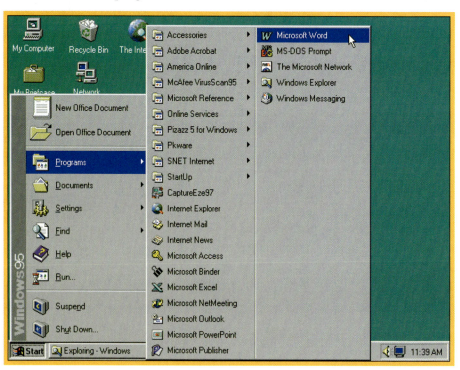

A-4

APPENDIX A ■ **WINDOWS TUTORIAL**

3. Point to a program that you want to open and then click. In a few seconds, the program will load and its first screen will appear. Notice that a button for the program appears in the taskbar. Keep the program open.

NOTE: Many items on the Program menu represent names for groups of programs. These group names have an arrow ▶ across from them on the right side of the menu. When you point to the group name, a submenu will appear listing programs that you can click to select.

Using the Taskbar

One of the major features of Windows is that it enables you to work with more than one program at a time. The taskbar makes it easy to switch between open programs.

The window in which you are working is called the *active* window. The title bar for the active window is highlighted, as is its taskbar button.

1. The program you opened in the preceding procedure should still be open. (If it's not, open a program now.) Open a second program using the Program command. Notice how the second program covers the first. The window containing the second program is now active. Its title bar is highlighted and its button on the taskbar is highlighted.

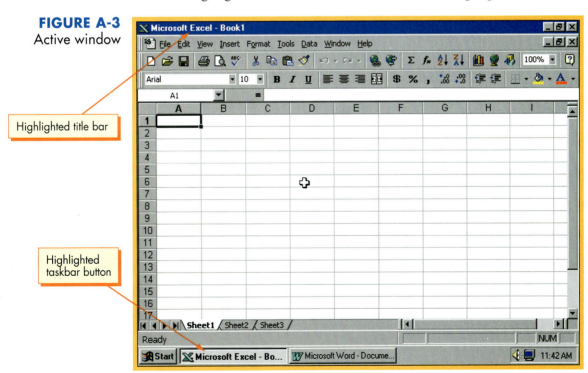

FIGURE A-3
Active window

Highlighted title bar

Highlighted taskbar button

A-5

APPENDICES

2. Click the button on the taskbar for the first program you opened. The program appears again.

3. Click the button on the taskbar for the second program to switch back to it.

Changing the Sizes of Windows

In Windows it's easy to adjust the size of your windows using the pointer. You can also use the Minimize button ▬, the Maximize button ◻, and the Restore button ❐ to adjust the size of windows.

TABLE A-2   Sizing Buttons

NAME	BUTTON	USE
Minimize button	▬	Reduces the window to a button on the taskbar.
Maximize button	◻	Enlarges the window to fill the desktop.
Restore button	❐	Returns the window to its previous size. (Appears when you maximize a window.)

1. In the open window, click ❐ at the right side of the title bar of the window. (If ◻ appears instead of ❐, the window has already been reduced. In that case, go on to step 2.)

2. Move the pointer to a window border. The pointer changes to a double-headed arrow ↔.

TIP: Sometimes the borders of a window can move off the computer screen. If you're having trouble with one border of a window, try another border.

3. When the pointer changes shape, you can drag the border to enlarge, reduce, or change the shape of the window.

4. Make the window smaller. Notice that the other open program appears behind the currently active window.

A-6

APPENDIX A ■ WINDOWS TUTORIAL

5. Click the window that had been behind the first window. It now appears in front of the first window because it has become the active window.

 6. Click ▬ to minimize the window to a button on the taskbar. The other program becomes active.

 7. Click the Close button ✗ at the top right corner of the window to close the current program. The desktop should now be clean.

8. Click the button on the taskbar for the other program you have open. Close the program by clicking . You have a clean desktop again.

Using the Documents Command

You can open an existing document by using the <u>D</u>ocument command on the Start menu. This command allows you to open one of the last 15 documents previously opened on your computer.

1. In the Start menu, point to <u>D</u>ocuments. The <u>D</u>ocuments submenu appears, showing documents that have been previously opened.

2. Click on a document. The document opens, along with the program in which the document was written (for example, if the document were a Word document, it would open within Word). A button for the document appears on the taskbar. You could now work on the document, if you wanted.

3. To close the document, click ✗ on the document window. Click ✗ to close the program window that contained the document.

FIGURE A-4
Close buttons

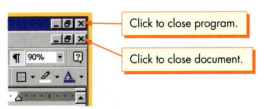

Using the Settings Command

You can change the way Windows looks and works by using the <u>S</u>ettings command. Be very careful when changing settings. Don't change them unless it's really necessary.

 NOTE: Before changing any settings, talk to your instructor.

A-7

FIGURE A-5
Settings submenu

1. Open the Start menu, and point to Settings. The Settings submenu appears.
2. Click the option that relates to the settings you want to change. Close any open windows and clear your desktop.

TABLE A-3 Settings options

OPTION	USE
Control Panel	Displays the Control Panel, which allows you to change screen colors, add or remove programs, change the date or time, and change other settings for your hardware and software.
Printers	Displays the Printer window, which allows you to add, remove, and modify your printer settings.
Taskbar	Displays the Taskbar Properties dialog box, which allows you to change the appearance of the taskbar and the way it works.

Using the Find Command

If you don't know where a document or folder is, you can use the Find command to find and open it.

FIGURE A-6
Find Submenu

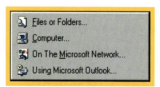

1. On the Start menu, point to Find. The Find submenu appears.
2. Click Files or Folders. The Find: All Files dialog box appears.

FIGURE A-7
Find: All Files dialog box

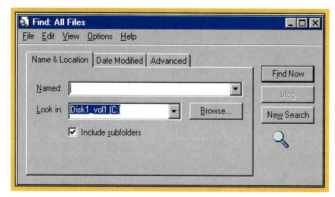

APPENDIX A ■ WINDOWS TUTORIAL

3. In the Named box, key the name of the file or folder you want to find.
4. Click the arrow next to the Look In box to specify where to search. (You could also check Browse.)

 TIP: You can use the Advanced tab to search files for specific text.

5. Click Find Now to start the search. Any matches for the file will be shown at the bottom of the dialog box.
6. To open a file that was found, double-click on the filename.
7. When you have finished viewing the file, close all open windows and clear your desktop.

Using the Run Command

If you know the name of the program you want to use, you can use the Run command to start it easily. This command is often employed to run a "setup" or "install" program that installs a new program on your computer.

1. In the Start menu, click Run. The Run dialog box appears.

FIGURE A-8
Run dialog box

2. If you know the name of a program you want to run, key the name and click OK. The program you specified will start. Otherwise, you can click Browse to look for the program.
3. When you're finished, close the program.

Using the Right Mouse Button

When the pointer is on an object in Windows and you click the right mouse button, a shortcut menu will typically appear. This menu provides you with the commands that would be most useful in working with the object to which you were pointing.

A-9

APPENDICES

A shortcut menu is available for Start. The shortcut menu options for Start are described in Table A-4.

FIGURE A-9
Shortcut menu for the Start button

1. Click Start with the right mouse button. The right mouse button Start menu appears.
2. Investigate the options on the right mouse button menu, and then close any open programs.

TABLE A-4 Shortcut menu for the start button

OPTION	USE
Open	Opens the Start Menu window. Double-click the Programs icon to open the Program window. Then, double-click the icon for the program you want to open.
Explore	Opens Windows Explorer (see Appendix E: "File Management").
Find	Opens the Find: All Files dialog box.

Using the Shut Down Command

You should always shut down Windows before you turn off or restart your computer. You can then be sure that your work will be saved and no files will be damaged.

1. In the Start menu, click Shut Down. The Shut Down Windows dialog box appears.

FIGURE A-10
Shut Down Windows dialog box

2. Click Yes. Windows will prompt you to save changes to any open documents, and will then shut down your computer.

A-10

APPENDIX B

Using the Mouse

Although you can use a keyboard with Windows, you'll probably find yourself using the mouse. Typically, you roll the mouse on a *mouse pad* (or any flat surface). A *pointer* shows your on-screen location as the mouse moves.

To select items on the computer screen using a mouse, you usually press the left button on the mouse. (Whenever you're told to "click" or "double-click" the mouse button, use the left mouse button. In those cases where you should use the right button, you'll be told to do so.)

When using a mouse, you'll need to become familiar with these terms.

TABLE B-1   Mouse Terms

TERM	DESCRIPTION
Point	Move the mouse until the tip of the on-screen pointer is touching an item on the computer screen.
Click	Press the mouse button and then quickly release it.
Double-click	Press and quickly release the mouse button twice.
Triple-click	Press and quickly release the mouse button three times.
Drag (or drag-and-drop)	Point to an object, hold down the mouse, and move the mouse to a new position (dragging the object to the new position). Then release the mouse button (and drop the object in the new position).

The mouse pointer changes appearance depending on where it's located and what you're doing. Table B-2 shows the most common types of pointers.

TABLE B-2   Frequently Used Mouse Pointers

POINTER NAME	POINTER	DESCRIPTION
Pointer	↖	Used to point to objects.
I-beam	I	Used when keying, inserting, and selecting text.
2-headed arrow	↖↘	Used to change the size of objects or windows.
4-headed arrow	✥	Used to move objects.
Hourglass	⧗	Indicates the computer is processing a command.
Hand	☞	Used in Help to display additional information.

A-11

APPENDICES

APPENDIX C

Using Menus and Dialog Boxes

Menus

Menus throughout Windows applications use common features. To open a menu, click the menu name. An alternative method for opening a menu is to hold down [Alt] and key the underlined letter in the menu name.

 TIP: If you open a menu by mistake, click the menu name to close it.

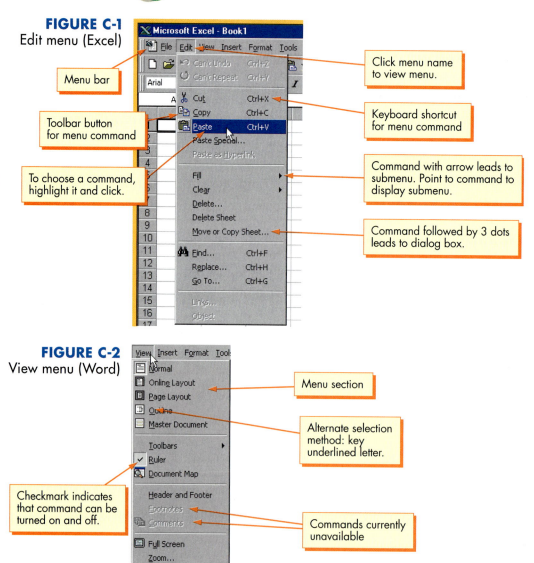

FIGURE C-1 Edit menu (Excel)

- Menu bar
- Toolbar button for menu command
- To choose a command, highlight it and click.
- Click menu name to view menu.
- Keyboard shortcut for menu command
- Command with arrow leads to submenu. Point to command to display submenu.
- Command followed by 3 dots leads to dialog box.

FIGURE C-2 View menu (Word)

- Checkmark indicates that command can be turned on and off.
- Menu section
- Alternate selection method: key underlined letter.
- Commands currently unavailable

A-12

APPENDIX C ■ USING MENUS AND DIALOG BOXES

Dialog Boxes

Dialog boxes enable you to view all of the current settings for a command, as well as change them. Like menus in Windows, dialog boxes share common features. The following examples show the most frequently seen features.

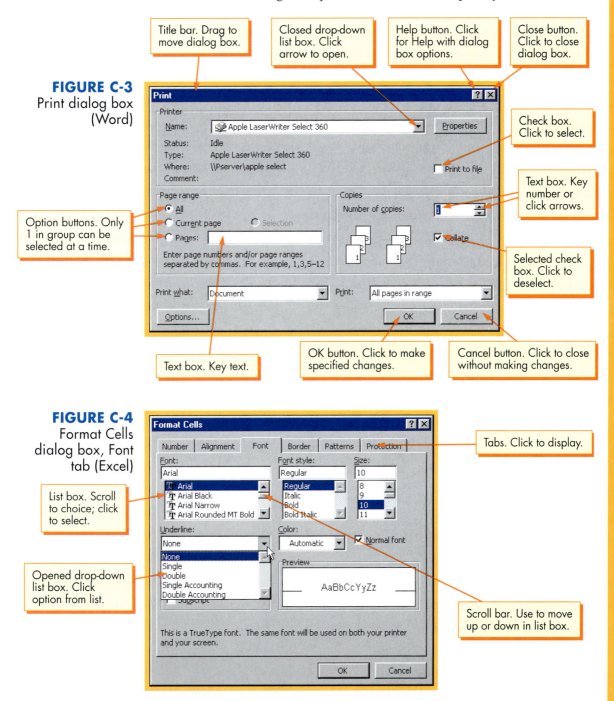

FIGURE C-3 Print dialog box (Word)

FIGURE C-4 Format Cells dialog box, Font tab (Excel)

A-13

APPENDICES

APPENDIX D

PowerPoint Toolbars

The following toolbars are most commonly used in PowerPoint:

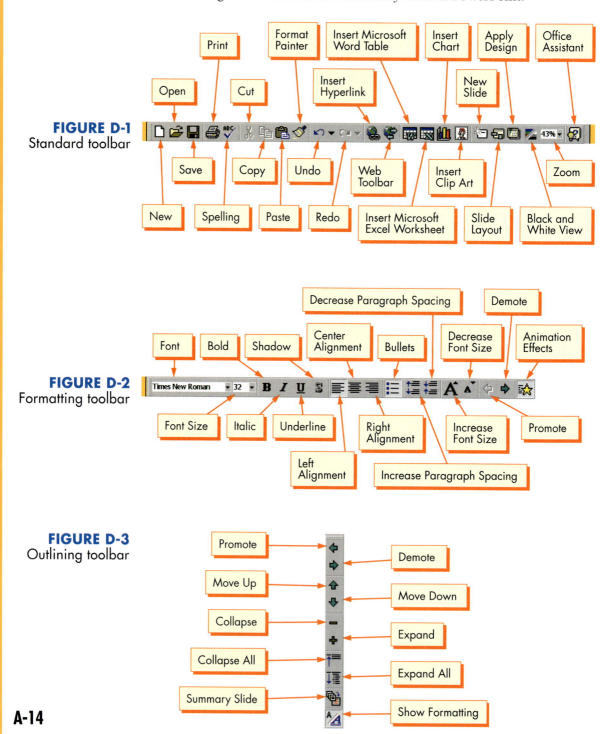

FIGURE D-1 Standard toolbar

FIGURE D-2 Formatting toolbar

FIGURE D-3 Outlining toolbar

A-14

APPENDIX D ■ POWERPOINT TOOLBARS

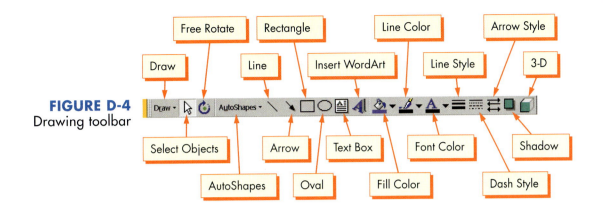

FIGURE D-4
Drawing toolbar

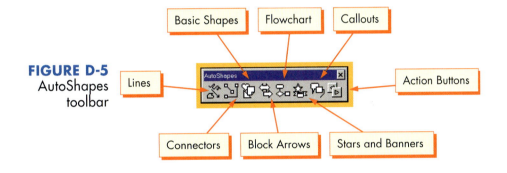

FIGURE D-5
AutoShapes toolbar

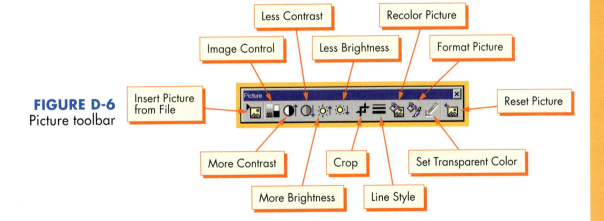

FIGURE D-6
Picture toolbar

A-15

APPENDICES

APPENDIX E

File Management

This Appendix briefly explains how information is stored in Windows. It also introduces one of the most useful tools for managing information in Windows—the Windows Explorer.

Files, Folders, and Paths

In Windows, the basic unit of storage is a *file*. The documents you create and use are files, as are the programs you use. These files are stored in *folders*, which can also contain other folders.

Windows supports filenames that can contain up to 250 characters. A filename also has a three-letter extension, which identifies the type of file. For example, the extension "doc" identifies a file as a Word document. The extension is separated from the filename by a period. For example: "Birthdays.doc."

> **NOTE:** In this course, we assume that your machine displays file extensions. If it doesn't, open Windows Explorer, select Option from the View menu, and make sure that the following option is *not* selected: "Hide MS-DOS file extensions for file types that are registered."

A file's *path* is its specific location on your computer or network. A file's path begins with the drive letter, followed by a colon and a backslash (example: c:\). The path then lists the folders in the order you would open them. Folders are separated by backslashes. The last item in the path is the filename.

For example: c:\My Documents\Letters\Reservations.doc

Windows Explorer

One of the most useful tools in Windows for managing files is the *Windows Explorer*, which gives you a view of your computer's components as a hierarchy, or "tree." Using Windows Explorer, you can easily see the contents of each drive and folder on your computer or network.

To open Windows Explorer, click the Start button with the right mouse button. Then click Explore in the Start button shortcut menu.

Table E-1 describes how to accomplish common file management tasks using Windows Explorer and shortcut menus.

APPENDIX E ■ FILE MANAGEMENT

FIGURE E-1
Windows Explorer

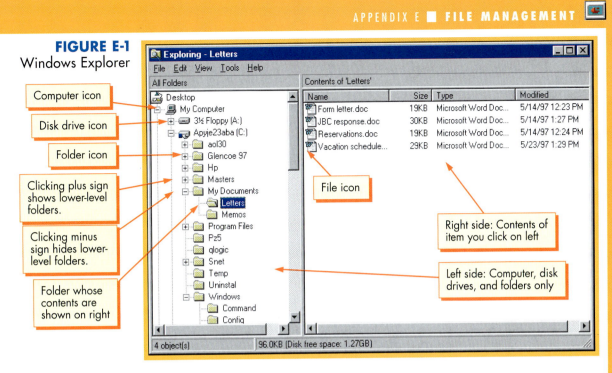

TABLE E-1 **Common File Management Tasks**

TASK	HOW TO DO
Copy file or folder	Right-click file or folder to be copied and click Copy, then right-click folder in which you want to copy file and click Paste. (Alternative: Drag and drop a file from one folder to another.)
Move file or folder	Same method as above, but using Cut and Paste.
Delete a file or folder	Point to icon for file to be deleted and press Delete.
Create a new folder	Choose New from File menu, and then choose Folder. Creates new folder at current position.
Copy file to floppy disk	Point to icon for file to be copied and press right mouse button. Point to Send To and click floppy disk drive in submenu.
Edit/rename file	Point to icon for file you want to rename, press right mouse button, and click Rename.
Open file	Double-click icon for file.
Print file	Point to icon for file to be printed, press right mouse button, and click Print.

A-17

APPENDIX F

Proofreader's Marks

PROOFREADER'S MARK		DRAFT	FINAL COPY
⌒	Delete space	to gether	together
#	Insert space	It may be	It may be
∽	Transpose	beleivable	believable
◯	Spell out	② years ago	two years ago
∧	Insert a word	How much it? (is)	How much is it?
⟋ OR —	Delete a word	it may not be true	it may be true
∧ OR ⟋	Insert a letter	temperture (a)	temperature
⟋ OR ⊃	Delete a letter and close up	commitment to buny	commitment to buy
⟋ OR —	Change a word	and if you won't (but / can't)	but if you can't
stet	Stet (don't delete)	I was very glad	I was very glad
/	Make letter lowercase	Federal Government	federal government
≡	Capitalize	Janet L. greyston	Janet L. Greyston
⊙	Insert a period	Mr Henry Grenada	Mr. Henry Grenada
∧	Insert a comma	a large old house	a large, old house
∨	Insert an apostrophe	my childrens car	my children's car
∨∨	Insert quotation marks	he wants a loan	he wants a "loan"
=	Insert a hyphen	a first rate job	a first-rate job
—	Insert underscore	an issue of Time	an issue of <u>Time</u>
ital	Set in italic	ital The New York Times	*The New York Times*
bf	Set in boldface	bf the Enter key	the **Enter** key
rom	Set in roman	rom the *most* likely	the most likely
{ }	Insert parentheses	left today May 3	left today (May 3)
⊐	Move to the right	$38,367,000	$38,367,000
⊏	Move to the left	⊏ Anyone can win!	Anyone can win!

A-18

APPENDIX G ■ MULTIMEDIA PACK AND GO

APPENDIX G

Multimedia and Pack and Go

Imagine being able to add full-motion video and high-quality sound to your presentation. With adequate screen resolution, hard disk space, and a sound card, all you need is the video clip and sound bite files. Check the Valupack folder on the Microsoft Office CD ROM for **.avi** video files and **.wav** audio files.

Once you place multimedia files in your presentation, use the Pack and Go feature to compress the files into a single package so you can show the presentation at another location.

Adding Video Clips

One way to add a video clip to a slide is to choose a slide AutoLayout that includes a media clip object. You then activate the object and insert the clip. Alternatively, you can use the Insert menu (Movies and Sounds command or Object command) or the Microsoft Clip Gallery (Videos tab) to insert a video clip on any slide layout.

FIGURE G-1
Text & Media Clip
AutoLayout

1. Insert a new slide with the Text & Media Clip AutoLayout. (Scroll through the New Slide dialog box to find the AutoLayout.)

2. Double-click the media clip placeholder to open the Insert Movie dialog box.

3. Locate the drive and folder that contains the desired video clip (with the **.avi** extension). To preview the video, right-click the filename and choose Play.

4. Select the file and click OK. The video clip is inserted into the placeholder. You can size and move the clip as you would any other object.

5. To control the timing and appearance of the video clip, select it and choose Custom Animation from the Slide Show menu. Click the Play Settings tab in the Custom Animation dialog box.

6. Click the Play using animation order check box. Choose either Pause slide show (to have the slide show stop while the video plays) or Continue slide show (to have the video play through the slide show). If you choose the latter option, choose a stop playing option. (See Figure G-2 on the next page.)

7. Click More Options to open the Play Options dialog box. Here you can choose to loop (play) the video over and over again or rewind the video when it's done playing.

A-19

APPENDICES

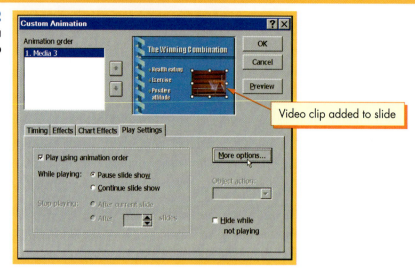

FIGURE G-2
Adding a video clip

8. Use the Effects tab in the Custom Animation dialog box to add builds and effects to the video clip.

Adding Audio Clips

You worked with sound effects in your presentations before, but not as individual audio clips. You can insert an audio clip as a stand-alone object on a slide, to be played manually or as part of a build effect. There are several ways to insert stand-alone audio clips, including the Insert menu, the media clip AutoLayout, and the Microsoft Clip Gallery. The latter method is demonstrated below.

1. Click the Insert Clip Art button and click the Sounds tab in the Microsoft Clip Gallery dialog box.
2. Use the vertical scroll bar to view the audio files, which are displayed as speaker icons with filenames.

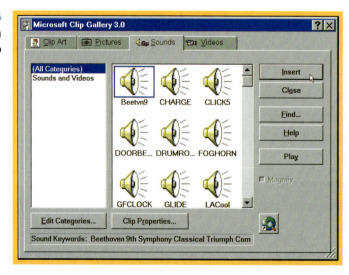

FIGURE G-3
Choosing an audio clip

APPENDIX G ■ MULTIMEDIA PACK AND GO

3. To preview an audio clip, select it and click the Play button. To insert a selected file, click Insert. The audio clip is inserted into the slide as a small icon. You can size and move this icon as you would any other object.

4. Once the file is inserted, right-click the icon to edit it, play it, or apply Custom Animation settings to coordinate it with your other slide objects.

FIGURE G-4
Slide with audio and video clips

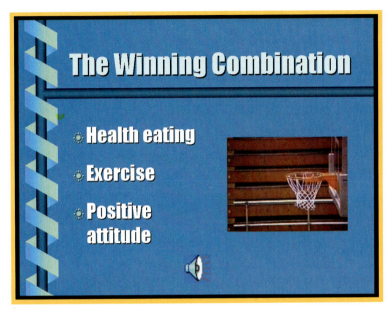

Using Pack and Go

Using the Pack and Go Wizard in PowerPoint you can pack up your entire presentation, including linked video and audio files, and save it to a floppy disk (or disks). You can then show the presentation on a computer that doesn't have PowerPoint installed.

1. Choose Pack and Go from the File menu to open the Pack and Go Wizard opening dialog box.

FIGURE G-5
Pack and Go Wizard opening dialog box

A-21

2. Click Next and specify the presentation to be packaged. The current presentation is selected by default.

3. Click Next and specify where the presentation should be stored.

4. Insert a blank formatted diskette into the drive and select the appropriate drive.

5. Click Next. Check the options to Include linked files and Embed TrueType fonts so your presentation will always run as you created it.

6. Click Next. The Pack and Go Wizard allows you to include the PowerPoint Viewer, which enables you to show a slide show on a computer that does not have PowerPoint installed.

7. Click Next and click Finish. Pack and Go compresses your presentation onto one or more blank disks, depending on the size of your presentation.

NOTE: To run a presentation compressed by the Pack and Go Wizard, use the Windows Explorer to find the file with the **.exe** extension on your diskette. This executable file installs the presentation in the folder you specify on your hard drive. You can then run the presentation.

Glossary

Adjustment handle Yellow diamond that appears in some AutoShape objects when they are selected, which is used to change angles, roundness, and points of the object. (6)

Animate Add special visual or sound effects to slide objects. (14)

Aspect ratio Relationship between the height and width in an image. If the aspect ratio is locked, when you change either the height or the width the corresponding dimension is automatically adjusted. (6)

AutoShapes Groups of ready-made shapes that you can resize, rotate, color, and combined with other shapes. (5)

Axis Line that borders one side of the chart plot area. A value axis displays a range of numbers and a category axis displays category names. (11)

Build Successively add elements to a slide. (14)

Cell Box formed by the intersection of a row and column in a table or spreadsheet. (12)

Chart box Rectangular box in an organization chart that contains space for one or more lines of information, such as a name and a title. (13)

Chart placeholder Box with a dotted line that appears on a slide showing the size and position of a chart. (11)

Connection sites Blue handles that appear on an AutoShape when the connector tool is active or when a connector is selected. Connection sites indicate places where a connector can be attached to an AutoShape. (13)

Connector line Straight, curved, or angled line with special endpoints that can lock onto connection sites on an AutoShape. (13)

Constrain Control the movement or drawing of an object in precise increments or proportions. When you constrain a rectangle as you draw it, it becomes a square; a constrained oval becomes a circle. (6)

Cropping Trimming the vertical or horizontal edges of a picture. (6)

Data series Group of data on a chart that relate to a common object or category such as product, geographic area, or year. (11)

Demote To indent one heading level. (3)

Design template Custom design that you apply to a presentation to give it a uniform color scheme and a particular "look." (3)

First line indent Paragraph indent style in which the first line is indented to the right of the body of the paragraph. (9)

Format Painter Tool used to copy the characteristics of one object to another. (7)

Gradient fill Coloring of an object in which one color fades into another. (7)

Guides Dotted horizontal and vertical lines used to place objects on a slide or measure the distance between objects. (10)

Handout Printouts that contain 2, 3, or 6 PowerPoint slides per page. (1)

Hanging indent Paragraph indent style in which the first line extends to the left of the body of the paragraph. This style is most often used with bullets. (9)

HTML (Hypertext Markup Language) Text format for documents used on the World Wide Web. (15)

GLOSSARY

Hyperlink In PowerPoint, colored and underlined text or a graphic object that you click to go to another slide, a file, or a location on the Internet. (1, 14)

Hypertext document Type of document used by sites on the World Wide Web that may contain pictures, sounds, movies, and hyperlinks which connect to other hypertext documents. (15)

Indent markers Two small triangles that appear on the ruler when a text box is selected. The lower triangle controls the left indent setting of the text box and the top triangle controls the first line indent setting. (9)

Legend Box showing the colors and patterns assigned to the data series or categories in a chart. (11)

Master Slide that contains formatted placeholders as well as any background items that appear on all slides in the presentation. (5)

Normal indent Paragraph indent style in which all the lines of a paragraph are moved the same amount to the right. A normal indent has an even left margin. (9)

Placeholder Box with dotted lines that holds a place on a slide for text, clip art, or another object. (1)

Promote To raise or "unindent" one heading level. (3)

Proportional sizing Changing the size of an object while retaining its height and width ratio. (6)

Resize handle Square handle that appears at each corner and along the sides of the rectangular area surrounding a selected object. Dragging a resize handle resizes the object. (5)

Scale Specifies the range of values on the value axis and the interval between values. (11)

Selection rectangle Dotted box that you draw by dragging the mouse pointer to select objects on a slide. (8)

Table Systematic arrangement of data in rows and columns, generally used for reference. (12)

Text box Container for text on a slide. (1)

Thumbnail Miniaturized version of a graphic image. (6)

Tick marks Small measurement marks, similar to the marks on a ruler, that cross a value or category axis. (11)

Transition effect Visual or sound effect that determines the manner in which a slide appears during a slide show. (14)

URL (Uniform Resource Locator) Combination of characters that comprise the location or address of a site on the World Wide Web. (15)

Vertex Reshaping handle used to edit the points on a freeform, scribble, or curve drawing. (10)

Wizard Online guide that helps you complete a specific task. (2)

Index

A

abbreviations, expanding, 46
Action Settings, 432
adding slides in Outline view, 104
adjustment handles, 187
aligning
    bullets, 140
    column headings (table), 375
    contents of table, 374–376
    flowchart elements, 393–394
    nudge, 314
    numbers in tables, 375
    objects, 241–244
    snap to grid, 314
    text, using tabs, 286
    titles and subtitles, 140
anchor
    freeform drawing, 317
    text anchor point, 291
animation, 84, 412–422
    in charts, 418
    in templates, 419
    object animations, 417–418
    text animations, 415–417
annotating charts with text, 353
arrowheads, 208–209
    adding to straight lines, 208–209
    placement of arrows, 208
aspect ratio, 173
attributes, 135–141
    alignment attributes, 140
    font attributes, 144
audio effects, 22, 171, 412, 414
AutoContent Wizard, 39–41, 55
AutoCorrect, 45
AutoLayout, 77, 342
    Table AutoLayout, 368
AutoShapes, 143, 186–188
    arrows and stars, 186
    callouts, 186
    flowcharts, 186, 390–391
        changing AutoShapes, 392–393
        connecting AutoShapes, 391–394
    Format AutoShape, 186
    formatting AutoShapes using text box options, 293–294
    multiple shapes, 184
    resizing proportionally, 188
    symmetrical shapes, 188
AutoShapes menu, 182
    Connectors, 392
    Flowchart, 391
axis titles (chart), 352

B

background
    color, 221
    shading effects, 215

Black and White view, 311
borders
    active text box border, 135
    adding borders to tables, 373–374
    adding borders to text placeholders, 207
    changing line style, 207
    removing borders from objects, 210
browser, 431, 432
    browser frame page layouts, 437
    browsing the Web, 433–435
        downloading files, 433–435
    Microsoft Internet Explorer, 431
    Netscape Navigator, 431
building, 415
bullets, 80–82, 138–140
    adding bullets, 42
    aligning bullets, 140
    bullet characters, 139
    bullet shape, 80
    bullet spacing, 284
    bullet text box, 136
    bulleted text placeholder, 135
    color and shape, 139–140
    demoting bullets, 80
    level of importance, 80
    promoting bullets, 80
    selecting bulleted text, 42
    turning on and off, 138–139
buttons
    3-D button, 182, 247
    Action buttons, 420
    Add to Favorites button, 13
    alignment buttons, 241
    Animation Effects button, 417
    Apply Design button, 83
    Arrow button, 182
    Arrow Style button, 182, 208
    AutoShapes button, 187
    Black and White View button, 86
    Bold button, 132
    Border Color button, 374
    brightness buttons, 175
    Bullets button, 139
    By Column button, 348
    By Row button, 348
    Callouts button, 187
    Center Alignment button, 140
    Center button, 375
    Chart Type button, 354
    chart-related buttons, 344–345
    Close buttons, 15, 26, 133
    Collapse All button, 111
    Collapse button, 105, 112
    Commands and Settings button, 13
    Copy button, 50
    Crop button, 175
    Cut button, 49
    Dash Style button, 182, 207
    Demote button, 80, 105
    Details button, 13

Direction button, 249
Distribute Columns Evenly button, 373
Drawing button, 353
Drawing toolbar buttons, 182
Expand All button, 112
Expand button, 105, 112
Fill Color button, 210, 349
Font Color button, 133, 145, 373
font size buttons, 15, 132
Format button, 350
Format Painter button, 215, 216
Format Picture button, 173
Free Rotate button, 181, 182
Handout Master Layout button, 297
Import File button, 344
Insert Chart button, 354
Insert Clip Art button, 171
Insert Hyperlink button, 431
Insert WordArt button, 182
Italic button, 132, 351
Left Alignment button, 140
Legend button, 345
Line button, 182
Line Color button, 207
Line Style button, 207
List button, 13
Look in Favorites button, 13
Maximize button, 51
Microsoft Word Table button, 368
move up/down buttons, 105, 109
New button, 77
New Slide button, 78, 105
Next Slide button, 16, 17
Notes Page View button, 20
nudge buttons, 315
Outline View button, 18, 19, 103
Oval button, 182
paragraph spacing buttons, 289
Paste button, 50, 111
Preview button, 12, 84, 143, 209
Previous Slide button, 17
Print button, 24
Promote button, 80, 105
Properties button, 13
Recolor Picture button, 218
Rectangle button, 182
Redo button, 81
Relative to Slide button, 242, 243
Round Rectangular Callout button, 187
Save button, 23
Search the Web button, 13
Select Object button, 182
Shading Color button, 373
Shadow button, 145, 182, 247
Shadow Color button, 248
Show Formatting button, 105
Show/Hide ¶ button, 370
Slide Layout button, 82, 148, 285
Slide Show button, 21, 413

I-1

INDEX

Slide Sorter View button, 19
Slide Transition button, 413
Slide View button, 19, 144, 147
Spelling button, 44
Start button, 11
Summary Slide button, 105, 420
Tab Type button, 285, 375
Text Box button, 178, 182, 353
To Grid button, 314
Underline button, 134
Undo button, 81
Up One Level button, 12
View buttons, 14
View Datasheet button, 346
Web Toolbar button, 434
WordArt Shape button, 177

C

callouts, 187
case of text, 134–135
    cycling through cases, 134
    lowercase, 134
    sentence case, 134
    title case, 134
    toggle case, 135
    uppercase, 134
cells (datasheet), 343
cells (table), 375
    adding fill color, 373
    changing cell indents, 375–376
    changing cell's font color, 373
    selecting cells, 371
charts, 342–357
    adding animation effects, 418
    adding shapes, 353–354
    adding text objects, 353–354
    annotating charts with text, 353
    background color, 349
    chart animations, 418
    chart layout, 343
    chart legend, 352
    chart objects, 344
    chart placeholder, 342
    chart type, 345, 348
    colors, patterns, 348–349
    column charts, 347
    data labels, 355
    data series, 347
    editing charts, 347–348
    formatting category axis, 351
    formatting chart item, 344
    formatting charts, 348–353
    formatting value axis, 350
    importing data from
        spreadsheet or text file, 344
    inserting axis titles, 352
    inserting charts, 342–343
    keying new chart data, 346
    line formatting, 348–349
    parts of chart, 350
    pie chart, 354–367
        exploding a slice, 356
        formatting pie plot area, 356
        pie chart labels, 355

sample chart, 343
sample data
    changing sample data, 343–346
    deleting sample data, 345
scale, 350
special effects, 353
tick marks, 350
viewing new charts, 346
clip art, 171–174
    aspect ratio, 173
    clip art images
        disassembling, 251–252
        formatting parts of, 252
        regrouping, 252–270
    clip art placeholder, 171
    colors of clip art objects, 218
    cropping, 174–176
    cutting, copying, pasting, 49–51
    editing, 251–253
    inserting, 172
    moving, 172–174
    position, 172–174
    proportional sizing, 173
    recoloring, 218
    resizing, 172
    rotating, 180–181, 252–270
    selecting, 173
    settings, 174–175
    size, 172–174
    thumbnails, 172
Clipboard, 49, 178
closing presentations, 26
color
    256 color bitmaps, 218
    background color, 221, 349
    black and white settings, 222
    bullets, 139–140
    color of objects, 209–210
    color view, 223
    colored borders around tables, 373–374
    fill color, 345
        Fill Color floating menu, 349
        gradient fill, 211
        in cells, 373
        in objects, 182
        removing, 210
    font color, 133, 145, 373
    hyperlink color, 433
    lightening or darkening, 211
    line color, 207
    object's outline, 182
    PowerPoint versus Word colors, 377
    recoloring Word table in
        PowerPoint, 376–377
    selected text, 182
    standard colors, 377
    uniform color in presentations, 83
color schemes, 219–222
    copying between presentations, 221
    creating new color scheme, 221
    template color scheme, 85
columns (table)
    column headings, 288
        aligning, 375
    column sizes, 372–373

    distributing columns, 372–373
    selecting columns, 371
command summaries
    AutoShapes, 190
    borders, 224
    bullets, 88, 150
    charts, 357
    clip art and pictures, 190
    closing, 27
    cut, copy and paste, 55
    datasheets, 357
    design template, 88
    duplicating objects, 253
    expand, collapse, 117
    fills, 224
    grouping objects, 253
    guides, 323
    headers and footers, 55
    Internet hyperlinks, 441
    move up, move down, 117
    next or previous slide, 27
    notes and handouts, 297
    nudge feature, 323
    org charts, 401
    outlines, 117
    paragraph spacing, 297
    printing, 27
    promote, demote, 117
    repeat, 150
    saving, 27
    selecting objects, 253
    show formatting, 117
    slide transition, 422
    slides, 88, 117
    speaker notes, 88
    spelling checker, 55
    style checker, 55
    tables, 378
    text alignment, 150
    text attributes, 150
    text boxes, 190
    undo, redo, 88
    WordArt, 190
    zoom control, 27
constrained objects, 184
Copyright notice, 436
creating
    borders, 206
    curved drawings, 321–323
    freeform drawings, 316–319
    new color schemes, 221
    overlapping objects, 246–247
    own drawings, 182–186
    presentations, 39–55
    tabbed tables, 287
    Word tables, 368–369
cropping, 174–176
curved drawings, 321–323
Cut, Copy, and Paste, 49–51

D

data (chart)
    data labels, 355
    data series, 345, 347

I-2

INDEX

keying new data, 346
data (table), 368–378
datasheets, 343
   title bar, 343
   viewing, 345
date and time, 52–53
Default Design, 83, 84
deleting objects, 183
demoting bulleted items, 105–107
demoting slide titles, 105–107
design elements, 144
design templates, 83–86
diagrams. *See* charts
dialog boxes
   Action Settings dialog box, 419
   Additional Clips dialog box, 172
   Apply Design dialog box, 84
   AutoCorrect dialog box, 46
   Background Color dialog box, 220
   Background dialog box, 217
   Bullet dialog box, 139
   Change Case dialog box, 134
   Chart Options dialog box, 352
   Color Scheme dialog box, 85, 220
   Fill Effects dialog box, 211, 212
   Find Clip dialog box, 172
   Font dialog box, 133, 134
   Format AutoShape dialog box, 141–150, 180, 210, 318, 391
   Format Axis dialog box, 350, 352
   Format Legend dialog box, 352
   Format Object dialog box, 376
   Format Picture dialog box, 173
   Format Plot Area dialog box, 356
   Format Text Box dialog box, 181
   Header and Footer dialog box, 52, 55, 149
   Hyperlink to Slide dialog box, 420
   Hyperlink to URL dialog box, 432
   Insert Hyperlink dialog box, 431
   Insert Outline dialog box, 114
   Insert Word Table dialog box, 369
   Line Spacing dialog box, 289
   Microsoft Clip Gallery dialog box, 171
   New Slide dialog box, 77, 342
   Open dialog box, 12
   Open Internet Address dialog box, 434
   Output options dialog box, 40
   Page Setup dialog box, 295
   Presentation options dialog box, 41
   Presentation style dialog box, 40
   Presentation type dialog box, 40
   Print dialog box, 25, 54–68, 112
   Recolor Picture dialog box, 218
   Replace Font dialog box, 137
   Save As dialog box, 23, 138
   Set Up Show dialog box, 422
   Slide Color Scheme dialog box, 221
   Slide Finder dialog box, 116
   Slide Layout dialog box, 82, 148
   Slide Transition dialog box, 421
   Speaker Notes dialog box, 87
   Spelling dialog box, 44
   moving out of way, 45
   Style Checker dialog box, 47
   Text & Line Color dialog box, 221
   WordArt Gallery dialog box, 177
disks and drives, 23–24, 84, 138
dissolve effect, 416–417
docked toolbars, 15
Draw menu, 182
   Align or Distribute, 377
   Change AutoShape, 392
   Edit Points, 320
   Group, 244, 253
   Nudge, 323
   Ungroup, 251, 253
drawing
   drawing freeform, 316–319
   drawing lines
      constrained lines, 185
      diagonal lines, 185
      horizontal lines, 185
      lines at an angle, 185
      multiple lines, 184
      straight lines, 182
      vertical lines, 185
   drawing shapes
      arrows and arrowheads, 182
      circles, 182, 184
      irregular shapes, 316–319
      multiple shapes, 184
      ovals, 182
      rectangles, 182
      squares, 182, 184
   drawing techniques, 310–323
   drawing text boxes, 182
   drawing tools, 182–186
   drawn objects
      aligning, 182
      duplicating, 250–251
      flipping, 182
      grouping, 182
      resizing, 186
      rotating, 182
Drawing toolbar
   3-D button, 247, 249
   Arrow Style button, 208
   AutoShapes, 317
   AutoShapes button, 187
   buttons, table of, 182
   Dash Style button, 207
   Draw, 314, 315
   Draw button, 241, 243, 247, 292
   Fill Color button, 210
   Font Color button, 133
   Free Rotate button, 181
   Free Rotate tool, 180
   in chart window, 353–354
   Insert WordArt tool, 176
   Line Color button, 207
   Line Style button, 207
   Line tool, 183
   Oval tool, 183
   Rectangle tool, 183
   Shadow button, 247
   show or hide, 345
   Text Box button, 178
duplicating objects, 250–251

E

e-mail. *See* World Wide Web
Edit menu
   Copy, 55
   Cut, 55, 399
   Duplicate, 250, 253
   Paste, 55
   Paste Boxes, 399
   Redo, 88
   Redo Demote, 82
   Repeat, 150
   Repeat Slide Layout, 148
   Replace, 48
   Select All, 239, 253, 414
   Undo, 88, 399
   Undo Demote, 81
editing, 17–18
   charts, 347–348
   clip art, 251–253
   freeform drawings, 320–321
   methods of editing, 44
   placeholder text, 42–44
   table text, 377–378
embedding TrueType fonts, 138
Excel, 343, 419
exiting PowerPoint, 26
expanding slides, 107–108

F

File menu
   Close, 26, 27
   Exit, 27
   New, 40, 436
   Page Setup, 295
   Print, 24, 27, 54, 87, 440
   Save, 23, 27
   Save As, 23, 27, 138
   Save as HTML, 436, 437
   Update, 398
files, 22–24
   different types of files, 22
   filename extensions, 22
      .doc, 22
      .ppt, 22
   filenames, 22, 24
fill, 373
   fill color, 345
   gradient fill, 211, 318
   marble and wood grain fill, 214
Fill Color floating menu, 349
Find and Replace, 48
floating text boxes, 178–180
floating toolbars, 15, 133
flowcharts
   aligning elements, 393–394
   example of flowchart, 394
   flowchart AutoShapes, 390–391
      changing, 392–393
      connecting, 391–394
fonts, 371
   embedding fonts, 137
   font attributes, 144
   font color, 145

I-3

INDEX

font face, 131
font size, 131, 137
font style, 131
Monotype Sorts font, 139
Symbol font, 139
TrueType fonts, 138
Wingdings font, 139
footers and headers, 51–53
    slide numbers, 148
Format AutoShape, 143–144
Format menu
    Alignment, 140, 150
    Apply Design, 83, 88
    Background, 217, 348
    Bullet, 150
    Change Case, 134, 150
    Colors and Lines, 207, 213, 224
    Font, 150
    Line Spacing, 289, 297
    Paragraph, 372
    Replace Fonts, 137
    Selected Axis, 350
    Slide Color Scheme, 220
    Slide Layout, 82, 88
Format Painter tool, 214–215, 221
formatting
    category axis (chart), 351
    chart items, 344
    charts, 348–353
    checkerboard formatting, 215
    copying formatting, 214
        one object to another, 215
        one slide to another, 215
    numbers, 148
    org chart boxes, 398–411
    pie plot area (chart), 356
    text, 144–149
    value axis (chart), 350
Formatting toolbar, 132
    Bullets button, 139
    Decrease Paragraph Spacing button, 289
    Font box, 132
    Font drop-down list, 138
    Increase Paragraph Spacing button, 289
    Italic button, 351
    Shadow tool, 182
    Underline button, 134
Formatting toolbar (Word)
    alignment buttons, 375
    Font Color button, 373
freeform drawings
    creating, 316–319
    editing, 320–321

G

graphics. *See* clip art
grayscale, 222
grid, 314
gridlines (chart)
    category axis gridlines, 345
    value axis gridlines, 345
gridlines (table), 373

grouping objects, 244–245
guides
    hiding, 312
    measuring objects, 310–313
    positioning objects, 310–313
    removing, 312
    temporarily disabling, 315

H

handles
    adjustment handles, 187
    corner handles, 188
    reshaping handles, 320
    resize handles, 141, 173, 187, 216, 240
    round green handles, 181
    small blue handles, 391
    small white boxes, 141
    vertexes (edit points), 320
    yellow diamond handles, 186
handouts, 24–26, 51–55, 296–297
    customizing, 296–297
    handout master, 296
    printing, 24–26, 54
headers and footers, 51–53
    slide numbers, 148
Help
    black and white print options, 224
    color schemes, 88
    creating Web pages, 441
    drawing objects, 190
    exporting PowerPoint outlines to Word, 117
    Help topics, 56
    manipulating objects, 254
    master slides, 150
    Office Assistant, 27
hiding slides, 414
HTML, 436
    HTML files, 438
    Save as HTML Wizard, 437
    viewing presentations in HTML format, 438–440
hyperlinks, 21, 109, 208, 419–421.
    See also Internet
    color, 433
    connecting to:
        another slide, 431
        Internet location, 431
    Internet hyperlinks
        creating, 430–432
        using, 432–433
    summary slide, 419
hypertext document, 430
Hypertext Markup Language. *See* HTML
Hypertext Transport Protocol, 431

I

icons
    AutoContent Wizard icon, 40, 436
    blank title slide icon, 103

    Bulleted List layout icon, 83
    chart icon, 343
    printer icon, 25
    slide icon, 42
    subordinate box icon, 396
    table icon, 369
    yellow file folder icon, 12
importing
    data from spreadsheet, 344
    data from text file, 344
    files, 344
    Word outlines, 113–116
indents, 283–284
    changing cell indents, 375–376
    first line indents, 283
    hanging indents, 283
    indent markers, 283, 284
    left indent, 284
Insert menu
    Clip Art, 171
    Hyperlink, 441
    New Slide, 78, 88
    New Title Master, 147
    Outline command, 113
    Picture, 172
    Slides from Files, 115, 117
    Slides from Outline, 117
Internet, 430–440. *See also* World Wide Web
    browser, 431, 432
        Microsoft Internet Explorer, 431, 433
        Netscape Navigator, 431
    contacting your local Internet service provider, 440
    if connection not active, 434
    Internet hyperlinks
        creating, 430–432
        using, 432–433
    Internet service provider, 431
        Microsoft Network, 431
    modem, 431
    publishing presentations, 436–440

K

keying text
    in tables, 370–371
    on slides, 17–18

L

labels (chart), 355
landscape orientation, 294
layers of objects, 246–247
layout
    chart layout, 343
    org chart layout, 394
    slide layout, 88, 147
    Title Slide layout, 148
legend (chart), 352
lines
    dotted lines, 181
    flowchart connector lines, 391–394

I-4

INDEX

guides, 310
line color, 207
removing from objects, 210
style, 182
thickness, 182
wavy red underline, 19, 44

M

margins, 140
   text box margins, 293
master slides, 144-149
   applying fill effect to object, 215
   changing color of object, 216
maximizing presentations, 51
measuring objects, 310-313
menu bar, 13, 16, 18
menus
   floating, 208
   gray bar at top, 208
Microsoft Clip Gallery, 171
Microsoft Graph, 343-346
Microsoft Office, 218
Microsoft Organization Chart, 394
   editing screen, 395
Microsoft Word, 368
   Word tables, 368-369
      enhancing appearance, 371-374
   Word toolbars, 369
modem, 431

N

navigating in PowerPoint, 13-17
New Slide button, 104
notes, 86-87, 296-297
   creating notes, 86-87
   customizing, 296-297
   editing speaker notes, 87
   notes master, 296
   printing, 54, 86-87
Notes and Handouts tab, 53
Notes Page view, 20-21, 86
Nudge option, 315
   precisely positioning objects, 315
numbers
   aligning numbers in tables, 374
   page numbers, 52
   slide numbers, 52, 148-149

O

objects, 170-190, 238-253
   3-D effects, 182, 249-250
   adding fill effect to master slide object, 215
   aligning objects, 241-244
      horizontally, 241-242
      relative to slide, 243
      vertically, 241-242
   centering objects, 243
   changing fill color, 209-210
   chart objects, 344
   colors of clip art objects, 218
   constrained objects, 184
   copying formatting from one object to another, 215
   deleting objects, 183
   deselecting all objects, 239
   distributing objects, 241-244
      horizontally, 242
      vertically, 242
   drawn objects
      aligning, 182
      flipping, 182
      grouping, 182
      resizing, 186
      rotating, 182
   duplicating objects, 250-251
   fill patterns, 213
      textured fill, 214
   flipping objects, 241-244
   graphic objects
      placing text in, 188-190
   group of selected objects
      removing items from, 239-240
   grouping objects, 244-245
   guides, using to measure, 310-313
   guides, using to position, 310-313
   layers of objects, 246-247
   master slide object
      changing color, 216
   mirror images, 241
   multiple objects
      rotating: grouped versus ungrouped, 252
      selecting, 239
   Nudge option, 315
   object animations, 417-418
   overlapping objects, 246-247
   removing fill colors, 210
   removing lines, 210
   rotated objects
      editing text in, 189
   selected objects
      exact placement of, 288
      selection rectangle, 240-241
   shading effects, 212
   shadow effects, 247-248
   Snap to Grid option, 314
   spacing objects evenly, 241
   text objects
      adding to charts, 353-354
   ungrouping objects, 245-246
   vertexes (edit points), 320
   WordArt object, 182
Office Assistant, 14, 15, 27, 40, 88
   Hide Assistant, 15
opening existing presentations, 12
org charts, 390, 394-401
   adjusting chart size in window, 398
   hierarchy, 394
   org chart boxes, 394
      assistant box, 395
      box style, 399
      co-worker box, 395
      demoting, 399-411
      fill colors, fonts, shadows, 400
      formatting, 398-411
      level, 394
      manager box, 395
      promoting, 399
      rearranging, 398-411
      stacking boxes, 399
      subordinate box, 395
   placeholder boxes
      adding new boxes, 396-398
      deleting boxes, 398
      inserting assistant boxes, 397
      inserting co-worker boxes, 397
      inserting subordinate boxes, 396
      keying text in boxes, 397-398
   reducing or magnifying, 395
organization charts. *See* org charts
Outline view, 18-19, 41, 102-117
   adding new slides, 104
   changing text attributes, 134
   creating new presentations, 103
   moving bulleted items, 109-111
   moving slides, 111-113
outlines
   importing Word outlines, 113-116
   printing outlines, 54
   turning off formatting applied by template, 112

P

page numbers, 52
page setup options, 294-296
   page orientation, 294-295
paragraph marks, 370
patterns, 210
pictures, 171-174. *See also* clip art
placeholders, 17
   active placeholder, 135
   bulleted text placeholder, 42, 79, 135
      adding additional bullets, 42
   chart placeholder, 342
   clip art placeholder, 171
   date placeholder, 297
   dotted placeholder, 144
   editing placeholder text, 42
   header placeholder, 297
   notes text placeholder, 86
   number placeholder, 148
   org chart placeholder, 395
   placeholder boxes, 395
   subtitle placeholder, 78
   text placeholder
      adding borders, 207
      applying attributes to, 135-137
      black and white settings, 223
      distance between bullets and text, 284
      editing sample text, 42-44
      line spacing, 290
      more than one bullet level, 284
      position of, 140-144
      selecting, 135
      shaded fill, 212
      size of, 140-144
      spacing between paragraphs, 290

I-5

INDEX

title placeholder, 41, 79, 132, 145
   editing sample text, 41–42
pointers
   arrow pointer, 17, 48, 85, 135, 396, 400
   circling arrow pointer, 181
   cropping tool pointer, 175
   cross pointer, 141, 179, 187, 420
   crosshair pointer, 317, 320
   double-headed arrow pointer, 141, 173, 186, 346
   drag-and-drop pointer, 48
   four circling arrows pointer, 181
   four-headed arrow pointer, 107, 135, 142, 173, 216, 312, 320
   I-beam pointer, 17, 42, 109, 110
   pencil shape pointer, 316, 372
   small arrowhead pointer, 187
   subordinate box icon pointer, 396
   two-headed arrow pointer, 107, 209
   white arrow pointer, 42, 110, 312
   white cross pointer, 344
points (line spacing), 290
portrait orientation, 295
positioning objects, 310–313
presentations
   adding interest to, 131–150
   adding new slides, 78–79
   animation effects, 84
   audio effects, 22, 171
   background effect, 217
   black and white v. color, 222–223
   changing fonts, 137–138
   closing presentation, 26
   color scheme, 219–222
      copying between presentations, 221
      converting to HTML Format, 437–438
   creating presentation, 39–55
   creating Web presentation, 436
   developing in Outline view, 103–104
   dissolve effect, 416–417
   embedding fonts, 137, 138
   hiding slides, 414–415
   identifying information, 52
   Internet hyperlinks, 432
   maximizing presentation, 51
   modifying Web presentations, 440
   naming presentation, 22–24
   new blank presentations
      creating in Outline view, 103
   publishing on the Web, 436–440
   saving, 22–24, 82, 137
      drives and diskettes, 23, 24
   speaker notes, 86–87
   starting with blank presentation, 76–88
   timing slides, 421–422
   transition effects, 412–415
   uniform color and design, 83
   viewing presentations in HTML format, 438–440
printing, 54–55
   handouts, 24–26, 54
   in black and white, 54, 222–223

in shades of gray, 54
notes, 54
outlines, 54
print options, 24, 54–68
Print Range, 54
slides, 24–26, 54
stopping a print job, 25
promoting bulleted items, 105–107
proportional sizing, 173

R

rearranging slides, 19, 48
Repeat, 148
resize handles, 141, 173, 187, 216
resizing drawn objects, 186
rotating
   AutoShapes, 180
   clip art, 180
   freeform drawings, 180
   multiple objects:
      grouped versus ungrouped, 252
   text, 180–181
   text boxes, 180
rows (table)
   row heights, 372
rulers, 242, 283–284, 287
   indent markers, 283

S

sample data, 343–346
sample text, 41–42
Save as HTML Wizard, 437
scale (chart), 350
screen resolution, 20
ScreenTips, 187, 208, 209, 349, 356
scroll bars, 14, 42
Search the Web, 13
selecting
   cells and columns (table), 371
   entire tables, 371
   text, methods of, 43
selection rectangle, 240, 400
shading effects, 210
shadow effects, 145
   on objects, 182, 247–248
   on text, 182
shape of bullets, 139–140
shapes, 143–144
   adding to charts, 353–354
   measurements, 184
   predefined shapes, 182
   spheres, shaded, 212
sizing handles. See resize handles
slide master, 144, 145
Slide Show menu
   Action Buttons, 420
   Action Settings, 432
   Custom Animation, 415
   Set Up Show, 422
   Slide Transition, 413
Slide Show view, 85, 415
slide shows, 18, 21–22, 412–422

adding animation effects:
   to charts, 418
   to templates, 419
object animations, 417–418
text animations, 415–417
timing slides, 421–429
Slide Sorter view, 19–20, 48–51, 81
   rearranging slides, 48
Slide view, 18, 42, 53–55, 78–79
   changing sample text, 41–44
   changing text attributes, 134
slides
   adding elements to slides, 415
   adding slides
      from another presentation, 115
      new slides, 78–79
   aligning objects relative to slide, 243
   black and white settings, 222
   changing slide layout, 88
   chart slide layout, 343
   choosing slide layouts, 77–78
   color scheme, 85
   copying color scheme between presentations, 221
   copying formatting from one to another, 215
   cutting, copying, pasting, 49–51
   deleting slides, 51
   demoting bulleted items, 105–107
   demoting slide titles, 105–107
   dimming text, 417
   displaying miniature versions, 48
   dissolve effect, 416–417
   expanding slides, 107–108
   flipping objects on slide, 243–244
   hiding slides, 414–415
   joining and splitting slides, 105
   master slides, 144–149, 215
   moving between presentations, 51
   moving by dragging, 48–49
   moving in Slide Sorter view, 49
   objects on a slide, 136
   Preview box, 53
   printing, 24–26, 54–68
   promoting bulleted items, 105–107
   removing master slide graphics, 217
   slide area, 14
   slide changer, 14
   slide icon, 42
   slide layouts, 77–78, 82–83
   slide master, 145, 176
      adding WordArt text objects, 176
      indent settings, changing, 285
      viewing, 145
   slide miniatures, 18, 19, 86, 103
   slide numbers, 42, 51–53, 148–149
   slide title, 112
   slide's contents, 76–78
   summary slides, 109, 419
   text build
      animating, 416
      applying, 415
   timing slides, 421–422
   title master, 147
      creating, 147
      viewing, 145

I-6

INDEX

title placeholder, 41
title slide, 41, 78
   title and body slides, 77
transition effects, 412–415
   global transition, 414–415
small black squares, 320
Snap to Grid option, 314
   temporarily disabling, 315
speaker notes, 86–87
special effects, 210, 414
   WordArt, 176–178
spelling checker, 44–45
   WordArt, 178
Standard toolbar
   Apply Design button, 83
   Black and White View button, 222
   By Column button, 348
   By Row button, 348
   Chart Type button, 354
   chart-related buttons, 344–345
   Clip Art button, 171
   Drawing button, 353
   Fill Color button, 349
   Format button, 350
   Format Painter tool, 215
   Insert Chart button, 354
   Insert Hyperlink button, 431
   Microsoft Word Table button, 368
   View Datasheet button, 346
   Web Toolbar button, 434
   Zoom drop-down list box, 86
Standard toolbar (Word)
   Show/Hide ¶ button, 370
   Tables and Borders button, 371
starting PowerPoint, 10
status bar, 14, 17, 25, 84, 145
   Default Designs, 84
style checker, 46–48, 135
   style checker options, 47
subtitles, 144
   alignment, 140
summary slides, 109
symmetrical AutoShapes, 188

T

Table AutoLayout, 368
Table menu
   Select Table, 371, 372
tables, 368–378
   active cell, 370
   adding colored borders, 373–374
   adding fill color to cells, 373
   adding rows, 369
   aligning contents, 374–376
   cells, 370
   column sizes, 372–373
   defining the structure, 369
   distributing columns, 372–373
   editing table text, 377–378
   enhancing appearance, 371–374
   gridlines, 373
   keying text, 370–371
   recoloring Word table in PowerPoint, 376–377

row heights, 372
rows and columns, 370
selecting entire tables, 371
tabbed tables, 287
text position in table row, 371–372
Word tables, 368–369
tabs, 285–289
   removing tab markers, 287
   setting tabs in text box, 286–287
   tabbed tables, 287
      column headings, 288
   types of tabs, 286, 375
templates, 84, 88
   adding animation effects, 419
   color scheme, 85
   design template, 83–86, 219
   outlines
      turning off formatting applied by template, 112
   Web-oriented template, 436
text, 131–150
   alignment of text, 140
   annotating charts with text, 353
   attributes, 131–135, 144
      bold, 131
      changing case, 134–135
      italic, 131
      underline, 131
   bulleted text, 138–139, 144
   color, 182
   cutting, copying, pasting, 49–51
   deleting text, 80
   editing in rotated objects, 189
   editing placeholder text, 42
   editing table text, 377–378
   editing text, methods, 44
   keying text in tables, 370–371
   placing text in graphic objects, 188–190
   promoting and demoting text, 80
   sample text, 41–44
   selecting text, methods, 43
   shadow effects, 131
   spacing
      line spacing, 289–290
      paragraph spacing, 289–290
   special effects
      3-D effects, 176
      rotating text, 180–181
      shading effects, 176
      stretching and curving text, 176–178
      text animations, 415–417
      WordArt, 176–178
      WordArt, spelling checker, 178
      WordArt, text shapes, 177
   subtitle text, 144
   text effect, 131
   text formatting, 132, 135–137
      using master slides, 144–149
   text manipulation, 282–297
      paragraph indents, 283–284
      tabs, 285–289
   text objects
      adding to charts, 353–354
   text position in table row, 371–372

text style, 131
text wrap, 291
title text, 144
text boxes, 17
   border of active text box, 135
   bullet text box, 136
   changing text box margins, 293
   fixed-width text box, 180
   floating text box, 178–180
   formatting AutoShapes, 293–294
   freeform text boxes, 178
   moving text boxes, 142
   resizing text boxes, 141
   resizing text boxes to fit, 292
   selecting text boxes, 135–137
   setting tabs, 286–287
   shape of text box, 141–142
   size of text box, 141–142
   text box settings, 290–294
   title text box, 136
text placeholder
   adding borders, 207
   applying attributes to, 135–137
   editing sample text, 42–44
   selecting text placeholder, 135
textures, 210
thumbnails, 172
tick marks (chart), 350
timing slides, 421–422
title bar, 13, 15, 24, 45, 50, 51
title master, 144, 147
   creating, 147
   viewing, 145
titles, 144
   aligning, 140
   axis titles (charts), 352
   org chart titles, 396
   subtitles, 144
   title placeholder, 41–42
toggle case, 135
toolbars, 13
   3-D Settings toolbar, 249
   Align or Distribute toolbar, 241
   AutoShapes toolbar, 187, 188
   Common Tasks toolbar, 15, 18, 82
   displaying and hiding, 15
   docked toolbars, 15
   Drawing toolbar, 145, 176
      buttons, table of, 182
   editing screen toolbar, 395
   floating toolbars, 15, 133
   Formatting toolbar, 15, 351
      Center Alignment button, 140
      Demote button, 80
      Left Alignment button, 140
      Promote button, 80
      Shadow button, 145
   Handout Master toolbar, 296
   Lines toolbar, 321
   Organization Chart toolbar, 395
   Outlining toolbar, 103, 105, 109
   Picture toolbar, 173, 175, 218
   Rotate or Flip toolbar, 243
   Shadow Settings toolbar, 248
   Slide Sorter toolbar, 413, 415, 421
   Standard toolbar, 20, 23

I-7

INDEX

Black and White View button, 86
Copy button, 50
Cut button, 49
New button, 77
New Slide button, 78, 104
Redo button, 81
Slide Layout button, 82
Spelling button, 44
Undo button, 81
Tables and Borders toolbar (Word), 371
Shading Color button, 373
Web toolbar, 433, 438
Word toolbars, 369
WordArt toolbar, 177
Toolbars menu, 15
Tools menu
AutoCorrect, 45
Expand Slide, 108
Hide Slide, 422
Options, 81
Slide Transition, 422
Spelling, 55
Style Checker, 47, 48, 55
ToolTips, 15
transition effects, 412–415
TrueType fonts, 138

U

ungrouping objects, 245–246
Uniform Resource Locator. *See* URL
URL, 430–432

V

vertexes (edit points), 320
adding, 320
deleting, 320
moving, 320
videos, 171
view buttons, using, 18
View menu
Datasheet, 346
Guides, 311, 323
Header and Footer, 52, 55, 148
Master, 144, 150, 178, 296, 297
Outline, 103, 117
Ruler, 242, 283
Slide, 19, 147
Slide Miniature, 18, 103
Slide Show, 422
Speaker Notes, 86, 87, 88
Toolbars, 15, 78, 218, 241
Zoom, 27
views
Black and White view, 223, 311
Color view, 223
Notes Page view, 20–21, 86
Outline view, 18–19, 41, 102–117, 134
Slide Show view, 85, 415
Slide Sorter view, 19–20, 48–51, 81, 84
Slide view, 18, 42, 53–55, 78–79

W

Web pages, 208
Window menu, 49
Arrange All, 50, 221
windows
datasheet window, 345
PowerPoint window, 14
Windows Explorer, 10
Windows taskbar, 10
Start button, 11
wizards, 39
AutoContent Wizard, 39–41, 55
Word tables, 368–369
enhancing appearance, 371–374
Tables and Borders toolbar, 371-374
WordArt objects, 176–178
menu of text shapes, 177
moving, 177
spelling checker, 178
World Wide Web, 430–440. *See also* Internet
browsing the Web, 433–435
to download files, 433–435
creating Web presentations using AutoContent Wizard, 436
hypertext documents, 430
Hypertext Transport Protocol, 431
index page, 437
linking to Web site, 430–432
modifying Web presentation, 440
navigation buttons, 437
presentations
converting existing presentation to HTML Format, 437–438
publishing presentations, 436–440
viewing presentations in HTML format, 438–440
Web address for Microsoft, 431
Web pages, 430, 432
creating own Web page, 436
Web-oriented template, 436

Z

zoom, 86, 148, 207, 245, 287, 313
placing objects precisely, 313
viewing objects in fine detail, 313
Zoom arrow, 314
Zoom box, 20
zoom percentage, 20, 21

Photo Credits

Page 2: Balterman/FPG; Page 4: Lang/FPG, Luria/FPG, Taylor/FPG, Gage/FPG; Page 9: Simpson/FPG; Page 75: Cummins/FPG; Page 169: Turner/FPG; Page 281: Weber/FPG; Page 341: Cummins/FPG; Page A-1: Hallinan/FPG